THE COMPLETE GUIDE
TO CHRISTIAN
QUOTATIONS

An Indispensable Resource for Writers, Pastors,
Teachers, Students—and Those Who Loves Books

THE COMPLETE GUIDE
TO CHRISTIAN
QUOTATIONS

MORE THAN 6,000 QUOTATIONS
NEARLY 500 CATEGORIES
SOURCE REFERENCES
SUBJECT AND AUTHOR INDEXES

BARBOUR
PUBLISHING

© 2011 by Barbour Publishing, Inc.

ISBN 978-1-60260-767-5

Published by Barbour Publishing, Inc., P.O. Box 719, Uhrichsville, Ohio 44683, www.barbourbooks.com

Our mission is to publish and distribute inspirational products offering exceptional value and biblical encouragement to the masses.

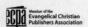 Member of the
Evangelical Christian
Publishers Association

Printed in the United States of America.

WELCOME TO
THE COMPLETE GUIDE
TO CHRISTIAN QUOTATIONS

Nearly seventy years ago, Bernard Darwin introduced *The Oxford Dictionary of Quotations* by writing, "Quotation brings to many people one of the intensest joys of living."

His assessment may be somewhat exaggerated—but if you're reading this introduction to *The Complete Guide to Christian Quotations,* you probably do find pleasure in the memorable words and phrases of others. A good quotation can provoke thought, encourage understanding, or support our most deeply held beliefs. An entire book of quotations can provide hours of agreeable reading.

This fresh new compilation comprises thousands of quotes from hundreds of individuals. The vast majority of these quotations are taken from books, sermons, hymns, and articles by evangelical Christian preachers, authors, and hymn writers of the past several centuries. Some quotations are from earlier church leaders, from the works of Catholic writers, even from people of non-Christian religious backgrounds. A few quotes originate with those who probably claimed no particular faith. But, to be included in this compilation, every quotation was deemed by our compilers and editors to be consistent with biblical truth.

The apostle Paul provides the precedent for quoting even non-Christian sources in a Christian work. As he preached to the "superstitious" men of Athens who had built an altar "to the unknown god" (Acts 17:22–23), Paul used the words of a Greek poet to make a point about the one true God:

> *For in him we live, and move, and have our being; as certain also of your own poets have said, For we are also his offspring. Forasmuch then as we are the offspring of God, we ought not to think that the Godhead is like unto gold, or silver, or stone, graven by art and man's device. And the times of this ignorance God winked at; but now commandeth all men every where to repent: Because he hath appointed a day, in the which he will judge the world in righteousness by that man whom he hath ordained; whereof he hath given assurance unto all men, in that he hath raised him from the dead.*
> ACTS 17:28–31

As informative and thought-provoking as quotations can be, they are still merely the words of imperfect human beings. The only text that is always completely reliable is the Bible—and for that reason, *The Complete Guide to Christian Quotations* includes a relevant scripture verse with each of its nearly 500 topics. We believe this regular reminder sets a helpful tone for the entire collection.

Barbour Publishing appreciates the efforts of our many compilers, whose names are listed in the back of this book. They scoured vast amounts of material—as often as possible, primary sources—to select the quotations that appear in this collection. We salute their efforts, and hope you as the reader benefit from them.

THE EDITORS

1 ABIDING

Abide in me, and I in you. As the branch cannot bear fruit of itself, except it abide in the vine; no more can ye, except ye abide in me.
JOHN 15:4

1 To abide with Christ—to stay with Him and to learn from Him—is to continually receive eyes to see, ears to hear, and a heart to obey.
Angela Thomas McGuffey
Tender Mercy for a Mother's Soul (2001)

2 Let other things come and go as they may, let other people criticize as they will, but never allow anything to obscure the life that is hid with Christ in God. Never be hurried out of the relationship of abiding in Him. It is the one thing that is apt to fluctuate but it ought not to.
Oswald Chambers
My Utmost for His Highest (1935)

3 Keep your life so constant in its contact with God that His surprising power may break out on the right hand and on the left. Always be in a state of expectancy, and see that you leave room for God to come in as He likes.
Oswald Chambers
My Utmost for His Highest (1935)

2 ABILITY (*see also* POWER; STRENGTH; TALENT)

If any man minister, let him do it as of the ability which God giveth.
1 PETER 4:11

1 Praise Him for dreaming up such a fantastically innovative, glorious, gracious plan whereby you and I can face anything this world can throw at us, not due to our ability but to His ability through us.
Bill Gillham
Lifetime Guarantee (1993)

2 You abound in talents, abilities, and skills. Which gifts of yours enrich you and the lives of those around you?
Virginia Ann Froehle
Loving Yourself More (1993)

3 Your gifts and abilities are part of God's purpose for your life. Not using them can lead to frustration, disappointment, and fatigue. So when you've pinpointed your strengths, it's important to look for opportunities and environments where you can use them.
Steve Stephens and Alice Gray
The Worn Out Woman (2004)

3 ABORTION

Thou hast covered me in my mother's womb.
PSALM 139:13

1 Aren't you glad your mother was pro-life?
Bumper Sticker

2 The greatest destroyer of peace is abortion because if a mother can kill her own child, what is left but for me to kill you and you to kill me? There is nothing between.
Mother Teresa
Nobel Peace Prize Lecture (1979)

3 Abortion is a glaring example of the difference worldview makes. Are not all children—Chinese babies or inner-city African American babies—worthy of protection?
Chuck Colson
BreakPoint Commentaries (2009)

4 ABSTINENCE (*see also* DISCIPLINE; SELF-CONTROL; TEMPERANCE)

Abstain from all appearance of evil.
1 THESSALONIANS 5:22

1 The perfect victory is to triumph over ourselves. For he that keepeth himself subject in

such sort that his sensual affections be obedient to reason, and his reason in all things obedient to Me; that person is truly conqueror of himself, and lord of the world.

Thomas à Kempis
The Imitation of Christ (15th century)

5 ABUNDANCE

I am come that they might have life, and that they might have it more abundantly.
JOHN 10:10

1 If you stay connected to Him, if you draw spiritual nourishment from Him, if you allow the power that flows through Him to flow through you, nothing will hold you back from reaching the most abundant life possible.

Bruce Wilkinson
Secrets of the Vine (2001)

2 Nothing in this world can bring you the fullness of life that God wants you to know. You were created by God and for God, and your life cannot be full without Him.

Colin Smith
Ten Keys to Unlock the Christian Life (2005)

3 Christ can be trusted to keep His Word that He will exchange our drab existence for joyous living, abundant life! And while true love, total acceptance and complete security are rare in our frantic world, the biblical evidence that our desires in these areas will be fulfilled in Christ is abundant.

Josh McDowell and Dale Bellis
Evidence for Joy (1984)

6 ACCEPTANCE

Wherefore we labour, that, whether present or absent, we may be accepted of him.
2 CORINTHIANS 5:9

1 Acceptance is an act of the heart. To accept someone is to affirm to them that you think it's a very good thing they are alive.

John Ortberg
Everybody's Normal Till You Get to Know Them (2003)

2 God's opinion is the only one that matters, and His pleasure isn't necessarily measured in book sales, income generated, or pats on the back from others.

Robin Chaddock
Discovering Your Divine Assignment (2005)

7 ACCOUNTABILITY

Submitting yourselves one to another in the fear of God.
EPHESIANS 5:21

1 Choosing to become accountable to others takes real courage.

Tom Eisenman
The Accountable Man (2004)

2 Accountability will not work unless there is real honesty and vulnerability between the men regarding their struggles and shortfalls.

Tom Eisenman
The Accountable Man (2004)

3 A boy who avoids accountability becomes a man who is answerable to no one—a recipe for disaster.

Rick Johnson
That's My Son (2005)

ACHIEVEMENT (*see* SUCCESS)

8 ADDICTION

All things are lawful for me, but I will not be brought under the power of any.
1 CORINTHIANS 6:12

1 God created us with a need to be fed and filled, yet our desires seemingly go unmet. In striving to find fulfillment, our longings

may swing wildly out of balance into realms of addiction. Left unchecked, our misplaced contentment crashes into our empty lives as we attempt to fill up on "treasures" that devastate not only our pocketbooks but also our souls.
Marsha Crockett
Dancing in the Desert (2003)

2   Someone has to come out of denial long enough to consider the possibility that we've all got addictive traits and symptoms.
David Hawkins
Breaking Everyday Addictions (2008)

3   We yearn for a free life.
David Hawkins
Breaking Everyday Addictions (2008)

4   This is our path out of denial and into freedom—through healing, accepting, and understanding the truth.
David Hawkins
Breaking Everyday Addictions (2008)

5   When any small adversity befalleth us, we are too quickly dejected, and turn ourselves to human comforts. If we would endeavor, like men of courage, to stand in the battle, surely we should feel the favorable assistance of God from heaven.
Thomas à Kempis
The Imitation of Christ (15th century)

6   Many seek to flee temptations, and fall more grievously into them. By flight alone we cannot overcome, but by patience and true humility we become stronger than all our enemies.
Thomas à Kempis
The Imitation of Christ (15th century)

7   None of us can afford addictions that kill pain for the moment but complicate our problems in the long run.
Mart DeHaan
"What Trust Looks Like" devotional (2009)

8   When men go into amusements that they cannot afford, they first borrow what they cannot earn, and then they steal what they cannot borrow. They go into embarrassment and then into theft; and when a man gets as far as that he does not stop short of the penitentiary. There is not a prison in the land where there are not victims of unsanctified amusements.
T. DeWitt Talmage
The Wisdom and Wit of T. DeWitt Talmage (19th century)

ADMONITION
(*see* CORRECTION; REBUKE)

9 ADOLESCENCE (*see also* YOUTH)
Let no man despise thy youth;
but be thou an example of the believers.
1 TIMOTHY 4:12

1   God designed us to go through developmental changes at all ages, and adolescence is simply one of them.
David Hawkins
When You're Living (2001)

2   The only bridge from childhood to adulthood is adolescence.
Lynn Anderson
If I Really Believe, Why Do I Have These Doubts? (1992)

3   Adolescence is a time of profound change and profound disappointment. Teenagers are learning their own limitations and the limitations of those around them.
Melissa Trevathan and Sissy Goff
The Back Door to Your Teen's Heart (2002)

4   Adolescents are living in a constant state of ambivalence. They long for intimacy but are afraid of it. They are trying to develop their own identity but still want to cling to their parents. They want freedom but within the confines of safety. They are

continually saying, "Come close, get away." In many ways, teenagers are not that much different from toddlers. They want their independence but are always checking to make sure we are watching.
Melissa Trevathan and Sissy Goff
The Back Door to Your Teen's Heart (2002)

10 ADOPTION

Ye have received the Spirit of adoption, whereby we cry, Abba, Father.
ROMANS 8:15

1 Save heaven itself there is nought more blissful than to enjoy that spirit of adoption.
Charles Spurgeon
"The Fatherhood of God" sermon (1858)

2 If I am adopted, I have become a child; God is no longer my judge, but my Father.
D. L. Moody
"The Eighth Chapter of Romans" sermon (19th century)

3 Adoption is a family idea, conceived in terms of love, and viewing God as father.
J. I. Packer
Knowing God (1993)

4 When society places a human life and its destiny irrevocably in your hands, it must be as certain as it is possible to determine that you will be worthy of this high and sacred trust.
C. W. Scudder
The Family in Christian Perspective (1962)

5 An adopted parent should possess heaping amounts of flexibility and patience.
C.W. Scudder
The Family in Christian Perspective (1962)

6 Adoption is not a substitute for parenthood, for it is parenthood.
C. W. Scudder
The Family in Christian Perspective (1962)

7 Adoption as gospel tells us about our identity, inheritance, and our mission as sons of God.
Russell Moore
Adoption for Life (2009)

8 That's adoption. We're part of a brand-new family, a new tribe, with a new story, a new identity.
Russell Moore
Adoption for Life (2009)

9 Our adoption means that we find a different kind of unity. In Christ, we find Christ.
Russell Moore
Adoption for Life (2009)

10 Because genuine faith is orphan-protecting, a culture of adoption and a culture of evangelism coexist together.
Russell Moore
Adoption for Life (2009)

11 Adoption is truly a labor of the heart!
Jayne Schooler and Thomas Atwood
The Whole Life Adoption Book (2008)

12 An adoptive family of blended cultures is a family because of their love and commitment to one another, just like any other family.
Jayne Schooler and Thomas Atwood
The Whole Life Adoption Book (2008)

13 Creating a positive, nurturing family environment requires a knowledge of what all people, not just adopted children, need.
Jayne Schooler and Thomas Atwood
The Whole Life Adoption Book (2008)

11 ADULTERY

Thou shalt not commit adultery.
EXODUS 20:14

1 There is something destructive about an affair—destroying one's inner integrity, a partner's self-esteem, and the possibility of

intimacy. And it reverberates through future generations, affecting our children and theirs.

J. Allan Petersen
The Myth of Greener Grass (1983)

2 What was once labeled adultery and carried a stigma of guilt and embarrassment now is an affair—a nice-sounding, almost inviting word wrapped in mystery, fascination, and excitement.

J. Allan Petersen
The Myth of the Greener Grass (1983)

3 Adultery is character assassination; it is the breaking of one's solemn promise; it is the treacherous betrayal of one's closest friend. Divorce involves the same kind of betrayal; it may be legal, but it is still nasty.

David Crabtree
Divorce: Is It the Answer? (2009)

ADVENT (*see* CHRISTMAS)

12 ADVERSITY (*see also* AFFLICTIONS; DIFFICULTIES; HARDSHIPS; TESTING; TRIALS; TROUBLES)

In the day of prosperity be joyful, but in the day of adversity consider: God also hath set the one over against the other, to the end that man should find nothing after him.
ECCLESIASTES 7:14

1 It is doubtful whether God can bless a man greatly until He has hurt him deeply.

A. W. Tozer
The Root of the Righteous (1955)

2 Thou hast brought me to the valley of vision, where I live in the depths but see thee in the heights.

Arthur Bennett (editor)
The Valley of Vision: A Collection of Puritan Prayers and Devotions (20th century)

3 Let me find thy light in my darkness, thy life in my death, thy joy in my sorrow, thy grace in my sin, thy riches in my poverty, thy glory in my valley.

Arthur Bennett (editor)
The Valley of Vision: A Collection of Puritan Prayers and Devotions (20th century)

4 Comfort and prosperity have never enriched the world as much as adversity has.

Billy Graham
The Leadership Secrets of Billy Graham (2005)

5 We must never limit God's ability to turn even the worst, most vile experience in our lives into something productive, beneficial and positive.

Charles Stanley
The Blessings of Brokenness (1997)

6 The things which hurt, instruct.

Benjamin Franklin
Poor Richard's Almanac (18th century)

7 The mature response to tough times is to affirm, by faith, that God has a purpose in everything he does or allows, even though that purpose might not be clear.

Jim Cymbala
You Were Made for More (2008)

8 Just as the faith of salvation comes through hearing a message of the gospel, so the faith to trust God in adversity comes through the Word of God alone.

Jerry Bridges
Trusting God: Even When Life Hurts (2008)

9 The reason so many of us struggle so intensely with adversity is that we have yet to adopt God's perspective and priorities.

Charles Stanley
How to Handle Adversity (1989)

10 There is nothing worse than a life filled with adversity from which nothing good ever comes.
Charles Stanley
How to Handle Adversity (1989)

11 Adversity removes the cloak of "what we are supposed to be" to reveal the truth of what we are.
Charles Stanley
How to Handle Adversity (1989)

12 If you are a child of God whose heart's desire is to see God glorified through you, adversity will not put you down for the count. There will be those initial moments of shock and confusion. But the man or woman who has God's perspective on this life and the life to come will always emerge victorious!
Charles Stanley
How to Handle Adversity (1989)

13 We simply can't trust God's power fully until we experience it in the midst of our crisis.
David Wilkerson
"Have Faith in God's Faithfulness" article (2009)

14 Whatever tragedy has befallen you—first, allow God to comfort your heart and then permit Him to use it as a way to point others to Christ.
Rebecca Lusignolo
Devotions for Difficult Days (2006)

15 We all come up against our own version of the Red Sea—Seas of Divorce, Debt, Death, Depression, Guilt, Fear, Loneliness or Hopelessness. And hey, if you're anything like me, you might look around for a boat when God wants to display His glory by parting the Sea instead.
Rebecca Lusignolo
Devotions for Difficult Days (2006)

16 There are certain things in this life that God can reveal to us only in the midst of adversity. There are hidden places deep in our souls He can reach only through our suffering.
Mary Nelson
Grace for Each Hour (2005)

17 Some needs and hurts are so deep they will respond only to a mentor's touch or a pastor's prayer.
George W. Bush
Inaugural Address (2001)

18 If our lives are easy, and if all we ever attempt for God is what we know we can handle, how will we ever experience His omnipotence in our lives?
Anne Graham Lotz
The Vision of His Glory (1996)

19 At the darkest moment in your life, you need to see that God is always in charge. He never loses control of the situation. He is always working behind the scene carrying out His plan.
Michael Youssef
Joseph: Portrait of a Winner (2008)

20 No matter how well we live our Christian life, circumstances will not always turn out the way we want.
Tullian Tchividjian
Do I Know God? (2007)

21 When we are in the midst of bewildering circumstance, that is not the time to make conclusions about what God is like.
Henry and Richard Blackaby
Hearing God's Voice (2002)

22 That which we sow in weakness shall be raised in strength.
Daniel Webster
Speeches and Forensic Arguments (19th century)

23 Anger and bitterness are misplaced responses when you understand that when "the worst thing that could happen" happens, God is still there.
  Stan Guthrie
  The Spiritual Uses of Unemployment (2009)

24 Life can take the legs right out from under our faith.
  Andy Stanley
  It Came from Within! (2001)

25 God has entrusted every single person with a measure of adversity.
  James MacDonald
  Replace a Complaining Attitude (2009)

26 God is not an escapist. . . . He walks us through the storms of life.
  Rich Mendola
  "The Storm Part 2" sermon (2009)

27 Are you in a storm? Well, if not, they will come.
  Rich Mendola
  "The Storm Part 2" sermon (2009)

28 In the midst of a storm, people need to see what real faith looks like.
  Rich Mendola
  "The Storm Part 2" sermon (2009)

29 Adversity—It can drive us to our knees in despair and depression or it can drive us to our knees in humble recognition of our dependence on the Father. It's our choice.
  Rebecca Lusignolo
  Bitter-Sweetness (2009)

30 Everybody has secret pain. Everybody has something that hurts.
  Beth Moore
  "Who Do You Trust?" teaching series (2007)

31 If we are not disposed meekly to bear injuries, we are not fitted to live in the world, for in it we must expect to meet with many injuries from men.
  Jonathan Edwards
  "Charity Disposes Us Meekly to Bear the Injuries Received from Others" sermon (1738)

32 Calamity is the perfect glass wherein we truly see and know ourselves.
  William D'Avenant
  The Dramatic Works of Sir William D'Avenant (17th century)

33 We are not trying to avoid our dilemmas. Rather Jesus Christ is showing us a way to overcome them.
  Merlin Carothers
  Prison to Praise (1970)

34 It is always unpleasant to be spoken against, and forsaken, and lied about, and to stand alone. But there is no help for it. The cup which our Master drank must be drunk by His disciples.
  J. C. Ryle
  Holiness: Its Nature, Hindrances, Difficulties, and Roots (19th century)

35 For this life, being a continual warfare, we must never expect to have rest from our spiritual adversary the devil, or to say, our combat with him is finished, till, with our blessed master, we bow down our heads, and give up the ghost.
  George Whitefield
  Selected Sermons of George Whitefield (18th century)

36 But if the path we tread be rough and lowly, it is that in which our great Exemplar has gone before. Going down into the valley of humiliation we walk in His footsteps.
  John Dawson
  The Saviour in the Workshop (1868)

ADVERSITY

37 Chaos is energy and power, untamed and unformed, but not bad. It can be shaped and channeled, tamed and reinterpreted in ways that bring new creation to life.
Patricia Livingston
This Blessed Mess (2000)

38 Prosperity is the blessing of the Old Testament; adversity is the blessing of the New.
Francis Bacon
Of Adversity (16th century)

39 Times of adversity are always times of opportunity.
Warren Wiersbe
God Isn't in a Hurry (1994)

13 ADVICE (*see also* GUIDANCE)
Ask counsel, we pray thee, of God.
JUDGES 18:5

1 Whose advice are you taking and whose example are you watching?
Anne Graham Lotz
God's Story (1997)

2 I find it amazing that those who sit on the sidelines seem to be so qualified to make decisions for those risking their lives as they play the game.
Bill Wilson
Christianity in the Crosshairs (2005)

3 Relationships take time. When we suggest that high-quality advice can be given under rushed conditions, we undercut what we can offer people—a calm place to carefully explore their situations. Furthermore, we are likely to harm people if, while we are ignorant about many aspects of their lives, we jump in with radical advice and grandiose plans to transform them.
Mary Pipher
Letters to a Young Therapist (2003)

14 AFFIRMATION
Finally, be ye all of one mind, having compassion one of another, love as brethren.
1 PETER 3:8

1 We tend to become what the most important person in our life thinks we will become. Think the best, believe the best, and express the best in others. Your affirmation will not only make you more attractive to them, but you will help play an important part in their personal development.
John Maxwell
Be a People Person (1989)

2 Next to spiritual commitment and physical survival, the greatest need of a human being is to be understood, affirmed, and appreciated.
J. Allan Petersen
Before You Marry (1974)

15 AFFLICTIONS (*see also* ADVERSITY; DIFFICULTIES; HARDSHIPS; TESTING; TRIALS; TROUBLES)
That no man should be moved by these afflictions: for yourselves know that we are appointed thereunto.
1 THESSALONIANS 3:3

1 They who dive in the sea of affliction, bring up rare pearls.
Charles Spurgeon
"The Golden Key of Prayer" sermon (1865)

2 God, who foresaw your tribulation, has specially armed you to go through it, not without pain but without stain.
C. S. Lewis
The Letters of C. S. Lewis (2003)

3 Like a rose whose fragrance is sweetest when its petals are crushed, the fragrance of Christ is made sweeter in our lives by affliction.
Anne Graham Lotz
The Daily Light Journal (2004)

4   Storms can be God's messengers.
Anne Graham Lotz
I Saw the Lord (2006)

5   An affliction rightly borne does us good.
Matthew Henry
Commentary on the Whole Bible (1706)

6   Most of us would have a hard time
saying, "It was good for me to be afflicted."
By definition, affliction is painful to endure.
How could we ever call it good? Yet that is
exactly what the psalmist said about his own
suffering.
Ray Pritchard
The God You Can Trust (2003)

7   Now let us thank the Eternal Power:
convinced that Heaven but tries our virtue by
affliction.
John Brown
Barbarossa (1754)

8   Good when He gives, supremely good;
Nor less when He denies:
Afflictions, from His sovereign hand,
Are blessings in disguise.
Brother Lawrence
The Practice of the Presence of God
(17th century)

9   Have courage then: make a virtue of
necessity: ask of GOD, not deliverance from
your pains, but strength to bear resolutely, for
the love of Him, all that He should please, and
as long as He shall please.
Brother Lawrence
The Practice of the Presence of God
(17th century)

10   No man hath affliction enough that is not
matured and ripened by it, and made fit for
God by that affliction.
John Donne
Devotions Upon Emergent Occasions (1623)

11   Sometimes God gives us a gentle push of
courage; sometimes He mercifully numbs us
so we don't experience the full intensity of our
pain; at other times He carries us when we
cannot take another step on our own.
Bruce Carroll
Sometimes Miracles Hide (1999)

12   The Lord's mercy often rides to the door of
our hearts on the black horse of affliction.
Charles Spurgeon
All of Grace (19th century)

13   Sometimes we question the love of God,
because we have no affliction, and anon because
we have nothing but affliction; as if God were not
the God of the valleys as well as of the mountains.
Thomas Manton
*One Hundred and Ninety Sermons on the
Hundred and Nineteenth Psalm*
(17th century)

14   The dark moments of our life will last only
as long as is necessary for God to accomplish
His purpose in us.
Charles Stanley
30 Life Principles Study Guide (2008)

15   Affliction is the opener of the
understanding.
Elisabeth Elliot
A Path Through Suffering (1990)

16   Do not try to fathom the effect and
purpose of affliction now. Eternity alone will
reveal its grandeur.
Paul Billheimer
Don't Waste Your Sorrows (1977)

AFFLUENCE (*see* MONEY; RICH, THE; WEALTH)

16 AFTERLIFE (*see also* HEAVEN)
*Godliness is profitable unto all things,
having promise of the life that now is,
and of that which is to come.*
1 TIMOTHY 4:8

1   In the end that Face which is the delight or the terror of the universe must be turned upon each of us either with one expression or with the other, either conferring glory inexpressible or inflicting shame that can never be cured or disguised.
    C. S. Lewis
    The Weight of Glory (1949)

17 AGING (*see also* ELDERLY, THE; MIDDLE AGE; OLD AGE)
With us are both the grayheaded and very aged men, much elder than thy father.
JOB 15:10

1   Old! I wish you all felt as young as I do tonight. Why, I am only sixty-two years old! If you meet me ten million years hence, then I will be young.
    D. L. Moody
    "The Eighth Chapter of Romans" sermon (19th century)

2   Don't let the age on your driver's license determine your season in life. Everyone's growing seasons look a bit different.
    Vicki Kuyper
    Be Patient, God Isn't Finished with Me Yet (2003)

3   Many mature adults, because their priorities are different than they were at an earlier age, worry less about little irritations and become less rigid and more accepting of each other.
    Grace Ketterman and Kathy King
    Caring for Your Elderly Parent (2001)

4   The extent to which the second half of your life is significant depends on how you read your story up to this point.
    Bob Buford
    Game Plan (1997)

5   We are persons in transition. There is more of life before us, and we are God's agents to each other in encouragement and development. Even in aging we need not cease to grow in different areas of life.
    Myron and Esther Augsburger
    How to Be a Christ-Shaped Family (1994)

6   Continual involvement with life is a major requirement for successful aging. Getting older is like waterskiing: When you slow down, you go down. So...keep on going!
    George Sweeting
    The Joys of Successful Aging (2002)

7   You are as young as your faith, as old as your doubt; as young as your self-confidence, as old as your fear; as young as your hope, as old as your despair.
    Samuel Ullman
    Youth (19th century)

8   Ambition has been called one of the major ingredients for keeping people from aging.
    William Krutza
    101 Ways to Enrich Your Marriage (1982)

9   It has often been said that the happiest people in retirement are those who touch life at the greatest number of points.
    Ted Engstrom and Norman Rohrer
    Welcome to the Rest of Your Life (1994)

10 Look, my feet hurt some mornings, and my body is less forgiving when I exercise more than I am used to. But I love my life more, and me more. I'm so much juicier. And as that old saying goes, it's not that I think less of myself, but that I think of myself less often. And that feels like heaven to me.
    Anne Lamott
    Plan B: Further Thoughts on Faith (2005)

11 You're either going to end up a bitter old person or you're going to end up a faithful old person.
    Rich Mendola
    "Journey: Simeon and Anna" sermon (2009)

12 If we live aright; the older, the happier.
T. DeWitt Talmage
The Wisdom and Wit of T. DeWitt Talmage
(19th century)

13 Longevity never cures impenitency.
T. DeWitt Talmage
The Wisdom and Wit of T. DeWitt Talmage
(19th century)

14 In spite of the aging process, we can be optimistic because—other things remaining the same—our basic temperament doesn't change in old age. It can however, be improved upon, and we can become more like Christ by living a Spirit-controlled life to His glory.
Peter Mustric
The Joy of Growing Older (1979)

18 AGNOSTICISM (*see also* ATHEISM)
The fool hath said in his heart, There is no God.
PSALM 14:1

1 Even skeptics have faith. They have faith that skepticism is true. Likewise, agnostics have faith that agnosticism is true. There are no neutral positions when it comes to beliefs.
Norman Geisler, Frank Turek, and David Limbaugh
I Don't Have Enough Faith to Be an Atheist (2004)

2 The one who raises the question against God in effect plays God while denying He exists.
Ravi Zacharias
The Undeluded Truth? (2008)

3 Do you not feel at least some theistic force to such a staggering array of complexity? If I were an atheist, this would keep me awake at night.
Paul Copan
"Atheistic Goodness Revisited" article (2007)

4 Is there any specifiable condition (or conditions) under which you might possibly allow for God to be the source of objective moral values? Or have you cordoned off all such possibilities from consideration?
Paul Copan
"Atheistic Goodness Revisited" article (2007)

5 The atmosphere of suspicion that surrounds the questions of skeptics, I think in many cases, is no more than an excuse for them not to take the Bible seriously.
J. I. Packer
J. I. Packer Answers Questions for Today (2001)

19 ALCOHOL
Wine is a mocker, strong drink is raging:
and whosoever is deceived thereby
is not wise.
PROVERBS 20:1

1 No one thinks he will become a slave to alcohol.
Jerry Dunn
God Is for the Alcoholic (1965)

2 O Lord! how long shall Christian people continue to support, by their silence and their ballots, the greatest form of slavery now known in America?
Charles Sheldon
In His Steps (1896)

3 The environment does have a good deal to do with the character.
Charles Sheldon
In His Steps (1896)

20 AMBITION
But rather seek ye the kingdom of God; and all
these things shall be added unto you.
LUKE 12:31

AMBITION

1   What's my goal? What's my ambition? Is it my happiness or my holiness?
    Kay Arthur
    As Silver Refined (1998)

2   Ambition must be tempered by self-control. It isn't somebody else's job to hold your ambition in check.
    Mark Elfstrand
    10 Passions of a Man's Soul (2006)

3   I charge thee, fling away ambition; By that sin fell the angels.
    William Shakespeare
    King Henry VIII (17th century)

4   The way of the dreamer is difficult—but anything less is hardly living at all!
    Bruce Wilkinson
    The Dream Giver (2003)

5   Until you decide to pursue your dream, you are never going to love your life the way you were meant to.
    Bruce Wilkinson
    The Dream Giver (2003)

AMERICA (*see* UNITED STATES)

21 AMUSEMENT
. . .lovers of pleasures more than lovers of God.
2 TIMOTHY 3:4

1   There is an unlawful use of amusement, but the difference between the man Christian and the man un-Christian is that the former masters the world, while in the latter case, the world masters him.
    T. DeWitt Talmage
    The Wisdom and Wit of T. DeWitt Talmage (19th century)

22 ANGELS
For it is written, He shall give his angels charge over thee, to keep thee.
LUKE 4:10

1   Angels minister to us personally. Many accounts in Scripture confirm that we are the subjects of their individual concern.
    Billy Graham
    Angels (1975)

2   We may not always be aware of the presence of angels. We can't always predict how they will appear. But angels have been said to be our neighbors. Often they may be our companions without our being aware of their presence. We know little of their constant ministry.
    Billy Graham
    Angels (1975)

3   God's restoring servants, His heavenly messengers, have encouraged, sustained and lifted the spirits of many flagging saints; and they have changed many hopeless circumstances into bright prospects.
    Billy Graham
    Angels (1975)

4   Angels are watching; they mark your path. They superintend the events of your life and protect the interest of the Lord God, always working to promote His plans and to bring about His highest will for you.
    Billy Graham
    Angels (1975)

5   For fools rush in where angels fear to tread.
    Alexander Pope
    Essay on Criticism (1709)

6   Angels, being the ministers appointed to execute the commands of God, must, of course, be admitted to be his creatures, but to stir up questions concerning the time or order in which they were created bespeaks more perverseness than industry.
    John Calvin
    Institutes of the Christian Religion (16th century)

23 ANGER

*Be ye angry, and sin not: let not the sun
go down upon your wrath.*
EPHESIANS 4:26

1   Angry words are lightly spoken,/Bitterest thoughts are rashly stirred,/Brightest links of life are broken,/By a single angry word.
   Horatio Palmer
   "Angry Words" (1867)

2   Men are not angered by mere misfortune but by misfortune conceived as injury.
   C. S. Lewis
   The Screwtape Letters (1942)

3   The peculiarity of ill temper is that it is the vice of the virtuous. It is often the one blot on an otherwise noble character.
   Henry Drummond
   The Greatest Thing in the World (1891)

4   You know that when we lose our temper it always seems right to us at the time, but later we realize we were wrong.
   R. T. Kendall
   The Parables of Jesus (2004)

5   Allowing anger to seethe on the back burner will lead to a very large lid blowing off a very hot pot.
   Charles Swindoll
   Man to Man (1996)

6   I don't know of anything more frustrating to deal with than anger (it makes me mad!).
   Charles Swindoll
   Man to Man (1996)

7   Destructive anger will be transformed into righteous anger as we grow in hatred of evil and love of good. To be righteously angry, we must be consumed by a holy fear of God.
   Dan Allender and Tremper Longman III
   The Cry of the Soul (1994)

8   When anger wins, love always loses.
   Willard Harley Jr.
   His Needs, Her Needs for Parents (2003)

9   Anger is like a homemade bomb strapped around one's waist. Whoever detonates the bomb becomes a suicide bomber. They not only injure anyone in the near vicinity, but they go up as well. Anger destroys their reputation, devastates friendships and, worst of all amputates their potential.
   Wayne Cordeiro
   The Dream-Releasers (2002)

10 We all get angry, and at times we should. What's important is that we find constructive outlets for that anger, whether it's an electronic sign in the rear window, the letter we never mail, or the golf balls we smash with a vengeance.
   Mort Crim
   Good News for Tough Times (2002)

11 When anger is the rule in a person's life, spirits of anger, hate, malice, resentment, bitterness, jealously, rage, and the like are drawn to them like flies are drawn to honey.
   Eddie and Alice Smith
   Spiritual Housecleaning (2003)

12 Anger is an expression of frustration, fear and hurt, and these feelings turn into anger in order to disguise what we are really feeling. Anger is a form of dishonest emotional expression.
   H. Norman Wright
   The Marriage Checkup (2002)

13 There is no greater anger than when God is silent, and talks not with us, but suffers us to go on in our sinful works, and to do all things according to our own passions and pleasure.
   Martin Luther
   Table Talk (16th century)

14 Better it were that God should be angry with us, than that we be angry with God, for he can soon be at an union with us again, because he is merciful; but when we are angry with him, then the case is not to be helped.
  Martin Luther
  Table Talk (16th century)

15 Speaking in anger is classified as careless because when we speak in anger, we are not thinking of the consequences of our words.
  Rhonda Rizzo Webb
  Words Begin in Our Hearts (2003)

16 The wrath of God is as pure as the holiness of God.
  Stuart Briscoe
  What Works When Life Doesn't (2004)

ANXIETY (*see* WORRY)

24 APATHY
So then because thou art lukewarm, and neither cold nor hot, I will spue thee out of my mouth.
REVELATION 3:16

1 You can be sure that your deepest desires reveal important truths about your spiritual condition.
  Tullian Tchividjian
  Do I Know God? (2007)

2 We tell men what Christ hath done and suffered for their souls, and it scarce moves them.
  Richard Baxter
  The Causes and Danger of Slighting Christ and His Gospel (17th century)

3 The heart is naturally hard, and grows harder by custom in sin, especially by long abuse of mercy, neglect of the means of grace, and resisting the Spirit of Grace.
  Richard Baxter
  The Causes and Danger of Slighting Christ and His Gospel (17th century)

4 Though our eyes, in what direction soever they turn, are forced to behold the works of God, we see how fleeting our attention is, and how quickly pious thoughts, if any arise, vanish away.
  John Calvin
  Institutes of the Christian Religion (16th century)

25 APOSTASY
And they shall turn away their ears from the truth, and shall be turned unto fables.
2 TIMOTHY 4:4

1 A state of apostasy is worse than a state of ignorance.
  Matthew Henry
  Commentary on the Whole Bible (1706)

2 The apostate drops as a wind-fall into the devil's mouth.
  Thomas Watson
  A Body of Practical Divinity (1838)

26 ARGUING
(*see also* CONFLICT; DISPUTING)
How forcible are right words! but what doth your arguing reprove?
JOB 6:25

1 Relationships live or die by their arguments, by the positive or negative way grievances are aired. The difference lies in whether your arguments simply escalate the family tension or lead eventually to feelings of resolution.
  Greg and Michael Smalley
  Communicating with Your Teen (2003)

2 If you want to stop an argument, close your mouth.
  Charles Swindoll
  Hand Me Another Brick (1981)

3 Getting into arguments is part of being human; it's not wrong. Enjoying the arguments, actively seeking them out for the pleasure of arguing, is wrong.
Suzette Haden Elgin
How to Turn the Other Cheek (1997)

4 We hurt most who we love the most. Bad grammar, painful truth.
Andy Stanley
It Came from Within! (2001)

5 Arguing and arguing about arguing takes a tremendous effort and uses up precious time.
Michele Weiner-Davis
Divorce Busting (1992)

6 Don't get a reputation for always being against everything: be for something.
Alex and Brett Harris
Do Hard Things (2008)

27 ARROGANCE (*see also* BOASTING)
Backbiters, haters of God, despiteful, proud, boasters...
ROMANS 1:30

1 Just because God gives us eternal life—just because God befriends us—it doesn't qualify us to tell Him what to do, how to do it and when to do it.
Michael Youssef
Joseph: Portrait of a Winner (2008)

2 What an indecent self-exaltation and arrogance it is, in poor, fallible, dark mortals, to pretend that they can determine and know, who are really sincere and upright before God, and who are not!
Jonathan Edwards
A Treatise Concerning Religious Affections (18th century)

ART (*see* CREATIVITY)

28 ASPIRATIONS
(*see also* GOALS; PLANS)
Be of good courage, and he shall strengthen your heart, all ye that hope in the LORD.
PSALM 31:24

1 Our dreams shape us. When unleashed upon a world, a dream is a powerful thing. If we don't express our dreams, we become frustrated.
Steve and Janie Sjogren
101 Ways to Reinvest Your Life (2003)

2 Resolve to pursue the dream God put in your heart. This involves coming to the place where you declare, "Now is the time. This is the place. I am the person." Perhaps you've thought about your dream for years. At other times it was impossible for you to say yes to your dream. "Later" may not work either. Go for it now while the time is right, while the door is open before you.
Steve and Janie Sjogren
101 Ways to Reinvest Your Life (2003)

3 Millions of men and women have died with their aspirations yet unleashed, their dreams now forever trapped beneath the turf.
Wayne Cordeiro
The Dream Releasers (2002)

4 Dreams are important. Dreams are visions for what we do not yet have, so they give us something to aim for in the future. A dream serves as that bright North Star that beckons and guides us through our days and nights.
Carol Kuykendall
Five-Star Families (2005)

5 Perhaps the deadliest poison of criticism comes when it is aimed toward someone's aspirations.
Les Parrott III
High-Maintenance Relationships (1996)

6   Don't allow your critics to snuff out your dreams. Protect yourself from this folly by associating with people who support and nurture your ideas. Keep your dreams alive.
Les Parrott III
High-Maintenance Relationships (1996)

7   Let us not flutter too high, but remain by the manger and the swaddling clothes of Christ.
Martin Luther
Table Talk (16th century)

8   The primary limitation in life is our low expectations for ourselves and others. When we expect minimum results, that's usually what we get.
John Maxwell
Breakthrough Parenting (1996)

9   Our minds, like the needle in that compass, can focus on a variety of subjects throughout the day. But in the end, they're left alone to settle, they'll focus on the objects of our greatest affection.
Bill Hybels
Laws of the Heart (1985)

10 There is no safer place for your hopes and dreams than in the loving hands of your faithful Father.
Leslie Ludy
Sacred Singleness (2009)

11 Whatever it is you dream about with regularity, you will begin to hope for. Hope stimulates planning. Planning produces behavior designed to move you forward. This brings progress. It all begins with a dream!
Neil Clark Warren
The Triumphant Marriage (1998)

12 If a dream that God has given you dies, it may be that God wants to see what's more important to you. The dream or Him.
Phil Vischer
"When Your Dream Dies" teaching (2008)

13 Dreams are made of strongly desired goals for the future or the fulfillment of an intensely desired purpose. Dreams have to do with satisfying our wishes for something good. Without dreams, we begin to wither up and die emotionally.
Carol Kent
A New Kind of Normal (2007)

14 Opening up our desire in God's presence—even when we're not sure which parts are true and which are false—is humbling, but it gives God a chance to help us sort it all out.
Ruth Haley Barton
Sacred Rhythms (2006)

29 ASSURANCE
These things have I written unto you that believe on the name of the Son of God; that ye may know that ye have eternal life.
1 JOHN 5:13

1   It is not God's design that men should obtain assurance in any other way, than by mortifying corruption, and increasing in grace, and obtaining the lively exercises of it.
Jonathan Edwards
A Treatise Concerning Religious Affections (18th century)

2   When we receive Christ as our Savior, we receive absolute assurance that we will spend eternity with God. That assurance gives us the hope and the courage to endure sorrow, disappointment, and dangerous, difficult times.
Joel Rosenberg
Epicenter (2003)

ASTROLOGY (see OCCULT)

30 ATHEISM (see also AGNOSTICISM)
For the invisible things of him from the creation of the world are clearly seen, being understood by the things that are made, even his eternal power and Godhead; so that they are without excuse.
ROMANS 1:20

1   God Doesn't Believe in Atheists.
Bumper Sticker

2   If there be a God, a man cannot by
obstinate disbelief of him, make him cease to
be, anymore than a man can put out the sun by
winking.
John Tillotson
The Wisdom of Being Religious (1819)

3   For when men live as if there were no
God, it becomes expedient for them that there
should be none: and then they endeavor to
persuade themselves so and will be glad to
find arguments to fortify themselves in this
persuasion.
John Tillotson
The Wisdom of Being Religious (1819)

4   To be disobedient to the commands of
God is a great contempt, but to deny his
Being, and to make sport of his word, and to
endeavour to render it ridiculous by turning
the wise and weighty sayings of that Holy
Book into raillery, is a direct affront to the
God that is above.
John Tillotson
The Wisdom of Being Religious (1819)

5   Having killed God, the atheist is left with
no reason for being, no morality to espouse, no
meaning to life, and no hope beyond the grave.
Ravi Zacharias
The Real Face of Atheism (2004)

6   I Don't Have Enough Faith to Be an
Atheist.
Norman Geisler, Frank Turek,
and David Limbaugh book title (2004)

7   A little philosophy inclineth man's mind
to atheism, but depth in philosophy bringeth
men's minds about to religion.
Francis Bacon
Of Atheism (17th century)

8   The atheist assumes that if one has no
evidence for God's existence, then one is
obligated to believe that God does not exist—
whether or not one has evidence against God's
existence.
Paul Copan
"The Presumptuousness of Atheism"
article (2007)

9   What the atheist fails to see is that atheism
is just as much a claim to know something
("God does not exist") as theism ("God exists").
Paul Copan
"The Presumptuousness of Atheism" article
(2007)

10 To place belief in Santa Claus or mermaids
and belief in God on the same level is
mistaken. The issue is not that we have no
good evidence for these mythical entities;
rather, we have strong evidence that they do
not exist.
Paul Copan
"The Presumptuousness of Atheism" article
(2007)

11 The existence of objective morality
provides further evidence for belief in God.
Paul Copan
"The Presumptuousness of Atheism" article
(2007)

12 If widow-burning or genocide is really
wrong and not just cultural, then it is difficult
to account for this universally binding
morality, with its sense of "oughtness," on
strictly naturalistic terms.
Paul Copan
"The Presumptuousness of Atheism" article
(2007)

13 Satan teaches men first to doubt and then
to deny; he makes them sceptics first, and so
by degrees makes them atheists.
Matthew Henry
Commentary on the Whole Bible (1706)

14 The man who is trying to be an atheist is trying to free himself from the laws of his being. He might as well try to free himself from liability to hunger or thirst.
Charles Hodge
What Is Darwinism? (1874)

15 A godless philosophy produces some people who give up on life and others who try to keep themselves going by filling their nagging emptiness with banal trivialities.
Stuart Briscoe
What Works When Life Doesn't (2004)

31 ATONEMENT
We also joy in God through our Lord Jesus Christ, by whom we have now received the atonement.
ROMANS 5:11

1 God, in abandoning His Son, is treating Jesus as a sinner so that He can treat you and me—who are sinners—as if we were righteous.
C. J. Mahaney
Christ Our Mediator (2004)

2 His blood sets us free from guilt, and we are now free for gratitude-centered service that truly seeks to praise and magnify his glorious grace.
Jerry Bridges and Bob Bevington
The Great Exchange (2007)

3 Justice must be served to a holy God; the payment cannot be simply overlooked.
Jerry Bridges and Bob Bevington
The Great Exchange (2007)

4 Genuine obedience of faith is always evidenced in the obedience of life.
Jerry Bridges and Bob Bevington
The Great Exchange (2007)

5 No man can give a satisfactory reason for the hope that is in him if he is a stranger to the "Blood."
D. L. Moody
Wondrous Love (1876)

6 Why, we should say the beggar had gone mad to be running away from the Prince of Wales with the bag of gold. Sinner, that is your condition. The Prince of Heaven wants to give you eternal life, and you are running away from Him.
D. L. Moody
Wondrous Love (1876)

32 ATTITUDE
(*see also* EMOTIONS; FEELINGS)
Keep thy heart with all diligence; for out of it are the issues of life.
PROVERBS 4:23

1 The very way in which we close a door or lay down a book may be a victory or a defeat, a witness to Christ's keeping or a witness that we are not truly being kept.
Frances Ridley Havergal
Kept for the Master's Use (1879)

2 No matter how daunting the circumstances of your life may be, the greatest battle you wage against failure occurs on the inside, not the outside. How do you fight that battle? You start by cultivating the right attitude.
John Maxwell
Failing Forward (2000)

3 Never allow negative thinking to keep you from God's best.
Joel Osteen
Your Best Life Begins Each Morning (2008)

4 No matter where you find yourself in life, you're in a season of celebration.
Vicki Kuyper
Be Patient; God Isn't Finished with Me Yet (2003)

5 You have the power to decide what your attitude will be.
H. Norman Wright
Communication: Key to Your Marriage (2000)

6   It's not that we don't have problems, that we are never defensive or preoccupied. This is part of life. But with the right attitude, things take their proper place. By being more spiritually sensitive, we are better able to both receive and share God's love.
  Robert Wicks
  Everyday Simplicity (2000)

7   When we are striving to live out a spiritual attitude, our behavior during the entire day is more likely to reflect God's will.
  Robert Wicks
  Everyday Simplicity (2000)

8   Do you envy people who are able to find something positive in every negative experience? Actually, this isn't just some natural ability. It's learned. We can teach ourselves to take life's setbacks, turn them right side up, and recognize their value.
  Mort Crim
  Good News for Tough Times (2002)

9   Perhaps the main reason being optimistic is worthwhile is that it simply feels better.
  Susan Vaughan
  Half Empty, Half Full (2000)

10   Optimists allow themselves to feel sad when they see suffering around them, but can still conceive of finding happiness around the next bend. Pessimists often find themselves worrying in advance about when the next big plunge will come.
  Susan Vaughan
  Half Empty, Half Full (2000)

11   We choose our attitudes.
  James MacDonald
  Replace a Complaining Attitude (2009)

12   No pessimist ever became a great leader.
  Ted Engstrom
  The Making of a Christian Leader (1978)

13   The pessimist sees a difficulty in every opportunity; the optimist sees an opportunity in every difficulty.
  Ted Engstrom
  The Making of a Christian Leader (1978)

14   When your attitude is wrong—the correctness of your opinion is of little importance.
  Steve Campbell
  "What to Say When You Shouldn't Say Anything" sermon (2009)

15   How we think about life's hard knocks can actually determine their impact on us more than the events themselves.
  David Hazard
  Reducing Stress (2002)

16   We may not be able to choose our temperament, our native intelligence, or our physical appearance, but we do get to choose our attitude.
  John Maxwell
  Breakthrough Parenting (1996)

17   I have discovered there is always the possibility of discovery just beyond irritation and annoyance.
  Michael Yaconelli
  Dangerous Wonder (1998)

18   There is nothing to be gained by fighting the inevitable.
  Ted Engstrom and Norman Rohrer
  Welcome to the Rest of Your Life (1994)

19   It is in the attitudes and reactions, in the things that happen too fast for thought, in that flash of anger or of pride that the real person is seen.
  Jim Petersen and Mike Shamy
  The Insider (2003)

20 Life is full of problems. Learn to be happy in spite of them, because they aren't going away. Yes, many will go away, but only to be replaced by other problems. Be happy with the problems you have, because the ones that are coming may be worse. Meanwhile, the feast of life has been prepared just for you. Sit down and enjoy.
Mike Mason
Champagne for the Soul (2003)

21 It doesn't take a major calamity to get us down; a petty annoyance will do nicely. A day, an entire week, indeed a lifetime, can be spoiled by a series of light and momentary troubles. While one believer praises God in the midst of terminal illness, another grumbles because of a runny nose. What's the difference between these two lives? Attitude.
Mike Mason
Champagne for the Soul (2003)

22 Find the gold. Whatever has happened to you in the past, and whatever is happening in your life now, look for the hidden blessing, the lesson to be learned, or the character trait to be forged. Trust that, since God has allowed these experiences, somewhere there is gold for you.
Elizabeth George
Loving God With All Your Mind (1994)

23 Life to the cheerful is as one perpetual banquet, whether he be poor or rich.
F. C. Cook
Bible Commentary: Proverbs-Ezekiel (19th century)

24 Real hardness of heart, in the Bible use of the phrase, means stubbornness of will.
Charles Finney
"The Sinner's Excuses Answered" sermon (19th century)

25 The attitude with which you take a stand says just as much as the stand itself.
Alex and Brett Harris
Do Hard Things (2008)

26 We are committing an unspeakable crime against ourselves when we drown ourselves in negative thinking.
Maxie Dunnam
Let Me Say That Again (1996)

27 We commit suicide on the installment plan when we harbor resentment, cultivate self-pity, nourish shame, and refuse to forgive.
Maxie Dunnam
Let Me Say That Again (1996)

28 We make the decision as to whether the events of our life will serve as stepping stones or stumbling blocks.
Maxie Dunnam
Let Me Say That Again (1996)

29 The reality is that you may not be able to control your environment; you may have to deal with sickness, an alcoholic spouse, a teenager on drugs, a mother who abandoned you, a father who abused you, a spouse who is irresponsible, aging parents, etc. You can however, control your attitude toward your environment. And your attitude will greatly influence your behavior.
Gary Chapman
Desperate Marriages (2008)

33 AUTHORITY

I exhort therefore, that, first of all, supplications, prayers, intercessions, and giving of thanks, be made for all men; For kings, and for all that are in authority.
1 TIMOTHY 2:1–2

1 A properly functioning family also is the birthplace of respect for authority.
Bill Hybels
Laws of the Heart (1985)

2 Life can be lived only in absolute and disciplined submission to its authority.
Charles Colson
Faith on the Line (1994)

AVARICE (*see* GREED)

**34 BACKSLIDING (*See also*
CARNALITY; WORLDLINESS)**
*Return, ye backsliding children,
and I will heal your backslidings.*
JEREMIAH 3:22

1   A high regard for the things of this world
always signals a lowering regard for God.
  Beth Moore
  Daniel (2006)

2   When we turn from the Lord, He does not
fight for us but allows us to be distressed by
those who oppose us.
  Erwin Lutzer
  The Truth About Same-Sex Marriage (2004)

3   To espouse the truth, and then to fall away,
brings an ill report upon the gospel, which will
not go unpunished.
  Thomas Watson
  Body of Practical Divinity (1838)

4   For every one that definitely turns his back
on Christ, there are hundreds who drift from
Him. Life's ocean is full of currents, any one
of which will sweep us past the harbor-mouth
even when we seem nearest to it, and carry us
far out to sea.
  F. B. Meyer
  The Way into the Holiest (1893)

35 BAPTISM (*see also* SACRAMENTS)
*Buried with him in baptism, wherein also ye are
risen with him through the faith of the operation
of God, who hath raised him from the dead.*
COLOSSIANS 2:12

1   Let whatsoever will or can befall me, I will
surely cleave by my sweet Saviour Christ Jesus,
for in him am I baptized; I can neither do nor
know anything but only what he has taught me.
  Martin Luther
  Table Talk (16th century)

2   Most of what we do in worldly life is
geared toward our staying dry, looking good,
not going under. But in baptism, in lakes
and rain and tanks and fonts, you agree to
do something that's a little sloppy because at
the same time it's also holy, and absurd. It's
about surrender, giving in to all those things
we can't control; it's a willingness to let go of
balance and decorum and get drenched.
  Anne Lamott
  Traveling Mercies (1999)

36 BEAUTY
*Deck thyself now with majesty and excellency;
and array thyself with glory and beauty.*
JOB 40:10

1   Beauty is to the spirit what food is to the
flesh.
  Frederick Buechner
  *Beyond Words: Daily Readings in the ABC's
of Faith* (2004)

2   We hunger for beauty because it is a
beautiful God whom we serve.
  Michael Card
  Scribbling in the Sand (2002)

3   Do not allow the daily demands to
interfere with seeing the colors of the day or
the shadows of the night.
  John Cowan
  Small Decencies (1992)

4   The most beautiful kind of woman is the
woman with a meek, gentle, peaceful, calm,
quiet disposition.
  John MacArthur
  How to Win Your Unsaved Spouse (1990)

5   Shape and height, texture and color are
determined by the amazing genes that the Lord
implanted in you as He designed you in the
womb. These were His gifts to you. Be assured

that God likes what He created you to be, in all your physical features. You are beautiful to Him.

Pat Warren
Weighed by the Word (2009)

6 We sell ourselves short if we think that the joy of the Lord can be captured in a cosmetically whitened smile.

Jonathan Wilson-Hartgrove
God's Economy (2009)

7 Be honest about it. Would you take all these pains about your looks if every body was blind?

Charles Finney
Lectures of Revivals of Religion (1835)

8 Beauty brings us into places of healing, as well as into God's presence.

Jane Rubietta
Between Two Gardens (2001)

37 BEHAVIOR

Ye are witnesses, and God also, how holily and justly and unblameably we behaved ourselves among you that believe.
1 THESSALONIANS 2:10

1 Our conduct has a direct influence on how people think about the gospel. The world doesn't judge us by our theology; the world judges us by our behavior.

Carolyn Mahaney
Feminine Appeal (2004)

2 More often people who claim to be Christian pursue the same selfish ambitions, worship the same worthless idols, enjoy the same sinful pleasures, watch the same ungodly entertainments, and grasp for the same greedy possessions as everyone else. There is shockingly little difference between the way that Christians and non-Christians behave.

Richard Phillips, Philip Ryken, and Mark Dever
The Church: One, Holy, Catholic, and Apostolic (2004)

3 Behaviors have consequences.

Henry Cloud and John Townsend
Boundaries (1992)

4 What we know ourselves to be helps us behave the way we're supposed to behave.

Warren Wiersbe
A Gallery of Grace (2002)

5 God has endued the soul of man not only with an understanding to discern, and direct, but also a will to govern, moderate, and over-rule the actions of life.

John Flavel
Pneumatologia (1698)

6 The will, like an absolute sovereign, reigns over the body.

John Flavel
Pneumatologia (1698)

7 Each of us has a story behind our behavior.

Valerie Hess and Marti Watson Garlett
Habits of a Child's Heart (2004)

38 BELIEF

Verily, verily, I say unto you, He that believeth on me hath everlasting life.
JOHN 6:47

1 Staying in the race takes something more substantial than not wanting to quit.

Jennifer Rothschild
Lessons I Learned in the Dark (2002)

2 It's amazing how many people think something doesn't exist because they don't believe in it.

Ray Comfort
What Hollywood Believes (2002)

3 Foundations to be reliable must always be unshakable.

Hannah Whitall Smith
The God of All Comfort (1906)

4   What you continually hear is what you will believe.
> Michelle McKinney Hammond
> *Ending the Search for Mr. Right* (2005)

5   People are generally persuaded by the reasons that themselves have discovered than by those which have come into the mind of others.
> Blaise Pascal
> *Pensées* (17th century)

6   You never know how much you really believe anything until its truth or falsehood becomes a matter of life and death to you.
> C. S. Lewis
> *A Grief Observed* (1961)

7   If all creeds are equally true, then since they are contradictory to one another, they are all equally false, or at least equally uncertain.
> J. Gresham Machen
> *Christianity and Liberalism* (1923)

8   Man lost life by unbelief—by not believing God's word; and we get life back again by believing—by taking God at His word.
> D. L. Moody
> *The Way to God* (1884)

9   The most credulous men in the world are unbelievers.
> Charles Hodge
> *What Is Darwinism?* (1874)

39 BELONGING
Because ye belong to Christ...
MARK 9:41

1   When God dwells at the center of our lives, peace and contentment will belong to us just as surely as we belong to God.
> Beth Moore
> *Prayers and Promises for Women* (2003)

2   Mankind is like a king or queen in exile, and we cannot be happy until we have recovered our true state.
> John and Stasi Eldredge
> *Captivating* (2005)

3   The New Covenant is our guarantee of belonging, of never being forsaken, of never being alone.
> Kay Arthur
> *Our Covenant God* (1999)

4   No one is too messed up for God to use, and no task is too unimportant to matter to God.
> Stephen Arterburn and Jack Felton
> *Toxic Faith* (1991)

5   God accepts us, and that is much more important than being accepted by others. Because God accepts us, we can face rejection by others.
> Stephen Arterburn and Jack Felton
> *Toxic Faith* (1991)

BEREAVEMENT
(*see* GRIEF; SORROW)

40 BETRAYAL
The Son of man is betrayed into the hands of sinners.
MARK 14:41

1   Betrayal by someone you trust is like an earthquake. The very ground beneath you is suddenly unstable.
> Barbara Bartocci
> *From Hurting to Happy* (2002)

41 BIBLE MEMORY
Thy word have I hid in mine heart, that I might not sin against thee.
PSALM 119:11

1   To run God's thoughts through your mind often will make your mind grow like God's mind.
> Henry H. Halley
> *Pocket Bible Handbook* (1948)

2   Memorization is a very valuable tool in the Christian life, and God will use it in a mighty way if we choose to memorize His Word.
  Carole Lewis
  Choosing Change (2001)

42 BIBLE STUDY
Search the scriptures.
JOHN 5:39

1   Nobody would think of mutilating Milton's poems so, taking a few lines out of *Paradise Lost,* and then imagining that he could really get at the heart of the poet's power. So, always look at texts in the connection in which they stand.
  Charles Spurgeon
  "The Unchangeable Christ" sermon (1888)

2   The greatest gift you will ever give your child will be to teach him to develop the habit of purposefully reading, studying, and applying God's Word daily. It will affect every area of his life every day of his life.
  Robin Sampson
  What Your Child Needs to Know When (2000)

3   It is typically human to turn to the Bible for selfish reasons. Instead of seeking simply to know God and His purposes, we approach our Bibles for life application at the expense of adoration and praise.
  Franklin Graham
  All for Jesus (2003)

4   It is not the quantity that is read, but the manner of reading, that yields us profit.
  François Fénelon and Jeanne Guyon
  Spiritual Progress (17th century)

5   Those who read fast, reap no more advantage than a bee would by only skimming over the surface of the flower, instead of waiting to penetrate into it, and extract its sweets. Much reading is rather for scholastic subjects, than divine truths.
  Jeanne Guyon
  Spiritual Progress (17th century)

6   It is proper here to caution beginners against wandering from truth to truth, and from subject to subject; the right way to penetrate every divine truth, to enjoy its full relish, and to imprint it on the heart, is to dwell upon it whilst its savor continues.
  Jeanne Guyon
  Spiritual Progress (17th century)

7   Others must learn how to study His Word for themselves so that they won't be carried about by every wind of doctrine and cunning craftiness of this evil world, which lies in wait to deceive.
  Kay Arthur
  Speak to My Heart, God (1993)

8   I challenge you—dig deep in God's Word and find the nugget of God's glory on every page.
  Tim Walter
  "Filled with God's Grace and Glory" sermon (2009)

9   Believers who don't live with a scheduled diet of God's Word will fail to stay competitive spiritually.
  Tony Evans and Jonathan Evans
  Get in the Game (2006)

10 Bibles laid open, millions of surprises.
  George Herbert
  Sin (17th century)

11 Read the Bible, first and foremost, always, every day, unremittingly and often with a concordance, until the history and prophecy and the wisdom literature of the Old Testament get into our very bones; and until the Gospels and Epistles of the New

Testament become the foundation blocks of our thinking and way of life.

John Higgins
"Ten Commandments for Preachers"
article (1985)

12 Ultimately, the goal of personal Bible study is a transformed life and a deep and abiding relationship with Jesus Christ.

Kay Arthur
How to Study Your Bible (1994)

13 When you know what God says, what He means, and how to put His truths into practice, you will be equipped for every circumstance of life.

Kay Arthur
How to Study Your Bible (1994)

14 Our primary goal—our driving passion—should be to know truth and then adjust our beliefs accordingly.

Kay Arthur
How to Study Your Bible (1994)

15 Prayer is crucial to Bible study.

Kay Arthur
How to Study Your Bible (1994)

16 Be very wary if in your Bible study you find something that no one else has ever seen before. God probably would not blind godly men to truth for almost 2,000 years and suddenly reveal it to you.

Kay Arthur
How to Study Your Bible (1994)

17 Ignorance of Scripture is the mother of error, not of devotion.

Thomas Watson and Samuel Lee
The Bible and the Closet (1842)

18 Many come rashly to the reading of the word, and no wonder if they come without preparation, they go away without profit.

Thomas Watson and Samuel Lee
The Bible and the Closet (1842)

19 Labor to remember what you read. Satan would steal the word out of our mind; not that he intends to make use of it himself, but lest we should make use of it.

Thomas Watson and Samuel Lee
The Bible and the Closet (1842)

20 We should read the Bible as those who listen to the very speech of God.

F. B. Meyer
The Way into the Holiest (1893)

21 If you long to have a deeper relationship with God, then find a quiet spot and a small portion of Scripture and spend time with those words every day for several days.

Valerie Hess and Marti Watson Garlett
Habits of a Child's Heart (2004)

22 We must be on guard against reading what we want into Scripture. We cannot randomly flip through the Bible and declare that whatever page we land on will provide us our answers.

Michael Youssef
"Your Spiritual Instruction Manual" article (2009)

23 Our Bibles aren't meant to sit on our shelves in pristine condition but are meant to be worn down with daily use.

Michael Youssef
"Your Spiritual Instruction Manual" article (2009)

43 BIBLE, THE

For the word of God is quick, and powerful, and sharper than any twoedged sword, piercing even to the dividing asunder of soul and spirit, and of the joints and marrow, and is a discerner of the thoughts and intents of the heart.

HEBREWS 4:12

1   The Bible is a statement, not of theories, but of actual facts. . .things are not true because they are in the Bible, but they are only in the Bible because they are true.
   Hannah Whitall Smith
   God of All Comfort (1906)

2   We believe the Bible to be, not man's account of his effort to find God, but rather an account of God's effort to reveal Himself to man.
   Henry H. Halley
   Pocket Bible Handbook (1948)

3   The Bible is all One Story. The last part of the last book in the Bible reads like the close of the story begun in the first part of the first book.
   Henry H. Halley
   Pocket Bible Handbook (1948)

4   There is no substitute for the Bible.
   Henry H. Halley
   Pocket Bible Handbook (1948)

5   The Bible must be the most popular yet least-read book in the world! . . .And yet it's the greatest story ever told, the ultimate love story, the biography of God himself.
   John Pritchard
   The 100-Minute Bible (2006)

6   God doesn't at all mind proving His own people wrong to prove His Word right.
   Beth Moore
   Believing God (2004)

7   Blessed Bible! thou art all truth.
   Charles Spurgeon
   "The Bible" sermon (1855)

8   Is there anything more powerful than the sword of the Spirit? That has not pierced the man's heart; is there anything else which will do it?
   Charles Spurgeon
   "Final Perseverance" sermon (1856)

9   Christianity does not teach that only the Bible contains truth. It only affirms that the Bible is true and that everything that contradicts it is false, since contradictions cannot both be true.
   Norman Geisler
   Who Made God? (2003)

10   People who say the Bible isn't relevant today obviously don't know the Author.
   Stormie Omartian
   Just Enough Light for the Step I'm On (1999)

11   For the Christian, the speed of sound (the Word that we hear) is in a sense greater than the speed of light (the things we can actually see).
   Mark Dever
   Nine Marks of a Healthy Church (2004)

12   Faith grows by reading and meditating upon the Word of God.
   E. M. Bounds
   The Necessity of Prayer (19th century)

13   From the first word of Genesis to the last word of Revelation, God's word is true and trustworthy. All we need do is obey the words of Jesus and abide in that Word and we'll have an answer for any lie or temptation Satan throws our way.
   Tony Evans
   God Cannot Be Trusted (And Five Other Lies of Satan) (2005)

14   If a book has errors, it is not the Word of God. If a book is the Word of God, it does not have errors. We cannot have a book that is both the Word of God and errant.
   R. C. Sproul
   One Holy Passion (1987)

15   Surely, it is possible to think of a book that is partly errant and partly the Word of God. But I do not think the Bible is that sort of book.
   R. C. Sproul
   One Holy Passion (1987)

16 The Bible is God's inspired Word—not a mere collection of various writers' opinions, ideas, philosophies, or "inspired" thoughts.
John MacArthur
Nothing But the Truth (1999)

17 If the Bible is perfect and without error, it follows logically that we must present it as the most authoritative book in the world—the one document that contains the last word on truth.
John MacArthur
Nothing But the Truth (1999)

18 All the infinities of God and the eternal world dwell in the Word as the seed of eternal life. And as the full-grown oak is so mysteriously greater than the acorn from which it spring, so God's words are but seeds from which God's mighty wonders of grace can grow up.
Andrew Murray
Prayers' Inner Chamber (19th century)

19 We are defenders of the ultimate truth. If we believe God is who He says He is, then His words are true. They are the truth, not some here-today, gone-tomorrow fad of thought. And that's exactly why God asks us to be defenders of His Word, the eternal truth.
Alex McFarland
The 10 Most Common Objections to Christianity (2007)

20 His words are truth—not lies, like the enemy's. They're the daily bread which nourishes our soul so we can confront and manage each day and all that He allows that day to bring.
Kay Arthur
Speak to My Heart, God (1993)

21 We have to take the Word of God just as it is; and if we are going to take it, we have no authority to take out just what we like, what we think is appropriate, and let dark reason be our guide.
D. L. Moody
Secret Power (1881)

22 When you stand before the Word of God, you are not merely encountering a concept; you are standing face-to-face with God. Your response to him will be radically different from standing before a book. The moment you choose to read his Word, you choose to come into his presence, face-to-face.
Henry and Tom Blackaby
The Man God Uses (1999)

23 Whatever your particular problem (or problems), the Bible does have the answer for you. There is hope.
Jerry Bridges
The Pursuit of Holiness (1996)

24 In the word of God there is sweet and wholesome nourishment, milk for babies, honey for those that are grown up.
Matthew Henry
Commentary on the Whole Bible (1706)

25 The Bible does not give us a road map for life, but it does give us a compass.
Gordon S. Jackson
Destination Unknown (2004)

26 There is a supernatural component to the Bible that elevates it far above the millions of other books written and published through the centuries.
Mike Macintosh
Falling in Love with the Bible (2005)

27 We may read other books that are exciting or insightful or helpful—but only the Bible is the Holy Spirit–inspired, life-giving, joy-producing revelation from heaven.
Mike Macintosh
Falling in Love with the Bible (2005)

28 The more you read the Bible, the more you understand yourself, the world you live in, and the One who made both.
Mike Macintosh
Falling in Love with the Bible (2005)

29 The Bible is a book of faith, and a book of doctrine, and a book of morals, and a book of religion, of especial revelation from God.
Daniel Webster
Speech at Completion of Bunker Hill Monument (1843)

30 The English Bible—a book which if everything else in our language should perish, would alone suffice to show the whole extent of its beauty and power.
Thomas Babington
On John Dryden (1828)

31 In teaching me the way to live/It taught me how to die.
George Pope Morris
My Mother's Bible (19th century)

32 If anyone can convince me that what I've written contradicts Scripture, I will "be the first to seize my writings and commit them to the flames," but if I'm not convinced, it would be wrong for me as a Christian to recant beliefs that are biblical.
Martin Luther
Address to the Diet at Worms (1521)

33 We must compare the words of Christ in Scripture to the teachings of any man, and if the man contradicts Christ he understands nothing.
Jeff Baldwin
Thinking Biblically (2005)

34 The standard for truth is not the majority, or an elite consensus—it is the Word of God, which may be plainly understood.
Jeff Baldwin
Thinking Biblically (2005)

35 If I am not convinced by proof from Holy Scripture, or by cogent reasons, if I am not satisfied by the very text I have cited, and if my judgment is not in this way brought into subjection to God's Word, I neither can nor will retract anything.
Martin Luther
Address to the Diet of Worms (1521)

36 The Word of God is the absolute authority in the life of a Christian.
Dutch Sheets
Watchman Prayer (2000)

37 The power of the word is not in people's ability to summarize the message they've heard. Rather it is the power of God's word piercing the soul.
R. C. Sproul
Saved from What? (2002)

38 The Bible is not a difficult book to understand. It was written by men of common sense and by the application of common sense to its teachings you will understand most of it, if not all of it.
Billy Sunday
The Best of Billy Sunday (1965)

39 The Bible is the means God has chosen to reach out in human language, reveal the essence of His rational heart, and elate the Good News of His redemptive plan.
Josh McDowell and Bob Hostetler
Beyond Belief to Conviction (2002)

40 The Scripture passages remind me that God loves me very much and has a plan for me.
Susan McCarthy Peabody
Alphabet Soup for Christian Living (2007)

41 Infinite potentates have raged against this book, and sought to destroy and uproot it—King Alexander the Great, the princes of Egypt and of Babylon, the monarchs of Persia,

of Greece, and of Rome, the emperors Julius and Augustus—but nothing prevailed; they are all gone and vanished, while the book remains.
Martin Luther
Table Talk (16th century)

42 The Holy Scripture is the highest and best of books, abounding in comfort under all afflictions and trials.
Martin Luther
Table Talk (16th century)

43 We ought not to criticize, explain, or judge the Scriptures by our mere reason, but diligently, with prayer, meditate thereon, and seek their meaning.
Martin Luther
Table Talk (16th century)

44 Let us not lose the Bible, but with diligence, in fear and invocation of God, read and preach it.
Martin Luther
Table Talk (16th century)

45 God has given us His Word to help us make decisions for daily living. The Scriptures are immensely practical, answering many of the questions that haunt us about how we should conduct our lives.
David Hawkins
When Life Makes You Nervous (2001)

46 The Bible warns that faith without works is dead. And dead faith, like road kill, stinks. It's not much to look at either. The meaningful life is a life of action.
Todd Hafer and Jeff Hafer
Wake Up and Smell the Pizza (2005)

47 The Bible is the book that makes fools of the wise of this world; it is only understood by the plain and simple hearted.
Martin Luther
Table Talk (16th century)

48 Esteem this book as the precious fountain that can never be exhausted.
Martin Luther
Table Talk (16th century)

49 In it thou findest the swaddling-clothes and the manger whither the angels directed the poor, simple shepherds; they seem poor and mean, but dear and precious is the treasure that lies therein.
Martin Luther
Table Talk (16th century)

50 The Holy Scripture of itself is certain and true; God grant me grace to catch hold of its just use.
Martin Luther
Table Talk (16th century)

51 The Bible is full of examples of people who dreamed big, and God blessed them.
Tracie Peterson
The Eyes of the Heart (2002)

52 Here is knowledge enough for me. Let me be *homo unius libri* [A man of one book].
John Wesley
Sermons on Several Occasions (18th century)

53 The Bible really doesn't care if we're offended when we read it.
Thor Ramsey
A Comedian's Guide to Theology (2008)

54 If I had no other reason for believing this book called the Bible, I would believe it for this reason: it is the only book I know of that tells me the plain, unvarnished truth about myself—the only one.
Martyn Lloyd-Jones
Compelling Christianity (20th century)

55 The Bible presents true truth, truth that is unchanging, truth that fits in with what exists, truth that answers the questions of life.
Edith Schaeffer
Common Sense Christian Living (1983)

56 The word is called "an hammer." Every blow of the hammer is to fasten the nails of the building; the preacher's words are but to fasten you the more to Christ.
Thomas Watson
A Body of Practical Divinity (1838)

57 They who slight the word written, slight God himself, whose stamp it bears.
Thomas Watson and Samuel Lee
The Bible and the Closet (1842)

58 The Scripture prescribes excellent recipes, but sin lived in, poisons all.
Thomas Watson and Samuel Lee
The Bible and the Closet (1842)

59 The Scripture is the library of the Holy Ghost; it is a code of divine knowledge, an exact model, and platform of religion.
Thomas Watson and Samuel Lee
The Bible and the Closet (1842)

60 The Scripture is the breeder and feeder of grace.
Thomas Watson and Samuel Lee
The Bible and the Closet (1842)

61 The world is full of religious books; but the man who has fed his religious life upon the Bible will tell in a moment the difference between them and the Scriptures of the Old and New Testaments.
F. B. Meyer
The Way into the Holiest (1893)

62 The Bible has been one of the greatest motivators of those who believe its content.
Elmer Towns
Core Christianity (2007)

63 God did not give us His Word to satisfy our curiosity but to change our lives.
Charles Swindoll
"Our Library of Living Truth" sermon (1978)

64 The Bible tells us everything we need to know about life.
Kay Arthur
God, Are You There? (1994)

65 Scripture does not tell us about the enemy in order for us to live anxious lives; we are told so we can prepare ourselves to win great victories.
Chip Ingram
The Invisible War (2006)

66 As Christians, we have the responsibility to seek out the truth and know it for ourselves. How often do we misinterpret and misquote Scripture because we fail to go to the Bible and understand its message?
Thelma Wells and Traci Mullins
Extravagant Grace (2000)

67 Approach God's Word like the divine, supernatural, power-packed text it is.
Beth Moore
Voices of the Faithful (2005)

68 Satan knows that the only offensive weapon we have to raise against him is the sword of the Spirit, the Word of God. He can't keep it from being powerful, but if he can tempt us to think little of it, he knows it will never be powerful in us.
Beth Moore
Voices of the Faithful (2005)

69 If the Bible be excluded, upon the most diligent and extensive search we have been able to make, no sufficient reason has been found, or can be given, for a hope of a good adequate to the capacity and desires of man.
Samuel Hopkins
"The Reason of the Hope of a Christian" sermon (1803)

70 Never to attempt to search after God anywhere but in his sacred word, and never to

speak or think of him farther than we have it for our guide. . .
John Calvin
Institutes of the Christian Religion
(16th century)

71 In reading the Scriptures we should constantly direct our inquiries and meditations to those things which tend to edification, not indulge in curiosity, or in studying things of no use.
John Calvin
Institutes of the Christian Religion (16th century)

72 Though every statement in the Scripture cannot be regarded as absolutely essential to salvation, yet everything there is essential to some other wise and important end, else it would not find a place in the good Word of God.
Thomas Witherow
The Apostolic Church: What Is It? (1990)

73 The Bible is essentially a Book in which God asks man many questions, and man in turn asks God many questions.
Tim Hansel
Eating Problems for Breakfast (1988)

44 BIGOTRY

Thou shalt neither vex a stranger, nor oppress him: for ye were strangers in the land of Egypt.
EXODUS 22:21

1 Christ knows how to reshape a prejudiced heart.
Charles Ware
Prejudice and the People of God (2001)

2 Just as prejudice blinds unbelievers to the only way of eternal life, it blinds believers to the preciousness of every soul.
Charles Ware
Prejudice and the People of God (2001)

3 Presumption and bigotry are incompatible with any serious concern for truth and with worship of the God of truth.
John Stott
Between Two Worlds:
The Challenge of Preaching Today (1982)

4 When it comes to racial and cultural and ideological boundaries, Jesus just doesn't get it. And His perspective is what matters. No dividing lines we draw can be significant after Christ shed his priceless blood for every human being on the planet.
Stephen Mosley
Secrets of Jesus' Touch (2003)

BIRTH (*see* NEW BIRTH)

45 BITTERNESS

Looking diligently lest any man fail of the grace of God; lest any root of bitterness springing up trouble you.
HEBREWS 12:15

1 There is only one cure for the cancer of bitterness. That is to forgive the perceived offender once and for all, with God's help.
James Dobson
When God Doesn't Make Sense (1993)

2 The heaviest thing to carry is a grudge.
L. James Harvey
701 More Sentence Sermons (2002)

3 It is wasted energy to stew over a wrong that has been made right.
Steve Campbell
"Jonah—Is This the End or Just the Beginning?" sermon (2009)

4 Time and anger are intertwined. The longer an offense goes unresolved, the more deep-seated it becomes. Then the heart becomes a hotbed for a root of bitterness.
Lisa Bevere
Be Angry But Don't Blow It! (2000)

5 Bitterness is like a boomerang. You send it soaring out toward the person or situation that has wronged you, and it comes back. You're the one who is hurt.

Barbara Bartocci
From Hurting to Happy (2002)

6 Bitterness cannot be contained. It always spreads.

Andy Stanley
Louder Than Words (2004)

7 Relinquishing bitterness is an open invitation for the Holy Spirit to give you His peace, His joy, and the knowledge of His will.

R. T. Kendall
Total Forgiveness (2002)

8 Bitterness is paralysis.
David Augsburger
70 x 7: The Freedom of Forgiveness (1970)

46 BLESSINGS

Blessed be the God and Father of our Lord Jesus Christ, who hath blessed us with all spiritual blessings in heavenly places in Christ.
EPHESIANS 1:3

1 He has made Christ heir of all things, and he has made you joint-heir with him; and hence he has given you everything.

Charles Spurgeon
"God in the Covenant" sermon (1856)

2 Scripture again and again points to God the Father as the headwaters of a constant stream of blessing for us.

Bill Gothard
The Power of Spoken Blessings (2004)

3 When we center our lives on Christ and allow His Spirit to control us, we find ourselves wanting to do all we can for those we love most—to give them the highest and best gifts we can. And nothing is higher and better than God's blessing.

Bill Gothard
The Power of Spoken Blessings (2004)

4 A bell isn't a bell until you ring it. A blessing isn't a blessing until you say it.

Bill Glass
Champions for Life (2005)

5 Seek the welfare of others. Find out how you can be a blessing. Pray for the city you live in right now and its people, for its welfare and your welfare. This is one of the fundamental keys. As you become a blessing, you set yourself up to be blessed.

Tony Evans
God Is Up to Something Great (2002)

6 God's blessings are dispersed according to the riches of his grace, not according to the depth of our faith.

Max Lucado
A Gentle Thunder (1995)

7 God doesn't bless us so that we'll know He's faithful—we trust in His faithfulness and then discover His blessings.

Karon Phillips Goodman
You Still Here, Lord? (2004)

8 No matter where we are, we can experience God's blessings to the extent that his hand of power is with us.

Jim Cymbala and Stephen Sorenson
The Church God Blesses (2002)

9 God wants you to enjoy His blessings— and to use them to make a difference in the world around you.

Bruce Wilkinson
Beyond Jabez (2005)

10 Learning and planning how to transmit blessing to our children involves as real a

decision as arranging their inheritance of material things via a will.
  Jack Hayford
  Blessing Your Children (2002)

11 When God at first made man
Having a glass of blessings standing by,
"Let us," said He, "pour on him all we can:
Let the world's riches, which dispersed lie,
Contract into a span."
  George Herbert
  The Pulley (17th century)

12 To be "blessed" is to be full of joy and hope in relationship with God. Blessed are those who have directed their attention from earthly rewards, who have gone deeper than superficial thinking.
  Susan McCarthy Peabody
  Alphabet Soup for Christian Living (2007)

13 We cannot have too much in so good and faithful a Friend, who will never fail us in this world nor in the next.
  Brother Lawrence
  The Practice of the Presence of God
  (17th century)

14 Let him [God], for ever so short a while, keep back the sun, so that it shine not, or lock up air, water, or fire, ah! how willingly would we give all our wealth to have the use of these creatures again.
  Martin Luther
  Table Talk (16th century)

15 Our blessings include life and health, family and friends, freedom and possessions... the gifts we receive from God are multiplied when we share them.
  Beth Moore
  Prayers and Promises for Women (2003)

16 Spiritual comforts which have always God's stamp upon them, are his gold, and temporal comforts, when they have his stamp upon them, are his silver, but comforts of our own coining, are counterfeit, are copper.
  John Donne
  "Sermon Preached at Lincoln's Inn"
  (17th century)

17 People who truly desire God's blessing must resist the devil and his schemes. That means before we have a right to expect God to bless us, we must turn away from the evil that hinders that blessing.
  John MacArthur
  Can God Bless America? (2002)

18 God blesses only one thing: saving faith in His Son, the Lord Jesus Christ.
  John MacArthur
  Can God Bless America? (2002)

47 BLINDNESS, SPIRITUAL

In whom the god of this world hath blinded the minds of them which believe not, lest the light of the glorious gospel of Christ, who is the image of God, should shine unto them.
2 CORINTHIANS 4:4

1 The same world that rejected the true Christ and hung Him on a cross is ripe for the rise of the Antichrist.
  Mark Hitchcock
  Iran—The Coming Crisis (2006)

2 The world that rejected the Light of the World will gladly embrace the Prince of Darkness.
  Mark Hitchcock
  Iran—The Coming Crisis (2006)

3 The world that couldn't tolerate the presence of the Holy One will welcome the Man of Sin.
  Mark Hitchcock
  Iran—The Coming Crisis (2006)

4   The unrenewed part of mankind is rambling through the world like so many blind men, who will neither take a guide, nor can guide themselves.

Thomas Boston
Human Nature in Its Fourfold State (1830)

48 BOASTING (*see also* ARROGANCE)

Where is boasting then? It is excluded.
ROMANS 3:27

1   If our hearts are full of our own wretched "I ams" we will have no ears to hear His glorious, soul-satisfying "I am."

Hannah Whitall Smith
God of All Comfort (1906)

2   What do we have more to boast about than the cross of Christ, by which God has satisfied his love and his justice, his mercy and his holiness, and displayed it to all the world as he saves all who trust in him?

Mark Dever
Twelve Challenges Churches Face (2008)

3   If we are not careful, wealth, wisdom, and strength quickly become grounds for boasting.

Alistair Begg
Pathway to Freedom (2003)

4   The ones who need to boast of personal accomplishments, such as impressive talk about academic degrees, about their latest achievements, trying to get recognition and appreciation in public, may really be telling us that they never felt that their competence was acknowledged as a child.

Gordon MacDonald
There's No Place Like Home (1990)

5   God has never heard anything so ludicrous as the empty boastings of. . .human beings who are rebelling against Him.

Stuart Briscoe
What Works When Life Doesn't (2004)

6   The great misfortune of the modern English is not at all that they are more boastful than other people (they are not); it is that they are boastful about those particular things which nobody can boast of without losing them.

G. K. Chesterton
Heretics (1905)

49 BODY OF CHRIST (*see also* CHURCH)

Now ye are the body of Christ.
1 CORINTHIANS 12:27

1   The Christian does not go to the temple to worship. The Christian takes the temple with him or her. Jesus lifts us beyond the building and pays the human body the highest compliment by making it His dwelling place, the place where He meets with us.

Ravi Zacharias
Jesus Among Other Gods (2000)

50 BOLDNESS

According to the eternal purpose which he purposed in Christ Jesus our Lord: In whom we have boldness and access with confidence by the faith of him.
EPHESIANS 3:11–12

1   Stand up to your obstacles and do something about them. You will find that they haven't half the strength you think they have.

Norman Vincent Peale
The Power of Positive Thinking (1952)

2   External confidence does not always indicate internal confidence.

Jerry White
Dangers Men Face (1997)

BONDAGE (*see* SLAVERY)

51 BORN AGAIN (see also CONVERSION; NEW BIRTH; REDEMPTION; REGENERATION; SALVATION)

Jesus answered and said unto him, Verily, verily, I say unto thee, Except a man be born again, he cannot see the kingdom of God.
JOHN 3:3

1   I strove, indeed, but strove in vain;
"The sinner must be born again"
Samson Occom
"Awaked by Sinai's Awful Sound" hymn
(1760)

2   When you come to Christ, you do not come to give, you come to receive. You do not come to try your best, you come to trust. You do not come just to be helped, but to be rescued. You do not come to be made better (although that does happen), you come to be made alive!
Erwin Lutzer
How You Can Be Sure That You Will Spend Eternity with God (1996)

3   No matter who you are or what your life has been like so far, the rest of your life's journey can be different. With God's help you can begin again.
Billy Graham
The Journey (2006)

4   Seest thou the necessity of that inward change, that spiritual birth, that life from the dead, that holiness? And art thou thoroughly convinced, that without it no man shall see the Lord?
John Wesley
"Awake, Thou That Sleepest" sermon (1743)

5   Justifying faith implies, not only a divine evidence or conviction that "God was in Christ reconciling the world unto himself," but a sure trust and confidence that Christ died for my sins, that he loved me, and gave himself for me.
John Wesley
"Justification by Faith" sermon
(18th century)

6   Hear this, and be astonished: He can create you a second time; He can cause you to be born again. This is a miracle of grace, but the Holy Ghost will perform it.
Charles Spurgeon
All of Grace (19th century)

7   Regret for a sinful past will remain until we truly believe that for us in Christ that sinful past no longer exists.
A. W. Tozer
That Incredible Christian (1960s)

8   Heaven is filled with a company of those who have been TWICE BORN.
D. L. Moody
The Way to God (1884)

BORROWING (see DEBT)

52 BROKENNESS

The sacrifices of God are a broken spirit: a broken and a contrite heart, O God, thou wilt not despise.
PSALM 51:17

1   God wants you to know that when everything else is gone, that makes more room for Him, and every time there is more room for Him, you are blessed.
Angela Thomas
A Beautiful Offering (2004)

2   What is true brokenness? Someone has said that brokenness, like a fragrance, is easier to detect than to define.
Nancy Leigh DeMoss
Brokenness: The Heart God Revives (2002)

3 Brokenness is not a feeling or an emotion. Rather, it requires a choice, an act of the will.
Nancy Leigh DeMoss
Brokenness: The Heart God Revives (2002)

4 Brokenness is the shattering of my self-will—the absolute surrender of my will to the will of God. It is saying "Yes, Lord!"—no resistance, no chaffing, no stubbornness—simply submitting myself to His direction and will in my life.
Nancy Leigh DeMoss
Brokenness: The Heart God Revives (2002)

5 Brokenness causes us to persevere in prayer.
Tim Walter
"Farthest Horizon—God's Unchanging Character" sermon (2009)

6 Brokenness is never an easy experience.
Michael Youssef
"A Prayer of Brokenness" article (2009)

7 Brokenness is God's requirement for maximum usefulness.
Charles Stanley
30 Life Principles Study Guide (2008)

8 There is just one basic dealing which can enable man to be useful before God: brokenness.
Watchman Nee
The Release of the Spirit (1965)

9 Stubbornness and self-love give way to beauty in one who has been broken by God.
Watchman Nee
The Release of the Spirit (1965)

10 If there is a cry coming up from a heart broken on account of sin, God will hear that cry.
D. L. Moody
Heaven (1881)

11 Somebody said that realizing we are broken is the beginning of healing.
Donald Miller
To Own a Dragon (2006)

12 Some of us would never have looked up had we not hit bottom.
Beth Moore
Breaking Free (1999)

BURDENS (*see* CARES)

53 BUSINESS

Seest thou a man diligent in his business? he shall stand before kings; he shall not stand before mean men.
PROVERBS 22:29

1 Our only business is to love and delight ourselves in God.
Brother Lawrence
The Practice of the Presence of God (17th century)

2 Let us thus think often that our only business in this life is to please God, that perhaps all besides is but folly and vanity.
Brother Lawrence
The Practice of the Presence of God (17th century)

3 It is a grand thing to have a man with whom God is, to entrust one's business to.
Andrew Murray
Master's Indwelling (1895)

54 BUSYNESS (*see also* STRESS)

And Jesus answered and said unto her, Martha, Martha, thou art careful and troubled about many things: But one thing is needful: and Mary hath chosen that good part.
LUKE 10:41–42

1 There is no necessary correlation between how busy you are and how productive you are. Being busy isn't the same as being productive.
Andy Stanley
The Next Generation Leader (2003)

2 Those who have stations of importance to fill, have generally so many indispensable duties to perform, that without the greatest care in the management of their time, none will be left to be alone with God.
François Fénelon and Jeanne Guyon
Spiritual Progress (17th century)

3 Don't get distracted by the busyness. Instead of dreading all those things you have to do, consider that those activities are part of what you are doing for the people you love.
Bruce Bickel and Stan Jantz
Simple Matters (2001)

4 Silence and solitude are not instant cures to busyness. They are lifetime commitments worked out in the real world of schedules and flawed human beings.
Michael Yaconelli
Dangerous Wonder (1998)

5 The restless, high-pressure hurry in which men live endangers the very foundations of personal religion.
J. C. Ryle
The Upper Room (19th century)

6 Cloaked by overactivity, a typical day in the life of many of us is marked with avoidance and escape.
Phileena Heuertz
Pilgrimage of a Soul (2010)

55 CALLING

*Who hath saved us, and called us
with an holy calling...*
2 TIMOTHY 1:9

1 The place God calls you to is the place where your deep gladness and the world's deep hunger meet.
Frederick Buechner
Listening to Your Life (1992)

2 Our call is to a holy confidence and humble dependence: We are to walk through life with our heads high, knowing it is Jesus who loves us and qualifies us for His purposes.
Susie Larson
Alone in Marriage (2007)

3 Lord, thou hast called me forth, I turn and call on thee.
George MacDonald
Diary of an Old Soul (1880)

4 All Christians are called to develop God-given talents, to make the most of their lives, to develop to the fullest their God-given powers and capacities.
Henry Blackaby
Spiritual Leadership (2001)

5 In a world that sees little value in Jesus, your calling, along with the calling of your fellow believers, is to declare His praise. This task—this grand purpose—cannot be delegated. Believers are the only people who can do on earth what the angels do in heaven.
Colin Smith
Ten Keys to Unlock the Christian Faith (2005)

6 If you want to satisfy your calling, follow the desires of your heart as God gives opportunity and directs your spirit. The Holy Spirit is the Person of God who gives you internal guidance. The closer you draw to God, the closer He gets to you through the Holy Spirit. That's how you validate your ambitions.
Mark Elfstrand
10 Passions of a Man's Soul (2006)

7 Let's rise to the occasion and embrace the incredible invitation to be co-laborers with God...to be carriers of His awesome Holy Spirit and ambassadors for His great kingdom. Let's represent Him. Awaken us to our destiny, Lord.
  Dutch Sheets
  Intercessory Prayer (1996)

8 The call of the Christian is to do as Jesus did, obeying the will of God no matter the cost and no matter the loss, being mindful of the reward and gain to come.
  Brent Barnett
  "The Man Who Went Against the Grain" article (2009)

9 Our main calling is to live in fellowship with Christ and to labor with him in extending his kingdom.
  Jim Cymbala and Stephen Sorenson
  The Church God Blesses (2002)

10 Do you feel inadequate for the tasks to which God has called you? God expects great things of us, but He rarely equips us in the ways we would choose.
  Ginger Garrett
  Couples Who Long for Children (2003)

11 There are people whose lives are waiting to be affected by what God has placed within you. So evaluate yourself. Define and refine your gifts, talents, and strengths. Choose today to look for opportunities to exercise your unique, God-endowed, God-ordained gifts and calling.
  John Mason
  An Enemy Called Average (2000)

12 There is no higher calling or privilege in life than to know Him and make Him known to others.
  Bill Bright and John Damoose
  Red Sky in the Morning (1998)

13 This is the work which I know God has called me to; and sure I am that His blessing attends it.
  John Wesley
  The Journal of John Wesley (18th century)

14 There is no man living who can do the work God has for me to do. No one can do it but myself.
  D. L. Moody
  The Faithful Saying (1877)

15 I've been writing about faith in one way or another for a long time. Now it's time to start living it.
  Stan Guthrie
  The Spiritual Uses of Unemployment (2009)

16 We cannot escape it—in Christian service we are called to excellence.
  Ted Engstrom
  The Making of a Christian Leader (1978)

17 Has God ever called you to do something you think is bigger than who you are?
  Dave Lusignolo
  "The Call to Service" sermon (2009)

18 God wants us to be ourselves so that we can fulfill the call He has placed on our lives.
  Joyce Meyer
  Do It Afraid! (1996)

CALVARY (*see* CROSS, THE)

56 CARES

Take heed to yourselves, lest at any time your hearts be overcharged with surfeiting, and drunkenness, and cares of this life...
LUKE 21:34

1 If you feel that the weight of your circumstances is too heavy to bear, maybe it's because the burden is yours, not His.
  Jennifer Rothschild
  Lessons I Learned in the Dark (2002)

2   Sometimes we get tired of the burdens of life, but we know that Jesus Christ will meet us at the end of our life's journey—and that makes all the difference.
   Billy Graham
   Answers to Life's Problems (1994)

3   May we allow His faithfulness to beam through us and lighten the burdens of others.
   Bruce Carroll
   Sometimes Miracles Hide (1999)

4   Our friends hurt because we hurt. And their love flows into us. That is burden-bearing.
   Luci Shaw
   God in the Dark (1989)

CARING (*see* COMPASSION)

57 CARNALITY (*see also* BACKSLIDING; WORLDLINESS)
Because the carnal mind is enmity against God.
   ROMANS 8:7

1   The consequence for not drinking deeply of God is to eventually lose the ability to drink at all.
   Ben Patterson
   Deepening Your Conversation with God (1991)

58 CHANGE
Behold, I shew you a mystery; We shall not all sleep, but we shall all be changed.
   1 CORINTHIANS 15:51

1   Change comes only with willful movement. Impact follows on the heels of action.
   Bill Hybels
   Descending into Greatness (1993)

2   No man can tell until he is moved by the Divine Spirit what he may do, or how he may change the current of a lifetime of fixed habits of thought and speech and action.
   Charles Sheldon
   In His Steps (1896)

3   Though many of us desire deeper relationships with others, we often are resistant to change. Out of our own resistance to the unfamiliar we keep ourselves from the love we want.
   Cheryl and Paul Meier
   Unbreakable Bonds (2002)

4   We long for something lasting in a world that constantly moves, shifts, and changes.
   Thomas and Nanette Kinkade
   The Many Loves of Marriage (2002)

5   We invest our energy in keeping life the way it is. We resist growth. We become reactors rather than making things happen. We stay in the holes of our discouragement. When we don't risk stepping out, we risk missing the life-abundant changes God has in store for us.
   H. Norman Wright
   Real Solutions for Overcoming Discouragement, Rejection and the Blues (2001)

6   Change is an easy thing to decide and a difficult thing to do.
   Steven Goldstein and Laurie Ashner
   Could It Be. . .Perimenopause? (1998)

7   Change occurs when we get involved, when we face the music.
   Charles Swindoll
   Growing Wise in Family Life (1988)

8   When we change for the better, we usually feel better.
   Larry Crabb
   Connecting (1997)

9   Once we examine ourselves and stop trying to shape up others, we open our hearts to change.
Florence Littauer
After Every Wedding Comes a Marriage (1981)

10   People can change and God is merciful to show us how.
Paul and Nicole Johnson
Random Acts of Grace (1995)

11   God is interested in hearts because that's where real and lasting change takes place.
Scott Turansky and Joanne Miller
Parenting Is Heart Work (2006)

12   You can find out if something is fixable only by getting busy and fixing it.
Henry Cloud
9 Things You Simply Must Do (2004)

13   Change takes place when truth is presented in relationship.
Larry Crabb
Encouragement: The Key to Caring (1984)

14   When you're through changing, you're through.
John Maxwell
Developing the Leader within You (1993)

15   As Christians we should never fear change. We must believe in change so long as it is change oriented toward godliness. The Christian life is a life of continual change.
Jay Adams
Godliness Through Discipline (1972)

16   A transition is a time to retool, rediscover, and redefine who you are.
Poppy Smith
I'm Too Young to Be This Old! (1997)

17   The truth is, any major move or change in our lives can leave us disoriented and insecure. Oddly enough, however, it is in these very

situations that you and I may encounter God as never before. These are the times to seek His face and His will with renewed intensity.
Jack Hayford
Pursuing the Will of God (1997)

18   Different words and different actions will produce different effects.
Dan Allender and Tremper Longman III
Breaking the Idols of Your Heart (1998)

19   The way things were is no longer the way things are.
David Gudgel
Before You Live Together (2003)

20   One means of pursuing change is by studying what we tell ourselves.
Shelly Beach
The Silent Seduction of Self-Talk (2009)

21   Change involves pain. Change involves suffering.
David Stoop
Seeking Wise Counsel (2002)

59 CHARACTER
Judge me, O LORD;
for I have walked in mine integrity.
PSALM 26:1

1   Character is not given to us; we build it ourselves.
Mabel Hale
Beautiful Girlhood (1922)

2   Character is everything.
Scott and Kris Wightman
College without Compromise (2005)

3   Conduct is what we do, character is what we are.
E. M. Bounds
The Necessity of Prayer (19th century)

4   Character is the root of the tree, conduct, the fruit it bears.
E. M. Bounds
The Necessity of Prayer (19th century)

5   Tomorrow's character is made out of today's thoughts. Temptation may come suddenly, but sin doesn't.
Randy Alcorn
The Purity Principle (2003)

6   We don't define a person's true character by the image that person wishes to convey or the reputation he or she hides behind, but by the choices and decisions that person has made and makes each day.
Joshua Harris
I Kissed Dating Goodbye (1997)

7   It is not what you do as a Christian that determines who you are; it is who you are that determines what you do.
Neil Anderson
Victory Over the Darkness (1990)

8   A major goal of raising children is to help them develop the character that will make their future go well.
Henry Cloud and John Townsend
Boundaries with Kids (1998)

9   Character is always more caught than taught.
Chip Ingram
Effective Parenting in a Defective World (2006)

10   Intentionally building character means that we resolve to develop Christlike character: that is, we actively engage in putting certain character traits into our lives.
Christine Wood
Character Witness (2003)

11   God wants His character and likeness to be reflected in your life.
Colin Smith
Unlocking the Bible Story (2002)

12   It is not what men do that is the vital matter, but rather what they are.
Hannah Whitall Smith
The Christian's Secret of a Happy Life (1888)

13   God is always most interested in the building and developing of our character. He wants more than anything for us to love Him, worship Him, and grow to love others more purely.
Ray and Nancy Kane
From Fear to Love (2002)

14   Authentic character counts!
Connie Grigsby and Kent Julian
How to Get Your Teen to Talk to You (2002)

15   Nothing in all the world can be hidden from God.
Steve Campbell "The Primary Importance" sermon (2009)

16   Bodily vigor is good, and vigor of intellect is even better, but far above both is character.
Theodore Roosevelt
The Strenuous Life (1899)

17   Character is shown in peace no less than in war. As the greatest fertility of invention, the greatest perfection of armament, will not make soldiers out of cowards, so no mental training and no bodily vigor will make a nation great if it lacks the fundamental principles of honesty and moral cleanliness.
Theodore Roosevelt
The Strenuous Life (1899)

18   Without God, we have the ability to manufacture character, but it's counterfeit and cheap. We can produce love, but it's

conditional; happiness, but it's temporary; peace, but it's circumstantial.
Jeff Kinley and MercyMe
I Can Only Imagine (2002)

19 Character is not just about how you do business, what you do when no one is looking, or the rules you use for proper societal behavior. It's more important than that. You are to be the light of your family, your work, your neighborhood, and your company.
David Edwards
Living Christ's Character from the Inside Out (2002)

20 Charisma requires some effort to develop, but it's easier to develop than character. Character exists within the person before it shows up on the outside. Genuine character actually produces its own charisma; however, manufactured charisma does not produce character.
David Edwards
Living Christ's Character from the Inside Out (2002)

21 Any relationship built without character will always be superficial because it is built on an image without anything to back it up. The same is true for our relationship with God. In fact, character is a prerequisite for every one of our relationships: our parents, our friends, our coworkers, whom we date, and whom we marry. Character is the thing that makes relationships work.
David Edwards
Living Christ's Character from the Inside Out (2002)

22 Our words reveal our character.
Rhonda Rizzo Webb
Words Begin in Our Hearts (2003)

23 There in the midst of unjust treatment and seemingly undeserved pain, the true character of a man or woman is revealed. Pretense is peeled away.
Andy Stanley
Louder Than Words (2004)

24 Your character is who you really are.
Andy Stanley
Louder Than Words (2004)

25 Good character is never fickle.
William Coleman
Before I Give You Away (1995)

26 Character will exhibit itself in the face.
William Elbert Munsey
Eternal Retribution (1951)

27 Today, there are far too many men with reputation (what men say about you) and far too few men with integrity (what God knows about you).
Rick Scarborough
Enough Is Enough (1996)

28 When we actively seek to expand His life in ours, His character gradually becomes ours.
Bruce Wilkinson
Experiencing Spiritual Breakthroughs (1999)

29 A farm is not a place for growing corn, it is a place for growing character, and a man has no character except what is built up through the medium of the things that he does from day to day.
Henry Drummond
A Life for a Life and Other Addresses (1893)

30 You may be poor, but you need not be impure. You may have to discharge lowliest duties, but you need never do a mean thing.
John Dawson
The Saviour in the Workshop (1868)

31 Your character is a product of the choices you make, and the reaction you have toward the circumstances in your life.
> Tim Burns
> *Forged in the Fire* (2003)

32 When we get squeezed by difficult circumstances, what comes out of us reveals our heart.
> Rebecca Lusignolo
> "Squeezed by Life" article (2007)

60 CHARITY
(*see also* GENEROSITY; GIVING)
And the King shall answer and say unto them, Verily I say unto you, Inasmuch as ye have done it unto one of the least of these my brethren, ye have done it unto me.
MATTHEW 25:40

1 To feed others with charity is to feed them with the Bread of Life, who is Christ, and to teach them also to love with a love that knows no hunger.
> Thomas Merton
> *No Man Is an Island* (1955)

2 Be charitable before wealth make thee covetous, and lose not the glory of the mite.
> Thomas Brown
> *Christian Morals* (17th century)

3 Thou seest a needy person, and thou turnest away thine eye; but it is the Prince of Darkness that casts this mist upon thee.
> John Donne
> "Sermon Preached at Lincoln's Inn" (1620)

4 Still thou sayest to the poor, I have not for you, when God knows, a great part of that which thou hast, thou hast for them, if thou wouldst execute God's commission, and dispense it accordingly, as God hast made thee his steward for the poor. Give really, and give gently; Do kindly, and speak kindly too, for that is bread, and honey.
> John Donne
> "Sermon Preached at Lincoln's Inn" (1620)

61 CHASTITY
(*see also* INTEGRITY; PURITY)
Teach the young women to be sober, to love their husbands, to love their children, to be discreet, chaste. . .
TITUS 2:4–5

1 Are you toying with sin? If so, for your self, your family, and your Lord—stop. Don't put yourself in a position of compromise.
> Chuck Colson
> "The Bewilderment of Sin" article (2009)

62 CHEER
(*see also* ENCOURAGEMENT)
Jesus spake unto them, saying, Be of good cheer; it is I; be not afraid.
MATTHEW 14:27

1 God often places someone at a camp, a club, or a church as a certain intersection to build you up: Someone to say something that you'll never forget or to encourage you at a moment of need.
> Gregg Matte
> *The Highest Education: Becoming a Godly Man* (2000)

2 Give a little of yourself, even though you feel stretched already. One certain way to receive encouragement, hope, or companionship is to give it.
> Gretchen Thompson
> *God Knows Caregiving Can Pull You Apart* (2002)

CHEERFULNESS (*see* HAPPINESS)

CHILDREARING (*see* PARENTING)

63 CHILDLIKE FAITH
Verily I say unto you, Whosoever shall not receive the kingdom of God as a little child, he shall not enter therein.
MARK 10:15

1   God is seeking childlikeness in everyone; and there is something about the dependence of thirsting after righteousness and the simplicity of submitting to the Holy Spirit's supernatural work that humbles us all like children.
  Jack Hayford
  Glory on Your House (1991)

2   To be a blessing to our children, we simply need to become childlike ourselves—to believe God's call and to receive God's grace for the task.
  Jack Hayford
  Blessing Your Children (2002)

3   I may have destroyed my own future, but God is always the perfect past, present and future. He still desires to restore childlikeness to my battered, aged soul. "Let's play," he calls. "Where are you?"
  Karen Burton Mains
  The God Hunt (2003)

4   The strong and lively exercises of a spirit of childlike, evangelical, humble love to God, give clear evidence of the soul's relation to God as his child; which does very greatly and directly satisfy the soul.
  Jonathan Edwards
  A Treatise Concerning Religious Affections (18th century)

64 CHILDREN

Lo, children are an heritage of the LORD: and the fruit of the womb is his reward.
PSALM 127:3

1   Our goal is not that children be happy, fulfilled, and successful. Granted, we may desire these things for them. But our highest objective should be that our children would repent from their sins, put their trust in Jesus Christ, and reflect the gospel to the world around them.
  Carolyn Mahaney
  Feminine Appeal (2004)

2   The sooner children learn how to be thoughtful, the easier they are to raise, and the more successful they'll become as adults.
  Willard Harley, Jr.
  His Needs, Her Needs for Parents (2003)

3   The passing on of our fears usually goes unnoticed by the adult. We may even think our children have not caught on that we are afraid. But children are very perceptive mirrors.
  Melissa Trevathan and Sissy Goff
  The Back Door to Your Teen's Heart (2002)

4   The earliest blessing a child can receive from those influencing his or her life is to answer the question, How can I cultivate an atmosphere of God's order and love in our home and form an understanding mind-set that life is not to be lived for oneself but in the interest of others?
  Jack Hayford
  Blessing Your Children (2002)

5   The children you and I can influence are more open to the things of the Spirit than adults often realize.
  Jack Hayford
  Blessing Your Children (2002)

6   Too many kids, lacking a parent's proper care and influence, are creating chaos in homes today, where God's order has not been established because children have been left to themselves.
  Jack Hayford
  Blessing Your Children (2002)

7   Children are spoiled not only by an overabundance of food, toys, clothing, and other material things. Many parents spoil them simply by giving in to their whims.
  Johann Christoph Arnold
  Endangered: Your Child in a Hostile World (2000)

8 It is a beautiful thing to see a child thoroughly absorbed in his play; in fact, it is hard to think of a purer, more spiritual activity.
   Johann Christoph Arnold
   Endangered: Your Child in a Hostile World (2000)

9 Puppies and children are so alike. They look around their world with amazement. "Wow! What a place to explore and conquer!" And they both want to feel safe and secure.
   H. Norman Wright
   Everything I Know About Parenting I Learned from My Puppy (2002)

10 Children have more need of example than criticism.
   Carol Kuykendall
   Learning to Let Go (1985)

11 Next time your child runs out of enthusiasm before running out of work, resist the urge to step in and erase the consequences. It's better to lose points on a book report than to develop the bad habit of quitting halfway up the hill.
   Craig and Janet Parshall
   Traveling a Pilgrim's Path (2003)

12 When kids respect others, they don't use or betray them. We need to teach kids that sex outside of marriage betrays both the other person and God Himself.
   Craig and Janet Parshall
   Traveling a Pilgrim's Path (2003)

13 Our world may be dark, dangerous, and desperate, but that's not the end of the story. There's light at the end of the tunnel, despite the bleak philosophy that dominates the culture in which our kids find themselves. Christ has provided them with a key to the dungeon and promised to stand beside them.
   Craig and Janet Parshall
   Traveling a Pilgrim's Path (2003)

14 When intimacy and attention are absent from the home, kids will be more vulnerable to outside influences.
   Walt Mueller
   Understanding Today's Youth Culture (1999)

15 No matter what they look like or how they act, all teenagers are yearning for adult love and acceptance. Kids who give in easily to peer pressure and go wrong are typically kids who lack the input, love, and acceptance of a significant adult in their lives.
   Walt Mueller
   Understanding Today's Youth Culture (1999)

16 We must teach our children that the real measure of their success in life is how much they'd be worth if they had absolutely nothing.
   Walt Mueller
   Understanding Today's Youth Culture (1999)

17 Our children will discover that if they are willing to sacrifice their own desires—whether popularity, possessions, position, and even family—to love, worship, and obey God, they will eventually learn that intimacy with God is more important than anything else.
   David and Anne Harper
   Light Their Fire for God (2001)

18 We must show our children by example the importance of finding common ground with those who are different than we are. Children can learn to look past differences in personalities, looks, backgrounds, and cultures to find common ground.
   David and Anne Harper
   Light Their Fire for God (2001)

19 Like all human beings, our children are unique, eternal individuals. Like us, they have their own private little worlds, their own thoughts, feelings, beliefs, experiences, and decisions that are taking place inside them all the time. Whether or not they share those

worlds with us depends upon how much we value them as individuals and to what degree we honor and respect their private lives.
John Burns
Miracle in Daddy's Hug (2003)

20 Caring for children is an extremely valuable skill that is scarce these days. It may be the most significant gift you could choose to spend your life giving.
Valerie Bell
Reaching Out to Lonely Kids (1994)

21 Childhood memories are one of the most reliable explanations of "why you are the way you are." These memories are like tapes playing in your head and they combine with the basic life-style you learned as a child to determine how you will respond to what happens to you every day.
Kevin Leman
Bringing Up Kids Without Tearing Them Down (1995)

22 Good behavior is convenient for us as parents, but we must not confuse it with a will submitted to God.
Christine Field
Help for the Harried Homeschooler (2002)

23 The soul of the poorest child is of equal dignity with the soul of Adam.
John Flavel
Pneumatologia (1698)

24 Our little ones won't be with us forever. When they're grown, they won't remember whether they had size one designer jeans or a solid-maple crib. But they will remember, even subconsciously, whether they were loved and protected.
Sandra Aldrich
Upward Glances (2000)

25 Our children will learn and become what their parents, their teachers and their culture impart to them.
Tony Evans
Guiding Your Family (1991)

26 The home marks a child for life.
Howard Hendricks
Heaven Help the Home (1973)

27 Is it like the Son of man to pick out the beautiful child, and leave the common child unnoticed?
George MacDonald
"The Child in the Midst" sermon
(19th century)

65 CHOICES
(*see also* DECISION-MAKING)
Choose you this day whom ye will serve; . . .
as for me and my house,
we will serve the Lord.
JOSHUA 24:15

1 You are free to choose what you surrender to, but you are not free from the consequences of that choice.
Rick Warren
The Purpose-Driven Life (2002)

2 We have every right to make choices, but no right to choose the consequences.
Anne Graham Lotz
The Daily Light Journal (2004)

3 When we choose to sin, there will be consequences. However, that's where our choice in the matter ends. We choose to sin, but God is the One who chooses the consequences. He decides what happens because of our sin, how many times it will happen, and how long it will last.
Tony Evans
God Cannot Be Trusted
(And Five Other Lies of Satan) (2005)

4   Every choice we make in life has the possibility of changing our lives forever.
    Jimmy Houston
    Hooked for Life (1999)

5   We need to realize that we are in control of our choices, no matter how we feel.
    Henry Cloud and John Townsend
    Boundaries (1992)

6   The Lord is forever faithful to His decision to give us free will. It's always our choice what we allow into our lives.
    Karon Phillips Goodman
    You Still Here, Lord? (2004)

7   Once to every man and nation,
    comes the moment to decide,
    In the strife of truth with falsehood,
    for the good or evil side.
    James Lowell
    "Once to Every Man and Nation" poem (1845)

8   No matter what you've experienced, remember this: There are people who've had it better than you and done worse. And there are people who've had it worse than you and done better. The circumstances really have nothing to do with getting over your personal history. Past hurts can make you bitter or better—the choice is yours.
    John Maxwell
    Failing Forward (2000)

9   Run not into extremities from whence there is no regression.
    Thomas Brown
    Christian Morals (17th century)

10 Poor choices, whether morally, relationally or spiritually, lead to unrest, stress and anxiety.
    John DeMarco
    New Man Magazine (2003)

11 You can only serve one master. . .and you need to decide who it's gonna be.
    Steve Campbell
    "Three Things That Will Destroy a Christian" sermon (2009)

12 And I create the world I live in
    By each and every choice I make today.
    And when all is said and done
    I'm the only oneWho can make the world
    A better place to stay.
    Martin Bell
    The Way of the Wolf (1968)

13 Your choices on earth have direct consequences on your life in eternity.
    Bruce Wilkinson
    A Life God Rewards (2002)

14 You can't make up your mind now to break off from all sin. If this be really so, then you cannot make up your mind to obey God, and you may as well make up your mind to go to hell! There is no alternative!
    Charles Finney
    "The Sinner's Excuses Answered" sermon (1850)

15 Life is made up of choices. Who you are sitting here today is the sum total of your choices.
    James MacDonald
    "Wise Up About Wisdom" sermon (2009)

16 The power to exercise the will has been delegated to us and God will not usurp it.
    Elisabeth Elliot
    These Strange Ashes (1989)

17 It is true, that men may have Christ whenever they are willing to comply with his terms. But if you are not willing now, how can you think you shall be willing hereafter?
    Richard Baxter
    The Causes and Danger of Slighting Christ and His Gospel (17th century)

18 You cannot control all the details or length of your life, but you can have something to say about its width and depth.
   Tim Burns
   Forged in the Fire (2003)

19 The choices we make determine the shape and color of our lives.
   Luis Palau
   Heart After God (1978)

66 CHRIST
(*see also* JESUS; MESSIAH; SAVIOR)
For unto you is born this day in the city of David a Saviour, which is Christ the Lord.
LUKE 2:11

1   Hold on to Christ with your teeth if your hands get crippled.
   Elizabeth Prentiss
   More Love to Thee—The Life and Letters of Elizabeth Prentiss (1882)

2   So Christ is not the channel merely through which all God's mercies descend to us, and by which all our prayers ascend to Him—He is the supply itself.
   Evan Henry Hopkins
   Thoughts on Life and Godliness (1883)

3   Whatever communion there is between our souls and Christ, it is he who begins the discourse.
   Matthew Henry
   Commentary on the Whole Bible (1706)

4   We are totally accepted in Christ! It's not necessarily a feeling; it's a fact. It is primarily believed, not felt.
   Bill Gillham
   Lifetime Guarantee (1993)

5   Receive Christ's works on the cross, the energy of his Spirit, his lordship over your life, his unending unfailing love. Drink deeply and often. And out of you will flow rivers of living water.
   Max Lucado
   Come Thirsty (2004)

6   We are taught from the very first moment to discover Christ under the distressing disguise of the poor, the sick, the outcasts. Christ presents himself to us under every disguise: the dying, the paralytic, the leper, the invalid, the orphan.
   Mother Teresa
   Loving Jesus (1991)

7   No matter what trials we face, Christ never leaves us. He is with us every step of the way!
   Billy Graham
   Hope for Each Day (2006)

8   Christ is at all times totally sufficient for the office He has undertaken.
   Jonathan Edwards
   "Jesus Christ, the Same Yesterday, Today and Forever" sermon (1744)

9   Christ does not exist in order to make much of us. We exist in order to enjoy making much of Him.
   John Piper
   Seeing and Savoring Jesus Christ (2004)

10 Christ is not only beloved by all believing souls, but is their well-beloved, their best-beloved, their only beloved.
   Matthew Henry
   Commentary on the Whole Bible (1706)

11 You will never have true pleasure or peace or joy or comfort until you have found Christ.
   D. L. Moody
   "Excuses" sermon (1880)

12 Christ presides over the supreme court of the universe. If He settles your case, there is no other place of appeal. There is no higher authority. There are no other proceedings. There can be no overruling.
Colin Smith
Unlocking the Bible Story (2002)

13 Christ is looking for those who will love him and be loved by him. So watch and pray. Take a few risks. Stay wide awake. And jump in the river—let it flow.
Robert Stofel
God, How Much Longer? (2005)

14 While Christians may disappoint you, Christ won't.
James Emery White
A Search for the Spiritual (1998)

15 The kingdom of Christ is a kingdom of grace, mercy, and of all comfort.
Martin Luther
Table Talk (16th century)

16 Christ desires nothing more of us than that we speak of him.
Martin Luther
Table Talk (16th century)

17 I know no other Christ than he who was crucified, and who in his Word is pictured and presented unto me.
Martin Luther
Table Talk (16th century)

18 We should consider the histories of Christ three manner of ways; first, as a history of acts or legends; secondly, as a gift or a present; thirdly, as an example, which we should believe and follow.
Martin Luther
Table Talk (16th century)

19 He is the prop which underpins creation. Christ, and not fate. Christ, and not nature.
F. B. Meyer
The Way into the Holiest (1893)

20 To experience the Christ is to run headlong into the path of a hurricane.
Martin Bell
The Way of the Wolf (1968)

21 Christ is the most gigantic figure of history.
Henry Drummond
"Why Christ Must Depart" sermon (19th century)

22 Christ ought to be as near to us as if He were still here. Nothing so simplifies the whole religious life as this thought.
Henry Drummond
"Why Christ Must Depart" sermon (19th century)

23 Christ has died, Christ has risen, Christ will come again. Nothing can undermine those facts.
Elisabeth Elliot
Be Still My Soul (2003)

24 To preach Christ means to set him forth as the One who, through his cross, sets men right with God again. To put faith in Christ means relying on him, and him alone, to restore us to God's fellowship and favor.
J. I. Packer
Evangelism and the Sovereignty of God (2008)

25 Regardless of the intensity of our storm, we are safest in the middle of the storm with Christ than any other place without Him.
Jude D'Souza
"From Fear to Awe" sermon (2009)

26 Christ arouses antagonism in the human heart and heroism does not. Everybody welcomes a hero. The minority welcome Christ. We do resent His absolute command. We do resent parting completely with ourselves. We do resent Christ.
Peter Taylor Forsyth
The Work of Christ (1909)

27 Christ did not go to His death with His eyes shut. He died because He willed to die, having counted the cost with the greatest, deepest moral vision in the world.
Peter Taylor Forsyth
The Work of Christ (1909)

28 As all the rivers are gathered into the ocean, which is the meeting-place of all the waters in the world, so Christ is that ocean in which all true delights and pleasures meet.
John Flavel
Christ Altogether Lovely (17th century)

29 Creatures, like pictures, are fairest at a certain distance, but it is not so with Christ; the nearer the soul approaches him, and the longer it lives in the enjoyment of him, still the sweeter and more desirable he becomes.
John Flavel
Christ Altogether Lovely (17th century)

30 He feels all our sorrows, needs, and burdens as his own. This is why it is said that the sufferings of believers are called the sufferings of Christ.
John Flavel
Christ Altogether Lovely (17th century)

31 Christ doesn't want a place in your life; He wants it all. He doesn't want you to fit Him into your plans; He wants to fit you into His.
J. Budziszewski
How to Stay Christian in College (2004)

32 Christ is a most meek, tender, compassionate, forgiving friend. If he did not excel in these things to an infinite degree, he could not be our friend. We have injured him more than any other person in the universe; and have done more to affront him, and provoke him to anger, than ever was done to any other.
Samuel Hopkins
"The Friendship between Jesus Christ and Believers" sermon (1803)

33 The correct perspective is to see following Christ not only as the necessity it is, but as the fulfillment of the highest human possibilities and as life on the highest plane.
Dallas Willard
The Spirit of the Disciplines (1988)

34 By the power of the gospel the covetous man may become generous, the egotist lowly in his own eyes. The thief may learn to steal no more, the blasphemer to fill his mouth with praises unto God. But it is Christ who does it all.
A. W. Tozer
That Incredible Christian (1960s)

35 We are only poor for this reason, that we do not know our riches in Christ.
Richard Sibbes
The Bruised Reed (1630)

36 None are damned in the church but those that are determined to be, including those who persist in having hard thoughts of Christ, that they may have some show of reason to fetch contentment from other things.
Richard Sibbes
The Bruised Reed (1630)

37 In view of the wide prevalence of Buddhism and Mahometanism, it may seem bold to call Christ the Light of the World, and as if modesty required us to be content with the ascription to Him of a merely provincial

authority. But no Christian can acquiesce in this compromise.

Alexander Balmain Bruce
Apologetics, or Christianity Defensively Stated (1892)

38 Christ is God's Forgiveness.
George MacDonald
"It Shall Not Be Forgiven" sermon
(19th century)

39 God's nature is infinitely contrary to sin, and so He cannot delight in a sinner out of Christ.
Joseph Alleine
A Sure Guide to Heaven (1671)

40 When you rest on the certainty that is in Jesus Christ, you are depending upon the dependable one who, in Scripture, speaks clearly, the one whose yes is yes and whose no is no.
Jay Adams
Christ and Your Problems (1971)

41 The Christ we believe, the Christ we trust, must be true if we are to be redeemed. A false Christ or substitute Christ cannot redeem. If it is thought unlikely that the biblical Christ can redeem, it is even less likely that the speculative Christ of human invention can redeem. Apart from the Bible we know nothing of consequence concerning the real Jesus. Ultimately our faith stands or falls with the biblical Jesus.
R. C. Sproul
Following Christ (1991)

42 It is a solemn thing to think that Christ does not remain as an uninvited guest.
D. L. Moody
Short Talks (19th century)

43 When we approach Christ, open our clenching fists, and lay down our armor of work and fatigue, we find again that oneness with Him, that irreplaceable rhythm of trust and toil.
Jane Rubietta
Between Two Gardens (2001)

67 CHRISTIANITY

And the disciples were called Christians first in Antioch.
ACTS 11:26

1 Banish forever from your minds the idea that religion is subtraction. It does not tell us to give things up, but rather gives us something so much better that they give themselves up.
Henry Drummond
The Greatest Thing in the World (1891)

2 A Christian is one who points at Christ and says, "I can't prove a thing, but there's something about his eyes and his voice. There's something about the way he carries his head, his hands, the way he carries his cross—the way he carries me."
Frederick Buechner
Listening to Your Life (1992)

3 Christ did not come to earth to teach Christianity—Christ is Christianity.
Josh McDowell
The Last Christian Generation (2006)

4 Remove Christ from Christianity, and you lose the entire meaning of Biblical faith.
Josh McDowell
The Last Christian Generation (2006)

5 Christianity is not merely a religion; it is a relationship with a Person.
Henry Blackaby
Experiencing God (2007)

CHRISTIANITY

6 If Christianity is dull and boring, if it is a burden and not a blessing, then most likely we are involved in a project, not a Person—a system not a Savior, rules rather than a relationship.
Joseph Stowell
Following Christ (1996)

7 The heart of Christian worship is the authentic preaching of the Word of God.
Albert Mohler Jr.
He Is Not Silent (2008)

8 I believe in Christianity as I believe the Sun has risen, not only because I see it, but because by it I see everything else.
C. S. Lewis
The Weight of Glory (1949)

9 The Christian walk is a journey. As we continue on our path, we come to know a deepening of our faith. We can eventually see God in everything and take great comfort in knowing He is there, even when we don't understand all that is happening.
Bettie Youngs and Debbie Thurman
A Teen's Guide to Christian Living (2003)

10 Christianity is the great antiseptic of society.
Henry Drummond
Stones Rolled Away and Other Addresses to Young Men (1893)

11 One thing that has especially appealed to me is that the Christian faith is not a blind, ignorant belief but rather an intelligent faith.
Josh McDowell
More Than a Carpenter (1977)

12 You can laugh at Christianity; you can mock and ridicule it. But it works. It changes lives. If you trust Christ, start watching your attitudes and actions, because Jesus Christ is in the business of changing lives.
Josh McDowell
More Than a Carpenter (1977)

13 A cheap Christianity, without a cross, will prove in the end a useless Christianity, without a crown.
J. C. Ryle
Holiness: Its Nature, Hindrances, Difficulties, and Roots (19th century)

14 "All are not Israelites that are of Israel," so when applied to Christianity, all are not real Christians that are nominally such.
George Whitefield
Selected Sermons of George Whitefield (18th century)

15 No duty is more imperative on the Christian teacher than that of showing that instead of Christianity being simply one theory among the rest, it is really the higher truth which is the synthesis and completion of all the other, that view which, rejecting the error, takes up the vitalizing elements in all other systems and religions, and unites them into a living organism with Christ as head.
James Orr
The Christian View of God and the World (1908)

16 If apologetic is to be spoken of, this surely is the truest and best form of Christian apology: to show that in Christianity, as nowhere else, the severed portions of truth found in all other systems are organically united, while it completes the body of truth by discoveries peculiar to itself.
James Orr
The Christian View of God and the World (1908)

17 Christianity, it is sometimes said by those who represent this view, is a life, not a creed; it is a spiritual system, and has nothing to do with dogmatic affirmations.
James Orr
The Christian View of God and the World (1908)

18 Christianity, it will be here said, is a fact-revelation: it has its centre in a living in Christ, and not a dogmatic creed.

James Orr
The Christian View of God and the World (1908)

19 Christianity without Christ is a frame without a picture, a body without breath.

John Stott
Christian Basics (1991)

20 A Christian is, literally, "Christ's one," someone who is not just vaguely influenced by Christian teaching, but one who has switched his or her most fundamental allegiance to Jesus. Christians understand the all-or-nothing choice that is forced upon us by the magnitude of Jesus' claims.

Timothy Keller
The Reason for God (2008)

21 God's creatively constructed household of faith resembles an art gallery.

Joy Sawyer
Dancing to the Heartbeat of Redemption (2000)

68 CHRISTIAN LIFE, THE

But as he which hath called you is holy,
so be ye holy in all manner of conversation.
1 PETER 1:15

1 It is a glorious thing to be a Christian.
Henry H. Halley
Pocket Bible Handbook (1948)

2 The Christian life was intended not to be a sitting still, but a race, a perpetual motion.
Charles Spurgeon
"Final Perseverance" sermon (1856)

3 The Christian idea has not been tried and found wanting. It has been found difficult and left untried.
G. K. Chesterton
The Homelessness of Man (1910)

4 We are not the Moral Majority. We are the Forgiven Few.
Jon Courson
Application Commentary (2003)

5 There is no suggestion here that religion will absolve any man from bearing burdens. That would be to absolve him from living, since it is life itself that is the burden. What Christianity does propose is to make it tolerable.
Henry Drummond
The Greatest Thing in the World (1891)

6 For the very essence of the Christian life is the giving of self to God. And we give ourselves to Him by giving ourselves to His children here on earth.
Agnes Sanford
The Healing Light (1947)

7 At the end of the day we are all simply beggars telling other beggars where we found bread.
Matt Smith
"The 'Me' Centered Church" article (2008)

8 Walking with God involves deliberately choosing to immerse ourselves in His ways, with His people, and in His kingdom.
Thomas Blackaby
Encounters with God Daily Bible (2008)

9 The Christian life is not a competition with others; we have a common goal and we grow together in the strength and grace of the body of believers.
George Verwer
Come! Live! Die! (1972)

10 Authentic Christianity is not just about keeping and protecting the faith and keeping the rules. It is even more than living to deepen your relationship with Jesus. Authentic Christianity, the real deal, is about embracing all of these important elements.
Joseph Stowell
The Trouble with Jesus (2003)

11 Dear Christian, the Lord never intended you to try your best to live the Christian life. He placed His Spirit within you to live His life through you to bring glory and honor to Himself. He does His work of ministry on earth through you. The battle is the Lord's.
Billy Graham
Lifetime Guarantee (1993)

12 Our Lord wants His true followers to be distinct, unlike the majority who follow the herd. In solving conflicts, doing business, and responding to difficulties, Jesus' people are not to maintain the same attitudes or choose the priorities of the majority.
Charles Swindoll
Simple Faith (1991)

13 A true Christian experience has its source in and is motivated by a personal relationship with Christ. Not just a personal relationship that saves me, but a relationship that determines my behavior, responses, thoughts, and actions in ways that would be particularly pleasing to Him.
Joseph Stowell
Fan the Flame (1986)

14 To be a Christian is to be like Christ.
Matthew Kelly
A Call to Joy (1997)

15 It is possible to live the Christian life just on the surface, knowing only enough to carry on an intelligent conversation in the church foyer with another equally uninformed believer. But when that happens you are vulnerable to the attack of the deceiver.
David Jeremiah
Spiritual Warfare (1995)

16 It is possible to be at the top of Christian service, respected and admired, and not have that indispensable ingredient by which God has chosen to work in His world today—the absolute sacrificial agape love of the Eternal God.
David Jeremiah
The Power of Love (1994)

17 I have heard of a great many people who think if they are united to the church, and have made one profession, that will do for all the rest of their days. But there is a cross for every one of us daily.
D. L. Moody
"Where Art Thou" sermon (1880)

18 Authentic living in the light of God's glory is not about being perfect but about living grace filled lives.
Chip Ingram
Effective Parenting in a Defective World (2006)

19 When the rams are following their shepherd and looking to him, their woolies rub each other companionably; but when they look at one another they see only each other's horns.
Neil Anderson and Charles Mylander
Blessed Are the Peace Makers (2002)

20 To have peace with God one must intentionally die to self, to all self ambition, until you are only living for Jesus.
Kathryn Kuhlman
Kathryn Kuhlman (1976)

21 We may never be martyrs but we can die to self, to sin, to the world, to our plans and ambitions.
Vance Havner
Messages on Revival (1958)

22 If we can just understand that the Golden Rule way of living is the only correct method, and the only Christlike method, this will settle all of our difficulties that bother us.
George Washington Carver (1940)
quoted in *George Washington Carver in His Own Words*

23 The first step toward becoming a Christian involves total honesty and the self-awareness that you are a sinner before a holy God.
James Emery White
A Search for the Spiritual (1998)

24 Our Christian faith is not so much about doing as it is about being—being in a relationship. And this must precede anything we try to do or it will prove to be little more than pretence.
Monte Swan
Romancing Your Child's Heart (2002)

25 God deals with godly Christians much as with the ungodly, yea, and sometimes far worse.
Martin Luther
Table Talk (16th century)

26 The first thing a worker has to learn is how to be God's noble man or woman amid a crowd of paltry things. A Christian worker must never make this plea—"If only I were somewhere else!"
Oswald Chambers
Approved Unto God (20th century)

27 Whoever sees me sees I would be a Christian. Therefore are my ways not like other men's ways.
John Wesley
The Journal of John Wesley (18th century)

28 David lived by a very simple principle. Nothing to prove and nothing to lose.
Charles Swindoll
"David and the Dwarf" sermon (2009)

29 You hear the word, and believe it in theory, while you deny it in practice. I say to you, that "you deceive yourselves."
Charles Finney
Lectures to Professing Christians (1837)

30 One has to do a great deal more than display his Christianity. He must not only talk it, but live it.
Henry Drummond
Stones Rolled Away and Other Addresses to Young Men (1893)

31 Our duty as Christians is always to keep heaven in our eye and the earth under our feet.
Matthew Henry
Commentary on the Whole Bible (1706)

32 All aspects of life are intertwined, and each must be given proper attention and effort. We all tend to become one-dimensional creatures, focusing primarily on only one aspect of life. Becoming lopsided we bump down the road— out of balance—increasing our wear and tear, our stress and distress.
J. Allan Petersen
Before You Marry (1974)

33 Man's capacity for spiritual life is a trinity in unity: intellect, sensibilities and conduct.
William Elbert Munsey
Eternal Retribution (1951)

34 It is time we stand up for what we believe and teach those eternal truths to our children.
James Dobson
Bringing Up Boys (2001)

35 Why couldn't Jesus command us to obsess about everything, to try to control and manipulate people, to try not to breathe at all, or to pay attention, stomp away to brood when people annoy us, and then eat a big bag of Hershey's Kisses in bed?
Anne Lamott
Plan B: Further Thoughts on Faith (2005)

36 It takes the deep water and the hot fire and the dark valley to teach us the walk of faith.
Elisabeth Elliot
Be Still My Soul (2003)

37 It's not about being comfortable, it's about being useful.
Steve Campbell
Garden Church meeting (2009)

38 I grant freely that it costs little to be a mere outward Christian.
J. C. Ryle
Holiness: Its Nature, Hindrances, Difficulties, and Roots (19th century)

39 To be a Christian it will cost a man his love of ease.
J. C. Ryle
Holiness: Its Nature, Hindrances, Difficulties, and Roots (19th century)

40 The peculiarity in the Christian consciousness is that everything in it is referred back upon Jesus Christ, and the Redemption accomplished through Him.
James Orr
The Christian View of God and the World (1908)

41 The vigor, and power, and comfort of our spiritual life depends on the mortification of the deeds of the flesh.
John Owen
Of the Mortification of Sin in Believers (1656)

42 The Christian man, simply by virtue of the life that is in him—not by attempting much in the way of forcing it upon others—but by his own spontaneous nature can so work upon men that they cannot but feel that he has been with Jesus.
Henry Drummond
A Life for a Life and Other Addresses (1893)

43 Men would sooner believe that the gospel is from heaven, if they saw more such effects of it upon the hearts and lives of those who profess it.
Richard Baxter
The Reformed Pastor (17th century)

44 A practicing Christian must above all be one who practices the perpetual return of the soul into the inner sanctuary, who brings the world into its Light and rejudges it, who brings the Light into the world with all its turmoil and its fitfulness and re-creates it.
Thomas Kelly
A Testament of Devotion (1992)

45 To glorify God is, having His character impressed upon you, to manifest it by acting in a Godlike manner in all that you do.
John Dawson
The Saviour in the Workshop (1868)

46 Very often the inertia and repugnance which characterize the so-called "spiritual life" of many Christians could perhaps be cured by a simple respect for the concrete realities of every-day life.
Thomas Merton
Contemplative Prayer (1969)

47 Presidents do not always act presidentially, diplomats do not always act diplomatically, kings do not always act kingly—but they are still presidents, diplomats, and kings. Christians do not always act like Christians, but they are still Christians.
John MacArthur
1 Corinthians (1984)

48 With due reverence, but very plainly, let it be said that God can do nothing for the man with shut hand and shut life. There must be an open hand and heart and life through which God can give what He longs to.
Samuel Gordon
Quiet Talks on Prayer (1904)

49 Remember—when we clearly understand who we are in Christ, we'll be eager to do what we can for Christ.
Bob Moorehead
A Passion for Victory (1996)

50 It is by willing, prayerful, and persistent obedience to the requirements of the Scriptures that godly patterns are developed and come to be a part of us. When we read about them we then ask God by His grace to help us live accordingly.
Jay Adams
Godliness Through Discipline (1972)

51 You have an exceptional calling—to be the very best you God created you to be. Your goal is to unwrap this gift and use all that you've been given in the pursuit of what matters most—loving God and loving other people.
Kerry and Chris Shook
One Month to Live (2008)

52 At the end of the day, living the Christian life requires us to deeply and profoundly give up on ourselves and trust God and his Word.
Mark Dever
"Psalms: Wisdom for Spiritual People" sermon (1997)

53 Don't presume to direct your own life on your own terms. Discovering the will of your creator and Savior—and walking in that will may not be the most "secure" way to live, according to the world's standards. But I assure you of this: It will be the most fulfilling thing that could ever happen to you.
Jack Hayford
Pursuing the Will of God (1997)

54 Living as God's poetry is countercultural in a society that largely neglects the mission of loveliness.
Joy Sawyer
Dancing to the Heartbeat of Redemption (2000)

55 It is the relationship that Christ is stressing.
J. B. Phillips
Your God Is Too Small (1952)

56 This is the mystery of the Christian life: to receive a new self, a new identity, which depends not on what we can achieve, but on what we are willing to receive.
Donald McNeill, Douglas Morrison, and Henri Nouwen
Compassion (1982)

69 CHRISTLIKENESS (*see also* GODLINESS; GOODNESS)

For even hereunto were ye called: because Christ also suffered for us, leaving us an example, that ye should follow his steps.
1 Peter 2:21

1 When God brings us to salvation, the most remarkable thing we see is that he transforms our hungers. He changes not just what we do but what we want to do.
Ravi Zacharias
The Grand Weaver (2007)

2 Focusing intently on Christ naturally results in a lifestyle of greater and greater selflessness.
Charles Swindoll
So You Want to Be Like Christ? (2005)

3 As no darkness can be seen by anyone surrounded by light, so no trivialities can capture the attention of anyone who has his eyes on Christ.
Gregory of Nyssa (4th century) quoted in *The Wisdom of the Saints: An Anthology*

4 What a contrast! Nothingness strives to be something, and the Omnipotent becomes nothing! I will be nothing with Thee, my Lord!
François Fénelon and Jeanne Guyon
Spiritual Progress (17th century)

5 The beauty of believers consists in their resemblance to Jesus Christ.
Matthew Henry
Commentary on the Whole Bible (1706)

6   Contemplative awareness of the risen Jesus shapes our resemblance to Him and turns us into the persons God intended us to be.
   Brennan Manning
   Abba's Child (1994)

7   Father, strip away from me whatever is blocking people's view of You in my life.
   Tim Walter
   "Filled with God's Grace and Glory" sermon (2009)

8   How grimy did God get when he reached down to clean you up? How grimy are you willing to get in order to be an "imitator of God"?
   Max Lucado
   Just Like Jesus (1998)

9   All our spiritual disciplines should be practiced in pursuit of Christ-likeness.
   Donald S. Whitney
   Simplify Your Spiritual Life (2003)

10   Let the heirs of the kingdom behave themselves suitably to their character and dignity.
   Thomas Boston
   Human Nature in Its Fourfold State (1830)

11   The true Christian is one who knows God's power working in himself, and finds it his true joy to have the very life of God flow into him, and through him, and out from him to those around.
   Andrew Murray
   Working for God (1901)

12   The priorities and intentions—the heart or inner attitudes—of disciples are forever the same. In the heart of a disciple there is a desire, and there is decision or settled intent. The disciple of Christ desires above all else to be like him.
   Dallas Willard
   The Spirit of the Disciplines (1988)

13   Know that if ye be like unto Him in sorrow, ye shall also be like unto Him in glory.
   The Lutheran Witness (1885)

14   In spending time with non-Christians, we walk in the footsteps of Christ. We make his pattern our pattern and His practice our practice. To be Christlike, we must spend time with non-Christians.
   R. Larry Moyer
   21 Things God Never Said (2004)

70 CHRISTMAS
Now the birth of Jesus Christ was on this wise. . .
MATTHEW 1:18

1   The perfect Christmas is a myth. After all, the first Christmas was hardly perfect. It was glorious and difficult, miraculous and earthy, sublime and sweaty, tender and harsh.
   Dave Meurer
   Good Spousekeeping (2004)

2   Who could have dreamed that this little baby would change the course of the world?
   Martin Bell
   The Way of the Wolf (1968)

71 CHURCH
(*see also* BODY OF CHRIST)
That he might present it to himself a glorious church, not having spot, or wrinkle, or any such thing; but that it should be holy and without blemish.
EPHESIANS 5:27

1   The Church was founded, not as an institution of authority to compel the world to live up to Christ's teachings, but only as a witness-bearing institution to Christ, to hold Him before the people.
   Henry H. Halley
   Pocket Bible Handbook (1948)

2   I would rather be a deacon of a church than Lord Mayor of London.
   Charles Spurgeon
   "Divine Sovereignty" sermon (1856)

3   Before the first star was kindled, before the first living creature began to sing the praise of its Creator, he loved his Church with an everlasting love.
Charles Spurgeon
"The Unchangeable Christ" sermon (1888)

4   My friends, it is one thing to go to church or chapel; it is quite another thing to go to God.
Charles Spurgeon
"Salvation to the Uttermost" sermon (1856)

5   God's children should learn to rid the church of problems, not to add problems to the church.
Watchman Nee
Not I But Christ (1948)

6   Whether your Christian life began yesterday or thirty years ago, the Lord's intent is that you play an active and vital part in his body, the local church.
Thabiti Anyabwile
What Is a Healthy Church Member? (2008)

7   In the final analysis, church members are the people who generally make or break a local church. And making or breaking a church has a lot to do with the membership's attitudes and actions toward its leaders.
Thabiti Anyabwile
What Is a Healthy Church Member? (2008)

8   The uniqueness of the church is her message—the Gospel. The church is the only institution entrusted by God with the message of repentance of sins and belief in Jesus Christ for forgiveness.
Mark Dever and Paul Alexander
The Deliberate Church (2005)

9   A church is not a Fortune 500 company. It's not simply another nonprofit organization, nor is it a social club. In fact, a healthy church is unlike any organization that man has ever devised, because man didn't devise it.
Mark Dever and Paul Alexander
The Deliberate Church (2005)

10   The words of God in Scripture are the building blocks of the church. As pastors and church leaders, then, our first priority is to make sure that the Gospel enjoys functional centrality in the church.
Mark Dever and Paul Alexander
The Deliberate Church (2008)

11   There is one God. He is holy and has given himself in love. His church, therefore, should reflect his own character; we should be united and holy and loving or else we lie about him!
Mark Dever
Twelve Challenges Churches Face (2008)

12   There is but one church, with one faith, and if we want to commend it to our generation to the glory of our Lord, then we must walk, like those before us, in a manner worthy of Christ and of the calling to which we have been called.
Richard Phillips, Philip Ryken, and Mark Dever
The Church: One, Holy, Catholic, and Apostolic (2004)

13   The church is a kingdom with citizens drawn from other nations. The church is the household of God—a family of faith. The church is a holy temple in which God dwells by his Spirit. Three images of the church: kingdom, household, temple.
Richard Phillips, Philip Ryken, and Mark Dever
The Church: One, Holy, Catholic, and Apostolic (2004)

14   External criteria such as affluence, numbers, money, or positive response have never been the biblical measure of success in

ministry. Faithfulness, godliness, and spiritual commitment are the virtues God esteems.
John MacArthur
Ashamed of the Gospel (1993)

15 Church was never intended to be an exclusive club focused inward.
Joseph Stowell
The Trouble with Jesus (2003)

16 There is no such thing as a powerful church without prayer.
David Jeremiah
The Prayer Matrix (2004)

17 The church needs both unity and diversity if it is to function in this world.
Warren Wiersbe
A Gallery of Grace (2002)

18 Yes, I see the Church as the body of Christ. But, oh! How we have blemished and scarred that body through social neglect and through fear of being nonconformists.
Martin Luther King Jr.
Letter from Birmingham Jail (1963)

19 The church is primarily the community of the resurrection, a community in which we can live the new life of the Spirit.
Josh and Sean McDowell
Evidence for the Resurrection (2009)

20 Jesus could not pay the price for our sin by hiding in the safety of the upper room, and we cannot remain in the safety of the sanctuary.
Charles Swindoll
The Darkness and the Dawn (2001)

21 Churches can run without prayer. Whole denominations can run without prayer. The question is: Is what they're doing worth doing if they can do it without prayer?
Ben Patterson
Deepening Your Conversation with God (1991)

22 The church is simply a community of love.
Janet Hagberg and Robert Guelich
The Critical Journey (1995)

23 A church's capacity to love and serve its community is directly proportional to its members' ability to befriend visitors one at a time.
Brad Berglund
Reinventing Sunday (2001)

24 Churches are in the business of creating a new heaven and a new earth, not satisfying share holders.
Brad Berglund
Reinventing Sunday (2001)

25 It was never in God's revealed plan that the Christian churches would degenerate to the point that they would begin functioning as social clubs.
A. W. Tozer
Whatever Happened to Worship?
(20th century)

26 Ah, I believe that the Church of Christ suffers more to-day from trusting in intellect, in sagacity, in culture, and in mental refinement, than from almost anything else.
Andrew Murray
Master's Indwelling (1895)

27 The church is looking for better methods; God is looking for better men.
E. M. Bounds
Power Through Prayer (1906)

28 Let the Church awake to her calling to train the feeblest of her members to know that Christ counts upon every redeemed one to live wholly for His work. This alone is true Christianity, is full salvation.
Andrew Murray
Working for God (1901)

29 Those who attack the Church most seriously, and disbelieve in it most thoroughly, are not proposing simply to level the Church to the ground in the sense of destroying any religious society. What they want to do is to put some other kind of society in the place of the Church.
    Peter Forsyth
    The Work of Christ (1909)

30 The fellowship of the church has degenerated into a social fellowship with a mild religious flavor.
    A. W. Tozer
    "Who Is the Holy Spirit?" sermon
    (20th century)

31 The church is one of the few organizations in the world that does not exist for the benefit of its own members.
    Ed Stetzer and David Putman
    Breaking the Missional Code (2006)

32 A church is theologically sound and missionally appropriate when it remains faithful to the gospel and simultaneously seeks to contextualize the gospel (to the degree it can) in the worldview container of its hearers.
    Ed Stetzer and David Putman
    Breaking the Missional Code (2006)

33 This principle seems clear: the further one goes into the avant-garde frontier of creative ministry, the more important it becomes that we be deeply rooted in the biblical, theological, and historical tradition.
    Ray Bakke
    A Theology as Big as the City (1997)

34 A deaf church is a dead church: that is an unalterable principle.
    John Stott
    Between Two Worlds: The Challenge of Preaching Today (1982)

35 I am dreaming for communities of faith to go on a "journey" together instead of being satisfied to just pull off good meetings.
    David Ruis
    Inside Out Worship (2005)

36 Like the church in America today, the Laodicean church was affluent but asleep. . . materially rich but spiritually poor. . .outwardly impressive but spiritually empty.
    Douglas Bennett
    The Minimization of the Gospel (2009)

72 CIRCUMSTANCES
The LORD gave, and the LORD hath taken away; blessed be the name of the LORD.
JOB 1:21

1 God has never had a people who were at the mercy of circumstances. His wisdom always anticipates hell's worst and provides for heaven's best. So it is with high confidence that we may look to Him, notwithstanding the bleakness of the present scene surrounding us.
    Jack Hayford
    Glory on Your House (1991)

2 Occasions of adversity best discover how great virtue or strength each one hath. For occasions do not make a man frail, but they reveal what he is.
    Thomas à Kempis
    The Imitation of Christ (15th century)

3 Circumstances don't make a man, they reveal him. Like teabags, our real strength comes out when we get into hot water.
    J. Allan Petersen
    The Myth of the Greener Grass (1983)

4 Our lives are shaped less by what actually happens to us than by the meaning we ascribe to these events.
    Michele Weiner-Davis
    Divorce Busting (1992)

5   What kids and many adults alike need to learn is that complaining is a reaction to events, and while many events cannot be controlled, reactions can.
  Dean Merrill
  Wait Quietly (1994)

6   Frame your picture of God based on who He really is, not through the lenses of your circumstances.
  Tim Burns
  Forged in the Fire (2003)

7   Every creature of God is given something that could be called an inconvenience, I suppose, depending on one's perspective.
  Elisabeth Elliot
  Let Me Be a Woman (1976)

8   Sometimes when you are going forward spiritually, you go backwards in the natural because when our natural circumstances don't suit us, that's when we press in spiritually with God.
  Joyce Meyer
  "Overcoming Fear with Faith" sermon (2009)

9   There is nothing accidental in the life of an obedient child of God.
  Paul Billheimer
  Don't Waste Your Sorrows (1977)

10   No one remains untouched by chaos.
  Patricia Livingston
  This Blessed Mess (2000)

73 CITIZENSHIP

Put them in mind to be subject to principalities and powers, to obey magistrates, to be ready to every good work.
TITUS 3:1

1   Christians must not forget their identity: Christians are first and foremost citizens of the Kingdom of Heaven.
  Franklin Graham
  The Name (2002)

2   The fact that we have our citizenship in heaven ought to make us better citizens on earth, no matter under what form of government we may live.
  Warren Wiersbe
  A Gallery of Grace (2002)

3   Let a man's opinions and conduct be what they may, yet, provided he be sincerely continued that they are right, however the exigencies of civil society may require him to be dealt with amongst men, in the sight of God he cannot be criminal.
  William Wilberforce
  A Practical View of the Prevailing Religious System of Professed Christians (1815)

4   Great indeed are our opportunities, great also is our responsibility.
  William Wilberforce
  A Practical View of the Prevailing Religious System of Professed Christians (1815)

5   Whatever makes men good Christians makes them good citizens.
  Daniel Webster
  Speeches and Forensic Arguments (19th century)

6   The Christian is to have his gaze turned towards the future with eager longing and zeal for righteousness; he is even now to be a citizen of the heavenly country.
  Paul Wernle
  The Beginnings of Christianity (1903)

7   Christians are best equipped to take action and make a difference if they're informed.
  Deborah Dewart
  Death of a Christian Nation (2010)

74 CLERGY

How then shall they call on him in whom they have not believed? and how shall they believe in him of whom they have not heard? and how shall they hear without a preacher?
ROMANS 10:14

1 Those who hold God's word never need add something untrue in speaking to men. The sturdy truth of God touches every chord in every man's heart.
   Charles Spurgeon
   "The Holy Ghost—The Great Teacher" sermon (1855)

2 A sense of sin is all we have to look for as ministers. We preach to sinners; and let us know that a man will take the title of sinner to himself, and we then say to him, "Look unto Christ, and ye shall be saved."
   Charles Spurgeon
   "Sovereignty and Salvation" sermon (1856)

3 Gentlemen, pull the velvet out of your mouths; speak God's word.
   Charles Spurgeon
   "The Bible" sermon (1855)

4 If churches are to be healthy, then pastors and teachers must be committed to discovering the meaning of Scripture and allowing that meaning to drive the agenda with their congregations.
   Thabiti Anyabwile
   What Is a Healthy Church Member? (2008)

5 Our failure is that preachers ignore the Cross, and veil Christ with sapless sermons and superfine language.
   D. L. Moody
   Secret Power (1881)

6 Ministers are the church's teeth; like nurses, they chew the meat for the babes of Christ.
   Matthew Henry
   Commentary on the Whole Bible (1706)

7 As God can send a nation or people no greater blessing, than to give them faithful, sincere, and upright ministers; so the greatest curse that God can possibly send upon a people in this world, is to give them over to blind, unregenerate, carnal, lukewarm, and unskilful guides.
   George Whitefield
   "On the Method of Grace" sermon (1741)

8 God very wonderfully entrusts his highest office to preachers that are themselves poor sinners who, while teaching it, very weakly follow it.
   Martin Luther
   Table Talk (16th century)

9 Always bear in mind, that you are set for the edification of believers, and the conversion of sinners, especially the latter; and that only in the measure in which these results follow, are your labours successful.
   Peter Barron
   The United Presbyterian magazine (1856)

10 The character as well as the fortunes of the gospel are committed to the preacher. He makes or mars the message from God to man.
   E. M. Bounds
   Power Through Prayer (1906)

11 The preacher's strongest and sharpest preaching should be to himself.
   E. M. Bounds
   Power Through Prayer (1906)

12 If you go after the money and don't care about the people, we're hirelings and not shepherds.
   A. W. Tozer
   "In Everything by Prayer" sermon (20th century)

13 Our task as preachers, then, is neither to avoid all areas of controversy, nor to supply slick answers to complex questions in order to save people the bother of thinking.
   John Stott
   Between Two Worlds: The Challenge of Preaching Today (1982)

14 He cannot succeed in healing the wounds of others who is himself unhealed by reason of neglecting himself.
Richard Baxter
The Reformed Pastor (17th century)

15 One word of seasonable, prudent advice, given by a minister to persons in necessity, may be of more use than many sermons.
Richard Baxter
The Reformed Pastor (17th century)

16 'Tis hard preaching a Stone into Tears, or making a Rock to tremble.
Richard Baxter
The Causes and Danger of Slighting Christ and His Gospel (17th century)

75 COMFORT

Who comforteth us in all our tribulation, that we may be able to comfort them which are in any trouble, by the comfort wherewith we ourselves are comforted of God.
2 CORINTHIANS 1:4

1 As I strengthen myself by being in the Word every day, the Holy Spirit comes into my life with His wisdom, discernment, power, and comfort. Comfort is not the absence of problems; comfort is the strength to face my problems.
Ken Hutcherson
Before All Hell Breaks Loose (2001)

2 God knows that life can throw us up against a wall with no options and that the pain can be intense. But He stands vigil over us like a pillar of cloud and fire. We are beautiful to Him, and His eye is continually upon us. He will be our strength and refuge while we wait in the dark. He will hold us as a Father holds His wounded child.
Angela Thomas
Do You Think I'm Beautiful? (2003)

3 God doesn't comfort us to make us comfortable, but to make us comforters.
Billy Graham
Facing Death—and the Life After (1987)

4 Come ye famishing souls, who find nought to satisfy you; come, and ye shall be filled! Come, ye poor afflicted ones, bending beneath your load of wretchedness and pain, and ye shall be consoled! Come, ye sick, to your physician, and be not fearful of approaching him because ye are filled with diseases; show them, and they shall be healed!
François Fénelon and Jeanne Guyon
Spiritual Progress (17th century)

5 We must set our faces like a flint to believe, under each and every sorrow and trial, in the divine Comforter, and to accept and rejoice in His all-embracing comfort.
Hannah Whitall Smith
The God of All Comfort (1906)

6 We must choose to be comforted.
Hannah Whitall Smith
The God of All Comfort (1906)

7 For the heartsick, bleeding soul out there today who is desperate for a word of encouragement, let me assure you that you can trust this Lord of heaven and earth. There is security and rest in the wisdom of the eternal Scriptures.
James Dobson
When God Doesn't Make Sense (1993)

8 God comforts us in our troubles, not out of them.
Gary and Mona Shriver
Unfaithful (2005)

9 Sometimes He quiets the storms in our lives, and sometimes He allows them to rage. But regardless of the weather, He always calms and comforts His children.
Lisa Harper
Every Woman's Hope (2001)

10 God knows your need to be comforted. He knows you need to be reminded regularly you are not alone or forgotten. You need a pick-me-up. You need to be held. You need to be encouraged. God gives of Himself to comfort you.
Margaret Feinberg
God Whispers (2002)

11 See! and confess, one comfort still must rise
'Tis this—Though man's a fool, yet God is wise.
Alexander Pope
An Essay on Man (17th century)

12 You'll live much more peacefully and comfortably if you live transparently, not doing anything you wouldn't want God to see.
Bob Barnes
Walking Together in Wisdom (2001)

13 No matter how great our burdens or how deep our pain, God is able to comfort us. No matter how severe the pressures of daily life, they can't separate us from the tenderness and compassion of our Heavenly Father.
Luis Palau
Stop Pretending (2003)

14 He only that stills the stormy seas, can quiet the distressed and tempestuous soul.
John Flavel
Pneumatologia (1698)

15 The best creature-comfort apart from Christ is but a broken cistern. It cannot hold one drop of true comfort.
John Flavel
Christ Altogether Lovely (17th century)

16 You do not need to continue dealing with your own burdens and sorrows and grief. You may turn them over to Jesus, who stands ready to receive them. It is His will to comfort and heal all who come to Him in faith.
Rubye Goodlett
Gathered Fragments (1986)

76 COMMITMENT
O Timothy, keep that which is committed to thy trust.
1 TIMOTHY 6:20

1 Through commitment, we can find the courage to live creatively and to die confidently.
Maxine Hancock
The Forever Principle (1980)

77 COMMON SENSE
But the wisdom that is from above is first pure, then peaceable, gentle, and easy to be intreated, full of mercy and good fruits, without partiality, and without hypocrisy.
JAMES 3:17

1 Common sense is not faith and faith is not common sense; they stand in the relation of the natural and the spiritual; of impulse and inspiration. Nothing Jesus Christ ever said is common sense, it is revelation sense, and it reaches the shores where common sense fails.
Oswald Chambers
My Utmost for His Highest (1935)

78 COMMUNICATION (*see also* CONVERSATION; LISTENING; SPEECH; TONGUE, THE)
Let him that is taught in the word communicate unto him that teacheth in all good things.
GALATIANS 6:6

1 When men bring up a topic for conversation, they actually intend to talk about that topic.
Bill and Pam Farrel
Men Are Like Waffles, Women Are Like Spaghetti (2001)

2 Words can be a powerful, rejuvenating tonic! If you love your spouse, child, parent, or friend, tell him or her. How often people regret not doing so—particularly after the person is gone.
Kenneth Boa and Gail Burnett
The Art of Living Well (1999)

3   Communication is the lifeblood of a relationship. As long as we communicate openly and honestly, our relationship will be alive with oneness.
   Dick Purnell
   Finding a Lasting Love (2003)

4   Verbal compliments, or words of appreciation, are powerful communicators of love.
   Gary Chapman
   The Five Love Languages (1995)

5   We have the capability of giving one sentence a dozen different meanings just by changing our tone.
   H. Norman Wright
   Helping Those Who Hurt (2003)

6   In order to form a habit of conversing with God continually, and referring all we do to Him; we must at first apply to Him with some diligence: but that after a little care we should find His love inwardly excites us to it without any difficulty.
   Brother Lawrence
   The Practice of the Presence of God
   (17th century)

7   We ought to act with God in the greatest simplicity, speaking to Him frankly and plainly, and imploring His assistance in our affairs, just as they happen.
   Brother Lawrence
   The Practice of the Presence of God
   (17th century)

8   We need only to recognize God intimately present with us, to address ourselves to Him every moment.
   Brother Lawrence
   The Practice of the Presence of God
   (17th century)

9   There is not in the world a kind of life more sweet and delightful than that of a continual conversation with God.
   Brother Lawrence
   The Practice of the Presence of God
   (17th century)

10 All miscommunication results from differing assumptions.
   James Dobson
   Straight Talk (1995)

11 Once communication lines are down, you'll find that it's extremely difficult to restore them.
   Gary Chapman
   The World's Easiest Guide to Family Relationships (2001)

12 The transition from mind to mouth sometimes breaks down because the words we use do not correctly convey our message. Do you always mean what you say and say what you mean?
   H. Norman Wright and Marvin Inmon
   Dating, Waiting, and Choosing a Mate
   (1978)

13 Never communicate information you consider to be important without first creating a burning curiosity within the listener.
   Gary Smalley
   For Better or for Best (1979)

14 Lectures during stressful times only create more stress.
   Gary Smalley
   If Only He Knew (1979)

15 It is not good enough to communicate so that you can be understood. You should communicate so clearly that you cannot be misunderstood.
   Ken Sande
   The Peacemaker (1991)

16 It has been said that men use conversation as a means of communicating information, but women use conversation as a means of bonding.
   Shannon Ethridge
   Every Woman's Battle (2003)

17 Listening is the essence of patient and unselfish communication.
Dallas and Nancy Demmitt
Can You Hear Me Now? (2003)

79 COMMUNITY
*And all that believed were together,
and had all things common.*
ACTS 2:44

1 You can't do life alone, and you don't have to. Life is meant to be a partnership, lived in community with family and friends.
Stan Toler
Minute Motivators for Men (2004)

2 No man is an island, entire of itself; every man is a piece of the continent, a part of the main.
John Donne
Devotions Upon Emergent Occasions (1623)

3 Any man's death diminishes me, because I am involved in mankind, and therefore never seemed to know for whom the bell tolls; it tolls for thee.
John Donne
Devotions Upon Emergent Occasions (1623)

4 Communities heal when they focus on releasing what's good.
Larry Crabb
Connecting (1997)

5 Biblical community is the unity in diversity of people who embrace their own and each other's uniqueness, becoming God's arms, feet, and hands on earth.
Janet Hagberg and Robert Guelich
The Critical Journey (1995)

6 People are yearning to discover community. We have had enough loneliness, independence and competition.
Thea Jarvis
Everyday Hospitality (2007)

7 Without forgiveness, community is only possible where people are safely and cautiously superficial.
David Augsburger *Caring Enough to Forgive—Caring Enough Not to Forgive* (1981)

8 In community, the particular talents of the individual members become like the little stones that form a great mosaic. The fact that a little gold, blue, or red piece is part of a splendid mosaic makes it not less but more valuable because it contributes to an image much greater than itself.
Donald McNeill, Douglas Morrison, and Henri Nouwen
Compassion (1982)

80 COMPASSION
And Jesus went forth, and saw a great multitude, and was moved with compassion toward them, and he healed their sick.
MATTHEW 14:14

1 What are we made for, if not to bear each other's burdens?
Elizabeth Prentiss
More Love to Thee—The Life and Letters of Elizabeth Prentiss (1882)

2 Compassion is. . .the sometimes-fatal capacity for feeling what it's like to live inside somebody else's skin.
Frederick Buechner
Beyond Words: Daily Readings in the ABC's of Faith (2004)

3 Helping others means our ears and our eyes are open.
H. Norman Wright
Helping Those Who Hurt (2003)

4 Compassion is living within the skin of another person, if only temporarily. Walking a mile in their proverbial moccasins. It involves responding to their weaknesses with a little

extra understanding, rather than simply "reacting" to those words and actions that so irritate you or try your patience.

Thomas and Nanette Kinkade
The Many Loves of Parenting (2003)

5   One of the most powerful ways to gain entrance into someone's heart is to serve them.

Melody Rossi
May I Walk You Home? (2007)

6   The Son of God passed by the mansions and went down into a manger, that he might sympathize with the lowly.

D. L. Moody
The Faithful Saying (1877)

7   Let's learn something very important. What is a Goliath to a person is a Goliath.

Charles Swindoll
"David and the Dwarf" sermon (2009)

8   If you want to get a man on his feet again, the thing to do is not to preach or read the Bible to him, but to get him out of the cellar in which he lives. Take him by the hand, and he will be led away from his former life.

Henry Drummond
Stones Rolled Away and Other Addresses (1893)

9   Sometimes our life experiences help us find ways to be compassionate.

Kim Moore and Pam Mellskog
A Patchwork Heart (2002)

10   True compassion must flow from a river of gratitude that swells its bank with thankfulness over sins forgiven, hope restored, and wounds healed.

Kim Moore and Pam Mellskog
A Patchwork Heart (2002)

11   God's compassion is not something abstract or indefinite, but a concrete, specific gesture in which God reaches out to us.

Donald McNeill, Douglas Morrison, and Henri Nouwen
Compassion (1982)

12   God's compassion is a compassion that reveals itself in servanthood.

Donald McNeill, Douglas Morrison, and Henri Nouwen
Compassion (1982)

81 COMPLAINING
(*see also* MURMURING)

*And when the people complained,
it displeased the LORD.*
NUMBERS 11:1

1   God of all comfort, keep me from complaining if my burden seems heavy. Help me to follow in your footsteps and endure every weakness without the sin of resentment or complaint.

Joni Eareckson Tada
Pearls of Great Price (2006)

2   Christ was willing to suffer and be despised, and darest thou complain of anything?

Thomas à Kempis
The Imitation of Christ (15th century)

3   For as thankfulness is an express acknowledgement of the goodness of God towards you, so repining and complaints are as plain accusations of want of God's goodness towards you.

William Law
A Serious Call to a Devout and Holy Life (1729)

4   Have you developed a habit of complaining? Do you gripe about every little thing or about the same thing over and over again? If so, you need to realize that your

constant griping is an offense to God, a poor testimony to the lost, and a detriment to your personality. Determine to break your habit. Ask Jesus to transform your personality, and begin today to avoid complaining.

Bob and Rusty Russell
Jesus: Lord of Your Personality (2002)

5   If you think you accomplish anything positive by complaining or nagging, God's Word says otherwise. By complaining, you just put yourself in judgment's way.

Rhonda Rizzo Webb
Words Begin in Our Hearts (2003)

6   Complaining is not just those things that we say but those things that we think.

James MacDonald
Replace a Complaining Attitude (2009)

7   Those who choose complaining as their lifestyle will spend their lifetime in the wilderness. Complaining is sin.

James MacDonald
Replace a Complaining Attitude (2009)

8   You are forfeiting the grace that could help you through that trial by complaining about it instead of embracing it as a messenger from God to keep you humble and to keep you close to Him.

James MacDonald
Replace a Complaining Attitude (2009)

82 COMPROMISE

Why even of yourselves judge ye not what is right?
LUKE 12:57

1   Compromising Christians are always weak Christians.

Frances Ridley Havergal
Kept for the Master's Use (1879)

2   It is no coincidence that the fear of God largely disappeared from our culture at about the same time that relativism and subjective believing became prevalent.

Josh McDowell
The Last Christian Generation (2006)

3   We must be free from fanaticism on one hand and too much caution on the other.

Charles Sheldon
In His Steps (1896)

4   Compromise is a gift to human relationships.

David Augsburger
Caring Enough to Confront (2009)

CONCEIT (*see* ARROGANCE; BOASTING; SELFISHNESS)

83 CONFESSION

My son, give, I pray thee, glory to the LORD *God of Israel, and make confession unto him.*
JOSHUA 7:19

1   Confession means that we agree with God. We agree that we have sinned. We agree that we are responsible for our sins. And we agree that God has the right to rid us of this sin.

Erwin Lutzer
After You've Blown It (2004)

2   What is not confessed can't be forgiven.

Henry Cloud and John Townsend
Safe People (2005)

3   Nothing so much brings one person in contact with another as the confession of sin. When a friend tells us of his success, he stands at a distance from our heart; when he tells of his guilt with tears, he is very near.

Fulton Sheen
Life of Christ (1958)

4   To confess your sins to God is not to tell God anything God doesn't already know. Until you confess them, however, they are the abyss

between you. When you confess them, they become the Golden Gate Bridge.
Frederick Buechner
Beyond Words: Daily Readings in the ABC's of Faith (2004)

5   The Lord, brethren, stands in need of nothing; and He desires nothing of any one, except that confession be made to Him.
Clement
The First Epistle of Clement to the Corinthians (1st century)

6   Confession follows conviction.
D. L. Moody
Wondrous Love (1876)

7   Let your confession be as wide as your transgression.
D. L. Moody
Weighed and Wanting (19th century)

84 CONFLICT
(*see also* ARGUING; DISPUTING)
From whence come wars and fightings among you? come they not hence, even of your lusts that war in your members?
JAMES 4:1

1   Deeper connection is the treasure buried in conflict.
Greg and Michael Smalley
Communicating with Your Teen (2003)

2   Conflict is inevitable; it's a natural part of all relationships, healthy or unhealthy. All relationships—with our teenagers, colleagues, friends, extended family, church acquaintances, or neighbors—will experience conflict because people differ so greatly as individuals. And we should value those differences! Because we're different, it's only natural that we disagree.
Greg and Michael Smalley
Communicating with Your Teen (2003)

3   Fair fighting. . .means learning not to demean or belittle the other person's opinions.
Les Parrott III
The Control Freak (2000)

4   Though conflict can be uncomfortable, you must remember this: God is greater than annoyance, He is mightier than evil. And He can take anything and use it for His good.
Heather Whitestone McCallum
Let God Surprise You (2003)

5   Conflict provides opportunities to glorify God, to serve others, and to grow to be like Christ.
Ken Sande
The Peacemaker (1991)

6   Most family conflicts can be resolved effectively if there is concern, communication, commitment. . .and large helpings of simple courtesy.
Gigi Graham Tchividjian
Currents of the Heart (1996)

85 CONFRONTATION
And Nathan said to David, Thou art the man.
2 SAMUEL 12:7

1 Only people who keep short accounts of their own failures, sins and weaknesses have earned the right to assist others with those things in their lives. Vulnerable, humble, transparent individuals make the best confronters.
Charles Swindoll
Simple Faith (1991)

86 CONSCIENCE
(*see also* CONVICTION)
Pray for us: for we trust we have a good conscience, in all things willing to live honestly.
HEBREWS 13:18

1   All men alike stand condemned, not by alien codes of ethics, but by their own, and all men therefore are conscious of guilt.
  C. S. Lewis
  The Problem of Pain (1947)

2   Conscience is God present in man.
  Victor Hugo
  Intellectual Autobiography (19th century)

3   Conscience is the authentic voice of God to you.
  Rutherford B. Hayes
  Letter to Scott Hayes (1892)

4   People can have deepened convictions and still be tragically wrong if the things they believe with conviction are wrong beliefs.
  Josh McDowell and Bob Hostetler
  Beyond Belief to Conviction (2002)

5   We cannot live in conflict with our conscience, which hopefully has been tuned to righteous standards.
  David Hawkins
  When Life Makes You Nervous (2001)

6   Conscience is the soul of freedom, its eyes, its energy, its life. Without conscience, freedom never knows what to do with itself.
  Thomas Merton
  No Man Is an Island (1955)

7   The voice of conscience is the voice of God; for it is his vicegerent and representative.
  John Flavel
  Pneumatologia (1698)

8   A strong, stable, religious life can be built up on no other ground than that of intelligent conviction.
  James Orr
  The Christian View of God and the World (1908)

9   All the worldly goods which I so carefully gathered, would I now give for a good conscience, which I so carelessly neglected.
  Lewis Bayly
  The Practice of Piety (1611)

10 Conscience can be so easily perverted or morbidly developed in the sensitive person, and so easily ignored and silenced by the insensitive, that it makes a very unsatisfactory god.
  J. B. Phillips
  Your God Is Too Small (1952)

87 CONSECRATION
(*see also* DEDICATION; DEVOTION; LOYALTY)
Who then is willing to consecrate his service this day unto the LORD?
1 CHRONICLES 29:5

1   The people who make a durable difference in the world are not the people who have mastered many things, but who have been mastered by one great thing.
  John Piper
  Don't Waste Your Life (2003)

2   Literally, a consecrated life is and must be a life of denial of self.
  Frances Ridley Havergal
  Kept for the Master's Use (1879)

3   Again and again God has shown that the influence of a very average life, when once really consecrated to Him, may outweigh that of almost any number of merely professing Christians.
  Frances Ridley Havergal
  Kept for the Master's Use (1879)

4   Satan sometimes suggests that an offering will satisfy God, when in fact He is demanding our all.
  Corrie ten Boom
  Not Good If Detached (1957)

CONTENTMENT

CONSOLATION (*see* COMFORT)

88 CONTENTMENT

*But godliness with contentment
is great gain.*
1 TIMOTHY 6:6

1 The Lord of the universe stands ready to pick up your life and give it significance, a sense of fulfillment beyond anything you have ever experienced. Your heart has got eternity in it...and you will not be fulfilled until you know you are making an eternal difference with the one life you have.
  Ron Hutchcraft
  Called to Greatness (2001)

2 God knows very well what happens to people when they are caught up in envy. What God really intends for us is that we would be content with who we are and what we have. Content with Him.
  Ron Mehl
  Right with God (2003)

3 When Christ becomes our central focus, contentment replaces our anxiety as well as our fears and insecurities.
  Charles Swindoll
  Laugh Again (1995)

4 Contentment, like a flawless diamond, is a valuable and scarce commodity. Talk to ten people at random, and you will be hard pressed to find even one or two who are truly content.
  Dennis and Barbara Rainey
  Pressure Proof Your Marriage (2003)

5 We must never be content with who we are, only with what we have.
  James MacDonald
  Lord, Change My Attitude (2001)

6 No matter what happens to you, a positive attitude comes from within. Your circumstances and your contentment are unrelated.
  John Maxwell
  Failing Forward (2000)

7 The godly person has found that what the greedy or envious or discontented person always searches for but never finds. He has found satisfaction and rest in his soul.
  Jerry Bridges
  The Practice of Godliness (1996)

8 Whether it is our past accomplishments or hurts, our future desires or fears, or the sight of who we truly are, these personal obstacles may keep contentment at bay as we allow them to lord themselves over us.
  Marsha Crockett
  Dancing in the Desert (2003)

9 God warns us that seeking our own brand of contentment apart from Him is futile, for "the bed is too short to stretch out on, the blanket too narrow to wrap around you."
  Marsha Crockett
  Dancing in the Desert (2003)

10 True contentment begins as a holy discontentment, a longing planted in our hearts by God Himself.
  Marsha Crockett
  Dancing in the Desert (2003)

11 No one can decide to make you content in your financial situation but you.
  Ellie Kay
  The Debt Diet (2005)

12 Scripture says God doesn't exist to serve us, but instead we exist to serve Him. Though He is giving and generous, He doesn't cater to our every wish.
  Jeff Kinley and MercyMe
  I Can Only Imagine (2002)

13 The first step toward contentment is thankfulness. And thankfulness is an attitude, an approach to life. Thankfulness leads to contentment and overcoming overload.
   Steve and Mary Farrar
   Overcoming Overload (2003)

14 Contentment is a Christian virtue that requires development, for it does not emerge fully formed at conversion.
   Donald S. Whitney
   Simplify Your Spiritual Life (2003)

15 We can be content in Christ, regardless of our circumstances, because in Him we have everything we need, for now and forever.
   Donald S. Whitney
   Simplify Your Spiritual Life (2003)

16 Contentment only comes from being truly content in your present circumstances.
   Brenda Armstrong
   The Single Mom's Workplace Survival Guide (2002)

17 Endeavor, my son, rather to do the will of another than thine own. Choose always to have less rather than more. Seek always the lowest place, and to be inferior to every one. Wish always, and pray, that God's will may be perfectly fulfilled in you.
   Thomas à Kempis
   Imitation of Christ (15th century)

18 By trying to grab fulfillment everywhere, we find it nowhere.
   Elisabeth Elliot
   Passion and Purity (1984)

19 You cannot rise above your present position in life? Make sure, then, that you beautify it, and shed all around it a pleasant fragrance.
   John Dawson
   The Saviour in the Workshop (1868)

20 Men in general would rather be somewhere else than where God in His providence has placed them.
   John Dawson
   The Saviour in the Workshop (1868)

21 Looking to another person for fulfillment (or wealth, power, position, or children) will never work. It is like pouring water through a sieve. The wire mesh gets wet indeed, but it does not hold the water. You must take responsibility for your own fulfillment.
   Stephen Arterburn
   Finding Mr. Right (2003)

22 We were made for God and nothing else will really satisfy us.
   Brennan Manning
   The Rabbi's Heartbeat (2003)

89 CONTROL

I the LORD search the heart, I try the reins, even to give every man according to his ways, and according to the fruit of his doings.
JEREMIAH 17:10

1 The more we try to gather the control of our lives, the more everything in our lives falls apart. God did not create us to control; He created us to live in agreement.
   David Edwards
   The God of Yes (2003)

2 While we can achieve a significant level of control, keeping all the plates spinning is no more possible than grasping the wind.
   Dan Allender and Tremper Longman III
   Breaking the Idols of Your Heart (1998)

90 CONVERSATION (see also COMMUNICATION; LISTENING; SPEECH; TONGUE, THE)

*My lips shall not speak wickedness,
nor my tongue utter deceit.*
JOB 27:4

1   Unkind words have tremendous power to sting.
Kenneth Boa and Gail Burnett
The Art of Living Well (1999)

2   Words are powerful because they evoke emotional, psychological, spiritual, and intellectual meaning.
Karen Burton Mains
You Are What You Say (1988)

3   What power words can hold! Properly presented, they can paint an absolutely credible picture of a person's heart.
Gary Smalley
Secrets to Lasting Love (2000)

4   Sometimes, brevity with emotion can say much more than just a mass of verbiage.
Ravi Zacharias
"A Nation in Decay" sermon (1979)

5   When we answer before listening, we prove to others that we are both stupid and rude.
Dallas and Nancy Demmitt
Can You Hear Me Now? (2003)

91 CONVERSION (see also BORN AGAIN; REDEMPTION; REGENERATION; SALVATION)

*Repent ye therefore, and be converted,
that your sins may be blotted out,
when the times of refreshing shall come
from the presence of the Lord.*
ACTS 3:19

1   God creates out of nothing—wonderful, you say, yes, to be sure, but he does what is still more wonderful, He makes saints out of sinners.
Søren Kierkegaard (19th century)
Quoted in *Fundamentals of the Faith*

2   There is a vast difference between intellectual belief and the total conversion that saves the soul.
Billy Graham
Peace with God (1984)

3   O when once the heart is gained, how easily is all the rest corrected! This is why God, above all things, requires the heart.
François Fénelon and Jeanne Guyon
Spiritual Progress (17th century)

4   Conversion brings with it a new capacity with which we may now serve God and righteousness. Before salvation, we were servants of sin, but now we may be servants of righteousness. The unsaved man has only one capacity, but the Christian has two.
Charles Ryrie
Balancing the Christian Life (1969)

5   I was just a mere boy when converted, hardly ten years old. There isn't much of a story to it. God just came into my heart one afternoon while I was alone in the "loft" of our big barn while I was shelling corn to carry to the mill to be ground into meal.
George Washington Carver (1930)
Quoted in George Washington Carver in His Own Words

6   Some people do not believe in sudden conversion. I should like them to answer me when was Zaccheus converted? He was certainly in his sins when he went up into that tree; he certainly was converted when he came down.
D. L. Moody
Best Thoughts and Discourses of D. L. Moody (1876)

7 If you will believe God, believe this: there is but one of these two ways for every wicked man, either conversion or damnation.

Richard Baxter

A Call to the Unconverted, to Turn and Live (17th century)

8 The convert's first duty, the first point that he was bound to clear up for himself, was that during the whole of his previous life he had been pursuing a wrong course, and that now he was in the right one.

Paul Wernle

The Beginnings of Christianity (1903)

9 Till men are deeply humbled, they can part with Christ and salvation for a lust, for a little worldly gain, for that which is less than nothing. But when God hath enlightened their consciences, and broken their hearts, then they would give a world for Christ.

Richard Baxter

The Causes and Danger of Slighting Christ and His Gospel (17th century)

10 It is one thing to have sin alarmed only by convictions, and another to have it crucified by converting grace.

Joseph Alleine

A Sure Guide to Heaven (1671)

11 Conversion then, in short, lies in the thorough change both of the heart and life.

Joseph Alleine

A Sure Guide to Heaven (1671)

12 The act of the heart in choosing Jesus Christ is not always performed in a single moment, nor is it always performed calmly and clearheadedly.

J. I. Packer

J. I. Packer Answers Questions for Today (2001)

92 CONVICTION
(*see also* CONSCIENCE)

And they which heard it, being convicted by their own conscience, went out one by one.

JOHN 8:9

1 Core convictions are revealed by our daily actions, by what we actually do. They are what might be called the "mental map."

John Ortberg

Faith and Doubt (2008)

2 When God convicts us of sin, the easiest thing to do is say "yes." Silence, excuses, rationalization, and deflection don't work. Forgiveness comes through confession.

Dave Earley

The 21 Most Effective Prayers of the Bible (2005)

3 If there is anything in your life which you know to be wrong, do not sleep until you have the thing settled with God.

D. L. Moody

Short Talks (19th century)

93 CORRECTION (*see also* REBUKE)

My son, despise not the chastening of the LORD; neither be weary of his correction.

PROVERBS 3:11

1 He that won't be counsell'd, can't be help'd.

Benjamin Franklin

Poor Richard's Almanac (18th century)

2 Being confronted on character issues isn't pleasant. It hurts our self-image. It humbles us. But it doesn't harm us. Loving confrontation protects us from blindness and self-destructiveness.

Henry Cloud and John Townsend

Safe People (2005)

3 Loving correction is part of love.
Dean Merrill
Wait Quietly (1994)

94 COUNSELING

For unto us a child is born, unto us a son is given. . .and his name shall be called Wonderful, Counsellor.
ISAIAH 9:6

1 Sometimes people ask if it is depressing to spend all day listening to problems. I tell them, "I am not listening to problems. I am listening for solutions."
Mary Pipher
Letters to a Young Therapist (2003)

95 COURAGE

Be strong and of a good courage; be not afraid, neither be thou dismayed: for the LORD thy God is with thee whithersoever thou goest.
JOSHUA 1:9

1 Be brave. Cowards always get hurt. Brave men generally come out unharmed.
A. B. Simpson
Days of Heaven Upon Earth (1897)

2 There is wide difference between wise caution and perverse squeamishness.
John Calvin
Bible Commentaries (16th century)

3 Many define courage as the lack of fear. We consider the lack of fear as a sign of anything but courage. Indeed, we see fearlessness as the hallmark of someone who lacks good sense!
Tim Clinton and Gary Sibcy
Attachments (2002)

4 When people see how courageous and optimistic you are during your troubled times, they will be drawn to Christ.
Josh McDowell and Bob Hostetler
Beyond Belief to Conviction (2002)

5 The first step of courage isn't taken in the midst of a battle; it's taken when you're willing to walk onto the battlefield and face the unknown.
Steven Curtis Chapman
The Great Adventure (2001)

6 The question is not can you dream, but do you have the courage to act on it?
Jentezen Franklin
Believe That You Can (2008)

7 Courage: The inner commitment to pursue a worthwhile *goal* without giving up *hope*.
Gary Smalley
For Better or for Best (1979)

8 Having courage for the long haul means embracing God's love in the face of unrelenting difficulty.
Carol Kent
A New Kind of Normal (2007)

9 Courage is simply doing what needs to be done even though you are scared and tired.
Rick Johnson
That's My Son (2005)

10 Courage is fear that has said its prayers.
Anne Lamott
Traveling Mercies (1999)

11 True freedom from fear consists of totally resigning one's life into the hands of the Lord.
David Wilkerson
"Resigned into God's Care" sermon (2010)

12 Courage is not the absence of fear.
Alex and Brett Harris
Do Hard Things (2008)

13 Positive attitudes, affirmation, appropriate discipline, stable relationships and love cultivate the soil of confidence.
Jerry White
Dangers Men Face (1997)

COURTESY (*see* RESPECT)

96 COVETOUSNESS (*see also* GREED)
Thou shalt not covet thy neighbour's house, thou shalt not covet thy neighbour's wife, nor his manservant, nor his maidservant, nor his ox, nor his ass, nor any thing that is thy neighbour's.
EXODUS 20:17

1 At the root of covetousness is a rejection of God's sufficiency.
James MacDonald
Lord, Change My Attitude (2001)

2 Our nation is absolutely submerged and drowning in a sea of covetousness. I'm part of it and you're part of it.
James MacDonald
Replace My Covetous Attitude (2009)

3 Materialism and covetousness are spreading across our land like a black plague.
James MacDonald
Replace My Covetous Attitude (2009)

4 Covetousness inflates the pleasure. Dwelling on the desire inflates its importance. It causes us to lose all perspective on what is real.
James MacDonald
Replace My Covetous Attitude (2009)

5 Yea, such a power of deceit is there in this sin that many times, when everybody else can see the man's worldliness and covetousness, he cannot see it himself, but has so many excuses and pretences for his eagerness after the world, that he blinds his own eyes and perishes in his self-deceit.
Joseph Alleine
A Sure Guide to Heaven (1671)

97 COWARDICE (*see also* FEAR)
And he said unto them, Why are ye so fearful? how is it that ye have no faith?
MARK 4:40

1 Will you let the fear of a false world, that has no love for you, keep you from the fear of that God, who has only created you, that he may love and bless you to all eternity?
William Law
A Serious Call to a Devout and Holy Life (1729)

2 Men trust an ordinary man because they trust themselves. But men trust a great man because they do not trust themselves. And hence the worship of great men always appears in times of weakness and cowardice; we never hear of great men until the time when all other men are small.
G. K. Chesterton
Heretics (1905)

98 CREATION (*see also* EVOLUTION)
In the beginning God created the heaven and the earth.
GENESIS 1:1

1 All nature's works His praise declare, to Whom they all belong;
There is a voice in every star, in every breeze a song.
Henry Ware Jr.
"All Nature's Works His Praise Declare" (1822)

2 If the universe is not eternal, it needs a cause. On the other hand, if it has no beginning, it does not need a cause of its beginning. Likewise, if a God exists who has no beginning, it is absurd to ask, "Who made God?"
Norman Geisler
Who Made God? (2003)

3 It is a category mistake to ask, "Who made the Unmade?" or "Who created the

Uncreated?" One may as well ask, "Where is the bachelor's wife?"
Norman Geisler
Who Made God? (2003)

4   Man forgets that our world is not as God made it. God made the world good. Sin corrupted it.
Billy Graham
Peace with God (1984)

5   When you see a beautiful painting, praise the artist. When you hear a beautiful song, praise the composer. When you experience beauty in nature, praise the Creator.
Bruce Bickel and Stan Jantz
God Is in the Small Stuff (1998)

6   The biblical doctrine of origins, as contained in the Book of Genesis, is foundational to all other doctrines of Scripture. Refute or undermine in any way the biblical doctrine of origins, and the rest of the Bible is compromised.
Ken Ham
The Lie: Evolution (1987)

7   Creation is an outpouring of love—an overflow of love from the heavens to earth. Creation not only declares the inventiveness and resourcefulness of God but reveals the abundance of his love.
David Benner
Surrender to Love (2003)

8   In the beginning, God made Adam out of a piece of clay, and Eve out of Adam's rib: he blessed them and said: "Be fruitful and increase"—words that will stand and remain powerful to the world's end.
Martin Luther
Table Talk (16th century)

9   The universe owes its existence to his will.
Charles Hodge
What Is Darwinism? (1874)

10 That design implies an intelligent designer, is a self evident truth.
Charles Hodge
What Is Darwinism? (1874)

11 We are not distinguished from brutes by our senses, but by our understanding.
John Flavel
Pneumatologia (1698)

12 Nothing is more injurious to the honour of the Eternal Mind than the supposition of eternal matter.
Matthew Henry
Commentary on the Whole Bible (1706)

13 Creation is the vesture of Christ. He wraps himself about in its ample folds.
F. B. Meyer
The Way into the Holiest (1893)

14 Before there was when, before there was where, you spoke. And creation became.
Martin Bell
Street Singing and Preaching (1991)

15 Design demands a designer.
Steve and Laura Goad
"Awesome Design" article (2009)

16 The one inescapable and highly improbable fact about the world is that we, as reflective human beings, are in fact here.
Alister McGrath and Joanna Collicutt McGrath
The Dawkins Delusion (2007)

17 It is virtually impossible to quantify how improbable the existence of humanity is.
Alister McGrath and Joanna Collicutt McGrath
The Dawkins Delusion (2007)

18 The Bible gives a clear and cogent account of the beginnings of the cosmos and humanity. There is absolutely no reason for an intelligent

mind to balk at accepting it as a literal account of the origin of our universe. Although the biblical account clashes at many points with naturalistic and evolutionary hypotheses, it is not in conflict with a single scientific fact.
John MacArthur
The Battle for the Beginning (2001)

99 CREATIVITY
*Write thee all the words
that I have spoken unto thee in a book.*
JEREMIAH 30:2

1   Men do not write well unless they have some end in writing. To sit down with paper and ink before you, and so much space to fill up, will ensure very poor writing.
Charles Spurgeon
"The Blessing of Full Assurance" sermon (1888)

2   I never sat down to write without first praying that I might not be suffered to write anything that would do harm, and that, on the contrary, I might be taught to say what would do good.
Elizabeth Prentiss
More Love to Thee—The Life and Letters of Elizabeth Prentiss (1882)

3   While we may never go more than a few hundred miles from our home, our written words can go around the world and make a difference for eternity.
Marlene Bagnull
Write His Answer (1990)

4   The only thing you have to risk by being a creative instrument of God is your image of yourself. God is secure in his image of you.
Alice Bass
The Creative Life (2001)

5   If the roots of your creative life are in Christ, then you are safe to experience the farthest reaches of your imagination.
Alice Bass
The Creative Life (2001)

6   The goal of a creative life is expression, not perfection; you have the freedom to pour out your heart to God, regardless of how well you do it.
Alice Bass
The Creative Life (2001)

7   We make, but thou art the creating core.
George MacDonald
Diary of an Old Soul (1880)

8   No human being should ever say, "I'm not creative," for this is denying a very important element of being made in the image of God. One of the special things about us is creativity, the ability to make and do things beyond mere functional purposes, things with meaning. It is important to help our children understand this by guiding them to use their imagination in making things.
Myron and Esther Augsburger
How to Be a Christ-Shaped Family (1994)

9   Writing forces us to articulate our innermost feelings.
Ingrid Trobisch
Keeper of the Springs (1997)

10 Being able to think, have ideas, and then to choose to make or do something, is essential to creativity.
Edith Schaeffer
What Is a Family? (1975)

11 Creativity can be constructive, and take what "is" and cause something new to spring forth which will be fulfilling and helpful and give birth to more beauty, to fresh ideas in another person or persons.
Edith Schaeffer
What Is a Family? (1975)

12 The choice in creativity goes in one direction or another, in that individual creative works can be constructive or destructive.
Edith Schaeffer
What Is a Family? (1975)

13 Constructive creativity not only affects other human beings, but brings glory to God by being in the stream of His creativity.
  Edith Schaeffer
  What Is a Family? (1975)

14 Artists have long understood the beauty of the relationship between the nurturer and the nurtured.
  Valerie Bell
  Reaching Out to Lonely Kids (1994)

15 Creativity is not about me. It is not about you. It is not us somehow acting like little gods, creating on our own in the same way God creates. Although he asks us to imitate him, we are not imitators of God in this dimension. The most we can hope for is to respond appropriately and creatively to who God is and what he means. Creativity is a response.
  Michael Card
  Scribbling in the Sand (2002)

16 Perhaps we struggle to see the connection between worship and the call to be creative precisely because they are so intimately linked. We have forgotten that the call to creativity is a call to worship.
  Michael Card
  Scribbling in the Sand (2002)

17 Creative activity of whatever kind is a never-failing source of deep fulfillment.
  Edith Margaret Clarkson
  So You're Single! (1978)

18 I do believe that creativity involves transcendence. Many a philosopher and theologian has stated that we most resemble the divine when we create. Imagine then, the power we tap into when we say yes to our creative gifts.
  Vinita Hampton Wright
  The Soul Tells the Story (2005)

19 When you take the stuff of life and rearrange it so that it matters, so that it does good things, you're acting creatively.
  Vinita Hampton Wright
  The Soul Tells the Story (2005)

20 The creative genius will likely never be understood completely, but our creativity will give us clues if we learn to be attentive.
  Vinita Hampton Wright
  The Soul Tells the Story (2005)

21 Be in the company of good books, beautiful pictures, and charming, delightful and inspiring music; and let all that one hears, sees, reads and thinks lift and inspire the higher.
  Henry Drummond
  Stones Rolled Away and Other Addresses to Young Men (1893)

22 It sometimes happens that a man, in giving to the world the truths that have most influenced his life, unconsciously writes the truest kind of a character sketch.
  D. L. Moody
  A Life for a Life and Other Addresses (1897)

23 Creativity is essential when it comes to our congregational worship. It's a sign of abundant life.
  Matt Redman
  Inside Out Worship (2005)

24 A writer learns more from what he writes than the reader, and often applies the perspective after the book is written.
  Donald Miller
  To Own a Dragon (2006)

25 As far as I can see, the reproduction of chaos is neither art, nor is it Christian.
  Madeline L'Engle
  Walking on Water (1980)

26 The artist is a servant who is willing to be a birth-giver.
  Madeline L'Engle
  Walking on Water (1980)

100 CRITICISM (*see also* FAULT-FINDING; JUDGING; SELF-RIGHTEOUSNESS)
Who art thou that judgest another?
JAMES 4:12

1 When unforgiveness is in the heart, criticism will be on the lips.
James MacDonald
Lord, Change My Attitude (2001)

2 If you never get criticized, chances are you aren't getting anything done.
Charles Swindoll
Hand Me Another Brick (1981)

3 Be open to hearing what your critics have to say. However, if you perceive that complaints come from blatantly mean-spirited critics, tune them out. Their criticisms say more about them than about you.
Les Parrott III
High-Maintenance Relationships (1996)

4 Always accept criticism, but never accept judgment.
James Richards
How to Stop the Pain (2001)

5 I've never answered critics. I have to answer only to God.
Kathryn Kuhlman
Kathryn Kuhlman (1976)

6 Criticism is like dripping water. The annoyance gradually wears on you, making you irritable as it breaks down your resistance and leaves you fully discouraged.
Bill Wilson
Christianity in the Crosshairs (2005)

7 No one likes to be criticized, regardless of how much truth lies behind the criticism.
Gary Smalley
For Better or for Best (1979)

8 I can think of nothing that demoralizes a man faster than criticism in front of his peers.
Gary Smalley
For Better or for Best (1979)

9 Although we cannot all be writers, we all want to be critics.
Martin Luther
A Treatise on Good Works (1520)

101 CROSS, THE

And he bearing his cross went forth into a place called the place of a skull, which is called in the Hebrew Golgotha.
JOHN 19:17

1 Let Me Dwell on Golgotha
John Newton
hymn title (1779)

2 At the Cross There's Room
Fanny Crosby
hymn title (19th century)

3 Christ's death on the cross was no tragedy but a glorious event.
Christopher Catherwood
The Cross (1986)

4 Before the foundation of the world was laid, God, in His divine sovereignty, planned to send His own Son to the cross to be our Savior.
Anne Graham Lotz
Just Give Me Jesus (2002)

5 It was at the cross that the omnipotent Creator died for the human creature's sin.
Anne Graham Lotz
Just Give Me Jesus (2002)

6 Man's sin reached its full horror and its most awful expression at Calvary. Not only had we disobeyed God's commandments and defied God's name, but now we were crucifying God's Son.
Colin Smith
Ten Keys for Unlocking the Bible (2002)

7 We believe that Calvary and the Resurrection are earth's greatest event as far as man is concerned. Even further, are not Calvary and the Resurrection the greatest events in God's eternities?
> Lance Latham
> *The Two Gospels* (1984)

8 We do not stand on what we do or how we behave. We stand on the finished work of the Cross.
> Jon Courson
> *Application Commentary* (2006)

9 What's not so popularly understood is that the cross was intended to work two ways: vertically, to heal our irreconcilable differences with God, and horizontally, to heal our irreconcilable differences with each other. The cross must stand between us and the Heavenly Father, but the cross also must stand between you and me.
> Gary Kinnaman
> *Learning to Love the One You Marry* (1997)

10 What is the cross? It is a minus turned into a plus!
> Robert Schuller
> *The Be (Happy) Attitudes* (1985)

11 The cross is simultaneously the most divisive and the most unifying event in human history.
> Albert Mohler Jr.
> *He Is Not Silent* (2008)

12 The thanks the world now gives to the doctrine of the gospel, is the same it gave to Christ, namely, the cross; 'tis what we must expect.
> Martin Luther
> *Table Talk* (16th century)

13 No man understands the Scriptures, unless he be acquainted with the cross.
> Martin Luther
> *Table Talk* (16th century)

14 The Cross was a shameful thing; the proclamation of a crucified Messiah appeared, therefore, to the devout Pharisee as an outrageous blasphemy.
> J. Gresham Machen
> *The Origin of Paul's Religion* (1921)

15 The cross is the key to heaven.
> Sadhu Sundar Singh
> *At the Master's Feet* (20th century)

16 This is the greatest sight you will ever see. Son of God and Son of Man, there He hangs, bearing pains unutterable, the just for the unjust, to bring us to God. Oh, the glory of that sight!
> Charles Spurgeon
> *All of Grace* (19th century)

17 There is no place like Calvary for creating confidence. The air of that sacred hill brings health to trembling faith.
> Charles Spurgeon
> *All of Grace* (19th century)

18 To the children, the manger is the chief thought, to us who are older (though we are all children together at Christmas-time) the Cross always stands near the manger. It is the background to every picture, invisible, but there.
> Amy Carmichael
> *Edges of His Ways* (1955)

19 Some of us know well that in order to go on with God we have many a time to go against the voice of the soul—our own or other people's—and to let the Cross come in to silence that appeal for self-preservation.
> Watchman Nee
> *Normal Christian Life* (20th century)

20 At bottom, the death on the Cross is not a means of propitiating God, but a symbol of His grace for men.
> Paul Wernle
> *The Beginnings of Christianity* (1903)

21 The Cross which consummated and crowned Christ came in its fullness of time.
>   Peter Taylor Forsyth
>   *The Work of Christ* (1909)

22 Take a long look at what happened at Calvary. The agony there was of the just for the unjust.
>   Elisabeth Elliot
>   *These Strange Ashes* (1989)

23 Nothing reveals the gravity of sin like the cross.
>   John Stott
>   *The Cross of Christ* (1986)

24 People want the benefit of the cross but they do not want the control of the cross.
>   A. W. Tozer
>   "Don't Beg God for the Holy Spirit" sermon (20th century)

25 The devil claimed a victory that afternoon, but only so Jesus could win victory forever.
>   Dave Earley
>   *The 21 Most Dangerous Questions of the Bible* (2007)

26 It is the Cross's power over my meaningless story that draws me to it.
>   Calvin Miller
>   *Once Upon a Tree* (2002)

27 Poets and composers may raise the Cross to the center of art and literature, but only our need and hunger can raise it to the center of our lives.
>   Calvin Miller
>   *Once Upon a Tree* (2002)

CULTURE (*see* SOCIETY)

102 DATING

There be three things which are too wonderful for me, yea, four which I know not: The way of an eagle in the air; the way of a serpent upon a rock; the way of a ship in the midst of the sea; and the way of a man with a maid.
PROVERBS 30:18–19

1 By anchoring yourself with the qualities of wisdom, optimism, discernment, spirituality, joyfulness, gratitude, and empathy, you are sure to avoid some of the dizzying motion of dating. And you are far more likely to find true love.
>   Les Parrott III
>   *7 Secrets of a Healthy Dating Relationship* (1995)

2 A date is often a showcase, designed to show only our best side and conceal our shortcomings.
>   Les Parrott III
>   *7 Secrets of a Healthy Dating Relationship* (1995)

3 While getting to know each other takes time, it's important to make every effort in the earliest stages of a relationship to show your true self to someone with whom you want to build a close relationship.
>   Les Parrott III
>   *7 Secrets of a Healthy Dating Relationship* (1995)

4 Sometimes the need to feel loved is so great that we attach ourselves to anyone, without first determining whether the relationship is a good idea.
>   Skip McDonald
>   *And She Lived Happily Ever After* (2005)

5 If marriage were a career, dating would be the internship.
>   Gary Chapman
>   *The World's Easiest Guide to Family Relationships* (2001)

6   People who are easily irritated while they are going together become more easily irritated after they get married.
William Coleman
Before I Give You Away (1995)

7   Couples who don't put energy and focus into their dating relationship settle for second best in their marriage bond.
Jim and Cathy Burns
Closer (2009)

8   You can impact your future partner if you're an encourager rather than a critic, a forgiver rather than a collector of hurts, an enabler rather than a reformer.
H. Norman Wright
Finding the Right One for You (1995)

9   Courting is not simply the invention of a romanticized society of a bygone day. It is native to the human heart and even corresponds to the heart of God, who courts, woos, and wins (and wins back) his bride Israel.
R. Paul Stevens
Down-to-Earth Spirituality (2003)

103 DAUGHTERS

*I will receive you. And will be a Father unto you,
and ye shall be my sons and daughters,
saith the Lord Almighty.*
2 CORINTHIANS 6:17–18

1   We live in a society that emphasizes preparation and education for everything but marriage, motherhood, and homemaking. Therefore, we must give this profession our highest attention when it comes to preparing our daughters for their futures.
Carolyn Mahaney
Feminine Appeal (2004)

2   We dads need to value our girls for all of their positive characteristics—their charm and grace, their intelligence, their athleticism,

their leadership abilities, or whatever it is that makes them who they are.
Bill McCartney
4th and Goal (2002)

3   When a daughter gets married, if her relationship with her mother is good, she may still look to her mother for a kind of nurturing she doesn't get from her husband.
Carol Kuykendall
Five-Star Families (2005)

4   Having a proper relationship with your married daughter requires a proper relationship with your son-in-law.
Michael Farris
What a Daughter Needs (2004)

104 DEATH

*Precious in the sight of the LORD
is the death of his saints.*
PSALM 116:15

1   The wicked man, when he dies, is driven to his grave, but the Christian comes to his grave.
Charles Spurgeon
"The Death of the Christian" sermon (1855)

2   We are kidding ourselves when we romanticize death as the beautiful climax of life well lived. It is an enemy. It is an ever greater enemy to the unbeliever, for death then becomes his threshold to hell.
Joni Eareckson Tada
Pearls of Great Price (2006)

3   I hunted all through the four Gospels trying to find one of Christ's funeral sermons, but I couldn't find any. I found He broke up every funeral He ever attended! Death couldn't exist where He was.
D. L. Moody
"The Ninety-First Psalm" sermon
(19th century)

4   It is strange that men will prepare for everything except death.
    Billy Graham
    Peace with God (1984)

5   Facing a serious illness and the certainty of death is a humbling experience. . .and one that wakes us up by shattering the illusion of security and health that surrounds our modern world.
    Ken Ham
    How Could a Loving God. . . ? (2007)

6   Christians are not immune to the fear of death.
    Billy Graham
    Facing Death—and the Life After (1987)

7   Death to a good man, is his release from the imprisonment of this world, and his departure to the enjoyments of another world.
    Matthew Henry
    Commentary on the Whole Bible (1706)

8   There is nothing more certain than death. There is nothing more uncertain than the time of death.
    Jeffrey Dean
    One-Liner Wisdom for Today's Guys (2006)

9   Everyone you know has one thing in common: Everyone you know will either go to Heaven or Hell.
    Jeffrey Dean
    One-Liner Wisdom for Today's Guys (2006)

10 Your heart beats about 100,000 times in a twenty-four hour period. One day, one of those beats will be your last. Does that thought concern you?
    Mark Cahill
    One Heartbeat Away (2005)

11 We don't put "Death" on our day planner, but one day it just shows up.
    Mark Cahill
    One Heartbeat Away (2005)

12 Death is like a dark valley that we all have to pass through. It is a dark place, but for the Christian it is a safe place. Christ has cleared out the enemies who lurked there.
    Colin Smith
    Unlocking the Bible Story (2002)

13 When you die—you die! There are no second chances. We always hear people say, "well, you only live once!" I am here to tell you, you only die once!
    Lisa Mendenhall
    "You Only Die Once" article (2009)

14 Five minutes after you die you will either have had your first glimpse of heaven with its euphoria and bliss or your first genuine experience of unrelenting horror and regret. Either way, your future will be irrevocably fixed and eternally unchangeable.
    Erwin Lutzer
    How You Can Be Sure That You Will Spend Eternity with God (1996)

15 Do you know how to die victoriously? Quit keeping score of the injustices that have happened to you.
    John Maxwell
    Be a People Person (1989)

16 From the time of Adam to the time of Christ, death had a way in but no way out. People went into death, but they could not emerge from it. But when Jesus died, He cut a hole in death itself.
    Colin Smith
    Unlocking the Bible Story (2002)

17 Die empty! My goal is to give the graveyard nothing but a vacant carcass of a used-up life!
    Wayne Cordeiro
    The Dream Releasers (2002)

18 When we develop an understanding of the life-death-life cycle we come to see that none of us is immune from loss and the suffering that accompanies it.

Joan Guntzelman
God Knows You're Grieving (2001)

19 Though death is a universal human experience, we should not then assume that it is a natural human experience. It is not what God intended. It is a result of the Fall, of things being corrupted from the way they were meant to be. Death is an enemy because it runs counter to Life. God is life. All that lives comes from the life-giving Spirit of God. Death is the enemy of life because it disrupts the life that God intended.

Albert Hsu
Grieving a Suicide (2002)

20 I thank my God for graciously granting me the opportunity. . .of learning that death is the key which unlocks the door to our true happiness.

Wolfgang Amadeus Mozart
Letter to his father (1787)

21 Death is always terrible to the wicked! . . .
The launch of an immortal spirit into the realms of an unchangeable and a never-ending eternity of bliss or woe; this brings with it serious reflections, solemn thoughts. Death gives things their true characters, and calls them by right names.

James Thomas Holloway
The Analogy of Faith (1836)

22 How does the wise man die? As does the fool.

Jonathan Edwards
"Sinners in the Hands of an Angry God" sermon (1741)

23 Choose any life but the life of God and heaven, and you choose death, for death is nothing else but the loss of the life of God.

William Law
The Spirit of Prayer (1750)

24 Death is a glorious event to one going to Jesus. Whither does the soul wing its way? What does it see first? There is something sublime in passing into the second stage of our immortal lives if washed from our sins.

David Livingstone (19th century)
Quoted in *David Livingstone: His Life and Letters*

25 If I live, I must succeed in what I have undertaken; death alone will put a stop to my efforts.

David Livingstone (19th century)
Quoted in *David Livingstone: His Life and Letters*

26 How many sorts of deaths are in our bodies? Nothing is therein but death.

Martin Luther
Table Talk (16th century)

27 We should always be ready when God knocks, prepared to take our leave of this world like Christians.

Martin Luther
Table Talk (16th century)

28 Though sickness, or trouble, or even death itself, should come to our house, and claim our dearest ones, still they are not lost, but only gone before.

D. L. Moody
Wondrous Love (1876)

29 We're so occupied with today that we take no thought for our future and eternity—that is, until somehow we're brought face to face with the specter of death.

Kay Arthur
Lord, Give Me a Heart for You (2001)

30 Death may be the final destination in our earthly journey, but it is merely the tunnel that transports us to the very real world beyond.
Charles Swindoll
"Visiting the Real Twilight Zone" sermon (1985)

31 Many long for life to be done that they may rest, as they say, in the quiet grave. Let no cheap sentimentalism deceive us. Death can only be gain when to have lived was Christ.
Henry Drummond
"To Me to Live Is Christ" sermon (19th century)

32 I do not wait for the undertaker, but for the Uptaker.
Corrie ten Boom
Not Good if Detached (1957)

33 I can not die for sin like Christ, but I can and I must die to sin like Christ. Christ died for me. In that He stands alone. Christ died to sin, and in that I have fellowship with Him.
Andrew Murray
Master's Indwelling (1895)

34 Death, and judgment, and eternity are not fancies, but stern realities. Make time to think about them. Stand still, and look them in the face. You will be obliged one day to make time to die, whether you are prepared or not.
J. C. Ryle
The Upper Room (19th century)

35 Since Adam, death has seized upon the sovereignty and reigns supreme. There are no exceptions.
Paul Wernle
The Beginnings of Christianity (1903)

36 Even the stoutest sinners will hear us on their death-bed, though they scorned us before.
Richard Baxter
The Reformed Pastor (17th century)

37 How often have I been warned of this doleful day by the faithful preachers of God's word, and I made but a jest of it! What profit have I now of all my pride, fine house, and gay apparel? What is become of the sweet relish of all my delicious fare?
Lewis Bayly
The Practice of Piety (1611)

38 The grave taketh away all civil differences; skulls wear no wreaths and marks of honour.
Thomas Manton
A Practical Commentary on the Epistle of James (17th century)

39 "To die is gain!" (Philippians 1:21). That kind of talk is absolutely foreign to our modern, spiritual vocabularies. We have become such life worshippers, we have very little desire to depart to be with the Lord.
David Wilkerson
"The Life Is Not in the Shell" sermon (2010)

40 Death is but a mere breaking of the fragile shell.
David Wilkerson
"The Life Is Not in the Shell" sermon (2010)

41 God may give us the miracle of an unexpected healing, or God may give us the miracle of a prepared and peaceful passing into His kingdom.
Bill Kemp and Diane Kerner Arnett
Going Home (2005)

105 DEBT

Be not thou one of them that strike hands, or of them that are sureties for debts.
PROVERBS 22:26

1 It's important to learn to live debt-free, and this includes borrowing from parents, friends, or siblings.
Susan Alexander Yates
And Then I Had Teenagers (2001)

2   We are a nation of consumers with credit instantly available to help us gratify our desires and medicate our insecurities.
Deborah Smith Pegues
30 Days to Taming Your Finances (2006)

106 DECEIT (*see also* LYING)
He that worketh deceit shall not dwell within my house: he that telleth lies shall not tarry in my sight.
PSALM 101:7

1   We know what a strong propensity men have to falsehood, so that they not only have a natural desire to be deceived, but each individual appears to be ingenious in deceiving himself.
John Calvin
Bible Commentaries (16th century)

2   A less-than-honest person is somewhere between a pain and a catastrophe.
Henry Cloud and John Townsend
Boundaries with Kids (1998)

3   Satan has a definite strategy, and it can be understood in one word: deception.
Tony Evans
Tony Evans Speaks Out (2000)

4   Therefore, in the name of God I exhort you, keep close every moment to the unction of the Holy One! Attend to the still, small voice! Beware of hearkening to the voice of a stranger!
John Wesley
The Works of the Rev. John Wesley (18th century)

5   O speak nothing, act nothing, think nothing, but as you are taught of God!
John Wesley
The Works of the Rev. John Wesley (18th century)

6   Satan cannot create anything new, cannot create anything at all. He must steal what God has created. Thus he twists love and God's wonderful gift of sex into lust and sadism and myriad perversions. He disfigures the heart's deep desire to worship God and persuades us to bow before lesser gods of lust or money or power.
Catherine Marshall
Something More (1974)

7   Perhaps the greatest self-deceit is to tell ourselves that we can be self-sufficient.
Joseph Stowell
Following Christ (1996)

8   Such fair and glorious colors do the ungodly ever bear in this world, while in truth and deed they are condemners, scoffers, and rebels to the Word of God.
Martin Luther
Table Talk (16th century)

107 DECISION-MAKING (*see also* CHOICES)
Butter and honey shall he eat, that he may now to refuse the evil, and choose the good.
ISAIAH 7:15

1   God speaks to us today because we need His definite and deliberate direction for our lives, as did Joshua, Moses, Jacob or Noah. We need His counsel for effective decision making.
Charles Stanley
How to Listen to God (1985)

2   Apart from the Holy Spirit in your life, the greatest power you possess is the power to choose.
Neil Anderson
Victory Over the Darkness (1990)

3   Indecision is sometimes a decision in itself.
Harry Jackson
In-laws, Outlaws, and the Functional Family (2002)

4   Like it or not, some things are simply
up to us.
    Beth Moore
    Get Out of That Pit (2007)

5   Five minutes before you see Jesus face
to face, what will you wish you had done
differently today? Do it!
    Anne Graham Lotz
    "No One Knows about That Day" article
    (2009)

6   Are you in a dilemma, wondering if you
should tell the truth or not? The question to
ask in such moments is, Will God bless my
deceit? Will he, who hates lies, bless a strategy
built on lies? Will the Lord, who loves the
truth, bless the business of falsehoods?
    Max Lucado
    Just Like Jesus (1998)

7   For the Christian, there is one thing and
one thing only that should be our baseline—
Scripture.
    Steve Campbell
    "The Primary Importance" sermon (2009)

8   We humans, you see, have an infinite
capacity for self-rationalization.
    Chuck Colson
    "The Bewilderment of Sin" article (2009)

9   Most of us don't give much thought to
the plethora of decisions we make as we
go through each day. Yet, the decisions we
make today will affect our children, our
grandchildren, and the generations to come.
    Joel Osteen
    Becoming a Better You (2007)

10   Sometimes we're pushing on the door we
want God to open, while his sign says "Pull."
    Martha Bolton
    If the Tongue's a Fire, Who Needs Salsa?
    (2002)

11   At the end of the day, direction, not
intention, determines destination.
    Andy Stanley
    The Principle of the Path (2008)

12   No one gets to the place where he no
longer needs wise counsel. Nobody.
    Andy Stanley
    The Principle of the Path (2008)

13   Every decision has an outcome and every
path has a destination.
    Andy Stanley
    The Principle of the Path (2008)

14   Immediate necessity makes many things
convenient, which if continued would grow
into oppressions.
    Thomas Paine
    Common Sense (1776)

15   Expedient and right are different things.
    Thomas Paine
    Common Sense (1776)

16   An ounce of prevention is worth a lifetime
of heartache.
    Jo Berry *Beloved Unbeliever* (1981)

17   It's sobering to think how quickly the
smallest personal decision can escalate into a
large group concern.
    Ted Engstrom and Robert Larson
    Integrity (1987)

18   Many would save themselves much sorrow
and trouble if they would only remember the
question, "What does it cost?"
    J. C. Ryle
    Holiness: Its Nature, Hindrances,
    Difficulties, and Roots (19th century)

19   Lives hinge on decisions forged in the heat
of crisis.
    Luis Palau
    Heart After God (1978)

108 DEDICATION
(*see also* CONSECRATION)

Not slothful in business;
fervent in spirit; serving the Lord.
ROMANS 12:11

1   We cannot be lukewarm; we have to be on fire with the cause of Christ.
D. L. Moody
The Faithful Saying (1877)

DEEDS (*see* GOOD WORKS)

109 DEFEAT (*see also* FAILURE; LOSS)

If any man's work shall be burned,
he shall suffer loss: but he himself
shall be saved; yet so as by fire.
1 CORINTHIANS 3:15

1   The Bible teaches that there are no lost causes. No permanent pit-dwellers except those who refuse to leave.
Beth Moore
Get Out of That Pit (2007)

2   I beg you to see that your enemy has a tremendous investment not only in digging and camouflaging a pit in your pathway but also, should you tumble down, in convincing you to stay there after you fall in.
Beth Moore
Get Out of That Pit (2007)

3   You never can't do it. . . . You just haven't done it yet.
Steve Campbell
"Just Keep Trying" sermon (2009)

4   God's purpose in your life is not to make everything easy. Our lives are meant to have meaning.
Beth Moore
"Who Do You Trust?" teaching series (2007)

110 DELIVERANCE

Thou art my hiding place; thou shalt preserve me
from trouble; thou shalt compass me about
with songs of deliverance.
PSALM 32:7

1   The hardest part about letting God fight your battle is that He sometimes waits until the eleventh hour so you will have no doubt of where the power is coming from.
Stormie Omartian
Just Enough Light for the Step I'm On (1999)

2   No storm is so great, no wave is so high, no sea is so deep, no wind is so strong, that Jesus cannot either calm it or carry us through it.
Anne Graham Lotz
The Daily Light Journal (2004)

3   God promises us forgiveness for what we have done, but we need His deliverance from what we are.
Corrie ten Boom
He Cares, He Comforts (1977)

4   When God sends destruction on the ungodly, he commands deliverance for the righteous.
Matthew Henry
Commentary on the Whole Bible (1706)

5   If we're willing to let truth speak louder than our feelings, and long enough that our feelings finally agree, we can be far more than okay. We can be delivered to a place where the air is crisp, the enemy whipped, and the view is magnificent.
Beth Moore
Get Out of That Pit (2007)

6   Those that keep themselves pure in times of common iniquity God will keep safe in times of common calamity.
Matthew Henry
Commentary on the Whole Bible (1706)

7   Once we begin to flee the things that threaten and burden us, there is no end to fleeing. God's solution is surprising. He offers rest. But it's a unique form of rest. It's to rest in him in the midst of our threats and our burdens. It's discovering, as David did in seasons of distress, that God is our rock and refuge right in the thick of our situation.
Mark Buchanan
The Rest of God (2006)

8   God's rescue plan—to be delivered, you have to let go.
Sheila Walsh
Let Go (2008)

9   When the Lord suspends the promised deliverance, the godly suspect not the truth of his word but the darkness of their own unbelieving hearts.
Thomas Manton
One Hundred and Ninety Sermons on the Hundred and Nineteenth Psalm (17th century)

10   As far as the Lord is concerned, the time to stand is in the darkest moment. It is when everything seems hopeless, when there appears no way out, when God alone can deliver.
David Wilkerson
"Right Song, Wrong Side" sermon (2009)

11   The great need of the present hour is Christians who have learned to sing the song of deliverance on the testing side of trouble.
David Wilkerson
"Right Song, Wrong Side" sermon (2009)

111 DEMONS

Thou believest that there is one God; thou doest well: the devils also believe, and tremble.
JAMES 2:19

1   When, love, joy, and peace rule a person's life, demons are repelled and God is blessed.
Eddie and Alice Smith
Spiritual Housecleaning (2003)

2   Demons operate through "slasher" movies, pornography, and heavy metal music, all designed to arouse the human emotions to violence and destruction.
Anne Graham Lotz
God's Story (1997)

3   A balancing word of caution: Some individuals become overly suspicious of people, and others become overly demon or devil conscious. Remember, we are to be watchmen, not watchdogs.
Dutch Sheets
Watchman Prayer (2000)

112 DEPRAVITY OF MAN

But we are all as an unclean thing, and all our righteousnesses are as filthy rags; and we all do fade as a leaf; and our iniquities, like the wind, have taken us away.
ISAIAH 64:6

1   Upon a poor polluted worm He makes His graces shine.
Isaac Watts
"Awake My Heart, Arise My Tongue" hymn (18th century)

2   Christ takes it for granted that people are bad. Until we really feel this assumption of His to be true, though we are part of the world He came to save, we are not part of the audience to whom His words are addressed.
C.S. Lewis
The Problem of Pain (1947)

3   The fact that after Satan is loosed at the end of the thousand years and some people will still follow him proves how depraved man can be.
David Jeremiah
Escape the Coming Night (1990)

4   Only those who see themselves drowning in sin will cry out, "God have mercy on me!"
Ray Comfort
Hell's Best Kept Secret (1989)

DEPRAVITY OF MAN

5   God has provided no remedy from the obstinacy of men; but if they will choose to be fools and to be miserable, he will leave them to inherit their own choice and to enjoy the portion of sinners.
John Tillotson
The Wisdom of Being Religious (1819)

6   I don't just commit sin. Apart from God, I am sinful. My problem is not just what I do; it's who I am without His nature.
Beth Moore
Jesus: 90 Days with the One and Only (2007)

7   The flesh is willing to flatter itself, and many who now give themselves every indulgence, promise to themselves an easy entrance into life. Thus men practice mutual deception on each other and fall asleep in wicked indifference.
John Calvin
Bible Commentaries (16th century)

8   If one evil thought, if one evil word, if one evil action, deserves eternal damnation; how many hells, my friends, do every one of us deserve, whose lives have been one continual rebellion against God.
George Whitefield
"A Sermon, Preached on Sabbath Morning" (1741)

9   Ye may do things materially good, but ye cannot do a thing formally and rightly good; because nature cannot act above itself. It is impossible that a man that is unconverted can act for the glory of God.
George Whitefield
"A Sermon, Preached on Sabbath Morning" (1741)

10   I know, by sad experience, what it is to be lulled asleep with a false peace. Long was I lulled asleep; long did I think myself a Christian, when I knew nothing of the Lord Jesus Christ.
George Whitefield
"A Sermon, Preached on Sabbath Morning" (1741)

11   Man is fallible and apart from God's grace can know nothing for certain. But if Christ is Who He says He is, then man can depend upon Him to know things for certain.
Jeff Baldwin
Thinking Biblically (2005)

12   None can trust in the merits of Christ, till he has utterly renounced his own.
John Wesley
Salvation by Faith (1738)

13   Good men avoid sin from the love of virtue: Wicked men avoid sin from a fear of punishment.
John Wesley
The Almost Christian (1741)

14   Having no spiritual senses, no inlets of spiritual knowledge, the natural man receiveth not the things of the Spirit of God; nay, he is so far from receiving them, that whatsoever is spiritually discerned, is mere foolishness unto him. He is not content with being utterly ignorant of spiritual things, but he denies the very existence of them.
John Wesley
"Awake, Thou That Sleepest" sermon (1743)

15   No works are good, which are not done as God hath willed and commanded them to be done.
John Wesley
Justification by Faith (1744)

16   No human being has the resources, the power, the money, or the merit to save himself.

The necessary power for rescue is not in us. It must come from God.

R. C. Sproul
Saved from What? (2002)

17 When finally summoned to the bar of God, to give an account of our stewardship, what plea can we have to urge in our defence, if we remain willingly and obstinately ignorant of the way which leads to life, with such transcendent means of knowing it, and such urgent motives to its pursuit?

William Wilberforce
A Practical View of the Prevailing Religious System of Professed Christians (1815)

18 Wherever we direct our view, we discover the melancholy proofs of our depravity; whether we look to ancient or modern times, to barbarous or civilized nations, to the conduct of the world around us, or to the monitor within the breast; whether we read, or hear, or act, or think, or feel, the same humiliating lesson is forced upon us.

William Wilberforce
A Practical View of the Prevailing Religious System of Professed Christians (1815)

19 Till the understanding of a man be enlightened to see the deformity of sin, and the beauty of holiness, he will never heartily loathe and grieve for the former, love and long for the latter.

George Swinnock
Works of George Swinnock (17th century)

20 Here is a major announcement brought to you by the God of the universe: Lost people are going to act lost—because they are lost!

Andy Stanley and Stuart Hall
Max Q Student Journal (2004)

21 The effects of Adam's choice to disobey God have traveled down through successive generations as a hideous moral cancer.

Richard Abanes
Harry Potter and the Bible (2001)

22 The spiritually blind people in the world are always looking for some problem outside themselves.

Martyn Lloyd-Jones
Compelling Christianity (20th century)

23 Get rid forever of the notion that becoming a Christian simply means being forgiven or trying to be a little bit better than you were before; you cannot be.

Martyn Lloyd-Jones
Compelling Christianity (20th century)

24 The soul, which was made upright in all its faculties, is now wholly disordered.

Thomas Boston
Human Nature in Its Fourfold State (1830)

25 Surely that corruption is ingrained in our hearts, interwoven with our very natures, has sunk into the marrow of our souls, and will never be cured but by a miracle of grace.

Thomas Boston
Human Nature in Its Fourfold State (1830)

26 First, I am to confirm the doctrine of the corruption of nature; to hold the glass to your eyes, wherein you may see your sinful nature; which, though God takes particular notice of it, many do quite overlook.

Thomas Boston
Human Nature in Its Fourfold State (1830)

27 We may conclude, that the natural darkness of our minds is such, as there is no cure for, but from the blood and Spirit of Jesus Christ, whose eye-salve only can make us see.

Thomas Boston
Human Nature in Its Fourfold State (1830)

28 If any saved person will dwell long enough upon the peril and wretchedness of any man out of Christ and the worth of his soul in God's sight as seen in the death of God's Son to save him, a feeling of intense desire for that man's salvation is almost certain to follow.
R. A. Torrey
How to Bring Men to Christ (1893)

29 Sinful unregenerate people will do evil things—it is their nature to do so—and laws will never change that.
Douglas Bennett
The Minimization of the Gospel (2009)

30 All you have got to do is, to prove that you are a sinner, and I will prove that you have got a Saviour. And the greater the sinner, the greater need you have of a Saviour.
D. L. Moody
Best Thoughts and Discourses of D. L. Moody (1876)

31 The reason why wicked men and devils hate God is, because they see him in relation to themselves. Their hearts rise up in rebellion, because they see him opposed to their selfishness.
Charles Finney
Lectures to Professing Christians (1837)

32 The fallen soul hath the nature of hell in it.
William Law
An Appeal to All That Doubt (18th century)

33 Apart from Jesus Christ, then, the chasm between God and us is impassable. It is our human finitude on the one hand, and our self-centered rebellion on the other. By ourselves we can neither know God nor reach him.
John Stott
Life in Christ (2003)

34 Mankind are all rebels against God, and are sunk into total moral depravity, in which they have a strong, fixed, and incurable propensity to rebellion, and a proportionable aversion from God and holiness, and will not come to Christ that they might be saved.
Samuel Hopkins
"An Improvement of the Subject"
sermon (1803)

35 God finds nothing in man to turn His heart, but enough to turn His stomach; He finds enough to provoke His loathing, but nothing to excite His love.
Joseph Alleine
A Sure Guide to Heaven (1671)

36 The Bible teaches us that man by nature is lost and guilty, and our experience confirms this.
D. L. Moody
The Way to God (1884)

37 People are like food. If left to their own devices, they can get a little rotten.
Martha Bolton and Phil Callaway
It's Always Darkest Before the Fridge Door Opens (2006)

DEPRESSION (*see* SADNESS)

113 DESPAIR

Yea, though I walk through the valley of the shadow of death, I will fear no evil: for thou art with me.
PSALM 23:4

1 I am convinced that the heart of the Lord is drawn to those who hold fast to their faith in such times of despair.
James Dobson
When God Doesn't Make Sense (1993)

2 Despair can open the heart to taste hope in God.
Dan Allender and Tremper Longman III
The Cry of the Soul (1994)

3   Actions you take (and decisions you make) in the darkness of confusion and despair will likely be mistakes.
Todd Hafer and Jeff Hafer
Wake Up and Smell the Pizza (2005)

4   Desperation does not make good decisions.
Beth Moore
"Overcoming Insecurity" teaching series (2006)

5   There is no place that we have been more deeply hurt in life than at the root of our distrust.
Beth Moore
"Who Do You Trust?" teaching series (2007)

6   If there is an area where you distrust God, underneath it is a place you've been wounded and we want Him to heal it.
Beth Moore
"Who Do You Trust?" teaching series (2007)

7   Hopelessness becomes debilitating.
Jay Kesler
Is Your Marriage Really Worth Fighting For? (1989)

8   God does not depend on our willpower and commitment to transform a hopeless situation.
Henry Cloud and John Townsend
God Will Make a Way (2002)

9   Occasions of desperation prepare the way for the recognition of Christ Himself.
Elisabeth Elliot
A Path Through Suffering (1990)

10   As strange as it may sound, desperation is a really good thing in the spiritual life. Desperation causes us to be open to radical solutions, willing to take all manner of risk in order to find what we are looking for.
Ruth Haley Barton
Invitation to Solitude and Silence (2004)

11   Perhaps in the desperation of a seemingly dead-end situation, our only recourse is to batter against the door of our fear, disbelief and inability, discovering to our surprise that it opens with the golden key of the prayer of faith.
Luci Shaw
The Crime of Living Cautiously (2005)

DESPISING (*see* HATRED)

114 DESTINY
There is a way that seemeth right unto a man, but the end thereof are the ways of death.
PROVERBS 16:25

1   He who is almost persuaded is almost saved, and to be almost saved is to be entirely lost.
I. Brundage
Memoirs of Philip P. Bliss (1877)

2   Have you considered, this short uncertain life is the time appointed for you to choose, whether you must be happy forever, or miserable forever?
Thomas Wilson
Private Thoughts (1828)

3   There is no true fulfillment in trying to shape our own destiny or make up our own god.
Richard Abanes
The Purpose That Drives Him (2005)

115 DEVIL
Put on the whole armour of God, that ye may be able to stand against the wiles of the devil.
EPHESIANS 6:11

1   The power of the devil is, after all, nothing but a usurped power.
Martyn Lloyd-Jones
The Cross (1968)

2   The devil never points out the abundant blessings of God in your life. The devil always points out what is missing, lacking, or negative.
Charles Stanley
When the Enemy Strikes (2004)

3   Satan is the prince of this world. He's like a roaring lion that goes to and fro looking for whom he can devour. Anyone without the protection of God is in trouble if Satan comes after him. Lost people have no defense. None.
Ken Hutcherson
Before All Hell Breaks Loose (2001)

4   When it comes to lying, deceiving, and twisting the truth, the devil is truly in a class all his own. He's a liar by nature, and his entire motivation—his reason for being—is to lie and deceive.
Tony Evans
*God Cannot Be Trusted
(And Five Other Lies of Satan)* (2005)

5   Satan is a liar, a deceiver, and a counterfeiter. And it's important for all of us to know that he's real and that he's doing everything he can to make our walk with Jesus and our witness for Him ineffective.
Tony Evans
God Cannot Be Trusted (And Five Other Lies of Satan) (2005)

6   Satan is the master of accusation.
Beth Moore
Praying God's Word (2000)

7   We have a cunning adversary, who watches to do mischief, and will promote errors, even by the words of Scripture.
Matthew Henry
Commentary on the Whole Bible (1706)

8   Satan is not mainly interested in causing us misery. He is mainly interested in making Christ look bad. He hates Christ. And he hates the glory of Christ. He will do all he can to keep people from seeing Christ as glorious.
John Piper
God Is the Gospel (2005)

9   Satan, who is a wonderful contriver of delusions, is constantly laying snares to entrap ignorant and heedless persons.
John Calvin
Bible Commentaries (16th century)

10 The Bible says that Satan's purpose is to blind sinners and beguile Christians, and to hurt and discourage those who belong to God. He will do anything to disturb the mind, deceive the heart, and defeat life.
David Jeremiah
Spiritual Warfare (1995)

11 For all his power, Satan is neither omnipotent, omniscient, nor omnipresent. His power has limitations, and he can only act within the limits imposed upon him by God. God is greater than Satan and his evil, which will never be able to separate Christians from God's love.
David Jeremiah
Spiritual Warfare (1995)

12 The devil works in many ways—sometimes openly, more often indirectly. But his goal is always the same: to turn us away from God.
Billy Graham
The Journey (2006)

13 No sooner is a temple built to God, but the Devil builds a chapel hard by.
George Herbert
Jacula Prudentum (17th century)

14 The Devil will use our words and his dictionary.
Adrian Rogers
Unmasking False Prophets (2007)

15 When you look for Satan, never fail to look in the pulpit.
   Adrian Rogers
   Unmasking False Prophets (2007)

16 Satan wants your desires to master you, rather than you mastering your desires.
   Tony Evans
   Tony Evans Speaks Out (2000)

17 It is foolish to underestimate the power of Satan, but it is fatal to overestimate it.
   Corrie ten Boom
   Amazing Love (1953)

18 The devil and temptations also afford us occasion to learn and understand the Scriptures, by experience and practice.
   Martin Luther
   Table Talk (16th century)

19 He that believes God's Word overcomes all, and remains secure everlastingly, against all misfortunes; for this shield fears nothing, neither hell nor the devil.
   Martin Luther
   Table Talk (16th century)

20 Satan is hoping that the present situation that you are in will send you over the edge.
   Beth Moore
   A Beautiful Mind (2009)

21 Satan's biggest lie is that sin is not destructive.
   Henry and Richard Blackaby
   Hearing God's Voice (2002)

22 Thus is the devil ever God's ape.
   Martin Luther
   Table Talk (16th century)

23 The devil can affright, murder, and steal; but God revives and comforts.
   Martin Luther
   Table Talk (16th century)

24 God scorns and mocks the devil, in setting under his very nose a poor, weak, human creature, mere dust and ashes, yet endowed with the first-fruits of the Spirit, against whom the devil can do nothing.
   Martin Luther
   Table Talk (16th century)

25 We cannot vex the devil more than by teaching, preaching, singing and talking of Jesus.
   Martin Luther
   Table Talk (16th century)

26 The Lord said to Christ: "Rule in the midst of thine enemies." On the other hand, the devil claims to be prince and God of the world.
   Martin Luther
   Table Talk (16th century)

27 'Tis impossible for Jesus Christ and the devil ever to remain under the same roof. The one must yield to the other—the devil to Christ.
   Martin Luther
   Table Talk (16th century)

28 The wrath is fierce and devouring which the devil has against the Son of God, and against mankind.
   Martin Luther
   Table Talk (16th century)

29 The devil assaults the Christian world with highest power and subtlety, vexing true Christians through tyrants, heretics, and false brethren, and instigating the whole world against them.
   Martin Luther
   Table Talk (16th century)

30 Satan indeed, that cruel jailer, secures his captives in the dark dungeon of ignorance.
   George Swinnock
   Works of George Swinnock (17th century)

31 The devil now layeth all the blocks he can possibly in the soul's way to hinder its journey to Christ.
George Swinnock
Works of George Swinnock (17th century)

32 Surrounded as we are today with so many hostile, as well as subtly deceptive, viewpoints, we must always be aware that one of Satan's oldest and most diabolical strategies is to convince humans that God cannot be trusted.
Fritz Ridenour
So What's the Difference (1967)

33 This world is a puppet, and Satan holds the strings.
Tony Evans
Theology You Can Count On (2008)

34 Satan offers you what he cannot give; he is a liar, and has been from the foundation of the world.
D. L. Moody
Best Thoughts and Discourses of D. L. Moody (1876)

35 Satan quoted Scriptures even in Jesus' time. He still does, and really doesn't mind when we do. But he would like to see us forget about the cross, the blood, and the resurrected Jesus.
Merlin Carothers
Prison to Praise (1970)

36 Christians who take Satan lightly are ignoring Biblical instructions. He is a formidable foe. We need to have a healthy respect for him. We are not more formidable than Satan, but God is. Our proper attitude is to understand the capabilities of this angelic being and to depend on God's strength for victory.
Chip Ingram
The Invisible War (2006)

37 Satan is not a metaphor for evil. He is a powerful angel who committed treason against his Creator and convinced a third of the angels to rebel along with him. He now seeks to destroy all that is good and God-ordained, and his strategy ever since the fall has been to tempt with the same agenda he had—to be like God.
Chip Ingram
The Invisible War (2006)

38 What he is most remarkable for is, his subtlety: for not having power given him from above, to take us by force, he is obliged to wait for opportunities to betray us, and to catch us by guile.
George Whitefield
Selected Sermons of George Whitefield (18th century)

39 The more powerful the testimony, the more powerfully he'll try to take it. The devil wants no one more than a whole-hearted, sincerely devoted follower of Christ.
Beth Moore
Voices of the Faithful (2005)

40 The enemy of our souls knows where our flesh is the weakest and he will put temptations in our paths at our most vulnerable points.
Stormie Omartian
The Power of a Praying Wife (1997)

41 Satan's goal is to deafen us to God's voice so that we embrace his thinking as easily and naturally as if it were God's very own.
Shelly Beach
The Silent Seduction of Self-Talk (2009)

42 We have forgotten that moral confusion is the enemy's favorite weapon.
Charles Colson
Faith on the Line (1994)

116 DEVOTION
(*see also* CONSECRATION; DEDICATION; LOYALTY)
Stablish thy word unto thy servant,
who is devoted to thy fear.
PSALM 119:38

1 Without devotion prayer is an empty form.
E. M. Bounds
The Essentials of Prayer (19th century)

2 The spirit of devotion puts God in all things.
E. M. Bounds
The Essentials of Prayer (19th century)

3 God loves you unconditionally, Beloved. The question is: Do you love Him unconditionally?
Kay Arthur
Beloved (1994)

4 When our deepest desire is not the things of God, or a favor from God, but God himself, we cross a threshold.
Max Lucado
It's Not About Me (2004)

5 Never should we so abandon ourselves to God as when He seems to abandon us.
François Fénelon and Jeanne Guyon
Spiritual Progress (17th century)

6 The focus needs to be on God, not on my life.
Henry Blackaby
Experiencing God (2007)

7 Christ is concerned with more than what we do. He is initially concerned about why we do what we do. Christ wants our external activities to be produced out of a personal relationship with Him. He demands something deeper than habit, more significant than ritual, more delightful than duty for duty's sake.
Joseph Stowell
Fan the Flame (1983)

8 The mercies of God, the basis for our dedication, are far greater than those of any human master, and blessings of a life dedicated in service to God are far more certain in their richness. Why so many hesitate to dedicate themselves to Him is difficult to understand.
Charles Ryrie
Balancing the Christian Life (1969)

9 Prayer, giving, and fasting are private acts of worship, and therefore should be done privately. We should do them out of love for God, not because we crave the world's praise. If we do these things for the praise of the world, then that is all the blessing we will receive.
Charles Stanley
Handle with Prayer (1987)

10 Our commitment is always a response to God's grace.
Colin Smith
Unlocking the Bible Story (2002)

11 We seem to forget that God desires more than our works, our sacrifices or our constant busyness in His behalf.
Sue Monk Kidd
God's Joyful Surprise (1987)

12 That there needed neither art nor science for going to God, but only a heart resolutely determined to apply itself to nothing but Him, or for His sake, and to love Him only.
Brother Lawrence
The Practice of the Presence of God (17th century)

13 I renounced, for the love of Him, everything that was not He; and I began to live as if there was none but He and I in the world.
Brother Lawrence
The Practice of the Presence of God (17th century)

14 Do not always scrupulously confine yourself to certain rules, or particular forms of devotion; but act with a general confidence in God, with love and humility.
> Brother Lawrence
> *The Practice of the Presence of God*
> (17th century)

15 Let all our employment be to know God: the more one knows Him, the more one desires to know Him.
> Brother Lawrence
> *The Practice of the Presence of God*
> (17th century)

16 Whatever is done or suffered, yet if the heart is withheld from God, there is nothing really given to him.
> Jonathan Edwards
> "The Greatest Performances or Sufferings in Vain without Charity" sermon (1738)

17 Commitment is the one and only way by which we may know the Christ.
> Martin Bell
> *The Way of the Wolf* (1968)

18 We cannot expect a tailor to make us a coat if we do not give him any cloth, nor a builder to build us a house if we let him have no building material; and in just the same way we cannot expect the Lord to live out His life in us if we do not give Him our lives in which to live.
> Watchman Nee
> *Normal Christian Life* (20th century)

19 To carry piety to the point of superstition is to destroy it.
> Blaise Pascal
> *Pensées* (17th century)

20 Good people who have not as yet attained to devotion fly toward God by their good works but do so infrequently, slowly, and awkwardly. Devout souls ascend to God more frequently, promptly, and with lofty heights. In short, devotion is simply that spiritual agility by which charity works in us or by aid of which we work quickly and lovingly.
> Francis de Sales
> *Introduction to the Devout Life*
> (17th century)

21 Eternal Father of my soul, let my first thought today be of You, let my first impulse be to worship You, let my first speech be Your name, let my first action be to kneel before You in prayer.
> John Baillie
> *A Diary of Private Prayer* (1949)

22 Before we can experience even a little of God's love, we must be really turned to him, and, in mind at least, be wholly turned from every earthly thing.
> Richard Rolle
> *The Fire of Love* (14th century)

117 DIFFICULTIES (*see also* ADVERSITY; AFFLICTIONS; HARDSHIPS; TESTING; TRIALS; TROUBLES)

Many are the afflictions of the righteous: but the Lord delivereth him out of them all.
PSALM 34:19

1 When God wants to bring more power into our lives, He brings more pressure. He is generating spiritual force by friction.
> A. B. Simpson
> *Days of Heaven Upon Earth* (1897)

2 Focusing on difficulties intensifies and enlarges the problem. When we focus our attention on God, the problem is put into its proper perspective and it no longer overwhelms us.
> Charles Stanley
> *How to Listen to God* (1985)

3   Let us watch against unbelief, pride, and self-confidence. If we go forth in our own strength, we shall faint, and utterly fall; but having our hearts and our hopes in heaven, we shall be carried above all difficulties, and be enabled to lay hold of the prize of our high calling in Christ Jesus.
   Matthew Henry
   Commentary on the Whole Bible (1706)

4   Whatever clouds you face today, ask Jesus, the light of the world, to help you look behind the cloud to see His glory and His plans for you.
   Billy Graham
   Hope for Each Day (2006)

5   We can rest in the reassurance that the difficulties of this life are only for a time. We have a promise and a hope to hold when times are hard and understanding is dim—one day we will be home, where tears and fears are no more, joy and delight are forever ours, leaning into the loving arms of our heavenly Father.
   Tamara Boggs
   And Then God Gave Us Kids (2003)

6   Difficult times? These provide us a chance to grow. Limitations? Opportunities for improvement. New challenges? These build strength and character. Mistakes? Yes, our mistakes can be assets. If we use them wisely, they can teach us valuable lessons.
   Mort Crim
   Good News for Tough Times (2002)

7   In difficulties we need only have recourse to Jesus Christ, and beg His grace, with which everything became easy.
   Brother Lawrence
   The Practice of the Presence of God (17th century)

8   We look around us and we think that people look like they've got it so together and we're just absolutely sure we're the only one that's a wreck in the room, and that is not true!
   Beth Moore
   "Who Do You Trust?" teaching series (2007)

9   No matter how big the giant might be in anyone's life—God is greater than that giant.
   Charles Swindoll
   "David and the Dwarf" sermon (2009)

10 Our difficulties are always matched by God's mercy.
   Bruce Carroll
   Sometimes Miracles Hide (1999)

11 The impossible faces us all.
   Jack Hayford
   Prayer Is Invading the Impossible (2002)

12 It is a great mistake to be looking at obstacles when we have such a God to look at.
   D. L. Moody
   Short Talks (19th century)

13 God is always calling on us to do the impossible.
   Madeline L'Engle
   Walking on Water (1980)

14 Life gets hold of us in the guise of difficult people we must strain against and circumstances that disrupt our peace.
   Patricia Livingston
   This Blessed Mess (2000)

118 DILIGENCE
And beside this, giving all diligence, add to your faith virtue; and to virtue knowledge...
2 PETER 1:5

1   To do one's best every time he does anything is to increase his power and prepare him for larger things.
   Henry Hopkins
   Half-Hour Talks on Character Building (1910)

2 She was inspired to be something which was not what the rest were, and to be that something different and laborious, for the sake of the rest.
Charles Dickens
Little Dorrit (1857)

119 DISAPPOINTMENT
(*see also* DISCOURAGEMENT; FRUSTRATION; STRUGGLES)
Sorrow is better than laughter: for by the sadness of the countenance the heart is made better.
ECCLESIASTES 7:3

1 The Bible never belittles human disappointment, but it does add one key word: temporary. What we feel now, we will not always feel.
Philip Yancey
Disappointment with God (1992)

2 The suffering caused by shattered dreams must not be thought of as something to relieve if we can or endure if we must. It's an opportunity to be embraced, a chance to discover our desire for the highest blessing God wants to give us, an encounter with Himself.
Larry Crabb
Shattered Dreams (2001)

3 We will enter into seasons of disappointment. But waiting for us there is a choice that determines if this season will make or break us, empty or empower us.
Susie Larson
Alone in Marriage (2007)

4 Disappointment can take our breath away, but in due time and at the right time, God will restore our breath, redirect us, and put wind in our sails.
Susie Larson
Alone in Marriage (2007)

5 The solution to our disappointments is never found in answering the question why—it is found in trusting God in the midst of our whys.
Hank Hanegraaff
The Covering (2002)

6 There can be no deep disappointment where there is not deep love.
Martin Luther King, Jr.
Letter from Birmingham Jail (1963)

7 This habit, too, of seeking some sort of recompense in the discontented boast of being disappointed, is a habit fraught with degeneracy. . . . To bring deserving things down by setting undeserving things up, is one of its perverted delights; and there is no playing fast and loose with the truth, in any game, without growing the worse for it.
Charles Dickens
Little Dorrit (1857)

8 Let not disappointment cause despondency, nor difficulty despair.
Thomas Brown
Christian Morals (17th century)

120 DISCERNMENT
For to one is given by the Spirit the word of wisdom; to another the word of knowledge by the same Spirit; To another faith by the same Spirit; to another the gifts of healing by the same Spirit; To another the working of miracles; to another prophecy; to another discerning of spirits.
1 CORINTHIANS 12:8–10

1 We do not believe all that Job's friends said.
Charles Spurgeon
"The Death of the Christian" sermon (1855)

2   The safest way to insure that no one misleads us is to see that we do not mislead ourselves.
Francis Frangipane
The Three Battlegrounds (1989)

3   We must not trust every saying or suggestion, but warily and patiently ponder things according to the will of God.
Thomas à Kempis
The Imitation of Christ (15th century)

4   The crowds have come to have their ears tickled not their consciences rattled.
David Jeremiah
Escape the Coming Night (1990)

5   We best oppose error by promoting a solid knowledge of the word of truth; and the greatest kindness we can do to children, is to make them early to know the Bible.
Matthew Henry
Commentary on the Whole Bible (1706)

6   Where there is not discernment, the behavior even of the purest soul may in effect amount to coarseness.
Henry David Thoreau
Essay on Love (1852)

7   We must not accept new trends (or old traditions) without first testing them to see if they meet with God's approval.
John MacArthur
Fool's Gold? (2005)

8   For it is a great part of wisdom not to be moved with every blast of words, nor to give ear to an ill, flattering siren; for thus we shall go on securely in the way we have begun.
Thomas à Kempis
The Imitation of Christ (15th century)

9   If we don't understand what the Church is and ignore the New Testament epistles,

humanism will pass for the Church, psychic readers will pass for prophets, mind-power and familiar spirits will pass for the Holy Spirit, positive thinking will pass for faith, and Satan's supernatural ability will pass for God's presence and power.
T. D. Jakes
Intimacy with God (2000)

10   The true saints have not such a spirit of discerning that they can certainly determine who are godly, and who are not. For though they know experimentally what true religion is, in the internal exercises of it; yet these are what they can neither feel, nor see, in the heart of another.
Jonathan Edwards
A Treatise Concerning Religious Affections (18th century)

121 DISCIPLESHIP
(*see also* LEARNING)
And when it was day, he called unto him his disciples: and of them he chose twelve, whom also he named apostles.
LUKE 6:13

1   When Jesus walked among humankind, there was a certain simplicity to being a disciple. Primarily it meant to go with him, in an attitude of study, obedience, and imitation.
Dallas Willard
The Spirit of the Disciplines (1988)

2   Nondiscipleship costs abiding peace, a life penetrated throughout by love, faith that sees everything in the light of God's overriding governance for good, hopefulness that stands firm in the most discouraging of circumstances, power to do what is right and withstand the forces of evil. In short, it costs exactly that abundance of life Jesus said he came to bring.
Dallas Willard
The Spirit of the Disciplines (1988)

122 DISCIPLINE (*see also* ABSTINENCE; SELF-CONTROL; TEMPERANCE)

I know thy works, and thy labour, and thy patience.
REVELATION 2:2

1   The rule that governs my life is this: Anything that dims my vision of Christ, or takes away my taste for Bible study, or cramps my prayer life, or makes Christian work difficult, is wrong for me, and I must, as a Christian, turn away from it.
    J. Wilbur Chapman
    The Spirit of the Disciples (1988)

2   Every spiritual habit begins with difficulty and effort and watchfulness.
    A. B. Simpson
    Days of Heaven Upon Earth (1897)

3   Responding to God's discipline brings immediate benefits. When we allow discipline to train us, we not only escape our sin, but we also grow in maturity.
    Bruce Wilkinson
    Secrets of the Vine (2001)

4   The most fruitful and the most joy-filled Christians are the most pruned Christians.
    Bruce Wilkinson
    Secrets of the Vine (2001)

5   Discipline without direction is drudgery.
    Donald Whitney
    Spiritual Disciplines for the Christian Life (1991)

6   Disciplined people can do the right thing at the right time in the right way for the right reason.
    John Ortberg
    The Life You've Always Wanted (2002)

7   God disciplines those who He loves, but He does not stop loving those He disciplines.
    Colin Smith
    Unlocking the Bible Story (2002)

8   Discipline entails more than catching a child in the act and punishing him. Far more important is nurturing his will for the good, which means supporting him whenever he chooses right over wrong—or, as my mother used to put it, "winning him for the good."
    Johann Christoph Arnold
    Your Child in a Hostile World (2000)

9   There is an old saying: Champions don't become champions in the ring—they are merely recognized there. That's true. If you want to see where someone develops into a champion, look at his daily routine.
    John Maxwell
    Leadership 101 (2002)

10 No matter how gifted a leader is, his gifts will never reach their maximum potential without the application of self-discipline.
    John Maxwell
    Leadership 101 (2002)

11 Divine discipline is God's merciful expression of his love for children who deserve his wrath but will never receive it.
    Bryan Chapell
    Holiness by Grace (2001)

12 A God who had no love for me would allow me to sin myself into oblivion. In the same way, letting my child run amok is not love. It is irresponsible.
    Christine Field
    Help for the Harried Homeschooler (2002)

13 Spiritual disciplines prepare our minds and hearts for obedience, like all rehearsal.
    Gregory Spencer
    Awakening the Quieter Virtues (2010)

DISCIPLING (*see* TEACHING)

**123 DISCOURAGEMENT
(*see also* DISAPPOINTMENT;
FRUSTRATION; STRUGGLES)**
*The LORD God of thy fathers hath said unto thee;
fear not, neither be discouraged.*
DEUTERONOMY 1:21

1 Discouraged people don't need critics.
Charles Swindoll
Encourage Me (1982)

2 For the future to be different, we need
to reach and we need to hope. When we're
discouraged, we don't have hope. But hope is
an antidote to discouragement.
H. Norman Wright
Real Solutions (2001)

3 Depressed, discouraged Christian, let me
urge you to take God at His word. No matter
how dark the night may seem—the morning
will come. With the darkness there is also
light. There is Christ; and in Him is light, light
that will enable you to endure it.
Jay Adams
Christ and Your Problems (1971)

DISCRIMINATION (*see* BIGOTRY)

**DISGRACE (*see* EMBARRASSMENT;
GUILT; SHAME)**

DISHARMONY (*see* DIVISION)

DISHONESTY (*see* LYING)

**124 DISPUTING
(*see also* ARGUING; CONFLICT)**
Do all things without murmurings and disputings.
PHILIPPIANS 2:14

1 If you must dispute, stay till you are master
of the subject; otherwise you will hurt the
cause you would defend.
George Whitefield
Memoirs of Rev. George Whitefield (1741)

**125 DIVERSION (*see also* AMUSEMENT;
ENTERTAINMENT; MEDIA, THE)**
*For all that is in the world, the lust of the flesh,
and the lust of the eyes, and the pride of life,
is not of the Father, but is of the world.*
1 JOHN 2:16

1 If the aspect of the world now dazzles your
eyes, the last day will cure you of this folly, but
it will be too late.
John Calvin
Bible Commentaries (16th century)

126 DIVISION
*Whereas there is among you envying,
and strife, and divisions, are ye not carnal,
and walk as men?*
1 CORINTHIANS 3:3

1 Some people seem to naturally create strife.
They complain all the time about what others
are doing or not doing. They blame others for
their own problems. They strike matches to
any kindling that exists anywhere and leave a
trail of relational fires behind them. Instead of
these people, we should seek friends who are
reconcilers, forgivers, lovers. We should seek
graceful people, peacemakers.
Tom Eisenman
The Accountable Man (2004)

2 Is it any wonder that Satan—who knows
full well what a church praying "in one accord"
and empowered by the Holy Spirit can
accomplish—does everything in his power to
cause rancor and division among Christians
and to entice them to sin?
Pat Robertson
Six Steps to Spiritual Renewal
(2002)

127 DIVORCE
*For the LORD, the God of Israel,
saith that he hateth putting away.*
MALACHI 2:16

DIVORCE

1 How I wish that those who profess to be His children would consult His Word to see what His heart is on the subject before they even begin to entertain the thought of leaving their mate.
Kay Arthur
Speak to My Heart, God (1993)

2 Whether your marriage is average or awful, it has the potential to be awesome. Don't give up too soon. Don't bail out! And since you brought it up, don't let some secular counselor talk you into throwing in the towel. As long as God is alive, there is hope.
Fred Lowery
Covenant Marriage (2002)

3 One of the great ironies of divorce is that people believe they are swapping their worn-out love relationship for something better. But in truth, marriage is the better thing.
Gary and Barbara Rosberg
Divorce-Proof Your Marriage (2002)

4 If you're constantly beating up on yourself as a result of this breakup—feeling worthless and just plain crummy—remember that you are a person of inestimable value.
H. Norman Wright
Let's Just Be Friends (2002)

5 Divorce these days is a religious vow, as if the proper offspring of marriage.
Tertullian
Apologeticus (2nd century)

6 What children lose when their parents split is their family. It is a fallacy to think of divorce as something between a husband and wife.
Michele Weiner-Davis
Divorce Busting (1992)

7 Desperately unhappy people search for ways out of their unhappiness.
Michele Weiner-Davis
Divorce Busting (1992)

8 Divorce represents our inability to hold to Jesus' command. It's giving up on what Jesus calls us to do...yes, this spouse might be difficult to love at times, but that's what marriage is for—to teach us how to love. Allow your marriage relationship to stretch your love and enlarge your capacity for love—to teach you to be a Christian.
Gary Thomas
Sacred Marriage (2000)

9 You are going through an agonizing experience. God describes marriage as two separate people becoming one flesh. Divorce is the process of taking apart that oneness and turning it back into two. How could being torn apart be anything but painful?
Winston Smith
Divorce Recovery (2008)

10 God doesn't promise to put your marriage back together, but he does promise to put you back together.
Winston Smith
Divorce Recovery (2008)

11 No matter how badly you were wounded by your spouse, you will grieve the end of your marriage.
Winston Smith
Divorce Recovery (2008)

12 No matter what your spouse has done or might do to you, no matter how your divorce affects your life, the all-powerful God of the universe promises to use all things for good in your life.
Winston Smith
Divorce Recovery (2008)

13 While circumstances—such as physical abuse—may make divorce a necessary evil, it is still a tragedy, and like any other misfortune, divorce causes pain.
Chris Stollar
Divorce: Is It the Answer? (2009)

14 Even if you're escaping a terrible situation, the effects of divorce can be devastating.
Brad Lewis
Healing the Wounds of Divorce (2009)

15 We have exactly two alternatives when we are burdened by unfathomable circumstances, of which divorce is no exception. We can sink into despair or we can rise up in praise and rejoice.
Kristin Armstrong
Happily Ever After (2007)

16 It is easier to clean up the physical damage of a tornado than the emotional damage caused by divorce.
Steve Grissom and Kathy Leonard
DivorceCare (2005)

17 The pain of divorce is much deeper and more soul wrenching than most people can imagine unless they have been through it themselves.
Steve Grissom and Kathy Leonard
DivorceCare (2005)

18 You may feel a deep need for a mate, a partner, a companion to ease your loneliness. Be patient; now is not the time. First you must learn to be single.
Steve Grissom and Kathy Leonard
DivorceCare (2005)

19 Divorce hurts your pride, and wounded pride leads to anger.
Steve Grissom and Kathy Leonard
DivorceCare (2005)

20 Where there is death, there is grief. You have experienced the death of your relationship, and once the initial shock wears off, you must grieve.
Steve Grissom and Kathy Leonard
DivorceCare (2005)

21 Like a broken bone, the emotional wounds of divorce need to be x-rayed, reset, and given time to heal properly.
Rose Sweet
Healing the Heartbreak (2001)

22 Following a death, people come over with casseroles and cookies and the insurance settlement is promptly paid. After a divorce, people avoid you and getting regular child support from a living ex-spouse is an ongoing nightmare.
Rose Sweet
Healing the Heartbreak (2001)

23 Where death is the end, divorce is the beginning of a steady stream of rejection, pain and loss administered like an ongoing emotional IV drip, poisoning the entire family.
Rose Sweet
Healing the Heartbreak (2001)

24 In divorce we tend to stay in denial, that first stage of the grieving process, because we desperately want to avoid the pain of rejection.
Rose Sweet
Healing the Heartbreak (2001)

128 DOCTRINE
I give you good doctrine, forsake ye not my law.
PROVERBS 4:2

1 Indifferentism about doctrine makes no heroes of the faith.
J. Gresham Machen
Christianity and Liberalism (1923)

2 The doctrine of God and the doctrine of man are the two great presuppositions of the gospel.
J. Gresham Machen
Christianity and Liberalism (1923)

3 Right doctrine and beliefs are only as good as they issue forth in transformed lives.
Keith Meyer
Whole Life Transformation (2010)

DOGMA (see DOCTRINE)

129 DOUBT (see also UNBELIEF)
I will therefore that men pray every where, lifting up holy hands, without wrath and doubting.
1 TIMOTHY 2:8

1   The chief reason we doubt, is that we don't appreciate the God we're dealing with.
    Jerry Dunn
    God Is for the Alcoholic (1965)

2   Unbelief is the parent disease of all our ailments—it is the disease that so readily affects us, just as it is the sin that so easily besets us.
    Evan Henry Hopkins
    Thoughts on Life and Godliness (1883)

3   Learn to expect, not to doubt. In so doing you bring everything into the realm of possibility.
    Norman Vincent Peale
    The Power of Positive Thinking (1952)

4   Doubt sees the obstacles; faith sees the opportunities.
    James MacDonald
    Lord, Change My Attitude (2001)

5   Let me, O my God, stifle forever in my heart, every thought that would tempt me to doubt thy goodness.
    François Fénelon and Jeanne Guyon
    Spiritual Progress (17th century)

6   A wavering Christian is a Christian who trusts in the love of God one day and doubts it the next, and who is alternately happy or miserable accordingly.
    Hannah Whitall Smith
    The God of All Comfort (1906)

7   I can have only compassion for those who sincerely bewail their doubt, who regard it as the greatest of misfortunes, and who, sparing no effort to escape it, make of this inquiry their principle and most serious occupations.
    Blaise Pascal
    Pensées (17th century)

8   I would have far more fear of being mistaken, and of finding that the Christian religion was true, than of not being mistaken in believing it true.
    Blaise Pascal
    Pensées (17th century)

9   Who has tried to make you feel ignorant and foolish and oh, so naïve for taking God at His Word? Whoever it is and whatever approach that person is using, the temptation to doubt God's Word is as old as Creation and comes straight from that old serpent, the Devil.
    Anne Graham Lotz
    God's Story (1997)

10 There never was a doubt in the world that didn't come straight from the devil.
    Billy Sunday
    The Real Billy Sunday (1914)

11 It is not about never doubting, it is about coming out on the other side with twice the faith you had going into your doubt.
    Beth Moore
    "Wrestling with God" teaching series (2009)

12 The whole point is not not ever doubting or questioning. It is that we walk it through and we find our God faithful.
    Beth Moore
    "Wrestling with God" teaching series (2009)

13 The more we distrust God, the heavier our hearts will get. You know why? Because, somewhere along the way, we determined to be God for ourselves.
    Beth Moore
    "Who Do You Trust?" teaching series (2007)

14 Defence presupposes a foe, but the foe is not the dogmatic infidel who has finally made up his mind that Christianity is a delusion, but anti-Christian thought in the believing man's own heart.

Alexander Balmain Bruce
Apologetics, or Christianity Defensively Stated (1892)

15 Even the disciples doubted.
Mary Nelson
Grace for Tough Times (2006)

DRUGS
(*see* ALCOHOL; DRUNKENNESS; SUBSTANCE ABUSE)

130 DRUNKENNESS
(*see also* ALCOHOL; SUBSTANCE ABUSE)

Let us walk honestly, as in the day; not in rioting and drunkenness.
ROMANS 13:13

1 To an alcoholic who feels totally unlovable, the message that God loves him comes as good news.
Jerry Dunn
God Is for the Alcoholic (1965)

2 Drunkenness is a sin that never goes alone, but carries men into other evils; it is a sin very provoking to God.
Matthew Henry
Commentary on the Whole Bible (1706)

131 DUTY (*see also* RESPONSIBILITY)

So likewise ye, when ye shall have done all those things which are commanded you, say, We are unprofitable servants: we have done that which was our duty to do.
LUKE 17:10

1 It is not only prayer that gives God glory but work. Smiting on an anvil, sawing a beam, whitewashing a wall, driving horses, sweeping, scouring, everything gives God some glory if being in his grace you do it as your duty.
Gerard Manley Hopkins
The Principle or Foundation (19th century)

2 Let us have faith that right makes might; and in that faith let us to the end, dare to do our duty as we understand it.
Abraham Lincoln
Address at Cooper Union (1860)

3 I looked to God with great earnestness day after day, to be directed; asking him to show me the path of duty, and give me grace to ride out the storm.
Charles Finney
Memoirs of Rev. Charles G. Finney (1876)

4 The right, practical divinity is this: Believe in Christ, and do thy duty in that state of life to which God has called thee.
Martin Luther
Table Talk (16th century)

5 It is men's duty to love all whom they are bound in charity to look upon as the children of God, with a vastly dearer affection than they commonly do.
Jonathan Edwards
A Treatise Concerning Religious Affections (18th century)

6 No man ever can tell what duty rightly discharged may issue in the most far-reaching and God-glorifying results.
John Dawson
The Saviour in the Workshop (1868)

7 Be it yours, brethren, to glorify God in the sphere in which He has placed you, by the diligent discharge of all your every-day duties.
John Dawson
The Saviour in the Workshop (1868)

8   It's when things get tough that the true level of commitment is evident.
H. Norman Wright
Finding the Right One for You (1995)

DYING (*see* DEATH)

132 EASE (*see also* LEISURE)

And I will say to my soul, Soul, thou hast much goods laid up for many years; take thine ease, eat, drink, and be merry. But God said unto him, Thou fool, this night thy soul shall be required of thee.
LUKE 12:19–20

1   Must I be carried to the skies
On flowery beds of ease,
While others fought to win the prize,
And sailed through bloody seas?
Isaac Watts,
"Am I a Soldier of the Cross?" hymn
(18th century)

2   Jesus did not die on the cross so we could have comfortable lives.
Rick Warren
The Purpose-Driven Life (2002)

133 EASTER

Why seek ye the living among the dead? He is not here, but is risen.
LUKE 24:5–6

1   The lamb of the Passover finds its ultimate fulfillment in the Person of Jesus Christ.
Franklin Graham
All for Jesus (2003)

EATING (*see* GLUTTONY)

EDUCATION (*see* LEARNING)

134 ELDERLY, THE
(*see also* AGING; OLD AGE)

Thou shalt rise up before the hoary head, and honour the face of the old man, and fear thy God.
LEVITICUS 19:32

1   Children who grew up well-nurtured tended to love the old.
Mary Pipher
Another Country (1999)

2   We live in a time when community reconstruction is what will save us. If we give our elders our time and our respect, they can teach us how to do it. They can teach us about civility, accountability, and connection.
Mary Pipher
Another Country (1999)

3   Instead of racking our brains to think of programs for seniors, we can draw them into existing activities that will bring them close to all ages.
Catharine Brandt
Forgotten People (1978)

4   Our parents and grandparents knew how to endure. When the going got rough, they hung tough. They didn't pull over to the side of life's road and whine about how tricky the lane changes were or how many times they got cut off by another driver.
Martha Bolton
Growing Your Own Turtleneck (2005)

5   If there is anything on earth beautiful to me, it is an aged woman, her white locks flowing back over the wrinkled brow—locks not white with frost, as the poets say, but white with the blossoms of the tree of life, in her voice the tenderness of gracious memories, her face a benediction.
T. DeWitt Talmage
The Wisdom and Wit of T. DeWitt Talmage (19th century)

6   Perhaps the greatest resource available to us after retirement is prayer.
Peter Mustric
The Joy of Growing Older (1979)

7 With the experiences of life to guide us and God leading us, the elderly years can be the most meaningful of all.
Peter Mustric
The Joy of Growing Older (1979)

135 EMBARRASSMENT
(*see also* GUILT; SHAME)

My confusion is continually before me, and the shame of my face hath covered me.
PSALM 44:15

1 A wicked man may be troubled for scandalous sins; a real convert laments heart sins.
Thomas Watson
The Doctrine of Repentance (1668)

136 EMOTIONS
(*see also* ATTITUDE; FEELINGS)
I cried with my whole heart; hear me, O LORD.
PSALM 119:145

1 Sentiment is shifting sand. You can have warm feelings toward God without faith, you can have feelings of optimism without hope, and you can have feelings of sympathy without love. Our God is not sand; he's a Rock.
Ravi Zacharias and Norman Geisler
Is Your Church Ready? (2003)

2 One of the greatest gifts we are given is our emotions; we need not fear our emotions.
Rich Hurst
Courage to Connect (2002)

3 We fear to face some horrible things that once hurt us, and we stuff it into the black holes of our unconsciousness where we suppose it cannot hurt us. But it only comes back disguised; it is like a demon wearing an angel's face. It lays low for a while only to slug us later, on the sly.
Lewis Smedes
Forgive and Forget (1986)

4 If unguarded, desire turns into desperation.
Beth Moore
"Overcoming Insecurity" teaching (2006)

5 Devastation has a way of leading to isolation.
Beth Moore
"Living Forgiving Offenses That Devastate" teaching (2008)

6 We have little control over our emotions but tremendous control over our actions.
J. Allan Petersen
The Myth of the Greener Grass (1983)

7 The soul can imprint itself on us outwardly. Fear, grief, or anger can etch themselves upon a face after years of expressing physically the inner turmoil of the soul.
Lisa Bevere
You Are Not What You Weigh (1998)

8 Exude calmness. Even when you don't feel calm, learn to act calm. Anxiety, anger, and despair are infectious. Model emotional control.
Mary Pipher
Letters to a Young Therapist (2003)

9 We cannot determine our emotions, but we can choose our attitudes and actions.
Gary Chapman
Hope for the Separated (1982)

10 The fact is—and both Scripture and experience make this clear—that no man or woman can completely fill another person's emotional tank. That's a God-sized task meant for. . .well God.
Cindi McMenamin
When Women Walk Alone (2002)

11 We are, indeed, watchmen for our own souls—our minds and emotions. It is critical that we act as gatekeepers or doorkeepers of our hearts.
Dutch Sheets
Watchman Prayer (2000)

EMPATHY (*see* COMPASSION)

137 ENCOURAGEMENT
(*see also* CHEER)

But charge Joshua, and encourage him, and strengthen him.
DEUTERONOMY 3:28

1 To encourage someone is to inspire them to have courage.
Patrick Morley
The Man in the Mirror (1992)

2 The most beneficial context in which men can encourage one another to be everything they can be in God is always a nonjudgmental environment of unconditional love, forgiveness, and encouragement.
Tom Eisenman
The Accountable Man (2004)

3 Encouragement is vital in the community of faith. It can uplift us in the midst of difficult work, cheer us when we feel alone, inspire us when we wonder if we are up to the task at hand. In times of distress, encouragement can come as a deep remedy for our pain.
Stephen Doughty
Discovering Community (1999)

4 Encouragement in Christ arises from the heart. It is prayerfully given, sometimes with many words but more often, I suspect, with few.
Stephen Doughty
Discovering Community (1999)

5 Pray and encourage one another.
Donna Partow
A 10-Week Journey to Becoming a Vessel God Can Use (1996)

6 Genuinely encouraging words are ones that communicate the idea, I know who you are;
I care about you, and I'm here to help you.
Gary Chapman
The World's Easiest Guide to Family Relationships (2001)

7 I have come to believe strongly that people can never be encouraged too much.
Hans Finzel
Empowered Leaders (1998)

8 In all of us, the potential to be good is there, if only someone will take the time to help us discover it and make it bloom.
Mary Pipher
Letters to a Young Therapist (2003)

9 Encouragement is the kind of expression that helps someone want to be a better Christian, even when life is rough.
Larry Crabb
Encouragement: The Key to Caring (1984)

10 Encouragement is not a technique to be mastered; it is a sensitivity to people and a confidence in God that must be nourished and demonstrated.
Larry Crabb
Encouragement: The Key to Caring (1984)

11 God's encouragement runs counter-intuitive to everything our bodies tell us to do.
Kim Moore and Pam Mellskog
A Patchwork Heart (2002)

138 END TIMES
(*see also* SECOND COMING)

But the day of the Lord will come as a thief in the night.
2 PETER 3:10

1 Not yet the thunderbolt! Not yet the riven heavens and the reeling earth! Not yet the great white throne, and the day of judgment; for he is very pitiful, and beareth long with men!
Charles Spurgeon
"God's Longsuffering" sermon (1887)

2   We are being given the opportunity to be firsthand observers to the staging of events that will precede the ultimate coming of Christ to this earth. Events written centuries ago are now unfolding right before our eyes and are telling us that our patient anticipation will soon be rewarded.
David Jeremiah
What in the World Is Going On? (2008)

3   Today as never before, we are beginning to see signs of our Lord's impending return.
David Jeremiah
What in the World Is Going On? (2008)

4   Nothing could be more dramatic than the contrast between our Lord's first and second comings: In His first coming the door of the inn was closed to Him. In His second coming the door of the heavens will be open to Him.
David Jeremiah
What in the World Is Going On? (2008)

5   The world only thinks it has seen tribulation.
Tim LaHaye
The Rapture (2002)

6   There is no question that the Lord Jesus Christ is coming again to this earth. It is a prophetic fact, guaranteed by the eternal Word of God. The deity and credibility of God demands it.
Tim LaHaye
The Rapture (2002)

7   The future that Daniel described is now.
Grant Jeffrey
Countdown to the Apocalypse (2008)

8   At no time in ancient history was a nation, or even a large confederation of nations, capable of raising an army numbering two hundred million men. But in our last-days generation, it is entirely possible.
Grant Jeffrey
Countdown to Apocalypse (2008)

9   Future events are casting their shadows before them.
Mark Hitchcock
Iran—The Coming Crisis (2006)

10   I fear the axe is laid to the root of the tree, soon to cut it down. God of his infinite mercy take us graciously away, that we may not be present at such calamities.
Martin Luther
Table Talk (16th century)

11   I believe the prophetic end-times clock, after almost two thousand years of silence, began ticking in 1948. It's been ticking louder and faster ever since.
Dave Earley
The 21 Most Dangerous Questions of the Bible (2007)

ENDURANCE
(*see* PERSEVERANCE)

139 ENEMIES
I will call upon the LORD, who is worthy to be praised: so shall I be saved from mine enemies.
PSALM 18:3

1   There is no little enemy.
Benjamin Franklin
Poor Richard's Almanac (18th century)

2   Noise and distraction. These remain some of the enemy's stock-in-trade.
Beth Moore
Jesus: 90 Days with the One and Only (2007)

3   Our opponents always seem to have the edge. But all that is false. We are never outnumbered. We are never outmanned, or outgunned.
David Roper
A Beacon in the Darkness (1995)

4   Sometimes the worst of times are designed by the enemy to get you to give up on God's

clear direction because he knows of the powerful and wondrous blessings that are ahead.
Chip Ingram
The Invisible War (2006)

ENJOYMENT (*see* PLEASURE)

ENMITY (*see* HATRED)

140 ENTERTAINMENT (*see also* AMUSEMENT; DIVERSION; MEDIA, THE)

A time to weep, and a time to laugh; a time to mourn, and a time to dance...
ECCLESIASTES 3:4

1   People have become so empty that they can't even entertain themselves. They have to pay other people to amuse them, to make them laugh, to try to make them feel warm and happy and comfortable for a few minutes.
Billy Graham
Peace with God (1984)

2   You will come to believe, and be influenced by, whatever you choose to listen to on a regular basis.
Steve Campbell
"Why More Aren't Healed" sermon (2009)

3   We are overwhelmed with stimulation, but we are often left feeling empty.
Gregory Spencer
Awakening the Quieter Virtues (2010)

4   Watching passively encourages uncritical acceptance and discourages discernment.
Gregory Spencer
Awakening the Quieter Virtues (2010)

5   Communication between family members has, in many cases, almost been destroyed by television.
Don Meredith
Becoming One (1999)

6   Television has proved a mix blessing. Like many other inventions that have great potential for good, television has been exploited—one could say prostituted— by greedy and unprincipled people for selfish and often evil purposes. One of its destructive effects is that habitual viewers seldom communicate with one another in a meaningful way. Superficial viewing habits are formed that inhibit intelligent conversation and deep thought.
J. Oswald Sanders
Facing Loneliness (1988)

141 ENVY (*see also* JEALOUSY)

For wrath killeth the foolish man, and envy slayeth the silly one.
JOB 5:2

1   Just when you catch up with the Joneses, they move.
Karen O'Connor
Addicted to Shopping (2005)

2   One-upmanship is a lonely road that leads to destruction, because everyone is either above us or below us.
Robert Stofel
God, Are We There Yet? (2004)

3   Envy and strife have overthrown great cities and rooted up mighty nations.
Clement
The First Epistle to the Corinthians (1st century)

4   Whenever you attempt a good work you will find other men doing the same kind of work, and probably doing it better. Envy them not.
Henry Drummond
The Greatest Thing in the World (1874)

5   We all have seeds of jealousy and envy in us. The question is, who among us will acknowledge it?
David Wilkerson
"Seeds of Envy and Jealousy" article (2009)

6   Envy is a sin that commonly carries with it its own punishment, in the rottenness of the bones.
Matthew Henry
Commentary on the Whole Bible (1706)

7   Envy is the reverse side of a coin called vanity. Nobody is ever envious of others who is not first proud of himself.
John Stott
The Cross of Christ (1986)

142 ETERNAL LIFE

And this is life eternal, that they might know thee the only true God, and Jesus Christ, whom thou hast sent.
JOHN 17:3

1   Hold fast to eternal salvation through the eternal covenant carried out by eternal love unto eternal life.
Charles Spurgeon
"The Blessing of Full Assurance" sermon (1888)

2   You know, eternal life does not start when you go to heaven. It starts the moment you reach out to Jesus. That is where it all begins!
Corrie ten Boom
He Cares, He Comforts (1977)

3   We are all the time coming to the end of things here—the end of the week, the end of the month, the end of the year, the end of school days. It is end, end, end all the time. But, thank God, He is going to satisfy us with long life; no end to it, an endless life.
D. L. Moody "The Ninety-First Psalm" sermon (late 19th century)

4   No doubt Christ's way to eternal life is a way of pleasantness. But it is folly to shut our eyes to the fact that His way is narrow, and the cross comes before the crown.
J. C. Ryle
Holiness: Its Nature, Hindrances, Difficulties, and Roots (18th century)

143 ETERNITY

The meek shall eat and be satisfied: they shall praise the LORD that seek him: your heart shall live for ever.
PSALM 22:26

1   May I view all things in the mirror of eternity.
Arthur Bennett (editor)
The Valley of Vision: A Collection of Puritan Prayers and Devotions (20th century)

2   May I speak each word as if it were my last, and walk each step as my final one.
Arthur Bennett (editor)
The Valley of Vision: A Collection of Puritan Prayers and Devotions (20th century)

3   Every act of our lives strikes some chord that will vibrate in eternity.
Rick Warren
The Purpose-Driven Life (2002)

4   God is working for eternity, and He has been working from eternity. He's not in a hurry, and we shouldn't be either.
Mark Dever and Paul Alexander
The Deliberate Church (2005)

5   The point right now isn't why death and suffering exist, or why some seem to suffer more or die sooner than others. . .the point is that you will die, and you need to be prepared for eternity.
Ken Ham
How Could a Loving God. . . ? (2007)

6   Eternity is just a breath away!
Anne Graham Lotz
I Saw the Lord (2006)

7   God rules from the perspective of eternity.
Kay Arthur
Beloved (1994)

8 Three-hundred million years from now, the only thing that will matter is whether you're in Heaven or in Hell.
   Mark Cahill
   One Thing You Can't Do in Heaven (2002)

9 He who provides for this life but takes no care for eternity is wise for a moment but a fool forever.
   John Tillotson
   The Wisdom of Being Religious (1819)

10 Since we are all part of the ultimate statistic—ten out of ten people die—where we go when we die, and who will be there with us, is something we all should think about.
   Mark Cahill
   One Heartbeat Away (2005)

11 Eternity will be here before we know it.
   Jon Courson
   Application Commentary (2006)

12 He only is safe for eternity who is sheltered behind the finished work of Christ.
   D. L. Moody
   "There Is No Difference" sermon (1880)

13 No one can know everything with absolute certainty. Just make sure you know the consequences of each side of the argument. Then choose wisely. Your eternity is at stake.
   Robert Stofel
   God, How Much Longer? (2005)

14 Nothing is so important to man as his own state, nothing is as formidable as his eternity; and thus it is not natural that there should be men indifferent to the loss of their existence and the perils of everlasting suffering.
   Blaise Pascal
   Pensées (17th century)

15 It concerns all our life to know whether the soul may be mortal or immortal.
   Blaise Pascal
   Pensées (17th century)

16 Make haste. Eternity is at hand. Eternity depends on this moment. An eternity of happiness, or an eternity of misery!
   John Wesley
   "Awake, Thou That Sleepest" sermon (1743)

17 Everything Christ did and taught has eternity in view. Most of us give a nod of our theology to heaven and then live as though this world is all we have.
   Joseph Stowell
   Following Christ (1996)

18 With Christ as your Companion, you are a creature of eternity.
   Edith Margaret Clarkson
   So You're Single! (1978)

19 There are two bidders for your soul to-night. It is for you to decide which shall have it.
   D. L. Moody
   Best Thoughts and Discourses of D. L. Moody (1876)

20 Answer the big question of eternity, and the little questions of life fall into perspective.
   Max Lucado
   The Applause of Heaven (1990)

21 We need a new breed of men who have the ability to focus on the unseen—the eternal—as well as the seen.
   Dennis and Barbara Rainey
   Moments Together (2004)

22 There will be no second chance after death. The time to prepare is now.
   Charles Swindoll
   "Visiting the Real Twilight Zone" sermon (1985)

23 In the perspective of Eternity, all lives will seem poor, and small, and lost, and self-condemned beside a life for Christ.
Henry Drummond
"To Me to Live Is Christ" sermon
(19th century)

24 As the womb is preparation for our bodies here on earth, so our time on earth is preparation for our time in eternity.
Pat Warren
Weighed by the Word (2009)

25 Heaven is a place and condition of perfect fellowship with God; hell is a place and condition of absolute separation from God.
J. Budziszewski
How to Stay Christian in College (2004)

26 Deep within us all there is an amazing inner sanctuary of the soul, a holy place, a Divine Center, a speaking Voice, to which we may continuously return. Eternity is at our hearts, pressing upon our time-torn lives, warming us with intimations of an astounding destiny, calling us home unto Itself.
Thomas Kelly
A Testament of Devotion (1992)

27 It is better to go bruised to heaven than sound to hell.
Richard Sibbes
The Bruised Reed (1630)

28 If we prepare months in advance for a vacation get-a-way or years in advance for a comfortable retirement, surely we can spend some quality time planning, or at the very least contemplating, our eternal destiny.
Rebecca Lusignolo
"Am I Saved?" article (2007)

29 The longest time man has to live has no more proportion to eternity than a drop of dew has to the ocean.
D. L. Moody
Heaven (1881)

30 Man's instinct is vertical—a yearning after the high, the lasting, the eternal.
Michael Phillips
A God to Call Father (1994)

144 EVANGELISM (*see also* GOSPEL, THE; MISSIONARIES; WITNESSING)
The fruit of the righteous is a tree of life; and he that winneth souls is wise.
PROVERBS 11:30

1 Men of God, if you are indeed the Lord's, and feel that you are his, begin now to intercede for all who belong to you. Never be satisfied unless they are saved too.
Charles Spurgeon
"Consecration to God" sermon (1868)

2 If you are following Jesus, you will be doing what He came to do: You would be rescuing the dying, whatever it takes.
Ron Hutchcraft
Called to Greatness (2001)

3 Apologetics as the handmaiden of evangelism must lead to a clear presentation of the gospel.
Ravi Zacharias and Norman Geisler
Is Your Church Ready? (2003)

4 Are today's Christians convinced that placard-carrying, slogan-bearing demonstrations can replace soul winning?
David Jeremiah
Escape the Coming Night (1990)

5 It takes more than boldness, bravery, and blood to make the name of Jesus known throughout the earth. We must be willing to

invest our most valuable resources and expend consistent, intense effort to advance His Name to the ends of the earth.
Franklin Graham
The Name (2002)

6   I never see important people—or anyone else—without having the deep realization that I am—first and foremost—an ambassador of the King of kings and Lord of lords. From the moment I enter the room, I am thinking about how I can get the conversation around to the Gospel.
Billy Graham
Just As I Am (1997)

7   These days, I'm more convinced than ever that the absolute highest value in personal evangelism is staying attuned to and cooperative with the Holy Spirit.
Bill Hybels
Just Walk Across the Room (2006)

8   Someday, friends, there comes a harvest. Someday there is a payoff. Someday sinners become saints. And between now and then, we get to keep spreading the message. We get to keep playing the roles we are meant to play. We get to keep planting seeds, trusting that God will bring the increase. Because in due time—oh, the increase he brings!
Bill Hybels
Just Walk Across the Room (2006)

9   There's nothing in life that's as exciting as befriending, loving, and leading wayward people toward faith in Christ. Nothing.
Bill Hybels and Mark Mittelberg
Becoming a Contagious Christian (1996)

10   Being gracious stems from having our lives and relationships with others marked by God's grace—His steadfast, unconditional love. In evangelism, this means that our thoughts,

emotions and behavior toward non-Christians are marked by graciousness as we seek to bring them to Jesus and commit to serve Him as King.
Christine Wood
Character Witness (2003)

11   Evangelism depends on focus, and the task of evangelism becomes much easier when we develop a credo based on our unique personality, natural talents and spiritual gifts.
Christine Wood
Character Witness (2003)

12   Come away, my dear brethren, fly, fly, fly for your lives to Jesus Christ; fly to a bleeding God, fly to a throne of grace; and beg of God to break your heart; beg of God to convince you of your actual sins; beg of God to convince you of your original sin; beg of God to convince you of your self-righteousness; beg of God to give you faith, and to enable you to close with Jesus Christ.
George Whitefield
"A Sermon, Preached on Sabbath Morning" (1741)

13   My business this morning, the first day of the week, is to tell you that Christ is willing to be reconciled to you. Will any of you be reconciled to Jesus Christ?
George Whitefield
"A Sermon, Preached on Sabbath Morning" (1741)

14   All evangelism is a form of witnessing, but not all witnessing is a form of evangelism. How we live serves as a foundation for evangelism, not as a substitute.
Douglas Cecil
The 7 Principles of an Evangelistic Life (2003)

15   If you know Jesus Christ, you already have a heart for evangelism. You do not need to try and manufacture a heart for evangelism.

Because of the indwelling ministry of the Holy Spirit, sharing Jesus Christ with the lost world is already a part of your life!
Douglas M. Cecil
The 7 Principles of an Evangelistic Life (2003)

16 There is no impact without contact. Evangelism is a contact sport.
Douglas M. Cecil
The 7 Principles of an Evangelistic Life (2003)

17 My friends, you cannot take palsied souls to a better place than the feet of Jesus.
D. L. Moody
The Faithful Saying (1877)

18 The one who would have real success in bringing others to Christ must himself be *a thoroughly converted person.*
R.A. Torrey
How to Bring Men to Christ (1893)

19 We must always bear in mind that the primary purpose of our work, is not to get persons to join the church or to give up their bad habits or to do anything else than this, to accept Jesus Christ, as their Saviour.
R. A. Torrey
How to Bring Men to Christ (1893)

20 Every man's conscience is on our side.
R. A.Torrey
How to Bring Men to Christ (1893)

21 It is irresponsible to evangelize without even giving thought to how someone will continue growing and progressing in their newfound Christian life.
Scott Hinkle
Recapturing the Primary Purpose (2005)

22 With the birth of each generation comes a fresh wave of humanity that needs to hear the gospel of Jesus Christ.
Scott Hinkle
Recapturing the Primary Purpose (2005)

23 While God may use you in great ways as an influence, ultimately it's the Holy Spirit's job to change hearts.
Nancy Kennedy
When He Doesn't Believe (2001)

24 Oh is it not a magnificent thing to be privileged thus, in any small measure, to spread the glorious tidings of our Blessed Lord!
Amy Carmichael
From Sunrise Land: Letters from Japan (1895)

25 Reaching one person at a time is still the best way to reach the world.
Lloyd John Ogilvie
Life without Limits (1975)

26 Christians must not only know what they believe, but they must likewise explain why.
James Eckman
Biblical Ethics (2004)

27 We're not trying to develop "clients"; we're trying to develop friends and relationships.
Steve Campbell
Discussion on church growth (2009)

28 To withhold a warning of death and disaster is cruel and unacceptable.
Jeff Chapman
"Fishing for Men" article (2009)

29 Being a soul winner is elementary Christianity.
Jeff Chapman
"Fishing for Men" article (2009)

30 Christ's command means that we all should be devoting all our resources of

ingenuity and enterprise to the task of making the gospel known in every possible way to every possible person.

    J. I. Packer
    Evangelism and the Sovereignty of God
    (2008)

31 The glory and efficiency of the gospel are staked on the men who proclaim it.
    E. M. Bounds
    Power Through Prayer (1906)

32 Because sinners are not converted by direct contact of the Holy Ghost, but by the truth, employed as a means. To expect the conversion of sinners by prayer alone, without the employment of truth, is to tempt God.
    Charles Finney
    Lectures of Revivals of Religion (1835)

33 The great majority of those who are counted believers are doing nothing towards making Christ known to their fellow-men.
    Andrew Murray
    Working for God (1901)

34 It is a remarkable truth that the same God who worked "through Christ" to achieve the reconciliation now works "through us" to announce it.
    John Stott
    The Cross of Christ (1986)

35 The Christian life is a pilgrimage from earth to heaven, and our task is to take as many as possible with us as we make this journey.
    Warren Wiersbe
    Be What You Are (1988)

36 The pressure of bringing people to Christ is God's. We can only bring Christ to people. The only pressure we ought to feel is the pressure to make the gospel clear.
    R. Larry Moyer
    21 Things God Never Said (2004)

145 EVIL

*The imagination of man's heart
is evil from his youth.*
GENESIS 8:21

1 The reality is that it is impossible to distinguish evil from good unless one has an infinite point that is absolutely good. The infinite reference point for distinguishing good from evil can be found only in the person of God, for God alone can exhaust the definition of "absolutely good."
    Norman Geisler
    Who Made God? (2003)

2 There is no evil so dark and so obscene. . . but that God can turn it to good.
    Frederick Buechner
    Listening to Your Life (1992)

3 Evil is not abstract. An intelligent being is the source of evil, and he assigns the administration of his works to real angelic creatures.
    David Jeremiah
    Escape the Coming Night (1990)

4 Evil is not a thing; it is a lack in a thing. Evil is a lack of perfection.
    Charles Stanley
    Winning the War Within (1988)

5 Evil is real. But the problem of evil has ultimately one source: our rebellion against God's holiness.
    Ravi Zacharias and Kevin Johnson
    Jesus Among Other Gods—Youth Edition
    (2000)

146 EVOLUTION (*see also* CREATION)

*For by him were all things created, that are
in heaven, and that are in earth, visible and
invisible, whether they be thrones, or dominions,
or principalities, or powers: all things were
created by him, and for him.*
COLOSSIANS 1:16

1 If it's unreasonable to believe that an encyclopedia could have originated without intelligence, then it's just as unreasonable to believe that life could have originated without intelligence.
Jonathan Sarfati
Refuting Evolution (1999)

2 A God who "created" by evolution is, for all practical purposes, indistinguishable from no God at all.
Jonathan Sarfati
Refuting Evolution (1999)

3 It is a fallacy to believe that facts speak for themselves—they are always interpreted according to a framework. The framework behind the evolutionists' interpretation is naturalism—it is assumed that things made themselves, that no divine intervention has happened.
Jonathan Sarfati
Refuting Evolution (1999)

4 As long as the creationist ministry exists in this world, it will be divisive. The truth always is!
Ken Ham
Why Won't They Listen? (2002)

5 Churches haven't trained their people to defend the Bible against the onslaughts of evolutionary humanism; instead they've been influenced by it.
Ken Ham
Why Won't They Listen? (2002)

6 Evolution is a religious position that makes human opinion supreme.
Ken Ham
The Lie: Evolution (1987)

7 Evolution is a religion which enables people to justify writing their own rules.
Ken Ham
The Lie: Evolution (1987)

8 If chance alone operates, why should that which exists (including biological structure) move toward a consistent increase in complexity?
Francis Schaeffer
How Should We Then Live? (1976)

9 The concept of an unbroken line from molecule to man, on the basis of only time plus chance, leaves these crucial questions of how and why unanswered.
Francis Schaeffer
How Should We Then Live? (1976)

10 Suggest the presence of something outside of and greater than the universe we know, and Darwinists get all but hysterical.
Chuck Colson
"A Passion for Truth" commentary (2007)

11 The first hurdle is that we have the problem of why there is something rather than nothing.
Paul Copan
"Atheistic Goodness Revisited" article (2007)

12 Being cannot come into existence from non-being since no such potentiality or productive cause yet exists. This is not simply a matter of some culture-bound "intuition," but hard metaphysics.
Paul Copan
"Atheistic Goodness Revisited" article (2000)

13 This banishing God from the world is simply intolerable, and, blessed be his name, impossible.
Charles Hodge
What Is Darwinism? (1874)

14 Life cannot come gradually—health can, structure can, but not Life.
Henry Drummond
Natural Law in the Spiritual World (19th century)

15 Naturalism is not a scientifically deduced fact but rather a philosophical presupposition.
Terrell Clemmons
"Questioning the Quantum Leap" article (2009)

16 It is the same impossibility for a thing to be created out of nothing, as to be created by nothing.
William Law
An Appeal to All That Doubt (18th century)

17 The evolutionary lie is so pointedly antithetical to Christian truth that it would seem unthinkable for evangelical Christians to compromise with evolutionary science in any degree.
John MacArthur
The Battle for the Beginning (2001)

147 EXAMPLE
I have given you an example,
that ye should do as I have done to you.
JOHN 13:15

1 Of all commentaries on the Scriptures, good examples are the best.
John Donne
Sermon LXXXI (1627)

2 If you know Jesus Christ personally, you have not only a rock, but a role model. And this rock and role model isn't just any old version—this One is perfect.
Steve Farrar
Point Man (1990)

3 It is your business to restore the integrity and the righteousness in the high places of this land, and let the people see examples which will be helpful to them in their Christian life.
Henry Drummond
A Life for a Life and Other Addresses (1893)

4 Do you seriously wish to travel the road to devotion? If so, look for a good person to guide and lead you.
Francis de Sales
Introduction to the Devout Life (17th century)

148 EXCELLENCE
Hear; for I will speak of excellent things;
and the opening of my lips shall be right things.
PROVERBS 8:6

1 The world has us under a magnifying glass. As a result, everything we do has to be that much better. God calls on us to live with excellence.
John Tesh
An Invitation to Pray and Worship (2003)

149 EXCUSES
And they all with one consent
began to make excuse.
LUKE 14:18

1 Don't be good at making excuses.
Bruce Bickel and Stan Jantz
God Is in the Small Stuff (1998)

2 Nothing can be a more grievous abomination in the sight of God than excuses made by a sinner who knows they are utterly false and blasphemous.
Charles Finney
"Men Often Highly Esteem What God Abhors" sermon (19th century)

3 An explanation for someone's behavior should never turn into an excuse for the things he does wrong.
Jan Silvious
Foolproofing Your Life (1998)

150 FAILURE (*see also* DEFEAT; LOSS)
For a just man falleth seven times,
and riseth up again: but the wicked
shall fall into mischief.
PROVERBS 24:16

1   Often we assume that God is unable to work in spite of our weaknesses, mistakes, and sins. We forget that God is a specialist; He is well able to work our failures into His plans.
Erwin Lutzer
Failure: The Back Door to Success (1975)

2   Failure does not have to be final.
Anne Graham Lotz
The Daily Light Journal (2004)

3   Failure can be your friend because it's a great teacher.
John Townsend
It's Not My Fault (2007)

4   Lesson number one about failure is this: whatever you wish to do, you will fail at it in the beginning. Accept that reality.
John Townsend
It's Not My Fault (2007)

5   When we have done something wrong, we must suppress our natural instinct to run and hide and instead come into God's presence as we are, without excuses or pretense.
Erwin Lutzer
After You've Blown It (2004)

6   What's amazing is that the grace of God is so far-reaching and profound that He can use your failures.
Tony Evans
God Is Up to Something Great (2002)

7   There is always life after lapses.
Karon Phillips Goodman
Grab a Broom, Lord—There's Dust Everywhere! (2003)

8   See the other person's failures in trustworthiness as opportunities to build your own forgiving disposition.
Everett Worthington
Forgiving and Reconciling (2003)

9   See your own failures as opportunities to practice humility.
Everett Worthington
Forgiving and Reconciling (2003)

10 In God's economy, nothing is wasted. Through failure, we learn a lesson in humility which is probably needed, painful though it is.
Bill Wilson
As Bill Sees It (1967)

11 Many Christians don't fail, they just quit before they get ripe.
Gary Thomas
Authentic Faith (2002)

12 God, who wants us to discover his love and be joyful, will not let us fail.
Susan McCarthy Peabody
Alphabet Soup for Christian Living (2007)

13 The fear of failure is crippling because it holds people back from acting on their desires, and it will certainly hinder you from fulfilling your destiny.
Joyce Meyer
Never Give Up! (2008)

14 One of the greatest obstacles we face in attempting to reach our potential is the fear of making a mistake, the very human fear of failure. And yet excellence is based on failure, usually one failure after another.
Ted Engstrom
The Pursuit of Excellence (1982)

15 The accuser of the brethren waits, like a vulture, for you to fail in some way.
David Wilkerson
Don't Be Afraid of Failure (2009)

16 Something much worse than failure is the fear that goes with it.
David Wilkerson
Don't Be Afraid of Failure (2009)

17 The best way to go on after a failure is to learn the lesson and forget the details.
John Mason
The Impossible Is Possible (2003)

18 More people fail from lack of purpose than from lack of talent.
Billy Sunday
The Sawdust Trail (1932)

19 Our perception of success and failure may, in fact be inaccurate. . .perhaps the almighty God has chosen to work through us without letting us know. We may find out years later that what we saw as failure was actually God's success.
Alice Fryling
Disciplemakers' Handbook (1989)

20 I find that all is failure that has not its base on the Rock Christ Jesus.
Smith Wigglesworth
Faith That Prevails (1938)

21 Moses—a great man of God—went backwards before he went forwards.
Joyce Meyer
"Overcoming Fear with Faith"
sermon (2009)

22 Someone has defined failure as succeeding at something that doesn't really matter.
Martha Bolton and Phil Callaway
It's Always Darkest before the Fridge Door Opens (2006)

23 Failure is impossible to avoid and very difficult to manage.
David Hawkins
The Relationship Doctor's Prescription for Living Beyond Guilt (2006)

24 To acknowledge your imperfections does not mean you are a failure; it is an admission that you are human.
Gary Chapman
Desperate Marriages (2008)

151 FAIRNESS

*Moreover the LORD answered Job, and said,
Shall he that contendeth with the
Almighty instruct him?*
JOB 40:1–2

1 We step out of bounds when we conclude that anything God does isn't fair.
John MacArthur
Ashamed of the Gospel (1993)

2 The God of Christianity never claims to be fair. He goes beyond fair. The Bible teaches that he decided not to give us what we deserve—that's mercy. In addition, God decided to give us exactly what we didn't deserve—we call that grace.
Andy Stanley
How Good Is Good Enough? (2003)

3 Is Christianity fair? It is certainly not fair to God. Christians believe that God sent his Son to die for your sins and mine. Fairness would demand that we die for our own sins.
Andy Stanley
How Good Is Good Enough? (2003)

4 Be fair with your children—and that doesn't mean be equal.
David and Claudia Arp
Answering the 8 Cries of the Spirited Child (2004)

5 Our sense of fairness tells us people should pay for the wrong they do. But forgiving is love's power to break nature's rule.
Sharon Jaynes
Becoming the Woman of His Dreams (2005)

6 God is utterly fair.
Edith Schaeffer
Common Sense Christian Living (1983)

152 FAITH

For we walk by faith, not by sight.
2 CORINTHIANS 5:7

1 Walking by sight is just this: "I believe in myself." Whereas walking by faith is: "I believe in God."
   Charles Spurgeon
   "Faith Versus Sight" sermon (1866)

2 Great faith believes in God even when he plays his hand close to his vest, never showing all his cards. He has his reasons for doing so. God wants to increase your "measure of faith." He does this whenever he conceals a matter, and you trust him nevertheless.
   Joni Eareckson Tada
   Pearls of Great Price (2006)

3 It seems we need an occasional blast of storm or fiery trial, if our faith is to mature.
   Joni Eareckson Tada
   Pearls of Great Price (2006)

4 The smallest grain of faith is a deathless and incorruptible germ which will yet plant the heavens and cover the earth with harvests of imperishable glory.
   A. B. Simpson
   Days of Heaven Upon Earth (1897)

5 Delay is often the test and the strength of faith.
   E. M. Bounds
   The Necessity of Prayer (19th century)

6 Faith gathers strength by waiting and praying.
   E. M. Bounds
   The Necessity of Prayer (19th century)

7 Faith deals with God, and is conscious of God.
   E. M. Bounds
   The Necessity of Prayer (19th century)

8 Faith is not believing just anything; it is believing God.
   E. M. Bounds
   The Necessity of Prayer (19th century)

9 Faith recognizes that God is in control, not man. Faith does it God's way, in God's timing—according to His good pleasure. Faith does not take life into its own hands, but in respect and trust places it in God's.
   Kay Arthur
   When Bad Things Happen (2002)

10 You must see with the eyes of faith, beyond the moment, beyond the situation, to your God.
   Kay Arthur
   Beloved (1994)

11 The circumstances of life will either shrink or stretch your faith.
   James MacDonald
   Lord, Change My Attitude (2001)

12 Faith is not a part of the Christian life; it's the whole thing.
   James MacDonald
   Lord, Change My Attitude (2001)

13 Faith is not having the answers to our suffering (the book of Job teaches this!). Faith is trusting God despite our suffering.
   Ravi Zacharias and Norman Geisler
   Is Your Church Ready? (2003)

14 God loves it when you and I step into the pitch-black night of this world with the candle of His presence.
   Angela Thomas
   A Beautiful Offering (2004)

15 In relationship to God, it is not enough to go on what feels right or what we sincerely believe is true. To have eternal life, we must relate to God on His terms, not ours. He is, after all, God. So, the test of any faith's validity is whether it conforms to his standard.
   Franklin Graham
   The Name (2002)

16 Faith opens all the windows to God's wind.
George MacDonald
Diary of an Old Soul (1880)

17 Faith is only as good as the object in which it is placed.
Erwin Lutzer
How You Can Be Sure That You Will Spend Eternity with God (1996)

18 Faith lets other people do their thing without getting anxious and worried. It leaves its case in God's hands.
Jim Cymbala and Dean Merrill
Fresh Faith (2003)

19 Faith is not generated by a kind of repetitious self-hypnosis; rather, it is strengthened through a knowledge of the one in whom it is placed, and that kind of knowledge comes through studying God's Word and through experiences with Him as we go through life.
Charles Ryrie
Balancing the Christian Life (1969)

20 Never try to have more faith—just get to know God better. And because God is faithful, the better you know him, the more you'll trust him.
John Ortberg
If You Want to Walk on Water, You've Got to Get Out of the Boat (2001)

21 Faith is believing what God says to the extent that it influences your thinking and your behavior.
Gary and Mona Shriver
Unfaithful (2005)

22 Faith sees beyond the difficulties and counts on God.
Colin Smith
Unlocking the Bible Story (2002)

23 It takes no faith to hear or obey an audible voice. But it takes faith to pay attention to the still small inner voice and witness of the Holy Spirit.
Steve Sampson
You Can Hear the Voice of God (1993)

24 Sight is not faith, and hearing is not faith, neither is feeling faith; but believing when we can neither see, hear, nor feel, is faith.
Hannah Whitall Smith
The Christian's Secret of a Happy Life (1888)

25 Radical faith doesn't mean that you are not afraid. Radical faith just means that you are willing to act despite your fears.
Chip Ingram
Holy Ambition (2002)

26 God is not limited by our chains, but we are limited by our faith.
Gary Kinnaman
Learning to Love the One You Marry (1997)

27 Faith is believing in things when common sense tells you not to.
George Seaton
Miracle on 34th Street (1947)

28 Faith is the simple belief that God will keep His promises.
Steve Campbell
Who God Will Heal (2009)

29 Faith is different from proof; the one is human, the other is gift of God.
Blaise Pascal
Pensées (17th century)

30 Faith puts Christ between itself and circumstances so that it cannot see them.
F. B. Meyer
The Shepherd Psalm (1889)

31 Faith is the hand by which my soul touches God.
Billy Sunday
The Best of Billy Sunday (20th century)

32 It is not great faith that we need, but faith in a great God.
   Corrie ten Boom
   Amazing Love (1953)

33 Faith is trusting God even when you cannot trace God. It is believing that no matter what you're going through, God is for you.
   Tullian Tchividjian
   Do I Know God? (2007)

34 When the Divine Light penetrates the soul, it is united with God as light with light. This is the light of faith.
   Meister Eckhart
   Meister Eckhart's Sermons (14th century)

35 The faith toward God in Christ must be sure and steadfast, that it may solace and make glad the conscience, and put it to rest. When a man has this certainty, he has overcome the serpent.
   Martin Luther
   Table Talk (16th century)

36 But faith is a thing in the heart, having its being and substance by itself, given of God as his proper work, not a corporal thing, that may be seen, felt, or touched.
   Martin Luther
   Table Talk (16th century)

37 Following a set of man-made rules isn't the key to eternal life; faith in Christ is.
   Lisa Harper
   Relentless Love (2002)

38 All we can truly rely on is faith in a God who is in control.
   Jane Jarrell
   Secrets of a Mid-Life Mom (2004)

39 For faith to be present, action is required.
   Jane Jarrell
   Secrets of a Mid-Life Mom (2004)

40 Faith proves itself by its obedience to the Lord.
   Jane Jarrell
   Secrets of a Mid-Life Mom (2004)

41 Faith grows when it is fed. It gets fat and sassy when it is shred.
   Tracie Peterson
   The Eyes of the Heart (2002)

42 Faith at first standeth but on one weak foot.
   George Swinnock
   Works of George Swinnock (17th century)

43 The gift of faith is the ability to envision what needs to be done and to trust God to accomplish it even though it seems impossible to most people.
   Aubrey Malphurs
   Maximizing Your Effectiveness (2006)

44 Preach faith till you have it; and then, because you have it, you will preach faith.
   John Wesley, quoting Peter Bohler
   The Journal of John Wesley (18th century)

45 The hardest part of faith is the last half hour.
   David Wilkerson
   World Challenge Pulpit Series (2000)

46 The key to understanding faith is understanding what it is anchored in. It is not based in our own wisdom or knowledge but in Christ.
   Steven Curtis Chapman
   The Great Adventure (2001)

47 Faith is believing right here with your head no matter how your heart feels.
   Beth Moore "Who Do You Trust?" teaching series (2007)

48 I don't want any of those things I fear to happen, but this I know, if they do, my God will take care of me, my God will take care of me!
> Beth Moore
> "Who Do You Trust?" teaching series (2007)

49 Step out of the boat no matter how the "weather" looks.
> Scott Hinkle
> *Recapturing Your Primary Purpose* (2005)

50 Faith must always be in the present tense. The most succinct statement of the principle is in Mark: "So I tell you, whatever you pray for and ask, believe you have got it, and you shall have it."
> Catherine Marshall
> *Beyond Ourselves* (1961)

51 One of God's most astounding characteristics is that even the ability to have faith in Him comes from Him.
> Laura Petherbridge
> *When Your Marriage Dies* (2005)

52 Faith is a quiet certainty that God keeps His promises.
> Mary Southerland
> *Experiencing God's Power in Your Ministry* (2006)

53 Faith has been reduced to a comfortable system of beliefs about God instead of an uncomfortable encounter with God.
> Michael Yaconelli
> *Dangerous Wonder* (1998)

54 True faith, real and pure faith, cannot be practiced in moderation.
> Stephen Arterburn and Jack Felton
> *Toxic Faith* (1991)

55 Faith is the condition in the covenant of grace; death required on Christ's part, faith required on man's part.
> Stephen Charnock
> *Discourse of God's being the Author of Reconciliation* (17th century)

56 Faith begins where the will of God is known. Faith must rest on the will of God alone, not on our desires or wishes.
> F. F. Bosworth
> *Christ the Healer* (1924)

57 Faith includes noticing the mess, the emptiness and discomfort, and letting it be there until some light returns.
> Anne Lamott
> *Plan B: Further Thoughts on Faith* (2005)

58 Faith occupies the position of a channel or conduit pipe. Grace is the fountain and the stream; faith is the aqueduct along which the flood of mercy flows down to refresh the thirsty sons of men.
> Charles Spurgeon
> *All of Grace* (19th century)

59 Great messages can be sent along slender wires, and the peace-giving witness of the Holy Spirit can reach the heart by means of a thread-like faith which seems almost unable to sustain its own weight.
> Charles Spurgeon
> *All of Grace* (19th century)

60 What is faith? It is made up of three things—knowledge, belief, and trust.
> Charles Spurgeon
> *All of Grace* (19th century)

61 The Puritans were accustomed to explain faith by the word "recumbency." It meant leaning upon a thing. Lean with all your weight upon Christ. It would be a better illustration still if I said, fall at full length, and lie on the Rock of Ages.
> Charles Spurgeon
> *All of Grace* (19th century)

62 You cannot turn anywhere in life without seeing faith in operation between man and man, or between man and natural law.
Charles Spurgeon
All of Grace (19th century)

63 As it is fabled of Midas that he turned everything into gold by his touch, so it is true of faith that it turns everything it touches into good.
Charles Spurgeon
All of Grace (19th century)

64 The Christian's faith isn't a leap into the dark. It is a well-placed trust in the Light of the world, Jesus.
Ravi Zacharias and Kevin Johnson
Jesus Among Other Gods—Youth Edition (2000)

65 Faith won't do you any good if the God you follow, worship, and commit your life to isn't real.
Ravi Zacharias and Kevin Johnson
Jesus Among Other Gods—Youth Edition (2000)

66 Faith goes beyond cerebral recognition and opens the door of the heart to Jesus Himself. It is at this heart level that the believer must be deeply rooted or, better yet, firmly established in His love.
Jack and Dona Eggar
Shaping Your Family's Faith (2007)

67 As gold that is tried in the fire, is purged from its alloy, and all remainders of dross, and comes forth more solid and beautiful; so true faith being tried as gold is tried in the fire, becomes more precious, and thus also is "found unto praise, and honor, and glory."
Jonathan Edwards
A Treatise Concerning Religious Affections (18th century)

68 Our circumstances should never be deeper than our faith.
Jeff Huff
"Storms" sermon (2009)

69 Faith opens the eyes to see the blessedness of God's service, the sufficiency of the strength provided, and the rich reward.
Andrew Murray
Working for God (1901)

70 It is a great strengthening of faith with understanding to begin every action in the name of God.
Lewis Bayly
The Practice of Piety (1611)

71 Our beliefs are not just estimates of probabilities. They are also the instruments that guide our actions.
John Ortberg
Faith and Doubt (2008)

72 Faith involves certain beliefs. Faith involves an attitude of hope and confidence. But at its core, faith is trusting a person.
John Ortberg
Faith and Doubt (2008)

73 Faith rests upon the character of God, not upon the demonstrations of laboratory or logic.
A. W. Tozer
That Incredible Christian (1960s)

74 The real secret of faith's power lies not in the faith itself but in its object, Jesus Christ.
John Stott
Life in Christ (2003)

75 Faith is a divine gift, but it is never forced upon us. And it doesn't happen through convincing proof or by witnessing miracles.
Lynn Anderson
*If I Really Believe,
Why Do I Have These Doubts?* (1992)

76 Do you count it a great faith to believe
what God has said? It seems to me, I repeat, a
little faith, and, if alone, worthy of reproach. To
believe what he has not said is faith indeed, and,
blessed. For that comes of believing in Him.
> George MacDonald
> "The Higher Faith" sermon (19th century)

77 They are blessed to whom a wonder is not
a fable, to whom a mystery is not a mockery,
to whom a glory is not an unreality—who are
content to ask, "Is it like Him?"
> George MacDonald
> "The Higher Faith" sermon (19th century)

78 We may have faith to believe in God as
Lord of the calm—but do we also have faith to
believe in Him as Lord of the storm?
> Matt and Beth Redman
> *Blessed Be Your Name* (2005)

79 The world is marked by unbelief; the
kingdom of God is marked by faith.
> Mark Dever "The Whole Bible: What
> Does God Want of Us?" sermon (2000)

80 Faith that does not act is a faith that is just
an act.
> Lois Evans
> *Stones of Remembrance* (2006)

81 Let us never limit God.
> Charles Colson
> *Faith on the Line* (1994)

153 FAITHFULNESS
*It is a faithful saying: For if we be dead with him,
we shall also live with him: If we suffer, we shall
also reign with him: if we deny him, he also will
deny us: If we believe not, yet he abideth faithful:
he cannot deny himself.*
2 TIMOTHY 2:11–13

1 Simply put, we need churches that are self-
consciously distinct from the culture. We need
churches in which the key indicator of success
is not evident results but persevering biblical
faithfulness.
> Mark Dever
> *Nine Marks of a Healthy Church*
> (2004)

2 You don't have to be any more talented,
any richer, any slimmer, any smarter, any more
or less of anything to partner with God. All
you have to be is willing to be used by him in
everyday ways.
> Bill Hybels
> *Just Walk Across the Room* (2006)

3 Would that we had the faith to look upon
every trying circumstance, from every fretting
worry, from every annoyance and temptation,
into the face of our Guide, and say, "It is the
right way, Thou great Shepherd of the sheep;
lead Thou me on!"
> F. B. Meyer
> *The Shepherd Psalm* (1889)

4 What if God was only faithful when he felt
like it, only dependable part of the time, only
loving on special occasions? Thank goodness,
He is always faithful to His own nature. The
world desperately needs to see that same kind
of faithfulness in our lives.
> Lloyd John Ogilvie
> *The Magnificent Vision* (1980)

5 Having resolved to make the love of God
the end of all his actions, he had found reasons
to be well satisfied with his method.
> Brother Lawrence
> *The Practice of the Presence of God*
> (17th century)

6 He is training us to a kind of faithfulness
whose high quality is unattained by any other
earthly means.
> Henry Drummond
> "Why Christ Must Depart"
> sermon (19th century)

7   Peace of conscience, liberty of heart, the sweetness of abandoning ourselves in the hands of God, the joy of always seeing the light grow in our hearts, finally, freedom from the fears and insatiable desires of the times, multiply a hundredfold the happiness which the true children of God possess in the midst of their crosses, if they are faithful.

François Fénelon
Christian Perfection (17th century)

8   In our darkest times, we must proclaim Jesus as the One who is powerful enough to heal and merciful enough to rescue. But all the time, underneath must be a conviction that even if for some reason we are not relieved of our struggle, our worship will not falter.

Matt and Beth Redman
Blessed Be Your Name (2005)

9   God entrusts great power only to those who have proven themselves faithful.

Rick Renner
Living in the Combat Zone (1989)

10 Faithfulness is the foundation for usefulness in God's Kingdom.

Rick Renner
Living in the Combat Zone (1989)

11 You have been created by God and for God, and someday you will stand amazed at the simple yet profound ways He has used you even when you weren't aware of it.

Kay Arthur
As Silver Refined (1998)

12 The greatest glory we can give to God is to distrust our own strength utterly, and to commit ourselves wholly to His safe-keeping.

Brother Lawrence
The Practice of the Presence of God (17th century)

13 God is faithful. You will never invest more in Him than He will in you. God's Word tells us to whom much is given, much is required (Luke 12:48), but I am also convinced that to whom much is required, much is surely given.

Beth Moore
Believing God (2004)

14 As Christians, we need to know that God will continue to care for us, and that His continuing care is based not on our faithfulness but on His.

Mark Dever
Nine Marks of a Healthy Church (2004)

15 I have experienced His presence in the deepest hell that man can create. I have really tested the promises of the Bible, and believe me, you can count on them.

Corrie ten Boom
He Cares, He Comforts (1977)

16 Let me tell you that God, who began a good work in you, is not about to stop now.

Jim Cymbala and Dean Merrill
Fresh Faith (2003)

17 Our faith is not meant to get us out of a hard place or change our painful condition. Rather, it is meant to reveal God's faithfulness to us in the midst of our dire situation.

David Wilkerson
"Have Faith in God's Faithfulness" article (2009)

18 God is faithful. If He has allowed a trial into your life, you can bank on the fact that He has a reason for having done so. Trust Him with your pain. Trust Him that He has a plan.

Rebecca Lusignolo
Adversity (2007)

19 Before we decided to look for God, God had already been looking for us.

John Stott
Basic Christianity (1958)

154 FALL, THE

And he said, Who told thee that thou wast naked?
Hast thou eaten of the tree, whereof I commanded
thee that thou shouldest not eat?
Genesis 3:11

1   Since the world was created, man has
imitated Satan; the creature of a day, the
ephemera of an hour, has sought to match
itself with the Eternal.
Charles Spurgeon
"Sovereignty and Salvation" sermon (1856)

2   When man fell in the garden, manhood
fell entirely; there was not one single pillar in
the temple of manhood that stood erect.
Charles Spurgeon
"Human Inability" sermon (1858)

3   One of the greatest sorrows which came
to human beings when Adam and Eve left the
Garden was the loss of memory, memory of all
God's children are meant to be.
Madeline L'Engle
Walking on Water (1980)

155 FALSE GODS

Turn ye not unto idols, nor make to yourselves
molten gods: I am the Lord your God.
Leviticus 19:4

1   It is an ill day for a people when their gods
are worse than themselves.
Charles Spurgeon
"Forgiveness Made Easy" sermon (1878)

2   False religion may cause persons to be loud
and earnest in prayer.
Jonathan Edwards
A Treatise Concerning Religious Affections
(18th century)

156 FALSEHOOD (*see also* LYING)

How then comfort ye me in vain, seeing in your
answers there remaineth falsehood?
Job 21:34

1   Fallacies do not cease to be fallacies
because they become fashions.
G. K. Chesterton
The Illustrated London News (1930)

2   The plunder is deep when the soul
is captured by a belief that is rooted in
falsehood.
Ravi Zacharias
Recapture the Wonder (2003)

3   If you say it doesn't matter what you
believe as long as you are sincere, you miss a
very important point: You can be sincerely
wrong.
James Emery White
A Search for the Spiritual (1998)

4   No greater mischief can happen to a
Christian people, than to have God's Word
taken from them, or falsified, so that they no
longer have it pure and clear.
Martin Luther
Table Talk (16th century)

5   Over the years I have learned something
about images or facades. They use up entirely
too much energy in their maintenance, leaving
us drained and void of the power to change or
develop the real.
Lisa Bevere
You Are Not What You Weigh (1998)

157 FAME

And when the queen of Sheba heard of the fame of
Solomon, she came to prove Solomon
with hard questions at Jerusalem.
2 Chronicles 9:1

1   It is all right when God sends us the
approval of our fellow men; however, we must
never make that approval a motive in our life.
A. B. Simpson
Days of Heaven Upon Earth (1897)

2 A great deal of our life is wrapped up in the image we want to project to all those around us. We want people to admire us and give us their approval. We imagine that popularity somehow equals success in our lives, yet Jesus calls His disciples to give up the popularity of the world for the praise of His Father.
Bill Gothard
Our Jealous God (2003)

3 I've come to the conclusion that I would rather labor in obscurity for God than be famous for doing something insignificant with my life.
Rory Noland
The Heart of the Artist (1999)

158 FAMILY
Children, obey your parents in all things: for this is well pleasing unto the Lord.
COLOSSIANS 3:20

1 Concentrate on the things you like about your loved ones and ignore the trivial.
Bill Glass
Champions for Life (2005)

2 If you want a spiritually healthy family, you must make sure that each member consumes a healthy diet of the everlasting Word of God.
Dennis and Barbara Rainey
Growing a Spiritually Strong Family (2002)

3 God designed the family to be a spiritual garden that grows flowers for today and seeds for tomorrow.
Dennis and Barbara Rainey
Growing a Spiritually Strong Family (2002)

4 If I can't love and serve my mother and sister today, what makes me think I'll be ready to love and serve a wife in the future?
Joshua Harris
I Kissed Dating Goodbye (1997)

5 Family should be the place where we best express who we are and develop our God-given talents on new levels. Ironically, many times it becomes the place where we are imprisoned, unable to be who we really are.
Dan Seaborn
26 Words That Will Improve the Way You Do Family (1997)

6 A boy who has a father who is committed to his mother will have a tremendous advantage when he becomes a husband. He will have an intuitive understanding that his commitment in marriage is not a right to be happy, but to demonstrate a willingness to be responsible. Even when it's inconvenient. Even when it crowds out his personal happiness.
Steve Farrar
Point Man (1980)

7 A family shapes itself through the time it spends together. At the most basic level, if there is no family time, it can be argued that there is no family.
Wayne and Mary Sotile
Beat Stress Together (1998)

8 Bringing two families together doesn't necessarily result in a sweet strawberry shake. Sometimes the results are more like vinegar and oil. The two don't naturally mix and they have to be shaken up often to combine the flavors into a palatable experience.
Maxine Marsolini
Blended Families (2000)

9 Divorce-proofing is the greatest hedge of protection you can place around your family. It is within the boundary of protection that you can design the ultimate plan for a relationship in which you are known, understood, honored, protected, and esteemed to the point that your deepest love needs are fulfilled.
Gary and Barbara Rosberg
Divorce-Proof Your Marriage (2002)

10 I believe that ministering to our families includes ministering to our parents, our in-laws, and other members of our extended families. Although we have to accomplish this with balance and much God-given wisdom, not caring for our family members is a sin.
Gigi Graham Tchividjian
For Women Only (2001)

11 Your family can experience the real and living God, but you must approach this relationship like others that you value.
Bruce Bickel and Stan Jantz
God Is in the Small Stuff for Your Family (1999)

12 With a family, there is a sense of belonging. Your family ties give you a sense of identity and a sense of being connected to something larger than yourself.
Bruce Bickel and Stan Jantz
God Is in the Small Stuff for Your Family (1999)

13 The family is in the business of people-making, of building each other, of being constructive and encouraging.
Myron and Esther Augsburger
How to Be a Christ-Shaped Family (1994)

14 Ritual is an ancient tool to honor patterns in God's creation. It is a way to celebrate our lives, to create and to keep family feeling.
Ingrid Trobisch
Keeper of the Springs (1997)

15 You don't choose your family. They are God's gift to you, as you are to them.
Desmond Tutu Address (1986)

16 Traditions pull us together when outside forces threaten to push us apart.
David and Claudia Arp
Where the Wild Strawberries Grow (1996)

17 The family is a crucial unit of growth, instruction, and discipline—a warm, secure incubator for producing wise adults.
Bob Barnes
Walking Together in Wisdom (2001)

18 Let us encourage you to never end a family relationship—even if you feel deep hurts from past offenses by family members. Realize over time things change. If you cut off the relationship and refuse reconciliation, the seeds of bitterness will remain and your heart will harden. Your anger and frustration will not go away just because you refuse to forgive or seek forgiveness.
David and Claudia Arp
Loving Your Relatives (2003)

19 There is not a glue that sticks a family closer together than a mutual awareness of the Creator and His workmanship.
Thomas and Nanette Kinkade
The Many Loves of Parenting (2003)

20 Healthy families are built through good communication, which is more than hearing and understanding. Good communication involves creating a safe atmosphere that allows family members to express their thoughts and feelings.
Teresa Langston
Parenting Without Pressure (2001)

21 God created us to be in families, which become either the place of our connectedness or our bondage.
Ted Roberts
Pure Desire (1999)

22 You are loved by a God who will never forget about you even when you feel he is far away. Build upon these bedrock truths and be proud of the things you accomplish with your family. And while you're at it, enjoy your children every chance you get.
Mike Klumpp
The Single Dad's Survival Guide (2003)

23 The me-ism of our times has taken a serious toll on the family.
Charles Swindoll
The Darkness and the Dawn (2001)

24 God is looking within each family for one intercessor who will "stand in the gap" and "put up a hedge" for the entire household. I encourage you to be the one who makes the decision to be subject to God for the purpose of peace, harmony, and unity.
Germaine Copeland
Prayers That Avail Much (1989)

25 Family treasures don't have to cost much or even be worth much monetarily. What's important is the emotional value each thing holds.
Florence Littauer, Marita Littauer, and Lauren Littauer Briggs
Making the Blue Plate Special (2006)

26 Obviously, families need rules for living together—rules that are probably few in number but inviolable in observance.
Gordon MacDonald
There's No Place Like Home (1990)

27 If we hope to do more than fantasize about family life, we need to sink our teeth into stuff that will stick to our ribs. What good is it if the family is "in" but God's timeless wisdom is "out"?
Charles Swindoll
Growing Wise in Family Life (1988)

28 God's desire is that there be a conscious, consistent transfer of God's truth from the older to the younger in the family.
Charles Swindoll
Growing Wise in Family Life (1988)

29 What is true of a nation and what is true of people in the Bible is also true of families.
Charles Swindoll
Growing Wise in Family Life (1988)

30 There are no shortcuts when it comes to building a healthy, loving and caring family.
Tony Evans
Guiding Your Family (1991)

31 Proximity on the family tree has very little to do with the nearness one feels to relatives.
Howard Hendricks
Heaven Help the Home (1973)

32 From Genesis to Revelation, God's relationship to mankind is constantly described in terms of a family illustration.
Jay Kesler
Is Your Marriage Really Worth Fighting For? (1989)

33 Whatever church God has guided you to, whoever your Christian family is, get your heart together with theirs! Guard your unity! Attend to them, love them, care for them! Help them, strengthen them in God, teach them, be taught by them.
Anne Ortlund
Disciplines of the Beautiful Woman (1977)

34 While families are imperfect institutions, they are also our greatest source of meaning, connection, and joy.
Mary Pipher
Letters to a Young Therapist (2003)

35 If there be but one in a home in touch with God, that one becomes God's door into the whole family.
Samuel Gordon
Quiet Talks on Prayer (1904)

36 Every home has its share of conflicts. The question is how do we win—or better yet, avoid—the battles?
Sonya Haskins
Homeschooling for the Rest of Us (2010)

37 When siblings stand up for each other, they learn to trust one another, laying the foundation for a positive relationship as the years go by.
Sonya Haskins
Homeschooling for the Rest of Us (2010)

38 The stresses of marriage and the home are designed to produce brokenness, to wean one from self-centeredness, and to produce the graces of sacrificial love and gentleness.
Paul Billheimer
Don't Waste Your Sorrows (1977)

39 Family life itself is a spiritual discipline (not simply the locale for devotions and family religious practices); it is a furnace of transformation.
R. Paul Stevens
Down-to-Earth Spirituality (2003)

159 FASTING

But thou, when thou fastest, anoint thine head, and wash thy face; That thou appear not unto men to fast, but unto thy Father which is in secret.
MATTHEW 6:17–18

1 If Jesus could have accomplished all He came to do without fasting, why would He fast?
Jentezen Franklin
Fasting (2008)

2 Without being combined with prayer and the Word, fasting is little more than dieting.
Jentezen Franklin
Fasting (2008)

3 Fasting itself is a continual prayer before God.
Jentezen Franklin
Fasting (2008)

4 Fasting and labour both exhaust and subdue the body.
Francis de Sales
Introduction to the Devout Life (17th century)

160 FATHERHOOD
(*see also* GOD, AS FATHER)

And, ye fathers, provoke not your children to wrath: but bring them up in the nurture and admonition of the Lord.
EPHESIANS 6:4

1 There is often more love in an angry father's heart than there is in the heart of a father who is too kind.
Charles Spurgeon
"The Fatherhood of God" sermon (1858)

2 Fatherhood is the very heart of masculinity. We are never stronger that when we grip the hands of those who look to us for strength.
Stu Weber
The Heart of a Tender Warrior (2002)

3 Men, the years go by quickly, don't they? The little boy who sat on your lap and asked you to read a book to him—the child who imitated your every move—is now asking for the car keys. And one day the little girl who called you Daddy and demanded a kiss every morning and a hug every night will bring home a boy whom she calls honey. We can't miss the opportunity to enjoy these years. We should take advantage of this time to be close to our children—or grandchildren. We'll never regret time spent with children. Not for a moment.
Bill McCartney
4th and Goal (2002)

4 Dads differ in that they have a more action-oriented love and thus need to play more with their kids. Roughhousing (pillow fights, wrestling), tag, hide-and-seek, kickball, hunting, and fishing are just a few examples of what we mean. When a dad connects with his child in this way, the bonds of love are formed. He becomes a harbor of safety, someone who is warm and can be trusted, especially in times of trouble.
Tim Clinton and Gary Sibcy
Attachments (2002)

5   Everyone makes mistakes in business and in personal life. Fathers are allowed room to make mistakes without failing their children. If your mistakes are understood in the context of love, they can be used as lessons your children can grow from.

Connie Neal
Your Thirty-Day Journey to Being a World-Class Father (1992)

6   You can win at home. By being consistent, committed, involved, and authentic you can be a hero to your wife and children.

Paul Pettit
Dynamic Dads (2003)

7   Are you ready and willing to be a hero? Obviously it's not easy; nothing worthwhile ever is. But if you long to become a hero by acting heroically, I personally know of no better way to accomplish that task than to be a hero at home. How? Work hard each day at becoming a servant leader in your home. Honor your wife. Interact with your children at a deep level. And commit yourself to great character and integrity.

Paul Pettit
Dynamic Dads (2003)

8   If you've neglected your family, you may need to run into the burning building that is your home. I guarantee the enemy of your soul is working overtime to destroy your wife and children.

Paul Pettit
Dynamic Dads (2003)

9   Reach a father, reach a family. Reach a family, reach a neighborhood. And on it goes.

Paul Pettit
Dynamic Dads (2003)

10 Children whose dad has regularly changed their diapers, burped them and rocked them to sleep, and read to them enjoy a reserve

of strength in dealing with stress and the frustrations of everyday life.

Kyle Pruett
Fatherneed (2000)

11 There is an expectation among children whose father was involved in their daily life that diligence of effort pays off and that frustrations need not defeat.

Kyle Pruett
Fatherneed (2000)

12 Fathering during adolescence has a lesser, though still significant, impact on sons than on daughters. Adolescent sons face the task of separating somewhat from their father and challenging his authority while still needing and appreciating his support from the sidelines.

Kyle Pruett
Fatherneed (2000)

13 There's power in a father's gentleness.
Steven Lawson
The Legacy (1998)

14 What a difference self-motivation makes. The challenge for us as fathers is to teach our children to have that same "good will" toward their work as they have toward their play.

Steven Lawson
The Legacy (1998)

15 When lawgiving is balanced with nurturing, a father helps his children learn to make decisions about right and wrong for themselves. It is not just a matter of "following orders."

David Stoop
Making Peace with Your Father (2004)

16 When it comes to rules and standards of behavior, children operate on a "show me, don't tell me" basis. They need to see morality modeled, struggled with, confronted, and dealt with realistically and honestly. A father who is

comfortably balanced in his lawgiving role is able to demonstrate his sense of integrity and morality by the way he relates to his children, not just proclaim it to them.
David Stoop
Making Peace with Your Father (2004)

17 A father demonstrates his love for his child through the love and commitment he shows to his wife.
John Burns
Miracle in a Daddy's Hug (2003)

18 Realize that God is the ultimate good Father. He not only can redeem the damage done in your own life by your very imperfect father, He can take up the slack where you fail as a father. But if you really come to know Him as your Father, you'll find yourself failing less and less as a dad.
Nick Harrison and Steve Miller
Survival Guide for New Dads (2003)

19 Our dads are our first heroes (and, decades later, our last).
John Thorn
Baseball: Our Game (1995)

20 Being an effective father to his kids is one of the most important tasks a man will face during his lifetime.
Ken Canfield
Beside Every Great Dad (1993)

21 A father holds awesome power in the lives of his children, for good or ill.
James Dobson
Bringing Up Boys (2001)

22 Fathering is not a sprint; it is a marathon.
Ken Canfield
The Heart of a Father (1996)

23 Fathering is a relationship, not a regimen.
Ken Canfield
The Heart of a Father (1996)

24 A father has enormous power. About this, he has no choice. For good or for bad, by his presence or absence, action or inaction, whether abusive or nurturing, the fact remains: a father is one of the most powerful beings on the face of the earth.
Ken Canfield
The Heart of a Father (1996)

25 The yearning of many men today to become good fathers is rooted in our past—we are all children who want our fathers. Something in us yearns to honor fatherhood.
Ken Canfield
The Heart of a Father (1996)

26 Your commitment to be a good father can be greater than any negative effects resulting from a poor relationship with your dad.
Ken Canfield
The Heart of a Father (1996)

27 Fatherhood may be the most frightening job in the world, but it is also the most important and most rewarding job a man can tackle.
Josh McDowell
The Father Connection (1996)

28 Fathering is indeed a privilege given by the Lord—a matchless opportunity to pour our lives into those we love so dearly.
Josh McDowell
The Father Connection (1996)

29 A father who does not communicate love and acceptance to his child is not a neutral influence in his child's life, but a negative one.
Josh McDowell
The Father Connection (1996)

30 Helping our kids internalize God's standard of honesty is a priority for any father who seeks to reflect the image of God the Father.
Josh McDowell
The Father Connection (1996)

31 Many of us make mistakes and break promises as fathers because we don't recognize how serious our promises to our children are.
Josh McDowell
The Father Connection (1996)

161 FAULT-FINDING
(*see also* CRITICISM; JUDGING; SELF-RIGHTEOUSNESS)

And why beholdest thou the mote that is in thy brother's eye, but considerest not the beam that is in thine own eye?
MATTHEW 7:3

1 Wink at small faults—remember thou hast great ones.
Benjamin Franklin
Poor Richard's Almanac (18th century)

2 Whenever we are angry, we are fault-finding—we choose to play God by judging or blaming the other person for being wrong or deserving of punishment.
David Hawkins
9 Critical Mistakes Most Couples Make (2005)

3 God blesses the one who does away with the pointing of the finger.
R. T. Kendall
Total Forgiveness (2002)

4 By focusing on the faults of others, we can manage to avoid looking at ourselves. Sometimes we're even guilty of the very acts we criticize in others.
Bruce Narramore
Guilt and Freedom (1974)

5 We do too much watching of our neighbor's garden, too little weeding in our own.
William George Jordan
The Kingship of Self-Control (1898)

162 FAVORITISM

My brethren, have not the faith of our Lord Jesus Christ, the Lord of glory, with respect of persons.
JAMES 2:1

1 To show favoritism is sin; it desecrates God's standard of love.
James Eckman
Biblical Ethics (2004)

163 FEAR (*see also* COWARDICE)

Fear not, little flock; for it is your Father's good pleasure to give you the kingdom.
LUKE 12:32

1 Awake, Our Souls! Away, Our Fears!
Isaac Watts hymn title (18th century)

2 Every fear is distrust, and trust is the remedy for fear.
A. B. Simpson
Days of Heaven Upon Earth (1897)

3 Fear of God can deliver us from the fear of man.
John Witherspoon
"Ministerial Character and Duty" sermon (18th century)

4 Always remember that, every time you step out of your comfort zone, you step into God's comfort zone.
Mark Cahill
One Thing You Can't Do in Heaven (2002)

5 What you can't face, you can't fix.
Karen O'Connor
Addicted to Shopping (2005)

6 Dare to step out of your comfort zone today. God has so much more in store. Keep pursuing and keep believing.
Joel Osteen
Your Best Life Begins Each Morning (2008)

7 Fear disrupts faith and becomes the biggest obstacle to trusting and obeying God.
  John Ortberg
  If You Want to Walk on Water,
  You've Got to Get Out of the Boat (2001)

8 When we jump in too soon to fix our children's struggles—or the problems of those whom we love—we are often simply revealing our own fears.
  Tamara Boggs
  And Then God Gave Us Kids (2003)

9 Most children are not born afraid. They learn the concept of fear either by experience (something happening to them) or by example.
  Melissa Trevathan and Sissy Goff
  The Back Door to Your Teen's Heart (2002)

10 When fears arise in all of our lives, let us recognize and resist the temptation to numb our feelings by seeking wealth, prestige, power, or beauty.
  Ray and Nancy Kane
  From Fear to Love (2002)

11 Fear can be conquered only by faith, and faith thrives on truth.
  Brendan O'Rourke and DeEtte Sauer
  Hope of a Homecoming (2003)

12 Slavish fear of God is to be put away. The right fear is the fear of losing God.
  Meister Eckhart
  Meister Eckhart's Sermons (14th century)

13 Fear is useful if it drives us to our knees and makes us cry out to God for power and courage to deal with the problems in our church.
  Jan Winebrenner and Debra Frazier
  When a Leader Falls (1993)

14 Listen, nothing makes us more manic than when we're tempted to panic.
  Beth Moore
  "A Beautiful Mind" teaching series (2009)

15 Panic is fear on steroids.
  Beth Moore
  "A Beautiful Mind" teaching series (2009)

16 Not only does fear talk us into trading power for powerlessness, but fear trades love for lust.
  Beth Moore
  "A Beautiful Mind" teaching series (2009)

17 Fear trades self-control for a controlling spirit, every single time.
  Beth Moore
  "A Beautiful Mind" teaching series (2009)

18 For God hath not given us the spirit of fear; but of power, and of love, and of a sound mind. . . . When we are driven by a spirit of fear, we will act out the antithesis or perversion of all three of those.
  Beth Moore
  Overcoming Insecurity (2006)

19 The feeling of fear is a very painful emotion, but in its nature very different from remorse.
  Archibald Alexander
  The Misery of the Lost (19th century)

20 Imagine what your life will look like when you have broken the bondage of fear.
  Bruce Wilkinson
  The Dream Giver (2003)

21 Never agree to do something in order to impress people or because you fear what they may think or say about you if you don't.
  Joyce Meyer
  Never Give Up! (2008)

22 Fear takes one giant and turns it into a whole population.
  Charles Swindoll
  "David and the Dwarf" sermon (2009)

23 There is that fear of the Lord which is the beginning of wisdom, which is founded in love. There is also a slavish fear, which is a mere dread of evil, and is purely selfish.
Charles Finney
Lectures to Professing Christians (1837)

24 It's time to loosen your white-knuckle grip on life and enjoy the ride.
John DeMarco
New Man magazine (2003)

25 The one thing we all have in common is fear.
Lloyd John Ogilvie
The Bush Is Still Burning (1980)

26 People who hide aspects of their lives end up being fearful, often in areas unrelated to what they are hiding.
Lloyd John Ogilvie
The Bush Is Still Burning (1980)

27 Fear has always been one of the principle enemies of a growing faith. It has a way of clouding our thinking and obscuring the facts.
Andy Stanley
Fields of Gold (2004)

28 Confidence in God's presence is our basic weapon against fear.
Mary Southerland
Experiencing God's Power in Your Ministry (2006)

29 Committing our fears to God means crawling up into His lap until the storm passes.
Mary Southerland
Experiencing God's Power in Your Ministry (2006)

30 Fear is contagious, and if you catch it, it will make your life a wasteland.
Jim Petersen and Mike Shamy
The Insider (2003)

31 Fear arises when we imagine that everything depends on us.
Elisabeth Elliot
The Music of His Promises (2000)

32 I can usually remember that we have to dread things only one day at a time.
Anne Lamott
Plan B: Further Thoughts on Faith (2005)

33 Sometimes the fear of doing something is much worse than doing it, and the fear of it torments you much more than the actual doing of it.
Joyce Meyer
Do It Afraid! (1996)

34 When you make friends with fear, it can't rule you.
Anne Lamott
Traveling Mercies (1999)

35 Fear paralyzes faith.
Jude D'Souza
"From Fear to Awe" sermon (2009)

36 Fear always hides the truth. Fear magnifies our weaknesses and it hides our potential.
Lynne Hybels
Nice Girls Don't Change the World (2005)

37 Did you know that denial is rooted on fear and pride? "I'm scared to face reality...and I refuse to trust God to help me make it through."
Rose Sweet
Healing the Heartbreak (2001)

38 The most audacious despiser of God is most easily disturbed, trembling at the sound of a falling leaf.
John Calvin
Institutes of the Christian Religion (16th century)

39 There is a difference in being afraid and being immobilized by fear.
> H. Norman Wright
> *Freedom from the Grip of Fear* (1989)

40 The fear of life is actually more debilitating than the fear of death.
> H. Norman Wright
> *Freedom from the Grip of Fear* (1989)

41 An exaggerated fear is equipped with binoculars; it tends to magnify dangers that are a great distance away, making small threats appear large.
> H. Norman Wright
> *Freedom from the Grip of Fear* (1989)

42 Sometimes faith is the absence of fear. Other times faith may be choosing to believe God even when your heart is melting with fear.
> Beth Moore
> *Breaking Free* (1999)

43 Denial of fear is as foolish as fear itself.
> Luci Shaw
> *The Crime of Living Cautiously* (2005)

FEEBLENESS (see WEAKNESS)

164 FEELINGS (see also ATTITUDE; EMOTIONS)

For we have not an high priest which cannot be touched with the feeling of our infirmities; but was in all points tempted like as we are, yet without sin.
HEBREWS 4:15

1 It would be fine to follow our feelings if we could always be sure they're faithful to reality. But they aren't: their perspective on reality typically has huge blind spots.
> C. J. Mahaney
> *Christ Our Mediator* (2004)

2 It's a frightening experience to sit with individuals who actually insist that what they feel is ultimately more authoritative to them than what's written clearly in Scripture.
> C. J. Mahaney
> *Christ Our Mediator* (2004)

3 I don't always feel His presence. But God's promises do not depend upon my feelings; they rest upon His integrity.
> R. C. Sproul
> *One Holy Passion* (1987)

4 If someone arrives late for an appointment and we need reassurance that she cares about us, we may feel hurt. If instead, our need is to spend time purposefully and constructively, we may feel frustrated. If, on the other hand, our need is for thirty minutes of quiet solitude, we may be grateful for her tardiness. Thus, it is not the behavior of the other person, but our own need that causes our feeling.
> David Hawkins
> *9 Critical Mistakes Most Couples Make* (2005)

5 The fulfillment of our heart's desire cannot take anything or anybody belonging to someone else.
> Catherine Marshall
> *Beyond Ourselves* (1961)

6 Lead with actions and let the feelings follow.
> Charles Swindoll
> *Insight for Living* broadcast (2009)

7 The surest road to failure in life is to follow your feelings.
> Gary Chapman
> *Hope for the Separated* (1982)

165 FELLOWSHIP

And when James, Cephas, and John, who seemed to be pillars, perceived the grace that was given unto me, they gave to me and Barnabas the right hands of fellowship.
GALATIANS 2:9

1   The bumble bee makes no honey alone, but if it falls among bees it works with them. Our own devout life will be materially helped by intercourse with other devout souls.

Francis de Sales
Introduction to the Devout Life
(17th century)

2   Blest be the tie that binds
Our hearts in Christian love;
The fellowship of kindred minds
Is like to that above.

John Fawcett
"Blest Be the Tie That Binds" hymn (1782)

3   We don't relate to Christ on our terms. We find him where He is, and fellowship means being there with Him.

Joseph Stowell
Following Christ (1996)

4   That man is right who loves all men as himself.

Meister Eckhart
Meister Eckhart's Sermons (14th century)

166 FEMININITY (*see also* WOMEN)

In like manner also, that women adorn themselves in modest apparel, with shamefacedness and sobriety; not with broided hair, or gold, or pearls, or costly array; But (which becometh women professing godliness) with good works.
I TIMOTHY 2:9–10

1 At the heart of mature femininity is a freeing disposition to affirm, receive, and nurture strength and leadership from worthy men in ways appropriate to a woman's differing relationships.

John Piper and Elisabeth Elliot
What's the Difference? (1990)

167 FLESH, THE

And they that are Christ's have crucified the flesh with the affections and lusts.
GALATIANS 5:24

1   Who hath a greater combat than he that laboureth to overcome himself?

Thomas à Kempis
The Imitation of Christ (15th century)

2   Your flesh, creative and cool as it is, will invariably remind you of a dozen ways to rationalize around the wrong of your lust. And there is a name for those who listen to those reasons: victim.

Charles Swindoll
Man to Man (1996)

3   The Lord is determined to strip us of all confidence in the flesh, leaving us with total confidence in him.

David Wilkerson
"Hold on to Your Confidence" article (2010)

168 FLEXIBILITY

I know both how to be abased, and I know how to abound: every where and in all things I am instructed both to be full and to be hungry, both to abound and to suffer need.
PHILIPPIANS 4:12

1   The really happy man is the one who can enjoy the scenery when he has to take a detour.

Gary Stanley
How to Make a Moose Run (2001)

2   How dull a life it would be if everything happened as anticipated!

Ted Engstrom and Norman Rohrer
Welcome to the Rest of Your Life (1994)

169 FOOLISHNESS

The foolishness of man perverteth his way: and his heart fretteth against the LORD.
PROVERBS 19:3

1 There is no fool like the sinner, who every moment ventures his soul, and lays his everlasting interest at stake.
John Tillotson
The Wisdom of Being Religious (1819)

2 I pity the man who is living on the devil's promises.
D. L. Moody
Best Thoughts and Discourses of D. L. Moody (1876)

3 To use a precious stone where a pebble would be sufficient, is not less foolish than to give honour to a fool.
F. C. Cook
Bible Commentary (19th century)

4 The Bible teaches you're only young once but you can be a fool for life.
James MacDonald
"Wise Up About Wisdom" sermon (2009)

5 The Devils never had a Saviour offered to them, but you have; and do you yet make light of him?
Richard Baxter
The Causes and Danger of Slighting Christ and His Gospel (17th century)

6 It is relational suicide to assume you can ever win over a fool by argument, sweet reasonableness, or any other common wisdom.
Jan Silvious
Foolproofing Your Life (1998)

170 FORGIVENESS

To the Lord our God belong mercies and forgivenesses.
DANIEL 9:9

of God

1 God has forgiven us continuously. He not only forgave us at the first all our sins, but he continues daily to forgive, for the act of forgiveness is a continuous one.
Charles Spurgeon
"Forgiveness Made Easy" sermon (1878)

2 The hardest person to forgive is yourself. If it seems impossible to do, remember that God forgives everyone, over and over, so for you to refuse yourself forgiveness is to set yourself above God.
Barbara Bartocci
From Hurting to Happy (2002)

3 I know beyond the shadow of doubt my debt of sin has been wiped out.
Corrie ten Boom
Amazing Love (1953)

4 Repentance is the key that accesses the door of forgiveness.
Steve Campbell
"Forgiving Other People" sermon (2009)

5 He casts our sins behind His back, He blots them out; He says that though they be sought for, they shall not be found.
Charles Spurgeon
All of Grace (19th century)

6 "Well," say you, "it would be a great miracle if the Lord were to pardon me." Just so. It would be a supreme miracle, and therefore He is likely to do it; for He does "great things and unsearchable" which we looked not for.
Charles Spurgeon
All of Grace (19th century)

7 To be forgiven is an immeasurable favor.
Charles Spurgeon
All of Grace (19th century)

8 The chief of sinners need not be a whit behind the purest of the saints. Believe for this, and according to your faith shall it be unto you.
Charles Spurgeon
All of Grace (19th century)

for Others

9   Every one says forgiveness is a lovely idea, until they have something to forgive.
    C. S. Lewis
    Mere Christianity (1952)

10 You forgive me, and I forgive you, and we forgive them, and they forgive us, and so a circle of unlimited forbearance and love goes round the world.
    Charles Spurgeon
    "Forgiveness Made Easy" sermon (1878)

11 Forgiveness is not an elective in the curriculum of servanthood. It is a required course, and the exams are always tough to pass.
    Charles Swindoll
    Improving Your Serve (1981)

12 In apology, let us be generous rather than stingy.
    Watchman Nee
    Not I But Christ (1948)

13 Release offenses, let go, and enjoy the freedom God gives to those who refuse to hold grudges.
    Barb Albert
    The 100 Most Important Bible Verses for Mothers (2006)

14 Everyone who has received God's forgiveness should be highly motivated to reconcile with those he or she has wronged.
    Erwin Lutzer
    After You've Blown It (2004)

15 Our generous and constant forgiveness of others should be the natural result of our embracing the forgiveness God has extended to us.
    Greg Laurie
    Wrestling with God (2003)

16 Yes, we never touch the ocean of God's love as much as when we love our enemies. It is such a joy to accept forgiveness, but it is almost a greater joy to give forgiveness.
    Corrie ten Boom
    He Cares, He Comforts (1977)

17 If you agree to bury the hatchet, don't leave the handle sticking out.
    Bruce Bickel and Stan Jantz
    God Is in the Small Stuff (1998)

18 Sometimes the only way to forgive ourselves is by remembering our humanity.
    Robert Jeffress
    When Forgiveness Doesn't Make Sense (2000)

19 The best remedy for painful memories is not forgetting the offense, but remembering your decision to forgive. If you're going to remember a wrong, make sure you also remember how you dealt with the wrong.
    Robert Jeffress
    When Forgiveness Doesn't Make Sense (2000)

20 Repentance is our offender's responsibility; forgiveness is our responsibility.
    Robert Jeffress
    When Forgiveness Doesn't Make Sense (2000)

21 Forgiveness is the obligation of the forgiven—and we are the forgiven.
    Robert Jeffress
    When Forgiveness Doesn't Make Sense (2000)

22 Differentiate between forgiving and trusting.
    Henry Cloud and John Townsend
    Boundaries Face to Face (2003)

23 Having found what we've been looking for, we now have the joy of giving it away.

Forgiving people instead of judging them. Seeing others as God sees them: in need of his love, in need of his truth.

Liz Curtis Higgs
Embrace Grace (2006)

24 A heart of forgiveness becomes a test of our own faith. We must take on a Christlike attitude that says, "Even though you blew it, I forgive you." It's crucial to a healthy relationship.

Gregg Matte
The Highest Education: Becoming a Godly Man (2000)

25 It's not so much that we are unable to forgive, but rather we are afraid of what forgiveness might cost us.

Gary and Mona Shriver
Unfaithful (2005)

26 The most crucial issue in a marriage is not that a couple communicate, but what they communicate. Let the thing communicated be forgiveness.

Walter Wangerin Jr.
As for Me and My House (1990)

27 Forgiveness is God's invention for coming to terms with a world in which, despite their best intentions, people are unfair to each other and hurt each other deeply.

Sharon Jaynes
Becoming the Woman of His Dreams (2005)

28 Forgiveness has little to do with what was done to us, but much to do with what we choose to do with it. I believe it is the ultimate expression of love.

Sharon Jaynes
Becoming the Woman of His Dreams (2005)

29 Forgiveness is powerful and beneficial. When we forgive someone for hurting us, it frees us from feeling like victims or feeling we are under the power of the person who hurt us.

Grace Ketterman and Kathy King
Caring for Your Elderly Parent (2001)

30 If you forget, you will not forgive at all. You can never forgive people for things you have forgotten about.

Lewis Smedes
Forgive and Forget (1986)

31 When transgressions rip apart relationships, forgiveness is the seamstress who reweaves the jagged tear in trust, thread by thread.

Everett Worthington
Forgiving and Reconciling (2003)

32 Forgiveness restores the unraveled seam of love and irons out the wrinkles of residual anger.

Everett Worthington
Forgiving and Reconciling (2003)

33 If I am required by God to be a forgiving person, then my ability to forgive must rest solely with me. It does not require the other person's participation.

David Stoop
Forgiving the Unforgivable (2001)

34 Forgiveness is a gift we give ourselves and others.

David Stoop
Forgiving the Unforgivable (2001)

35 Forgiveness means the offense is gone. I may remember the offense, but I will "remember it against them no more!"

David Stoop
Forgiving the Unforgivable (2001)

36 Perhaps one of the greatest benefits we can experience when we forgive is the possibility of a restored relationship.

David Stoop
Forgiving the Unforgivable (2001)

37 When it comes to forgiveness, one of our problems is that most of us have better memories than God has.
H. Norman Wright
Let's Just Be Friends (2002)

38 Forgiveness is not passivity, dear one. It is power.
Beth Moore
Get Out of That Pit (2007)

39 Relationships don't thrive because the guilty are punished but because the innocent are merciful.
Max Lucado
Just Like Jesus (1998)

40 Why should we hold on to the sins of others while our own sins have been cast into the depths of the sea?
Corrie ten Boom
Amazing Love (1953)

41 Forgiveness does not mean ignoring what has been done or putting a false label on an evil act. It means, rather, that the evil act no longer remains as a barrier to the relationship.
Johann Christoph Arnold
Why Forgive? (2000)

42 Far from leaving us weak and vulnerable, forgiveness is empowering, both to the person who grants it and the one who receives it.
Johann Christoph Arnold
Why Forgive? (2000)

43 In bringing true closure to the most difficult situations, forgiveness allows us to lay aside the riddles of retribution and human fairness, and to experience true peace of heart.
Johann Christoph Arnold
Why Forgive? (2000)

44 Forgiveness sets into motion a positive chain reaction that passes on the fruits of our forgiveness to others.
Johann Christoph Arnold
Why Forgive? (2000)

45 Forgiveness is the oil that lubricates family relationships, and nowhere is it more needed than among siblings.
David and Claudia Arp and John and Margaret Bell
Loving Your Relatives (2003)

46 Forgiveness is the touchstone that distinguishes love from infatuation.
John Cowan
Small Decencies (1992)

47 Simply put, forgiveness is the decision to cancel a debt.
Andy Stanley
It Came from Within! (2001)

48 Some of the sweetest words in the world, no matter what language, are those that say, "I forgive you."
Kay Arthur
Lord, Give Me a Heart for You (2001)

49 When we refuse to have a heart for the God who commands us to forgive, then we're open targets for Satan's schemes.
Kay Arthur
Lord, Give Me a Heart for You (2001)

50 In a perfect world, there would be no need for apologies. But because the world is imperfect, we cannot survive without them.
Gary Chapman and Jennifer Thomas
The Five Languages of Apology (2006)

51 The need for apologies permeates all human relationships.
Gary Chapman and Jennifer Thomas
The Five Languages of Apology (2006)

52 Real love does not keep score. We are never more like God than when we put down our score cards—and forgive.

  Paul and Nicole Johnson
  Random Acts of Grace (1995)

53 Christians are the most forgiven people in the world. Therefore, we should be the most forgiving people in the world.

  Ken Sande
  The Peacemaker (1991)

54 Forgiveness is both an event and a process.

  Ken Sande
  The Peacemaker (1991)

55 Forgiveness means to give up our resentment for the omission or commission of something that hurts us. Forgiveness grants relief to the person who "owes" us for what they have done to us or allowed to happen to us. In its most complete form, true forgiveness means we cease to feel resentment against the person who inflicted the pain.

  Carol Kent
  A New Kind of Normal (2007)

56 As a born-again believer, I have accepted God's forgiveness in the salvation of Jesus Christ, and I can freely forgive others and joyfully move on.

  Barbara Johnson
  She Who Laughs, Lasts (2000)

57 Forgiving someone who did us wrong does not mean we tolerate the wrong he did.

  Lewis Smedes
  The Art of Forgiving (1996)

58 Forgiving surrenders the right to vengeance, it never surrenders the claims of justice.

  Lewis Smedes
  The Art of Forgiving (1996)

59 If you recognize how large an offense God forgave you, your gratefulness will enable you to more easily forgive someone's offense against you.

  Scott Turansky and Joanne Miller
  Parenting Is Heart Work (2006)

60 It is not enough to forgive others. We must also learn to forgive ourselves—and to accept the gift of God's forgiveness.

  Steve Stephens and Alice Gray
  The Worn Out Woman (2004)

61 The Bible has a simple but rich solution to bitterness: forgiveness.

  Winston Smith
  Divorce Recovery (2008)

62 Give back better than you are given.

  Henry Cloud
  9 Things You Simply Must Do (2004)

63 All marriage authorities say the same thing: A healthy marriage is one in which forgiveness is practiced. To develop a closer relationship it is vital to give forgiveness but also receive forgiveness with grace.

  Jim and Cathy Burns
  Closer (2009)

64 A man will say: "I forgive, but I cannot forget. Let the fellow never come in my sight again." To what does such a forgiveness reach? To the remission or sending away of the penalties which the wronged believes he can claim from the wrong-doer. But there is no sending away of the wrong itself from between them.

  George MacDonald
  "It Shall Not Be Forgiven" sermon
  (19th century)

65 Almost no concept is more important to the Christian faith than forgiveness. The Gospel itself is a message about God's

forgiveness, and Christ's teaching was full of exhortations to His people to be forgiving to one another. He set an incredibly high standard, teaching us to forgive even the most stubborn offenders.

John MacArthur
The Freedom and Power of Forgiveness (1998)

66 God is the consummate forgiver. And we depend every day on His ongoing forgiveness for our sins. The least we can do is emulate His forgiveness in our dealings with one another.

John MacArthur
The Freedom and Power of Forgiveness (1998)

67 Forgiveness. Nothing is more foreign to sinful human nature. And nothing is more characteristic of divine grace.

John MacArthur
The Freedom and Power of Forgiveness (1998)

68 Our response to an offense determines our future. There are too many wonderful opportunities awaiting us when we take the way of escape from the dungeon of resentment.

Dave Earley
The 21 Most Effective Prayers of the Bible (2005)

69 The people we have wronged may not always be able to tell us that they forgive us, but we need to forgive ourselves.

Bill Kemp and Diane Kerner Arnett
Arnett Going Home (2005)

70 Forgiveness refuses superiority.

David Augsburger
*Caring Enough to Forgive—
Caring Enough Not to Forgive* (1981)

71 Genuine forgiveness in ongoing relationships is not a unilateral action, but a mutual interaction.

David Augsburger
*Caring Enough to Forgive—
Caring Enough Not to Forgive* (1981)

72 He taught us how to forgive each other, just as He forgives us. It's the glue that helps hold us together.

Bettie Youngs and Debbie Thurman
A Teen's Guide to Christian Living (2003)

73 Forgiveness never just overlooks or winks at sin.

David Augsburger *70 x 7:
The Freedom of Forgiveness* (1970)

74 God paid the immeasurable cost of your forgiveness. How can you hesitate to pay the infinitely smaller cost of forgiving your brother—or your enemy?

David Augsburger
70 x 7: The Freedom of Forgiveness (1970)

FRAILTY (*see* WEAKNESS)

171 FREEDOM

*And ye shall know the truth,
and the truth shall make you free.*
JOHN 8:32

1 Do not linger in the shame of sin as if such suffering will bring in holiness.

Watchman Nee
Not I But Christ (1948)

2 Freedom is not just freedom from restraint; freedom is freedom to do what God has empowered you to do.

Mel Lawrenz
Jubilee (2008)

3 When God gave us the gift of freedom, He placed it within a framework. He also gave us a well-defined guideline for the effective use of this gift.
Gigi Graham Tchividjian
For Women Only (2001)

4 A fish is free as long as it stays in the water. If it suddenly declares that it wants its freedom to fly in the air like a bird, disaster occurs. A train is free as long as it stays on the track. However, if it demands freedom to take off down a major highway, the result is destruction and devastation. We too can only experience true freedom in its fullest if we remain within the framework of freedom. Often this requires accepting responsibility and practicing discipline.
Gigi Graham Tchividjian
For Women Only (2001)

5 For if the soul remain in the purity in which God created her, neither angel nor devil may rob her of her freedom.
Meister Eckhart
Meister Eckhart's Sermons (14th century)

6 And where the Spirit of the Lord is, there is liberty; such liberty from the law of sin and death, as the children of this world will not believe, though a man declare it unto them.
John Wesley
A Plain Account of Christian Perfection (18th century)

7 God is committed to freeing His children from every present lie, snare, and bondage.
Lisa Bevere
You Are Not What You Weigh (1998)

8 The opposite of a slave is not a free man. It's a worshiper. The one who is most free is the one who turns the work of his hands into sacrament, into offering. All he makes and all he does are gifts from God, through God, and to God.
Mark Buchanan
The Rest of God (2006)

9 Most of the time we like the idea of our own freedom. There are times when we do not at all like the idea of the freedom of others. If we suffer because of their freedom, let us remember that they suffer because of ours.
Elisabeth Elliot
These Strange Ashes (1989)

10 Freedom in God's world never comes apart from structure. When one is free to live as God intended, he is truly free indeed.
Jay Adams
Christian Living in the Home (1972)

11 Humans love freedom like fish love water. They pretty much have to have it.
Stephen Arterburn and John Shore
Midlife Manual for Men (2008)

172 FRIENDSHIP

*A friend loveth at all times,
and a brother is born for adversity.*
PROVERBS 17:17

1 A person is made better or worse by his friends.
Mabel Hale
Beautiful Girlhood (1922)

2 Your best friends will criticize you privately and encourage you publicly.
Bruce Bickel and Stan Jantz
God Is in the Small Stuff (1998)

3 What you tolerate is what you will get.
Henry Cloud and John Townsend
Boundaries Face to Face (2003)

4 Write injuries in dust, benefits in marble.
Benjamin Franklin
Poor Richard's Almanac (18th century)

5 If I will lie for you, I will lie to you. If I will cheat for you, I will cheat on you. If I will be

mad at someone for you, I will be mad at you for someone else. If I will do it for you, I will do it to you.
   Justin Lookadoo and Hayley DiMarco
   Dateable (2006)

6   Those who draw together for mere temporal profit, have no right to call their union friendship; it is not for love of one another that they unite, but for love of gain.
   Francis de Sales
   Introduction to the Devout Life
   (17th century)

7   It is very proper for friends, when they part, to part with prayer.
   Matthew Henry
   Commentary on the Whole Bible (1706)

8   There is a world of difference between being friendly to someone because they're useful to you and being someone's friend.
   John Ortberg
   Everybody's Normal Till You Get to Know Them (2003)

9   We can handle pressure better if we know that there's at least one other person who understands what we're going through.
   David and Claudia Arp
   Answering the 8 Cries of the Spirited Child (2004)

10   It's interesting. You sign a contract for marriage, a license to drive a car, a mortgage to own a house, a W-2 form for a job, an agreement to join a health club, a birth certificate for your kids, but there are no documents to bind you to a friendship. No sealed stamp of commitment. No official guidelines, unless you consider God's Word.
   Traci Mullins
   Celebrating Friendship (1998)

11   Life is partly what we make it, and partly it is made by the friends we choose.
   Traci Mullins
   Celebrating Friendship (1998)

12   True friendship is like sound health; the value of it is seldom known until it be lost.
   Traci Mullins
   Celebrating Friendship (1998)

13   You will not have many true friends. In your entire life, you may not ever have more than ten or fifteen real, close friends. It isn't possible or practical. Thus, the first characteristic we could list about friends is that they are unique. They are unique to you, and in that way, special.
   Paul Jehle
   Dating vs. Courtship (1993)

14   Inconvenience does not exist between friends. It doesn't matter when it is, they will be there if needed.
   Paul Jehle
   Dating vs. Courtship (1993)

15   A friend is also intimate. Friends really know you, the way you really are, not the way you pretend to be in certain situations. A friend cuts through the mask. You can really confide in a friend and get intimate about the most serious things in your life.
   Paul Jehle
   Dating vs. Courtship (1993)

16   The ability to develop deep friendships determines the depth of emotional intimacy that we will experience in our relationships. I am not referring to mere acquaintances or people you occasionally hang out with but about friends in the real sense—people to whom you can open up your heart and life.
   Dick Purnell
   Finding a Lasting Love (2003)

17 What is it that makes you the best of friends? What is it about you that brings out the best in others? It could be your willingness to engage the lives of your friends wherever they are.
   G. A. Myers
   Hugs for Friends Book 2 (2003)

18 Respect is a prime element of friendship.
   F. Dean Lueking
   Let's Talk Marriage (2001)

19 I awoke this morning with a devout thanksgiving for my friends, the old and the new. Shall I not call God the Beautiful, who daily showeth himself to me in his gifts?
   Ralph Waldo Emerson
   Friendship (1841)

20 We take pains to conciliate the good will and friendship of men, that so they may show us a favorable countenance; how much the more ought we to conciliate our Lord Jesus, that so he may be gracious unto us.
   Martin Luther
   Table Talk (16th century)

21 Ultimately, friendships will determine the direction and quality of all of our lives.
   Andy Stanley
   The Seven Checkpoints (2001)

22 We almost never rise above the level of our closest friendships.
   John Maxwell
   Breakthrough Parenting (1996)

23 Our friendships flow in the deep waters of the heart where God dwells and transformation takes place.
   John and Stasi Eldredge
   Captivating (2005)

24 When God gives a friend, he is entrusting us with the care of another's heart.
   John and Stasi Eldredge
   Captivating (2005)

25 The bad will sooner debauch the good than the good reform the bad.
   Matthew Henry
   Commentary on the Whole Bible (1706)

26 Rubble is the ground on which our deepest friendships are built.
   Anne Lamott
   Plan B: Further Thoughts on Faith (2005)

27 I would do many things to please my friends; but to go to hell to please them is more than I would venture.
   Charles Spurgeon
   All of Grace (19th century)

28 It may be very well to do this and that for good fellowship; but it will never do to lose the friendship of God in order to keep on good terms with men.
   Charles Spurgeon
   All of Grace (19th century)

29 Friendship is like love. It cannot be demanded or driven or insisted upon. It must be wooed to be won.
   Laura Ingalls Wilder
   On Wisdom and Virtues (20th century)

30 Faithfulness is essential to the character of a friend: without this there can be no safety in intimacy with and confidence in him.
   Samuel Hopkins
   "The Friendship between Jesus Christ and Believers" sermon (1803)

31 Show me a man's closest companions and I can make a fairly accurate guess as to what sort of man he is, as well as what sort of man he is likely to become.
   Howard and William Hendricks
   As Iron Sharpens Iron (1995)

32 Friends will watch your back when you don't even know there are incoming arrows.
Martha Bolton and Phil Callaway
It's Always Darkest before the Fridge Door Opens (2006)

173 FRUIT, SPIRITUAL

But the fruit of the Spirit is love, joy, peace, longsuffering, gentleness, goodness, faith, meekness, temperance: against such there is no law.
GALATIANS 5:22–23

1 If we be like trees planted by the rivers of water, bringing forth our fruit in our season, it is not because we were naturally fruitful, but because of the rivers of water by which we were planted. It is Jesus that makes us fruitful.
Charles Spurgeon
"The Incarnation and Birth of Christ" sermon (1855)

2 All fruits grow—whether they grow in the soil or in the soul; whether they are the fruits of the wild grape or of the True Vine. No man can make things grow. He can get them to grow by arranging all the circumstances and fulfilling all the conditions. But the growing is done by God.
Henry Drummond
The Greatest Thing in the World (1891)

3 Let us pray God that he would root out of our hearts everything of our own planting, and set out there, with his own hands, the tree of life, bearing all manner of fruits.
François Fénelon and Jeanne Guyon
Spiritual Progress (17th century)

4 No one can have a heart in one condition and produce fruit of an opposite condition. The condition of your heart will affect your actions, and your actions will reflect your heart.
Henry and Tom Blackaby
The Man God Uses (1999)

5 The fruit of the Spirit was never intended to be a demonstration of our dedication and resolve. It is the evidence of our dependency on and sensitivity to the promptings of the Spirit.
Charles Stanley
The Wonderful Spirit-Filled Life (1992)

6 You can't be a born again child of God and produce fruit from hell all of your life.
Lisa Mendenhall
"You Only Die Once" article (2009)

7 Pulling weeds and planting seeds. That's the story of life. We are individual lots on which either weeds of selfishness or fruit of the Holy Spirit grows and flourishes.
Dennis and Barbara Rainey
Moments Together (2004)

8 The fruit of the Spirit is about our character, not our behavior or conduct. The fruit of the Spirit is about being not doing.
Michael Youssef
"A Healing Spirituality" article (2010)

174 FRUSTRATION

For the creature was made subject to vanity, not willingly, but by reason of him who hath subjected the same in hope, because the creature itself also shall be delivered from the bondage of corruption into the glorious liberty of the children of God.
ROMANS 8:20–21

1 Prayerless people cut themselves off from God's prevailing power, and the frequent result is the familiar feeling of being overwhelmed, overrun, beaten down, pushed around, defeated. Surprising numbers of people are willing to settle for lives like that.
Bill Hybels
Too Busy Not to Pray (1988)

2   Minor hurts that would ordinarily not call for forgiving can become major offenses by sheer repetition.
Lewis Smedes
Forgive and Forget (1986)

3   The broad path leads, not to fulfillment, but to futility.
Steven Lawson
Men Who Win (1992)

**FULFILLMENT
(*see* CONTENTMENT)**

175 FUTURE, THE
*Thus saith the Lord of hosts;
In those days it shall come to pass. . .*
ZECHARIAH 8:23

1   Our future is not about what we have or don't have, or about what might happen or what might not happen. Our future is all about Who we know and how well we know Him.
Cindi McMenamin
Letting God Meet Your Emotional Needs (2003)

2   The present is ours; the future belongs to God.
E. M. Bounds
The Necessity of Prayer (19th century)

3   God has your tomorrow covered even though you haven't been there yet.
Tony Evans
God Is Up to Something Great (2002)

4   We should be faithless indeed, and guilty of heathen distrust, did we desire to penetrate the future, which God has hidden from us; leave it to Him: let Him make it short or long, bitter or sweet; let Him do with it even as it shall please Himself.
François Fénelon
Spiritual Progress (17th century)

5   Future contingents cannot be certain to us, because we know them as such. They can be certain only to God whose understanding is in eternity above time.
Thomas Aquinas
Summa Theologiae (13th century)

6   The choices we make every hour of every day create our future.
Lori Salierno
Real Solutions for Ordering Your Private Life (2001)

7   I think God, in His mercy, doesn't let us see the future because we wouldn't be able to enjoy the present.
Carol Kent
A New Kind of Normal (2007)

8   The sorrows and perplexities of human existence must and will give way to eschatological joy in submission to the sovereign Lord of history and of the ages to come.
Eugene Merrill
Everlasting Dominion (2006)

176 GENDER
*So God created man in his own image,
in the image of God created he him;
male and female created he them.*
GENESIS 1:27

1   One of the fundamental differences between men and women is the way they express love. Men are goal-oriented and express love by doing, while women are relationship-oriented and express love by being.
Nancy Cobb and Connie Grigsby
How to Get Your Husband to Talk (2001)

2   Over the years I have come to see from Scripture and from life that manhood and womanhood are the beautiful handiwork of

a good and loving God. He designed our differences and they are profound.

John Piper and Elisabeth Elliot
What's the Difference? (1990)

3 We are adrift in a sea of confusion over sexual roles. And life is not the better for it.

John Piper and Elisabeth Elliot
What's the Difference? (1990)

177 GENEROSITY
(*see also* CHARITY; GIVING)
The liberal soul shall be made fat: and he that watereth shall be watered also himself.
PROVERBS 11:25

1 At the core of the generous person's heart is this penchant for Christ's love—the desire to receive it and to give it to everyone along the way who is in need.

Gordon MacDonald
Secrets of the Generous Life (2002)

2 Listening to God's voice with a joyful spirit, generous people seek wisdom concerning how and when to give. Once they make a commitment, they follow through promptly and keep their promises.

Gordon MacDonald
Secrets of the Generous Life (2002)

3 The most obvious lesson in Christ's teaching is that there is no happiness in having and getting anything, but only in giving.

Henry Drummond
The Greatest Thing in the World (1874)

4 By nature, the concept of generosity is in direct conflict with the concept of self-preservation.

Andy Stanley
Fields of Gold (2004)

5 The problem with giving leftovers is that your generosity can never exceed your ability to meet your own needs.

Andy Stanley
Fields of Gold (2004)

178 GENTLENESS
(*see also* HUMILITY; MEEKNESS)
Now I Paul myself beseech you by the meekness and gentleness of Christ. . .
2 CORINTHIANS 10:1

1 The rightness of your cause never justifies harshness in your spirit.
Colin Smith
Unlocking the Bible Story (2002)

2 Contrary to popular opinion, it takes strength to be gentle.
Lloyd John Ogilvie
The Magnificent Vision (1980)

179 GIFTS, SPIRITUAL
Now there are diversities of gifts, but the same Spirit.
1 CORINTHIANS 12:4

1 Some convert the lost. Some encourage the saved. And some keep the movement going. All are needed.
Max Lucado
A Gentle Thunder (1995)

2 Exhibit God with your uniqueness. When you magnify your Maker with your strengths, when your contribution enriches God's reputation, your days grow suddenly sweet.
Max Lucado
Cure for the Common Life (2005)

3 Spiritual gifts are bestowed upon believers according to the purposes of God and distributed by the sovereign wisdom of God. Our spiritual gifts never belong to us; they're

an expression of the Holy Spirit doing the Father's will.
> Henry and Mel Blackaby
> *What's So Spiritual About Your Gifts?* (2004)

4 Which way soever a man's genius lies, he should endeavor to honour God and edify the church with it.
> Matthew Henry
> *Commentary on the Whole Bible* (1706)

5 Our gifts and talents are the things people celebrate about us, but we find to be no big deal, because the ability comes naturally to us. That is why it is called a gift.
> Michelle McKinney Hammond
> *Ending the Search for Mr. Right* (2005)

6 One good thing about God's gifts and calling is that they are permanent and enduring.
> John Mason
> *An Enemy Called Average* (1990)

7 Gifts and talents are really God's deposits in our personal accounts, but we determine the interest on them.
> John Mason
> *An Enemy Called Average* (1990)

8 Never underestimate the power of the gifts that are within you. Gifts and talents are given to us not only so that we can fulfill to the fullest the call in our own lives, but also so that we can reach the souls who are attached to those gifts.
> John Mason
> *An Enemy Called Average* (1990)

9 Whether your gift is mighty or humble, whether you exercise it in the marketplace or at the podium, in the executive suite or in the schoolroom, in the office or at home, your main task or gift or ministry is to be a light in a dark world.
> Gigi Graham Tchividjian
> *For Women Only* (2001)

10 Blessedness is a gift of God, which cannot be taken away by the chances and changes of this life, because it has been given by God.
> Susan Johnson
> *A New Dating Attitude* (2001)

11 Your gifts make you valuable, but not necessarily famous.
> Fred Hartzler
> "Nehemiah" sermon (2010)

12 God's gifts are given to serve others.
> Tim Walter
> "Otherness, the Lifestyle of Jesus" sermon (2009)

13 God's gift to me is my potential. My gift back to God is what I do with my potential.
> John Maxwell
> *Developing the Leader within You* (1993)

14 It's an insult to God when we focus on the gifts and passions we don't have and try to develop only our weak areas. Our greatest potential lies in the areas of our greatest strengths.
> Kerry and Chris Shook
> *One Month to Live* (2008)

180 GIVING (*See also* CHARITY; GENEROSITY)

Every man according as he purposeth in his heart, so let him give; not grudgingly, or of necessity: for God loveth a cheerful giver.
2 CORINTHIANS 9:7

1 Wouldn't it be well to give some of your bouquets before a man dies, and not go and load down his coffin? He can't enjoy them then.
> D. L. Moody
> "Mary and Martha" sermon (19th century)

2 Giving is a giant level positioned on the fulcrum of this world, allowing us to move

mountains in the next world. Because we give, eternity will be different—for others and for us.
Randy Alcorn
The Treasure Principle (2001)

3 The act of giving is a vivid reminder that it's all about God, not about us. It's saying I am not the point. He is the point. He does not exist for me. I exist for Him.
Randy Alcorn
The Treasure Principle (2001)

4 Ironically, many people can't afford to give precisely because they're not giving. If we pay our debt to God first, then we will incur His blessing to help us pay our debts to men. But when we rob God to pay men, we rob ourselves of God's blessing.
Randy Alcorn
The Treasure Principle (2001)

5 If we would get from God, we must give to others.
R. A. Torrey
How to Pray (1900)

6 We never outgrow our need for others. In fact, giving ourselves to help others is even more life building than receiving help from others. The law of living is giving.
George Sweeting
The Joys of Successful Aging (2002)

7 I do not believe one can settle how much we ought to give. I am afraid the only safe rule is to give more than we can spare.
C. S. Lewis
Words to Live By (20th century)

8 All of Christ's reasons for loving the church are concerned with what He can do for the church, not with what the church does for Him.
Bruce Wilkinson
Experiencing Spiritual Breakthroughs (1999)

9 Beyond giving of our material possessions, God calls upon us to give our selves away—our time, energy, and passion.
Jill Briscoe
8 Things That Will Change a Woman's Life (2004)

10 God has promised us that when we give, He will give back to us, then add some more.
Joel Osteen
Your Best Life Now (2004)

11 Practice giving more than you get.
William Coleman
Engaged (1980)

181 GLORY, GOD'S

Behold, the LORD our God hath shewed us his glory and his greatness.
DEUTERONOMY 5:24

1 We must prefer God before ourselves, and endeavor to will our own happiness for his glory.
François Fénelon and Jeanne Guyon
Spiritual Progress (17th century)

2 Let it be God's glory and not our own that we seek, and when we get to that point, how speedily the Lord will bless us for good.
D. L. Moody
Secret Power (1881)

3 The glory of God is the beautiful brightness of God. There is no greater brightness. Nothing in the universe, nor in the imagination of any man or angel, is brighter than the brightness of God.
John Piper
God Is the Gospel (2005)

4 God created you so that you might spend eternity glorifying Him by enjoying Him forever.
John Piper
The Dangerous Duty of Delight (2001)

5   If anything has been accomplished through my life, it has been solely God's doing, not mine, and He—not I—must get the credit.
Billy Graham
Just As I Am (1997)

6   All of creation was created to glorify God. God intended that we would join the created world in reflecting the beauty and strength of His magnificent character. Pain and trouble are the graffiti that Satan scrawls across the face of God's glory.
Joseph Stowell
Through the Fire (1985)

7   As the capstone of God's creation in this world, mankind exists to glorify God. The fact that sin entered the human race in the Garden of Eden did not change the purpose for our existence. It simply meant that God would glorify Himself through man in a completely unique manner.
James Odens
Lighting the Way to God (1999)

8   The main point of our spirituality, according to the Bible, is the furthering of God's glory, not the fixing of our lives. In other words, God does not exist for us; we exist for Him.
Dwight Edwards
Revolution Within (2001)

9   The glory of God is a silver thread which must run through all our actions.
Thomas Watson
A Body of Practical Divinity (1838)

10 Glorifying of God consists in four things: 1st. Appreciation, 2d. Adoration, 3d. Affection, 4th. Subjection. This is the yearly rent we pay to the crown of heaven.
Thomas Watson
A Body of Practical Divinity (1838)

11 God counts himself glorified when he is loved.
Thomas Watson
A Body of Practical Divinity (1838)

12 This is the one purpose of God, the great worker in heaven, the source and master of all work, that the glory of His love and power and blessing may be shown.
Andrew Murray
Working for God (1901)

13 I'm often reminded of God's glory when I see fireworks exploding in the night sky, illuminating everything around with breathtaking beauty and power.
Preston Parrish
Windows into the Heart of God (2007)

14 Let us therefore not seek our own, but that which pleases the Lord and is helpful to the promotion of his glory.
John Calvin
On the Life of the Christian Man (1550)

182 GLUTTONY
For the drunkard and the glutton
shall come to poverty.
PROVERBS 23:21

1   A glutton is one who raids the icebox for a cure for spiritual malnutrition.
Frederick Buechner
Listening to Your Life (1992)

183 GOALS
(*see also* ASPIRATIONS; PLANS)
The preparations of the heart in man, and the
answer of the tongue, is from the LORD.
PROVERBS 16:1

1   It is better to aim at the impossible than to be content with the inferior.
Mabel Hale
Beautiful Girlhood (1922)

2   Perhaps a racer's goal is to qualify for a race for the first time or become a national champion. But remember the obvious—you cannot become a champion after the first race; therefore, your season must become a series of smaller goals, that hopefully, lead to your ultimate objective.
Ken Owen
Faith in the Fast Lane (2002)

3   Think about what you want to become. Think about the process of time and the pathway of choices that will help you reach that goal. Then get revved-up and put the pedal to the metal on an exciting life of growth. That always makes you a winner!
Ken Owen
Faith in the Fast Lane (2002)

4   The primary idea in all of my work was to help the farmer and fill the poor man's empty dinner pail. . . . My idea is to help the "man farthest down." This is why I have made every process just as simple as I could to put it within his reach.
George Washington Carver
George Washington Carver in His Own Words (1929)

5   When you lay aside your personal goals, desires, and ambitions, that is when God will reveal the goals, desires, and ambitions that He has for you.
Greg Laurie
The Upside Down Church (1999)

6   Remember, the most satisfaction comes from pursuing the goal, not simply from achieving it!
Ted Engstrom
The Pursuit of Excellence (1982)

7   When you set goals, it doesn't necessarily mean you'll achieve all of them, but at least you have an idea of where you're going.
Sonya Haskins
Homeschooling for the Rest of Us (2010)

8   We must be sure to set goals within our reach. Attempting the impossible will destroy our motivation overnight. Rome wasn't built in a day. Neither is a career. . .nor a life that's worth living.
Ted Engstrom
Motivation to Last a Lifetime (1984)

184 GOD
The LORD appeared to Abram, and said unto him, I am the Almighty God; walk before me, and be thou perfect.
GENESIS 17:1

General

1   To allow God to be God we must follow him for who he is and what he intends, and not for what we want and what we prefer.
Ravi Zacharias
The Grand Weaver (2007)

2   Taking delight in random encounters that come our way is a wonderful reminder that God is in control.
Mel Lawrenz
Jubilee (2008)

3   For all those dark times, here's a word of hope: God meets us where we are. Even if we aren't looking in his direction, he is always looking in ours.
Liz Curtis Higgs
Embrace Grace (2006)

4   It is deeply insulting to God for us to open the Bible, and seeing many things about Him that we do not like, decide to reshape God into a more pleasing image. God is not whoever you want Him to be. He is who He is!
Colin Smith
Unlocking the Bible Story (2002)

5 If you think God is boring, you have never encountered the God of the Bible.
Colin Smith
Unlocking the Bible Story (2002)

6 Many people, both believers and unbelievers, are confidently gripping an image of God that simply doesn't square with the God of the Bible.
Dwight Edwards
Revolution Within (2001)

7 Security is not the absence of danger, but the presence of God.
Miriam Iwashige
Keepers At Home (1997)

8 There are many claims that various gods exist, but only one God cared enough to become a man and die on our behalf.
Josh and Sean McDowell
Evidence for the Resurrection (2009)

9 God tends to choose and use people outside their comfort zones.
Douglas Cecil
The 7 Principles of an Evangelistic Life (2003)

10 God accomplishes extraordinary things through ordinary people who believe God can and will use them—imperfections and all.
Donna Partow
A 10-Week Journey to Becoming a Vessel God Can Use (1996)

11 If there is not Dream Giver, there is no dream.
Cindi McMenamin
When a Woman Discovers Her Dream (2005)

12 Other people's opinions do not determine your potential. What they said or what they think about you does not change what God has placed on the inside.
Joel Osteeen
Becoming a Better You (2007)

13 God will not accept a divided heart. He must be absolute monarch.
D. L. Moody
Weighed and Wanting (19th century)

14 God is as near as your next breath, and He is in control.
Beth Moore
Prayers and Promises for Women (2003)

15 If we pursue our relationship with God, we will have invested wisely.
David Hawkins
Breaking Everyday Addictions (2008)

16 There is a universal longing in the human heart to see God and make Him tangible.
Elmer Towns
Core Christianity (2007)

17 Get alone with God and tell him your thoughts. Be unreservedly honest. Scream, cry, yell, let it all out. God is big enough to handle your anger. Your rage won't shock him—you're talking with the One who knows how many hairs you have on your head. He identifies with your agony and comprehends your pain.
Laura Petherbridge
When Your Marriage Dies (2005)

18 God requires of me that I now regard all my members, all my faculties, as belonging wholly to Him.
Watchman Nee
Normal Christian Life (20th century)

19 God is like nothing we could have imagined.
J. Budziszewski
How to Stay Christian in College (2004)

20 What the Christian apologist is concerned to show is not that a God of some sort exists, but that the Christian idea of God is worthier

to be received than that of the pantheist or the deist, or of any rival theory of the universe.
  Alexander Balmain Bruce
  Apologetics, or Christianity Defensively Stated (1892)

21 When he chooses to worship wood and stone rather than be thought to have no God, it is evident how very strong this impression of a Deity must be; since it is more difficult to obliterate it from the mind of man, than to break down the feelings of his nature.
  John Calvin
  Institutes of the Christian Religion (16th century)

Attributes of

22 God cannot be all things to all people. He can only be those things that are consistent with Himself. He is truth; therefore, He cannot lie. He is eternal; therefore He cannot cease. While we choose to love or be merciful, God is quite different. God doesn't choose to love or to be merciful. God is loving. God is merciful.
  Joseph Stowell
  Through the Fire (1985)

23 God's trustworthy character is the key to the Christian life of faith, nothing else.
  James Odens
  Lighting the Way to God (1999)

24 God never changes who He is. He is always consistent. He is not fickle. He was not a different God in the Old Testament or to your grandparents. He is and always has been the same God. He is holy (He keeps His promises). He is righteous (He always does what's right). He is good (He loves us and is always working in us and for us). These things never change.
  David Edwards
  The God of Yes (2003)

25 We have a God who is infinitely gracious, and knows all our wants.
  Brother Lawrence
  The Practice of the Presence of God (17th century)

26 The truths of God can both comfort the afflicted and afflict the comfortable.
  Skip Heitzig
  Relationships (1997)

27 Just as a parent, spying her child wearing Mother's shoes and party dress, delights in the love that is offered, so God delights in the affection of His children.
  Gordon MacDonald
  Secrets of the Generous Life (2002)

28 The Spirit of God is given to the true saints to dwell in them, as his proper lasting abode; and to influence their hearts, as a principle of new nature or as a divine supernatural spring of life and action.
  Jonathan Edwards
  A Treatise Concerning Religious Affections (18th century)

29 We must remember that God always acts like Himself. He has never at any time anywhere in the vast universe acted otherwise than in character with His infinite perfections.
  A. W. Tozer
  That Incredible Christian (1964)

30 He is to us everything which is good and comforting for our help. He is our clothing who wraps and enfolds us for love, embraces us and shelters us, surrounds us for his love which is so tender that he may never desert us.
  Julian of Norwich
  Revelations of Divine Love (14th century)

31 It is thus not always just the display of his attributes that constitutes a theological understanding of God but their withdrawal as well.
Eugene Merrill
Everlasting Dominion (2006)

32 Through all the ages you have been the Lord and giver of life, the source of all knowledge, the fountain of all goodness.
John Baillie
A Diary of Private Prayer (1949)

Beyond Human Beings

33 We must understand God by His revelation of Himself, not by our own hunches, not by our own wishes, not by the way we like to think of God.
Mark Dever
Nine Marks of a Healthy Church (2004)

34 Become lost in God's grandeur. There can be nothing better, more productive, or more rewarding in your life than to become lost in great thoughts about a great God.
Charles Stanley
How to Listen to God (1985)

35 When we acknowledge God's greatness in our lives, our hearts are humbled and we are reminded of who He is and His great love for us.
Dennis and Barbara Rainey
Two Hearts Praying As One (2002)

36 Only the God of the Bible is omniscient, omnipotent, and omnipresent, and the bottom line is that we are not.
Ken Ham
How Could a Loving God. . . ? (2007)

37 He is so big. . .and we are so nothing.
Anne Graham Lotz
I Saw the Lord (2006)

38 Our God specializes in working through normal people who believe in a supernormal God who will do His work through them.
Bruce Wilkinson
The Prayer of Jabez (2000)

39 All created beings shrink to nothing in comparison with the Creator.
Matthew Henry
Commentary on the Whole Bible (1706)

40 The deeper our despair of entering aright into the thoughts of God, the greater the confidence of expectancy may be. God wants to make his Word true in us.
Andrew Murray
Prayer's Inner Chamber (1912)

41 Things we call good are often God's evil things, and our evil is His good. But, however things may look, we always know that God must give the best because he is God and could do no other.
Hannah Whitall Smith
The God of All Comfort (1906)

42 We can only delve so far into the infinite mind of the Maker before we run out of marbles.
James Dobson
When God Doesn't Make Sense (1993)

43 We serve a Most High God, and His dream for your life is so much bigger and better than you can even imagine.
Joel Osteen
Your Best Life Begins Each Morning (2008)

44 If God can make a billion galaxies, can't he make good out of our bad and sense out of our faltering lives? Of course he can. He is God.
Max Lucado
3:16: The Numbers of Hope (2007)

45 No one knows the mind of God. . . . If we did, He wouldn't be God.
   Darlene Mindrup
   Brides of the Empire (1996)

46 The next time you wonder if God knows what He's doing, think about just how much distance is between the earth and the heavens above. A million miles? Ten million? More? That's how much more your heavenly Father sees than you see.
   Mary Nelson
   Grace for Each Hour (2005)

47 The bottom line is this—God is God and man is man.
   Michael Youssef
   Joseph: Portrait of a Winner (2008)

48 It is enough to know that God is God.
   A. W. Tozer
   Knowledge of The Holy (1961)

49 With the goodness of God to desire our highest welfare, the wisdom of God to plan it, and the power of God to achieve it, what do we lack?
   A. W. Tozer
   Knowledge of The Holy (1961)

50 As God's people, we are chosen to be trophies of God's amazing grace.
   Henry and Richard Blackaby and Claude King *Fresh Encounter* (2007)

51 People do not "figure God out." God reveals himself to people.
   Henry and Richard Blackaby
   Hearing God's Voice (2002)

52 Imagine what God could do with our minds if we obediently allowed Him to fill them with those things that are of true importance.
   Carole Lewis
   Choosing Change (2001)

53 Sometimes the greatest gift God can give us is to get in the way of our dreams.
   Jonathan Wilson-Hartgrove
   God's Economy (2009)

54 It is through us that God accomplishes what he pleases. He, of course, does not need to work out his will in such a way. But He chooses to do so.
   Richard Abanes
   The Purpose That Drives Him (2005)

55 None but God can satisfy the longings of an immortal soul; that as the heart was made for Him, so He only can fill it.
   Richard Chenevix Trench
   Notes on the Parables (1856)

56 Grace in the hearts of the saints, being therefore the most glorious work of God, wherein he communicates of the goodness of his nature, it is doubtless his peculiar work, and in an eminent manner above the power of all creatures.
   Jonathan Edwards
   A Treatise Concerning Religious Affections (18th century)

57 Although no creature can define what God is, because he is incomprehensible and dwelling in inaccessible light, yet it has pleased his majesty to reveal himself to us in his word, so far as our weak capacity can best conceive him.
   Lewis Bayly
   The Practice of Piety (1611)

58 Nothing is more limiting than the self-imposed boundaries we clamp around our own lives when we require God to fit into our expectations.
   Jack Hayford
   Prayer Is Invading the Impossible (2002)

59 For how can the human mind which has not yet been able to ascertain of what the body of the sun consists, though it is daily presented

to the eye, bring down the boundless essence of God to its little measure?

John Calvin
Institutes of the Christian Religion
(16th century)

60 If there is one thing I am now absolutely certain of, it is that no human minds or committees will ever capture the powerful reality we call God with human words or formulas or creeds.

Timothy Johnson
Finding God in the Questions (2004)

61 When we come to worship the Living God, we get involved with something far too deep for our minds to comprehend.

Matt Redman
Facedown (2004)

62 We lack language and imagery by which to describe and understand both God and the behavior of subatomic particles.

Luci Shaw
God in the Dark (1989)

63 No figure in history, however splendid and memorable, can possibly satisfy the mind which is seeking the living contemporary God.

J. B. Phillips
Your God Is Too Small (1952)

Creator

64 Incredible as it seems, the Creator of the universe desires an intimate, loving fellowship with the people He created.

Bill Gothard
The Power of Crying Out (2002)

65 There is no more foundational message than God is Creator. After all, if God is not Creator, then nothing else matters. All is meaningless.

Ken Ham
Why Won't They Listen? (2002)

66 If God is not the communicator, if He's no longer the creator, and if He's renounced as the arbitrator between right and wrong, then the result is chaos.

Alex McFarland
The 10 Most Common Objections to Christianity (2007)

67 God enjoys His creation.
A. W. Tozer
Knowledge of The Holy (1961)

68 Our Creator God has created us distinct and very different from one another. When we accept those differences as God-given and even blessed by Him, we will experience the rewards of more positive attitudes, better relationships, mutual respect, and godly character.

Bob and Emilie Barnes
Simple Secrets Couples Should Know (2008)

69 God hath made the same organ for seeing and weeping.

George Swinnock
Works of George Swinnock (17th century)

70 Everything that God has created is like an orchestra praising Him.

Oswald Chambers
Approved Unto God (20th century)

71 Nothing that God does is unstructured.
Elisabeth Elliot
The Mark of a Man (1981)

72 God is the Creator and the protector and the lover. For until I am substantially united to him, I can never have perfect rest or true happiness, until, that is, I am so attached to him that there can be no created thing between my God and me.

Julian of Norwich
Revelations of Divine Love (14th century)

73 The foundation of human knowledge is the character of God as Creator.

James Sire
The Universe Next Door (1976)

74 Think about it: If there is a Creator who knows us and cares about how we live, then our lives should be profoundly affected.

Timothy Johnson
Finding God in the Questions (2004)

Dependence on

75 Begin your day by acknowledging your dependence upon God and your need for God. Purpose by grace that your first thought of the day will be an expression of your dependence on God, your need for God, and your confidence in God.

C. J. Mahaney
Humility: True Greatness (2005)

76 Those who know God have no need to protect their rights. Because they believe in Him, they learn to bear the Cross daily and to rely upon Him for the outcome.

Watchman Nee
Changed into His Image (1967)

77 When we are defeated and God does not speak, He is leading us to the end of ourselves and to a complete confidence in Him.

Watchman Nee
Changed into His Image (1967)

78 God didn't make a mistake when He made us weak and dependent on Him.

Karon Phillips Goodman
Grab a Broom, Lord—
There's Dust Everywhere! (2003)

79 Independence is not an option for us. God existed without us, not vice versa.

Henry Cloud and John Townsend
How People Grow (2001)

80 The essential thing in Christian living is not where you are going or what you are doing, but in whose strength you are living.

George Verwer
Come! Live! Die! (1972)

81 Life is not a do-it-yourself project. Our toolbox isn't adequate. We need to bring in the heavy equipment. God says love Me first. Make Him Number One.

Al Hartley
It Takes a Family (1996)

82 The Bible teaches us that we were created for God; that is, we were created to relate to Him and to serve Him. Everything that we are and everything that we have has been given to us to reflect His greatness through our lives and to make us useful in the lives of others. If we can only learn that lesson, then everything in life, even our tragedies, can be turned into a source of joy and growth.

Thomas Jones
Single Again Handbook (1993)

83 We may think that we can do many things all on our own. But that is not true. Jesus taught that without Him, we can do nothing. He meant that all of life is the gift of God.

Thomas Jones
Single Again Handbook (1993)

84 It is God's manner of dealing with men, to "lead them into a wilderness, before he speaks comfortably to them," and so to order it, that they shall be brought into distress, and made to see their own helplessness and absolute dependence on his power and grace, before he appears to work any great deliverance for them, is abundantly manifest by the Scripture.

Jonathan Edwards
A Treatise Concerning Religious Affections (18th century)

85 You get to know God real good when He's all ya' got.

Joyce Meyer
"Overcoming Fear with Faith" sermon (2009)

86 There is an absolute and universal dependence of the redeemed on God.
> Jonathan Edwards
> "God Glorified in Man's Dependence" sermon (18th century)

87 No man can survey himself without forthwith turning his thoughts towards the God in whom he lives and moves; because it is perfectly obvious, that the endowments which we possess cannot possibly be from ourselves; nay, that our very being is nothing else than subsistence in God alone.
> John Calvin
> Institutes of the Christian Religion (16th century)

88 He knows that unless we honor Him as our ultimate need-meeter, we will entrust our needs to fallible humans who will be unable to meet them.
> Bill and Lynne Hybels
> Fit to Be Tied: Making Marriage Last a Lifetime (1991)

89 Though I may become increasingly mature as a son in God's purpose, I never will get past being a child in my need of Him!
> Jack Hayford
> Pursuing the Will of God (1997)

Eternality of

90 He sees ages pass, but with him it is ever now.
> Charles Spurgeon
> "The Immutability of God" sermon (1855)

91 n whatever condition you find yourself wherever you are. . .remember that God is faithful and that His love is eternal.
> Beth Moore
> Prayers and Promises for Women (2003)

Generosity of

92 God's bounty is limited only by us, not by His resources, power, or willingness to give.
> Bruce Wilkinson
> The Prayer of Jabez (2000)

93 God gives us fantastic gifts, but He wants us to remember that everything belongs to Him. He wants to be our only possession.
> Michael Card
> Immanuel, Reflections on the Life of Christ (1990)

Faithfulness of

94 Oh Lord! Thou knowest how busy I must be this day: If I forget Thee, do not Thou forget me.
> Jacob Astley
> Prayer before the Battle of Edgehill, English Civil War (1642)

95 When you finally meet the One who made you, and examine the lifelines he has sent along the way, you will at last understand how every detail made sense in the swirling reality of life's blessings and threats.
> Ravi Zacharias
> The Grand Weaver (2007)

96 God never started anything to fail, and you won't fail at the purpose He's given you now unless you stop.
> Karon Phillips Goodman
> You're Late Again, Lord! (2002)

97 What God promises is that He always, always comes. He always shows up. He always saves. He always rescues. His timing is not ours. His methods are usually unconventional. But what we can know, what we can settle in our soul, is that He is faithful to come when we call.
> Angela Thomas
> Do You Think I'm Beautiful? (2003)

98 When your friends and loved ones fail you, God remains by your side, steadfast and true.
    Liz Curtis Higgs
    Embrace Grace (2006)

99 We do not become what God wants or obey what God commands by trying harder or doing more. It is the faithfulness of God working in us to will and do His good pleasure that brings about faithful, godly living.
    James Odens
    Lighting the Way to God (1999)

100 God will not let you go.
    Max Lucado
    3:16: The Numbers of Hope (2007)

101 God promises not to give us more than we can take. However, life piles misery on our heads until it feels like every last breath of our faith will be choked off. God is ever-present and faithful even in the screaming silence, and never leaves our side.
    Bonnie Keen
    God Loves Messy People (2002)

102 What God begins, He always completes.
    Anne Graham Lotz
    Heaven, My Father's House (2002)

103 You can have full confidence in God no matter what season of life you're in right now.
    Donna Partow
    Becoming the Woman God Wants Me to Be (2008)

104 It's not your intelligence or your hard work that will lead you through—it is God's faithfulness.
    Simi Mary Chacko
    personal testimony (2009)

105 God never leaves us. It is we who leave God.
    Janet Hagberg and Robert Guelich
    The Critical Journey (1995)

106 God never gives up on you.
    T. D. Jakes
    Intimacy with God (2000)

107 One of the most powerful, though difficult, lessons we all need to learn on our spiritual pilgrimage is that even when bad things happen and we do not understand why, we can trust God to be present and working on our behalf.
    Henry Cloud and John Townsend
    God Will Make a Way (2002)

108 You and I can go to God when we are too tired, too lazy, too uncommitted, too sick, or feeling too sorry for ourselves. In fact, moments like these are precisely when we need to call upon God and be filled with His faithfulness.
    Elizabeth George
    God's Garden of Grace (1996)

109 The next time you wonder if the Lord is really going to help you, just ask.
    Mary Nelson
    Grace for Tough Times (2006)

as Father

110 I dare not say, "Our father which art in heaven," till I am regenerated. I cannot rejoice in the fatherhood of God towards me till I know that I am one with him, and a joint heir with Christ.
    Charles Spurgeon
    "Divine Sovereignty" sermon (1856)

111 God's children are God's children anywhere and everywhere, and shall be even unto the end. Nothing can sever that sacred tie, or divide us from his heart.
    Charles Spurgeon
    "The Fatherhood of God" sermon (1858)

112   Our Father: our Preserver; who day by day, sustains the life he has given; of whose continuing love we now and every moment receive life and breath and all things.
> John Wesley (18th century)
> quoted in *John and Charles Wesley—Selected Writings and Hymns*

113   We are still His children, even when we disobey. We feel guilty and ashamed, and sometimes we simply want to hide. But God still loves us, and He wants to forgive us and welcome us back!
> Billy Graham
> *The Journey* (2006)

114   Every time we let loneliness take over our feelings, we have lost sight of that personal caring and loving Father: He is "Abba," our Papa.
> Michael Card *Immanuel,*
> *Reflections on the Life of Christ* (1990)

115   You wouldn't let your children go hungry. Your heavenly parent loves you and longs for you to be spiritually fed, growing, healthy, and content!
> Tamara Boggs
> *And Then God Gave Us Kids* (2003)

116   Don't fall into the trap of self-defeat. Let God untangle the web of lies you've believed about yourself and set you free to find who you are in Him—a daughter of the King, worthy because of His shed blood, forgiven by His grace, and strengthened by His strong hand.
> Laurie Lovejoy Hilliard and Sharon Lovejoy Autry
> *Hold You, Mommy* (2006)

117   Our Heavenly Father has to rebuke us (through His Word and our leaders) to expose us to ungodliness and to keep Satan's devices from bringing us harm.
> Juanita Bynum
> *My Spiritual Inheritance* (2004)

118   I considered myself before Him as a poor criminal at the feet of his judge; at other times I beheld Him in my heart as my *Father*.
> Brother Lawrence
> *The Practice of the Presence of God*
> (17th century)

119   You see, it's one thing to accept him as Lord, another to recognize him as Savior—but it's another matter entirely to accept him as Father.
> Max Lucado
> *He Still Moves Stones* (1993)

Fear of

120   The fear of God is a profound respect for his holiness, which includes a fear of the consequences of disobeying Him.
> Randy Alcorn
> *The Purity Principle* (2003)

121   The fear of God shouldn't scare us out of our wits; it should scare us into them.
> Randy Alcorn
> *The Purity Principle* (2003)

122   If there is no fear of God, then there is no fear of the consequences of sin—there is no fear of Judgment Day or eternal damnation in hell.
> Ray Comfort
> *How to Bring Your Children to Christ* (2005)

123   The greatness of God rouses fear within us, but His goodness encourages us not to be afraid of Him.
> A. W. Tozer
> *Knowledge of The Holy* (1961)

124   The fear of God is reverential awe and respect for Him. It is a heartfelt conviction that He is not only loving and personal but also holy and just.
> Dennis and Barbara Rainey
> *Moments Together* (2004)

125   Without the reverential fear and awe of God, we quickly become people pleasers instead of God pleasers.
Joyce Meyer
Do It Afraid! (1996)

126   The fear of the Lord is the only way to be released from the fear of man.
Joy Dawson
Intimate Friendship with God (1986)

127   Whom then shall I hear, God or man?
John Wesley
The Journal of John Wesley (18th century)

Fellowship with

128   God desires to fellowship with us just as much as He fellowshipped with the people in the Old and New Testament. If our relationship with Him is a one-way trip and there is no communication or dialogue then there isn't much fellowship.
Charles Stanley
How to Listen to God (1985)

129   You are in danger of substituting prayer and Bible study for living fellowship with God, the living interchange of giving him your love, your heart, your life, and receiving from him his love, his life, his Spirit. Your needs and their expression, your desire to pray humbly and earnestly and believingly may so occupy you, that the light of his countenance and the joy of his love cannot enter you.
Andrew Murray
Prayer's Inner Chamber (1989)

130   God is not honored when we celebrate the high days of our relationship out of a mere sense of duty. He is honored when those days are our delight!
John Piper
The Dangerous Duty of Delight (2001)

131   God tells us that we are so significant to Him that He always keeps an eye on us. He manages to be so sensitive to our situation that He even keeps track of the hairs on our head.
Robert McGee
The Search for Significance (1998)

132   We're not called just to work for God. We are called to work with God.
John Ortberg
If You Want to Walk on Water, You've Got to Get Out of the Boat (2001)

133   To feast upon the Lord is to draw our nourishment from him. We look to him for all we need in life—spiritually, emotionally, mentally, and physically. We learn to rejoice in him regardless of our circumstances.
Skip McDonald
And She Lived Happily Ever After (2005)

134   You can't expect to develop a close friendship with someone whom you totally ignore. You need to acknowledge God's presence, recognize His activity in your lives, and appreciate His provisions.
Bruce Bickel and Stan Jantz
God Is in the Small Stuff for Your Family (1999)

135   You need to make room for God in your lives. When you do, you'll be amazed at the difference. You'll see God's hand directing you, you'll hear His voice comforting you, and you'll sense His spirit embracing you. He will be real to you.
Bruce Bickel and Stan Jantz
God Is in the Small Stuff for Your Family (1999)

136   We shouldn't ever hesitate to invite God in on the details of our days. He already knows them, and He cares enough to want to be a part of them.
Laurie Lovejoy Hilliard and Sharon Lovejoy Autry
Hold You, Mommy (2006)

137   Two prisoners whose cells adjoin communicate with each other by knocking on the wall. The wall is the thing which separates them but is also their means of communication. It is the same with us and God. Every separation is a link.
   Simone Weil
   Gravity and Grace (1947)

138   To be with God wondering, that is adoration. To be with God gratefully, that is thanksgiving. To be with God ashamed, that is contrition. To be with God with people and things we care about in our hearts, that is intercession. But the center of it in desire and in design will be the being with God.
   Michael Ramsey
   "The Heart of Prayer" article (1978)

139   It is the business of the shepherd to lead the willing sheep aright.
   F. B. Meyer
   The Shepherd Psalm (1889)

140   It is our part to allow as small a space as possible to intervene between His footsteps and our own.
   F. B. Meyer
   The Shepherd Psalm (1889)

141   It breaks God's heart that we run from instead of to him when we fail.
   Brennan Manning
   Posers, Fakers, and Wannabes (2003)

142   God can indeed use you to bring others into His kingdom.
   Greg Laurie
   How to Share Your Faith (1999)

143   What comes into our minds when we think about God is the most important thing about us.
   A. W. Tozer
   Knowledge of The Holy (1961)

144   Walking closely with God in covenant is a choice every generation must make.
   Henry and Richard Blackaby and Claude King
   Fresh Encounter (2007)

145   When you live in continual repentance, God purifies you so that there is nothing between you and Him, and you can experience the joy of His presence. You see, sin will not cut off your relationship with God, but it will hurt your fellowship with Him.
   Dee Brestin and Kathy Troccoli
   Living in Love with Jesus (2002)

146   With all your weakness and helplessness, with all your frailties and infirmities, with all your sorrows and cares, He invites you to come to Him.
   John Dawson
   The Saviour in the Workshop (1868)

147   Fundamental to any biblical spirituality is a real joy in God and in who he has revealed himself to be.
   Mark Dever
   "Psalms: Wisdom for Spiritual People" sermon (1997)

148   It is a great thing for a mighty God to permit sinful men like you and me to call upon Him. When men get great we cannot get a chance to call upon them, but it is not so with our God. He commands us to call.
   D. L. Moody
   Short Talks (19th century)

Goodness of

149   We need the whole song, all the verses and the choruses to serve us as our own story unfolds because—trust me—life is hard, but God is good.
   Gloria Gaither
   Then Sings My Soul, Book 2 (2004)

150   A root set in the finest soil, in the best climate, and blessed with all that sun, and air,

and rain can do for it, is not in so sure a way of its growth to perfection, as every man may be, whose spirit aspires after all that which God is ready and infinitely desirous to give him.
William Law
The Spirit of Prayer (1750)

151   Depart in the least degree from the goodness of God, and you depart into evil, because nothing is good but his goodness.
William Law
The Spirit of Prayer (1750)

152   The God of the Bible is totally perfect and complete in every way, which means that God can be trusted and counted on in ways that go beyond our human limitations.
James Emery White
A Search for the Spiritual (1998)

153   For the sun meets not the springing bud that stretches towards him, with half that certainty, as God, the source of all good, communicates himself to the soul that longs to partake of him.
William Law
The Spirit of Prayer (1750)

154   The goodness of God breaking forth into a desire to communicate good, was the cause and the beginning of the creation.
William Law
The Spirit of Prayer (1750)

155   God's kindness is not arbitrary. He touches us kindly, gently—and with purpose.
Amy Nappa
A Woman's Touch (2001)

156   Because of God's grace, there is nothing we can do that will make Him love us more than He already does. And there is nothing we can do or have done that will cause Him to love us any less.
Steven Curtis Chapman
The Great Adventure (2001)

157   Who can describe the tokens of God's goodness that are extended to the human race even in this life?
Augustine
The City of God (5th century)

158   The cross stands as the final symbol that no evil exists that God cannot turn into a blessing. He is the living Alchemist who can take the dregs from the slag-heaps of life—disappointment, frustration, sorrow, disease, death, economic loss, heartache—and transform the dregs into gold.
Catherine Marshall
Beyond Ourselves (1961)

159   If we feel overworked and someone tells us to take a rest—that's temporary. If he tells us to go on a vacation, we'll come back afterward to the same old rat race. If he tells us to go to God, we've found a permanent solution.
Anne Ortlund
Disciplines of the Beautiful Woman (1977)

160   Have you ever contemplated one of those long theological lists of God's attributes and concluded that he is above all beautiful? We rarely ponder His beauty, much less seek "to gaze upon it." Rarely does our theology include it in its outlines. But the beauty of God is a biblical reality. Throughout the Word of God he is recognized by and praised for being beautiful.
Michael Card
Scribbling in the Sand (2002)

161   God's not Superman. Do you understand what I'm saying? He's God!
Beth Moore
"Who Do You Trust?" teaching series (2007)

Holiness of

162   God's holiness is his separateness from all that smacks of evil.
James Sire
The Universe Next Door (1976)

Honesty with

163   If I wear a little mask before God and never let my guard down, if I keep on one of those ridiculous grins that we Christians seem to wear much of the time—which suggests that "nothing ever gets me down 'cause I'm a Christian," then I would probably never be present with God on a very deep level.
Sue Monk Kidd
God's Joyful Surprise (1987)

Image of

164   We are not only imitators of God's nature, but are actually participants in it.
Thomas Blackaby
Encounters with God Daily Bible (2008)

Imagined Quotations of

165   "My child, you believe Me for so little. Don't be so safe in the things you pray. Who are you trying to keep from looking foolish? Me or you?"
Beth Moore
Praying God's Word (2000)

166   "The true peace which is born of My presence in the hearts of true believers they are unable to see, but, feeling its power, they become happy in it."
Sadhu Sundar Singh
At the Master's Feet (20th century)

167   "Have you not asked to be made humble? See then I have placed you in the very school where the lesson is taught; your surrounding and companions are only working out my will."
Paul Billheimer
Don't Waste Your Sorrows (1977)

Knowledge of

168   He knew me before I knew myself; yea, he knew me before I was myself.
Charles Spurgeon
"The Incarnation and Birth of Christ" sermon (1855)

169   Remember that God is never surprised. He knows the future as thoroughly as He knows the past and has provided for us. He has everything in hand, and we should lean on Him. He will not fall over!
Jill Briscoe
The New Normal (2005)

170   That there exists in the human minds and indeed by natural instinct, some sense of Deity, we hold to be beyond dispute, since God himself, to prevent any man from pretending ignorance, has endued all men with some idea of his Godhead, the memory of which he constantly renews and occasionally enlarges, that all to a man being aware that there is a God, and that he is their Maker, may be condemned by their own conscience when they neither worship him nor consecrate their lives to his service.
John Calvin
Institutes of the Christian Religion (16th century)

171   But, as a heathen tells us, there is no nation so barbarous, no race so brutish, as not to be imbued with the conviction that there is a God.
John Calvin
Institutes of the Christian Religion (16th century)

172   God is even more eager to be known by you than you are to know Him.
Preston Parrish
Windows into the Heart of God (2007)

Listening to

173   Through Scripture, creation, the church, and by his Spirit, God fills the world with his voice. The only issue is, "Are we listening?"
John Loftness and C. J. Mahaney
Disciples for Life (1993)

174   A prayerful spirit is the spirit to which God will speak. A prayerful spirit will be a listening spirit waiting to hear what God says.
Andrew Murray
The Prayer Life (1912)

175   The highest blessedness of prayer will be our ceasing to pray, to let God speak.
Andrew Murray
The Prayer Life (1912)

176   When we hear His call and respond appropriately, there will be no limit to what God can and will do through His people. But if we do not even recognize when He is speaking, we are in trouble at the very heart of our relationship to Him.
Henry Blackaby
What the Spirit Is Saying to the Churches (2003)

177   Now, more than ever, we live in a world where we need to hear God's voice. There are so many voices vying for our attention.
Margaret Feinberg
God Whispers (2002)

178   God wants to speak into areas of your life you have never even considered. He wants to give you words and wisdom you didn't think were possible. He desires to do exceedingly more than you can hope or expect.
Margaret Feinberg
God Whispers (2002)

179   Whenever God whispers to you—whether it is a word of conviction, revelation, or intercession—He is ultimately trying to draw you closer to Himself. While the initial words may seem overwhelming, unclear, or even strange at first, if they are truly from Him then you will find yourself drawn back to the heart of God.
Margaret Feinberg
God Whispers (2002)

180   There is an old saying, "When the student is ready, the teacher appears." I like to think of God as being that teacher, but using books, tapes, speakers, or other incidents to be his messengers. Mentoring often comes in the form of truth being shared at just the right time. If we discipline ourselves to have "eyes that see and ears that hear" and to look up with expectant eyes, we will find God at work in many different ways throughout our lives.
Betty Southard
The Mentor Quest (2002)

181   When God speaks, human reason and sentimental feelings should be silent.
Archibald Alexander
The Misery of the Lost (19th century)

182   Some people are so busy expressing their own opinion that God's voice can't be heard over their own.
Steve Campbell
"What to Say When You Shouldn't Say Anything" sermon (2009)

183   Among the communication tools in God's hamper are nature, art, music, books and even, on occasion, current events. When we intentionally and deliberately learn from these things, God can use them to speak to us personally.
Valerie Hess and Marti Watson Garlett
Habits of a Child's Heart (2004)

184   We have to force ourselves to sit down, to breathe deeply, to listen. But when we do, God empowers us to rise up and accomplish great things for Him.
　　Dean Merrill
　　Wait Quietly (1994)

185   God delights in communicating with His people; therefore, we must seek to increase our ability to listen to what he is saying.
　　Jane Hamon
　　Dreams and Visions (2000)

186   This year I have started out trying to live all my waking moments in conscious listening to the inner voice, asking without ceasing, "What, Father, do you desire said? What, Father, do you desire done this minute?"
　　Frank Laubach
　　Letters by a Modern Mystic (1937)

187   Any hour of any day may be made perfect by merely choosing. It is perfect if one looks to God that entire hour, waiting for his leadership all through the hour and trying hard to do every tiny thing exactly as God wishes it done.
　　Frank Laubach
　　Letters by a Modern Mystic (1937)

Lordship of

188   "But, Lord. . ." is an oxymoron, isn't it? It's a contradiction in terms, because if Jesus is Lord, then we say, "Yes, Sir," not, "But, Lord."
　　Anne Graham Lotz
　　Why? Trusting God When You Don't Understand (2004)

189   God is not merely complementary to humankind and the world. God is necessary.
　　Maxie Dunnam
　　The Workbook of Intercessory Prayer (1979)

190   You've probably noticed that the person who owns something, whatever it is, has a certain pride that a mere observer never has. Ownership makes a difference. God owns us, so when He looks at our lives, He looks at them not as an observer, but as an investor.
　　John Maxwell
　　Be All You Can Be (1987)

191   When I put God first, He helps me with all my other priorities. He enables me to love my wife more. He brings a greater quality of love and life into the whole family. And it's not just love that's enriched. Every family today is faced with situations that call for the patience of Job and the wisdom of Solomon. Guess what? Where do you suppose they got those virtues?
　　Al Hartley
　　It Takes a Family (1996)

192   It is no accident that God has chosen to call us sheep.
　　W. Phillip Keller
　　A Shepherd Looks At Psalm 23 (1970)

193   The Christian lives in God's world, and He is lord thereof.
　　Paul Wernle
　　The Beginnings of Christianity (1903)

194   God never intended to compete with men for the devotion of women, nor with women for the delight of men.
　　Nancy Groom
　　Heart to Heart About Men (1995)

195   To make God the center of one's life is to focus heart, soul, mind, and strength on him; it is to be deeply in love with one's creator and redeemer. To make God the circumference of one's life is to adopt the lifestyle of a dedicated disciple; it is to know, affirm, and live within the parameters of heaven's revealed will.
　　Rubel Shelly
　　Written in Stone (1994)

Mercy of

196   Whoever defends himself will have himself for his defense, and he will have no other. But let him come defenseless before the Lord and he will have for his defender no less than God Himself.
  A. W. Tozer
  The Pursuit of God (1948)

197   I hate myself, that I cannot believe it so constantly and surely as I should; but no human creature can rightly know how mercifully God is inclined toward those that steadfastly believe in Christ.
  Martin Luther
  Table Talk (16th century)

198   God cries out, "I AM the God of the farthest horizon." There is no one too far from God that God does not want to bring them into relationship with Him.
  Tim Walter
  "Farthest Horizon—God's Unchanging Character" sermon (2009)

199   It is true, God hath been found of some who sought Him not. He hath cast himself in their way, who were quite out of his.
  Henry Scougal
  Life of God in the Soul of Man (17th century)

200   He takes ownership of the pain we entrust to his keeping.
  Ruth Graham and Stacy Mattingly
  In Every Pew Sits a Broken Heart (2004)

201   The omniscience of God is a wonder. The omnipotence of God is a wonder. God's spotless holiness is a wonder. None of these things can we understand. But the greatest wonder of all is the mercy of God.
  Andrew Murray
  Have Mercy Upon Me (1896)

202   If Christ be so merciful as not to break me, I will not break myself by despair, nor yield myself over to the roaring lion, Satan, to break me in pieces.
  Richard Sibbes
  The Bruised Reed (1630)

203   God is eagerly watching with hungry eyes for the quick turn of a human eye up to Himself.
  Samuel Gordon
  Quiet Talks on Prayer (1904)

204   God is both the Hound of Heaven and the Hound Calvary who pursues each of us through our particular corridor of time.
  Calvin Miller
  Once Upon a Tree (2002)

Name of

205   God's name is so important that in heaven the very mention of it evokes worship.
  Bill Bright
  The Joy of Faithful Obedience (2005)

Omnipresence

206   Well, then, wherever you are, you are near to God; he is a God at hand, and a God afar off.
  Thomas Manton
  A Practical Commentary on the Epistle of James (17th century)

Omniscience

207   There is not a desire that arises in thy soul, but the Lord takes notice of it.
  Thomas Brooks
  The Unsearchable Riches of Christ (1655)

208   God knows things we have no way of knowing. When we don't inquire of the Lord and ask in faith for guidance, we totally miss what he wants us to accomplish.
  Jim Cymbala and Dean Merrill
  Fresh Faith (2003)

209   God, the only good of all intelligent natures, is not an absent or distant God, but is more present in and to our souls, than our own bodies.
    William Law
    The Spirit of Prayer (1750)

210   He is the God of the supernatural—omnipotent, omnipresent, omniscient in this life and the next. We cannot believe this and also think that our God's no match for the evil of the world.
    Catherine Marshall
    Something More (1974)

211   If God is supernatural—beyond nature—why must He be understood only in natural terms?
    Fritz Ridenour
    So What's the Difference? (1967)

212   Let us consider ourselves under the all-seeing eye of that divine Majesty, as in the midst of an infinite globe of light, which compasseth us about both behind and before, and pierceth to the innermost corners of the soul.
    Henry Scougal
    Life of God in the Soul of Man
    (17th century)

213   Our days are in God's hands. He is all-sufficient to meet our needs, and the Savior is with us every step of the way.
    Elizabeth George
    God's Garden of Grace (1996)

214   Doubtless it is the glorious prerogative of the omniscient God, as the great searcher of hearts, to be able well to separate between sheep and goats.
    Jonathan Edwards
    A Treatise Concerning Religious Affections
    (18th century)

215   God reads the secrets of the heart. God reads its most intimate feelings, even those which we are not aware of.
    Jean-Nicholas Grou
    How to Pray (18th century)

216   Let us remember that God sees all from heaven, that the eyes of God are upon us at all times and in all places.
    Benedict of Nursia
    The Rule of St. Benedict (6th century)

Power of

217   You do not test the resources of God till you try the impossible.
    F. B. Meyer
    The Missionary Review of the World (1913)

218   So long as God is in the universe, every soul that's in the universe must feel His power. No space can be so wide, no time so long as to exhaust His influence.
    Phillips Brooks
    "An Evil Spirit from the Lord" sermon
    (1886)

219   When God speaks, things happen because the words of God aren't just as good as his deeds, they are his deeds.
    Frederick Buechner
    Listening to Your Life (1992)

220   The early Church knew they could not accomplish God's will without God's power.
    Tim Walter
    "The Acts of the Holy Spirit" sermon
    (2009)

221   Nothing transcends the power of God. Whether our difficulty is from Satan, others, self-inflicted, or experienced in the process

of our obedience, it is God's prerogative to rearrange, reconstruct, reinterpret, and realign the situation to bring glory and praise to His name.
Joseph Stowell
Through the Fire (1985)

222   There is no end to the power He wants to exhibit in our lives. . . . God can keep his people on fire for him, can keep them sharp and intense.
Jim Cymbala and Dean Merrill
Fresh Faith (2003)

223   It is God who rules over human careers and families and even national destinies.
Grant Jeffrey
Countdown to Apocalypse (2008)

224   No matter what has happened, it doesn't spell the end of God's ability to make it good. God is completely capable of taking leftovers and making a gourmet meal. He is never left without options. And He never leaves us hopeless.
David Edwards
The God of Yes (2003)

225   Our God is the Divine Alchemist. He can take junk from the rubbish heap of life, and melting this base refuse in the pure fire of His love, hand us back—gold.
Catherine Marshall
Something More (1974)

226 Do not ask "what can I do?" but "what can He not do?"
Corrie ten Boom
Amazing Love (1953)

227   Only God is able to humble us without humiliating us and to exalt us without flattering us.
Ravi Zacharias
Recapture the Wonder (2003)

228   All things are therefore possible to me, if I am united to Him Who can do all things.
Meister Eckhart
Meister Eckhart's Sermons (14th century)

229   All the remedies we know are insipid without God's power.
David Hawkins
Prescription for Living Beyond (2006)

230   God invites us to accept His power to overcome the secrets in our lives.
Serita Ann Jakes
The Princess Within (1999)

231   No matter how bad it seems, with God's help we can overcome. No matter how great the challenge seems, we can make it through. No matter how big the mountain, we can climb it. No matter how bad the odds seem, we can win. No matter the enemy we are facing, we must stand and proclaim, "That's all right. That's okay. We're going to beat you anyway."
Arron Chambers
Running on Empty (2005)

232   In all things, in the least creatures, and their members, God's almighty power and wonderful works clearly shine. For what man, how powerful, wise, and holy soever, can make out of one fig, a fig-tree?
Martin Luther
Table Talk (16th century)

233   Now, to give grace, peace, everlasting life, forgiveness of sins, to justify, to save, to deliver from death and hell, surely these are not the works of any creature, but of the sole majesty of God, things which the angels themselves can neither create nor give.
Martin Luther
Table Talk (16th century)

234   If you will give what you have to God,
He'll multiply it and give it back to you in a way
that you would never have believed possible.
   Carole Lewis
   Choosing Change (2001)

235   It is God-dishonouring to forget that
He still has power, although our armies are
defeated, and all seems dark and gloomy.
   D. L. Moody
   Wondrous Love (1876)

236   Your heart can depend totally upon the
Lord, for His strength never weakens, His might
never diminishes, and His power never fades.
   Roy Lessin
   The Loving Heart (2005)

237   The soldiers gasped. Saul sighed. Goliath
jeered. David swung. And God made His point.
"Anyone who underestimates what God can do
with the ordinary has rocks in his head."
   Max Lucado
   The Applause of Heaven (1990)

238   No one is too far for God to reach and
no one is too weak for God to use powerfully.
   Tim Walter
   "Farthest Horizon—God's Unchanging
   Character" sermon (2009)

239   Because He is God, He is able to weave
together every single aspect and event in your
life and produce something good.
   Elizabeth George
   Loving God with All Your Mind (1994)

240   Don't measure the size of the mountain;
talk to the One who can move it.
   Max Lucado
   Traveling Light (2001)

241   We serve a supernatural God. He is not
limited to the laws of nature. He can do what
human beings cannot do.
   Joel Osteen
   Your Best Life Now (2004)

242   The Power of God is that whereby he
can simply and freely do whatsoever he will.
   Lewis Bayly
   The Practice of Piety (1611)

243   The great power of God appears in
bringing a sinner from his low state, from the
depths of sin and misery, to such an exalted
state of holiness and happiness.
   Jonathan Edwards
   "God Glorified in Man's
   Dependence" sermon (18th century)

244   It is a more glorious work of power to
rescue a soul out of the hands of the devil, and
from the powers of darkness, and to bring it
into a state of salvation, than to confer holiness
where there was no prepossession or opposition.
   Jonathan Edwards
   "God Glorified in Man's Dependence"
   sermon (18th century)

245   There are undoubtedly professing
Christians with childish conceptions of God
which could not stand up to the winds of real
life for five minutes.
   J. B. Phillips
   Your God Is Too Small (1952)

Providence

246   Love to God disposes men to see his
hand in everything; to own him as the
governor of the world, and the director of
providence; and to acknowledge his disposal
in everything that takes place.
   Jonathan Edwards
   "Charity Disposes Us Meekly to Bear the
   Injuries from Others" sermon (1738)

247   Be thankful for the providence which
has made you poor, or sick, or sad; for by all
this Jesus works the life of your spirit and turns
you to Himself.
   Charles Spurgeon
   All of Grace (19th century)

248   The providence of God means that God oversees me, and my life is not a bundle of accidents.
   R. Paul Stevens
   Down-to-Earth Spirituality (2003)

Reverence of

249   Friendship with God is reserved for those who reverence Him.
   Ron Mehl
   Right with God (2003)

250   Until we see God in His terrifying size and limitless scope, we will never see ourselves as we really are. Nor will we fully appreciate the fact that He chose to love you and me.
   Joseph Stowell
   Why It's Hard to Love Jesus (2003)

251   By its being thus ordered, that the creature should have so absolute and universal a dependence on God, provision is made that God should have our whole souls, and should be the object of our undivided respect.
   Jonathan Edwards
   "God Glorified in Man's Dependence" sermon (18th century)

252   Unless everything peculiar to divinity is confined to God alone, he is robbed of his honour, and his worship is violated.
   John Calvin
   Institutes of the Christian Religion (16th century)

Righteousness of

253   Everything we know and hope for has its sure hope because God is righteous. He could be righteous and condemn us. How can He then justify us? Only by laying the whole burden of sin upon His Son on Calvary.
   Lance Latham
   The Two Gospels (1984)

254   If we desire to be a mature brother or sister, one of the keys is to recognize that God is right in all He does.
   Jon Courson
   Application Commentary (2006)

Serving

255   To be a servant of God, you must be moldable and remain in the hand of the Master.
   Henry Blackaby
   Experiencing God (2007)

256   The Lord doesn't have any trouble hitting a moving target. In fact, it's easier to steer a moving vehicle than one that is immobile.
   Charles Swindoll
   Hand Me Another Brick (1981)

257   The most important thing is not the work I can do for God. The most important thing is to make God the most important thing.
   Phil Vischer
   "When Your Dream Dies" teaching (2008)

258   The truth is, God is the most reasonable of all beings. He asks only that we should use each moment for Him, in labour, or in rest, whichever is most for His glory. He only requires that with the time, talents, and strength which He has given us, we should do all we can to serve Him.
   Charles Finney
   "The Sinner's Excuses Answered" sermon (1850)

Silence of

259   I cannot force God to give me the guidance or help I think I need. There may be a good reason for his remaining silent sometimes.
   John Ortberg
   God Is Closer Than You Think (2005)

260   God's silence doesn't mean His absence. Just because you can't see or hear God doesn't negate His presence and active work behind the scenes. Base your movement on who you know and what you know about Him, not on what you are seeing and feeling at the moment.
     Lois Evans
     Stones of Remembrance (2006)

Sovereignty of

261   The picture of divine sovereignty in Scripture is that God positively ordains whatsoever comes to pass. He always acts with a purpose. Even the wicked unwittingly do his bidding, and thus they fulfill His sovereign purpose in the end.
     John MacArthur
     The Truth War (2007)

262   While God rules specifically over His people, one day He will rule absolutely over all the people.
     Ed Dobson
     Finding God in the Face of Evil (2002)

263   We are all bound to the throne of the Supreme Being by a flexible chain which restrains without enslaving us. The most wonderful aspect of the universal scheme of things is the action of free beings under divine guidance.
     Joseph de Maistre
     Considerations on France (1796)

264   He's either in full control or He's not on the throne at all.
     Michael Youssef
     Joseph: Portrait of a Winner (2008)

265   Nothing comes to pass in time but what was decreed in eternity. If anything were done which he did not first know, he were not infinitely wise; if anything were done which he

did not first will, positively or permissively, he were not infinitely supreme and powerful.
     Stephen Charnock
     Discourse of God's Being the Author of Reconciliation (1652)

266   If you find yourself trying to rescue your friend or loved one, then ask God to help you let go of the burden. Rescue is not ultimately your responsibility; it is God's.
     Ruth Graham and Stacy Mattingly
     In Every Pew Sits a Broken Heart (2004)

267   Surely God is so sovereign as that comes to, that he may enable us to do our duty when he pleases, and on what occasion he pleases.
     Jonathan Edwards
     A Treatise Concerning Religious Affections (18th century)

268   If you believe in a God who controls the big things, you have to believe in a God who controls the little things. It is we, of course, to whom things look "little" or "big."
     Elisabeth Elliot
     Let Me Be a Woman (1976)

269   The Lord God Almighty, since before He spoke creation into being, has been orchestrating all things to harmoniously converge and culminate in the glory, honor, and worship of His Son, the Lord Jesus Christ. That's why history is His story.
     Preston Parrish
     Windows into the Heart of God (2007)

270   There are two boys, educated it may be in the same school, by the same master, and they shall apply themselves to their studies with the same diligence, but yet one shall far outstrip his fellow. Why is this? Because God hath asserted his sovereignty over the intellect as well as the body.
     Charles Spurgeon
     "Divine Sovereignty" sermon (1856)

271   We are God's own; to him, therefore, let his wisdom and will dominate all our actions. We are God's own; therefore let every part of our existence be directed towards him as our only legitimate goal.
  John Calvin
  On the Life of the Christian Man (1550)

Supremacy of

272   Perhaps our place is not at the center of the universe. God does not exist to make a big deal out of us. We exist to make a big deal out of him. It's not about you. It's not about me. It's all about Him.
  Max Lucado
  It's Not About Me (2004)

273   God wants us to seek Him more than anything else, even more than we seek answers to prayer. When we come to God in prayer, sometimes our hearts are so full of what we want that we leave God out. Our minds become consumed with the gift rather than the giver.
  Charles Stanley
  Handle with Prayer (1987)

274   Seeing God as merely an elevated form of ourselves sets us up for failure.
  Pam Farrel
  Woman of Confidence (2001)

275   I'd like us to consider that maybe we have difficulty discovering God's wonderful plan for our lives because, if the truth be told, He doesn't really intend to tell us what it is. And maybe we are wrong to expect Him to.
  Kevin DeYoung
  Just Do Something (2009)

276   People's opinions do not change the mind or essence of God.
  Michael Youssef
  "The Perfect Antidote" article (2009)

277   We must all know intellectually and experientially that God is first. He must be our lives—in a class all by himself. Everything in our lives must converge at that one point: Christ.
  Anne Ortlund
  Disciplines of the Beautiful Woman (1977)

278   According to Christian belief, man exists for the sake of God; according to the liberal church, in practice if not in theory, God exists for the sake of man.
  J. Gresham Machen
  Christianity and Liberalism (1923)

279   We had better throw ourselves back on God, for there will be a day when we will have nothing but God.
  A. W. Tozer
  "Who Is the Holy Spirit?" sermon (20th century)

280   If your concept of God is right and you see Him as Owner, Controller, and Provider, and beyond that as your loving Father, then you know you have nothing to worry about.
  John MacArthur
  Anxiety Attacked (1993)

281   Whatsoever excellency thou hast seen in any creature, it is nothing but a sparkle of that which is in infinite perfection in God.
  Lewis Bayly
  The Practice of Piety (1611)

282   Have you ever considered that God, being God, could put into place a plan that does not depend on your agreement for its success?
  Preston Parrish
  Windows into the Heart of God (2007)

Unchanging Nature

283   God is perpetually the same. He is not composed of any substance or material, but is

spirit—pure, essential, and ethereal spirit—and therefore he is immutable.

Charles Spurgeon
"The Immutability of God" sermon (1855)

284   God will be no different tomorrow than he is today. His love for us is the same. His power to meet our needs is unchanged.

Jim Cymbala and Dean Merrill
Fresh Faith (2003)

Will of

285   Our confidence rests in the fact that God's will may be delayed, but never thwarted.

Anne Graham Lotz
The Daily Light Journal (2004)

286 Our prayers become part of God's plan and will.

Maxie Dunnam
The Workbook of Intercessory Prayer (1979)

287   There is nothing in our lives that is accidental. Every day's happenings are measured by the Lord.

Watchman Nee
Not I But Christ (1948)

288   Even if you've missed God's plan entirely for years and years and years, that plan can still swing into operation the minute you're ready to step up and step in, with God at your side.

Tony Evans
God Is Up to Something Great (2002)

289   All that we are going to have has been planned for us—it is not an afterthought.

R. T. Kendall
The Parables of Jesus (2004)

290   Just because you have the power of God on your life does not mean that you are totally submitted to the will of God.

Juanita Bynum
My Spiritual Inheritance (2004)

291   I hope that when I have done what I can, He will do with me what He pleases.

Brother Lawrence
The Practice of the Presence of God
(17th century)

292   I have no pain or difficulty about my state, because I have no will but that of God, which I endeavour to accomplish in all things.

Brother Lawrence
The Practice of the Presence of God
(17th century)

293   God gives us one day at a time to discover and experience His good plan for our lives.

Thomas and Nanette Kinkade
The Many Loves of Marriage (2002)

294   When God asks us to do something, He prepares us to be able to do it (that doesn't necessarily mean we will feel prepared!).

Melody Rossi
May I Walk You Home? (2007)

295   Dreams do come true, and real people have lives that are better than fairy tales when they trust their decisions to God.

Serita Ann Jakes
The Princess Within (1999)

296   Doing the will of God means we say no to the desires of the flesh, the desires of the eyes and our pride in possessions.

Kevin DeYoung
Just Do Something (2009)

297   More than anything we can give for God, be for God, do for God, He simply wants our heart.

Donna Partow
This Isn't the Life I Signed Up For (2003)

298   It is God's purpose for us to live in harmony with others, but especially those who share our faith.

Bettie Youngs and Debbie Thurman
A Teen's Guide to Christian Living (2003)

299   I know of nothing which so quiets and enlivens my own spiritual life as the knowledge that "God knows what He is doing with me!"
W. Phillip Keller
A Shepherd Looks At Psalm 23 (1970)

300   When we pray and God's answer is "not yet," we must understand that God has his reasons for waiting.
Henry and Richard Blackaby
Hearing God's Voice (2002)

301   You will feel tremendous peace when you are in God's will and great unrest when you are not.
Henry and Richard Blackaby
Hearing God's Voice (2002)

302   God does not expect us to imitate Jesus Christ: He expects us to allow the life of Jesus to be manifested in our mortal flesh.
Oswald Chambers
Approved Unto God (20th century)

303   God wants you to be an "eagle Christian," one who can fly high, be bold, live with power, keep circumstances and relationships in perspective, live at peace, stay strong, and soar above the storms of life.
Joyce Meyer
Never Give Up! (2008)

304   Refuse to settle for anything less than everything God has for you.
Joyce Meyer
Never Give Up! (2008)

305   I would a thousand times rather that God's will should be done than my own.
D. L. Moody
Prevailing Prayer: What Hinders It? (1884)

306 God's will for your life will always line up with his law, his principles, and his wisdom.
Andy Stanley
The Principle of the Path (2008)

307   One never accomplishes the will of God by breaking the law of God, violating the principles of God, or ignoring the wisdom of God.
Andy Stanley
The Principle of the Path (2008)

308   The more one attempts to control the past via refusing to forgive, the less one is in control of one's own future. To allow God to handle unfinished business also allows God the freedom to guide and direct one's future.
John Splinter
The Complete Divorce Recovery Handbook (1992)

309   There are always consequences when one chooses to live outside of God's best plan.
John Splinter
The Complete Divorce Recovery Handbook (1992)

310   As we journey on the adventure of life, God leads us. He walks ahead. . .he's the point man out there blazing the trail.
Steven Curtis Chapman
The Great Adventure (2001)

311   God created you in His own image, and He wants you to experience His joy and abundance. But God will not force His joy upon you; you must claim it.
Beth Moore
Prayers and Promises for Women (2003)

312   Just when you think you have your whole life figured out; God will come along and change everything.
Jentezen Franklin
Believe That You Can (2008)

313   You need to keep doing what God told you to do.
Jentezen Franklin
Believe That You Can (2008)

GOD

314   No man acts rightly save by the assistance of divine aid; and no man or devil acts unrighteously save by the permission of the divine and most just judgment.
   Augustine
   The City of God (5th century)

315   It is true that wicked men do many things contrary to God's will; but so great is His wisdom and power, that all things which seem adverse to His purpose do still tend towards those just and good ends and issues which He Himself has foreknown.
   Augustine
   The City of God (5th century)

316   There is no greater protection than is found in the will of God.
   Rich Mendola
   "And So We Came to Rome" sermon (2009)

317   God has an individual plan for each person. If you will go to Him and submit to Him, He will come into your heart and commune with you. He will teach and guide you in the way you should go.
   Joyce Meyer
   If Not for the Grace of God (1995)

318   You will recognize the will of God and you will find that that is what your heart delights in alone. You will no longer even shed a tear in sympathy with the flesh.
   Watchman Nee
   Normal Christian Life (20th century)

Work of

319   Watch to see where God is working and join Him!
   Henry Blackaby
   Experiencing God (2007)

320 God is able to transform us. He knows what is best. He knows what it takes. He will, as the loving, all-powerful sculptor, chip away until Jesus is seen in the hardened hunk of our lives.
   Joseph Stowell
   Through the Fire (1985)

321   God handles the task, start to finish.
   Max Lucado
   3:16: The Numbers of Hope (2007)

322   Once you see God in an ordinary moment at an ordinary place, you never know where he'll show up next.
   John Ortberg
   God Is Closer Than You Think (2005)

323   If God took the time to design you as the wholly unique person you are, don't think for a minute He left out what He designed you to do and be. It's written on the fabric of your heart.
   Cindi McMenamin
   When a Woman Discovers Her Dream (2005)

324   Few of us dare to dream of what God might have had in mind when He made us the unique way that we are and breathed His life into us.
   Cindi McMenamin
   When a Woman Discovers Her Dream (2005)

325   We all get caught up in the daily details of life, and it can hinder our seeing the bigger plan God has for us. Our immediate problems overwhelm us and seem to obliterate God's promises. God, on the other hand, sees the bigger picture and wants us to focus in on what he is accomplishing in our lives. God's lessons are surrounding us daily, if only we are willing to set aside our busyness and open our "eyes to see and ears to hear."
   Betty Southard
   The Mentor Quest (2002)

326   All the works of God are unsearchable and unspeakable, no human sense can find them out.
   Martin Luther
   Table Talk (16th century)

327   Truly, if God were to give an account to every one of his works and actions, he were but a poor, simple God.
   Martin Luther
   Table Talk (16th century)

328   When God contemplates some great work, he begins it by the hand of some poor, weak, human creature, to whom he afterwards gives aid.
   Martin Luther
   Table Talk (16th century)

329   Where human help is at an end, God's help begins.
   Martin Luther
   Table Talk (16th century)

330   God is working in your attitudes and in your character in ways that will make you a gracious reflection of His holiness.
   Roy Lessin
   The Loving Heart (2005)

331   It is God's delight to make possible to us that which seems impossible, and when we reach a place where He alone has right of way, then all the things that have been misty and misunderstood are cleaned up.
   Smith Wigglesworth
   Faith That Prevails (1938)

332   God will do exceedingly abundantly above all we ask or think for us when He can bring us to the place where we can say with Paul, "I live no longer, and Another, even Christ, has taken the reigns and the rule."
   Smith Wigglesworth
   Faith That Prevails (1938)

333   When God sets his seal on a man's heart by his Spirit, there is some holy stamp, some image impressed and left upon the heart by the Spirit, as by the seal upon the wax.
   Jonathan Edwards
   A Treatise Concerning Religious Affections (18th century)

334   Don't ever think that God is not at work in your life. He's making things happen even when you don't realize it.
   Joel Osteen
   Your Best Life Now (2004)

Wrath of

335   There is no resisting, nor escaping God's anger. See the mischief sin makes; it provokes God to anger. And those not humbled by lesser judgments, must expect greater.
   Matthew Henry
   Commentary on the Whole Bible (1706)

336   Was not the wrath of God due to our souls?
   Stephen Charnock
   Discourse of God's Being the Author of Reconciliation (17th century)

185 GODLESSNESS
The triumphing of the wicked is short,
and the joy of the hypocrite but for a moment.
JOB 20:5

1   He that has not God, let him have else what he will, is more miserable than Lazarus, who lay at the rich man's gate, and was starved to death.
   Martin Luther
   Table Talk (16th century)

186 GODLINESS (*see also* CHRISTLIKENESS; GOODNESS)
Godliness is profitable unto all things,
having promise of the life that now is,
and of that which is to come.
1 TIMOTHY 4:8

1   Godliness is a life-long business. The working out of the salvation that the Lord, himself, works in you is not a matter of certain hours, or of a limited period of life. Salvation is unfolded throughout our entire sojourn here.
   Charles Spurgeon
   "The Watchword for Today—'Stand Fast'" sermon (1888)

2   A "godly" person is one who ceases to be self-centered in order to become God-centered.
   Charles Swindoll
   So You Want to Be Like Christ? (2005)

3   Love God, not godliness.
   Bruce Bickel and Stan Jantz
   God Is in the Small Stuff (1998)

4   There is no higher compliment that can be paid to a Christian than to call him a godly person.
   Jerry Bridges
   The Practice of Godliness (1996)

5   Godliness is more than Christian character: It is Christian character that springs from a devotion to God. But it is also true that devotion to God always results in godly character.
   Jerry Bridges
   The Practice of Godliness (1996)

6   When disaster comes—and it will come—our response is to demonstrate the hope, love, forgiveness, justice, holiness, and patience of the God we serve.
   Ed Dobson
   Finding God in the Face of Evil (2002)

7   Let us cleave, therefore, to those who cultivate peace with godliness, and not to those who hypocritically profess to desire it.
   Clement
   The First Epistle to the Corinthians (1st century)

8   One can know a great deal about godliness without much knowledge of God.
   J. I. Packer
   Knowing God (1993)

9   In seeking God we have to be prepared, not only to revise our ideas but to reform our lives.
   John Stott
   Basic Christianity (1958)

10 What God asks of us is a will which is no longer divided between him and any creature. It is a will pliant in his hands which neither seeks nor rejects anything, which wants without reserve whatever he wants, and which never wants under any pretext anything which he does not want.
   François Fénelon
   Christian Perfection (17th century)

11 You are never more like God than when you are living in relationships with God's people and working in partnerships for the re-creation and redemption of God's world.
   Ray Bakke
   A Theology as Big as the City (1997)

12 Godliness is the goal of the Christian life; we must please God by being, thinking, doing, saying, and feeling in the ways that He wants us to.
   Jay Adams
   Godliness Through Discipline (1972)

13 There is only one way to become a godly person, to orient one's life toward godliness, and that means, pattern by pattern. The old sinful ways, as they are discovered, must be replaced by new patterns from God's Word.
   Jay Adams
   Godliness Through Discipline (1972)

14 There is no easier path to godliness than the prayerful study and obedient practice of the Word of God.
   Jay Adams
   Godliness Through Discipline (1972)

GOLGOTHA (*see* **CROSS, THE**)

187 GOODNESS (*see also* **CHRISTLIKENESS; GODLINESS**)
For the fruit of the Spirit is in all goodness and righteousness and truth.
EPHESIANS 5:9

1 Let us seek to be useful. Let us seek to be vessels fit for the Master's use, that God, the Holy Spirit, may shine fully through us.
D. L. Moody
Secret Power (1881)

2 God can bring good out of the extremes of our own folly.
J. I. Packer
Knowing God (1993)

3 Love, goodness, and communication of good, is the immutable glory and perfection of the divine nature, and nothing can have union with God, but that which partakes of this goodness.
William Law
An Humble, Affectionate, and Earnest Address (1761)

4 The love that brought forth the existence of all things, changes not through the fall of its creatures, but is continually at work, to bring back all fallen nature and creature to their first state of goodness.
William Law
An Humble, Affectionate, and Earnest Address (1761)

188 GOOD WORKS
In all things shewing thyself a pattern of good works. . .
TITUS 2:7

1 The child of God knows his good works do not make him acceptable to God, for he was acceptable to God by Jesus Christ long before he had any good works.
Charles Spurgeon
"The Fatherhood of God" sermon (1858)

2 Do what you may, strive as earnestly as you can, live as excellently as you please, make what sacrifices you choose, be as eminent as you can for everything that is lovely and of good repute, yet none of these things can be pleasing to God unless they be mixed with faith.
Charles Spurgeon
"Faith" sermon (1856)

3 God does not only want right things done; He wants us to be the medium of right things that He is doing.
Watchman Nee
Changed into His Image (1967)

4 The New Testament comes right out and says what the Old Testament implies: No one will reach God by being good.
Andy Stanley
How Good Is Good Enough? (2003)

5 Regardless of what we say, it's what we do that reveals what we as a church or individual actually believe about God and His will for us.
Henry Blackaby
What the Spirit Is Saying to the Churches (2003)

6 If God is satisfied with the death of Christ, we should be too.
Erwin Lutzer
How You Can Be Sure That You Will Spend Eternity with God (1996)

7 The moral man is as guilty as the rest. His morality cannot save him.
D. L. Moody
Weighed and Wanting (19th century)

8 Let a man remember that the great thing is not to think about religion, but to do it.
Henry Drummond
Stones Rolled Away and Other Addresses to Young Men (1893)

9 I have heard it said many times: We must pray as if it all depends on God, and work as if it all depends on us. I believe that describes the mixture of faith and works that God honors... if it is done with a broken heart.

Rick Scarborough
Enough Is Enough (1996)

10 Spiritually sick men cannot sweat out their distemper with working.

John Owen
Of the Mortification of Sin in Believers (1656)

11 Practice comes first in religion, not theory or dogma. And Christian practice is not exhausted in outward deeds. They are the fruits, not the roots.

Thomas Kelly
A Testament of Devotion (1992)

12 Doing beats talking every time.

Maxie Dunnam
Let Me Say That Again (1996)

13 Neither silver, gold, precious stones, nor any rare thing has such manifold alloys and flaws as have good works, which ought to have a single simple goodness, and without it are mere color, show and deceit.

Martin Luther
A Treatise on Good Works (1520)

14 We ought first to know that there are no good works except those which God has commanded, even as there is no sin except that which God has forbidden.

Martin Luther
A Treatise on Good Works (1520)

15 The first and highest, the most precious of all good works is faith in Christ.

Martin Luther
A Treatise on Good Works (1520)

16 Some people wish to do without good works. I say, "This cannot be." As soon as the disciples received the Holy Ghost, they began to work.

Meister Eckhart
Meister Eckhart's Sermons (14th century)

17 The aim of man is not outward holiness by works, but life in God, yet this last expresses itself in works of love.

Meister Eckhart
Meister Eckhart's Sermons (14th century)

18 We are but the instruments or assistants, by whom God works.

Martin Luther
Table Talk (16th century)

189 GOSPEL, THE (*see also* EVANGELISM; MISSIONARIES; WITNESSING)

This gospel of the kingdom shall be preached in all the world for a witness unto all nations.
MATTHEW 24:14

1 If there's anything in life that we should be passionate about, it's the gospel. And I don't mean passionate only about sharing it with others. I mean passionate in thinking about it, dwelling on it, rejoicing in it, allowing it to color the way we look at the world.

C. J. Mahaney
The Cross Centered Life (2002)

2 The greatest need in the church today is the gospel. The gospel is not only news for a perishing world, it is a message that forms, sustains, and animates the church.

Thabiti Anyabwile
What Is a Healthy Church Member? (2008)

3 The amazing center of the Good News is this: I did the sinning; Jesus did the dying. Because of Him, we can trade in a death penalty we deserve for eternal life we don't deserve.

Ron Hutchcraft
The Battle for a Generation (1996)

4   The rod is the centerpiece of fishing. It's pretty hard to go fishing without one. The gospel is the centerpiece of Christianity. It's impossible to be a Christian without it.
Jimmy Houston
Hooked for Life (1999)

5   The ultimate good of the gospel is seeing and savoring the beauty and value of God. God's wrath and our sin obstruct that vision and that pleasure. The removal of this wrath and this rebellion is what the gospel is for. The ultimate aim of the gospel is the display of God's glory and the removal of every obstacle to our seeing it and savoring it as our highest treasure.
John Piper
God Is the Gospel (2005)

6   This is the heart of the gospel. Jesus stands under the judgment of God for our sins. Christ asks the Father to divert the punishment away from us, and He absorbs it in Himself. That is how forgiveness is released.
Colin Smith
Ten Keys for Unlocking the Bible (2002)

7   God-centered lives provide undeniable evidence of the truth of a God-centered gospel. On the other hand, nothing undermines the gospel more quickly or effectively than a messenger whose life denies the words that are spoken.
James Odens
Lighting the Way to God (1999)

8   The lesson is clear in my mind: labor to preach the gospel, to explain to people the truth of the finished work of Christ; let good and faithful works and the sacrifice of one's life be the result of the gospel.
Lance Latham
The Two Gospels (1984)

9   I don't think it's coincidental that the first two letters in "gospel" are "go."
Jon Courson
Application Commentary (2005)

10   Don't complicate the gospel.
Steve Sampson
You Can Hear the Voice of God (1993)

11   We need to stop shaping Jesus in some misguided effort to make Him appealing. Jesus doesn't need to be like us; we need to be like Him.
James MacDonald
Five Distortions of the Gospel (2007)

12   The Careful Gospel: Let's not upset anybody, just keep 'em comfortable and coming back; there's lots of time for folks to figure it out. The gospel of "get them to church, and in time everything will come together as long as we don't offend them" is a dangerous gospel. Well-intentioned is not enough. The gospel without urgency is not the gospel.
James MacDonald
"Five Distortions of the Gospel in Our Day" sermon (2007)

13   Our task is not to debate the Gospel; our task is to announce it.
David Roper
A Beacon in the Darkness (1995)

14   The gospel of Jesus Christ offers the only antidote to the ills that plague our society.
Bill Bright and John Damoose
Red Sky in the Morning (1998)

15   The glory of the Christian gospel is that God not only demanded that sacrifice, but He provided it as well.
Albert Mohler Jr.
He Is Not Silent (2008)

16   The resurrection of our Saviour Christ, in the preaching of the gospel, raises earthquakes in the world now, as when Christ arose out of the sepulchre bodily.
Martin Luther
Table Talk (16th century)

17 What is needed today is not a new gospel, but live men and women who can re-state the Gospel of the Son of God in terms that will reach the very heart of our problems.
Oswald Chambers
Approved Unto God (20th century)

18 Never offer men a thimbleful of Gospel.
Henry Drummond
The Greatest Thing in the World (1874)

19 The gospel is a rose; it cannot be plucked without prickles.
Thomas Watson
A Body of Practical Divinity (1838)

20 We will never impact the world for Jesus with a relativized, wimpy, fear-driven, people-pleasing "gospel."
Richard Ganz
Tabletalk magazine (2009)

21 The gospel is not a magic wand that makes our sins and vices disappear from one day to the next. It delivers us, a step at a time, as we walk with the Holy Spirit.
Jim Petersen and Mike Shamy
The Insider (2003)

22 The gospel is unknown, not from want of explanation, but from absence of personal revelation. This the Holy Ghost is ready to give, and will give to those who ask Him.
Charles Spurgeon
All of Grace (19th century)

23 The gospel starts by teaching us that we, as creatures, are absolutely dependent on God, and that he, as Creator, has an absolute claim on us. Only when we have learned this can we see what sin is, and only when we see what sin is can we understand the good news of salvation from sin.
J. I. Packer
Evangelism and the Sovereignty of God (2008)

24 The gospel of Christ does not move by popular waves.
E. M. Bounds
Power Through Prayer (1906)

25 When we proclaim the gospel, we must go on to unfold its ethical implications, and when we teach Christian behavior we must lay its gospel foundations.
John Stott
Between Two Worlds: The Challenge of Preaching Today (1982)

26 Happy am I to have so full a gospel to proclaim! Happy are you to be allowed to read it!
Charles Spurgeon
All of Grace (19th century)

27 The gospel is no mere proclamation of "eternal truths," but the discovery of a saving purpose of God for mankind, executed in time.
James Orr
The Christian View of God and the World (1908)

190 GOSSIP

The words of a talebearer are as wounds, and they go down into the innermost parts of the belly.
PROVERBS 26:22

1 No surer sign of an unprofitable life than when people give way to censoriousness and inquisitiveness into the lives of other men.
Francis de Sales
Introduction to the Devout Life (17th century)

2 Don't get sucked in to gossip or listen to slanderous remarks that are coming second- and third-hand.
Tom Eisenman
The Accountable Man (2004)

3   Few people would consider slander heinous enough to be included with murder, adultery, and stealing. That may be because we rarely stop to consider the long-range consequences of ruining another person's good name.

Kenneth Boa and Gail Burnett
The Art of Living Well (1999)

4   Let us remember that none of us will ever be more maligned or slandered than was our Lord.

Gary Thomas
Authentic Faith (2002)

191 GOVERNMENT

For rulers are not a terror to good works, but to the evil. Wilt thou then not be afraid of the power? do that which is good, and thou shalt have praise of the same.
ROMANS 13:3

1   Show me the nation that has ever crumbled into oblivion and decay that was governed by Christian beliefs.

Billy Sunday
"Nuts for Skeptics to Crack" sermon (1922)

2   History instructs us that this love of religious liberty, a compound sentiment in the breast of man, made up of the clearest sense of right, and the highest conviction of duty, is able to look the sternest despotism in the face, and with means apparently most inadequate, to shake principalities and powers.

Daniel Webster
Speeches and Forensic Arguments (1820)

3   Moral habits cannot be safely trusted on any other foundation than religious principle, nor any government be secure which is not supported by moral habits.

Daniel Webster
Speeches and Forensic Arguments (1820)

4   Of the motives which influenced the first settlers to a voluntary exile, induced them to relinquish their native country, and to seek an asylum in this then unexplored wilderness, the first and principal, no doubt were connected with Religion.

Daniel Webster
Speeches and Forensic Arguments (1820)

5   Society in every state is a blessing, but government even in its best state is but a necessary evil.

Thomas Paine
Common Sense (1776)

6   *Wherefore*, security being the true design and end of government, it unanswerably follows, that whatever *form* thereof appears most likely to ensure it to us, with the least expense and greatest benefit, is preferable to all others.

Thomas Paine
Common Sense (1776)

7   States that reject the idea of God tend either to tyranny or to open disorder. In either case, the end is disorder, because tyranny itself is a disorder.

Thomas Merton
No Man Is an Island (1955)

8   A King is not a King, because he is a good King, nor leaves being a King, as soon as he leaves being good. All is well summed by the Apostle, You must needs be subject, not only for wrath, but also for conscience sake.

John Donne
"Sermon Preached at Lincoln's Inn" (1620)

9   When law and morality contradict each other, the citizen has the cruel alternative of either losing his moral sense or losing his respect for the law.

Frederic Bastiat
The Law (1850)

10 America, of course, like every other human thing, can in spiritual sense live or die as much as it chooses. But at the present moment the matter which America has very seriously to consider is not how near it is to its birth and beginning, but how near it may be to its end.
G. K. Chesterton
Heretics (1905)

11 Democracy is not philanthropy; it is not even altruism or social reform. Democracy is not founded on pity for the common man; democracy is founded on reverence for the common man, or, if you will, even on fear of him.
G. K. Chesterton
Heretics (1905)

192 GRACE

*The grace of our Lord Jesus Christ
be with your spirit.*
PHILEMON 1:25

1 Grace, 'Tis a Charming Sound
Philip Doddridge hymn title (1740)

2 Grace, Enough for Me
Edwin Excell hymn title (1905)

3 Grace is something not which I improve, but which improves, employs me, works on me.
Charles Spurgeon
"Divine Sovereignty" sermon (1856)

4 Let people talk as they will about universal grace, it is all nonsense, there is no such thing, nor can there be. They may talk correctly of universal blessings, because we see that the natural gifts of God are scattered everywhere, more or less, and men may receive or reject them. It is not so, however, with grace.
Charles Spurgeon
"Divine Sovereignty" sermon (1856)

5 The new covenant, is not founded on works at all, it is a covenant of pure unmingled grace.
Charles Spurgeon
"God in the Covenant" sermon (1856)

6 Unless you're deeply aware of your sin, and of what an affront it is to God's holiness, and of how impossible it is for Him to respond to sin with anything other than furious wrath—you'll never appreciate grace, and it will never be amazing to you.
C. J. Mahaney
Christ Our Mediator (2004)

7 For me, grace is never more amazing than when I'm looking intensely at the cross, and I believe the same will be true for every child of God.
C. J. Mahaney
Christ Our Mediator (2004)

8 Only those who see themselves as utterly destitute can fully appreciate the grace of God.
Erwin Lutzer
Failure: The Back Door to Success (1975)

9 To accept grace is to admit failure, a step we are hesitant to take. We opt to impress God with how good we are rather than confessing how great he is.
Max Lucado
In the Eye of the Storm (1991)

10 Human efforts that seek to impress God or persuade Him to overlook sin are insults to a God of grace.
Franklin Graham
All for Jesus (2003)

11 Nowhere in Scripture do we find that loving Christ is the reason for forgiveness. True expressions of love for Him flow as a spontaneous and unstoppable response to forgiveness. Acts of authentic love are a response to Christ's amazing work of grace.
Joseph Stowell
Why It's Hard to Love Jesus (2003)

12 Preaching grace alone has left the sinner thinking lightly of sin.
Ray Comfort
Hell's Best Kept Secret (1989)

13 For grace is given not because we have done good works, but in order that we may be able to do them.
Augustine
Of the Spirit and the Letter (5th century)

14 God singles out the humble soul to fill him to the brim with grace, when the proud is sent away empty.
Thomas Brooks
The Unsearchable Riches of Christ (1655)

15 By his holiness and grace, God extends a complete pardon for our sins—past, present, and future.
Jonathan Campbell and Jennifer Campbell
The Way of Jesus (2005)

16 When a believer has been steeped in grace, all the members of his or her immediate society detect a refreshing fragrance.
Christine Wood
Character Witness (2003)

17 Just as a team provides its athletes all they need to perform on the field, even so grace gives us all the provisions to enable us to maximize our spiritual potential.
Tony Evans and Jonathan Evans
Get in the Game (2006)

18 Grace is absolute, inflexible, all-encompassing.
Philip Yancey
The Jesus I Never Knew (1995)

19 Why do we expect the best from a world steeped in pain? Continually we find ourselves blindsided by reality. Every new morning offers another chance to admit our inadequacy—once again for this new day, a chance to accept the bewildering ecstasy of God's grace. Why is it so difficult to accept such a love when His Grace is the one gift that can penetrate the messy corners of our worlds?
Bonnie Keen
God Loves Messy People (2002)

20 In their pride, the builders of Babel assumed they could work their way into God's Presence and He would accept them on the basis of what they had done. They were wrong then, and they are still wrong today.
Anne Graham Lotz
God's Story (1997)

21 Grace is a supernatural mixture of patience, help, forgiveness, and sympathy, and it is the internal expression of what our God is like.
Ed Young
From Bad Beginnings to Happy Endings (1994)

22 Blind as we are, we hinder God, and stop the current of His graces. But when He finds a soul penetrated with a lively faith, He pours into it His graces and favours plentifully.
Brother Lawrence
The Practice of the Presence of God (17th century)

23 We know also that we can do all things with the grace of God, which He never refuses to them who ask it earnestly.
Brother Lawrence
The Practice of the Presence of God (17th century)

24 Ah, how impious and ungrateful is the world, thus to condemn and persecute God's ineffable grace!
Martin Luther
Table Talk (16th century)

25 God's grace is just that—grace, unmerited favor. Nothing I will do can ever cause Him to love me more or less.
David Hawkins
Prescription for Living Beyond (2006)

26 Moments of awe are moments when we are the most vulnerable to grace. Without those moments, we are vulnerable to everything else.
Ken Gire
Reflections on Your Life (1998)

27 Grace is undeserved mercy.
James Scudder
Your Secret to Spiritual Success (2002)

28 The Spirit discovereth to the sinner, that though his wound be dangerous, because the God whom he hath provoked is resolved either to have his law satisfied, or his eternal wrath endured, yet that it is not desperate, for there is balm in Gilead, and a physician in Israel, that can heal his soul.
George Swinnock
The Door of Salvation Opened by the Key of Regeneration, and the Sinner's Last Sentence (17th century)

29 Living the Christian life in your own power nullifies the grace of God.
Tony Evans
Theology You Can Count On (2008)

30 Free grace will fix those whom free will shook down into a gulf of misery.
Thomas Boston
Human Nature in Its Fourfold State (1830)

31 Grace bestowed upon another is always grace imparted to you.
Martin Bell
Street Singing and Preaching (1991)

32 You cannot receive grace if you think it's a reward for something you have done.
Paul and Nicole Johnson
Random Acts of Grace (1995)

33 But graciousness is withholding certain facts you know to be true, so as to leave your enemy's reputation unscathed. Graciousness is shown by what you don't say, even if what you could say would be true.
R. T. Kendall
Total Forgiveness (2002)

34 I don't think anything concerns me more than using grace as a tool to justify sin.
Charles Swindoll
"Trouble at Home" sermon (2009)

35 Oh friend, the great grace of God surpasses my conception and your conception, and I would have you think worthily of it!
Charles Spurgeon
All of Grace (19th century)

36 Sound forth those words as with the archangel's trumpet: "By grace are ye saved." What glad tidings for the undeserving!
Charles Spurgeon
All of Grace (19th century)

37 Grace finds us in our poverty and presents us with the gift of an inheritance we didn't deserve. . . the gift of grace.
Patsy Clairmont and Traci Mullins
Extravagant Grace (2000)

38 Even though we still sin and often can't seem to stop, God declared us righteous when we believed and received Jesus. And because the sin thing stays with us like onions after lunch, we desperately need God's grace.
Patsy Clairmont and Traci Mullins
Extravagant Grace (2000)

39 God wants you to experience his grace whether you have faced your life with courage or with cowardice. Grace is not about us; it is about God. He will meet you wherever you are to help you take the next gutsy step.
Patsy Clairmont and Traci Mullins
Extravagant Grace (2000)

40 Grace empowers you to perform the tasks God has given you on earth, and to enjoy what he has called you to do.
Patsy Clairmont and Traci Mullins
Extravagant Grace (2000)

41 There is no way to travel from the state of sinfulness to the state of holiness except by the highway of grace.
Joyce Meyer
If Not for the Grace of God (1995)

42 Grace is the godly man's treasure.
Jonathan Edwards
A Treatise Concerning Religious Affections (18th century)

43 No promise of the covenant of grace belongs to any man, until he has first believed in Christ.
Jonathan Edwards
A Treatise Concerning Religious Affections (18th century)

44 To check therefore all suggestions to spiritual pride, let us consider, that we did not apprehend Christ, but were apprehended of him. That we have nothing but what we have received.
George Whitefield (18th century) quoted in *Selected Sermons of George Whitefield*

45 I do not at all understand the mystery of grace—only that it meets us where we are but does not leave us where it found us.
Anne Lamott
Traveling Mercies (1999)

46 God never allows a thorn but that He provides sufficient grace and strength in our weaknesses.
James MacDonald
"Strength in Weakness" sermon (2009)

47 Sufficient grace is not just enough to survive, but enough to have supernatural joy in the midst of anything He allows us to go through.
James MacDonald
"Strength in Weakness" sermon (2009)

48 If a small measure of grace in the saints makes them sweet and desirable companions, what must the riches of the Spirit of grace filling Jesus Christ without measure make him in the eyes of believers?
John Flavel
Christ Altogether Lovely (17th century)

49 God desires nothing from you but that you should really acknowledge your sin and cast yourself down before Him as a guilty sinner. Then you will certainly and speedily receive His grace.
Andrew Murray
Have Mercy Upon Me (1896)

50 Everything begins with God the Father. The initiative of grace is his alone.
John Stott
Life in Christ (2003)

51 If grace is or was best then, it is best now.
Richard Sibbes
The Bruised Reed (1630)

52 The grace of God in bestowing this gift is most free. It was what God was under no obligation to bestow.
Jonathan Edwards
"God Glorified in Man's Dependence" sermon (18th century)

53 It is by God's power that we are preserved in a state of grace.
Jonathan Edwards
"God Glorified in Man's Dependence" sermon (18th century)

54 God's grace does not come to people who morally outperform others, but to those who admit their failure to perform and who acknowledge their need for a Savior.
Timothy Keller
The Reason for God (2008)

55 A central message of the Bible is that we can only have a relationship with God by sheer grace. Our moral efforts are too feeble and falsely motivated to ever merit salvation.
Timothy Keller
The Reason for God (2008)

56 The fact that we are God's people says nothing good about our natures or us. We are God's people only by his grace, because our natures are entirely too prone to evil and rebellion.
Mark Dever
"Exodus: All the World's a Stage" sermon (2002)

57 God's grace will soak like a soothing balm into the heat of your pain.
Mary Nelson
Grace for Tough Times (2006)

58 Miracles convey the power of God, but time conveys the grace.
Kim Thomas
Living in the Sacred Now (2001)

193 GRANDPARENTS
Children's children are the crown of old men.
PROVERBS 17:6

1 The one obligation that a grandmother does have is the one stated in this principle: the obligation to be a safe haven.
Suzette Haden Elgin
The Grandmother Principles (1998)

2 The grandparent who impacts his grandchild's life is the one willing to kneel down to the child's level, to laugh at what he or she laughs at, to cry at what makes him or her tearful.
Eric Wiggin
The Gift of Grandparenting (2001)

194 GRATITUDE (*see also* THANKSGIVING)
Sing unto the LORD with thanksgiving; sing praise upon the harp unto our God.
PSALM 147:7

1 There is power in gratitude to heal us spiritually, emotionally, and relationally.
Kerry and Chris Shook
One Month to Live (2008)

195 GREATNESS
Whosoever therefore shall humble himself as this little child, the same is greatest in the kingdom of heaven.
MATTHEW 18:4

1 True greatness is found in simple surrender to God's plan for our lives.
Jim Cymbala
You Were Made for More (2008)

196 GREED (*see also* COVETOUSNESS)
He that is greedy of gain troubleth his own house.
PROVERBS 15:27

1 Today some people think they're "doing without" if they can't afford to buy dessert.
Martha Bolton
Growing Your Own Turtleneck (2005)

2 No matter how mature we become as Christ-followers, we are only a step away from yielding to the gravitational pull of greed.
Gordon MacDonald
Secrets of the Generous Life (2002)

197 GRIEF (*see also* SORROW)

Have mercy upon me, O LORD, for I am in trouble: mine eye is consumed with grief.
PSALM 31:9

1 Grieving is the natural way we go about adjusting to loss. It's the way we gradually come to know deep within ourselves—whether we like it or not—that the loss is real.
Joan Guntzelman
God Knows You're Grieving (2001)

2   We move toward healing when we choose to inch our foot out the door of our own grief and back into the day to day happenings of life.
    Joan Guntzelman
    God Knows You're Grieving (2001)

3   Christians sometimes think that we are not supposed to grieve, because our faith and theology provide us with confidence about heaven and eternal life. But while 1 Thessalonians 4:13 says that we are not to grieve as those without hope, we grieve nevertheless. Those without hope grieve in one way; those with hope grieve in another. Either way, grief is universal and not to be avoided. It is a legitimate response to loss.
    Albert Hsu
    Grieving a Suicide (2002)

4   Little sorrows are often loud and talkative, while deep grief is comparatively silent.
    James Thomas Holloway
    The Analogy of Faith (1836)

5   No one ever told me that grief felt so like fear.
    C. S. Lewis
    A Grief Observed (1961)

6 Grief is the emotional tool God placed in our hearts to enable us to release things we value.
    Scott Turansky and Joanne Miller
    Parenting Is Heart Work (2006)

7   We are a world in grief, and it is at once intolerable and a great opportunity. I'm pretty sure that it is only by experiencing that ocean of sadness in a naked and immediate way that we come to be healed.
    Anne Lamott
    Traveling Mercies (1999)

8   Grief is woven throughout the tapestry of life.
    Zig Ziglar
    Confessions of a Grieving Christian (1998)

9   The intensity of grief is directly related to the intensity of love.
    Zig Ziglar
    Confessions of a Grieving Christian (1998)

10 Tears are liquid love.
    Faye Landrum
    Acquainted with Grief (2006)

198 GROWTH, SPIRITUAL (*see also* MATURITY; SANCTIFICATION)
But grow in grace, and in the knowledge of our Lord and Saviour Jesus Christ.
2 PETER 3:18

1   Every experience God gives us, every person He puts in our lives is the perfect preparation for the future that only He can see.
    Corrie ten Boom
    The Hiding Place (1971)

2   Every disappointment is a trial of our faith... a test that proves the genuineness of your relationship with your God and His Word.
    Kay Arthur
    As Silver Refined (1998)

3   No matter what happens, beloved, no matter how disappointing it is, you must, in an act of the will, rejoice and pray and give thanks.
    Kay Arthur
    As Silver Refined (1998)

4   Perils as well as privileges attend the higher Christian life. The nearer we come to God, the thicker the hosts of darkness in heavenly places.
    A. B. Simpson
    Days of Heaven Upon Earth (1897)

5   Hall of Fame coach Vince Lombardi used to say, "Potential means you ain't done nothing yet." All of us have potential. God's not done with any of us yet.
    Bill Glass
    Champions for Life (2005)

6   Only you will ever limit what you are for God.
> Kay Arthur
> *Beloved* (1994)

7   When we become aware of our problems and character issues, God holds us responsible for dealing with them and facing the tough changes we need to make.
> Henry Cloud and John Townsend
> *Safe People* (1995)

8   Remember, you are the only one who can keep you from becoming the person God wants you to be.
> Neil Anderson
> *Victory Over the Darkness* (1990)

9   Just as in natural food, so in the spiritual: we must have food for growth as well as food for maintenance.
> Paul Brand
> *He Satisfies My Soul* (2008)

10 Don't kick against your loving Father's refining process. He is allowing your circumstances to chip away all your dependence on your own flesh and instead opt for your identity in Christ.
> Bill Gillham
> *Lifetime Guarantee* (1993)

11 Before the acorn can bring forth the oak, it must become itself a wreck. No plant ever came from any but a wrecked seed.
> Hannah Whitall Smith
> *The God of All Comfort* (1906)

12 Spiritual growth occurs as a result of intentional and appropriate effort.
> Jerry Bridges
> *Growing Your Faith* (2004)

13 In distinction from the physical realm, Christians should never stop growing spiritually.
> Jerry Bridges
> *Growing Your Faith* (2004)

14 Growth in godly character is not only progressive and always unfinished, it is absolutely necessary for spiritual survival. If we are not growing in godly character, we are regressing; in the spiritual life we never stand still.
> Jerry Bridges
> *The Practice of Godliness* (1996)

15 God is changing us by giving us the gift of an enlarged heart.
> Fawn Parish
> *Honor—What Love Looks Like* (1999)

16 The truth is, the more spiritually mature you grow, the more you will find your heart being drawn to people. You want to reach out to people, especially those neglected by society or far from God.
> John Ortberg
> *Everybody's Normal Till You Get to Know Them* (2003)

17 Newborns need to nurse long and often. And when we are newborn in Christ, we need frequent, lengthy feedings from Jesus for spiritual growth, emotional attachment, and immunity from spiritual disease.
> Tamara Boggs
> *And Then God Gave Us Kids* (2003)

18 Change in our lives is not brought about by our tense tinkering. It is brought about by the radiant, immeasurable energy of Christ, which has never left the world since He first said yes to God.
> John Maxwell
> *Be All You Can Be* (1987)

19 Growth in God comes by obedience. . . perpetual obedience.
> Steve Sampson
> *You Can Hear the Voice of God* (1993)

20 What does it take to play in the major leagues? Years of hard work, near perfection in the fundamentals of the game, and a high degree of success in the areas that count most. Likewise, the fully developed believer knows God at an ever-deeper level that has been pursued over a period of time.
    Tony and Jonathan Evans
    Get in the Game (2006)

21 God's will for us is to grow, to continue to learn and improve. The biggest room in our house is always the room for self-improvement.
    John Mason
    An Enemy Called Average (1990)

22 Personal maturity takes time, and it will not happen automatically. It must be thoughtfully planned and carefully considered. And don't forget to consider the spiritual side of your life when planning for any new season of your life.
    Ken Owen
    Faith in the Fast Lane (2002)

23 You can't shift directions until you see clearly and honestly where you are.
    Barbara Bartocci
    From Hurting to Happy (2002)

24 Someone once said that our problems can become our teachers. The hard part is admitting our deficiencies and then taking action to correct them.
    Robert Stofel
    God, Are We There Yet? (2004)

25 Until we learn to have an obedient nature—we will always be in "spiritual diapers."
    Steve Campbell
    "The Primary Importance" sermon (2009)

26 God is always ready, but we are very unready. God is near us, but we are far from Him. God is within, and we are without. God is friendly; we are estranged.
    Meister Eckhart
    Meister Eckhart's Sermons (14th century)

27 We should feed and nourish our souls with high notions of God; which would yield us great joy in being devoted to Him.
    Brother Lawrence
    The Practice of the Presence of God (17th century)

28 You will make much more progress in your spiritual life if you give high priority to your church life.
    James Scudder
    Your Secret to Spiritual Success (2002)

29 The closer we walk with God—the farther we walk away from sin.
    Steve Campbell
    "What to Do When We Sin" sermon (2009)

30 Let prayer, and the devotional study of the sacred writings, ever nourish the flame of piety in your bosom.
    Peter Barron
    The United Presbyterian Magazine (1856)

31 Oftentimes, the challenges in our life drive us to the sufficiency of Christ.
    Beth Moore
    "Who Do You Trust?" teaching series (2007)

32 Many times we want to escape from the pressure, when the pressure, if we yield to it, can shape Christ-likeness in us.
    Beth Moore
    "Who Do You Trust?" teaching series (2007)

33 Having accepted the Father's will over our own, we are then ready to face our own Calvary.

> Charles Swindoll
> *The Darkness and the Dawn* (2001)

34 If you are not growing in grace, becoming more and more holy, yielding yourselves up to the influence of the gospel, you are deceiving yourselves.

> Charles Finney
> *Lectures to Professing Christians* (1837)

35 There is no standing at a stay, He that goes not forward in godliness, goes backward, and he that is not better, is worse; but even in temporal things too there is a liberty given us, nay there is a law, an obligation laid upon us, to endeavour by industry in a lawful calling, to mend and improve, to enlarge ourselves, and spread, even in worldly things.

> John Donne
> "Sermon Preached at the Hague" (1619)

36 As we grow in our relationship with God, we should experience a revolutionary change in our attitudes toward people.

> Bill Hybels
> *Laws of the Heart* (1985)

37 In intellectual honesty, we should be willing to study and explore the spiritual life with all the rigor and determination we would give to any field of research.

> Richard Foster
> *Celebration of Discipline* (1978)

38 We are sometimes guilty of confining becoming a Christian to accepting by faith what was accomplished for us in the remote past. In all of this we prove to minimize what the resurrected Jesus wants to do to us and with us now through the ministry of the Holy Spirit.

> Tony Campolo
> *How to be Pentecostal Without Speaking in Tongues* (1991)

39 God expects us to grow spiritually. The end result is His responsibility. Our job is to cooperate with the process.

> Rory Noland
> *The Heart of the Artist* (1999)

40 Nothing will change in your life without knowledge of God's Word.

> Joyce Meyer
> *When, God, When?* (1994)

41 At different seasons of life, we will be growing in different areas. I try to see where God is at work in my life, and where he is at work in the lives of my friends, and then I pray for and encourage growth in those particular areas.

> Alice Fryling
> *Disciplemakers' Handbook* (1989)

42 Literal instruction is when we learn the truths contained in the word by rote, and talk one after another of Divine things. But spiritual illumination is when these things are revealed to us by the Spirit of God.

> Thomas Manton
> *One Hundred and Ninety*
> *Sermons on the Hundred and Nineteenth*
> *Psalm* (17th century)

43 Let go of as many expectations as possible... instead, ask God to make any necessary changes.

> Stormie Omartian
> *The Power of a Praying Wife* (1997)

44 At a certain point in the spiritual journey, God will draw a person from the beginning stage to a more advanced stage.... Such souls will likely experience what is called "the dark night of the soul." The "dark night" is when those persons lose all the pleasure that they once experienced in their devotional life. This happens because God wants to purify them and move them on to greater heights.

> John of the Cross (16th century)
> quoted in *Selected Writings*

45 God perceives the imperfections within us, and because of his love for us, urges us to grow up. His love is not content to leave us in our weakness, and for this reason he takes us into a dark night. He weans us from all of the pleasures by giving us dry times and inward darkness.

John of the Cross (16th century)
quoted in *Selected Writings*

46 Through the dark night pride becomes humility, greed becomes simplicity, wrath becomes contentment, luxury becomes peace, gluttony becomes moderation, envy becomes joy, and sloth becomes strength.

John of the Cross (16th century)
quoted in *Selected Writings*

47 How dangerous it is for our salvation, how unworthy of God and of ourselves, how pernicious even for the peace of our hearts, to want always to stay where we are! Our whole life was only given us to advance us by great strides toward our heavenly country.

François Fénelon
Christian Perfection (17th century)

48 Do not be content with a static Christian life. Determine rather to grow in faith and love, in knowledge and holiness.

John Stott
Christian Basics (1991)

49 We are born spiritually just as we were born physically, with everything complete and intact. We do not add arms or legs or organs as we mature physically. These grow and develop, but they are not added. Likewise when we are born spiritually, we are undeveloped but complete. We need spiritual food and exercise in order to grow, but we do not need and we will not be given additional spiritual parts.

John MacArthur
1 Corinthians (1984)

50 Far too often when we examine our heart, through either neglect or poor decisions, we find that it isn't in a growing mode.

Jim and Cathy Burns
Closer (2009)

51 It's not too late to become who God created you to be.

Kerry and Chris Shook
One Month to Live (2008)

52 Telling others about Christ is never a condition of salvation; it should be a result of salvation as we grow in His grace.

R. Larry Moyer
21 Things God Never Said (2004)

53 There is little appeal in becoming "spiritual vampires," sucking on the blood of Christ for forgiveness while being barely alive spiritually.

Keith Meyer
Whole Life Transformation (2010)

54 If our lives were gardens—and gardens in Scripture are often euphemisms for the soul— here we would look for brambles and briars, pests and parasites. Here we would deadhead, plucking off faded blooms to preserve energy for new blossoms.

Jane Rubietta
Between Two Gardens (2001)

55 Our being must precede our doing and consuming if we are to grow up into all the fullness of Christ.

Jane Rubietta
Resting Place (2005)

56 Spiritual anorexia (not taking in the food we need) and spiritual bulimia (not letting ourselves digest it after we have received it, however large the quantities) will keep us from real spiritual health and progress.

J. I. Packer
J. I. Packer Answers Questions for Today (2001)

57 Nothing in the spiritual life originates from us. It all originates with God.
   Ruth Haley Barton
   Sacred Rhythms (2006)

58 We cannot use shortcuts when it comes to understanding spiritual truth, building Christian character, or building the local church.
   Warren Wiersbe
   God Isn't in a Hurry (1994)

GRUDGES (*see* BITTERNESS)

GRUMBLING (*see* COMPLAINING; MURMURING)

199 GUIDANCE
If any of you lack wisdom, let him ask of God, that giveth to all men liberally, and upbraideth not; and it shall be given him.
   JAMES 1:5

1 I have often heard, that it is safer to hear and to take counsel, than to give it.
   Thomas à Kempis
   The Imitation of Christ (15th century)

2 The true and living God, the One who lives from eternity to eternity, desires more than anything that we humble ourselves and make Him our personal, one-and-only God. When we do that, He comes to us and lives within us, gives us direction, and teaches us His ultimate truth.
   Tony Evans
   God Cannot be Trusted (And Five Other Lies of Satan) (2005)

3 Because of the Holy Spirit's witness and illumination, you never have to be alone in your decisions—but this is true only as long as you're seeking the mind of God and wanting to do His will.
   Tony Evans
   The Fire That Ignites (2003)

4 It takes a lot of wisdom, a lot of mistakes, and a lot of prayer to figure out when to listen and when to offer advice.
   Susan Alexander Yates
   And Then I Had Teenagers (2001)

5 A friend gives you good and timely advice. They know what to say at the right time, and it can save you embarrassment and heartache. The advice can be trusted because you know they are looking out for your best interest.
   Paul Jehle
   Dating vs. Courtship (1993)

6 When you know a great deal, the temptation to share it by force is strong. Resist! Except when invited to lecture, and in actual emergencies.
   Suzette Haden Elgin
   The Grandmother Principles (1998)

7 If I have done anything in my life, it has been easy because the Master has gone before.
   Mary Slessor
   Mary Slessor of Calabar (1917)

8 Be guided, only by the healer of the sick, the raiser of the dead, the friend of all who were afflicted and forlorn, the patient Master who shed tears of compassion for our infirmities. We cannot but be right when we put all the rest away, and do everything in remembrance of Him. . . . There can be no confusion in following Him, and seeking for no other footsteps, I am certain!
   Charles Dickens
   Little Dorrit (1857)

9 Those that make their own bosoms their oracle, God is disengaged from being their guide: they need him not; but the snares they run into will soon show them how much they need him.
   Thomas Manton
   One Hundred and Ninety Sermons on the Hundred and Nineteenth Psalm (17th century)

10 Self-help is an oxymoron.
Henry Cloud
Concede Control (2006)

200 GUILT *(See also* EMBARRASSMENT; SHAME)
O God, thou knowest my foolishness; and my sins are not hid from thee.
PSALM 69:5

1 The Bible tells us that we have been washed clean from a guilty conscience to serve the living God. God does not want you to be engaged in morbid introspection all your life long. He wants you to enter joyously into His service as a full-fledged member of His holy family.
Pat Robertson
Six Steps to Spiritual Revival (2002)

2 The only real way to lose the guilt is by asking Christ for forgiveness. He's the only One who can let you off the hook. The good news is He can and will erase your wrong every time. You can start fresh, just as if it never happened. So if you feel guilty about some of the things you've done, bring them to Him. He'll always forgive you.
Claire and Curt Cloninger
E-mail from God for Teens (1999)

3 The ultimate remedy for living beyond guilt and shame is abiding in the protective love of Christ. All of our earthly maladies find respite in Him.
David Hawkins
Prescription for Living Beyond (2006)

4 Confession is a first step toward change.
Andy Stanley
It Came from Within! (2001)

5 As long as you are carrying a secret, as long as you are trying to ease your conscience by telling God how sorry you are, you are setting yourself up to repeat the past.
Andy Stanley
It Came from Within! (2001)

6 God will wipe off the guilt of your defects by the virtue of that precious blood which has been shed for your reparation.
Stephen Charnock
Discourse on the Cleansing Virtue of Christ's Blood (17th century)

7 When true Christians are in an ill frame, guilt lies on the conscience; which will bring fear, and so prevent the peace and joy of an assured hope.
Jonathan Edwards
A Treatise Concerning Religious Affections (18th century)

8 In spite of our "enlightened society," our "new morality," and our "psychological maturity," our era continues to be plagued by guilt.
Bruce Narramore
Guilt and Freedom (1974)

201 HABITS
Now when Daniel knew that the writing was signed, he went into his house; and his windows being open in his chamber toward Jerusalem, he kneeled upon his knees three times a day, and prayed, and gave thanks before his God, as he did aforetime.
DANIEL 6:10

1 Motivation can fade. Habits prevail.
Bruce Bickel and Stan Jantz
God Is in the Small Stuff (1998)

2 Generally, there is one desire or one habit that keeps us from enjoying and tasting the fullness of God.
Ravi Zacharias
"Is There Not a Cost?" sermon (2008)

3 There must be no dallying with an attachment which is incompatible with the Love of God.
Francis de Sales
Introduction to the Devout Life (17th century)

4   How do you break a habit? The same way you developed it. One incident at a time, five minutes at a time, one hour at a time, one day at a time.
   Lisa Bevere
   Be Angry But Don't Blow It! (2000)

5   Nagging about the bad habit may drive the habit underground, but it doesn't fix anything.
   Dave Meurer
   Good Spousekeeping (2004)

6   Don't just eliminate a particular habit and fail to replace it with something of value.
   James Scudder
   Your Secret to Spiritual Success (2002)

7   If you keep doing what you've always done, you're going to get what you've always gotten.
   David Hawkins
   Breaking Everyday Addictions (2008)

8   When you say no to one habit, you also have to say yes to a healthier new habit.
   David Hazard
   Reducing Stress (2002)

9   The only way to kill a habit is to starve it to death. Starving a bad habit can be painful, but not as painful as letting it rule over you.
   Shannon Ethridge
   Every Woman's Battle (2003)

10 No man can make a habit in a moment or break it in a moment. It is a matter of development, of growth. But at any moment man may begin to make or begin to break any habit.
   William George Jordan
   The Kingship of Self-Control (1898)

202 HAPPINESS
Happy is that people, whose God is the LORD.
PSALM 144:15

1   It is true that He desires our happiness, but that is neither the chief end of his work, nor an end to be compared with that of his glory.
   François Fénelon and Jeanne Guyon
   Spiritual Progress (17th century)

2   Thou should also know that the more a man sets himself to be receptive of divine influence, the happier he is: who most sets himself so, is the happiest.
   Meister Eckhart
   Meister Eckhart's Sermons (14th century)

3   There is no danger of developing eyestrain from looking on the bright side of things, so why not try it?
   Joyce Meyer
   Approval Addiction (2005)

4   When the dream planted in our heart is one that God has planted there, a strange happiness flows into us. At that moment all of the spiritual resources of the universe are released to help us.
   Catherine Marshall
   Beyond Ourselves (1961)

5   Happiness consists in finding out precisely what the "one thing necessary" may be, in our lives, and in gladly relinquishing all the rest. For then, by a divine paradox, we find that everything else is given us together with the one thing we needed.
   Thomas Merton
   No Man Is an Island (1955)

6   One reason so many people are unhappy is that, though they are busy pursuing happiness, they aren't all that sure what happiness is.
   Stuart Briscoe
   What Works When Life Doesn't (2004)

7   Happiness doesn't come to those who sit around waiting until life gets better. Happiness comes to those who grab hold of its proffered

hand in order to rise up and conquer their struggles.
Mike Mason
Champagne for the Soul (2003)

8 It takes wiliness to be happy. When cornered, we have to look at all the options and find a way out. We have to know how to outwit the heebie-jeebies, how to think faster than our blackest thought. . .often to be joyful we must go down—down through the noise of racing thoughts, down through the swirling chaos of circumstances, down through the deceptive appearances of life, down into the still waters and green pastures at the heart's core.
Mike Mason
Champagne for the Soul (2003)

203 HARDSHIPS (*see also* ADVERSITY; AFFLICTIONS; DIFFICULTIES; TESTING; TRIALS; TROUBLES)
Thou therefore endure hardness, as a good soldier of Jesus Christ.
2 TIMOTHY 2:3

1 God is more concerned with our condition than our comfort, and He will allow things to become uncomfortable in our lives to expose our true condition. He would rather have us temporarily uncomfortable than eternally tormented.
Lisa Bevere
Be Angry But Don't Blow It! (2000)

2 A crisis can blindside you, sabotaging your life, or it can provide a magical opportunity to pursue adventures and dreams never imagined.
Mary Ann Froehlich
When You're Facing the Empty Nest (2005)

3 If we had our way, probably none of us would ever choose hard times. Yet the hard experiences usually mold us into people of strength and character.
Thomas Jones
Single Again Handbook (1993)

4 No one can pilgrim to heaven without bearing the toils and hardships of the pilgrimage.
The Lutheran Witness (1885)

5 Crisis crushes. And in crushing, it often refines and purifies.
Charles Swindoll
Encourage Me (1982)

HARD WORK (*see* DILIGENCE)

204 HARMONY (*see also* UNITY)
Be of the same mind one toward another.
ROMANS 12:16

1 Is there any way to restore harmony to the world? It can be done only by someone coming in from eternity and stopping the false note in its wild flight.
Fulton Sheen
Life of Christ (1958)

2 My heart and mind were created to work in harmony together. Never has an individual been called upon to commit intellectual suicide in trusting Christ as Savior and Lord.
Josh McDowell
More Than a Carpenter (1977)

205 HATRED
Hatred stirreth up strifes: but love covereth all sins.
PROVERBS 10:12

1 A bond of hatred is just as strong as a bond of love. It just hurts more.
John Splinter
The Complete Divorce Recovery Handbook (1992)

2 In hatred, everybody loses.
David Augsburger
70 x 7: The Freedom of Forgiveness (1970)

3 Hidden hatred can sour a likable lady into a suspicious carper, a warm, understanding man into a caustic cynic.
David Augsburger
70 x 7: The Freedom of Forgiveness
(1970)

206 HEALING

Jesus went about all the cities and villages, teaching in their synagogues, and preaching the gospel of the kingdom, and healing every sickness and every disease among the people.
MATTHEW 9:35

1 You don't know how the Lord will redeem your life from the pit, but you must trust that He will. Like the little boy who offered the loaves and fish to the disciples without knowing how Jesus would use them, offer your circumstances to the Lord. He knows how to transform the worst of circumstances into miraculous healing.
Brendan O'Rourke and DeEtte Sauer
Hope of a Homecoming (2003)

2 I am not a faith healer because I've never healed anyone. It's just the mercy of God.
Kathryn Kuhlman
Kathryn Kuhlman (1976)

3 No, I do not know why all are not healed physically, but all can be healed spiritually, and that's the greatest miracle any human being can know.
Kathryn Kuhlman
Kathryn Kuhlman (1976)

4 Our Heavenly Healer often has to hurt us in order to heal us. We sometimes fail to recognize His mighty love in this, yet we are firmly held always in the Everlasting Arms.
Elisabeth Elliot
Secure in the Everlasting Arms (2002)

5 There are no short cuts to grief work. Healing takes time.
John Splinter
The Complete Divorce Recovery Handbook
(1992)

6 Reorient yourself to new circumstances. Let it hurt for a while. It will get better. Take your time. Heal slowly, from the inside out. Learn (or relearn) how to tap the amazing love and healing of Jesus Christ.
John Splinter
The Complete Divorce Recovery Handbook
(1992)

7 Truth with love brings healing.
David Augsburger
Caring Enough to Confront (2009)

8 Bridges can be built across the most troubled waters when Christ is the motivator.
Howard Hendricks
Heaven Help the Home (1973)

9 Because of covenant, wounds need not leave scars. They can become imprints for the expression of His grace if only you will take God at His word—a word that cannot be broken and that will never be changed.
Kay Arthur
Our Covenant God (1999)

10 Appropriating faith is not believing that God can but that He will. Those who claim to believe in healing, but say one word in favor of it and ten words against it, cannot produce faith for healing.
F. F. Bosworth
Christ the Healer (1924)

11 Jehovah Rapha, the God Who Heals, places His hand on the gaping wounds of our hearts and transforms the wounds into beautiful scars. Healing. . .it's what He does. Telling others about His healing power in our

lives. . .it's what He longs for us to do. That's how others will recognize His Son.

Sharon Jaynes
Your Scars Are Beautiful to God (2006)

12 There is a difference between being *forgiven* of a sin and being *healed* of a sin. Forgiveness is what takes place in God's heart. Healing is what happens in yours.

Joe Beam
Getting Past Guilt (2003)

207 HEALTH

Be not wise in thine own eyes: fear the LORD, and depart from evil. It shall be health to thy navel, and marrow to thy bones.
PROVERBS 3:7–8

1 As we practice the work of forgiveness, we discover more and more that forgiveness and healing are one.

Agnes Sanford
The Healing Light (1947)

2 Man frequently applies a remedy to the outward body, whilst the disease lies at the heart.

François Fénelon and Jeanne Guyon
Spiritual Progress (17th century)

3 It's the Lord who heals and He can use any method He chooses.

Jon Courson
Application Commentary (2005)

4 Cultivating a healthy spirit requires devoting time each day to the spiritual disciplines of Scripture memory, Bible reading, and praying.

Donna Partow
Becoming the Woman God Wants Me to Be (2008)

5 I wish you could convince yourself that God is often (in some sense) nearer to us and more effectually present with us, in sickness than in health.

Brother Lawrence
The Practice of the Presence of God (17th century)

6 Next to the office of him who ministers to men's souls, there is none really more useful and honorable than that of him who ministers to the soul's frail tabernacle—the body.

J. C. Ryle
The Upper Room (19th century)

208 HEAVEN

And I heard a great voice out of heaven saying, Behold, the tabernacle of God is with men, and he will dwell with them, and they shall be his people, and God himself shall be with them, and be their God.
REVELATION 21:3

1 Absent from flesh! then rise, my soul,
Where feet nor wings could never climb,
Beyond the heav'ns, where planets roll,
Measuring the cares and joys of time.

Isaac Watts
"Absent from Flesh! O Blissful Thought!" hymn (18th century)

2 What is heaven, but to be with God, to dwell with him, to realize that God is mine, and I am his?

Charles Spurgeon
"God in the Covenant" sermon (1856)

3 Talk of princes, and kings, and potentates: Their inheritance is but a pitiful foot of land, across which the bird's wing can soon direct its flight; but the broad acres of the Christian cannot be measured by eternity. He is rich, without a limit to his wealth. He is blessed, without a boundary to his bliss.

Charles Spurgeon
"The Fatherhood of God" sermon (1858)

4 Jesus is what makes heaven heaven.
Jon Courson
Application Commentary (2003)

5 Cemeteries interrupt the finest families.
Retirement finds the best employees. Age
withers the strongest bodies. With life comes
change. But with change comes the reassuring
appreciation of heaven's permanence.
Max Lucado
It's Not About Me (2004)

6 Our way to heaven lies through the
wilderness of this world.
Matthew Henry
Commentary on the Whole Bible (1706)

7 Earth is embittered to us, that heaven may
be endeared.
Matthew Henry
Commentary on the Whole Bible (1706)

8 I do not know how near it may be to us;
it may be that some of us will be ushered very
soon into the presence of the King. One gaze
at Him will be enough to reward us for all we
have had to bear. Yes, there is peace for the
past, grace for the present, and glory for the
future.
D. L. Moody
Twelve Select Sermons (1884)

9 Had Christ remained on earth, sight would
have taken the place of faith. In Heaven,
there will be no faith, because His followers
will see; there will be no hope, because they
will possess; but there will be love, for love
endureth forever!
Fulton Sheen
Life of Christ (1958)

10 If one Indian ruler could prepare
something as breathtakingly beautiful as
the Taj Mahal as a tomb for his wife of just
fourteen years, what must God be preparing
as a home where He will live forever and ever
with His people whom He loves?
Anne Graham Lotz
Heaven: My Father's House (2002)

11 Make no mistake about it! Heaven is a
home populated by the Lord and his loved
ones who have made the deliberate choice to
be there.
Anne Graham Lotz
Heaven: My Father's House (2002)

12 Based on your choices you have made, if
you were to die today, would you be inside or
outside of Heaven's gates?
Anne Graham Lotz
Heaven: My Father's House (2002)

13 Like a child who suddenly stops sobbing
when he is clasped in the arms of his mother,
such will be the grip of heaven upon our souls.
Ravi Zacharias
Recapture the Wonder (2003)

14 Heaven is as near to our souls, as this world
is to our bodies; and we are created, we are
redeemed, to have our conversation in it.
William Law
The Spirit of Prayer (1750)

15 If this world is all we have and there's no
hope for a world to come, we're doomed to
lives of misery.
Tullian Tchividjian
Do I Know God? (2007)

16 So that if in this life we would enjoy the
peace of paradise, we must accustom ourselves
to a familiar, humble, affectionate conversation
with Him.
Brother Lawrence
The Practice of the Presence of God
(17th century)

17 From the glimpses of heaven given us by
Jesus, we know that whatever else heaven is,
it's full of Joy.
Ken Gire
Reflections on Your Life (1998)

18 Heaven is not a state of mind. Heaven is reality itself.
C. S. Lewis
The Great Divorce (1946)

19 None will walk the celestial pavement of heaven but those washed in the blood.
D. L. Moody
Wondrous Love (1876)

20 If you don't enter the kingdom of heaven by God's way, you cannot enter at all.
D. L. Moody
Weighed and Wanting (19th century)

21 I want to know one thing—the way to heaven; how to land safe on that happy shore.
John Wesley
Sermons on Several Occasions (18th century)

22 When he came to expel Adam out of his forfeited paradise, he assures him of one that should open the gates of the heavenly paradise to him.
Stephen Charnock
Discourse of God's being the Author of Reconciliation (17th century)

23 He told us—and it is only because we are so accustomed to it that we do not wonder more at the magnificence of the conception—that when our place in this world should know us no more there would be another place ready for us.
Henry Drummond
"Why Christ Must Depart" sermon (19th century)

24 He that has long been on the road to Heaven finds that there was good reason why it was promised that his shoes should be iron and brass, for the road is rough.
Charles Spurgeon
All of Grace (19th century)

25 It will amaze the universe to see us enter the pearly gate, blameless in the day of our Lord Jesus Christ.
Charles Spurgeon
All of Grace (19th century)

26 Again I charge you, MEET ME IN HEAVEN.
Charles Spurgeon
All of Grace (19th century)

27 We have a glorious future awaiting us beyond death's door.
Kirk Cameron and Ray Comfort
Life's Emergency Handbook (2002)

28 The society of heaven will be select. No one who studies Scripture can doubt that.
D. L. Moody
Heaven (1881)

29 There are a good many kinds of aristocracy in this world, but the aristocracy of heaven will be holiness.
D. L. Moody
Heaven (1881)

209 HELL

If thy hand offend thee, cut it off: it is better for thee to enter into life maimed, than having two hands to go into hell, into the fire that never shall be quenched.
MARK 9:43

1 O brethren, above all things shun hypocrisy. If ye mean to be damned, make up your minds to it, and be damned like honest men; but do not, I beseech you, pretend to go to heaven while all the time you are going to hell.
Charles Spurgeon
"God, the All-Seeing One" sermon (1858)

2 The urgency of the gospel is utterly lost when the preacher denies the reality or severity of everlasting punishment.
John MacArthur
Ashamed of the Gospel (1993)

3 Some people seem to be under the delusion that hell has evaporated, or at least that all intelligent people have stopped believing in it.
D. James Kennedy
Why I Believe (1980)

4 The main reason we believe in hell is because Jesus Christ declares that it is so.
D. James Kennedy
Why I Believe (1980)

5 A lot of people talk about hell, use it to tell others where to go, but do not want to be confronted with the thought that it might be their destination.
Billy Graham
Facing Death and the Life After (1987)

6 Men are not sent to hell because of being murderers or liars, they are sent to hell because they are unrighteous.
David Jeremiah
Escape the Coming Night (1990)

7 While the Lord is well-pleased in saving sinners through the righteousness of Christ, he will also glorify his justice, by punishing all proud despisers.
Matthew Henry
Commentary on the Whole Bible (1706)

8 Sinners don't flee from the wrath to come because they don't believe there is a wrath to come.
Ray Comfort
Hell's Best Kept Secret (1989)

9 Hell is out of fashion today, but it is not out of business! Just because we don't like the idea of hell doesn't mean that it does not exist. Many people say they don't believe in hell, so hell can't exist. But remember: it doesn't matter what we believe; it matters what is true.
Mark Cahill
One Heartbeat Away (2005)

10 The unconverted walk over the pit of hell on a rotten bridge.
Jonathan Edwards
"Sinners in the Hands of an Angry God" sermon (1741)

11 Natural men are held in the hand of God over the pit of hell.
Jonathan Edwards
"Sinners in the Hands of an Angry God" sermon (1741)

12 There is nothing that keeps wicked men, at any one moment, out of hell, but the mere pleasure of God.
Jonathan Edwards
"Sinners in the Hands of an Angry God" sermon (1741)

13 One phrase summarizes the horror of hell. "God isn't there."
Max Lucado
Just Like Jesus (1998)

14 When one asked, where God was before heaven was created? St Augustine answered: He was in himself. When another asked me the same question, I said: He was building hell for such idle, presumptuous, fluttering and inquisitive spirits as you.
Martin Luther
Table Talk (16th century)

15 The same conscience there is in men of a future judgment, bears witness also of the truth of future punishments.
Thomas Boston
Human Nature in Its Fourfold State (1830)

16 As the saints in heaven are advanced to the highest pitch of happiness, so the damned in hell arrive at the height of misery.
Thomas Boston
Human Nature in Its Fourfold State (1830)

17 Men are punished by God for their sins often visibly, always secretly, either in this life or after death.
Augustine
The City of God (5th century)

18 It is He who gave to this intellectual nature free-will of such a kind, that if he wished to forsake God his blessedness, misery should forthwith result.
Augustine
The City of God (5th century)

19 The Hell of the Bible is horrible beyond description, and the hypotheses of this hour cannot exceed it.
William Elbert Munsey
Eternal Retribution (1951)

20 Without him, we are combustible matter before a consuming fire, and cannot approach to the throne of God with any success.
Stephen Charnock
Discourse on the Cleansing Virtue of Christ's Blood (17th century)

21 Hell is as real to those who die without Christ as heaven is to the child of God.
Charles Swindoll
"Visiting the Real Twilight Zone" sermon (1985)

22 What if God withdraw his patience and sustenation, and let you drop into hell while you are quarrelling with his word?—Will you then believe that there is no hell?
Richard Baxter
A Call to the Unconverted, to Turn and Live (17th century)

23 There is something so shocking in the consideration of eternal torments, and seemingly such an infinite disproportion between an endless duration of pain, and short life spent in pleasure, that men (some at least of them) can scarcely be brought to confess it as an article of their faith, that an eternity of misery awaits the wicked in a future state.
George Whitefield (18th century)
quoted in *Selected Sermons of George Whitefield*

24 That the torments reserved for the wicked hereafter, are eternal.
George Whitefield (18th century)
quoted in *Selected Sermons of George Whitefield*

25 There cannot be one argument urged, why God should reward his saints with everlasting happiness, which will not equally prove that he ought to punish sinners with eternal misery.
George Whitefield (18th century)
quoted in *Selected Sermons of George Whitefield*

26 Hell is God's tribute to the freedom he gave each of us to choose whom we would serve; it is a recognition that our decisions have a significance that extends far down the reaches of foreverness.
James Sire
The Universe Next Door (1976)

27 Philosophically there must be a hell. That is the name for the place where God is not; for the place where they will gather together who insist on leaving God out. God out! There can be no worse hell than that! God away! Man held back by no restraints!
Samuel Gordon
Quiet Talks on Prayer (1904)

28 Every man plots how he may escape damnation.
Jonathan Edwards
"Sinners in the Hands of an Angry God" sermon (1741)

210 HERESY
A man that is an heretick after the first and second admonition reject.
TITUS 3:10

1 There is as much danger from false brethren, as from open enemies.
Matthew Henry
Commentary on the Whole Bible (1706)

2   When false teaching goes unchallenged,
it breeds more confusion and draws still more
shallow and insincere people into the fold.
> John MacArthur
> *The Truth War* (2007)

3   It is better to be divided by Truth than be
united by error.
> Adrian Rogers
> *Unmasking False Prophets* (2007)

4   It is wrong to tell a lie. Even worse, to
teach a lie. But my friend, it is monstrous
to teach a lie about God. There is no greater
crime than to be a false prophet or to be a false
teacher. God does not take it lightly.
> Adrian Rogers
> *Unmasking False Prophets* (2007)

5   Some people tell us it does not make any
difference what a man believes if he is only
sincere. One church is just as good as another
if you are only sincere. I do not believe any
greater delusion ever came out of the pit of
hell than that.
> D. L. Moody
> *Wondrous Love* (1876)

211 HOLIDAYS
(*see also* CHRISTMAS; EASTER)
This day is holy unto our LORD: neither be ye sorry;
for the joy of the LORD is your strength.
NEHEMIAH 8:10

1   Another year is dawning, dear Father, let it be
In working or in waiting, another year with
Thee.
> Frances Ridley Havergal
> "Another Year Is Dawning" hymn (1874)

2   You set the course for the entire year by
what you do with those first few days of each
New Year.
> Jentezen Franklin
> *Fasting* (2008)

3   I see not a step before me as I tread on
another year;
But I've left the Past in God's keeping—the
Future
His mercy shall clear;
And what looks dark in the distance may
brighten as I draw near.
> Mary Gardiner Brainard
> "Not Knowing" poem (19th century)

212 HOLINESS
Give unto the LORD the glory due unto his name;
worship the LORD in the beauty of holiness.
PSALM 29:2

1   We must wear our piety, not as some
holiday garment, but as our everyday dress.
> Charles Spurgeon
> "Faith Versus Sight" sermon (1866)

2   Holiness and usefulness go hand in hand.
> Elizabeth Prentiss
> *More Love to Thee: The Life and Letters*
> *of Elizabeth Prentiss* (1882)

3   We are called to live lives that more
fully reflect God's character. Holiness is our
responsibility and our destiny. It is God's
work in us, work to which we are called as co-
laborers. What a blessing that is!
> Mark Dever
> *Twelve Challenges Churches Face* (2008)

4   You can't get holy in a hurry.
> Bruce Bickel and Stan Jantz
> *God Is in the Small Stuff* (1998)

5   For who does not know, that it is better to
be pure and holy, than to talk about purity and
holiness?
> William Law
> *A Serious Call to a Devout and Holy Life*
> (1729)

6 Nothing is pressed more earnestly in the Scriptures, than to walk as becomes those called to Christ's kingdom and glory.
Matthew Henry
Commentary on the Whole Bible (1706)

7 Holiness is not some nebulous thing. It's a series of right choices.
Stephen Arterburn, Fred Stoeker, and Mike Yorkey
Every Man's Battle (2000)

8 We cannot make ourselves holy. We can become holy only through the power of Christ and the working of the Holy Spirit in our lives. Through a pure and clean life, we reveal to our world the reality of holy God in our lives.
Henry and Tom Blackaby
The Man God Uses (1999)

9 Although God will grant Christlikeness to us when Jesus returns, until then He intends for us to grow toward Christlikeness. We aren't merely to wait for holiness, we're to pursue it.
Donald Whitney
Spiritual Disciplines for the Christian Life (1991)

10 It's dangerous to assume that because a man is drawn to holiness in his study that he is thereby a holy man. I am sure that the reason that I have a deep hunger to learn of the holiness of God is precisely because I am not holy.
R. C. Sproul
The Holiness of God (20th century)

11 Because God is holy, He cannot look on sin with indifference.
Josh and Sean McDowell
Evidence for the Resurrection (2009)

12 If you seek holiness of life, I encourage you to make a good friend of the Sermon on the Mount.
Richard Foster
Streams of Living Water (1998)

13 A true saint greatly delights in holiness; it is a most beautiful thing in his eyes; and God's work, in savingly renewing and making holy and happy, a poor, and before perishing soul, appears to him a most glorious work.
Jonathan Edwards
A Treatise Concerning Religious Affections (18th century)

14 He that would truly work for God must follow after holiness.
Andrew Murray
Working for God (1901)

15 God promises that if we pursue holiness, happiness will come.
J. I. Packer
J. I. Packer Answers Questions for Today (2001)

213 HOLY SPIRIT
The grace of the Lord Jesus Christ, and the love of God, and the communion of the Holy Ghost, be with you all.
2 CORINTHIANS 13:14

General

1 God has given His people what we need to fill up when we run low. It's the incredible gift of Himself, dwelling inside us. It's the person of God we call the Holy Spirit.
Jill Briscoe
A Little Pot of Oil (2003)

2 You may have no family, no food, no clothes, no future, no spouse, no health, or no children, yet be rich beyond your wildest dreams because you have the Holy Spirit in your life.
Jill Briscoe
A Little Pot of Oil (2003)

3 Jesus knows we need power to live and make courageous choices. He sent the Holy Spirit to inhabit the lives of true believers for the purpose of empowering us, guiding us, and teaching us how to live for God.
Dennis and Barbara Rainey
Pressure Proof Your Marriage (2003)

4   Being filled and led by the Spirit may take you places you never planned; but the will of God will never lead you where the grace of God cannot keep you.
    Neil Anderson
    Victory Over the Darkness (1990)

5   Walking by the Spirit is relationship, not regimentation.
    Neil Anderson
    Victory Over the Darkness (1990)

6 You cannot convince the Holy Spirit to do what He doesn't want to do, and He always wants to do the Father's will.
    Henry and Mel Blackaby
    What's So Spiritual About Your Gifts? (2004)

7   The Holy Spirit is the One who is poured out upon you like a healing balm—to sooth, to calm, and to comfort. He is the One who renews your strength, revives your spirit, refills your cup, restores your strength, and refreshes your spirit.
    Roy Lessin
    Today Is Your Best Day (2006)

8   The Holy Spirit of the living God is engaging all God's people with a renewing, reviving call to open to the glory of His grace in Holy Spirit fullness. The objective of this experience is not to introduce us to a glib, giddy kind of "charismania," but to equip, prepare, and fortify us against the spirits of darkness, deception, and destruction.
    Jack Hayford
    Glory on Your House (1991)

9   The Holy Spirit's power cannot be harnessed. His power cannot be used to accomplish anything other than the Father's will. He is not a candy dispenser. He is not a vending machine. He is not a genie waiting for someone to rub His lamp the right way. He is holy God.
    Charles Stanley
    The Wonderful Spirit-Filled Life (1992)

10 I have learned to be obedient to the Holy Spirit. I cannot use the Holy Spirit; He only uses me.
    Kathryn Kuhlman
    Kathryn Kuhlman (1976)

11 When God knocks, open the door and open your heart to the Holy Spirit.
    Susan McCarthy Peabody
    Alphabet Soup for Christian Living (2007)

12 Our blessed Saviour Christ himself preaches that the Holy Ghost is everlasting and Almighty God.
    Martin Luther
    Table Talk (16th century)

13 The Holy Spirit always upsets the status quo.
    Tony Campolo
    How to Be Pentecostal without Speaking in Tongues (1991)

14 The Holy Spirit does not flow through methods but through men.
    E. M. Bounds
    Power Through Prayer (1906)

15 We need words to make ourselves intelligible to other people but not to the Spirit.
    Jean-Nicholas Grou
    How to Pray (18th century)

Gifts of

16 If we seek the gifts of the Spirit and not the Holy Spirit Himself, we'll always focus on self. We must learn to understand that there are no gifts apart from an intimate relationship with the Spirit.
    Henry and Mel Blackaby
    What's So Spiritual About Your Gifts? (2004)

17 The Holy Spirit gives boldness. We don't even have to ask Him for it. It just comes with the Holy Spirit.
  Kathryn Kuhlman
  Kathryn Kuhlman (1976)

18 You can never be "good enough" on your own to please God. Only the Holy Spirit has what it takes to give us what it takes to please God: His essential goodness reproduced in us.
  Lloyd John Ogilvie
  The Magnificent Vision (1980)

19 When the believer does not know that Christ is living in him, does not know the Spirit and power of God working in him, there may be much earnestness and diligence, with little that lasts for eternity.
  Andrew Murray
  Working for God (1901)

Living in the

20 To live according to the Spirit means first of all to think in alignment with what the Spirit is thinking. It's to think in terms of what God says about everything, not what you're saying or thinking yourself or what anybody else says about you.
  Tony Evans
  The Fire That Ignites (2003)

21 How do you know when you're walking in the Spirit? You know it when you're living a life of prayer, because prayer is the proof of dependence on the Spirit.
  Tony Evans
  The Fire That Ignites (2003)

22 Those who have the gale of the Holy Spirit go forward even in sleep.
  Brother Lawrence
  The Practice of the Presence of God
  (17th century)

23 For we must first hear the Word, and then afterwards the Holy Ghost works in our hearts; he works in the hearts of whom he will, and how he will, but never without the Word.
  Martin Luther
  Table Talk (16th century)

24 Allow yourself to be led by the Spirit of God. That Spirit will unerringly conduct you to the end purpose for which your soul was created. . .the enjoyment of God.
  Jeanne Guyon
  Experiencing the Depths of Jesus Christ
  (1685)

25 No relationship, marriage, or family will ever be all that God intended unless its members are experiencing God at work in their lives through the enabling work of the Holy Spirit.
  Dennis and Barbara Rainey
  Moments Together (2004)

26 Without a complete dependence upon the Holy Spirit we can only fail.
  A. W. Tozer
  Whatever Happened to Worship?
  (20th century)

27 The Holy Spirit never enters a man and lets him live like the world. You can be sure of that.
  A. W. Tozer
  "Who Is the Holy Spirit?" sermon
  (20th century)

28 God permits troubles to beset His children, but He also refreshes them. He grants them respite when the heart is still and the soul joyous, and you will agree with me that such moments of the secret joy of the Spirit are far more precious than the highest pleasures this world can offer.
  The Lutheran Witness (1885)

Role of

29 The Holy Spirit's job is to make God's presence evident and perceptible in this world, and He does that most noticeably through the church.
Tony Evans
The Fire That Ignites (2003)

30 If the Christian life is simply a matter of doing our best, there was no need for God to send the Holy Spirit to help us.
Charles Stanley
The Wonderful Spirit-Filled Life (1992)

31 The Holy Spirit guides the believer in the way of wisdom. To refuse to live wisely is to ignore the leading of the Holy Spirit.
Charles Stanley
The Wonderful Spirit-Filled Life (1992)

32 The Holy Spirit is heaven's matchmaker. He brings us to Christ.
Colin Smith
Unlocking the Bible Story (2002)

33 Fire converts wood into its own likeness, and the stronger the wind blows, the greater grows the fire. Now by the fire understand love, and by the wind the Holy Spirit.
Meister Eckhart
Meister Eckhart's Sermons (14th century)

34 It is a ministry of the Holy Spirit to drive the deadness of our souls away and to banish the apathy that infects most other people.
Tony Campolo
How to Be Pentecostal without Speaking in Tongues (1991)

35 We must understand that the Holy Spirit lives in us to empower us to succeed at whatever God calls us to do.
T. D. Jakes
Intimacy with God (2000)

36 The Spirit of God is a holy spirit and His work is to make free from the power of sin and death.
Andrew Murray
Master's Indwelling (1895)

37 The Holy Spirit can cast out the evil spirit of the fear of man. He can make the coward brave.
Charles Spurgeon
All of Grace (19th century)

38 A man may easier see without eyes, speak without tongue, than truly mortify one sin without the Spirit.
John Owen
Of the Mortification of Sin in Believers (1656)

39 Most of us don't really know the deep thoughts and intentions of our own hearts; therefore we must rely upon the Spirit of God to try, to prove and to reveal that which is within us.
Jane Hamon
Dreams and Visions (2000)

40 The stirring of spiritual desire indicates that God's Spirit is already at work within us, drawing us to Himself.
Ruth Haley Barton
Sacred Rhythms (2006)

214 HOME
Let them learn first to shew piety at home...
1 TIMOTHY 5:4

1 Righteousness must not only be found in our pulpits, but in our homes. The home is the church in miniature.
Steve Farrar
Point Man (1990)

2 Seeing home as sacred space motivates us to invest our time and energy here.
Kathy Coffey
God Knows Parenting Is a Wild Ride (2002)

3   Home is the arena for our most influential work.
   Kathy Coffey
   God Knows Parenting Is a Wild Ride (2002)

4   It is essential to see that home is the place where we most often participate in God's holiness, and bring God's compassion and creativity to our most intimate world.
   Kathy Coffey
   God Knows Parenting Is a Wild Ride (2002)

5   When we build a house, we add paint and paper to the walls. When we build a home, we use family photos.
   Al Hartley
   It Takes a Family (1996)

6   There is no place like home when the people who live there make "building one another" their highest priority.
   Gordon MacDonald
   There's No Place Like Home (1990)

7   There's no place like home if those in charge care passionately for the moral and spiritual "messages" that are allowed in the door.
   Gordon MacDonald
   There's No Place Like Home (1990)

8   The Christian home must blossom in a field of weeds.
   Howard Hendricks
   Heaven Help the Home (1973)

9   The primary purpose of a home is to reflect and to distribute the love of Christ. Anything that usurps that is idolatrous.
   Ravi Zacharias
   Jesus Among Other Gods (2000)

10 A truly Christian home is a place where sinners live; but it is also a place where the members of that home admit that fact and understand the problem, know what to do about it, and as a result grow by grace.
   Jay Adams
   Christian Living in the Home (1972)

11 Home is the most important place for a man to be affirmed. If a man knows that his wife believes in him, he is empowered to do better in every area of his life. A man tends to think of life as a competition and a battle, and he can energetically duke it out if he can come home to someone who supports him unconditionally, who will wipe his brow and tell him he can do it.
   Shaunti Feldhahn
   For Women Only (2004)

215 HONESTY

That ye may walk honestly...
1 THESSALONIANS 4:12

1   Scrupulous truthfulness should always characterize everyone who stands up to proclaim the truth of God.
   Charles Spurgeon
   Autobiography (1897)

2   Honesty, or dishonesty, is shown in every little act of life.
   Mabel Hale
   Beautiful Girlhood (1922)

3   Sometimes, we withhold the truth because we're afraid our honesty will hurt someone's feelings. But we pay a high price when we hold things in, particularly when we know we've been dishonest on some level. We don't need ulcers and all kinds of other problems that result from a disturbed conscience. We certainly don't need to "tell all," especially if it would be unkind to do so, but dishonesty is never right.
   Dan Seaborn
   26 Words That Will Improve the Way You Do Family (2002)

4   Many of us mistakenly believe that God doesn't want us to be honest about our lives. We think that He will be upset with us if we tell Him how we really feel. But the Scriptures tell us that God does not want us to be superficial in our relationship with Him, with others, or in our own lives.
Robert McGee
The Search for Significance (1998)

5   Honesty is like a flu shot. It may give you a short, sharp pain, but it keeps you healthier in the long run.
Willard Harley Jr.
His Needs, Her Needs for Parents (2003)

6   Truthfulness is much more than the absence of lies. It is genuine communication of minds and hearts. Real truthfulness reflects the character of God, who is always exactly what He says he is, and who speaks painful but joyful truth, never any small talk to our hearts. Think of Jesus: ever kind, but relentlessly truthful.
Tim Stafford
Never Mind the Joneses (2004)

7   To be really truthful, we have to do more than stop lying. Really, most of the work is positively learning how to speak the whole truth in love. However, truthfulness has to begin with a process of purification. Insincerity, lies, and deception create such a hall of mirrors that truth, when someone speaks it, hardly registers.
Tim Stafford
Never Mind the Joneses (2004)

8   Always meet with God as a God who desires truth in the inward parts. In all your confession of sin, in all your religion, in your whole existence, let truth in the inward parts be your desire, as it is the desire of God.
Andrew Murray
Have Mercy Upon Me (1896)

216 HONOR (*see also* RIGHTEOUSNESS; VIRTUE)

He that followeth after righteousness and mercy findeth life, righteousness, and honour.
PROVERBS 21:21

1   "Honor all." The application of this command could significantly shatter hell's viselike grip on individuals and cultures and drastically affect how future generations view Christ and His claims.
Fawn Parish
Honor: What Love Looks Like (1999)

2   When honor is unleashed, it can reveal the heart of God to hardened individuals and to whole cultures, opening them up to their intended destiny of eternal intimacy with God.
Fawn Parish
Honor: What Love Looks Like (1999)

3   If the primary reason that we honor God is our profit, then we will discover there are many occasions where honoring him offers no apparent benefit. In those moments, we will turn from his ways unless what motivates us is a desire to honor God for his grace rather than a seeking after our own benefit.
Bryan Chapell
Holiness by Grace (2001)

4   True honor is not the honor that one claims for oneself, but rather it is the honor that is conferred on one by others.
J. Dwight Pentecost
The Parables of Jesus (1982)

217 HOPE

Why art thou cast down, O my soul? and why art thou disquieted within me? hope thou in God.
PSALM 42:11

1   All My Hope on God Is Founded.
Joachim Neander hymn title
(17th century)

2 What is there, what can there be, to make life worthwhile, apart from the Christian Hope?
Henry H. Halley
Pocket Bible Handbook (1948)

3 Hope sees a crown in reserve, mansions in readiness, and Jesus himself preparing a place for us, and by the rapturous sight she sustains the soul under the sorrows of the hour.
Charles Spurgeon
"The Holy Spirit's Intercession" sermon (1880)

4 Hope is one of the Theological virtues. This means that a continual looking forward to the eternal world is not (as some modern people think) a form of escapism or wishful thinking, but one of the things a Christian is meant to do.
C. S. Lewis
Mere Christianity (1952)

5 Given the choice of viewing life through the rose-colored glasses of hope rather than the dark blinders of sadness, anger, and worry, wouldn't it be far better to assume you'll find a foothold amid the chaos? After all, even if you go under, won't you have enjoyed the swim all the more if you sustain hope until the end rather than sinking into despair?
Susan Vaughn
Half Empty, Half Full (2000)

6 To lose hope has the same effect on our heart as it would be to stop breathing.
Brent Curtis
The Sacred Romance (1997)

7 Keep dreaming the dream that God has put into your heart.
Jentezen Franklin
Believe That You Can (2008)

8 At the bottom of the pit is not apathy, not hopelessness, not despair. At the bottom of the pit is the rule of God!
Martin Bell
Street Singing and Preaching (1991)

9 Is it not most hopeful for men that a Man is now on the throne of the universe?
Charles Spurgeon
All of Grace (19th century)

10 If the Christian hope be not founded upon reason and truth, but must be given up as fabulous and mere delusion, we are left without hope, and we must sink into the most gloomy darkness and despair.
Samuel Hopkins
"The Reason of the Hope of a Christian" sermon (1803)

11 In Jesus Christ, God experienced the greatest depths of pain. Therefore, though Christianity does not provide the reason for each experience of pain, it provides deep resources for actually facing suffering with hope and courage rather than bitterness and despair.
Timothy Keller
The Reason for God (2008)

12 Hope is like a magnet that draws you toward your goal.
H. Norman Wright
Freedom from the Grip of Fear (1989)

13 Hope lives even when the body is dying.
Bill Kemp and Diane Kerner Arnett
Going Home (2005)

HOPELESSNESS (*see* DESPAIR)

218 HOSPITALITY
Use hospitality one to another without grudging.
1 PETER 4:9

1 When we are willing to open our homes, our kitchens, our living rooms, and most of all our hearts to others, God can make exciting things happen.
Rachael Crabb and Raeann Hart
The Personal Touch (1990)

2 The emphasis in our practice of hospitality should be on how we give of ourselves to minister to others—not on how we perform to entertain others.

> Rachael Crabb and Raeann Hart
> *The Personal Touch* (1990)

3 Hospitality is the social staff of life, a starting point for discourse and interaction.

> Thea Jarvis
> *Everyday Hospitality* (2007)

4 Ideally, hospitality is the outward expression of an inner attitude, a virtue that erupts from the heart, spilling out toward others.

> Thea Jarvis
> *Everyday Hospitality* (2007)

5 Hospitality is contagious.

> Thea Jarvis
> *Everyday Hospitality* (2007)

219 HUMANITY

When I consider thy heavens, the work of thy fingers, the moon and the stars, which thou hast ordained; What is man, that thou art mindful of him? and the son of man, that thou visitest him?
PSALM 8:3–4

1 Man, but a particle of Thy creation. . .

> Augustine
> *Confessions* (4th century)

2 The world is a sort of macrocosm of which man is a microcosm, and what is true of the nations of the world is true of individuals.

> Martyn Lloyd-Jones
> *The Cross* (1986)

3 I have no sympathy with the doctrine of universal brotherhood, and universal fatherhood; I don't believe one word of it. If a man lives in the flesh and serves the flesh, he is a child of the devil. That is pretty strong language, but it is what Christ said.

> D.L. Moody
> "The Eighth Chapter of Romans" sermon (19th century)

4 If the human race in its present state moved into the New Jerusalem today, it would be hell by tomorrow.

> Vance Havner
> *Jesus Only* (1946)

5 Humanism places mankind at the center of all things and makes him the measure of all things.

> Bill Bright and John Damoose
> *Red Sky in the Morning* (1998)

6 And thus ever, by day and night, under the sun and under the stars, climbing the dusty hills and toiling along the weary plains, journeying by land and journeying by sea, coming and going so strangely, to meet and to act and react on one another, move all we restless travellers through the pilgrimage of life.

> Charles Dickens
> *Little Dorrit* (1857)

7 Each and every person has the same measure of value to God.

> Scott Hinkle
> *Recapturing the Primary Purpose* (2005)

8 He was made of the dust of the ground, a very unlikely thing to make man of; but the same infinite power that made the world of nothing made man, its masterpiece, of next to nothing. He was not made of gold-dust, powder of pearl, or diamond dust, but common dust, dust of the ground. Our fabric is earthly, and the fashioning of it like that of an earthen vessel. What have we then to be proud of?

> Matthew Henry
> *Commentary on the Whole Bible* (1706)

9   God raised Jesus from the dead to the end that we should be clear—once and for all—that there is nothing more important than being human. Our lives have eternal significance. And no one—absolutely no one—is expendable.
   Martin Bell
   The Way of the Wolf (1968)

10 We are not only undeserving, but ill-deserving.
   Thomas Manton
   One Hundred and Ninety Sermons on the Hundred and Nineteenth Psalm (17th century)

11 The highest angel has nothing of its own that it can offer unto God, no more light, love, purity, perfection, and glorious hallelujahs, that spring from itself, or its own powers, than the poorest creature upon earth.
   William Law
   An Humble, Affectionate, and Earnest Address (1761)

12 If man is not made for God, why is he not happy except in God? If man is made for God, why is he so opposed to God?
   Blaise Pascal
   Pensées (17th century)

13 You are more evil than you have ever feared, and more loved than you have ever hoped.
   Mark Driscoll and Gerry Breshears
   Death by Love (2008)

14 Minor shades of moral difference fade away before the one radical division of mankind into children of light and children of darkness.
   Alexander Balmain Bruce
   Apologetics, or Christianity Defensively Stated (1892)

15 All men are either sons of God or sons of the devil.
   Alexander Balmain Bruce
   Apologetics, or Christianity Defensively Stated (1892)

16 If you have a narrow view of people, go places you have never gone, meet the kind of people you do not know, and do things you have not done before.
   John Maxwell
   Winning with People (2004)

220 HUMAN NATURE
But Jesus did not commit himself unto them, because he knew all men, and needed not that any should testify of man: for he knew what was in man.
JOHN 2:24–25

1   The problem with a living sacrifice, is that it can crawl off the altar, and we often do that.
   Rick Warren
   The Purpose-Driven Life (2002)

2   Our inner "self" doesn't want to dump God entirely, just keep Him at a comfortable distance.
   Charles Swindoll
   Improving Your Serve (1981)

3   When it comes to accepting the truth about ourselves, things have not changed much since Adam first blamed Eve.
   Henry Cloud and John Townsend
   Boundaries Face to Face (2003)

4   Between the frailty of our bodies and the limitations of our minds, we humans have ample proof that we are not gods.
   Jeff Walling
   Until I Return (2000)

5   It seems to be a law of man's intelligent nature that when accused of wrong, either by his conscience or by any other agent, he must either confess or justify.
   Charles Finney
   "The Sinner's Excuses Answered" sermon (19th century)

6 There are no other principles, which human nature is under the influence of, that will ever make men conscientious, but one of these two, fear or love.

Jonathan Edwards
A Treatise Concerning Religious Affections (18th century)

7 It is not the design of Christ to take away our humanity, but to sanctify it.

Kim Thomas
Living in the Sacred Now (2001)

8 When a man fails in life he usually says, "I am as God made me." When he succeeds he proudly proclaims himself a "self-made man."

William George Jordan
The Kingship of Self-Control (1898)

221 HUMILITY (*see also* GENTLENESS; MEEKNESS)

The fear of the LORD is the instruction of wisdom; and before honour is humility.

PROVERBS 15:33

1 Jesus comes to little ones.

Charles Spurgeon
"The Incarnation and Birth of Christ" sermon (1855)

2 Be content to walk your weary way, through the fields of poverty, or up the hills of affliction; by-and-bye ye shall reign with Christ, for he has "made us kings and priests unto God, and we shall reign for ever and ever."

Charles Spurgeon
"Christ Exalted" sermon (1856)

3 Catch [a man] at the moment when he is really poor in spirit and smuggle into his mind the gratifying reflection, "By jove! I'm being humble," and almost immediately pride—pride at his own humility—will appear.

C. S. Lewis
The Screwtape Letters (1941)

4 As sinfully and culturally defined, pursuing greatness looks like this: Individuals motivated by self-interest, self-indulgence, and a false sense of self-sufficiency pursue selfish ambition for the purpose of self-glorification. Contrast that with the pursuit of true greatness as biblically defined: Serving others for the glory of God. This is the genuine expression of humility; this is true greatness as the Savior defined it.

C. J. Mahaney
Humility: True Greatness (2005)

5 It takes a lot of humility to cry aloud to God in our distress. And humility before the living God is precisely what we need.

Bill Gothard
The Power of Crying Out (2002)

6 A humble person is not one who thinks little of himself, hangs his head, and says, "I'm nothing." Rather, he is one who depends wholly on the Lord for everything, in every circumstance.

David Wilkerson
Revival on Broadway! (1996)

7 Humility retires itself from the public gaze.

E. M. Bounds
The Essentials of Prayer (19th century)

8 Humility never exalts itself.

E. M. Bounds
The Essentials of Prayer (19th century)

9 The preoccupation with self is the enemy of humility.

Franklin Graham
All for Jesus (2003)

10 Cost what it may, and in spite of my fears and speculations, I desire to become lowly and a fool, still more despicable in my own eyes than in those of the wise in their own conceit.

François Fénelon and Jeanne Guyon
Spiritual Progress (17th century)

11 True humility consists in a deep view of our utter unworthiness, and in an absolute abandonment to God, without the slightest doubt that He will do the greatest things in us.
François Fénelon and Jeanne Guyon
Spiritual Progress (17th century)

12 The truly humble soul is not surprised at its defects or failings; and the more miserable it beholds itself, the more it abandons itself to God, and presses for a more intimate alliance with Him, seeing the need it has of his aid.
François Fénelon and Jeanne Guyon
Spiritual Progress (17th century)

13 Humility gladly submits to God's rightful place as Lord. It produces a right spirit toward others and a grateful sense of submission to God's providing work on our behalf.
Joseph Stowell
Tongue in Check (1983)

14 Oh, how few be there who are low in their own eyes! The number of souls that are high in the esteem of God , and low in their own esteem, are very few.
Thomas Brooks
The Unsearchable Riches of Christ (1655)

15 An humble soul that lies low, oh what sights of God hath he! What glory doth he behold, when the proud soul sees nothing!
Thomas Brooks
The Unsearchable Riches of Christ (1655)

16 Humility is both a grace, and a vessel to receive grace. There is none who sees so much need of grace as humble souls.
Thomas Brooks
The Unsearchable Riches of Christ (1655)

17 Here is a wonder! God is on high; and yet the higher a man lifts up himself, the farther he is from God; and the lower a man humbles himself, the nearer he is to God.
Thomas Brooks
The Unsearchable Riches of Christ (1655)

18 An humble soul is like a violet, that by its fragrant smell draws the eye and the hearts of others to him.
Thomas Brooks
The Unsearchable Riches of Christ (1655)

19 Pride closes the door to spiritual growth, but humility opens the door of your life to more of God's grace. Pause for a moment to ponder this promise and let it sink in. God gives grace to the humble.
Colin Smith
Ten Keys to Unlock the Christian Life (2005)

20 When we've had a disagreement, we can show true character by walking into the room and apologizing honestly and humbly. Pride is not a virtue. Humility is. Pride can cost us valuable relationships, but humility costs us only pride. Men of character know how to apologize and how to forgive.
Bill McCartney
4th and Goal (2002)

21 The truly godly person never forgets that he was at one time an object of God's holy and just wrath. He never forgets that Christ Jesus came into the world to save sinners—and he feels along with Paul that he is himself the worst of sinners.
Jerry Bridges
The Practice of Godliness (1996)

22 If we are humble enough to accept someone's input, we can avoid stumbling along while we don't know what we don't know.
Bill McCartney
Blind Spots (2003)

23 Humility does demand that we carefully weigh the opinions of thoughtful men; we should refrain from depending solely on our own intellect.
Jeff Baldwin
Thinking Biblically (2005)

24 Let us then also pray for those who have fallen into any sin, that meekness and humility may be given to them, so that they may submit, not unto us, but to the will of God. For in this way they shall secure a fruitful and perfect remembrance from us.
> Clement
> *The First Epistle of Clement to the Corinthians* (1st century)

25 The humiliation leads to a greater glory.
> C. S. Lewis
> *The Weight of Glory* (1949)

26 When man humbles himself, God cannot restrain His mercy; He must come down and pour His grace into the humble man, and He gives Himself most of all, and all at once, to the least of all.
> Meister Eckhart
> *Meister Eckhart's Sermons* (14th century)

27 When unadorned, adorned the most.
> Brother Lawrence
> *The Practice of the Presence of God* (17th century)

28 Work on your humility. Come to terms with the fact that your skills are God given. You can only do what He equips you to do.
> Stan Toler
> *Minute Motivators for Men* (2004)

29 Don't put yourself on a pedestal. Appreciate the worth of others. Let others know that you have confidence in them.
> Stan Toler
> *Minute Motivators for Men* (2004)

30 Have we the humility to thank our Father for the gift of pain?
> Elisabeth Elliot
> *Secure in the Everlasting Arms* (2002)

31 He that can humble himself earnestly before God in Christ, has already won.
> Martin Luther
> *Table Talk* (16th century)

32 There are many willing to preach to thousands, but are not willing to take their seat beside one soul, and lead that soul to the blessed Jesus.
> D. L. Moody
> *The Faithful Saying* (1877)

33 It is a genuine act of humility to realize that we can learn from others who have gone before us.
> Richard Foster
> *Streams of Living Water* (1998)

34 Be humble, talk little, think and pray much.
> George Whitefield
> *Memoirs of Rev. George Whitefield* (1741)

35 Humility—to put a seal upon your lips and forget what you have done.
> Henry Drummond
> *The Greatest Thing in the World* (1874)

36 Let us remember, how great have been our advantages, and how little we have profited by them: and on the other hand, how many disadvantages others have had, and how little they are behind us after all.
> George Edward Jelf
> *The Secret Trials of the Christian Life* (19th century)

37 "What hast thou that thou didst not receive?" Apart from God, what are we?
> George Edward Jelf
> *The Secret Trials of the Christian Life* (19th century)

38 What we call our strong points will become the source of our most alarming weakness, if they are not tempered and sanctified by the increasing humility and ever-active faith, which are among the chief characteristics of a Christian.
> George Edward Jelf
> *The Secret Trials of the Christian Life* (19th century)

39 The most eminent saints have been of low stature in their own eyes; like the sun at the zenith, they showed least when they were at the highest.
Thomas Watson and Samuel Lee
The Bible and the Closet (1842)

40 You can see the world standing tall, but to witness the Savior, you have to get on your knees.
Max Lucado
The Applause of Heaven (1990)

41 A posture of humility will serve you better than an in-your-face swagger.
Alan Dowd
"Speaking Creatively" article (2009)

42 One can so easily become too great to be used by God. One can never be too small for His service.
Corrie ten Boom
Not Good If Detached (1957)

43 Humility is one of the great marks of a crucified man.
Andrew Murray
Master's Indwelling (1895)

44 Man is to be humbled to the dust by the thought of the glory of God as seen in the visible creation.
F. C. Cook
Bible Commentary (19th century)

45 Christ's people have frequently to humble themselves.
John Dawson
The Saviour in the Workshop (1868)

46 Humility is taught by hardship in the face of obedience. Humility is tested by the choices we make.
Tim Burns
Forged in the Fire (2003)

47 We do not want to be beginners. But let us be convinced of the fact that we will never be anything else but beginners.
Thomas Merton
Contemplative Prayer (1969)

48 No one that is not of a contrite and humble spirit will dwell with God in His high and holy place.
D. L. Moody
Heaven (1881)

49 When we are humble enough to allow God to fill us with His love, a miracle happens.
Kim Moore and Pam Mellskog
A Patchwork Heart (2002)

50 Faith, whether in God or in people, can only happen in utter humility.
Mike Mason
Practicing the Presence of People (1999)

51 There are three great motivations to humility: it becomes us as creatures; it becomes us as sinners; and it becomes us as saints.
Andrew Murray
Humility (1896)

52 Humility is not so much a grace or virtue along with; it is the root of all, because it alone assumes the right attitude before God and allows Him as God to do all.
Andrew Murray
Humility (1896)

53 The way of ascending is humility; the way of descending is pride.
Benedict of Nursia
The Rule of St. Benedict (6th century)

54 No matter where we are—whether doing the work of God, or in the garden, or on a journey—we should adopt the posture of reverence, ever mindful of who we are. Our attitude should be that of the publican in the

Gospel who said, with his eyes fixed on the ground, "Lord, I am a sinner and I am not worthy to lift my eyes up to heaven."

Benedict of Nursia
The Rule of St. Benedict (6th century)

222 HUMOR

*Thou wilt shew me the path of life:
in thy presence is fulness of joy.*
PSALM 16:11

1   That I have written in a semi-humorous vein needs no apology, since thereby sound moral teaching has gained a hearing from at least three hundred thousand persons. There is no particular virtue in being seriously unreadable.

Charles Spurgeon
John Ploughman's Talk (19th century)

2   People who live above their circumstances usually possess a well-developed sense of humor, because in the final analysis that's what gets them through.

Charles Swindoll
Laugh Again (1995)

3   Humor gives us power. We often cannot control situations or events, but we can control our response. Instead of discouragement or despair, we can claim power.

Anne Bryan Smollin
Tickle Your Soul (1999)

4   When it comes to last words, I'm afraid I won't be able to do it. As a writer, I know I'm going to keep wanting to do a rewrite.

Martha Bolton
Didn't My Skin Used to Fit? (2000)

5   A sense of humor helps us through many sticky problems.

Dennis Gibson
The Sandwich Years (1991)

223 HUNGER, SPIRITUAL

*Blessed are they which do hunger and thirst
after righteousness: for they shall be filled.*
MATTHEW 5:6

1   Today, as you hunger after His bread, remember that God is seeking the hungry; as you long for living waters, remember that He invites the thirsty to drink; as you seek His presence, remember that He bids you to draw near; as you commit to walk in His ways, remember that He is always on the alert, looking for those who are totally committed to Him.

Roy Lessin
Today Is Your Best Day (2006)

2   Spirituality is not a formula; it is not a test. It is a relationship. Spirituality is not about competency; it is about intimacy. Spirituality is not about perfection; it is about connection.

Michael Yaconelli
Messy Spirituality (2002)

3   The way of the spiritual life begins where we are now in the mess of our lives. Accepting the reality of our broken, flawed lives is the beginning of spirituality not because the spiritual life will remove our flaws but because we let go of seeking perfection and, instead, seek God, the one who is present in the tangledness of our lives. Spirituality is not about being fixed; it is about God's being present in the mess of our unfixedness.

Michael Yaconelli
Messy Spirituality (2002)

4   Collectively and individually, we are crying for the solace of reconnection with God.

Sue Patton Thoele
Heart Centered Marriage (1996)

5   Whether we feast through silence, through stillness, through meditation or contemplation, God longs to feed us.

Jane Rubietta
Resting Place (2005)

224 HUSBANDS

*Husbands, love your wives, even as Christ
also loved the church, and gave himself for it.*
EPHESIANS 5:25

1   God has placed husbands and fathers in
authority in their own homes, but He has also
placed them under authority of Jesus Christ.
Until we bow to His lordship and model His
sacrificial servanthood, we do not earn the
respect necessary to lead.
  Stu Weber
  The Heart of a Tender Warrior (2002)

2   Husbands, your wives need your
attention, your tenderness, your special care
as much as your lawns need water. If you
withdraw your lives and become preoccupied
with your own pursuits, they'll begin to
dry up inside. The life will flow right out of
them—and you will be held responsible for
that before God.
  Ken Hutcherson
  Before All Hell Breaks Loose (2001)

3   If, as a husband, I'm asked to be willing
to die for my wife, should I not be willing to
live for her? I continually examine my attitude
toward my wife to see if my actions represent
what Scripture has to say about the way I
should treat my wife. Am I her leader, her
protector, her provider, her security?
  Bob Barnes
  Men Under Construction (2006)

4   A pastor once asked a group of men on a
retreat, "Men, is your wife a better Christian
because she is married to you, or has your
marriage been a hindrance to her spiritual
growth?"
  Bob Barnes
  Men Under Construction (2006)

5   Home is the most important place for a
man to be affirmed. If a man knows that his
wife believes in him, he is empowered to do
better in every area of his life. A man tends
to think of life as a competition and a battle,
and he can energetically duke it out if he can
come home to someone who supports him
unconditionally, who will wipe his brow and
tell him he can do it.
  Shaunti Feldhahn
  For Women Only (2004)

6   Before a man can understand his role as
a husband, he must first understand what it
means to be a man.
  Bob Lepine
  The Christian Husband (1999)

7   To qualify as a husband, a man must be
more than just a man. He's got to be a godly
man—a man who fears God, who leads a
spiritually disciplined life, and who is marked
by a masculine expression of godly character.
He has to be more than a man's man—he has
to be a God's man.
  Bob Lepine
  The Christian Husband (1999)

225 HYPOCRISY

Thou shalt not be as the hypocrites are.
MATTHEW 6:5

1   If I, being what I am, can consider that I
am in some sense a Christian, why should the
different vices of those people in the next pew
prove that their religion is mere hypocrisy and
convention?
  C. S. Lewis
  The Screwtape Letters (1942)

2   A spoiled saint, a Pharisee, an inquisitor, or
a magician, makes better sport in Hell than a
mere common tyrant or debauchee.
  C. S. Lewis
  The Screwtape Letters (1941)

3   A shallow Christian is what the world calls a hypocrite—a stumbling block to those who are lost.

    Jimmy Houston
    Hooked for Life (1999)

4   Not only does hypocrisy in our lives bother God, it gives a watching world an excuse to reject Jesus. If our lives are not morally consistent with what we claim to be good and true, there is no hope of catching the attention of those in our lives.

    Joseph Stowell
    The Trouble with Jesus (2003)

5   It is a small matter to be devout and recollected for an hour or half hour, if the unction and spirit of prayer do not continue with us during the whole day.

    François Fénelon and Jeanne Guyon
    Spiritual Progress (17th century)

6   Do I worship God with my words while my actions belie the truth of my allegiance?

    Rebecca Lusignolo
    Devotions for Difficult Days (2006)

7   One of our consistent prayers should be for God to reveal the hypocrite in our hearts.

    Lisa Harper
    Relentless Love (2002)

8   God looks at our motives not just listens to our words.

    Beth Moore
    "Wrestling with God" teaching series (2009)

9   Pharisees—someone with 20/20 vision for your faults and legally blind for theirs.

    Martha Bolton
    If the Tongue's a Fire, Who Needs Salsa? (2002)

10 Before you act, know your motivation.

    Martha Bolton
    If the Tongue's a Fire, Who Needs Salsa? (2002)

11 There is something insincere about a man or woman who repeatedly tells God how much he or she loves Him while refusing to obey Him.

    Andy Stanley
    Louder Than Words (2004)

12 If we make a great show of respect and love to God, in the outward actions, while there is no sincerity in the heart, it is but hypocrisy and practical lying unto the Holy One.

    Jonathan Edwards
    "The Greatest Performances or Sufferings in Vain without Charity" sermon (1738)

13 To pretend to such respect and love, when it is not felt in the heart, is to act as if we thought we could deceive God.

    Jonathan Edwards
    "The Greatest Performances or Sufferings in Vain without Charity" sermon (1738)

14 To be a hypocrite, you must praise God while pretending God does not see or know the truth of your life.

    Richard Phillips
    Tabletalk magazine (2009)

15 Hypocrisy is the great enabler of sin.

    Richard Phillips
    Tabletalk magazine (2009)

16 There are two classes of hypocrites among professors of religion, those that deceive others and those that deceive themselves.

    Charles Finney
    Lectures to Professing Christians (1837)

17 There is a danger of the Christian fellowship becoming so sanctimonious that

those with deep unresolved problems are frightened into silence or hypocrisy.
Gary Collins
It's OK to Be Single (1976)

18 When once a hypocrite is thus established in a false hope, he has not those things to cause him to call his hope in question, that oftentimes are the occasion of the doubting of true saints.
Jonathan Edwards
A Treatise Concerning Religious Affections (18th century)

19 The hypocrite has not the knowledge of his own blindness, and the deceitfulness of his own heart, and that mean opinion of his own understanding that the true saint has.
Jonathan Edwards
A Treatise Concerning Religious Affections (18th century)

20 The devil does not assault the hope of the hypocrite, as he does the hope of a true saint.
Jonathan Edwards
A Treatise Concerning Religious Affections (18th century)

21 How great therefore may the resemblance be, as to all outward expressions and appearances, between a hypocrite and a true saint!
Jonathan Edwards
A Treatise Concerning Religious Affections (18th century)

22 If a Christian is overtaken by ever so small a fault, the world will say maliciously: There, see his hypocrisy.
The Lutheran Witness (1885)

23 Since we are all naturally prone to hypocrisy, any empty semblance of righteousness is quite enough to satisfy us instead of righteousness itself.
John Calvin
Institutes of the Christian Religion (16th century)

24 The difference between hypocrites and sinners is that sinners admit they sin.
Joe Beam
Getting Past Guilt (2003)

IDLENESS (*see* LAZINESS)

226 IDOLATRY (*see also* FALSE GODS)
Wherefore, my dearly beloved, flee from idolatry.
1 CORINTHIANS 10:14

1 We were made to know and treasure the glory of God above all things; and when we trade the treasure for images, everything is disordered.
John Piper
Seeing and Savoring Jesus Christ (2004)

2 "Golden calves" are built in every generation: "I want to worship my god—my way."
Tim Walter
"Filled with God's Grace and Power" sermon (2009)

3 Are we not rude and deserve blame, if we leave Him alone, to busy ourselves about trifles, which do not please Him and perhaps offend Him? 'Tis to be feared these trifles will one day cost us dear.
Brother Lawrence
The Practice of the Presence of God (17th century)

4 We easily fall into idolatry, for we are inclined thereunto by nature, and coming to us by inheritance, it seems pleasant.
Martin Luther
Table Talk (16th century)

5 Whoso hearkens not to God's voice, is an idolater, though he performs the highest and most heavy service of God.
Martin Luther
Table Talk (16th century)

6   Whatever preoccupies your thoughts and your schedule, is quite likely your "god."
Bill Bright
The Joy of Faithful Obedience (2005)

7   There are many ways we can practice idolatry without bowing before carved pieces of wood or stone.
Bill Bright
The Joy of Faithful Obedience (2005)

8   Those who are always ready to ask how little they may do for religion rather than how much they may do, are serving their own gods.
Charles Finney
Lectures to Professing Christians (1837)

9   What is it about us that causes us to withhold from God the reverence we lavish on human idols?
Charles Colson
Faith on the Line (1986)

10   Images dishonor God, for they obscure His glory.
J. I. Packer
Knowing God (1993)

ILLNESS (*see* SICKNESS)

227 IMAGE OF GOD

So God created man in his own image,
in the image of God created he him;
male and female created he them.
GENESIS 1:27

1   Who am I? Who are you? We are the crowning glory of the creation of God. You must never forget that you are created in the image of God as the crowning glory of his creation.
Voddie Baucham, Jr.
The Supremacy of Christ in a Postmodern World (2007)

2   Every human being is worthy of respect just because we are created in the image of God.
Gary and Mona Shriver
Unfaithful (2005)

3   The farther we move from God, the more we devalue man.
Ravi Zacharias
The Real Face of Atheism (2004)

4   Human beings need reminders that we are not "just mortals." We are created in the image of God with value and dignity.
Lynn Anderson
The Jesus Touch (2002)

5   When we touch others with the touch of Jesus, we remind people from all walks of life that they are created in the image of God, beings of dignity and value in the sight of heaven.
Lynn Anderson
The Jesus Touch (2002)

6   Love works the likeness of God into the soul.
Meister Eckhart
Meister Eckhart's Sermons (14th century)

7   Imagination is a wonderful gift, but when we use it to conjure up our own image of God it leads us astray.
Alistair Begg
Pathway to Freedom (2003)

8   To have no other parent but God, no other element but the breath of God, no other instrument but the purpose of God, this is to be the image of God.
John Donne
"Sermon Preached Before King Charles I" (1629)

228 IMMORALITY (*see also* LUST; SENSUALITY; SIN; TEMPTATION)
Flee fornication.
1 CORINTHIANS 6:18

1   Sexual impurity has become rampant in the church because we've ignored the costly work of obedience to God's standards as individuals, asking too often, "How far can I go and still be called a Christian?"
    Stephen Arterburn, Fred Stoeker, and Mike Yorkey
    Every Man's Battle (2000)

2   I am grieved with the loose walk of those that are Christians, that have had discoveries of Jesus Christ; there is so little difference betwixt them and other people, that I can scarce know which is the true Christian.
    George Whitefield
    "A Sermon, Preached on Sabbath Morning" (1741)

3   Bad behavior is never appropriate, and doing wrong is never okay—even with the right motivation.
    Mark Gregston
    What's Happening to My Teen? (2009)

IMMORTALITY
(*see* ETERNAL LIFE)

INDIFFERENCE (*see* APATHY)

229 INFLUENCE
And as he passed by, he saw Levi the son of Alphaeus sitting at the receipt of custom, and said unto him, Follow me. And he arose and followed him.
MARK 2:14

1   The people who influence you are people who believe in you.
    Henry Drummond
    The Greatest Thing in the World (1891)

2   When our lives are yielded to the Spirit's control, God is certain to work through us in leaving His mark on those around us.
    Henry and Mel Blackaby
    What's So Spiritual About Your Gifts? (2004)

3   The true legacy of a servant will not be determined by what he has done but by what others do as a result of what he has done.
    Wayne Cordeiro
    The Dream Releasers (2002)

4   Long after whatever personal investments you may leave your children are spent, a spiritual legacy will only compound daily and pay rich dividends throughout all eternity. The man who leaves only a financial inheritance for his children leaves them poor.
    Steven Lawson
    The Legacy (1998)

5   This is all the Inheritance I can give to my dear Family. The Religion of Christ can give them one which will make them rich indeed.
    Patrick Henry
    Last Will and Testament (1798)

6   Read David Brainerd today and yesterday, and find as usual my spirit greatly benefited by it. I long to be like him; let me forget the world and be swallowed up in a desire to glorify God.
    William Carey (19th century) quoted in
    Faithful Witness: The Life and Mission of William Carey

7   History is what comes before us; legacy is what comes after us. When you know your history—you know where you have come from—and you know your purpose, you are uniquely positioned to pass what you've learned on to others. You live your life with a sense of legacy—thinking about the differences you can make in the world and what people will say about you.
    Florence Littauer, Marita Littauer, and Lauren Littauer Briggs
    Making the Blue Plate Special (2006)

8   The thing we fear most is having lived our lives pleasantly, but to have made no measurable difference whatever.
    Lloyd John Ogilvie
    Life without Limits (1975)

9 When the qualities of courage, persistence, gratefulness, calmness, gentleness, and unselfish love are present in a person's character, it is easier to receive his words and to follow his instructions or example.

Gary Smalley
For Better or for Best (1979)

10 The impact God has planned for us does not occur when we're pursuing impact. It occurs when we're pursuing God.

Phil Vischer
"When Your Dream Dies" teaching (2008)

11 We don't have the power to change someone else, but we can influence them.

Henry Cloud and John Townsend
Boundaries in Marriage (1999)

12 Young dreams may be wild ones, but they are never corrected by ridiculing them. They must be steered by a loving voice that has earned the right to be heard, not one enforced by means of power.

Ravi Zacharias
Jesus Among Other Gods (2000)

13 The value of mentoring derives from the value of relationships.

Howard and William Hendricks
As Iron Sharpens Iron (1995)

14 Those around us impact us.

R. Larry Moyer
21 Things God Never Said (2004)

230 INSPIRATION

All scripture is given by inspiration of God, and is profitable for doctrine, for reproof, for correction, for instruction in righteousness.
2 TIMOTHY 3:16

1 Interruption is often divine inspiration.
Jon Courson
Application Commentary (2003)

2 There is inspiration in our longings, and sometimes we can even discover God's dream for us there.

Alice Bass
The Creative Life (2001)

3 Jesus is more than just an example to look at and try to follow; he is the source of inspiration and the fulfillment of abundant living.

Alice Bass
The Creative Life (2001)

4 Divine inspiration was essential to man's first created state. The Spirit of the triune God, breathed into, or brought to life in him, was that alone which made him a holy creature in the image and likeness of God.

William Law
An Humble, Affectionate, and Earnest Address (1761)

231 INTEGRITY
(*see also* REVELATION)

The integrity of the upright shall guide them,
PROVERBS 11:3

1 Let vile persons and vile ways be contemned in your eyes: be of more noble spirits than to be companions with them. Regard not their societies, nor their scorns; their flatteries or their frowns.

Charles Spurgeon
"God in the Covenant" sermon (1856)

2 No double dealing must the Christian man have, no playing fast and loose with God or man; no hypocritical professions, or false principles. He must be as transparent as glass.

Charles Spurgeon
"Consecration to God" sermon (1868)

3 The greatest obstacle to the impact of the gospel has not been its inability to provide answers, but the failure on our part to live it out.

Ravi Zacharias
Beyond Opinion (2007)

4 Satan never wastes a fiery dart by aiming at a spot covered by armor. The bull's eye is located dead center in our inconsistency. That's where the enemy plans to bring us down.

Beth Moore
Daniel (2006)

5 Our love for Christ is revealed in the trenches, not in the pew.

Joseph Stowell
Why It's Hard to Love Jesus (2003)

6 The world is looking for people who really believe and live what they say.

Kay Arthur
Speak to My Heart, God (1993)

7 Do the right thing not the comfortable thing.

L. James Harvey
701 More Sentence Sermons (2002)

8 God measures us at the heart level. Externals are only symptomatic, superficial, and cosmetic. Externally we can fool all the people most of the time. But God? Never!

Joseph Stowell
Fan the Flame (1986)

9 Even when we think no one is watching, we must be faithful to live for Him, in His way and His light.

Rebecca St. James
Wait for Me (2008)

10 Friend, if a man would not keep a sacred vow before Almighty God to his wife—I wouldn't trust him to keep any promise, any where, any time.

Adrian Rogers
"A Nation in Crisis" sermon (1996)

11 All spring and summer, each leaf's true color is masked over by green chlorophyll cells. When fall comes and the chlorophyll departs, the true color is no longer obscured. The "change" is really just an unveiling. The leaf doesn't become more colorful; it shows the world what it has been all along.

Dwight Edwards
Revolution Within (2001)

12 One can no more reconcile immorality in private with a call to public integrity than one can reconcile being a racist in private with being unprejudiced in public.

Ravi Zacharias
Deliver Us from Evil (1996)

13 What we believe is evidenced by how we live, not just by what we say.

Connie Grigsby and Kent Julian
How to Get Your Teen to Talk to You (2002)

14 Do well and right, and let the world sink.

George Herbert
Country Parson (17th century)

15 Integrity is a part of our character and is best known by three behaviors: Telling the truth; Keeping one's promises; Taking responsibility for one's behavior.

Ross Campbell
Parenting Your Adult Child (1999)

16 The blameless one rises each day with an eye toward living in accordance with the revelation offered by God. All other things find their proper order after this priority.

Gordon MacDonald
Secrets of the Generous Life (2002)

17 Nearly every grave moral failure begins with a small sin.

Charles Colson
"The Bewilderment of Sin" article (2009)

18 It is not enough that a man know what is right, but he must have the disposition to do what is right, or he will be a polluter of society, a firebrand in the State.

School Committee Public Documents of Massachusetts (1866)

19 Credible words reflect our integrity.

Rhonda Rizzo Webb
Words Begin in Our Hearts (2003)

20 When a man's understanding is convinced, and he admit the truth in its relation to himself, then there must be a hearty approbation of it in its bearing or relation to himself.

Charles Finney
Lectures to Professing Christians (1837)

21 While we can cherish the godly heritage or sterling reputation of those who have gone before, we need to live it out in our own lives.

Sandra Aldrich
Upward Glances (2000)

22 Simply put, integrity is doing what you said you would do.

Ted Engstrom and Robert Larson
Integrity (1987)

23 The world is better able to read the nature of religion in a man's life than in the Bible.

Richard Baxter
The Reformed Pastor (17th century)

24 Image is what people think we are. Integrity is what we really are.

John Maxwell
Developing the Leader within You (1993)

25 We should not profess one thing and do the opposite. No Christian has ever bought the friendship of the world without disloyalty to Christ.

D. L. Moody
Short Talks (19th century)

232 INTELLECT
(*see also* KNOWLEDGE)

And beside this, giving all diligence, add to your faith virtue; and to virtue knowledge.
2 PETER 1:5

1 That intellect is most needful, to offer to the heart the Word of God which the Holy Spirit can quicken. And yet it is absolutely impotent, either to impart, or quicken, the true life. It is but a servant that carries the food: it is the heart that must feed, and be nourished and live.

Andrew Murray
Prayer's Inner Chamber (1912)

2 So Godlike a gift is intellect, so wondrous a thing is consciousness, that to link them with the animal world seems to trifle with the profoundest distinctions in the Universe.

Henry Drummond
The Lowell Lectures on the Ascent of Man (1893)

3 A religion divorced from earnest and lofty thought has always, down the whole history of the Church, tended to become weak, jejune, and unwholesome; while the intellect, deprived of its rights within religion, has sought its satisfaction without, and developed into godless nationalism.

James Orr
The Christian View of God and the World (1908)

233 INTERCESSION (*see also* PRAYER)

I exhort therefore, that, first of all, supplications, prayers, intercessions, and giving of thanks, be made for all men.
1 TIMOTHY 2:1

1   Have you ever learned the beautiful art of letting God take care of you and giving all your thought and strength to pray for others and for the kingdom of God? It will relieve you of a thousand cares.
A. B. Simpson
Days of Heaven Upon Earth (1897)

2   And that is the ultimate purpose of all this intercession: not just to save our own from the world, but to save the world through our own.
Agnes Sanford
The Healing Light (1947)

3   If we have our eyes and hearts open, there are many who need our prayers each day. Just reading the newspaper or watching the evening news provides ample opportunity for intercessory prayers—prayers on behalf of others.
Debra Farrington
A Beginner's Guide to Unceasing Prayer (2002)

4   When you pray for unconverted people, you do so on the assumption that it is in God's power to bring them to faith. You entreat him to do that very thing, and your confidence in asking rests on the certainty that he is able to do what you ask.
J. I. Packer
Evangelism and the Sovereignty of God (2008)

5   When we hold up the life of another before God, when we expose it to God's love, when we pray. . .only then do we sense what it means to share in God's work, in his concern; only then do the walls that separate us from others go down and we sense that we are at bottom all knit together in a great and intimate family.
Douglas Steere
Prayer and Worship (1978)

6   There is no greater intimacy with another than that which is built through holding him or her up in prayer.
Douglas Steere
Prayer and Worship (1978)

7   In intercessory prayer, one seldom ends where one began.
Douglas Steere
Prayer and Worship (1978)

8   Despite disappointments, the Christian is obligated to pray for the sick because we are bidden to do so and because the crumb of our caring is but a morsel broken from the whole loaf of the Father's infinite and tender love.
Catherine Marshall
Something More (1974)

9   Never stop praying for "hopeless" cases.
Robert Morgan
Moments for Families with Prodigals (2003)

10   Intercessory prayer is an extension of the ministry of Jesus through His Body, the Church, whereby we mediate between God and humanity for the purpose of reconciling the world to Him, or between Satan and humanity for the purpose of enforcing the victory of Calvary.
Dutch Sheets
Intercessory Prayer (1996)

11   There was a man convicted and converted in answer to prayer. So if you are anxious about the conversion of some relative, or some friend, make up your mind that you will give God no rest, day or night, till He grants your petition.
D. L. Moody
Prevailing Prayer: What Hinders It? (1884)

12   A "prayer warrior" is a person who is convinced that God is omnipotent—that God has the power to do anything, to change anyone and to intervene in any circumstance. A person who truly believes this refuses to doubt God.
Bill Hybels
Too Busy Not to Pray (1988)

234 INTIMACY WITH GOD
(*see also* KNOWING GOD; PRESENCE OF GOD)

And the LORD spake unto Moses face to face, as a man speaketh unto his friend.
EXODUS 33:11

1   It matters not to me what I do, or what I suffer, so long as I abide lovingly united to God's will—that is my whole business.
Brother Lawrence
The Practice of the Presence of God (17th century)

2   When you read the Bible, the God of the universe is talking to you.
Beth Moore
Daniel (2006)

3   It is a great thing to enter the inner chamber, and shut the door, and meet the Father in secret. It is a greater thing to open the door again, and go out, in an enjoyment of that presence which nothing can disturb.
Andrew Murray
The Prayer Life (1912)

4   God didn't want me to do more for Him. He wanted me to be more with Him.
Bruce Wilkinson
Secrets of the Vine (2001)

5   Seeking the approval of others always leads us away from what matters. Jesus wants my heart. He's most concerned about my relationship to Him.
Joseph Stowell
Why It's Hard to Love Jesus (2003)

6   Thou art the life of my soul as my soul is the life of my body.
François Fénelon and Jeanne Guyon
Spiritual Progress (17th century)

7   Thou art more intimately present to me than I am to myself; this I, to which I am so attached and which I have so ardently loved, ought to be strange to me in comparison with Thee; Thou art the bestower of it.
François Fénelon and Jeanne Guyon
Spiritual Progress (17th century)

8   It is not necessary to descend into the depths nor to pass beyond the seas; it is not necessary to ascend into the heavens to find Thee; Thou art nearer to us than we are to ourselves.
François Fénelon and Jeanne Guyon
Spiritual Progress (17th century)

9   The turning point of our lives is when we stop seeking the God we want and start seeking the God who is.
Patrick Morley
The Man in the Mirror (1992)

10   God loves us by giving us himself to enjoy. The gospel is good news because it announces to us that God has acted in Christ not just that we may have heaven, but so that we may have God.
John Piper
God Is the Gospel (2005)

11   My Lord, I find that nothing else will do,
But follow where thou goest, sit at thy feet,
And where I have thee not, still run to meet.
George MacDonald
Diary of an Old Soul (1880)

12   Seeking God's face is far different from asking Him for something or presenting Him with a list of petitions. For me, seeking the Lord's face means praying over and over and over again that I might be close to Him, be led by Him, have the knowledge of His will, and be used in His plan.
Pat Robertson
Six Steps to Spiritual Survival (2002)

13 A gracious soul can reconcile itself to the poorest accommodations; if it may have communication with God in them.
Matthew Henry
Commentary on the Whole Bible (1706)

14 We can approach the Bible not as a dry manuscript or history text, but as a way to develop closeness with our Father. God inspired His Book to be written and given to us that we may know Him intimately.
Mike Macintosh
Falling in Love with the Bible (2005)

15 We cannot have intimacy with God or anyone else if we stay hidden and offer only who we think we ought to be or what we believe is wanted.
John and Stasi Eldredge
Captivating (2005)

16 Our intimacy with God—His highest priority for our lives—determines the impact of our lives.
Charles Stanley
30 Life Principles Study Guide (2008)

17 The first step is to slow down the pace. That allows you to be fully present, to be mindful, to be intentional, to create space, and to notice where God is working and join him in that work.
Keri Wyatt Kent
Breathe: Creating Space for God in a Hectic Life (2005)

18 Connection with God, which is the reason for any spiritual practice, begins with changing our focus (from ourselves and our problems to God and his sufficiency) and changing our pace (from hurried and distracted to deliberate and focused).
Keri Wyatt Kent
Breathe: Creating Space for God in a Hectic Life (2005)

19 Do not forget that the aim God has in view in His grace and your redemption is to restore the broken bond of fellowship and love between Him and the sinner. True religion consists in this, that the soul should find its highest happiness in personal communication with God.
Andrew Murray
Have Mercy Upon Me (1896)

20 A soul will never grow until it is able to let go of the tight grasp it has on God.
John of the Cross (16th century)
quoted in *Selected Writings*

21 Our fellowship with God is not meant to wait until we are in heaven. God's greatest desire, and our greatest need, is to be in constant fellowship with Him now, and there is no greater expression or experience of fellowship than prayer.
John MacArthur
Alone with God (1995)

22 Frequently, if we were sensitive and listening, there come clear insights of things to be done. Often they come in that receptive silent waiting after we have opened our needs and where we do nothing but wait for direction.
Douglas Steere
Prayer and Worship (1978)

23 It is very greatly pleasing to him that a simple soul should come naked, openly, and familiarly.
Julian of Norwich
Revelations of Divine Love (14th century)

24 Sometimes we forget that God has a personality and wants to engage us at a deeper level.
David Crowder
Praise Habit (2004)

25 The more we understand what God is really like, the prospect of the fulfillment of that concept becomes most exciting.
Joy Dawson
Intimate Friendship with God (1986)

26 To have a nodding acquaintance with the Creator of the universe is no small thought. But to be on intimate terms with Him is enough to give us heart flutters for the rest of our lives.
Joy Dawson
Intimate Friendship with God (1986)

27 In all times and places there have been those who seek to escape the bonds of flesh and ascend to be united with God. In Christian teaching, God descended into flesh in order to make that union possible.
David Downing
Into the Region of Awe (2005)

235 ISRAEL
Brethren, my heart's desire and prayer to God for Israel is, that they might be saved.
ROMANS 10:1

1 It is vitally important, therefore, that Christians become faithful in praying for the peace of Jerusalem every day, visit and tour Israel while they still can, and find new and creative ways to show Israel and the Jewish people how much the church loves and cares for them.
Joel Rosenberg
Epicenter (2006)

2 As the Creator of all things, God has an interest in the nations of the world that is so intense that his ultimate purpose for Israel, the seed of Abraham, was to serve as a redemptive medium to restore all the peoples of the earth to perfect fellowship with him.
Eugene Merrill
Everlasting Dominion (2006)

236 JEALOUSY (*see also* ENVY)
For jealousy is the rage of a man: therefore he will not spare in the day of vengeance.
PROVERBS 6:34

1 There is not a single soul that jealousy looks good on. Nobody! It looks ugly on everybody, and it makes us act ugly—it makes us act out of character.
Beth Moore
"A Beautiful Mind" teaching series (2009)

2 Nobody is drawn to hysteria, insecurity, and jealousy.
Beth Moore
"A Beautiful Mind" teaching series (2009)

3 You have to learn to be happy when other people get what you're still waiting for.
Joyce Meyer
"Overcoming Fear with Faith" sermon (2009)

4 One small seed of jealousy, once it takes root in the soil of the soul, can sprout overnight into a sprawling vine of poison ivy.
Luis Palau
Heart After God (1978)

237 JESUS
(*see also* CHRIST; MESSIAH; SAVIOR)
And she shall bring forth a son, and thou shalt call his name JESUS: for he shall save his people from their sins.
MATTHEW 1:21

General

1 Jesus was everything of humanity and nothing of superficiality; everything of godliness and nothing of religiosity. Jesus ministered the joy, life, love and health—the glory—of His Kingdom, and He did it in the most practical, tasteful ways.
Jack Hayford
Glory on Your House (1991)

2   After we have asked the Spirit to tell us what Jesus would do and have received an answer to it, we are to act regardless of the results to ourselves.
   Charles Sheldon
   In His Steps (1896)

3   Focus on Jesus, for he is the heart of the Christian faith.
   James Emery White
   A Search for the Spiritual (1998)

4   We have the way; we have the resources. If only we had the will, we could change the world for Jesus Christ.
   Bill Bright and John Damoose
   Red Sky in the Morning (1998)

5   Either He was a lunatic or God. And He was not a lunatic.
   C. S. Lewis
   The Weight of Glory (1949)

6 We have spread so many coats of whitewash over the historical Jesus that we scarcely see the glow of his presence anymore.
   Brennan Manning
   Posers, Fakers, and Wannabes (2003)

7   Jesus does not ask us to understand His ways and timing. He asks only for our trust.
   Greg Laurie
   Breakfast with Jesus (2003)

8   After two thousand years, no name has been scrutinized more, none abused or challenged more in the public media.
   Ravi Zacharias
   Christian Worldview interview (2008)

9   When I think about Jesus having to grow mentally, I am filled with hope.
   Carole Lewis
   Choosing Change (2001)

10 To give you an idea of the depth of Jesus' suffering, being abandoned by God is the definition of hell.
   Tony Evans
   Theology You Can Count On (2008)

11 His whole life was a continual suffering, but his death was the top and complement of his obedience, for in that he manifested the greatest love to God and the highest charity to man.
   Stephen Charnock
   Discourse on the Cleansing Virtue of Christ's Blood (17th century)

12 Jesus was not a people pleaser—He was a God pleaser.
   Rich Mendola
   "Farthest Horizon: Responding to Personal Attacks" sermon (2009)

13 Jesus promises us a satisfaction unlike anything else in life. In offering us Himself, Jesus is unlike any religious leader in the world.
   Ravi Zacharias and Kevin Johnson
   Jesus Among Other Gods— Youth Edition (2000)

14 Many will say that Jesus was a good moral teacher. Let's be realistic. How could he be a great moral teacher and knowingly mislead people at the most important point of his teaching—his own identity?
   Josh McDowell
   More Than a Carpenter (1977)

15 The presence and company of Christ will make amends for all we suffer here below.
   J. C. Ryle
   Holiness: Its Nature, Hindrances, Difficulties, and Roots (19th century)

16 He is bread to the hungry, water to the thirsty, a garment to the naked, healing to the wounded; and whatever a soul can desire is found in him.
   John Flavel
   Christ Altogether Lovely (17th century)

Advocate

17 Christ, our High-priest, is ascended into heaven, and sits on the right hand of God the Father, where, without ceasing, he makes intercession for us.
   Martin Luther
   Table Talk (17th century)

Birth of

18 Swaddling clothes camouflaged the King of Glory.
   Byron Stewart
   "Behold the Lion" sermon (2008)

Blood of

19 Our Lord Jesus did not die for imaginary sins, but His heart's blood was spilt to wash out deep crimson stains, which nothing else can remove.
   Charles Spurgeon
   All of Grace (19th century)

20 There is no death of sin without the death of Christ.
   John Owen
   Of the Mortification of Sin in Believers (1656)

Burden Bearer

21 An attitude that releases joy begins with your knowing Christ in a personal way and allowing Him to take the blows of life for you.
   Charles Swindoll
   Laugh Again (1995)

22 There is something about keeping him divine that keeps him distant, packaged, predictable. But don't do it. For heaven's sake, don't. Let him be as human as he intended to be. Let him into the mire and muck of our world. For only if we let him in can he pull us out.
   Max Lucado
   God Came Near (1986)

23 If we want to row against the storms of life, we can do it, and Jesus will let us row until our arms fall off. Or we can call upon the Lord and He will save us.
   Neil Anderson and Charles Mylander
   Blessed Are the Peacemakers (2002)

24 He has been where we are, and he walks with us and weeps with us. And with your tears he can water the seeds of character planted by pain.
   Stephen Arterburn and Jack Felton
   More Jesus, Less Religion (2000)

25 There will be no summons of sorrow which He will not be able to answer.
   Henry Drummond
   "Why Christ Must Depart" sermon (19th century)

26 Even Jesus wept in his trying hour; he knows our pain firsthand.
   David Wilkerson
   "Right Song, Wrong Side" sermon (2009)

27 In what Luther calls "the great exchange," the sinless Jesus so thoroughly took our place that he became the worst of what we are— rapists, thieves, perverts, addicts, liars, gluttons, gossips, murderers, adulterers, fornicators, homosexuals, and idolaters.
   Mark Driscoll and Gerry Breshears
   Death by Love (2008)

Following

28 Following Jesus simply means learning from him how to arrange my life around activities that enable me to live in the fruit of the Spirit.
   John Ortberg
   The Life You've Always Wanted (2002)

29 Doing something in Jesus' name means to do it in his character. It means doing it as Jesus himself would do it if he were in your place.
John Ortberg
The Life You've Always Wanted (2002)

30 Our motto will be, "What would Jesus do?" Our aim will be to act just as he would if he were in our places, regardless of immediate results.
Charles Sheldon
In His Steps (1896)

31 What has Jesus Christ ever asked you to do that wasn't for your own good?
Billy Sunday (20th century) quoted in
The Best of Billy Sunday

32 We should begin each day in fellowship with Jesus, walking with Him and listening to Him.
Greg Laurie
Breakfast with Jesus (2003)

33 Follow Jesus' example the next time you're faced with temptation. Remember what you know of God's word, then ask God to help you fight the battle. And guess what? You're on the winning side.
Greg Laurie
Breakfast with Jesus (2003)

34 Better to be with Jesus, in any circumstance, than to be anywhere else without Him.
Greg Laurie
Breakfast with Jesus (2003)

35 At all times we would be wise to walk a little closer to Christ.
W. Phillip Keller
A Shepherd Looks At Psalm 23 (1970)

36 Jesus, who was not lazy in any respect, calls us to follow His example.
Carole Lewis
Choosing Change (2001)

37 When He took upon Himself the common lot of men, Jesus showed once and for all how God expects His children to live and die.
Jay Adams
Christ and Your Problems (1971)

38 To follow Jesus doesn't remove us from the stuff of life. It is not resolution. It is tension and journey.
David Crowder
Praise Habit (2004)

39 We must be willing to be led.
F. B. Meyer
The Shepherd Psalm (1889)

40 One of the rewards of following Christ is the simplicity and wonder it brings to life.
Joseph Stowell
Following Christ (1996)

41 Following God is always the best choice. It is the safest choice, although it feels anything but safe in the chaos of change.
Mary Ann Froehlich
When You're Facing the Empty Nest (2005)

Humanity of

42 God Himself became a Man to give us a concrete, definite, tangible idea of what to think of when we think of God.
Henry H. Halley
Pocket Bible Handbook (1948)

43 You see, in becoming man, God made it possible for man to see God. When Jesus went home he left the back door open.
Max Lucado
God Came Near (1986)

44 They came at night; they touched him as he walked down the street; they followed him around the sea; they invited him into their homes and placed their children at his feet.

Why? Because he refused to be a statue in a cathedral or a priest in an elevated pulpit. He chose instead to be Jesus.

> Max Lucado
> *God Came Near* (1986)

45 If Jesus personally knows the pain of loss and suffering, he can comfort and encourage me in the midst of the turbulence that he himself warned is inevitable in a world corrupted by sin.

> Lee Strobel
> *The Case for Christ* (1998)

46 Everything that is done for the benefit of humanity, all charity, it all comes through the principles of Jesus Christ.

> Billy Sunday (20th century) quoted in
> *The Best of Billy Sunday*

47 As we look into that workshop at Nazareth, and see the Son of God, in lowly guise, toiling with hammer and hatchet, may we not learn how much He humbled Himself?

> John Dawson
> *The Saviour in the Workshop* (1868)

48 If God is infinite, he is beyond us. If he is beyond us, we cannot know him unless he chooses to make himself known. If he were to make himself known, he would surely do so in the highest terms intelligible to us, namely through human personality. It is exactly this that Christians believe he has done.

> John Stott
> *Christian Basics* (1991)

49 Jesus died with both a literal and metaphorical broken heart.

> Mark Driscoll and Gerry Breshears
> *Death by Love* (2008)

50 Jesus was the mixed-racial Savior of the world.

> Ray Bakke
> *A Theology as Big as the City* (1997)

51 Christian, no matter how serious your present problems may be, no matter how hopeless the situation may seem, take heart! You are not alone. You have a sympathetic high priest who can enter into all your problems, for they have been His problems too.

> Jay Adams
> *Christ and Your Problems* (1971)

Imagined Quotations from

52 "Many there are in this world who know about Me, but do not know Me; that is they have no personal relationship with Me, therefore they have no true apprehension of or faith in Me, and do not accept Me as their Saviour and Lord."

> Sadhu Sundar Singh
> *At the Master's Feet* (20th century)

53 "My children cannot find in this great garden of a world, so full of charming and beautiful things, any true joy until they find Me. I am their Emmanuel, who is ever with them, and I make Myself known to them."

> Sadhu Sundar Singh
> *At the Master's Feet* (20th century)

Lamb of God

54 The Lamb was, and always will be, the Lion.

> Byron Stewart
> "Behold the Lion" sermon (2008)

55 Our Lord will never be appreciated as the Lamb unless He's first encountered as the Lion.

> Dwight Edwards
> *Revolution Within* (2001)

56 Had not this Lamb offered himself to be slain, man had been cast into everlasting chains as well as the devils, who had no mediator, no lamb to be slain for them.

Stephen Charnock
Discourse on the Cleansing Virtue of Christ's Blood (17th century)

Lordship of

57 The first thing Jesus insists upon, at the very moment of the church's origination, is the claim that he alone is Lord.
Richard Phillips, Philip Ryken, and Mark Dever
The Church: One, Holy, Catholic, and Apostolic (2004)

58 We have to be careful that anything we undertake in the name of Jesus Christ we do for one ultimate purpose: His glory, not ours.
Franklin Graham
All for Jesus (2003)

59 Your reaction to Jesus reveals your spiritual condition.
Rich Mendola
"The Acts of the Holy Spirit: Wonders and Good News" sermon (2009)

60 No matter what authority Satan and his subjects have temporarily been allowed in this world system, Christ can pull rank any time He wants to.
Beth Moore
Jesus: 90 Days with the One and Only (2007)

61 When our world seems out of control and disaster comes our way, we can be confident that God has not abandoned us. He is still at work, moving all of creation toward His larger purpose—bringing it under the lordship of the Son, Jesus.
Ed Dobson
Finding God in the Face of Evil (2002)

62 Our Lord used the Word of God as His primary weapon against temptation. He did not use "executive privilege," but instead gave us a

model for winning our own spiritual battles.
Greg Laurie
Breakfast with Jesus (2003)

63 When Jesus is truly our Lord, he directs our lives and we gladly obey him. Indeed, we bring every part of our lives under his lordship—our home and family, our sexuality and marriage, our job or unemployment, our money and possessions, our ambitions and recreations.
John Stott
Christian Basics (1991)

64 If I proclaim Jesus to be Lord of my life, then He's Lord of my bank account, my speech, my sexual appetites, my eating habits, my thoughts and all the minutia of details that I encounter each and every day. He is Lord of all.
Rebecca Lusignolo
"Lord of All" devotional (2008)

Love of

65 Wherever you are spiritually, whatever you have been through emotionally, you are already wrapped in the Lord's embrace. Held by nail-scarred hands. Enfolded in the arms of One who believes in you, supports you, treasures you, and loves you.
Liz Curtis Higgs
Embrace Grace (2006)

66 Jesus will not love you any less or any more for all eternity than He loved you when He purchased your life with His own blood.
Bruce Wilkinson
A Life God Rewards (2002)

67 If Jesus loves me as he says, he has my best interests at heart. That means I have nothing to lose and everything to gain by committing myself to him and his purposes.
Lee Strobel
The Case for Christ (1998)

68 Never was any love lost that was bestowed upon Christ.
Matthew Henry
Commentary on the Whole Bible (1706)

69 When Jesus tells us to love our enemies, He Himself will give us the love with which to do it. We are neither factories nor reservoirs of His love, only channels. When we understand that, all excuse for pride is eliminated.
Corrie ten Boom
Amazing Love (1953)

70 The kind of love Jesus models is astonishing, so unlike our meager efforts to tolerate difficult people or to be nice to people who are not nice to us.
Lloyd John Ogilvie
The Magnificent Vision (1980)

71 Jesus' desire was not just to engage in their intellects but to capture their hearts.
Brent Curtis
The Sacred Romance (1997)

72 The Lord wants to be personally involved in our lives. He wants to be involved with us in the grocery store checkout line. He wants to be involved with us when we get caught in a traffic jam and can't move.
Joyce Meyer
If Not for the Grace of God (1995)

73 He that endeavours to check disease, to alleviate suffering, to lessen pain, to help the self-curative powers of nature, and to lengthen life, may surely take comfort in the thought, that, however much he may fail, he is at any rate walking in the footsteps of Jesus of Nazareth.
J.C. Ryle
The Upper Room (19th century)

74 Jesus Christ is an unchangeably faithful and everlasting friend.

Samuel Hopkins
"The Friendship between Jesus Christ and Believers" sermon (1803)

75 Jesus loved us through the cross before we loved him, and his love transforms us so that we can love him and love others.
Mark Driscoll and Gerry Breshears
Death by Love (2008)

Mediator

76 Only someone both fully divine and truly human can effectively mediate between God and men, and Jesus is exactly that.
C. J. Mahaney
Christ Our Mediator (2004)

77 Without Christ, God will not be found, known, or comprehended.
Martin Luther
Table Talk (16th century)

78 Since a mediator is not a mediator of one, but supposes in the notion of it two parties, there must be a consent on both sides. God's consent is manifested by giving, our consent is by receiving, which is a title given to faith.
Stephen Charnock
Discourse on the Cleansing Virtue of Chist's Blood (1652)

Messiah

79 The reason the Bible doesn't give us a list of behaviors that, if kept, will guarantee us a spot in heaven is because the forty-four authors of Scripture understood that mankind needs a savior, a Messiah, not a to-do list.
Andy Stanley
How Good Is Good Enough? (2003)

Power of

80 The Roman guard became the Keystone cops. Two hundred fighting men collapse

into a noisy pile of shields, swords, and lamps. Don't miss the symbolism here: When Jesus speaks, Satan falls.
> Max Lucado
> *A Gentle Thunder* (1995)

81 The best of Satan melts as wax before the presence of Christ.
> Max Lucado
> *A Gentle Thunder* (1995)

82 If Jesus has divine power, he has the supernatural ability to guide me and help me and transform me as I follow him.
> Lee Strobel
> *The Case for Christ* (1998)

83 There is still nothing in the world more revolutionary than a people moving together by the Spirit of Jesus.
> Jonathan Campbell and Jennifer Campbell
> *The Way of Jesus* (2005)

84 To show others Christ's sufficiency, you must—of necessity—at times be in a position of desperate need yourself.
> Rebecca Lusignolo
> *Adversity* (2007)

85 Jesus Christ is able to untangle all the snarls in your soul, to banish all your complexes, and to transform even your fixed habit patterns, no matter how deeply they are etched in your subconscious.
> Corrie ten Boom
> *Amazing Love* (1953)

86 No matter what critics may say, the Christ of the New Testament can change lives.
> Josh and Sean McDowell
> *Evidence for the Resurrection* (2009)

87 The words of our Saviour Christ are exceeding powerful; they have hands and feet; they outdo the utmost subtleties of the worldly-wise.
> Martin Luther
> *Table Talk* (16th century)

88 Because Jesus Christ is a man, He feels what we feel. Because He is God, He can do something about it.
> Tony Evans
> *Theology You Can Count On* (2008)

89 Set faith at work on Christ for the killing of your sin.
> John Owen
> *Of the Mortification of Sin in Believers* (1656)

Resurrection

90 We focus so much on the fact that Jesus died for us, we sometimes forget that He also lived for us and lives for us still.
> Michael Card
> *Immanuel: Reflections on the Life of Christ* (1990)

as Sacrifice

91 Make no mistake: Jesus can descend from the cross and save Himself at any moment. It isn't the nails that keep Him there. What keeps Him there is what placed Him there— His passion to do the will of His Father, and His love for sinners like you and me.
> C. J. Mahaney
> *Christ Our Mediator* (2004)

92 Who really killed Jesus? God did. That's who sent Him to the cross, crushing Him beneath the weight of our sins.
> C. J. Mahaney
> *Christ Our Mediator* (2004)

93 New things will always come along. Some will be good; some will be better. But according to God, only one thing will be

best. He sent His Son into the world to live a perfect life and go to the cross to bear His wrath for sinners like you and me.

C. J. Mahaney
The Cross Centered Life (2002)

94 If the concept of sin doesn't make sense, then someone dying for our sins is even more confusing and considered downright ridiculous by many.

Ravi Zacharias
Beyond Opinion (2007)

95 Jesus is always more ready to forgive than you are to confess.

Tony Evans
God Is Up to Something Great (2002)

96 Think of what Christ did: He left his heavenly home, in obedience to His Father, came to this earth to live and to be one of us. Remember, this was God in human form— Immanuel—God with us. His motives would be misunderstood. Jesus willingly suffered in order to identify with us. His whole purpose and reason for coming was to give everything for us—including His precious blood and life.

Franklin Graham
The Name (2002)

97 The agonies of God's Son were incomparable. No one ever suffered like this man. Through all eternity, we will contemplate the killing of the Son of God and sing, "Worthy is the Lamb who was slain."

John Piper
Seeing and Savoring Jesus Christ (2004)

98 Everyone else came into the world to live; Jesus came into the world to die.

Fulton Sheen
Life of Christ (1958)

99 Sometimes we might not even be aware of the loving sacrifices a friend is making on our behalf. That's what was so awesome about

Jesus' sacrifice: He gave His life to save those who didn't know Him or who rejected Him as their friend.

G. A. Myers
Hugs for Friends (2003)

100 The mystery of the humanity of Christ, that he sunk himself into our flesh, is beyond all human understanding.

Martin Luther
Table Talk (16th century)

101 The more I look at the sufferings of the Son of God, the more sure I am that they must meet my case. Why did He suffer, if not to turn aside the penalty from us?

Charles Spurgeon
All of Grace (19th century)

102 We face death, but thanks to Jesus, we only face its shadow.

Max Lucado
Traveling Light (2001)

103 Jesus' death is not a tragedy perpetuated by oppressive Roman soldiers but a self-initiated sacrifice, an offering he came to make.

Mark Driscoll and Gerry Breshears
Death by Love (2008)

as Savior

104 A good map can't catch the fish, but it can show you where they live. The Bible can't save you, but it can lead you to the One who can—Jesus.

Jimmy Houston
Hooked for Life (1999)

105 One of the best-kept secrets in Christianity is that God accepts us. True, He can't stand our sinful acts, but He loves us. He doesn't have us on performance-based acceptance; He has us on Jesus-based acceptance.

Bill Gillham
Lifetime Guarantee (1993)

106   Christ came down to save us from a terrible hell, and any man who is cast down to hell from here must go in the full blaze of the gospel, and over the mangled body of the Son of God.
D. L. Moody
"Christ Seeking Sinners" sermon (1880)

107   When Jesus died, heaven was opened for all who would come.
Colin Smith
Unlocking the Bible Story (2002)

108   Only the spirit and life of Christ Himself will satisfy a thirsting soul.
W. Phillip Keller
A Shepherd Looks at Psalm 23 (1970)

109   The religion of Paul was rooted altogether in the redeeming work of Jesus Christ. Jesus for Paul was primarily not a Revealer, but a Saviour.
J. Gresham Machen
The Origin of Paul's Religion (1921)

110   The loss of a soul! Christ knew what it meant. That is what brought Him from the bosom of the Father; that is what brought Him from the throne; that is what brought Him to Calvary.
D. L. Moody
Best Thoughts and Discourses of D. L. Moody (1876)

111   The end for which Christ lives, and for which he has left his church in the world, is the salvation of sinners.
Charles Finney
Lectures to Professing Christians (1837)

112   This mentality that "what is true for you is not necessarily what is true for me" is in direct contrast to the biblical Truth that Jesus Christ is the only way to heaven.
Michael Youssef
"The Perfect Antidote" article (2009)

113   If there is any trouble in your heart, if you are in darkness, or in the power of sin, I bring to you the Son of God, with the promise that He will come in and take charge.
Andrew Murray
Master's Indwelling (1895)

114   It is well for us that as sin lives, and the flesh lives, and the devil lives, so Jesus lives; and it is also well that whatever might these may have to ruin us, Jesus has still greater power to save us.
Charles Spurgeon
All of Grace (19th century)

115   Look to Jesus for all you need between Hell Gate and Heaven Gate.
Charles Spurgeon
All of Grace (19th century)

116   We do not realize what we owe Him until we realize that He has plucked us from the fearful pit, and the miry clay, and set us upon a rock of God's own founding.
Peter Taylor Forsyth
The Work of Christ (1909)

117   Christ comes with kingly power, to rescue sinners, as a prey from the mouth of the terrible one.
John Flavel
Christ Altogether Lovely (17th century)

118   When Christ cried out on Calvary, "It is finished!" He meant what He said. All that men have to do now is just accept the work of Jesus Christ.
D. L. Moody
The Way to God (1884)

Seeking the Lost

119   Just as we would look for our children, Jesus also continues "seeking" us until we are found. We would never say, "Oh, I have most

of my children. That's fine. We can go on without that one." Jesus doesn't want to leave any child behind either. He isn't concerned that we have crossed the boundary lines or done things that we shouldn't have done. His concern is that we are found.

Laurie Lovejoy Hilliard and Sharon Lovejoy Autry
Hold You, Mommy (2006)

120   If there is a man or woman in this audience to-night who believes that he or she is lost, I have good news to tell you—Christ is come after you.

D. L. Moody
Best Thoughts and Discourses of D. L. Moody (1876)

Servant

121   When Jesus came in the form of a servant, he was not disguising who God is. He was revealing who God is.

John Ortberg
The Life You've Always Wanted (2002)

122   The Gospel accounts show Him with a passion for helping those in trouble. He has not changed. The minute we need saving from anything, He stands ready in His role as Saviour.

Catherine Marshall
Something More (1974)

Son of God

123   If Jesus is the Son of God, his teachings are more than just good ideas from a wise teacher; they are divine insights on which I can confidently build my life.

Lee Strobel
The Case for Christ (1998)

Supremacy of

124   A prevalent obstruction to the centrality and supremacy of Jesus is our preoccupation with ourselves.

Joseph Stowell
The Trouble with Jesus (2003)

125   The older we get in the Lord, the simpler life becomes as we realize it's all about Jesus.

Jon Courson
Application Commentary (2005)

126   Our journey begins where the wise men's ended. Like them, we have found a Wisdom not to ponder but to worship, a wisdom that is not a matter of words but who is The Word.

Michael Card
Immanuel: Reflections on the Life of Christ (1990)

127   Jesus is the only One who can satisfy our longings. All other relationships will fall short. No one else is able to completely satiate our hunger for perfect love.

Lisa Harper
Every Woman's Hope (2001)

128   Jesus is the perfect model of endurance. During His ministry, He was pulled in a thousand different directions, constantly gave to others, and experienced rejection and suffering in return. Yet He knew His goal and kept a single focus to accomplish it. Though He made Himself available to others, He also knew how to set boundaries and found times for private spiritual renewal. Who can better understand your situation? When you are tired, weary, and don't know if you can keep going, look to Him.

Melody Rossi
May I Walk You Home? (2007)

129   Christ remains the measure of men, and His life of perfect integrity, as He lived before God for men and before men for God, remains our pattern and example.

Iain Campbell
Tabletalk magazine (2009)

130   Just as in science I should speak of protoplasm, of oxygen or carbonic acid gas, so in talking of religion I must talk about faith and Jesus Christ.
Henry Drummond
Stones Rolled Away and Other Addresses to Young Men (1893)

Teachings of

131   The Sermon on the Mount, like all the rest of the New Testament, really leads a man straight to the foot of the cross.
J. Gresham Machen
Christianity and Liberalism (1923)

Uniqueness of

132   Jesus Christ has no peers; there is no one to be compared with Him.
D. L. Moody
"The Transfiguration" sermon
(19th century)

133   There is only one safe and sure center of Christian experience, doctrine and testimony: Jesus Christ. Stand at any other point, no matter how good, and you will become lopsided. Stand with Him and you keep your balance, for by Him all things consist.
Vance Havner
Jesus Only (1946)

134   Jesus is not only Lord of creation in that He made everyone and everything. He is also Lord of redemption, the one who sacrificed Himself to die in the place of sinful men, taking the wages of sin upon Himself; the one who conquered sin and death by rising from the dead; the only one through whom a person can and must be delivered from sin.
James Odens
Lighting the Way to God (1999)

135   I wonder how many of us have turned away from Jesus, given up any hope of the spiritual life because we don't fit, because we aren't like everyone else, and because our Christianity seems so different and strange from the rest of the churches. I wonder if we realize how anxious Jesus is to reach out and walk with us arm in arm.
Michael Yaconelli
Messy Spirituality (2002)

136   Is there anyone more misquoted, misrepresented, or misinterpreted than Jesus Christ?
Joshua Youssef
"The Power of the Unaltered Word of God" article (2009)

137   I need Christ, not something that resembles Him.
C. S. Lewis
A Grief Observed (1961)

138   The distinct claims of Jesus to be God eliminate the popular ploy of skeptics who regard Jesus as just a good moral man or a prophet who said a lot of profound things.
Josh McDowell
More Than a Carpenter (1977)

139   No ordinary righteous man died on the Cross but the Son of God, the highest object of the divine love.
Paul Wernle
The Beginnings of Christianity (1903)

140   God, still fully God, became fully man as well so that He could pour Himself out on an executioner's cross as our representative. That's who Jesus was—both Son of God and Son of Man—and that's what Jesus did.
J. Budziszewski
How to Stay Christian in College (2004)

141   The Prince of the kings of the earth, the King of glory, stoops from the throne of the

universe, and takes His place in the workshop of perhaps the meanest village in the land! How Godlike!

John Dawson
The Saviour in the Workshop (1868)

142   The more we see of Jesus, the more we know there's still so much to be seen. The more He touches our lives, the more we realize our desperate need for Him to consume every part of us.

Matt Redman
The Unquenchable Worshipper (2001)

238 JOY

Be glad in the LORD, and rejoice, ye righteous: and shout for joy, all ye that are upright in heart.
PSALM 32:11

1   I know of no greater need today than the need for joy. Unexplainable, contagious joy. Outrageous joy.

Charles Swindoll
Laugh Again (1995)

2   Joy is a choice. It's a matter of attitude that stems from one's confidence in God—that He is at work, that He is in full control, that He is in the midst of whatever has happened, is happening and will happen. Either we fix our minds on that and determine to laugh again, or we wail and whine our way through life. We determine which way we will go.

Chuck Swindoll
Laugh Again (1995)

3   God created us to enjoy him because joy is the clearest witness to the worth of what we enjoy. It's the deepest reverberation in the heart of man of the value of God's glory.

John Piper
The Supremacy of Christ in a Postmodern World (2007)

4   We have no joy but in Christ.

Matthew Henry
Commentary on the Whole Bible (1706)

5   Happiness is when you are happy. Joy is when God has done so much in your life that you will bring happiness to others.

Gary Kinnaman
Learning to Love the One You Marry (1997)

6   Joy is for the journey, especially the most difficult parts of it, not just for the reflective moments after the storm.

Lloyd John Ogilvie
The Magnificent Vision (1980)

7   Now is the time to wake up to the possibilities each of us has to add joy and meaning to our daily lives through practicing the art of loving and being loved.

Cheryl and Paul Meier
Unbreakable Bonds (2002)

8   Joy is not the fruit of "favorable" circumstances. Rather, it's the outpouring of a contented heart.

Wendy Widder
Living Whole (2000)

9   Joy is more than a feeling; it is a deep peace, blended together with a solid hope that God has not left us. Joy is a delight in knowing there will be a better day. Can we have joy as our companion even when the road gets bumpy? Absolutely.

Karol Ladd
The Power of a Positive Woman (2002)

10   Joy requires single-mindedness. The world is full of reasons to be sad or distressed, but beauty and goodness also abound. Which to look at? What you see is what you get.

Mike Mason
Champagne for the Soul (2003)

11 I need God's joy—and I (and probably you as well) most need His joy when things are black. You and I need joy when we're suffering and misunderstood, when we're rejected and hated, and when we're in emotional or physical pain.
 Elizabeth George
 God's Garden of Grace (1996)

12 One of the greatest threats to our joy is disobedience to God's Word. When we live in disobedience, we become a fruitless and joyless Christian.
 Michael Youssef
 "Joy Through Christ" article (2010)

13 When Christ is the center of our lives, when His glory is our goal, when we refuse to be intimidated by life's obstacles, and when we live totally for Christ in obedience, we will find a joy that will carry us through the darkest of valleys.
 Michael Youssef
 "Joy Through Christ" article (2010)

14 The children of the world first joy, then must sorrow forever; but the children of God first sorrow, then rejoice forever.
 The Lutheran Witness (1885)

15 Evidence about God provides a basis for faith that meets your needs for being loved, accepted, and secure; and that kind of faith yields joy.
 Josh McDowell and Dale Bellis
 Evidence for Joy (1984)

16 Magnets help draw two surfaces together. And magnetic joy can draw people together.
 Martha Bolton and Phil Callaway
 It's Always Darkest before the Fridge Door Opens (2006)

17 Christians without joy are basically useless to the work of God. They will enter heaven when they die, but they will take no one with them. After all, who would want what they have?
 Joe Beam
 Getting Past Guilt (2003)

239 JUDGING (*see also* **CRITICISM; FAULT-FINDING; SELF-RIGHTEOUSNESS**)
Judge not according to the appearance, but judge righteous judgment.
JOHN 7:24

1 Jonah wanted his own way more than he wanted God's will. Before judging Jonah too quickly—are we guilty of the same?
 Steve Campbell
 "Jonah—Is This the End or Just the Beginning?" sermon (2009)

2 Sodom was warned and then destroyed, and God is sending a warning to America. America is embracing the same sins that God destroyed Sodom and Gomorrah for.
 Adrian Rogers
 Unmasking False Prophets (2007)

3 He...could never mount on wings of words to Heaven. Duty on earth, restitution on earth, action on earth: these first, as the first steep steps upward. Strait was the gate and narrow was the way; far straiter and narrower than the broad high road paved with vain professions and vain repetitions, motes from other men's eyes and liberal delivery of others to the judgment—all cheap materials, costing absolutely nothing.
 Charles Dickens
 Little Dorrit (1857)

4 The reason we see hypocrisy and fraud and unreality in others is because they are all in our own hearts. The great characteristic of a saint is humility—Yes, all those things and other evils would have been manifested in me but for the grace of God, therefore I have no right to judge.
 Oswald Chambers
 My Utmost for His Highest (1935)

5 Try not to judge what you hear too quickly. Wait. Watch. Listen. And maybe you will discover the thrill of God speaking to you in some way through the life of another person.
Ken Gire
Reflections on Your Life (1998)

6 Judgmentalism. . .is that ugly refusal to acknowledge that "there but for the grace of God go I."
Paul Copan
"Who Are You to Judge Others?" article (2001)

7 Our society would benefit from the courageous words of qualified people who display both firmness of conviction and civility or respect, which is what Ephesians 4:15 refers to—"speaking the truth in love."
Paul Copan
"Who Are You to Judge Others?" article (2001)

8 Behind the mask of an apparently sensitive and compassionate "open-mindedness," there often exists a moral gutlessness.
Paul Copan
"Who Are You to Judge Others?" article (2001)

9 We have to know the facts of a case if we want the privilege of having an opinion about it.
Lewis Smedes
Choices (1986)

10 Were we to think more of our own mistakes and offences, we should be less apt to judge other people.
Matthew Henry
Commentary on the Whole Bible (1706)

11 Men in a corrupt and carnal frame, have their spiritual senses in but poor plight for judging and distinguishing spiritual things.
Jonathan Edwards
A Treatise Concerning Religious Affections (18th century)

240 JUDGMENT, GOD'S

The judgments of the LORD are true and righteous altogether.
PSALM 19:9

1 We are very interested in death but we rarely speak about judgment.
Martyn Lloyd-Jones
Love So Amazing (1962)

2 The final judgment will be done to display and glorify the righteousness of God.
Jonathan Edwards
"The Final Judgment" sermon (1741)

3 One of the biggest lies Satan tells the lost is that they will be good enough for God on Judgment Day.
Mark Cahill
One Thing You Can't Do in Heaven (2002)

4 People today simply do not believe that there will be a day of judgment.
R. C. Sproul
Saved from What? (2002)

5 Who needs a Savior when there's no clear and present threat of judgment?
R. C. Sproul
Saved from What? (2002)

6 God judges sin because He loathes what it does to us and to others. He wants us to loathe sin, too—and be its executioner. If we don't, He will.
David Roper
A Beacon in the Darkness (1995)

7 This present scene, and all its cures and all its gaieties, will soon be rolled away, and "we must stand before the judgment seat of Christ."
William Wilberforce
A Practical View of the Prevailing Religious System of Professed Christians (1815)

8 Great as is the misery of a lost soul when separated from the body, this is probably small when compared with the exceeding weight of misery which shall overtake it at the Day of Judgment.
Archibald Alexander
The Misery of the Lost (19th century)

9 God is resolved that men shall feel sin either here or hereafter.
George Swinnock
Works of George Swinnock (17th century)

10 The eyes of the Lord are upon the righteous of the land, but the wicked cannot elude His vengeance.
Peter Barron
The United Presbyterian Magazine (1856)

11 What will you wish you had done, when the King comes?
Amy Carmichael
From Sunrise Land: Letters from Japan (1895)

12 It is the highest folly to regulate our actions by any other standard than that by which we must be judged.
Henry Scougal
Life of God in the Soul of Man (17th century)

13 You are but dead and damned men, except you will be converted. Should I tell you otherwise, I should deceive you with a lie.
Richard Baxter
A Call to the Unconverted, to Turn and Live (17th century)

14 Often, without being at all aware of it, men judge themselves, not by God's rule, but by their own.
Charles Finney
"Men Often Highly Esteem What God Abhors" sermon (19th century)

15 When God hath shaken your careless Soul out of your Body, and you must answer for all your Sins in your own Name; O then, what would you give for a Saviour!
Richard Baxter
The Causes and Danger of Slighting Christ and His Gospel (17th century)

16 If thou shalt thus condemn thyself, how shalt thou escape the just condemnation of God, who knows all thy misdeeds better than thyself?
Lewis Bayly
The Practice of Piety (1611)

17 Can we think that he that threw the angels out of heaven will suffer dust and worms' meat to run a contrary course, and to continue always so?
Richard Sibbes
The Bruised Reed (1630)

18 To hope that we shall be saved, though continuing unconverted, is to hope that we shall prove God a liar.
Joseph Alleine
A Sure Guide to Heaven (1671)

241 JUSTICE
*Defend the poor and fatherless:
do justice to the afflicted and needy.*
PSALM 82:3

1 Too often people fall into the trap of thinking that because God hasn't dealt with evil yet, He is not dealing with it at all.
Ronald Rhodes
Who Made God? (2003)

2 No cruelty, no crime, no injustice escapes the attention of God.
Kay Arthur
When Bad Things Happen (2002)

3 A holy God made the universe in such a way that actions true to His character, and the laws derived from His character, are always rewarded. Actions that violate His character,

however, are always punished. He rewards every act of justice; He punishes every act of injustice.

Randy Alcorn
The Purity Principle (2003)

4   God will not be mocked; that which a man soweth, that shall he also reap. And if ye will not be at peace with God, God will not be at peace with you. Who can stand before God when he is angry.

George Whitefield
"A Sermon, Preached on Sabbath Morning" (1741)

5   The bow of God's wrath is bent, and the arrow is made ready on the string, and justice bends the arrow at your heart.

Jonathan Edwards
"Sinners in the Hands of an Angry God" sermon (1741)

6   O sinner! Consider the fearful danger you are in: 'tis a great furnace of wrath, a wide and bottomless pit.

Jonathan Edwards
"Sinners in the Hands of an Angry God" sermon (1741)

7   We want justice for others, mercy for ourselves.

David Hawkins
Prescription for Living Beyond (2006)

8   None are ruined by the justice of God but those that hate to be reformed by the grace of God.

Matthew Henry
Commentary on the Whole Bible (1706)

9   Though justice be thy plea, consider this, That, in the course of justice, none of us Should see salvation: we do pray for mercy.

William Shakespeare
The Merchant of Venice (1598)

242 JUSTIFICATION

But for us also, to whom it shall be imputed, if we believe on him that raised up Jesus our Lord from the dead; Who was delivered for our offences, and was raised again for our justification.
ROMANS 4:24–25

1   If Abram, after years of holy living, is not justified by his works, but is accepted before God on account of his faith, much more must this be the case with the ungodly sinner who, having lived in unrighteousness, yet believeth on Jesus and is saved.

Charles Spurgeon
"Justification by Faith" sermon (1868)

2   In the Bible justification has to do with our legal standing before God. It is God's declaration that we are righteous at the bar of his justice.

Richard Phillips, Philip Ryken, and Mark Dever
The Church: One, Holy, Catholic, and Apostolic (2004)

3   Take heed thou destroy not thy own soul by pleading thy righteousness more or less. Go as altogether ungodly, guilty, lost, destroyed, deserving and dropping into hell; and thou shalt then find favour in his sight, and know that he justifieth the ungodly.

John Wesley
Justification by Faith (1744)

4   A not guilty is entered into the court of God when this blood is pleaded, and a not guilty inscribed upon the roll of conscience when this blood is sprinkled.

Stephen Charnock
Discourse on the Cleansing Virtue of Christ's Blood (17th century)

5   Only God can justify the ungodly; but He can do it to perfection.

Charles Spurgeon
All of Grace (19th century)

6 I venture to say that a sinner justified by God stands on even a surer footing than a righteous man justified by his works, if such there be.

Charles Spurgeon
All of Grace (19th century)

243 KINDNESS

Put on therefore, as the elect of God, holy and beloved, bowels of mercies, kindness. . .
COLOSSIANS 3:12

1 All who have received grace should learn to be gracious to others.

Watchman Nee
Not I But Christ (1948)

2 We must learn to value our fellow Christians and not engage in fault-finding or in exposing their weaknesses.

Watchman Nee
Changed into His Likeness (1967)

3 Without kindness, truth is just so much dogma. Without truth, kindness is mere sentimentality.

David Roper
A Beacon in the Darkness (1995)

4 By showing love through acts of kindness, we can point people toward the God who is both kindness and love.

Amy Nappa
A Woman's Touch (2001)

5 Pour honey into hearts instead of vinegar.

Amy Nappa
A Woman's Touch (2001)

6 You can be an instrument of God simply by speaking kind words that build people up.

Cindi McMenamin
When a Woman Discovers Her Dream (2005)

7 Everyone can be thoughtful, and even a small gesture can have a positive impact.

Rachael Crabb and Raeann Hart
The Personal Touch (1990)

244 KINGDOM OF GOD/HEAVEN

Repent ye: for the kingdom of heaven is at hand.
MATTHEW 3:2

1 The Kingdom of God is a Kingdom of limitless power, ceaseless joy, and unending peace. It is a Kingdom of righteousness, a Kingdom of love, and a Kingdom of right relationships.

Roy Lessin
Today Is Your Best Day (2006)

2 So great is the kingdom of Heaven that the things of this world pale into insignificance.

Matthew Kelly
A Call to Joy (1997)

3 The kingdom of God is like a playground. We're all in this big, worldwide community sharing equipment, choosing sides for games, running, resting, and learning how to get along with all the others on the playground.

Robin Chaddock
Discovering Your Divine Assignment (2005)

4 The doctrine of the Kingdom of Heaven, which was the main teaching of Jesus, is certainly one of the most revolutionary doctrines that ever stirred and changed human thought.

H. G. Wells
Outline of History (1920)

5 So, when I think on God's Kingdom, I am compelled to be silent because of its immensity, because God's Kingdom is none other than God Himself with all His riches.

Meister Eckhart
Meister Eckhart's Sermons (14th century)

6 Whoever knows and recognizes how near God's Kingdom is to him may say with Jacob, "God is in this place, and I knew it not."
Meister Eckhart
Meister Eckhart's Sermons (14th century)

7 What is the kingdom of Christ? A rule of love, of truth—a rule of service. The king is the chief servant in it.
George MacDonald
"The Child in the Midst" sermon
(19th century)

245 KNOWING GOD
(*see also* INTIMACY WITH GOD; PRESENCE OF GOD)
That ye might walk worthy of the Lord unto all pleasing, being fruitful in every good work, and increasing in the knowledge of God.
COLOSSIANS 1:10

1 Members of Christian churches continue to think small thoughts of God and great thoughts of man. This state of affairs reveals that too many Christians have neglected their first great calling: to know their God.
Thabiti Anyabwile
What Is a Healthy Church Member? (2008)

2 We have not been created for the purpose of finding our ultimate satisfaction in a job. There is no spouse whom we were ever meant to take as the ultimate concern in our life. We have been made for the purpose of knowing God.
Mark Dever
Twelve Challenges Churches Face (2008)

3 As the Mississippi flows through the middle of America and the tributaries feed into it on both sides, so when one seeks first the Kingdom of God and His righteousness, all else flows into the central purpose, to know Christ and to make Him known.
Vance Havner
Jesus Only (1946)

4 Learning Who God is is not a lecture but a lab.
Karon Phillips Goodman
You Still Here, Lord? (2004)

5 Getting to know God is not a task for the lazy among us. It's a full-time job!
Karon Phillips Goodman
You Still Here, Lord? (2004)

6 What men stand most in need of, is the knowledge of God.
François Fénelon and Jeanne Guyon
Spiritual Progress (17th century)

7 Awareness is not possible if our hearts are filled with preoccupation, with the desire to control, or with worry about our image.
Robert Wicks
Everyday Simplicity (2000)

8 God speaks and reveals Himself through His Word. He describes His character, qualities, desires, and plans. He gives us a glimpse into His background and "history." In short, He provides us with lots of information so we can know Him.
Mike Macintosh
Falling in Love with the Bible (2005)

9 He knows God rightly who knows Him everywhere.
Meister Eckhart
Meister Eckhart's Sermons (14th century)

10 No man desires anything so eagerly as God desires to bring men to the knowledge of Himself.
Meister Eckhart
Meister Eckhart's Sermons (14th century)

11 The eye with which I see God is the same with which God sees me. My eye and God's eye is one eye, and one sight, and one knowledge, and one love.
Meister Eckhart
Meister Eckhart's Sermons (14th century)

12 Knowledge about God is not a substitute for a relationship with God.
　Donna Partow
　This Isn't the Life I Signed Up For (2003)

13 Those who speak of the transformation wrought in Paul by the appearance of Jesus as magical or mechanical or inconceivable have never reflected upon the mysteries of personal intercourse.
　J. Gresham Machen
　The Origin of Paul's Religion (1921)

14 Knowledge of God without knowledge of our wretchedness makes for pride.
　Blaise Pascal
　Pensées (17th century)

15 The ardent desire of knowing God, is the surest testimony of our love to God, and of God's favour to us.
　Lewis Bayly
　The Practice of Piety (1611)

16 If God is the Supreme Good then our highest blessedness on earth must lie in knowing Him as perfectly as possible.
　A. W. Tozer
　That Incredible Christian (1960s)

17 To know God means knowing more than that He exists. It means knowing him as we know a brother, or better, our own father.
　James Sire
　The Universe Next Door (1976)

18 We can find God in our own questions; we don't have to settle for others' answers.
　Timothy Johnson
　Finding God in the Questions (2004)

19 It is impossible to know God, to obey Him, to function within His family, or to understand His Word if we are thinking incorrectly about who He is.
　Michael Phillips
　A God to Call Father (1994)

20 The degree to which man chooses to follow his God-hungry instinct will determine the extent to which mind, heart, soul, and will reach their fullness of maturity and potential, and whether they operate with unity and harmony inside him.
　Michael Phillips
　A God to Call Father (1994)

21 Desire and intention are the most dynamic of our faculties; they do work. They are the true explorers of the Infinite, the instruments of our ascents to God. Reason comes to the foot of the mountain; it is the industrious will urged by the passionate heart which climbs the slope.
　Evelyn Underhill
　The Essentials of Mysticism (1960)

246 KNOWLEDGE
(*see also* INTELLECT)
And I have filled him with the spirit of God, in wisdom, and in understanding, and in knowledge.
Exodus 31:3

1 It is not the study of theology, it is not reading books upon points of controversy, it is not searching into mysterious prophecy which will bless your soul, it is looking to Jesus crucified.
　Charles Spurgeon
　"Justification by Faith" sermon (1868)

2 There never has been a day when knowledge has been sweeping over the earth as it is at the present time. . . . But this doesn't mean that righteousness is increasing. Therefore, let us be wary.
　D. L. Moody
　"The Eighth Chapter of Romans" sermon (19th century)

3 But Eve was led astray by the desire for knowledge—"the fruit was to be desired to make one wise," and man got a knowledge of good without possessing it, a knowledge of it

only from the evil that was its opposite. And since that day man has ever sought his religion more in knowledge than in life.

Andrew Murray
Prayer's Inner Chamber (1912)

4   It was especially the desire for knowledge, in a way and at a time God had forbidden it, that led Eve astray. As the outcome of the temptation, to think that we can take the knowledge of God's truth for ourselves out of his Word as we will, is still our greatest danger.

Andrew Murray
Prayer's Inner Chamber (1912)

5   Books are wonderful mentors; they are available at any hour of the day or night. We can reread them and glean new insights throughout our lives. No doubt God has spoken to me through books more than through any other source.

Betty Southard
The Mentor Quest (2002)

6   Be a learner and a listener. Spend more time gaining wisdom and knowledge than giving it. Be proud of who you are. Your Creator has already affirmed you. He looked on all of His creation and declared it very good.

Stan Toler
Minute Motivators for Men (2004)

7   Knowledge is power, but power for evil as well as for good.

School Committee Public Documents of Massachusetts (1866)

8   If in our pursuit of higher knowledge, God seems to get smaller, we are being deceived.

Beth Moore
Voices of the Faithful (2005)

9   Since the Holy Spirit always instructs us in what is useful, but altogether omits, or only touches cursorily on matters which tend little to edification, of all such matters, it certainly is our duty to remain in willing ignorance.

John Calvin
Institutes of the Christian Religion (16th century)

10   Let us here remember that on the whole subject of religion one rule of modesty and soberness is to be observed, and it is this, in obscure matters not to speak or think, or even long to know, more than the Word of God has delivered.

John Calvin
Institutes of the Christian Religion (16th century)

LAST DAYS
(*see* END TIMES; SECOND COMING)

247 LAUGHTER (*see also* HUMOR)
A merry heart doeth good like a medicine.
PROVERBS 17:22

1   Laughter is not only necessary for special friendship bonding but for good health.

Sandra Aldrich
From One Single Mother to Another (1991)

2   Not only does laughter relieve daily tension, but it creates marvelous memories.

Sandra Aldrich
From One Single Mother to Another (1991)

3   Laughing at ourselves is a sign that our spirit transcends the present trouble. We believe that this life is not all there is. We believe that our God will look after us.

Anne Bryan Smollin
God Knows You're Stressed (2001)

4   Genuine, hearty laughter is one of the greatest gifts imparted to us by our Father. It has the amazing power to diminish our

pain, lift our souls in joyous good cheer, while providing bright hope for the unknown days ahead.
W. Phillip Keller
What Makes Life Worth Living? (1998)

5   Laughter was created for the good of the human body and spirit.
Donna VanLiere and Eddie Carswell
Sheltering Trees (2001)

6   Laughter removes all barriers. When people are laughing together, there are no age differences, no racial barriers, and no economic distinctions. It is just people enjoying their existence.
Bruce Bickel and Stan Jantz
Simple Matters (2001)

7   Play is an expression of God's presence in the world; one clear sign of God's absence in society is the absence of playfulness and laughter.
Michael Yaconelli
Dangerous Wonder (1998)

8   For those who love God, laughter isn't optional, it's scriptural.
Liz Curtis Higgs
She Who Laughs, Lasts (2000)

9   Laughter is the language of the young at heart and the antidote to what ails us.
Barbara Johnson
She Who Laughs, Lasts (2000)

248 LAW, THE (*see also* RULES)
Therefore by the deeds of the law there shall no flesh be justified in his sight: for by the law is the knowledge of sin.
ROMANS 3:20

1   The law sets before us our wretched state by sin, but there it leaves us. It discovers our disease, but does not make known the cure.
Matthew Henry
Commentary on the Whole Bible (1706)

2   Many such there have been, and are, who speak lightly of the restraints of God's law, and deem themselves freed from obligations to obey it. Let Christians stand at a distance from such.
Matthew Henry
Commentary on the Whole Bible (1706)

3   For the law rules and governs mankind; therefore the law judges mankind, and not mankind the law.
Martin Luther
Table Talk (16th century)

4   It is a favorite thing with infidels to set their own standard, to measure themselves by other people. But that will not do in the Day of Judgment. Now we will use God's law as a balance weight.
D. L. Moody
Weighed and Wanting (19th century)

5   Rebellion never goes without consequences.
Andy Stanley
The Seven Checkpoints (2001)

6   The law was not made for you to judge, but that you might be ruled and judged by it.
Richard Baxter
A Call to the Unconverted, to Turn and Live (17th century)

7   The law of God was more vindicated by the death of Christ than it would have been had all transgressors been sent to Hell.
Charles Spurgeon
All of Grace (19th century)

8   God's intent in giving us law is to restore us to harmonious relationships with ourselves, with others, and with Himself.
Judson Cornwall
Let Us Enjoy Forgiveness (1978)

9   Lawlessness, a condition of being without law, can bring only ruin.
>   Judson Cornwall
>   *Let Us Enjoy Forgiveness* (1978)

249 LAZINESS

Slothfulness casteth into a deep sleep; and an idle soul shall suffer hunger.
PROVERBS 19:15

1   A steadfast gaze into heaven may be to a devout soul a high order of worship, but if this filled up much of our working time it might become the idlest form of folly.
>   Charles Spurgeon
>   "The Ascension and the Second Advent Practically Considered" sermon (1884)

2   Idleness does not grow in the soil of fellowship with God. God created us for work so that by consciously relying on his power and consciously shaping the world after his excellence, we might be satisfied in him, and he might be glorified in us.
>   John Piper
>   *Don't Waste Your Life* (2003)

3   I was taught that laziness was one of the worst evils, and that there was dignity and honor in labor.
>   Billy Graham
>   *Just As I Am* (1997)

4   Be active, be diligent; avoid all laziness, sloth, indolence. Fly from every degree, every appearance, of it; else you will never be more than half a Christian.
>   John Wesley
>   *The Works of the Rev. John Wesley* (18th century)

5   An idle body is a disease in a state; an idle soul is a monster in a man.
>   John Donne
>   "Sermon Preached Before King Charles I" (1629)

6   Not a few regard all toil with utter aversion.
>   John Dawson
>   *The Saviour in the Workshop* (1868)

250 LEADERSHIP

Therefore now go, lead the people unto the place of which I have spoken unto thee. . .
EXODUS 32:34

1   A recognition of the fallen nature of authority and the possibility of its abuse is good and healthy. Power apart from God's purposes is always demonic. But a suspicion of all authority or an innate distrust of it is very bad.
>   Mark Dever
>   *A Display of God's Glory* (2001)

2   The leader who refuses to move until the fear is gone will never move. Consequently, he will never lead.
>   Andy Stanley
>   *The Next Generation Leader* (2003)

3   Acknowledging weakness doesn't make a leader less effective. On the contrary, in most cases it is simply a way of expressing that he understands what everyone else has known for some time. When you acknowledge your weaknesses to the rest of your team, it is never new information.
>   Andy Stanley
>   *The Next Generation Leader* (2003)

4   No man doth safely rule, be he that hath learned gladly to obey.
>   Thomas à Kempis
>   *The Imitation of Christ* (15th century)

5   One secret of successful leadership is knowing when you need help and being willing to get the best help available.
>   Connie Neal
>   *Your Thirty-Day Journey to Being a World-Class Father* (1992)

6   One of the most dangerous and terrifying trends in America today is the disregard for character as a central necessity in a leader's credentials.
Ravi Zacharias
Deliver Us from Evil (1996)

7   Can you imagine what would happen in the marketplace if everybody in the company treated everybody else like a VIP?
Bill Hybels
Descending into Greatness (1993)

8   The key to developing people is to catch them doing something right.
Ken Blanchard
Leadership Smarts (2004)

9   If you want to know why your people are not performing well, step up to the mirror and take a peek.
Ken Blanchard
Leadership Smarts (2004)

10   Accepting leadership responsibilities for the first time exposes an individual's level of maturity and sense of responsibility.
John Maxwell
Winning with People (2004)

11   Leaders do more than lead people; they cultivate other leaders.
Glenn Daman
Shepherding the Small Church (2002)

12   The way leaders cope with and accomplish change is through influence.
Aubrey Malphurs
Maximizing Your Effectiveness (2006)

13   If no one is following your leadership, then you have little or no influence.
Aubrey Malphurs
Maximizing Your Effectiveness (2006)

14   Good leaders are learners who continue to pursue growth in their expertise as leaders.
Aubrey Malphurs
Maximizing Your Effectiveness (2006)

15   Will you be the one influenced by others— or the one who influences others for Christ?
Andy Stanley and Stuart Hall
Max Q Student Journal (2004)

16   The friends you influence today are the world changers and world influencers of tomorrow.
Andy Stanley and Stuart Hall
Max Q Student Journal (2004)

17   The Christian leader never equates mediocrity with the things of God, but is always committed to the pursuit of excellence.
Ted Engstrom
The Making of a Christian Leader (1978)

18   No man is worthy to rule until he has been ruled; no man can lead well until he has given himself to leadership greater than his own.
Catherine Marshall
Beyond Ourselves (1961)

19   Being a leader takes time, discipline, and effort, but what good is it if you gain the world and lose your family?
Florence Littauer
After Every Wedding Comes a Marriage (1981)

20   Leadership is about influencing people for good. It is about accomplishing more through others than we could ever do on our own. People are what it is all about, and leadership is taking groups of people to exciting places they would not attempt on their own.
Hans Finzel
Empowered Leaders (1998)

21 Leaders need a compass now more than ever, and God has given us a most reliable one in His Word. The timeless truths we find in the Scriptures apply to today's complex world.
    Hans Finzel
    Empowered Leaders (1998)

22 Leadership is influence. Leadership is too much to do and not enough time. Leadership is everyone wanting a piece of your time. Leadership is unrealistic expectations. Leadership is pressure from followers that never lets up. Leadership is a balancing act.
    Hans Finzel
    Empowered Leaders (1998)

23 Sooner or later a leader wakes up and realizes that he can never meet everyone's expectations and that he must quit worrying about what other people think.
    Hans Finzel
    Empowered Leaders (1998)

24 Everyone is a leader because everyone influences someone. Not everyone will become a great leader, but everyone can become a better leader.
    John Maxwell
    Developing the Leader within You (1993)

25 Good leadership is a gift of God for the blessing of his people.
    Mark Dever
    "Amos: Does God Care?" sermon (2003)

26 The higher the leadership the deeper the servanthood.
    Steve Campbell
    "The Submission Principle" sermon (2010)

27 Leadership is an obligation and a privilege of every person, young and old, because it is based simply on what we do.
    Charlie "Tremendous" Jones
    Life Is Tremendous! (1968)

28 Anyone who is not leading others in life is not really living.
    Charlie "Tremendous" Jones
    Life Is Tremendous! (1968)

251 LEARNING

A wise man will hear, and will increase learning; and a man of understanding shall attain unto wise counsels.
PROVERBS 1:5

1 The highest science, the loftiest speculation, the mightiest philosophy, which can ever engage the attention of a child of God, is the name, the nature, the person, the work, the doings, and the existence of the great God whom he calls his Father.
    Charles Spurgeon
    "The Immutability of God" sermon (1855)

2 Almost anyone can gain scholastic achievement to become a doctor, businessman, etc. But is it truly an achievement if they become a crooked doctor, or businessman? What good is it to know five foreign languages if one does not have tongue control? What good is it to be proficient in accounting if one cheats on income taxes?
    Robin Sampson
    What Your Child Needs to Know When (2000)

3 It is of little value for our children to master chemistry or algebra if they don't know how to get along with their spouses or cannot discipline their children.
    Robin Sampson
    What Your Child Needs to Know When (2000)

4 Let us seek to have our minds prepared for receiving things hard to be understood, by putting in practice things which are more easy to be understood.
    Matthew Henry
    Commentary on the Whole Bible (1706)

5 In developing spiritual disciplines, or in teaching holy truth, we attempt to apply this teaching model: What is learned with pleasure is learned full measure.
Karen Burton Mains
The God Hunt (2003)

6 Education comes in many forms: from a conversation that picks up one well-placed comment or bit of information, a one-hour session at a nearby school, a brief article in a local newspaper, a few moments spent with a book, or a heart to heart talk with a friend.
Gretchen Thompson
God Knows Caregiving Can Pull You Apart (2002)

7 We can be thankful that we don't know everything. Turned right side up, this lack of knowledge becomes an opportunity to learn.
Mort Crim
Good News for Tough Times (2002)

8 For those intent on political and social transformation, a bleak version of history is better than a balanced one.
Lynne Cheney
Telling the Truth (1995)

9 An educated and virtuous people cannot be enslaved. An ignorant and vicious people cannot be free.
School Committee Public Documents of Massachusetts (1866)

10 The proper mental and moral training of the children holds the first place; and on every generation devolves the responsibility of giving them such education.
School Committee Public Documents of Massachusetts (1866)

11 When we consider that our free institutions are safe, and the Union impregnable for all coming time, only on the condition that the people of every generation shall be characterized by a broad intelligence and a high Christian morality...then we shall learn the value of our schools, where the foundation stones of character are laid, the principles which govern life are established, and the mental and moral habits are fixed.
School Committee Public Documents of Massachusetts (1866)

12 Yes, all the people must be solidly and properly educated as the only guarantee of perpetuated liberty.
School Committee Public Documents of Massachusetts (1866)

13 Education must have a religious basis, not sectarian except in the sense that the Bible is sectarian—broad but distinctively Christian. So our fathers thought, and so we think.
School Committee Public Documents of Massachusetts (1866)

14 The schools where our future citizens are preparing for their duties and responsibilities, should rest on the pure and broad religious basis of the Bible.
School Committee Public Documents of Massachusetts (1866)

15 Listening sets the stage whereby we can learn. It sets an atmosphere whereby another person begins to open up to us the treasures of his life.
Ralph Ransom Frederick
Steps on the Stairway (1981)

16 The Church, which only cares for saving souls, and the State, which only cares for educating minds, are both making a vast mistake.
J. C. Ryle
The Upper Room (19th century)

17 The most tremendous experience in life is the learning process. The saddest time is when a person thinks that he has learned enough.
Charlie "Tremendous" Jones
Life Is Tremendous! (1968)

252 LEGALISM

Woe unto you, scribes and Pharisees, hypocrites! for ye pay tithe of mint and anise and cummin, and have omitted the weightier matters of the law, judgment, mercy, and faith: these ought ye to have done, and not to leave the other undone.
MATTHEW 23:23

1 At its heart, legalism is a desire to appear holy. It is trying to be justified before men and not God.
David Wilkerson
Revival on Broadway! (1996)

2 When our faith becomes nothing more than a series of rules and regulations, joy flees and our love for Christ grows cold.
Billy Graham
The Journey (2006)

3 Heaven does not govern by outward rules and regulations etched in stone, but by the secret code written on our hearts. Dead, lifeless rules etched in stone are for dead, hard hearts.
Lisa Bevere
Be Angry But Don't Blow It! (2000)

4 On the playground of life, it's the justice we seek for those who are oppressed and victimized, it's the mercy we extend to those in need of earthly goods or spiritual comfort, and it's the faithfulness we exhibit to our relationships that are the real tests of what our faith is all about, not how well we keep the rules.
Robin Chaddock
Discovering Your Divine Assignment (2005)

5 There is no middle ground for snobs and Pharisees. They try to protect themselves from being contaminated by those below while elevating themselves to center stage.
Robert Stofel
God, Are We There Yet? (2004)

6 Rules will never set us free, just as fear and control will never keep us safe.
Lisa Bevere
Kissed the Girls and Made Them Cry (2002)

7 Can thy poor finite performances satisfy infinite justice for the violation of his righteous precepts?
George Swinnock
Works of George Swinnock (17th century)

8 Canst thou think that future obedience can satisfy for former disobedience?
George Swinnock
Works of George Swinnock (17th century)

9 We make a serious mistake when we substitute moralism for connection.
Larry Crabb
Connecting (1997)

10 Legalism is simply "behavior modification."
Elmer Towns
Core Christianity (2007)

11 When I extend my personal boundaries to another I am a legalist.
Jim Petersen and Mike Shamy
The Insider (2003)

12 Legalism forms when the rules get ahead of the relationship and begin to govern a person's life more than God's Spirit does.
Jeffrey Miller
The Hazards of Being a Man (2007)

13 Legalism does not understand the nature of divine commands, refuses to face the complexity of many ethical dilemmas, and waives any primary obligation for showing compassion.
Rubel Shelly
Written in Stone (1994)

253 LEISURE (*see also* EASE)

And he said unto them, Come ye yourselves
apart into a desert place, and rest a while:
for there were many coming and going,
and they had no leisure so much as to eat.
MARK 6:31

1 All of our leisure activities—our hobbies,
the things we do to relax and to express our
creativity—can be sacred times, times to
remember and enjoy the presence of God and
to be grateful for our gifts.
Debra Farrington
A Beginner's Guide to Unceasing Prayer
(2002)

LIBERTY (*see* FREEDOM)

254 LIFE

For what is your life? It is even a vapour,
that appeareth for a little time,
and then vanisheth away.
JAMES 4:14

General

1 Life is like the transition from class to class
in a school. If we fail to master the rudiments
of arithmetic before moving to the next level,
we will have problems.
Robert Stofel
God, How Much Longer? (2005)

2 New life, supernatural life, the abundant
life of the living Christ is imparted to the
person who in desperation turns from the
old, barren, bleak ways of the world to keep
company with Christ.
W. Phillip Keller
What Makes Life Worth Living? (1998)

3 To lead an unexamined life means to rush
from task to busy task, but not call enough

time-outs to reflect on life's larger meaning
and purpose.
Patrick Morley
Understanding Your Man in the Mirror
(1998)

4 Jesus is trying to get us to understand a key
dynamic principle. When we give up our tight
grasp on our own life, we discover life as it was
meant to be lived.
Greg Laurie
The Upside Down Church (1999)

5 When I am able to live according to His
purpose, to recognize that regardless of my
circumstance I have relinquished control
to Him (not lip service), then I am able to
connect with the joy that reality brings.
Cynthia Yates
Living Well in Retirement (2005)

6 Life is not a series of accidents but a
succession of divine appointments.
Mary Southerland
Sandpaper People (2005)

7 Use your imagination and do something
you've never done before. God wants you to
taste life, to sample all the goodies He has
made available. Venture out. See His creation.
Notice something you've never noticed before.
It's amazing how alive you will feel.
Michelle McKinney Hammond
Sassy, Single, and Satisfied (2003)

8 Whatever your personal experiences, you
are either paralyzed or empowered by them.
Michelle McKinney Hammond
How to Be Found by the Man You've Been
Looking For (2005)

9 Our lives are a voyage of discovery.
John Stott
Basic Christianity (1958)

10 Life is definite and resident; and Spiritual Life is not a visit from a force, but a resident tenant in the soul.
   Henry Drummond
   Natural Law in the Spiritual World
   (19th century)

11 Life without God. Senseless? Meaningless? Full of despair? Yes.
   Edith Schaeffer
   Common Sense Christian Living (1983)

12 We think it a great kindness in a man to spare our life, but what kindness is it in God to give us our life?
   Thomas Watson
   A Body of Practical Divinity (1838)

13 No matter how far along our spiritual pilgrimage we may have come, we need to be shown again and again that humble, ordinary things can be very holy and very full of God.
   Elisabeth Elliot
   A Path Through Suffering (1990)

14 The Declaration of Independence— America's birth certificate—acknowledges that persons are endowed by their Creator with certain inalienable rights, including the right to life.
   Deborah Dewart
   Death of a Christian Nation (2010)

15 We must bow to the seasons of order and disorder God establishes in our lives.
   Dan Allender and Tremper Longman III
   Breaking the Idols of Your Heart (1998)

16 We can never tame life.
   Dan Allender and Tremper Longman III
   Breaking the Idols of Your Heart (1998)

17 Life is a series of in-betweens.
   Kim Thomas
   Living in the Sacred Now (2001)

18 Duty looks at life as a debt to be paid; love sees life as a debt to be collected.
   William George Jordan
   The Kingship of Self-Control (1898)

19 Life isn't mainly a matter of doing what you like to do, it's doing what you ought to do and need to do!
   Charlie "Tremendous" Jones
   Life Is Tremendous! (1968)

20 We encounter God in the ordinariness of life: not in the search for spiritual highs and extraordinary mystical experiences but in our simple presence in life.
   Brennan Manning
   The Rabbi's Heartbeat (2003)

Brevity of

21 "Gone!" is the greatest part of our history. Scarcely have we time enough to tell the story, ere it comes to its finis.
   Charles Spurgeon
   "God, the All-Seeing One" sermon (1858)

22 When kings die, and in funeral pomp are carried to the grave, we are taught the lesson— "I am God, and beside me there is none else."
   Charles Spurgeon
   "Sovereignty and Salvation" sermon (1856)

23 The only thing that we can guarantee about our lives is that we have the current breath in our lungs. We cannot guarantee another breath. That comes with the permission of our Creator.
   Ray Comfort
   What Hollywood Believes (2002)

24 The years of our pilgrimage are all too short to master it triumphantly. Yet this is what Christianity is for—to teach men the art of life.
   Henry Drummond
   The Greatest Thing in the World (1891)

25 One unsettling word hangs over all those earth-things that give our lives some sense of greatness: temporary. No friendship, no championship. No scholarship, no relationship, no ownership, no fellowship can fully satisfy our God-given hunger for something that will be great forever.
Ron Hutchcraft
Called to Greatness (2001)

26 The brevity of life grants power to abide, not an excuse to bail. Fleeting days don't justify fleeing problems. Fleeting days strengthen us to endure problems.
Max Lucado
It's Not About Me (2004)

27 Between us and heaven or hell there is only life, which is the frailest thing in the world.
Blaise Pascal
Pensées (17th century)

28 To think that God in Christ is deeply concerned about me as a particular person immediately gives great purpose and enormous meaning to my short sojourn on this planet.
W. Phillip Keller
A Shepherd Looks At Psalm 23 (1970)

29 Slow down to look and listen. Life happens fast.
David Staal
Words Kids Need to Hear (2008)

30 I have thought, I am a creature of a day, passing through life as an arrow through the air. I am a spirit come from God, and returning to God: Just hovering over the great gulf; till, a few moments hence, I am no more seen; I drop into an unchangeable eternity!
John Wesley
Sermons on Several Occasions by John Wesley (18th century)

31 You have no guarantee that you will be alive this time tomorrow—none at all.
Martyn Lloyd-Jones
Compelling Christianity (20th century)

32 Those riches and honours, profits and pleasures, that must be buried with us, and cannot accompany us into another world, are but a wretched portion, and will leave men comfortless at long run.
Thomas Boston
Human Nature in Its Fourfold State (1830)

33 The second half of life is a chance to get our priorities straight. It's a time to realize that having the last word isn't as important as having a conversation.
Martha Bolton
Didn't My Skin Used to Fit? (2000)

34 It's time to realize that it's not going to matter how much money you leave your family when you die. What is important is how much of yourself you leave with them.
Martha Bolton
Didn't My Skin Used to Fit? (2000)

35 Each man has only a certain amount of life, of time, of attention—a definite measurable quantity. If he gives any of it to this life solely it is wasted.
Henry Drummond
Natural Law in the Spiritual World (19th century)

36 I heard some one in the inquiry-room telling a young person to go home and seek Christ in his closet. I would not dare to tell any one to do that. You might be dead before you got home.
D. L. Moody
Best Thoughts and Discourses of D. L. Moody (1876)

37 Life in the body to all men is short.
Henry Drummond
"Why Christ Must Depart" sermon (19th century)

38 Man's will is to live. Hence he feels his mortality as a hard slavery which causes him to sigh in deepest melancholy.
Paul Wernle
The Beginnings of Christianity (1903)

**LIFE EVERLASTING
(*see* ETERNAL LIFE)**

**255 LIGHT, SPIRITUAL
(*see also* DISCERNMENT;
UNDERSTANDING; WISDOM)**
The people that walked in darkness have seen a great light: they that dwell in the land of the shadow of death, upon them hath the light shined.
ISAIAH 9:2

1 God's light shines both within us and without us, and by learning to receive Him within we begin to perceive Him without.
Agnes Sanford
The Healing Light (1947)

2 There is a radiance hidden in your heart that the world desperately needs.
John and Stasi Eldredge
Captivating (2005)

3 Light may seem at times to be an impertinent intruder, but it is always beneficial in the end.
J. Gresham Machen
Christianity and Liberalism (1923)

4 None are so aware of corruption as those whose souls are most alive.
Richard Sibbes
The Bruised Reed (1630)

5 Christ is the true light of the world; it is through him alone that true wisdom is imparted to the mind.
Jonathan Edwards
"God Glorified in Man's Dependence" sermon (18th century)

6 The light of Christ burns away the shadow of the soul, throwing wide the windows of our lives, that others might enter in and they, too, find light and life.
Jane Rubietta
Between Two Gardens (2001)

7 This is the spiritual journey—to live into the fullness of Christ's life within us.
Phileena Heuertz
Pilgrimage of a Soul (2010)

8 Only in the chaos of darkness can the real power of light shine.
Patricia Livingston
This Blessed Mess (2000)

9 Light is dependable, yet so infinitely varied—the same each day, yet every day different. Like God maybe? Perhaps that's why he shows us himself in the metaphor of light.
Luci Shaw
God in the Dark (1989)

10 Just like the moonshine, our light is borrowed light.
D. L. Moody
Wondrous Love (1876)

**256 LISTENING
(*see also* COMMUNICATION;
CONVERSATION; SPEECH;
TONGUE, THE)**
*Bow down thine ear,
and hear the words of the wise. . .*
PROVERBS 22:17

1 If what you have to say to someone is very important, you will not let them continue their labors while you talk. You ask for their undivided attention. So also, God does not speak to us until we slow down, tune out the static, and give Him our attention.
Francis Frangipane
The Three Battlegrounds (1989)

2 Hearing is a sense formed to receive sounds, and is rather passive than active, admitting, but not communicating sensation; and if we would hear, we must lend the ear for that purpose. Christ, the eternal Word, who must be communicated to the soul to give it new life, requires the most intense attention to his voice, when He would speak within us.
François Fénelon and Jeanne Guyon
Spiritual Progress (17th century)

3 We listen with our facial expressions.
Sharon Jaynes
Becoming the Woman of His Dreams (2005)

4 Listening shows that someone cares.
Catharine Brandt
Forgotten People (1978)

5 What do we mean by listening? What do we mean by hearing? Is there a difference? Definitely. Hearing involves gaining content or information for your own purposes. This isn't helping. Listening involves caring for and being empathetic toward the friend who is talking. Hearing means that you are concerned about what's going on inside you during the conversation. We've all done this. Listening means that you're trying to understand the feelings of the other person and are listening for his or her sake. This is helping.
H. Norman Wright
Helping Those Who Hurt (2003)

6 Scripture often reminds us that it's not enough to have ears—we must use them.
Max Lucado
Just Like Jesus (1998)

7 Listening requires you to set aside preconceived ideas or judgments and convey a message of acceptance of the person.
Les and Leslie Parrott III
Questions Couples Ask (1996)

8 Listening opens up another's spirit.
Les and Leslie Parrott III
Questions Couples Ask (1996)

9 Not talking is one action. Listening is another action. Just because you're not talking doesn't mean you're listening.
Mark Gregston
What's Happening to My Teen? (2009)

10 The greatest enemy of listening is wanting to tell your own story.
Scott Turansky and Joanne Miller
Parenting Is Heart Work (2006)

11 People long to be heard, but few people know how to listen.
Dallas and Nancy Demmitt
Can You Hear Me Now? (2003)

257 LONELINESS
And the LORD God said, It is not good that the man should be alone.
GENESIS 2:18

1 God's love, pouring through the lonely life of Jesus, runs deeper, wider, and farther than any loneliness of the human heart. Prayers from our lonely, troubled lips mix with the prayers of the risen Christ on our behalf. He understands our expectations—and our grief when those expectations fail to materialize.
Bonnie Keen
God Loves Messy People (2002)

2 Regarding loneliness, we need to be a friend to others rather than waiting for others to reach out to us. This requires thoughtfulness and a conscious effort to help others.
George Sweeting
The Joys of Successful Aging (2002)

3 No worse fate can befall a man in this world than to live and grow old alone, unloving, and unloved.
Henry Drummond
The Greatest Thing in the World (1874)

4 Lonely people suffer from fear. They honor their anxiety. Instead of moving out to find and love others, even though this means tolerating some anxiety, they move away from others so they don't feel anxious about rejection or slights. By opting for temporary comfort instead of putting up with risk and anxiety, they keep themselves hurting from the infinitely greater pain of loneliness.

William and Candace Backus
Untwisting Twisted Relationships (1998)

5 When persons are first awakened to the divine life, because grace is weak and nature strong, God is often pleased to vouchsafe them some extraordinary illuminations of his Holy Spirit; but when they are grown to be more perfect men in Christ, then he frequently seems to leave them to themselves; and not only so, but permits a horrible deadness and dread to overwhelm them; at which times Satan will not be wanting to vex and tempt them to impatience, to the great discomfort of their souls.

George Whitefield
(18th century) quoted in
Selected Sermons of George Whitefield

6 The route to knowing God eventually passes directly through the valley of profound loneliness.

Larry Crabb
Encouragement: The Key to Caring (1984)

7 Not only does God's heart extend toward you when you feel alone in your pain, his healing hand extends toward you as well.

Cindi McMenamin
When Women Walk Alone (2002)

8 Loneliness is more readily experienced than defined.

J. Oswald Sanders
Facing Loneliness (1988)

9 It is no sin to be lonely, so there is no need to add a sense of guilt to the problem.

J. Oswald Sanders
Facing Loneliness (1988)

LONGSUFFERING (see PATIENCE)

LORD'S DAY
(see SABBATH; SUNDAY)

258 LORD'S SUPPER
(see also SACRAMENTS)
*The Lord Jesus the same night in which he was
betrayed took bread: And when he had given
thanks, he brake it, and said, Take, eat:
this is my body, which is broken for you:
this do in remembrance of me.*
1 CORINTHIANS 11:23–24

1 We need to come to the Table of the Lord with a sense of anticipation, believing that the Lord will meet us there in a unique way, that he will heal our hurts, bind up our wounds, and minister to our needs.

Robert Webber
Worship Is a Verb (1992)

2 The Lord's supper that Jesus instituted was not meant to be a slightly sentimental forget-me-not, but rather a service rich in spiritual significance.

John Stott
The Cross of Christ (1986)

259 LOSS (see also DEFEAT; FAILURE)
*Yea doubtless, and I count all things
but loss for the excellency of the knowledge
of Christ Jesus my Lord.*
PHILIPPIANS 3:8

1 All we have to do is look around us and we see that loss is one half of the process of life. New life can only come when there is a letting go of what was there before. This is the story of human existence from beginning to end.

Joan Guntzelman
God Knows You're Grieving (2001)

2 Most people don't have a choice in their loss, but everyone has a choice in their recovery.
H. Norman Wright
Let's Just Be Friends (2002)

3 The loss of a friend may lead to acquaintance with the Friend.
Brother Lawrence
The Practice of the Presence of God (17th century)

4 We cannot mourn losses until we understand clearly what we have lost.
David Stoop
Making Peace with Your Father (2004)

5 I am learning that none of the good gifts I have received belongs to me, and God is well within His rights to take them back. When He decides it's time to do so, there's much less pain if we offer them up willingly rather than cling tightly.
Stan Guthrie
The Spiritual Uses of Unemployment (2009)

260 LOVE
He that loveth not knoweth not God; for God is love.
1 JOHN 4:8

General

1 Love is greater than faith, because the end is greater than the means. What is the use of having faith? It is to connect the soul with God. And what is the object of connecting man with God? That he may become like God. But God is Love. Hence Faith, the means, is in order to Love, the end.
Henry Drummond
The Greatest Thing in the World (1891)

2 Love Is a Decision.
Gary Smalley book title (1989)

3 Genuine love is honor put into action regardless of the cost.
Gary Smalley
Love Is a Decision (1989)

4 Love never requires an act that is contrary to God's word. Love always places another's best interest first. Love never forces. Love always sticks around.
Jeffrey Dean
One-Liner Wisdom for Today's Guys (2006)

5 Love motivated by mere duty cannot hold out for very long.
Stephen Kendrick and Alex Kendrick
The Love Dare (2008)

6 I am a beast until I love as God doth love.
George MacDonald
Diary of an Old Soul (1880)

7 Love has no other message but its own. Every day we try to live out Christ's love in a very tangible way in every one of our deeds. If we do any preaching, it is done with deeds, not with words.
Mother Teresa
Loving Jesus (1991)

8 Divine love is not an emotional response, but an act of the will. Divine love is expressed not necessarily because we "feel" like it, but because we choose to love. If we wait to "feel" like loving someone, our love will be erratic and arbitrary.
Joseph Stowell
Tongue in Cheek (1983)

9 Love without distinction, without calculation. Love without procrastination. Just love.
David Jeremiah
The Power of Love (1994)

10 A love that cares, that goes out of its way to find what it can do to minister, makes a difference.
David Jeremiah
The Power of Love (1994)

11 The Bible says that love is a responsibility. We are commanded to love. God doesn't ask us if we feel like it, He tells us in His Word that it is our responsibility to love.
David Jeremiah
The Power of Love (1994)

12 Love is not a feeling, love is a response. Love is an action.
> David Jeremiah
> *The Power of Love* (1994)

13 The biggest disease today is not leprosy or tuberculosis, but rather the feeling of being unwanted, uncared for, and deserted by everybody. The greatest evil is the lack of love.
> Tim Clinton and Gary Sibcy
> *Attachments* (2002)

14 Real love proves itself in the face of overwhelming obstacles.
> Colin Smith
> *Unlocking the Bible Story* (2002)

15 What makes us human is not our mind but our heart, not our ability to think but our ability to love.
> Philip Yancey
> *The Jesus I Never Knew* (1995)

16 You were designed to love. That's where your happiness lies—not in an endless chase after selfish pleasures.
> Claire and Curt Cloninger
> *E-mail from God for Teens* (1999)

17 No one should crucify herself for wanting love. The longing for love is a natural human emotion. It is a spiritual instinct, built into the center of our soul by the Author of love Himself: God.
> Michelle McKinney Hammond
> *Ending the Search for Mr. Right* (2005)

18 We should desire to love and be loved. But the desire for love should not rule us to the point where we look for it in all the wrong places, trying to fulfill our longing with unhealthy alternatives, or becoming paralyzed by our yearning.
> Michelle McKinney Hammond
> *Ending the Search for Mr. Right* (2005)

19 We all need to love and accept the love of other people. Even though we talk about being self-sufficient, we are made by God with a need to connect with others.
> Dick Purnell
> *Finding a Lasting Love* (2003)

20 Christian love is practical; it doesn't just say words, it does what needs to be done.
> Warren Wiersbe
> *A Gallery of Grace* (2002)

21 To be awake in the world is to realize when opportunities to love and be loved are in our grasp. These are moments of great significance.
> Robert Stofel
> *God, How Much Longer?* (2005)

22 To love and to be loved expresses the greater privilege of humanness, of being persons who share the image of the Divine.
> Myron and Esther Augsburger
> *How to Be a Christ-Shaped Family* (1994)

23 Love that doesn't enter the other person's world is little more than a nice thought between your ears.
> Gary Stanley
> *How to Make a Moose Run* (2001)

24 When God measures a man, he puts the tape around his heart—not his head.
> Steven Lawson
> *The Legacy* (1998)

25 Ye see, beloved, how great and wonderful a thing is love, and that there is no declaring its perfection. Who is fit to be found in it, except such as God has vouchsafed to render so? Let us pray, therefore, and implore of His mercy, that we may live blameless in love, free from all human partialities for one above another.
> Clement
> *The First Epistle of Clement to the Corinthians* (1st century)

26 We're blessed when we learn to love and to respect others and to love and to honor the Lord with everything we are and with everything we have.
> Rhonda Rhea
> *Turkey Soup for the Soul* (2004)

27 We are born with a desire to create unbreakable bonds. This desire motivates us to make the effort to change and engage in a spiritual life of love, a life beyond mere animal instinct. When we truly feel connected with ourselves, with others, and with God, our lives become dynamic, exciting, and inspired.
Cheryl and Paul Meier
Unbreakable Bonds (2002)

28 With every loving action and every honest word, you'll make love and truthfulness a part of your character.
Bob Barnes
Walking Together in Wisdom (2001)

29 Love can't be forced. It flows out of fullness, not fear.
David and Janet Congo
Lifemates (2001)

30 If we're not telling God and our family that we love them, we just wasted a day of our life.
Ted Roberts
Pure Desire (1999)

31 Love is the fulfilling of the law, the end of the commandment.
John Wesley
A Plain Account of Christian Perfection (18th century)

32 We may die without the knowledge of many truths, and yet be carried into Abraham's bosom. But, if we die without love, what will knowledge avail? Just as much as it avails the devil and his angels!
John Wesley
Sermons on Several Occasions (18th century)

33 If love does not prompt all work, all work is for naught.
D. L. Moody
The Faithful Saying (1877)

34 If you love, you will unconsciously fulfil the whole law.
Henry Drummond
The Greatest Thing in the World (1874)

35 Without distinction, without calculation, without procrastination, love.
Henry Drummond
The Greatest Thing in the World (1874)

36 Whatever men may do or suffer, they cannot by all their performances and sufferings, make up for the want of sincere love in the heart.
Jonathan Edwards
"The Greatest Performances or Sufferings in Vain without Charity" sermon (1738)

37 Love never dies. Love is always now. There is no yesterday in love, and no tomorrow.
Don Osgood
Listening for God's Silent Language (1995)

38 Love is the most desired commodity in the world.
J. Allan Petersen
Before You Marry (1974)

39 Love is not static but dynamic, and, as such, it must grow and mature or it will diminish through neglect.
J. Allan Petersen
Before You Marry (1974)

40 Love is quiet. It's a thoughtful deed done for your spouse or children with no expectation of return.
Tony Evans
Guiding Your Family (1991)

41 God's Word continually commands us to love one another. In the Bible, love is not something you feel; love is something you do.
Jay Kesler
Is Your Marriage Really Worth Fighting For? (1989)

42 True love values individuals for who they are rather than for what they are able to do.
Stephen Arterburn and Jack Felton
Toxic Faith (1991)

43 Poets and prophets have long known that love conquers all, but the exciting thing is that there is currently a huge groundswell of grassroots advocacy for the idea of love as healer.
Sue Patton Thoele
Heart Centered Marriage (1996)

44 It helps to remember that as sinners we're all difficult people in our own ways. But God's love and grace have been extended to us all, and one of the requirements of following Him is that we extend grace to others.
Steve Stephens and Alice Gray
The Worn Out Woman (2004)

45 Love knows how to do without what it naturally wants. Love knows how to say, "What does it matter?"
Amy Carmichael
Edges of His Ways (1955)

46 Love works wisely and gently in a soul where he wills it, powerfully extinguishing short temper, envy, and all passions of anger and self-pity, bringing into the soul in their place the virtues of patience, mildness, peaceability and warmth toward one's fellow Christians.
Walter Hilton
Toward a Perfect Love (1985)

47 True love is quite capable of being angry, and must be angry and even sharp with its beloved children.
Peter Taylor Forsyth
The Work of Christ (1909)

48 Charity is spiritual fire, and when it burst into flames, it is called devotion.
Francis de Sales
Introduction to the Devout Life
(17th century)

49 Love can only be what it is meant to be when it is wedded first to the sacred.
Ravi Zacharias
Jesus Among Other Gods (2000)

50 Nothing is inexorable but love.
George MacDonald
"The Consuming Fire" sermon
(19th century)

51 Love is one, and love is changeless. For love loves unto purity.
George MacDonald
"The Consuming Fire" sermon
(19th century)

52 Love at first is not feeling. Love first can be expressed as giving. That is at the core of love. If one gives, the feeling of love will follow.
Jay Adams
Christian Living in the Home (1972)

53 We are ashamed to yearn for cherishing, but deadening our souls to avoid the pain of any additional disappointment has darkened and narrowed our world to a gray existence masquerading as life.
Nancy Groom
Heart to Heart About Men (1995)

54 The greatest of all motivators is love.
Jerry White
Dangers Men Face (1997)

55 Nothing is wrong with wanting to be loved, to be happy, or to have your needs met.
David Gudgel
Before You Live Together (2003)

56 Love can talk for an hour and never say anything.
William Coleman
Engaged (1980)

57 Love is one of the most enjoyable mysteries in life.
William Coleman
Engaged (1980)

58 It is never too late to speak of love.
Dennis Gibson
The Sandwich Years (1991)

59 Learning to love is not a matter of
following certain techniques, but of opening
the heart.
Mike Mason
Practicing the Presence of People (1999)

Brotherly Love

60 Say not "Our Father," and then look upon
thy brethren with a sneer or a frown. I beseech
thee, live like a brother, and act like a brother.
Charles Spurgeon
"The Fatherhood of God" sermon (1858)

61 Everyone feels benevolent if nothing
happens to be annoying him at the moment.
C. S. Lewis
The Problem of Pain (1947)

62 Christ bids us live in an atmosphere of love.
A. B. Simpson
Days of Heaven upon Earth (1897)

63 If you accuse, accuse from love. If you
correct, correct from love. If you spare, spare
from love. Let love be rooted deep in you, and
only good can grow from it.
Augustine (4th century) quoted in
Augustine and His World

64 Without distinction, without calculation,
without procrastination, love. Lavish it upon
the poor, where it is very easy; especially upon
the rich, who often need it most; most of all
upon our equals, where it is very difficult, and
for whom perhaps we each do least of all.
Henry Drummond
The Greatest Thing in the World (1891)

65 The gray matter of the brain will one day
crumble and decay, but the tenderness of the
heart is from everlasting to everlasting and in
touching it we have touched immortality.
Agnes Sanford
The Healing Light (1947)

66 Love is the essence of discipleship: it is
the wall that surrounds a disciple, the roof that
protects him, and the ground which supports him.
George Verwer
Come! Live! Die! (1972)

67 The basic human need to be accepted and
affirmed has not changed. Jesus offers to satisfy
this longing. He is looking to extend the
gracious offer through followers who practice
the happy art of sharing in an unusual and
enriching love for one another regardless.
John Stowell
The Trouble With Jesus (2003)

68 What do you see in the stare of a stranger?
Christ's love compels us to reach across
barriers.
Stephen Mosley
Secrets of Jesus' Touch (2003)

69 The closer we draw to one another, the
closer we are allowed to God's throne.
Dean Merrill
Wait Quietly (1994)

70 If we cannot show love for others, both for
our neighbor and for our brothers and sisters
in the Lord, it is a red flag that something is
very wrong in our relationship with God.
Dee Brestin and Kathy Troccoli
Living in Love with Jesus (2002)

71 To be good a person must have charity, and
to be devout, in addition to charity, he must
have great zeal and readiness in performing
charitable actions.
Francis de Sales
Introduction to the Devout Life
(17th century)

72 As it was love that first created humanity, so even human love, in proportion to its divinity, will go on creating the beautiful for its own outpouring.
George MacDonald
"The Consuming Fire" sermon
(19th century)

73 What a different world we would have if we could all see each other as children of God!
Timothy Johnson
Finding God in the Questions (2004)

74 Dwell in patience and in peace and love and unity one with another.
George Fox
Personal Letter (17th century)

of God

75 Richer, fuller, deeper,
Jesus' love is sweeter
Sweeter as the years go by.
Lelia Morris
"Sweeter As the Years Go By"
hymn (1912)

76 He saw thee ruined in the fall of thy father Adam, but his mind never changed from his purpose to save thee.
Charles Spurgeon
"The Infallibility of God's Purpose" sermon (1861)

77 Who shall counsel the Most High to cast off the darlings of his bosom, or persuade the Saviour to reject his spouse?
Charles Spurgeon
"The Infallibility of God's Purpose" sermon (1861)

78 When our Father sees us making strides toward home, He runs to meet us.
Jennifer Rothschild
Lessons I Learned in the Dark (2002)

79 It was a God of incomparable love who sent His own Son to die for the very ones who nailed Him to a cross.
Jon Courson
Application Commentary (2003)

80 God always seeks out those He loves. That is His nature, the nature of Love.
Thomas Blackaby
Encounters with God Daily Bible (2008)

81 While I knew God loved me unconditionally, I also knew He didn't unconditionally approve of my behavior.
Stephen Arterburn, Fred Stoeker, and Mike Yorkey
Every Man's Battle (2000)

82 Be assured, no one—man, woman, or child—says "I love you" with more certainty than the Lord. His regard for us goes far beyond kind words and warm feelings; his is a show-and-tell love, held up for the whole world to see.
Liz Curtis Higgs
Embrace Grace (2006)

83 We cannot drift from the love and care of an everlasting God.
Hannah Whitall Smith
The God of All Comfort (1906)

84 Trust God's love. His perfect love. Don't fear he will discover your past. He already has. Don't fear disappointing him in the future. He can show you the chapter in which you will. With perfect knowledge of the past and perfect vision of the future, he loves you perfectly in spite of both.
Max Lucado
Come Thirsty (2003)

85 The beautiful thing about God's love is that it is a giving love—a love that flows in

abundance with kindness, generosity, and goodness.
Roy Lessin
Today Is Your Best Day (2006)

86 Created out of God's love, our original design is to enjoy the fullness of this love in communion with the Creator, with one another and with all creation.
Jonathan Campbell and Jennifer Campbell
The Way of Jesus (2005)

87 One of the greatest truths of the Bible is that God loves us. And because He loves us, He wants to give us what is best for us.
Billy Graham
Answers to Life's Problems (1994)

88 God wants to teach you what true love is, as you come to experience and understand His love for you.
Billy Graham
Answers to Life's Problems (1994)

89 God wants us to adore Him, dance with Him, eat, drink, and sing with Him in the experience of His awesome, glorious love. The mystery of His desire is that an eternal, infinite, holy and utterly self-fulfilling Being wants us—and He is willing to go to any lengths whatsoever to disrupt, arouse and stop us from pursuing any other lover than Himself.
Dan Allender and Tremper Longman III
The Cry of the Soul (1994)

90 God did not create us out of need. He created us out of his love.
John Ortberg
Love Beyond Reason (1998)

91 The One who made you loves you most.
Michelle McKinney Hammond
Ending the Search for Mr. Right (2005)

92 When we humble ourselves, quit fast-forwarding past the bad parts, and admit

that we're lost without Him, we become His unlikely children. Desperate, imperfect people. . .completely adored, accepted, and beloved by a perfect God.
Lisa Harper
Every Woman's Hope (2001)

93 Every single person in our lives will disappoint us at some level. Some days they'll be busy when we need them to be still; other days they'll be self-centered when we need them to concentrate on us. Sometimes they'll bruise us with harsh words aimed right for the soft places in our soul. They won't meet all our emotional needs. They can't; they have too many needs of their own. They're sinners just like us. Only our Creator can love us perfectly, the way He created us to be loved. His love is the only thing that can define us without destroying us.
Lisa Harper
Every Woman's Hope (2001)

94 It is God who loved us first. His unceasing love sends Him after us. He is the seeking Lover, the one who has made us for Himself. From the very beginning we were created to be found and loved by Him. He has woven this secret into the very fibers of our soul and when we seek Him with all the longing He has planted in our hearts, in the end, we simply discover Him seeking us, loving us—in all times and all places.
Sue Monk Kidd
God's Joyful Surprise (1987)

95 I am in love with how God loves our messy world. In all our sloppy journeys, soul-worn seasons, good intentions gone belly-up, in all our stubborn tenacity to find the gold at the end of the rainbow, we are, every one of us, at some point, just messy people. You can dress us up and parade us around, but hidden under our well-coifed exteriors often lies a soul in

disarray. Yet we are loved. Loved in spite of our messy lives. Loved in the midst of them. Loved through the very places that cannot be explained away.

    Bonnie Keen
    God Loves Messy People (2002)

96 God relentlessly loves us in spite of all the mistakes we make. He is and always will be mankind's best and final hope.

    David Edwards
    The God of Yes (2003)

97 My car is not my identity; it is transportation. My identity is wrapped up in the astonishing fact that the God of the universe calls me His own. He loves me relentlessly, understands my weaknesses, and forgives my sins.

    Dave Meurer
    Good Spousekeeping (2004)

98 God pours His love through one generation after the other.

    Al Hartley
    It Takes a Family (1996)

99 One unquestioned text we read,
All doubt beyond, all fear above;
Nor crackling pile nor cursing creed
Can burn or blot it—God is love.

    Oliver Wendell Holmes
    "What We All Think" (1858)

100 To grasp fully the grace that daily restores our confidence in his love, we must keep our hands empty of any claim that God must bless us on the basis of our goodness. For if he loves us because of what is in our hands, then the days will come when we will believe that his affection has diminished because our works are small, or that his care has vanished because our deeds are wrong.

    Bryan Chapell
    Holiness by Grace (2001)

101 How can a man abide in love, when he does not keep God's commands which issue forth from love?

    Meister Eckhart
    Meister Eckhart's Sermons (14th century)

102 This King, full of mercy and goodness, very far from chastising me, embraces me with love, makes me eat at His table, serves me with His own hands, gives me the key of His treasures.

    Brother Lawrence
    The Practice of the Presence of God
    (17th century)

103 He converses and delights Himself with me incessantly, in a thousand and a thousand ways, and treats me in all respects as His favourite.

    Brother Lawrence
    The Practice of the Presence of God
    (17th century)

104 If we knew how much He loves us, we should be always ready to receive equally and with indifference from His hand the sweet and the bitter; all would please that came from Him.

    Brother Lawrence
    The Practice of the Presence of God
    (17th century)

105 Attentive love comes from God. He's the one who gives the ability to give and receive the right kind of love in all the right ways.

    Rhonda Rhea
    Turkey Soup for the Soul (2004)

106 The first command in Ephesians 5 tells us to be imitators of God by reflecting the way he loves us. Our love for others flows out of our sense of being deeply loved. Instead of constantly looking for the right person, God tells us to become the right person. Instead of

looking for love, God tells us to realize that love has already found us! God loves as no one else ever can.

Chip Ingram
Love, Sex, and Lasting Relationships (2003)

107   The best way for us to demonstrate that we have understood and accepted God's love is to learn to imitate him as closely as possible in the way we treat others.

Chip Ingram
Love, Sex, and Loving Relationships (2003)

108   God's love for us is constant, unconditional, and not dependent upon how good or bad we are, how well or poorly we keep the commandments.

Joseph Champlin
Should We Marry? (2001)

109   God bursts with love. He is far from being emotionally uninvolved with his creation. God's bias toward us is strong, persistent and positive. God chooses to be known as Love, and that love pervades every aspect of God's relationship with us.

David Benner
Surrender to Love (2003)

110   Love is God's character, not simply an emotion.

David Benner
Surrender to Love (2003)

111   There is no mystery about it. We love others, we love everybody, we love our enemies, because He first loved us.

Henry Drummond
The Greatest Thing in the World (1874)

112   He who wept over the city in olden time cares still, as He looks upon the sinning and the suffering of to-day.

Amy Carmichael
From Sunrise Land: Letters from Japan (1895)

113   There is another love, a higher love that is strong enough to build a lifelong relationship upon. It is, in fact, the very same love God had for us when He sacrificed His only Son to die in our place.

Eric and Leslie Ludy
When God Writes Your Love Story (1999)

114   God weeps over your anguish because you are precious to him.

Laura Petherbridge
When Your Marriage Dies (2005)

115   God does not love the rest of the world more than he loves you.

Stephen Arterburn and Jack Felton
More Jesus, Less Religion (2000)

116   Refresh me today in Your love, so that in Your coolness I may stand the heat.

Elisabeth Elliot
The Music of His Promises (2000)

117   God hath a tender regard unto the souls of men, and is infinitely willing to promote their welfare.

Henry Scougal
Life of God in the Soul of Man
(17th century)

118   He hath condescended to our weakness, and declared with an oath, that he hath no pleasure in our destruction.

Henry Scougal
Life of God in the Soul of Man
(17th century)

119   When our heart is filled with God's love, the Holy Spirit takes control. Good fruit springs forth in words and actions as the result of this loving relationship.

Jack and Dona Eggar
Shaping Your Family's Faith (2007)

LOVE

120   Nothing in me can surprise Him out of loving me. . .there is wonderful comfort in that.

> Amy Carmichael
> *Edges of His Ways* (1955)

121   We have no beauty, no goodness to make us desirable in his eyes; all the origins of his love to us are in his own breast.

> John Flavel
> *Christ Altogether Lovely* (17th century)

122   When we are experiencing ourselves as the beloved of God, accepted and cherished by him in all of our beauty and brokenness, our hard, rough edges start to soften. We begin to see others as beloved as well, and that is what gets reflected back to them when they look into our eyes. Not only does the love of God come to us in solitude, the love of God begins to pour through us to others.

> Ruth Haley Barton
> *Invitation to Solitude and Silence* (2004)

123   Knowing oneself loved by God is not a matter of knowing about God's love. It's not a matter of saying the right words or even claiming the right beliefs. It's about something that happens on a level deeper than words and ideas and knowledge and thoughts. It's something that gets inside one's soul and never leaves.

> Lynne Hybels
> *Nice Girls Don't Change the World* (2005)

124   The love of God, which will make us conscious of God's love for us, will give us wings to fly on his way and to raise us above all our troubles.

> François Fénelon
> *Christian Perfection* (17th century)

125   We are so preciously loved by God that we cannot even comprehend it. No created being can ever know how much and how sweetly and tenderly God loves them. It is only with the help of his grace that we are able to persevere in spiritual contemplation with endless wonder at his high, surpassing, immeasurable love which our Lord in his goodness has for us.

> Julian of Norwich
> *Revelations of Divine Love* (14th century)

126 God is no respecter of persons, He has no favorites. If He'll show Himself strong on behalf of Joseph or Job, He'll do the same for you.

> Rebecca Lusignolo
> "No Favorites" devotional (2010)

127   The power of God's love will never be contained nor understood.

> Tim Hansel
> *Eating Problems for Breakfast* (1988)

128   God's manner is not to bring comfortable texts of Scripture to give men assurance of his love, and that they shall be happy, before they have had a faith of dependence.

> Jonathan Edwards
> *A Treatise Concerning Religious Affections* (18th century)

for God

129   Get near to Christ, and you will never want to go back to the world. People may call you narrow, but God uses a narrow man and a narrow woman.

> D. L. Moody
> "The Transfiguration" sermon
> (19th century)

130   After loving God with all of our heart, soul, mind, and strength, there won't be any affection left over for other delights that compete with God.

> Bill Gothard
> *Our Jealous God* (2003)

286

131   God is a jealous God. He is a pursuing, passionate lover of all. Even in our best prayers and deepest desires, He wants to remain our greatest love.

Bonnie Keen
God Loves Messy People (2002)

132   The mind in love with God is engaged with God's thoughts and ways, just as a lover is engaged with the words and actions of the beloved.

Nancy Nordenson
Just Think (2003)

133   Our love for Christ is more important to Him than all of our service to Him. Strict obedience and service alone are not enough. Love for Jesus must come first.

Anne Graham Lotz
The Vision of His Glory (1996)

134   We ought not to be weary of doing little things for the love of God, who regards not the greatness of the work, but the love with which it is performed.

Brother Lawrence
The Practice of the Presence of God
(17th century)

135   The best life consists of directing all that we have, do, and are towards loving God. And then because of our love for him, we should love those around us rather than treating them as competition or the means to material ends.

Walt Mueller
Understanding Today's Youth Culture (1999)

136   Jesus said the entire Old Testament hangs on two commands: Love God and love the person next to you (Matthew 22:34–40). How can you love the person next to you and not open your heart to him? And how can you open your heart without letting yourself be vulnerable? Peter wrote, "Above all, love each other deeply" (1 Peter 4:8). Above all

ministries, business obligations, "Christian" stuff and evangelistic enterprises, we are to deeply, vulnerably love those next to us.

Russell Willingham
Relational Masks (2004)

137   Let your soul be filled with so entire a love to Him that you may love nothing but for his sake.

John Wesley
A Plain Account of Christian Perfection
(18th century)

138   Whom have I in heaven but thee? And there is none upon earth whom I desire besides thee.

John Wesley
A Plain Account of Christian Perfection
(18th century)

139   Anyone who loves God wants to please Him.

Joyce Meyer
Approval Addiction (2005)

140   Get up every day, love God, and do your best.

Joyce Meyer
Approval Addiction (2005)

141   Love to God is obedience, love to God is holiness. To love God and to love man is to be conformed to the image of Christ; and this is salvation.

Charles Spurgeon
All of Grace (19th century)

142   Loving God is the biblical foundation for all relationships.

Jack and Dona Eggar
Shaping Your Family's Faith (2007)

143   Do you continually remind those under your care, that the one rational end of all our studies, is to know, love, and serve the only

true God, and Jesus Christ whom he hath
sent?

John Wesley
Scriptural Christianity (1744)

144   How do we express love to God? We
express our love by placing Him at the center
of all that we are and hope to be and by
obeying Him unreservedly.

Jack and Dona Eggar
Shaping Your Family's Faith (2007)

145   A man must first love God or have his
heart united to him, before he will esteem
God's good his own, and before he will desire
the glorifying, and enjoying of God as his
happiness.

Jonathan Edwards
A Treatise Concerning Religious Affections
(18th century)

146   Men may love a God of their own
forming in their imaginations, when they are
far from loving such a God as reigns in heaven.

Jonathan Edwards
A Treatise Concerning Religious Affections
(18th century)

147   Perfect love of God with our heart,
soul, mind, and strength will not happen until
we are no longer compelled to think about
ourselves.

Bernard of Clairvaux
On the Love of God (12th century)

148   There is only one way to love God: to
take not a single step without him, and to
follow with a brave heart wherever he leads.

François Fénelon
Christian Perfection (17th century)

149   To sanctify the Lord in their hearts was
to love him supremely, and trust in him alone,
desiring that he might be exalted and glorified
above all creatures forever.

Samuel Hopkins
"The Reason of the Hope of a Christian"
sermon (1803)

150   A relationship with the Living God
shouldn't just fade away or wear out like an
old pair of shoes. It's meant to be new every
morning, just like the mercy it responds to.

Matt Redman
The Unquenchable Worshipper (2001)

151   Love for God and love for the world
cannot coexist in the same soul: the stronger
drives out the weaker, and it soon appears who
loves the world, and who follows Christ. The
strength of people's love is shown in what
they do.

Richard Rolle
The Fire of Love (14th century)

152   It is impossible to love God without
loving our neighbor.

Mother Teresa
Loving Jesus (1991)

261 LOYALTY
(*see also* CONSECRATION;
DEDICATION; DEVOTION)

*O LORD God of Abraham, Isaac, and of Israel,
our fathers, keep this for ever in the imagination
of the thoughts of the heart of thy people,
and prepare their heart unto thee.*
1 CHRONICLES 29:18

1   Our commitment to others will never
exceed our commitment to God.

Carter Conlon
"The Final Word Before the Lord Returns"
sermon (2009)

2   Friends are loyal. They are with you in
good and bad times. They do not leave when
the going gets rough or when you are rough.
They are not just friends when you are in a
good mood! This loyalty does not mean that

they will cover your faults and worship you. It means they will stand up for you, even if you are wrong and need correction.
Paul Jehle
Dating vs. Courtship (1993)

3 God bless loyal people—I love loyal people. People who will stick with you when all else is in turmoil. People who will still love you even when they know you. People who, despite your human failures, still believe in you. Those are the kind of people I want in my life.
Rick Johnson
That's My Son (2005)

LUCIFER (*see* DEVIL)

262 LUST (*see also* IMMORALITY; SENSUALITY; SIN; TEMPTATION)
Dearly beloved, I beseech you as strangers and pilgrims, abstain from fleshly lusts, which war against the soul.
1 PETER 2:11

1 When we consider that our culture as a whole regards the words love and sex as interchangeable, we shouldn't be surprised that many dating relationships mistake physical attraction and sexual intimacy for true love.
Joshua Harris
I Kissed Dating Goodbye (1997)

2 Lust is in opposition to love. It means to set your heart and passions on something forbidden.
Stephen Kendrick and Alex Kendrick
The Love Dare (2008)

3 Lust is the Devil's counterfeit for love. There is nothing more beautiful on earth than a pure love and there is nothing so blighting as lust.
D. L. Moody
Weighed and Wanting (19th century)

4 The body cannot thrive in a fever, nor can the soul under the feverish heat of lust.
Thomas Watson and Samuel Lee
The Bible and the Closet (1842)

5 If we wallow in the mire of any untamed, unfortified lust, what soever our evangelical professions may be, or howsoever we may fancy ourselves entered into a fellowship with the Father by the means of the mediator, it is but a lying imagination.
Stephen Charnock
Discourse on the Cleansing Virtue of Christ's Blood (17th century)

6 The loathsome carcase does not more hatefully swarm with crawling maggots, than an unsanctified soul with filthy lusts.
Joseph Alleine
A Sure Guide to Heaven (1671)

263 LYING (*see also* DECEIT)
Lie not one to another, seeing that ye have put off the old man with his deeds.
COLOSSIANS 3:9

1 It is possible for a person to repeat a falsehood so many times that he at length imposes it upon himself, and believes that he is stating the truth.
Charles Spurgeon
Autobiography (1897)

2 A lie is cowardly. After all that might be said to excuse an untruth, when you have sifted it down to its starting-point, you will find its real reason for being is cowardice.
Mabel Hale
Beautiful Girlhood (1922)

3 Those who deceive others, deceive themselves, as they will find at last, to their cost.
Matthew Henry
Commentary on the Whole Bible (1706)

4 The society we live in sets us up to excuse white lies. All you have to do is read the billboards on the highway and watch the commercials on television; easily half of them include white lies. Sure, there is probably a grain of truth in them, but sometimes it's a pretty small grain!
　　Dan Seaborn
　　26 Words That Will Improve the Way You Do Family (2002)

5 We have got nowadays so that we divide lies into white lies and black lies, society lies and business lies, etc. The Word of God knows no such letting-down of the standard.
　　D. L. Moody
　　Weighed and Wanting (19th century)

6 A man's face will often reveal that which his words try to conceal.
　　R. A.Torrey
　　How to Bring Men to Christ (1893)

7 One of the ways we befriend lies is to use words in ways that tangle their true meaning.
　　Karen Burton Mains
　　You Are What You Say (1988)

8 Understand now what lying is. Any species of designed deception. If the deception is not designed it is not lying. But if you design to make an impression contrary to the naked truth, you lie.
　　Charles Finney
　　Lectures of Revival of Religion (1835)

MAGIC (*see* OCCULT)

MANKIND (*see* HUMANITY)

264 MARRIAGE
Marriage is honourable in all.
HEBREWS 13:4

1 The biblical purpose for marriage, you see, is not man-centered or needs-centered. It's God-centered. It's profoundly mysterious and profoundly significant. Your marriage is meant to point to the truth of the crucified and risen Savior who will return for his Bride.
　　C. J. Mahaney *Sex, Romance, and the Glory of God* (2004)

2 Happiness and passion in marriage do not come from finding the right partner, but in being the right partner.
　　Bill and Pam Farrel
　　Men Are Like Waffles, Women Are Like Spaghetti (2001)

3 A woman marries a man expecting he will change and he doesn't. A man marries a woman expecting that she won't change and she does.
　　Bill and Pam Farrel
　　Men Are Like Waffles, Women Are Like Spaghetti (2001)

4 Marriage is between two people, a man and his wife. No one else should be a participant—not in person, in print, or on video.
　　Bill and Pam Farrel
　　Men Are Like Waffles, Women Are Like Spaghetti (2001)

5 God wants marriage to be a three-way, lifelong spiritual relationship between a man, a woman, and God.
　　Dennis and Barbara Rainey
　　Growing a Spiritually Strong Family (2002)

6 The keeping of a covenant is very important to almighty God. He keeps His word. He's a covenant keeper. So if we want to please Him and in the process create the relational environment where a marriage and family can flourish spiritually, we need to take the marriage covenant very seriously.
　　Dennis and Barbara Rainey
　　Growing a Spiritually Strong Family (2002)

7   If you want your marriage to go the distance and your family to be all that God intended, pray together as a couple every day.
>   Dennis and Barbara Rainey
>   *Two Hearts Praying As One* (2002)

8   Since marriage is a spiritual relationship involving husband, wife, and God, prayer together keeps communication flowing among all three.
>   Dennis and Barbara Rainey
>   *Two Hearts Praying As One* (2002)

9   Romance is the act of keeping your courtship alive long after the wedding day.
>   Gary Smalley
>   *Love Is a Decision* (1989)

10   Every enduring marriage involves an unconditional commitment to an imperfect person.
>   Gary Smalley
>   *Love Is a Decision* (1989)

11   Love doesn't feel all mushy. Love isn't sweaty palms and sleepless nights. Love is a decision you make to care for someone no matter how you feel. If they are disfigured in an accident or throwing up for hours on end, you still love them.
>   Justin Lookadoo and Hayley DiMarco
>   *Dateable* (2006)

12   Getting married is not the issue. Anyone can do that. It's staying married that is the goal.
>   Justin Lookadoo and Hayley DiMarco
>   *Dateable* (2006)

13   Marriage won't transform us into new people; it will only act as a mirror, showing what we already are.
>   Joshua Harris
>   *I Kissed Dating Goodbye* (1997)

14   When you were joined together as husband and wife, God gave you a wedding gift—a permanent prayer partner for life.
>   Stephen Kendrick and Alex Kendrick
>   *The Love Dare* (2008)

15   What is one of the greatest needs in your spouse's life right now? Is there a need you could lift from their shoulders today by a daring act of sacrifice on your part?
>   Stephen Kendrick and Alex Kendrick
>   *The Love Dare* (2008)

16   Eliminate the poison of unrealistic expectations in your home.
>   Stephen Kendrick and Alex Kendrick
>   *The Love Dare* (2008)

17   A wife may and should adorn herself according to her husband's wishes when he is present—if she does as much in his absence one is disposed to ask in whose eyes she seeks to shine?
>   Francis de Sales
>   *Introduction to the Devout Life*
>   (17th century)

18   In order to thrive, your marriage must be your number one priority—at the top of your list. And your spouse needs to see this every day. The principle is simple: If your partner doesn't feel she is special to you, sooner or later she'll be tempted to find someone who does make her feel special.
>   Steve Stephens
>   *20 (Surprisingly Simple) Rules and Tools for a Great Marriage* (2003)

19   It's not easy to keep marriage at the top of your priority list when there are so many other demands on your time: demanding jobs, demanding children, and other demanding responsibilities. While each has its place in your life, developing a healthy marriage is most

important and should be given more attention than your other responsibilities.
Steve Stephens
20 (Surprisingly Simple) Rules and Tools for a Great Marriage (2003)

20 If two people are not solidly committed to each other, their marriage will sooner or later fall apart. Trust is the foundation of a good marriage, and trust begins with commitment.
Steve Stephens
20 (Surprisingly Simple) Rules and Tools for a Great Marriage (2003)

21 A marriage is like a dance. No matter how careful you are, periodically you're going to step on your partner's feet.
Steve Stephens
20 (Surprisingly Simple) Rules and Tools for a Great Marriage (2003)

22 Our innate desire for intimacy comes, of course, from our Creator. It is no accident that we have a desire—some may call it a need—to draw close to one another and to God. We have been created for relationship. Jesus was an example to us of the Word becoming flesh. He taught us the gospel in the context of relationships. Intimacy with our mate was part of God's design.
David Hawkins
9 Critical Mistakes Most Couples Make (2003)

23 We do not need to shrink from our desire to be close. We need make no apologies from wanting to have someone to laugh with, share our day, and make fun and exciting plans with. The Creator Himself designed us to be in an intimate, joyful marriage.
David Hawkins
9 Critical Mistakes Most Couples Make (2003)

24 The typical wife doesn't understand her husband's deep need for sex any more than the typical husband understands his wife's deep need for affection.
Willard Harley Jr.
His Needs, Her Needs (1986)

25 Meet your spouse's needs as you would want your spouse to meet yours.
Willard Harley Jr.
His Needs, Her Needs (1986)

26 Caring partners converse in a caring way.
Willard Harley Jr.
His Needs, Her Needs (1986)

27 Honesty is the best marriage insurance policy.
Willard Harley Jr.
His Needs, Her Needs (1986)

28 Marriage begins when two people make the clear, unqualified promise to be faithful, each to the other, until the end of their days. That spoken promise makes the difference. A promise made, a promise witnessed, a promise heard, remembered, and trusted—this is the groundwork of marriage. Not emotions. No, not even love.
Walter Wangerin Jr.
As for Me and My House (1990)

29 Marriage is an unacknowledged cataclysm to lifestyles.
Walter Wangerin Jr.
As for Me and My House (1990)

30 Thriving partners treat each other with generosity. They regularly offer each other gifts that they know the other cherishes.
Wayne and Mary Sotile
Beat Stress Together (1998)

31 It is fascinating to note how much more couples know about each other early in their relationship than they do once they've been together for years. The reason? We stop paying attention. Remember: If you aren't learning something new about each other every week or two, you simply aren't paying close enough attention.
Wayne and Mary Sotile
Beat Stress Together (1998)

32 A happy marriage is a long conversation that always seems too short.
H. Norman Wright
Communication: Key to Your Marriage (2000)

33 In marriage you have a choice to respond with empathy, sympathy or apathy.
H. Norman Wright
Communication: Key to Your Marriage (2000)

34 To be loved and appreciated gives all of us a reason to live each day. . .in long-term marriages where one or both spouses are continually taken for granted, a wall of indifference arises between husband and wife.
H. Norman Wright
Communication: Key to Your Marriage (2000)

35 Remember: A thirty-five-year marriage does not guarantee year number thirty-six. Take nothing for granted just because you have it today.
H. Norman Wright
Communication: Key to Your Marriage (2000)

36 Spouses cling and cry, get angry and protest, or become withdrawn and detached when actually all they long for is closeness and to be valued.
David and Jan Stoop
The Complete Marriage Book (2002)

37 The need for closeness and the reactions to being disconnected are a natural part of being human in close relationships, especially in a marital relationship.
David and Jan Stoop
The Complete Marriage Book (2002)

38 One of the most important traits of couples who fight fair is the focus they put on the problem, not the person.
Les Parrott III
The Control Freak (2000)

39 I don't know of a single person who has ever changed a spouse through arguing.
Les Parrott III
The Control Freak (2000)

40 I'm convinced that the major reason Christian marriages are falling apart in epidemic proportion is that couples give up too soon.
Fred Lowery
Covenant Marriage (2002)

41 Persistence is one of the keys to achieving oneness in marriage.
Fred Lowery
Covenant Marriage (2002)

42 We all get tired, run down, and stressed out at times, and the future never looks very promising from that perspective. Those are the times when we have to rely upon knowledge rather than feelings, covenant rather than contract, and refuse to give up.
Fred Lowery
Covenant Marriage (2002)

43 Covenant is the heart of marriage, and sacrifice is the heart of covenant.
Fred Lowery
Covenant Marriage (2002)

44 Can you imagine what would happen if each husband said, "My wife is a very important person, and I am going to honor, respect, and encourage her." And if the wife said the same thing about her husband?
Bill Hybels
Descending into Greatness (1993)

45 Unless a marriage is kept fresh and nurtured, it will fade like an old photograph.
Gary and Barbara Rosberg
Divorce-Proof Your Marriage (2002)

46 Marriage is a dynamic love relationship between a man and a woman, and at every

moment that relationship is either growing deeper and richer or stagnating and decaying.

Gary and Barbara Rosberg
Divorce-Proof Your Marriage (2002)

47 God's primary solution to human aloneness is the oneness, companionship, and togetherness of having a spouse. When husbands and wives distance themselves from each other, they are fighting against God's plan for their marriage and missing out on the blessing of oneness that God designed for them.

Gary and Barbara Rosberg
Divorce-Proof Your Marriage (2002)

48 In a marriage where there is genuine oneness, the joy of one is the joy of the other, the unhappiness of one is the unhappiness of the other. Each partner, therefore, becomes a key resource to the other.

Ruthann Ridley
Every Marriage Is Different (1993)

49 What makes a husband or wife feel supported varies from one marriage to another—because every marriage is different. One husband says he feels supported by his wife when she communicates that she is available to him and lets him know she values his ideas.

Ruthann Ridley
Every Marriage Is Different (1993)

50 Mutual support is showing that we want 100 percent what is best for our spouse.

Ruthann Ridley
Every Marriage Is Different (1993)

51 Sometimes mutual support means listening; at other times it means getting involved in a practical way. But it always means being sensitive and willing to serve the other person right where he (or she) is. This is the essence of oneness.

Ruthann Ridley
Every Marriage is Different (1993)

52 Tell the truth! It all starts here. A marriage has so much to gain if both partners can rest assured that the truth, the whole truth, and nothing but the truth is the intended goal of every message they give each other.

Neil Clark Warren
Forever My Love (1998)

53 Marriage is about teamwork. Two separate individuals may see things differently and might make different decisions. But often the best solution will be a compromise in which neither of you gets everything you wanted.

Howard Markman, Scott Stanley, and Susan Blumberg
Fighting for Your Marriage (1994)

54 There are three levels on which truth-telling is crucial. The first is the verbal level. There must be no lies! Second, truth is crucial on the behavioral level. Both marital partners need to become known as people who do what they promise they'll do. Third, it's important to be truthful on the being level. Each partner needs to be himself, or be herself, in order to contribute to the relationship.

Neil Clark Warren
Forever My Love (1998)

55 Want a healthy marriage? Then tell the truth every chance you get. Talk the truth, behave the truth, and be the truth.

Neil Clark Warren
Forever My Love (1998)

56 It is easy in a demanding world for two people who are married to become distant and lost. Formulating a vision for your future together is an exercise that every couple needs to engage in—and preferably every year.

Neil Clark Warren
Forever My Love (1998)

57 Turn off the television, put life on "pause," and take time to refresh your relationship after a tiring day. Any couple, who takes even a half hour every day to check in, discuss anything

and everything, is going to see dramatic improvement in their communication.
Neil Clark Warren
Forever My Love (1998)

58 Although the Bible has much to say about the marriage relationship, it has even more to say about a vital, living, authentic relationship with God—the best foundation for a happy and successful marriage.
Dave Meurer
Good Spousekeeping (2004)

59 Marriage becomes what we create and put in instead of what we expect and take out.
Susanna McMahon
Having Healthy Relationships (1996)

60 There are few guarantees in life, but one of them is that any unresolved problems with your self will become marital problems.
Susanna McMahon
Having Healthy Relationships (1996)

61 Two damaged and problematic people make for a damaged and difficult marriage. Because life consists of problems and no one is free of them, it makes sense that marriage is also about problems. It provides us, then, with one of our greatest settings in which to become problem solvers. Life, marriage, and problem solving are all process.
Susanna McMahon
Having Healthy Relationships (1996)

62 "To have and to hold from this day forward" isn't just a license to hug—it's a promise to be kept.
Gary Stanley
How to Make a Moose Run (2001)

63 God wants our marriages to be living, breathing, public-service announcements declaring the brilliance of His plan for mankind.
Harry Jackson
In-laws, Outlaws, and the Functional Family (2002)

64 You and your spouse have a choice to be either a great, God-honoring couple or an average, mediocre one. You decide each day whether you will run the race in such a way as to get the prize or limp along in a halfhearted effort.
Harry Jackson
In-laws, Outlaws, and the Functional Family (2002)

65 Many people think marriage will be a magical cure for their problems, that their old struggles will disappear as soon as they tie the knot. And perhaps for a while the freshness and exhilaration of their relationship hides signs of trouble. The newlyweds think, it's a new beginning. We're going to leave the old problems behind and start over. But inevitably, marriage only intensifies problems.
Harry Jackson
In-Laws, Outlaws, and the Functional Family (2002)

66 You never hear of a man marrying a woman to reform her.
Billy Sunday
The Real Billy Sunday (1914)

67 Men or women who are wise enough to untie the anger knot in another's heart will learn to listen beyond the sharp words, to the hurt feelings behind the emotional outburst.
Gary and Greg Smalley
Winning Your Husband (2002)

68 If you cannot speak positively about your mate to others, then maintain gracious silence.
Gary and Greg Smalley
Winning Your Husband (2002)

69 Being married does not qualify either a husband or a wife to be a mind reader.
Gary and Greg Smalley
Winning Your Husband (2002)

70 Success in marriage doesn't come as the result of finding the right mate, but in the ability of both partners to adjust to the reality of the person they married.

David and Janet Congo
Lifemates (2001)

71 Marriage is a daily excursion with another person into the unknown. We cannot see beyond the frame of one moment at a time. Yet it is those hidden elements, those mysterious curves in the highway, that draw us along with a sense of anticipation and adventure. The truth is, you can allow that excursion to become flat and predictable, or you can glory in the quest and become explorers with shining eyes who delight in each day's trek.

Thomas and Nanette Kinkade
The Many Loves of Marriage (2002)

72 Wedlock should be a padlock. Getting married should be as permanent and secure as turning a lock and throwing away the key. Marriage means standing by the commitment we have made come what may.

Greg Laurie
Marriage + Connections (2002)

73 Marriage is all about commitment. And there is no secret greater than that.

Greg Laurie
Marriage + Connections (2002)

74 We hear way too much about marriages that are in trouble or don't make it. Yet there are many, many couples today who have fulfilling marriages, even exceptional ones. It is no accident that the strong marriages are the way they are. Good marriages don't just happen. The couples in exceptional marriages are willing to learn and grow; develop a positive, biblical attitude; and discover how to speak their spouse's language and celebrate differences.

H. Norman Wright
The Marriage Checkup (2002)

75 We can learn that it is impossible to understand and appreciate who your spouse is without understanding his or her God-given uniqueness.

H. Norman Wright
The Marriage Checkup (2002)

76 For many, marriage is seen as a convenient arrangement in which two individuals occupy the same house and share the same bed while living out their separate lives. In algebraic terms, this would be 1 + 1 = 2. In the Biblical view, however, marriage is meant to be the dissolution of two single lives, and the creation of a brand-new entity. God's marital math is 1 + 1 = 1. A husband and wife become "one flesh," which means not just physical intimacy, but a merging of lives and dreams, moving together even as they move toward God.

Len Woods
Marriage Clues for the Clueless (1999)

77 With no long-term vision, and no agreed-upon spiritual goals or direction, marriages tend to drift. The circumstances of life, like the waves of the sea, end up propelling aimless couples to places they'd rather not go. Imagine a crew on a sailing vessel embarking on a voyage without a definite destination and you begin to get the picture.

Len Woods
Marriage Clues for the Clueless (1999)

78 Marriage brings two sinners into close proximity, where their selfish desires rub against each other day after day. Friction increases when God adds "little sinners" to the mix! There is only one way to deal with this volatile mixture: with humble confession, loving confrontation, and genuine forgiveness—the three basic tools of the biblical peacemaker.

Ken Sande and Tom Raabe
Peacemaking for Families (2002)

79 If you want your children to glorify God, have fulfilling and enduring marriages, be fruitful in their careers, and contribute to their churches and the building of God's kingdom, teach them to be peacemakers!

Ken Sande and Tom Raabe
Peacemaking for Families (2002)

80 A companion in marriage is the human face of God.

Anthony Garascia
Rekindle the Passion (2001)

81 God created no closer relationship outside of one with Him than that of husband and wife.

Donna VanLiere and Eddie Carswell
Sheltering Trees (2001)

82 If God is kept at the center of our marriages, there will be no one who encourages, challenges, inspires, motivates, or believes in us like our spouses.

Donna VanLiere and Eddie Carswell
Sheltering Trees (2001)

83 On this side of heaven we will experience no greater love than that of a God-centered husband or wife.

Donna VanLiere and Eddie Carswell
Sheltering Trees (2001)

84 There is nothing so ugly as a husband or wife who bitterly attacks and demeans his mate. But nothing is so beautiful as a loving relationship that conforms to God's magnificent design.

James Dobson
Straight Talk (1995)

85 A man can never totally satisfy your craving for love. His humanity will not allow him to.

Michelle McKinney Hammond
How to Be Found by the Man You've Been Looking For (2005)

86 Fidelity is a calling to be faithful in every area of marriage.

Bob and Emilie Barnes
Simple Secrets Couples Should Know (2008)

87 Somewhere between the thrill of the engagement, the hectic preparations for the wedding, and the joy of the big day—and often despite excellent premarital counseling—the message gets lost, overlooked, or silenced. That message? Marriage takes effort and commitment.

Bob and Emilie Barnes
Simple Secrets Couples Should Know (2008)

88 Oneness doesn't mean sameness. Oneness refers to an agreement in commitment, mission in life, goals, and dreams.

Bob and Emilie Barnes
Simple Secrets Couples Should Know (2008)

89 No matter how depressing or irritating my spouse might be, my response is my responsibility.

Emerson Eggerichs
Love and Respect (2004)

90 A wife's unconditional respect for her husband reveals her reverence for Christ.

Emerson Eggerichs
Love and Respect (2004)

91 In the ultimate sense, your marriage has nothing to do with your spouse. It has everything to do with your relationship to Jesus Christ.

Emerson Eggerichs
Love and Respect (2004)

92 A wedding ring is a sign of loyalty. No husband should leave home without one.

Emerson Eggerichs
Love and Respect (2004)

93 Plain and simple, your husband's relationship with the Lord isn't dependent on you.

Nancy Kennedy
When He Doesn't Believe (2001)

94 Maintaining communication with your spouse will take a boatload of patience and persistence. There will be times when you'll feel like you're beating your head against a brick wall as you try to make yourself understood. Take some aspirin and keep pounding. Eventually your work will pay off.
Gary Chapman
The World's Easiest Guide to Family Relationships (2001)

95 Great or potentially great marriages all suffer if neglected.
J. Allan Petersen
The Myth of the Greener Grass (1983)

96 Marriage resembles a pair of shears, so joined that they cannot be separated; often moving in opposite directions, yet always punishing anyone who comes between them.
H. Norman Wright and Marvin Inmon
Dating, Waiting, and Choosing a Mate (1978)

97 Marriage does not demand perfection. But it must be given priority.
H. Norman Wright and Marvin Inmon
Dating, Waiting, and Choosing a Mate (1978)

98 Couples who have few or no mutual interests have little or no basis for enjoying their leisure time.
H. Norman Wright and Marvin Inmon
Dating, Waiting, and Choosing a Mate (1978)

99 Though marriage is the most significant human relationship of our life, often less time is given to preparing for it than we give to learning to drive, planning a vacation, or learning a language.
J. Allan Petersen
Before You Marry (1974)

100 Some of the greatest satisfaction you will ever receive in this life will come from your marriage.
William Coleman
Before I Give You Away (1995)

101 The potential in marriage is enormous. It is like a treasure chest. Every year you open the lid more and more to discover rare jewels you wouldn't dare dream of. Pity the person who is afraid to even peek inside.
William Coleman
Before I Give You Away (1995)

102 Accommodate is what you do, not what you do to your mate. . .or what you expect done by your mate.
William Krutza
101 Ways to Enrich Your Marriage (1982)

103 Divergent interests do not have to destroy a marriage. On the contrary, they can enhance one.
Michele Weiner-Davis
Divorce Busting (1992)

104 The more important a woman feels she is to her husband, the more she encourages him to do the activities she knows he enjoys— activities she used to resent.
Gary Smalley
If Only He Knew (1979)

105 Conveying a superior attitude is the biggest killer of marriage and produces the most frustration, hurt and fear within a marriage.
Gary Smalley
Secrets to Lasting Love (2000)

106 Praise your mate for the small things, because small things eventually add up to big changes.
Gary Smalley
Secrets to Lasting Love (2000)

107   Magnificent marriages involve two people who dream magnificently.
   Neil Clark Warren
   The Triumphant Marriage (1995)

108   If you want to become more like Jesus, I can't imagine any better thing to do than to get married. Being married forces you to face some character issues you'd never have to face otherwise.
   Gary Thomas
   Sacred Marriage (2000)

109   If the purpose of marriage was simply to enjoy an infatuation and make me "happy," then I'd have to get a "new" marriage every two or three years. But if I really wanted to see God transform me from the inside out, I'd need to concentrate on changing myself rather than changing my spouse.
   Gary Thomas
   Sacred Marriage (2000)

110   We need to remind ourselves of the ridiculousness of looking for something from other humans that only God can provide. . . . I believe that much of the dissatisfaction we experience in marriage comes from expecting too much from it.
   Gary Thomas
   Sacred Marriage (2000)

111   Marriage is more manageable with humor. Laughing relationships last longer, and couples who cut up create ties that bind for a lifetime.
   Liz Curtis Higgs
   She Who Laughs, Lasts (2000)

112   Too often they marry in haste and repent at leisure, and lay up misery for life by wedding an uncongenial partner.
   J. C. Ryle
   The Upper Room (19th century)

113   Eve was made to order. God saw the shape of Adam's need and designed the woman to fit it exactly in every way.
   Elisabeth Elliot
   The Mark of a Man (1981)

114   Marriage is not meant to be the place where one gets completed as a person.
   Henry Cloud and John Townsend
   Boundaries in Marriage (1999)

115   We must become more deeply concerned about our own issues than our spouse's.
   Henry Cloud and John Townsend
   Boundaries in Marriage (1999)

116   Don't wait for your spouse to take the first step. Assume the first move is always yours.
   Henry Cloud and John Townsend
   Boundaries in Marriage (1999)

117   Guys think of a woman as a swamp: You can't see where you're stepping, and sooner or later you just know you're going to get stuck in quicksand.
   Shaunti and Jeff Feldhahn
   For Men Only (2006)

118   It's common for men to think that pursuing goes with dating, not with marriage. But women don't see things that way. There is never that magic moment of closure, when they feel permanently, fully, deeply loved. They think that's what the rest of married life is for! That's why they need and deserve to be pursued every day.
   Shaunti and Jeff Feldhahn
   For Men Only (2006)

119   When the Bible teaches that men and women fulfill different roles in relation to each other, charging man with a unique leadership

role, it bases this differentiation not on temporary cultural norms but on permanent facts of creation.
John Piper and Elisabeth Elliot
What's the Difference? (1990)

120   Happiness in marriage is a choice, and we have found that if you take care of the special moments, the years will take care of themselves.
Jim and Cathy Burns
Closer (2009)

121   Just as women have the right to be offended by their husbands' wandering eyes, men have the right to be offended by their wives' wandering minds.
Shannon Ethridge
Every Woman's Battle (2003)

122   If a man's wife believes in him, he can conquer the world—or at least his little corner of it.
Shaunti Feldhahn
For Women Only (2004)

123   Whole, healthy marriages cannot be built on foundations of brokenness.
Bill and Lynne Hybels
Fit to Be Tied: Making Marriage Last a Lifetime (1991)

124   Spouses cannot be expected to be life preservers.
Bill and Lynne Hybels
Fit to Be Tied: Making Marriage Last a Lifetime (1991)

125   The holy state of matrimony—trampled and degraded in man's schemes—glistens as the crowning jewel of the perfect creation.
Jeanne Hendricks
A Woman for All Seasons (1977)

126 Marriage is not only workable; it is one of the highest forms of human fulfillment.
Jeanne Hendricks
A Woman for All Seasons (1977)

127   Marriage involves not so much love as will.
Jeanne Hendricks
A Woman for All Seasons (1977)

128   A successful marriage foundation requires two people who understand that there are only two avenues of effecting change in their mate: love and blessing. Both must confess the futility of human manipulation.
Don Meredith
Becoming One (1999)

129   The blessing of experiencing a great marriage is almost beyond words.
Don Meredith
Becoming One (1999)

130   Not only is marriage as an institution not hopeless, but it can be exceedingly successful above and beyond one's expectations.
Don Meredith
Becoming One (1999)

131   In and of themselves, all of the ifs matter in marriage.
David Gudgel
Before You Live Together (2003)

132   It is impossible to duplicate the process of marriage by living together.
H. Norman Wright
Finding the Right One for You (1995)

133   The glue that will keep marriage together is not love. There is a word that is becoming foreign in meaning and application to our culture in general—it's the word commitment.
H. Norman Wright
Finding the Right One for You (1995)

134   Marriage is an unconditional commitment and not a contract.
H. Norman Wright
Finding the Right One for You (1995)

135   Marriage solves almost no problems.
William Coleman
Engaged (1980)

136   I believe God designed marriage between a man and a woman here on earth to give us a glimpse of what a marriage with Christ can be like in heaven.
Cindi McMenamin
When Women Walk Alone (2002)

265 MARTYRDOM

They were stoned, they were sawn asunder, were tempted, were slain with the sword: they wandered about in sheepskins and goatskins; being destitute, afflicted, tormented; (Of whom the world was not worthy.)
HEBREWS 11:37–38

1   The blood of the martyrs, though not a sacrifice of atonement, yet was a sacrifice of acknowledgment to the grace of God and his truth.
Matthew Henry
Commentary on the Whole Bible (1706)

2   The love we bear to the blessed martyrs causes us, I know not how, to desire to see in the heavenly kingdom the marks of the wounds which they received for the name of Christ, and possibly we shall see them.
Augustine
The City of God (5th century)

3   The blood of the martyrs has been the seed of the church.
Matthew Henry
Commentary on the Whole Bible (1706)

266 MASCULINITY (*see also* MEN)
Watch ye, stand fast in the faith, quit you like men, be strong.
1 CORINTHIANS 16:13

1   At the heart of mature masculinity is a sense of benevolent responsibility to lead, provide for and protect women in ways appropriate to a man's differing relationships.
John Piper and Elisabeth Elliot
What's the Difference? (1990)

2   The image of a man as a warrior appeals to us because it resonates with—and ultimately distorts—something inside every man.
Bob Lepine
The Christian Husband (1999)

3   Instead of looking to the world for a definition of masculinity, we need to align our thinking to what God's Word says marks a man. Instead of being conformed, we need to be transformed.
Bob Lepine
The Christian Husband (1999)

267 MATERIAL THINGS
(*see also* POSSESSIONS; TREASURE)
Lay not up for yourselves treasures upon earth, where moth and rust doth corrupt, and where thieves break through and steal.
MATTHEW 6:19

1   Forbid it Lord, that our roots become too firmly attached to this earth, that we should fall in love with things.
Peter Marshall
The Prayers of Peter Marshall (1949)

2   If you believe for a moment that you own even a single possession, your contentment will be tied to it.
Bruce Bickel and Stan Jantz
God Is in the Small Stuff (1998)

3   The best things in life aren't things.
L. James Harvey
701 More Sentence Sermons (2002)

4 The god of the world is riches, pleasure, and pride, wherewith it abuses all the creatures and gifts of God.
    Martin Luther
    Table Talk (16th century)

5 What will your university education amount to, and all your wealth and honors if you go down through lust and passion and covetousness, and lose your soul at last?
    D. L. Moody
    Weighed and Wanting (19th century)

6 When we lose God's view of things, we lose perspective on everything else, too.
    Ben Patterson
    Deepening Our Conversation with God (1991)

7 When our possessions possess us—imprison us—risk and adventure become impossible.
    Michael Yaconelli
    Dangerous Wonder (1998)

8 Because we lack a divine Center, our need for security has led us into an insane attachment to things.
    Richard Foster
    Celebration of Discipline (1978)

9 It would be wonderful if we could stop accumulating so much stuff and start putting some of it to eternal use. The secret is keeping our worldly goods in spiritual perspective and maintaining a healthy balance.
    Jill Briscoe
    8 Choices That Will Change a Woman's Life (2004)

10 Wealth blunts, poverty sharpens, the critical power of the intellect.
    F. C. Cook
    Bible Commentary (19th century)

11 Living in this consumer-centered, commercial-filled world, we are constantly being told that we have a right for more and better. Such a message may make for effective advertisement, but it spells poor theology.
    Dave Earley
    The 21 Most Effective Prayers of the Bible (2005)

268 MATURITY (*see also* GROWTH, SPIRITUAL; SANCTIFICATION)

This also we wish, even your perfection.
2 CORINTHIANS 13:9

1 God's plan with most of us appears to be a design to make us flexible, twisting us this way and that, now giving, now taking; but always at work for and in us.
    Elizabeth Prentiss
    More Love to Thee—The Life and Letters of Elizabeth Prentiss (1882)

2 Maturity in Christ is about consistent pursuit in spite of the attacks and setbacks. Maturity in Christ is not about finally attaining some level of pseudo-perfection. It is about remaining in the arms of God. Abiding and staying, even in my weakness, even in my failure.
    Angela Thomas
    Do You Think I'm Beautiful? (2003)

3 Spiritual maturity has to do with wanting to do the Father's will for us—not only out of duty but out of overwhelming adoration and devotion. God measures maturity by the level of devotion we display.
    Joseph Stowell
    Why It's Hard to Love Jesus (2003)

4 Ask the advanced Christian what has made him go on and to grow, and he will not tell you ease and prosperity, freedom from care, exemption from danger, and inward toil. No, but the plague of his own heart, the strivings of sin, the power of temptation.
    James Thomas Holloway
    The Analogy of Faith (1836)

5 A man, and a Christian man too, may keep up all the outward appearances of religion; but if he has guilt on his conscience, or allows sin in his soul, he may frequent the Lord's house but it will be without profit; he may worship but it will be without peace.

James Thomas Holloway
The Analogy of Faith (1836)

6 If your relationship with God is only powerful enough to carry you through sunny days and overflowing bank accounts, it cannot and will not be a beacon of hope to a hopeless and hurting world.

Rebecca Lusignolo
Adversity (2007)

7 "What do you want with me ?" I want you, not to be a convert to my opinions, but to be a member of Christ, a child of God, and an heir of his kingdom.

John Wesley
The Works of the Rev. John Wesley
(18th century)

8 I have frequently observed that there are two very different ranks of Christians, both of whom may be in the favour of God—a higher and a lower rank. The latter avoid all known sin, do much good, use all the means of grace, but have little of the life of God in their souls, and are much conformed to the world. The former make the Bible their whole rule, and their sole aim is the will and image of God.

John Wesley
Personal Letter (1770)

9 We starve in the midst of plenty, groan under infirmities, with the remedy in our own hands.

William Law
The Spirit of Prayer (1750)

10 The discipline of life was meant to destroy this self, but that discipline having been evaded—and we all to some extent have opportunities, and too often exercise them, of taking the narrow path by the shortest cuts—its purpose is baulked. But the soul is the loser.

Henry Drummond
Natural Law in the Spiritual World (1884)

11 It is better to keep our eyes intent upon the goal, than to let them roam to mark how far some are behind us in the race.

George Edward Jelf
The Secret Trials of the Christian Life
(19th century)

12 We never arrive as being "finished products" as human beings. We have a lot yet to learn, daily.

Edith Schaeffer
Common Sense Christian Living (1983)

13 Kids give us glimpses of how we used to think or, for many of us, how we still think.

Dennis and Barbara Rainey
Moments Together (2004)

14 Just imagine how our world would change if all of us who claim the name of Christ could truly be said to possess a mature Christian faith.

Stephen Arterburn and Jack Felton
More Jesus, Less Religion (2000)

269 MEDIA, THE (*see also* AMUSEMENT; DIVERSION; ENTERTAINMENT)

When thine eye is evil,
thy body also is full of darkness.
LUKE 11:34

1 The constant bombardment of images shapes the perceptions of a whole generation and results in altered beliefs and lifestyles that make even the aberrant seem normal.

Ravi Zacharias
Deliver Us from Evil (1996)

2 Today's popular culture is filled with stories, video clips, lyrics and so forth that can help us to communicate the unchanging message in a relevant manner.
Walt Mueller
Engaging the Soul of Youth Culture (2006)

3 Children learn from ads that they are the most important person in the universe, that impulses should not be denied, that pain should not be tolerated and that the cure for any kind of pain is a product.
Mary Pipher
The Shelter of Each Other (1996)

4 The television, which Leonard Cohen called "that hopeless little screen," teaches values as clearly as any church.
Mary Pipher
The Shelter of Each Other (1996)

5 It is not the media's role to comfort the afflicted and to afflict the comfortable, even though this is taken as gospel in America's liberal newsrooms.
Bernard Goldberg
A Slobbering Love Affair (2009)

6 Let's be honest: we're only human. So no matter how fair we think we are, we process information through a filter of our own biases.
Bernard Goldberg
A Slobbering Love Affair (2009)

7 I find a lot of Western journalists intellectually cowardly here. They would never do with Mohammed what they do with Jesus.
Ravi Zacharias
Christian Worldview article (2008)

270 MEDITATION

I will meditate in thy precepts,
and have respect unto thy ways.
PSALM 119:15

1 Give every truth time to send down deep roots into the heart.
François Fénelon and Jeanne Guyon
Spiritual Progress (17th century)

2 Meditation teaches us to become like tea bags, soaking deeply and quietly in God and His Word so that we can better hear him speak to our hearts and minds.
Valerie Hess and Marti Watson Garlett
Habits of a Child's Heart (2004)

3 Meditation has no point unless it is firmly rooted in life.
Thomas Merton
Contemplative Prayer (1969)

4 In meditation we should not look for a "method" or a "system," but cultivate an "attitude," an "outlook": faith, openness, attention, reverence, expectation, supplication, trust, joy. All these finally permeate our being with love.
Thomas Merton
Contemplative Prayer (1969)

5 Contemplative prayer disciplines our soul to be attentive to God.
Phileena Heuertz
Pilgrimage of a Soul (2010)

6 Meditation is simply the art of thinking steadily and methodically about spiritual things.
Evelyn Underhill
The Essentials of Mysticism (1960)

7 I compel my mind to open straight out toward God. I wait and listen with determined sensitiveness. . . . I determine not to get out of bed until that mind set, that concentration upon God, is settled.
Frank Laubach
Letters by a Modern Mystic (1937)

271 MEEKNESS
(*see also* GENTLENESS; HUMILITY)
But thou, O man of God, flee these things;
and follow after righteousness, godliness,
faith, love, patience, meekness.
1 TIMOTHY 6:11

1 Meekness is born in situations that humble you.
Kay Arthur
As Silver Refined (1998)

272 MEMORIES
But call to remembrance the former days. . .
HEBREWS 10:32

1 We remember what we ought to forget and
forget what we ought to remember.
Charles Swindoll
"David and the Dwarf" sermon (2009)

2 Remembering becomes a tool that sees
us through present pain and difficulties
and propels us into new, faith-filled spaces,
preparing us for the future.
Lois Evans
Stones of Remembrance (2006)

273 MEN (*see also* MASCULINITY)
Wise men lay up knowledge.
PROVERBS 10:14

1 The measure of a married man is the
spiritual and emotional health of his family.
Stu Weber
The Heart of a Tender Warrior (2002)

2 The ability to make and keep promises is
central to manhood. It may be trite to say that
a man's word is his bond, but it is never trite to
see it in action.
Stu Weber
The Heart of a Tender Warrior (2002)

3 God's definition of real manhood is pretty
simple: It means hearing His Word and doing
it. That's God's only definition of manhood—a
doer of the Word. And God's definition of a
sissy is someone who hears the Word of God
and doesn't do it.
Stephen Arterburn, Fred Stoeker, and
Mike Yorkey
Every Man's Battle (2000)

4 Men, in particular, need others to help
them compensate for their blind spots. God
built a man to focus on a certain target; he
reaches that target by blocking off everything
else. But the same ability that allows him to
succeed also leads to blind spots.
Bill McCartney
Blind Spots (2003)

5 God has placed men in the lives of other
men and boys for a purpose—to push them
beyond what they think they can do, beyond
their zones of comfort.
Don Otis
Whisker Rubs (2007)

6 A boy never becomes a man simply by
going on an adventure. Rather, the adventure
itself reveals whether the boy is a man or will
ever become one.
Don Otis
Whisker Rubs (2007)

7 Perhaps the greatest weakness men face at
the turn of the twenty-first century is that they
tend to lead unexamined lives.
Patrick Morley
Understanding Your Man in the Mirror
(1998)

8 A good man is a gift to all who know
him—he's dependable like the sunrise, because
his goodness springs from inner strength, not
outward circumstances.
Bob Barnes
Men under Construction (2006)

9 For men, the name of the game is conquest.
James Dobson
Straight Talk (1995)

10 Despite what your eyes see, God is not limited in His reserve of men whom He has set aside for uncompromising women.
Michelle McKinney Hammond
How to Be Found by the Man You've Been Looking For (2005)

11 Men are highly motivated when they believe they can succeed.
Bill and Pam Farrel
The Marriage Code (2009)

12 For most of our lives, we men have trained ourselves to cut through the clutter of emotion in order to focus on the "real issue." Instead, we need to grasp the single most important key to being a good listener: For our wife, her negative feelings about a problems are the real issue. In other words, the feelings are what she is trying most to share and have understood, even more than the problem itself.
Shaunti and Jeff Feldhahn
For Men Only (2006)

13 Men are powerfully driven by the emotional need to feel desired by our wives, and we filter everything through that grid: Do I feel desired or not desired by my wife? If we feel our wife truly wants us sexually, we feel confident, powerful, alive, and loved. If we don't, we feel depressed, angry, and alone.
Shaunti and Jeff Feldhahn
For Men Only (2006)

14 Wherever you turn today, you will find men looking for a guide, a coach, a model, an advisor. They are looking for someone who knows about life.
Howard and William Hendricks
As Iron Sharpens Iron (1995)

15 An occupational hazard of men is to ignore experience and refuse to consult others, especially those older than us.
Jeffrey Miller
The Hazards of Being a Man (2007)

16 Relationships are sometimes messy, rarely predictable, and never easy to control. For these reasons, men avoid close relationships.
Jeffrey Miller
The Hazards of Being a Man (2007)

17 The variety of confusing messages from all directions is making it difficult for men to understand and embrace what it really means to be a man.
Bob Lepine
The Christian Husband (1999)

18 All men are running—either the rat race, or the right race. So we must be careful in which race we run. The race we choose will determine the course of our life today, and it will determine our eternal destiny tomorrow.
Steven Lawson
Men Who Win (1992)

19 Nothing looks weaker or wimpier than a man who uses power to keep others at bay so that he can stay where he is—with what little he has.
Stephen Arterburn and John Shore
Midlife Manual for Men (2008)

274 MENTORING
Rebuke not an elder, but intreat him as a father;
and the younger men as brethren;
The elder women as mothers;
the younger as sisters, with all purity.
1 TIMOTHY 5:1–2

1 Looking for a mentor is a bit like looking for love.
Howard and William Hendricks
As Iron Sharpens Iron (1995)

275 MERCY
That the Lord is very pitiful, and of tender mercy.
JAMES 5:11

1   It is the heartfelt cry that always reconnects the people back to God and His grace and His mercy.
Bill Gothard
The Power of Crying Out (2002)

2   Bow before the mercy seat. There the consciousness of your unworthiness will not hinder you, but be a real help in trusting God. There you may have the assured confidence that your upward look will be met by his eye, that your prayer can be heard, that his loving answer will be given.
Andrew Murray
Prayer's Inner Chamber (1912)

3   Mercy is not the ability to no longer feel the pain and heartache of living in this world. Mercy is knowing that I am being held through the pain by my Father.
Angela Thomas
Do You Think I'm Beautiful? (2003)

4   Everything in the gospel is ordered by God to extend the maximum grace and mercy to His people.
Jonathan Edwards
"The Final Judgment" sermon (1741)

5   Since Christ is the incarnate display of the wealth of the mercies of God, it is not surprising that his life on earth was a lavish exhibit of mercies to all kinds of people. Every kind of need and pain was touched by the mercies of Jesus in his few years on earth.
John Piper
Seeing and Savoring Jesus Christ (2004)

6   Guilt is darkness; mercy is light.
Lisa Bevere
Be Angry But Don't Blow It! (2000)

7   God's mercies come day by day. They come when we need them—not earlier and not later. God gives us what we need today.

If we needed more, He would give us more. When we need something else, He will give that as well. Nothing we truly need will ever be withheld from us. Search your problems, and within them you will discover the well-disguised mercies of God.
Ray Pritchard
The God You Can Trust (2003)

8   Today's mercies are for today's burdens. Tomorrow's mercies will be for tomorrow's problems.
Ray Pritchard
The God You Can Trust (2003)

9   God is merciful, but there is a limit to God's patience.
Anne Graham Lotz
The Vision of His Glory (1996)

10 Mercy begins with remembering our own deeds.
James Lucas
The Paradox Principle of Parenting (2003)

MESSIAH
(*see* CHRIST; JESUS; SAVIOR)

276 MIDDLE AGE (*see also* AGING)
We spend our years as a tale that is told.
PSALM 90:9

1   They say the mind is the first thing to go. . . at least I think that's what they say.
Laura Jensen Walker
Mentalpause (2001)

2   I don't remember ear hair plucking being part of the marriage vows. . .guess that would fall under "for better or worse."
Laura Jensen Walker
Mentalpause (2001)

3   Reassessment is the prevailing theme of the midlife crisis. He asks questions

about values—"Who am I? What do I want to be? Does my work have value? Am I accomplishing anything?"
Jim Conway
Men in Midlife Crisis (1978)

4   One major difference between the teen and the man in midlife crisis is that the teen wants to get older, while the man in the midlife crisis wants to stay young.
Jim Conway
Men in Midlife Crisis (1978)

5   Before a midlife crisis, it is possible to think of yourself as young.
Jim Conway
Men in Midlife Crisis (1978)

6   No man will successfully make it through the midlife transition until he can comfortably accept his aging and let go of the fantasy of being twenty-eight—or whatever is your favorite age.
Jim Conway
Men in Midlife Crisis (1978)

7   Perhaps the most basic need of the midlife man is to convince himself and the world around him that he is still young.
Jim Conway
Men in Midlife Crisis (1978)

8   Used wisely, mid-life can be your launching pad for personal and spiritual expansion.
Poppy Smith
I'm Too Young to Be This Old! (1997)

9   Midlife is the place where our former sense of our immortality collides with the realization that we will one day be a statistic on the obituary page.
Kim Thomas
Living in the Sacred Now (2001)

MIGHT (*see* ABILITY; POWER; STRENGTH)

277 MIND, THE
(*see also* THINKING; THOUGHTS)
Be renewed in the spirit of your mind.
EPHESIANS 4:23

1   We are to control our thoughts rather than have our thoughts control us.
Charles Stanley
When the Enemy Strikes (2004)

2   Fill the mind with thoughts of God rather than with thoughts of fear, and you will get back thoughts of faith and courage.
Norman Vincent Peale
The Power of Positive Thinking (1952)

3   Conditions are created by thoughts far more powerfully than conditions create thoughts.
Norman Vincent Peale
The Power of Positive Thinking (1952)

4   The mind of man is a busy thing; if it is not employed in doing good, it will be doing evil.
Matthew Henry
Commentary on the Whole Bible (1706)

5   If someone is deceived, he is thoroughly convinced that he is not deceived.
Nathaniel and Hans Bluedorn
The Fallacy Detective (2002)

6   Each of us leads a secret thought life, an invisible life known only to us—it is not known to others. This secret life is usually very different from the visible you—the you that is known by others. Yet it is the real you, the you that is known by our God.
Patrick Morley
The Man in the Mirror (1992)

7   The more selective you are about seeds, the more delighted you will be with the crop.
Max Lucado
Just Like Jesus (1998)

8 We can either decide to think with the mind of the natural man, which easily goes off to the left and down into the ditch of hysteria and insecurity and jealousy or I can decide I want the mind of Christ activated in me.
Beth Moore
"A Beautiful Mind" teaching series (2009)

9 We must use our minds; but we must admit their limitations.
John Stott
Basic Christianity (1958)

10 Where your mind goes, the rest of you soon follows.
Martha Bolton
If the Tongue's a Fire, Who Needs Salsa? (2002)

11 If we neglect the opportunities for cultivating the mind, how shall it escape ignorance and feebleness?
Henry Drummond
Natural Law in the Spiritual World (19th century)

12 Do nothing rashly. What are you doing? Where are you going? What will be the end and consequence of your present line of action? Stop and think. By thoughtless actions they created habits which have become second nature to them.
J. C. Ryle
The Upper Room (19th century)

13 Whatever fills our minds will come out in our actions and decisions.
Michael Youssef
"Remaining Spiritually Stable" article (2010)

14 The most far-reaching changes are taking place in the unseen chambers of our minds.
Poppy Smith
I'm Too Young to Be This Old! (1997)

15 As greater numbers of people crowd the earth, so greater amounts of information crowd men's minds.
Don Meredith
Becoming One (1999)

MINISTERS (*see* CLERGY)

278 MINISTRY

And I thank Christ Jesus our Lord, who hath enabled me, for that he counted me faithful, putting me into the ministry.
1 TIMOTHY 1:12

1 The "celebrity syndrome" so present in our Christian thought and activities just doesn't square with the attitudes and messages of Jesus.
Charles Swindoll
Improving Your Serve (1981)

2 You may not be involved in full-time ministry. And yet if you are a believer, your basic job description is the same as mine. It is to be full of the Holy Spirit and to pour yourself out to others in love and ministry, trusting in the Spirit to make that possible.
Jill Briscoe
A Little Pot of Oil (2003)

3 For Jesus, prayer was a vital element in making God's power available to people in need.
Jim Reapsome
10 Minutes a Day with Jesus (2008)

4 The devil seeks to totally paralyze your ministry.
Ray Comfort
Hell's Best Kept Secret (1989)

5 Enlarge my territory. I encourage you to pray this for all of your God-honoring pursuits. Much of what God wants us to do involves the expansion of not only literal territory, but influence as well.
Bruce Wilkinson
Beyond Jabez (2005)

6 The most important thing we can do in the service of our King is to become men and women of prayer.
Jon Courson
Application Commentary (2006)

7 Sometimes offering yourself as a vessel for the presence and work of God is costly.
John Ortberg
God Is Closer Than You Think (2005)

8 The very best thing we can do to help others is to help ourselves. We must develop our lives so that we are always motivated by love. We must be able to convey hope, confidence, and trust. We should help people feel loved and safe. We should become models for others to follow rather than experts who fix people.
James Richards
How to Stop the Pain (2001)

9 What God asks us to do, He equips us to do.
Dutch Sheets
Watchman Prayer (2000)

10 To serve God with fear is good; to serve Him out of love is better; but to fear and love Him together is best of all.
Meister Eckhart
Meister Eckhart's Sermons (14th century)

11 I shall have this good at least; that till death I shall have done all that is in me to love Him.
Brother Lawrence
The Practice of the Presence of God (17th century)

12 We must not be afraid to minister to one another. Even if the sheep in need is the one in the lead.
Jan Winebrenner and Debra Frazier
When a Leader Falls (1993)

13 Salvation is free. . . . But serving Christ will cost you.
Steve Campbell
"The Cost of Following Christ" sermon (2009)

14 If a man serves not God only, then surely he serves the devil.
Martin Luther
Table Talk (16th century)

15 He must be of a high and great spirit that undertakes to serve the people in body and soul, for he must suffer the utmost danger and unthankfulness.
Martin Luther
Table Talk (16th century)

16 When a man will serve God, he must not look upon that which he does; not upon the work, but how it ought to be done, and whether God has commanded it or no.
Martin Luther
Table Talk (16th century)

17 The key to determining what you can do in the body of Christ is discovering who you are—your ministry identity in Christ.
Aubrey Malphurs
Maximizing Your Effectiveness (2006)

18 He brought my life passion from my life pain.
Beth Moore
"Wrestling with God" teaching series (2009)

19 His servant I am, and, as such, am employed according to the plain direction of His Word.
John Wesley
The Journal of John Wesley (18th century)

20 Remember that you must do God's work according to His ways.
Bill Wilson
Christianity in the Crosshairs (2005)

21 A cup of cold water given to a disciple in sincere love, is worth more in God's sight, than all one's goods given to feed the poor, yea, than the wealth of a kingdom given away, or a body offered up in the flames without love.
Jonathan Edwards
"The Greatest Performances or Sufferings in Vain without Charity" sermon (1738)

22 I want to take the "mess" of my life and allow God to use it as the ministry of my life.
Rhonda Landers
Teaching on Addiction (2009)

23 To be in Christ is to be in ministry and to be in ministry is to communicate to people the joy and power of the new life in Christ.
Lloyd John Ogilvie
Life without Limits (1975)

24 A life that selflessly and sacrificially serves the least is a worthy goal worth pursuing.
Leslie Ludy
Sacred Singleness (2009)

25 Serving God is about doing—doing with every fiber of your passion and commitment.
Bruce Wilkinson
Experiencing Spiritual Breakthroughs (1999)

26 There is no role that is unimportant and no job that is trivial.
Rory Noland
The Heart of the Artist (1999)

27 The faithful servants of Jesus Christ are wont to prefer the public good to their own personal interests.
Matthew Henry
Commentary on the Whole Bible (1706)

28 An intense desire to be cleansed from every sin lies at the root of fitness for true service.
Andrew Murray
Working for God (1901)

29 If you are still breathing, you have a ministry. Whether at work, church or elsewhere, we have an obligation to serve and share Christ.
Frank Edelinski
"Be Blessed" sermon (2009)

30 For some persons there are who, though expert in spiritual ministry, go about it in a headstrong manner, and while acting intelligently, tread underfoot any good they do.
Richard Baxter
The Reformed Pastor (17th century)

31 If year after year our lives are consumed with activities we've been neither gifted nor impassioned to do, and we never have a chance to slide into the sweet spot of giving out of our true self, we pay a higher price in ministry than God is asking us to pay. And the saddest thing is, when we allow this to happen, nobody wins.
Lynne Hybels
Nice Girls Don't Change the World (2005)

32 The highest in repute and office in the church yet are still but servants.
Thomas Manton
A Practical Commentary on the Epistle of James (17th century)

33 When your own hands are in God's work, your eyes must be to Christ's hands for support in it.
Thomas Manton
A Practical Commentary on the Epistle of James (17th century)

34 Prayer is striking the winning blow at the concealed enemy. Service is gathering up the results of that blow among the men we see and touch.
Samuel Gordon
Quiet Talks on Prayer (1904)

35 The key to breaking the code of a community is to have the heart of the Father for that community.
Ed Stetzer and David Putman
Breaking the Missional Code (2006)

36 God isn't impressed in the least by job title, bank account, or standing in the community. God is searching for a servant's heart.
Luis Palau
Heart After God (1978)

MINISTRY

37 Whosoever gives a cup of cold water to a little one refreshes the heart of the Father.
George MacDonald
"The Child in the Midst" sermon
(19th century)

38 The heart posture of humility recognizes that God alone can do powerful and meaningful things. By His grace we may get involved with such ministry, but we are ever the carriers and never the cause.
Matt Redman
Inside Out Worship (2005)

39 Anyone who serves God will discover sooner or later that the great hindrance to his work is not others but himself.
Watchman Nee
The Release of the Spirit (1965)

40 God does not want us to simply forget the pain of the past. He wants us to be fruitful in the land of our suffering! Use it for good. Minister to others. Plant seeds of hope.
Sharon Jaynes
Your Scars Are Beautiful to God (2006)

41 Let my life today be the channel through which some little portion of Your divine love and pity may reach the lives that are nearest to my own.
John Baillie
A Diary of Private Prayer (1949)

279 MIRACLES
*And Stephen, full of faith and power,
did great wonders and miracles
among the people.*
ACTS 6:8

1 The spectacular and the supernatural are not necessarily related to one another.
Steve Sampson
You Can Hear the Voice of God (1993)

2 Everything that happened in the early church, we have a right to expect today.
Kathryn Kuhlman
Kathryn Kuhlman (1976)

3 Saying everything is a miracle destroys the concept of miracles as effectively as saying there are no such things.
David DeWitt
Answering the Tough Ones (1980)

4 God is a miracle-working God.
Joel Osteen
Your Best Life Now (2004)

5 The mightiest signs and wonders cannot change our hearts! Only the Spirit of God can do that!
Lynn Anderson
*If I Really Believe,
Why Do I Have These Doubts?* (1992)

6 If there is a Creator God, there is nothing illogical at all about the possibility of miracles. After all, if he created everything out of nothing, it would hardly be a problem for him to rearrange parts of it as and when he wishes.
Timothy Keller
The Reason for God (2008)

7 We are surrounded by the many miracles of life, and yet we fail to recognize them.
Tim Hansel
Eating Problems for Breakfast (1988)

280 MISSIONARIES
(*see also* EVANGELISM; GOSPEL, THE; WITNESSING)
*And a vision appeared to Paul in the night;
There stood a man of Macedonia,
and prayed him, saying,
Come over into Macedonia, and help us.*
ACTS 16:9

1 The aim of the missionary is to do God's will, not to be useful, not to win the heathen; he is useful and he does win the heathen, but that is not his aim. His aim is to do with will of his Lord.

Oswald Chambers
My Utmost for His Highest (1935)

MODERATION (*see* ABSTINENCE; SELF-CONTROL; TEMPERANCE)

281 MODESTY
(*see also* MORALITY; PURITY)
In like manner also, that women adorn themselves in modest apparel. . .
1 TIMOTHY 2:9

1 If you dress like a piece of meat, you're gonna get thrown on the BBQ.

Justin Lookadoo and Hayley DiMarco
Dateable (2006)

282 MONEY
(*see also* RICH, THE; WEALTH)
For the love of money is the root of all evil: which while some coveted after, they have erred from the faith, and pierced themselves through with many sorrows.
1 TIMOTHY 6:10

1 What is gold compared with thy God? Thou couldst not live on it; thy spiritual life could not be sustained by it. Apply it to thy aching head, and would it afford thee any ease?

Charles Spurgeon
"God in the Covenant" sermon (1856)

2 When you serve God, you are using God's money to accomplish His wishes. But when you serve money, you are using God's money to accomplish your wishes.

Bruce Wilkinson
A Life God Rewards (2002)

3 Money is useful, but the love, the attention, and the care we offer to others are the most important things.

Mother Teresa
Loving Jesus (1991)

4 We must learn to view money in a new way—as a means of exchange—not as a magic wand!

Karen O'Connor
Addicted to Shopping (2005)

5 How we use our money demonstrates the reality of our love for God. In some ways it proves our love more conclusively than depth or knowledge, length of prayers or prominence of service. These things can be feigned, but the use of our possessions shows us up for what we actually are.

Charles Ryrie
Balancing the Christian Life (1969)

6 We love money simply for the approval, self-esteem, and value it brings. It makes us important, it provides an outlet. Money quenches our ego for a moment, but leaves us thirsty for more.

Gregg Matte
The Highest Education: Becoming a Godly Man (2000)

7 Prosperity is really a matter of attitude, not an amount of money. Money doesn't cause problems. People who fall in love with it do. . . . Falling in love with it is like having an affair with your weed eater—not very fulfilling.

Vicki Kuyper
Be Patient, God Isn't Finished with Me Yet (2003)

8 When you realize that everything you buy is purchased with a portion of your life, it should make you more careful with the use of money.

James Dobson
Life on the Edge (1995)

9   Adult-like attitudes about money can be instilled throughout childhood.
   Michael Farris
   What a Daughter Needs (2004)

10   The quickest way to double your money is to fold it in half and put it back in your pocket.
   Cynthia Yates
   Living Well in Retirement (2005)

11   The writer of Proverbs points out that when character and maturity are absent, the destructive force of money erupts, and the potential good of that inheritance is squandered—spent recklessly, invested unwisely, lost swiftly. Not blessed!
   Gordon MacDonald
   Secrets of the Generous Life (2002)

12   We're a pluralistic culture struggling to find common beliefs, and unfortunately, our most central belief system is about the importance of money.
   Mary Pipher
   The Shelter of Each Other (1996)

13   Trust not to the omnipotency of gold, and say not unto it thou art my confidence.
   Thomas Brown
   Christian Morals (17th century)

14   You probably already know this, but God did not create the budget. Nowhere in the Bible will you find God putting one of his prophets on a budget. No, God is a loving and generous God. The budget is a human idea.
   Kathy Peel
   She Who Laughs, Lasts (2000)

15   There are two kinds of people in the world: savers and spenders. Savers keep a constant eye on the bottom line, always trying to cut costs and put a little more away for the future. . . . Spenders, on the other hand, love to visit car lots and watch QVC.
   Jonathan Wilson-Hartgrove
   God's Economy (2009)

16   We cannot live on bread alone—or pie alone, for that matter—and the same is true of money. No matter how much we have, it doesn't satisfy.
   Jonathan Wilson-Hartgrove
   God's Economy (2009)

17   Why, there is greater occasion for thankfulness just in the unimpaired possession of one of the five senses than there would be if someone left us a fortune.
   Laura Ingalls Wilder
   On Wisdom and Virtues (20th century)

18   The world says, "In everything by money." . . . The Church says, "In everything by prayer."
   A. W. Tozer
   "In Everything by Prayer" sermon (20th century)

19   Nothing puts more pressure on a marriage than financial irresponsibility, lack of money, and huge debt.
   Stormie Omartian
   The Power of a Praying Wife (1997)

20   As children of God we have a single goal—treasure in heaven; a single vision—God's purposes; and a single Master—God, not money.
   John MacArthur
   Anxiety Attacked (1993)

21   As the Bible says, there is nothing worse than the love of money (1 Timothy 6:10), for it means that one's heart is everlastingly bothering about the love of the transitory and not giving itself a chance to acquire devotion.
   Richard Rolle
   The Fire of Love (14th century)

283 MORALITY
(*see also* MODESTY; PURITY)
Wherefore lay apart all filthiness and superfluity of naughtiness, and receive with meekness the engrafted word, which is able to save your souls.
JAMES 1:21

1   Whenever you find a man who says he does not believe in a real Right and Wrong, you will find the same man going back on this a moment later. He may break his promise to you, but if you try breaking one to him he will be complaining "It's not fair" before you can say Jack Robinson.
C. S. Lewis
Mere Christianity (1943)

2   If Jesus sets the standard for morality, I can now have an unwavering foundation for my choices and decisions, rather than basing them on the ever-shifting sands of expediency and self-centeredness.
Lee Strobel
The Case for Christ (1998)

3   We are being told today that private morality can be disconnected from public service. . .that's not what God's Word says.
Adrian Rogers
"A Nation in Crisis" sermon (1996)

4   We are being told today that somehow public approval validates wrong behavior.
Adrian Rogers
"A Nation in Crisis" sermon (1996)

5   If there is no absolute moral standard, then one cannot say in a final sense that anything is right or wrong.
Francis Schaeffer
How Should We Then Live? (1976)

6   If there is no absolute beyond man's ideas, then there is no final appeal to judge between individuals and groups whose moral judgments conflict. We are merely left with conflicting opinions.
Francis Schaeffer
How Should We Then Live? (1976)

7   No man is justified in doing evil on the ground of expediency.
Theodore Roosevelt
The Strenuous Life (1899)

8   All true morality, inward and outward, is comprehended in love, for love is the foundation of all the commandments.
Meister Eckhart
Meister Eckhart's Sermons (14th century)

9   Morality is about doing things to people that result in their rights being respected and their needs being tended to.
Lewis Smedes
Choices (1986)

10 To claim there are absolute truths about right and wrong is viewed as being intolerant, bigoted or judgmental—the three "sins" of our postmodern secular culture.
Fritz Ridenour
So What's the Difference? (1967)

11 With no absolute measuring stick about right and wrong, the ultimate result is moral chaos.
Fritz Ridenour
So What's the Difference? (1967)

12 In an attempt to escape what they call the contradiction between a good God and a world of evil, atheists try to dance around the reality of a moral law (and hence, a moral law giver) by introducing terms like "evolutionary ethics."
Ravi Zacharias
"The Undeluded Truth?" essay (2008)

13 When we are planning for posterity, we ought to remember, that virtue is not hereditary.
Thomas Paine
Common Sense (1776)

14 Think not, that morality is ambulatory; that vices in one age are not vices in another; or that virtues, which are under the everlasting seal of right reason, may be stamped by opinion.
Thomas Brown
Christian Morals (17th century)

15 Let your resolve be that, by the grace of God enabling you, you will cultivate moral refinement, and everything that can truly exalt and ennoble character; and nothing whatever is there in your position in life, or the circumstances with which you are surrounded, to hinder you from carrying out this resolution.
John Dawson
The Saviour in the Workshop (1868)

16 Christ's moral ideal commands universal respect, and to lower its claims to adapt it to average capacity, a policy too often pursued, is only to expose Christianity to contempt.
Alexander Balmain Bruce
Apologetics, or Christianity Defensively Stated (1892)

17 We are not the measure of morality. God is.
James Sire
The Universe Next Door (1976)

18 Unless there is a God by whom "right" and "wrong" can be reliably assessed, moral judgments can be no more than opinion, influenced by upbringing, training, and propaganda.
J. B. Phillips
Your God Is Too Small (1952)

284 MORALS
But Peter and John answered and said unto them, Whether it be right in the sight of God to hearken unto you more than unto God, judge ye.
ACTS 4:19

1 Doing good for others does not come from a textbook, but from The Book, and the model of a surrendered life that serves Him always.
Scott and Kris Wightman
College without Compromise (2005)

2 Many a man has been brave physically who has flinched morally.
Henry Hopkins
Half-Hour Talks on Character Building (1910)

3 Ethical actions bring ethical reactions.
Jerry Fleming
Profit at Any Cost? (2003)

4 Developing and adhering to foundational ethical principles will give you confidence that your decisions are right, and you will sleep well knowing that you are living according to your deep beliefs.
Jerry Fleming
Profit at Any Cost? (2003)

5 For a society to flourish, people must have some common moral beliefs.
Mary Pipher
The Shelter of Each Other (1996)

6 The human moral symphony has many movements. We make moral judgments, not simply as carping critics humped against the forward flanks of moral evil, but as children of God who want life to be truly and fully human in all its features, as it was meant to be by its Creator.
Lewis Smedes
Choices (1986)

285 MOTHERHOOD
How often would I have gathered thy children together, even as a hen gathereth her chickens under her wings...
MATTHEW 23:37

1 The loss of a mother is never made up or atoned for.
Elizabeth Prentiss
More Love to Thee—The Life and Letters of Elizabeth Prentiss (1882)

2 Behind every great man has been a great mother.
Henry Hopkins
Half-Hour Talks on Character Building (1910)

3   There is no more important job in the
universe than to raise a child to love God,
live productively, and serve humanity. How
ridiculous that a woman should have to
apologize for wanting to fulfill that historic role!
James Dobson
Life on the Edge (1995)

4   Each of us is divinely chosen to be the
mother of each child under our care.
Elisa Morgan
Mom to Mom (1996)

5   A mother's love is unselfish and has no
limits this side of heaven.
Billy Sunday
The Sawdust Trail (1932)

6   I do not believe there are devils enough to
pull a boy or girl out of the arms of a Christian
mother.
Billy Sunday
The Sawdust Trail (1932)

7   Being a mother truly is an assignment
from God which He uses, for instance, to
make us more Christlike by giving us countless
opportunities to die to our self.
Elizabeth George
Loving God with All Your Mind (1994)

8   Mothers have vivid imaginations—
especially late at night when we're not sure
where our children are.
Gigi Graham Tchividjian
Currents of the Heart (1996)

286 MURMURING
(*see also* COMPLAINING)
*Do all things without murmurings
and disputings.*
PHILIPPIANS 2:14

1   Division among God's people gives Satan
a tremendous advantage in conquering our

usefulness, joy and peace. The destructive
influence of murmuring, contentious words
must be exchanged for words that produce
confidence in Christ and encouragement to
His people.
Joseph Stowell
Tongue in Check (1983)

287 MUSIC
*Let the word of Christ dwell in you richly in all
wisdom; teaching and admonishing one another
in psalms and hymns and spiritual songs,
singing with grace in your hearts to the Lord.*
COLOSSIANS 3:16

1   There is nothing like singing [God's] own
words. The preacher claims the promise, "My
Word shall not return unto Me void," and
why should not the singer equally claim it?
Frances Ridley Havergal
Kept for the Master's Use (1879)

2   As we sing a new song to the Lord, let's
not forget the old ones.
Robert Morgan
Then Sings My Soul (2003)

3   The music industry knows your kids. Get to
know your kids by getting to know their music.
Walt Mueller
Understanding Today's Youth Culture (1999)

4   If you want your child to be a long-term
worshiper, then you need to bring the joy of
music into these precious early years.
Patrick Kavanaugh
Raising Children to Adore God (2003)

5   When the Psalmist admonished God's
people to "sing a new song," the writer forgot
to say that the new song may be in a different
key.
Brad Berglund
Reinventing Sunday (2001)

288 NATURE

The heavens declare the glory of God;
and the firmament sheweth his handywork.
PSALM 19:1

1 The course of Nature is the art of God.
Edward Young
Night Thoughts (1742)

2 More and more as we come closer and closer
in touch with nature and its teachings are we
able to see the Divine and are therefore fitted to
interpret correctly the various languages spoken
by all forms of nature about us.
George Washington Carver
George Washington Carver in His Own
Words (1930)

3 Natural laws were created by Christ and
they alter at His bidding.
John Piper
Seeing and Savoring Jesus Christ (2004)

289 NEIGHBORS

Thou shalt love thy neighbour as thyself.
MATTHEW 22:39

1 A man must not choose his neighbour; he
must take the neighbour that God sends him.
In him, whoever he be, lies, hidden or revealed,
a beautiful brother.
George MacDonald
"Love Thy Neighbour" sermon
(19th century)

290 NEW BIRTH (*see also* BORN AGAIN; CONVERSION; REDEMPTION; REGENERATION; SALVATION)

Marvel not that I said unto thee,
Ye must be born again.
JOHN 3:7

1 We have no reason to expect pardon,
except we seek it by faith in Christ; and that
is always attended by true repentance, and
followed by newness of life, by hatred of sin,
and love to God.
Matthew Henry
Commentary on the Whole Bible (1706)

2 By faith we accept Christ Jesus as our
only hope and Savior. He comes, in Spirit,
to live in our heart, soul, and mind to do
the work of re-creating. By this work of re-
creation, God begins to fashion us into His
likeness, His workmanship, His treasure, His
masterpiece.
Angela Thomas McGuffey
Tender Mercy for a Mother's Soul (2001)

3 Receiving Christ into our lives is not the
end of something, but the beginning.
Jim Cymbala
You Were Made for More (2008)

4 In the new birth, God takes your unique
individuality and gives you a new disposition
so that you can begin to live for His glory.
There is no other Christian in the world
like you.
Colin Smith
Ten Keys to Unlock the Christian Life
(2005)

5 Life change for a Christian is not just a
matter of stopping things, of tearing out the
weeds that have grown in the garden of your
life. It is a matter of letting God start some
new things by planting seeds to grow a harvest
of righteousness.
David Jeremiah
Spiritual Warfare (1995)

6 We're not forgiven to be free to sin. We're
forgiven to be free from sin.
Steve Campbell
"Three Things That Will Destroy a
Christian" sermon (2009)

7 The eternal plan was not to bring God
down to man's level but for the Son to take
humanity up into God.
A. W. Tozer
Whatever Happened to Worship?
(20th century)

8 The only way to get into the human family is by birth, and the only way to get into God's family is by birth.
Warren Wiersbe
Be What You Are (1988)

9 As God's children through the new birth we are able to drink deeply from God's unending stream of joy–regardless of what life offers us!
Elizabeth George
God's Garden of Grace (1996)

NEWNESS (*see* REBIRTH)

NOTORIETY (*see* FAME)

**291 OBEDIENCE
(*see also* SURRENDER)**
*To obey is better than sacrifice,
and to hearken than the fat of rams.*
1 SAMUEL 15:22

1 Wherever you are, be all there. Live to the hilt every situation you believe to be the will of God.
Jim Elliot (20th century) quoted in *Through Gates of Splendor* by Elisabeth Elliot

2 I don't know a single person who truly seems to bear the mark of God's presence and power in his or her life who hasn't been asked by God to be obedient in a way that was dramatically painful.
Beth Moore
Believing God (2004)

3 Standing with our hands on our hips saying, "Okay, God, if you want to ruin me, go ahead," is not surrendering our dreams. It will definitely get God's attention, but it won't be the kind of attention we want.
Stormie Omartian
Just Enough Light for the Step I'm On (1999)

4 Did you ever think what Moses would have lost if God had excused him and let Aaron, or Caleb, or Joshua, or some one else take his place?
D. L. Moody
"The Transfiguration" sermon (19th century)

5 God knows best in what manner to let me live, and I desire to ask for nothing but a docile, acquiescent temper, whose only petition shall be, "What wilt Thou have me to do?" not how can I get most enjoyment along the way.
Elizabeth Prentiss
More Love to Thee—The Life and Letters of Elizabeth Prentiss (1882)

6 Only he who believes is obedient. Only he who is obedient believes.
Dietrich Bonhoeffer
The Cost of Discipleship (1937)

7 God expects to be believ'd in what He has Reveal'd, as well as obey'd in what He has commanded.
Thomas Wilson
Private Thoughts (1828)

8 Ask yourself, does my Heavenly Father set before me a path of obedience along which the Spirit and power of Christ cannot lead me?
Evan Henry Hopkins
Thoughts on Life and Godliness (1883)

9 The same inspired Word that reveals to us the Divine will as the path of obedience, declares also that there is for us the Divine power as the means of obedience. Let us not separate these two things.
Evan Henry Hopkins
Thoughts on Life and Godliness (1883)

10 The blessedness and the blessing of God's Word is only to be known by doing it.
Andrew Murray
Prayer's Inner Chamber (1912)

11 Christ's commands were meant to be obeyed. If this be not done, the accumulation of Scripture knowledge only darkens and hardens and works satisfaction with the pleasure which the acquisition of knowledge brings, which unfits us for the Spirit's teaching.
Andrew Murray
Prayer's Inner Chamber (1912)

12 But if obedience, Lord, in me do grow,
I shall one day be better than I know.
George MacDonald
Diary of an Old Soul (1880)

13 The formula to living the Spirit-filled life is simple: Obedience. We have no need of the Holy Spirit if we aren't willing to do what God has asked of us. The power of the Spirit will be seen at our first step of obedience.
Henry and Mel Blackaby
What's So Spiritual About Your Gifts? (2004)

14 Great expectations, if they are not accurate, can soon prove to be a source of great disillusionment. Expect only to place Him at the center of your life, and lovingly surrender to all that He is and all that He requires. Then let whatever blessing comes from that commitment be your unexpected blessing.
Joseph Stowell
Fan the Flame (1986)

15 We cannot rely on God's promises without obeying his commandments.
John Calvin
Bible Commentaries (16th century)

16 When we are calling to God to turn the eye of his favour towards us he is calling to us to turn the eye of our obedience towards him.
Matthew Henry
Commentary on the Whole Bible (1706)

17 Every time we say yes to God we will get a little more sensitive to hearing him the next time.
John Ortberg
God Is Closer Than You Think (2005)

18 God is willing to speak to those who have a heart to obey.
Rich Mendola
"Joy in the Holy Spirit. . .in the Desert" sermon (2009)

19 Whatever God shows you to do—obey it quickly.
Rich Mendola
"Joy in the Holy Spirit. . .in the Desert" sermon (2009)

20 In the Bible, power always follows obedience.
Sharon Jaynes
Becoming the Woman of His Dreams (2005)

21 The element that is missing in so many concepts of obedience is the idea that the desire to obey God is already inside us. It's like the Gatorade commercial that asks, "Is it in you?" If you are a believer, the answer is yes.
Tony Evans and Jonathan Evans
Get in the Game (2006)

22 Obedience means taking action—to love one another, to restore a relationship, to confront a person in sin.
Bill Hybels
Descending into Greatness (1993)

23 If you take the challenge of radical faith, you are going to be afraid. I guarantee it. I'm afraid. Yet it's okay to be afraid.
Chip Ingram
Holy Ambition (2002)

24 Commitment doesn't work unless it's preceded by surrender. Commitment often says, "I can," but surrender says, "Lord, I can't."
Tony Evans
Tony Evans Speaks Out (2000)

25 God's Word will judge your life, but it cannot change your life unless you obey it.
Steve Campbell
"The Primary Importance" sermon (2009)

26 Our obedience to God is the evidence of the quality of our relationship with God.
Steve Campbell
"The Primary Importance" sermon (2009)

27 God is interested in more than our recovery from a specific illness; He is intent on our learning how to obey Him in the totality of life.
Catherine Marshall
Something More (1974)

28 The inevitable consequence of obedience without delight is the erosion of holiness. We cannot continue to do our duty to God if we have no love for the task or the Taskgiver.
Bryan Chapell
Holiness by Grace (2001)

29 If you don't obey God's Word. . .He may choose someone else to do what He's called you to do.
Dave Ice
Sermon on 1 Samuel 15 (2009)

30 Choose God's ways at every opportunity.
Elizabeth George
A Woman after God's Own Heart (1997)

31 Obedience, when it flows out of a genuine love for Jesus Christ, is never wasted and never regretted.
Leslie Ludy
Sacred Singleness (2009)

32 On the other side of surrender, we will find the greatest joy!
Leslie Ludy
Sacred Singleness (2009)

33 Obedience to God's commands not only protects us from harm; it also allows God to provide for us, sometimes in breathtaking ways.
Josh McDowell and Bob Hostetler
Right from Wrong (1994)

34 Prayer is the first step in obedience.
Steve Campbell
"Foundations for Answered Prayer" sermon (2009)

35 Obedience reflects belief.
David Wilkerson
"The Ultimate Test of Faith" article (2009)

36 God assumes full responsibility for our needs when we obey Him.
Charles Stanley
30 Life Principles Study Guide (2008)

37 Obey God and leave all the consequences to Him.
Charles Stanley
30 Life Principles Study Guide (2008)

38 Until men feel that they owe everything to God, that they are cherished by his paternal care, and that he is the author of all their blessings, so that nought is to be looked for away from him, they will never submit to him in voluntary obedience; nay, unless they place their entire happiness in him, they will never yield up their whole selves to him in truth and sincerity.
John Calvin
Institutes of the Christian Religion (16th century)

39 But it is not obedience alone that our Lord will have, but obedience to the truth, that is, to the Light of the World, truth beheld and known.
George MacDonald
"The Child in the Midst" sermon (19th century)

40 Certainly God can and will forgive our sin. But He will not force us to have power over sin and enjoy obedience.

Keith Meyer
Whole Life Transformation (2010)

41 One does not have to understand to be obedient.

Madeline L'Engle
Walking on Water (1980)

42 When we disobey God, we always lose.

Zig Ziglar
Confessions of a Grieving Christian (1998)

43 Let me then put back into Your hand all that You have given me, rededicating to Your service all the powers of my mind and body, all my worldly goods, all my influence with others. All these, O Father, are Yours to use as You will.

John Baillie
A Diary of Private Prayer (1949)

44 Our first step should be to take leave of ourselves and to apply all of our powers to the service of the Lord. The service of the Lord does not only include implicit obedience, but also a willingness to put aside our sinful desires and to surrender completely to the leadership of the Holy Spirit.

John Calvin
On the Life of the Christian Man (1550)

45 No matter who you are, if you will yield your life to God, you can become a vessel God can use.

Donna Partow
A 10-Week Journey to Becoming a Vessel God Can Use (1996)

292 OCCULT

There shall not be found among you any one that maketh his son or his daughter to pass through the fire, or that useth divination, or an observer of times, or an enchanter, or a witch.

DEUTERONOMY 18:10

1 It's difficult to describe Wiccan beliefs comprehensively. This is part of its appeal—each practitioner can add or subtract beliefs at will.

Catherine Edwards Sanders
Wicca's Charm (2005)

2 Wicca is spiritually real, and kids are tapping into unseen supernatural forces when they practice it.

Catherine Edwards Sanders
Wicca's Charm (2005)

3 Perhaps Satan's cleverest tool has been false religions, especially those religious systems that make adherents feel as if they have control of the world around them.

Richard Abanes
Harry Potter and the Bible (2001)

4 The two underlying beliefs that seem to connect all forms of Satanism are selfish hedonism and nonconformity.

Richard Abanes
Harry Potter and the Bible (2001)

5 It is to Christ that spiritual truth-seekers must look. Occultism presents nothing but a distraction.

Richard Abanes
Harry Potter and the Bible (2001)

6 It is never easy to watch ungodly activity and unbiblical beliefs grow in popularity, nor is it ever comfortable to take a stand against such problems.

Richard Abanes
Harry Potter and the Bible (2001)

293 OLD AGE
(*see also* AGING; ELDERLY, THE)

They shall still bring forth fruit in old age; they shall be fat and flourishing.

PSALM 92:14

1   The trouble is, old age is not interesting until one gets there. It's a foreign country with an unknown language to the young and even to the middle-aged.
Mary Pipher
Another Country (1999)

2   By suffering, the old learn to endure; in sorrow they find wisdom.
Mary Pipher
Another Country (1999)

3   Like it or not, old age happens. We can allow it to make us helpless or grouchy, or mellow and ever more wise and loving.
Grace Ketterman and Kathy King
Caring for Your Elderly Parent (2001)

4   You know you're getting old when. . .you need a running start to go for a walk.
Martha Bolton
Didn't My Skin Used to Fit? (2000)

5   At some point we have to accept that we aren't teenagers anymore. We really do need diffused lighting.
Martha Bolton
Didn't My Skin Used to Fit? (2000)

6   Good stock and a healthy body are important gifts, but keeping in the will of God and having spiritual reserves to call upon in advanced age can be far more important.
Peter Mustric
The Joy of Growing Older (1979)

OPPONENTS (*see* ENEMIES)

294 OPPOSITION
(*see also* PERSECUTION)
For consider him that endured such contradiction of sinners against himself, lest ye be wearied and faint in your minds.
HEBREWS 12:3

1   God may be using people who disagree with you.
Bruce Bickel and Stan Jantz
God Is in the Small Stuff (1998)

2   Everyone who stands up to resist the flow of normal life will face opposition.
Bill Wilson
Christianity in the Crosshairs (2005)

3   When facing opposition you either become more dedicated or more discouraged. It's your choice.
Bill Wilson
Christianity in the Crosshairs (2005)

4   We can better bear any trouble from God, than injuries from men: "Oppression maketh a wise man mad."
Thomas Manton
One Hundred and Ninety Sermons on the Hundred and Nineteenth Psalm
(17th century)

PAIN (*see* SUFFERING)

PARADISE (*see* HEAVEN)

295 PARADOXES
For as the heavens are higher than the earth, so are my ways higher than your ways, and my thoughts than your thoughts.
ISAIAH 55:9

1   Let me learn by paradox that the way down is up, that to be low is to be high. . .that to have nothing is to possess all, that to bear the cross is to wear the crown. . .that the valley is the place of vision.
The Valley of Vision: A Collection of Puritan Prayers
(20th century)

2   God is known for taking the ordinary and making it extraordinary. Throughout scripture

God used ordinary men to affect his kingdom in extraordinary ways.
> Henry and Tom Blackaby
> *The Man God Uses* (1999)

3 Why is it that we remember with difficulty, and without difficulty forget, learn with difficulty, and without difficulty remain ignorant?
> Augustine
> *The City of God* (5th century)

4 The greatest truths are always the most loosely held.
> Henry Drummond
> *Natural Law in the Spiritual World* (19th century)

5 How strange it is, Lord, that we require the bitter-sweet force of adversity—in all its various forms—to fully ripen us in our walk with You.
> Rebecca Lusignolo
> "Bitter-Sweetness" devotional (2009)

6 The waters which broke down everything else bore up the ark. The more the waters increased the higher the ark was lifted up towards heaven.
> Matthew Henry
> *Commentary on the Whole Bible* (1706)

7 There is a poverty which makes a man rich for the kingdom of God.
> F. C. Cook
> *Bible Commentary* (19th century)

8 The greater the potential for good the greater the potential for evil.
> Elisabeth Elliot
> *Passion and Purity* (1984)

9 Strength is found in weakness. Control is found in dependency. Power is found in surrender.
> Dan Allender and Tremper Longman III
> *Breaking the Idols of Your Life* (1998)

10 On and through commitment, we experience the central paradox of the Gospel: We lose our lives to find them.
> Maxine Hancock
> *The Forever Principle* (1980)

11 To live in the tension of being a divine vessel (temptation: pride) and an earthen vessel (temptation: shame) is the paradoxical dance of belief.
> Joy Sawyer
> *Dancing to the Heartbeat of Redemption* (2000)

296 PARENTING
Provoke not your children to wrath: but bring them up in the nurture and admonition of the Lord.
EPHESIANS 6:4

1 Mothers and fathers are granted a single decade to lay a foundation of values and attitudes by which their children cope with the pressures and problems of adulthood.
> James Dobson
> *The New Hide or Seek* (1999)

2 A parent's voice is a megaphone straight to the heart of a child.
> Bill Glass
> *Champions for Life* (2005)

3 There are many ways to show your family that you are serious about following in the footsteps of Jesus Christ, but two in particular really count: Admitting your mistakes and asking for forgiveness when you mess up in a relationship—especially with one of your children.
> Dennis and Barbara Rainey
> *Growing a Spiritually Strong Family* (2002)

4 If we want to raise godly children, the best way to achieve this is to be godly parents.
> Ray Comfort
> *How to Bring Your Children to Christ* (2005)

5   We should value the eternal welfare of our children, rather than our own temporal anxiety when it comes to applying discipline.
Ray Comfort
How to Bring Your Children to Christ (2005)

6   God is the composer of life itself, so listen to His words and His words alone, and then be blessed by refusing to walk in "the counsel of the ungodly," particularly when it comes to raising your precious children.
Ray Comfort
How to Bring Your Children to Christ (2005)

7   If you skip around the Law, your kids may just skip around the cross.
Ray Comfort
How to Bring Your Children to Christ (2005)

8   We'll never regret time spent with children. Not for a moment.
Bill McCartney
4th and Goal (2002)

9   Respect for parents has to be learned in the home because popular culture sure doesn't teach it. Not only do your kids need to learn to respect you, but you, as parents, need to be worthy of their respect.
Bill McCartney
4th and Goal (2002)

10   God begins to take away our selfishness by giving us children for whom we would do things we would never do for anyone else.
Steve Farrar
Point Man (1990)

11   We are easily guided by the land mines we want our kids to avoid rather than the character we want them to develop.
Chip Ingram
Effective Parenting in a Defective World (2006)

12   One of the rich blessings in this season of parenting teens is that you can begin to explain some things to them and they will begin to "get it." Wisdom is coming!
Susan Alexander Yates
And Then I Had Teenagers (2001)

13   Sometimes we just need to open our ears and hearts and save the advice for the family dog! It's not enough to hear our children's words; we need to listen for the meaning of those words.
David and Claudia Arp
Answering the 8 Cries of the Spirited Child (2004)

14   We should never assume that we know what our children mean simply because we heard what they said.
David and Claudia Arp
Answering the 8 Cries of the Spirited Child (2004)

15   Encouraging our children to do their best is important, but then we have to back off. It is my experience, as a parent and an educator, that we get the most frustrated over things we truly cannot control in our children's lives.
David and Claudia Arp
Answering the 8 Cries of the Spirited Child (2004)

16   Adolescence is our time to encourage the questions, the struggles, and the longings and to help guide these kids to something far greater than the childhood they are leaving behind.
Melissa Trevathan and Sissy Goff
The Back Door to Your Teen's Heart (2002)

17   If you pretend to be perfect and demand that your children join in the pretense, they will not be able to turn to you when they fail.
Connie Neal
Your Thirty-Day Journey to Being a World-Class Father (1992)

18 For a child to be appropriately molded, parents need to look at the model they're displaying before their children. Children mimic well.

Maxine Marsolini
Blended Families (2000)

19 If a person's character makeup determines his future, then child rearing is primarily about helping children to develop character that will take them through life safely, securely, productively, and joyfully.

Henry Cloud and John Townsend
Boundaries with Kids (1998)

20 We teach our children that they must try every sport at least once, and we sign them up for as many personal interest classes as our bank accounts and palm pilots allow. In doing so, we falsely assume that we elevate their sense of self-worth. But what we may be teaching them is that they can never be truly happy and fulfilled without grasping every opportunity presented by the world.

Marsha Crockett
Dancing in the Desert (2003)

21 When a parent, after a particularly harsh day, is too tired to listen to a child, the situation may be just that: an honest fatigue. If that same parent repeatedly shuts out the young life begging for attention, the link between parent and child surely will fracture under the strain.

Steven Doughty
Discovering Community (1999)

22 It's in the day-to-day, run-of the-mill activities of our life that we impact our children the most. Habits, routines, and heroes are made in the normal days, not at the annual visit to the theme park.

Paul Pettit
Dynamic Dads (2003)

23 There's a principle that effective parents have learned to follow. If they want to be heard by their children more, they talk less. The greater the amount of verbiage that comes from us, the more it closes a child's ears and mouth.

H. Norman Wright
Everything I Know About Parenting I Learned from My Puppy (2002)

24 Nothing encourages troubled parents more than the support of other parents who have lived long enough to see their anguished prayers for their own children answered.

Robert Morgan
Moments for Families with Prodigals (2003)

25 The way we parent is making a huge difference in the life of a person who will someday take an important place in this society.

Kathy Coffey
God Knows Parenting Is a Wild Ride (2002)

26 Parenting is taxing, exhausting, difficult, and maddening. It is also wonderful, fulfilling, important, and a divine call.

Dave Meurer
Good Spousekeeping (2004)

27 This prodigal child thing hurts. Tell the truth to yourself and your friends. Stop trying to hide the pain. Don't be a martyr and suffer alone. When your child begins to stray from the hopes and dreams you had for her, face the fact that she is changing everything in your world too.

Brendan O'Rourke and DeEtte Sauer
Hope of a Homecoming (2003)

28 Give your children the luxury of seeing one parent who loves the other unconditionally. This will serve them well when they face the challenges of marriage themselves. Give your mate a place of honor in your home.

Connie Grigsby and Kent Julian
How to Get Your Teen to Talk to You (2002)

29 Love and respect your children and expect the same from them.
William Coleman
If I Could Raise My Kids Again (1996)

30 A searing burn teaches us not to touch the stove. When someone else hurts our feelings, we learn not to hurt others' feelings. Our children will not have the freedom to learn these lessons unless we let go of them. We let go in obedience to God because we cannot control their lives; most importantly, we let go because we love them.
Carol Kuykendall
Learning to Let Go (1985)

31 As parents, we need to help our children discover what they do well. We need to train them in the way God made them to go, not the way we want them to go or the way the nosey neighbor thinks they should go. We need to train them up according to the individual gifts that God gave them.
Carol Kuykendall
Learning to Let Go (1985)

32 The way we respond to our children's mistakes today is the way they'll assume we'll respond in the future. And what they find in us is much of what they expect to find in God.
Elisa Morgan
Mom to Mom (1996)

33 Master parents dispense justice and mercy evenly, with both hands.
James Lucas
The Paradox Principle of Parenting (2003)

34 There are qualities in your special youngster that you may not have seen before. Find them. Cultivate them. And then give God time to make something beautiful in their little life.
James Dobson
Parenting Isn't for Cowards (1987)

35 The goal of a consequence is to have children make choices and learn from those choices in order to shape their own behavior. Therefore, when you determine consequences, always check your motive. Power, control, or revenge should never be a factor in determining consequences. Use consequences only to modify or change a child's behavior.
Teresa Langston
Parenting Without Pressure (2001)

36 Parenting is an art that must be developed and honed.
Valerie Bell
Reaching Out to Lonely Kids (1994)

37 Praise your child's character in the presence of others.
Darrell Hines
Resolving Conflict in Marriage (2001)

38 Bless your child's individuality. Don't stifle his or her creativity; rather, find a way to channel it into positive activities and expressions.
Darrell Hines
Resolving Conflict in Marriage (2001)

39 If we demonstrate unconditional love, daily prayer, persistent faith, and adherence to God's laws, we give our children a gift. If we teach them that good deeds and kind words are expressions of the Spirit, we are on track toward living more like Jesus.
Jane Jarrell
Secrets of a Mid-Life Mom (2004)

40 Can my child look at my life as a worthy example to emulate?
Pam Foster
A Checklist for Parents (1992)

41 According to the values which govern my life, my most important reason for living is to get the baton—the gospel—safely in the hands of my children.
James Dobson
Straight Talk (1995)

42 When a parent makes it a point to understand what his or her child likely feels in a situation—rather than simply focusing on the situation itself—then that parent gains an excellent opportunity to speak life-changing words.
David Staal
Words Kids Need to Hear (2008)

43 Noticing a child's efforts will provide you with better, more abundant fodder than waiting for accomplishments.
David Staal
Words Kids Need to Hear (2008)

44 If you've trusted God with your child during the good times, why is it hard to trust Him with your teen during the hard times?
Mark Gregston
What's Happening to My Teen? (2009)

45 Praise causes the tail to want to wag the dog.
Kevin Leman
Bringing Up Kids Without Tearing Them Down (1995)

46 Parenting is an art with certain guiding principles.
Jayne Schooler and Thomas Atwood
The Whole Life Adoption Book (2008)

47 Parenting of the external produces faulty results, but parenting of the internal will help our children grow up loving God and loving one another.
Michael Youssef
Leading the Way (2009)

48 Right behavior will always follow right beliefs. Never the other way around.
Michael Youssef
Leading the Way (2009)

49 Shaming children into outward conformity strikes at the very core of their identity in Christ. . . . It is wrong.
Michael Youssef
Leading the Way (2009)

50 Be careful what you criticize your children for doing because they won't want to do it any more.
Michelle Duggar
The Duggars: 20 and Counting! (2008)

51 Be careful what you praise your children for doing, because they'll do a lot of it.
Michelle Duggar
The Duggars: 20 and Counting! (2008)

52 Parenting is the ultimate form of discipleship.
Christine Field
Help for the Harried Homeschooler (2002)

53 We must let our children know that a standard is a standard, anywhere, anytime, under any circumstances.
Christine Field
Help for the Harried Homeschooler (2002)

54 Make sure your children know they are loved, whether or not their performance pleases you.
Christine Field
Help for the Harried Homeschooler (2002)

55 Being a parent is better than a course on theology. Being a father is teaching me that when I am criticized, injured, or afraid, there is a Father who is ready to comfort me.
Max Lucado
The Applause of Heaven (1990)

56 It is never too early to train a child to hear God's voice. As we make prayer a part of everyday life, we show our children that prayer

is a normal function like eating and not just a boring religious ritual.

Florence Littauer, Marita Littauer, and Lauren Littauer Briggs
Making the Blue Plate Special (2006)

57 If you want to change the children, change the parent. Any growth plan for your family must begin with you.

John Maxwell
Breakthrough Parenting (1996)

58 It's important to God, and therefore to us, that we be intentional about how we train our children, especially in light of the way our culture would mislead them.

Tony Evans
Guiding Your Family (1991)

59 Children are not looking for perfect parents; but they are looking for honest parents.

Howard Hendricks
Heaven Help the Home (1973)

60 God has had your mission of raising godly kids in His mind from the beginning of time, and He wants you to succeed even more than you do.

Bruce Wilkinson
Experiencing Spiritual Breakthroughs (1999)

61 There is no greater privilege in living than bringing a tiny human being into the world and then trying to raise him or her properly during the next eighteen years.

James Dobson
Bringing Up Boys (2001)

62 The ultimate goal for people of faith is to give each child an understanding of Scripture and a lifelong passion for Jesus Christ.

James Dobson
Bringing Up Boys (2001)

63 You must never make your child believe you believe he is destined for failure and rejection. He will believe you!

James Dobson
Bringing Up Boys (2001)

64 Being overly concerned about potential parenting problems in the future will sap our energy and our joy and interfere with our efforts as parents today. God calls us to handle each day one at a time. Today is real, and God will enable us to deal with what today holds.

Elizabeth George
Loving God with All Your Mind (1994)

65 The mother who yields weakly is as guilty as abandoning the child she spoils, as if she cast him forth.

F. C. Cook
Bible Commentary (19th century)

66 A parent's main task is to receive a child as a charge from the Lord and then to dedicate the child to God's ways.

Rick Johnson
That's My Son (2005)

67 I want my children to trust me enough to know that if I let them suffer for even a millisecond that I had a reason for it. . .a really good reason. Our Father deserves no less from me.

Becky Lusignolo
"Super Saint?" teaching (2009)

68 May God help us who are parents to pray continually for our children, that God will preserve them from the corrupting influences of those amongst whom they are thrown. But it is folly to pray for our children if we follow Lot's example, and run right into the devil's camp.

D. L. Moody
Short Talks (19th century)

69 The role of parenting was never meant for one person alone.
Cindi McMenamin
When Women Walk Alone (2002)

70 Neither God nor our children expect us to be perfect. But we can become examples of men and women who genuinely love God and seek to follow Him with a whole and earned heart.
Gigi Graham Tchividjian
Currents of the Heart (1996)

71 For a combination of excitement and terror, nothing quite matches the birth of one's first child.
Preston Parrish
Windows into the Heart of God (2007)

72 If we live for our children, we will be bitterly disappointed.
R. Paul Stevens
Down-to-Earth Spirituality (2003)

297 PARENTS
Honour thy father and thy mother: that thy days may be long upon the land which the LORD thy God giveth thee.
EXODUS 20:12

1 God wanted a family—sons and daughters who could personally relate to Him, and vice versa. So He made our original parents similar to Himself.
Dutch Sheets
Intercessory Prayer (1996)

2 If a child can't learn to obey a parent who is visible, he'll never learn to obey a God who isn't.
Chip Ingram
Effective Parenting in a Defective World (2006)

3 My advice for parents is simple. If you want to be good parents, you need to care for each other first.
Willard Harley Jr.
His Needs, Her Needs for Parents (2003)

4 Parents should do whatever it takes to love each other for their children's sake.
Willard Harley Jr.
His Needs, Her Needs for Parents (2003)

5 Forgiving our parents frees us to appreciate the gifts they are giving our children.
Grace Ketterman and Kathy King
Caring for Your Elderly Parent (2001)

6 Pampered children are the product of pampered parents—parents who insist on getting their own way, and whose lives are structured around the illusion that instant gratification brings happiness.
Johann Christoph Arnold
Endangered: Your Child in a Hostile World (2000)

7 When someone loses a parent, he loses a person who for many years has been the most influential person in his life. For most of us, losing a parent means losing someone who loved us and cared for us in a way no one else does or ever will again. We can no long gain our parent's approval, praise, or permission. Feelings of attachment to a parent are unique.
H. Norman Wright
Helping Those Who Hurt (2003)

8 Parents can get away with many mistakes if their children see them as a solid, loving alliance.
Scott Larson
When Teens Stray (2002)

9 Parenting means daily involvement. It means fighting the battle for the hearts and minds and futures of the boys and girls, the young men and women, God has placed in your charge.
Thomas and Nanette Kinkade
The Many Loves of Parenting (2003)

10 Parents have a hard time letting go of their children. Even when they know their little darling is marrying a sweet, caring, Christian, there is still that lingering feeling that "No one is good enough for my son/daughter!" or "No one will love him/her like we do." Try to understand these normal parental instincts. But more than that, do everything in your power to convince your future in-laws that you are the best thing to happen to their child.

Len Woods
Marriage Clues for the Clueless (1999)

11 God matches our offering to the need of our child and the need of our child to our offering.

Elisa Morgan
Mom to Mom (1996)

12 We need to restore the social model of married parents bringing into the world a desired child, a child to be loved and nurtured, to be taught a sense of right and wrong, to be educated to his or her maximum potential in a society that provides opportunities for work and a fulfilling life. Simple to say; difficult to achieve; yet the ideal toward which we must never stop striving.

Colin Powell
My American Journey (1995)

13 Wise parents do not seek to solve the problems of their married children. They are there to make loving suggestions if these are asked for, but they do not impose themselves on their children's lives. They give their children space to build their own lives. They allow them the freedom to say no to invitations or requests that conflict with their plans or wishes. They relate to their children in ways that will foster their growth as individuals and as a couple.

Ross Campbell and Gary Chapman
Parenting Your Adult Child (1999)

14 God created us to empower children through a relationship, not to make a product of them according to a preprogrammed packaged deal.

Judy and Jack Balswick
Relationship-Empowerment Parenting (2003)

15 Have you invited God to help you carry out your work as parents? Do you deliberately ask for His wisdom when you make decisions, His strength when you're tired, His peace when you're concerned? Do you ask Him for patience when you're at the brink of frustration, or joy when you're facing discouragement?

Nick Harrison and Steve Miller
Survival Guide for New Dads (2003)

16 You'll find that including God in all that you do as parents definitely makes the work more manageable and more fulfilling.

Nick Harrison and Steve Miller
Survival Guide for New Dads (2003)

17 The first and biggest down payment on [a child's] image insurance is a parent's time.

Kevin Leman
Bringing Up Kids Without Tearing Them Down (1995)

18 When we're enjoying a right relationship with God and a right relationship with our parents, we have the most important relationships in life in order—and the freedom to establish a right relationship with the world.

Bill Hybels
Laws of the Heart (1985)

19 Parents spend two years teaching children how to stand up and speak for themselves. Then they spend another eighteen years teaching them to sit down and be quiet.

Ted Engstrom and Robert Larson
Integrity (1987)

20 From the birth of your child onward, you as a parent are a craftsman for God.
Bruce Wilkinson
Experiencing Spiritual Breakthroughs (1999)

21 When moms and dads concentrate too much on their parental roles, they forget their relationship as husband and wife.
Dennis Gibson
The Sandwich Years (1991)

PARTIALITY (*see* FAVORITISM)

298 PASSION
But it is good to be zealously affected always in a good thing.
GALATIANS 4:18

1 This is true zeal for God—to know Him and love Him with a deep and consuming love, and to serve others in the same way we would serve Jesus. Anything else is an imitation.
Keith Green
"Zeal—The Good, the Bad, and the Ugly" article (1980)

2 How is it that we're so zealous to put on outward, heroic shows of loyalty for our faith—and so reluctant to set aside our own agenda and do what Jesus wants us to do?
Keith Green
"Zeal—The Good, the Bad, and the Ugly" article (1980)

3 If it doesn't mean anything to you, it won't mean anything to God.
Jentezen Franklin
Fasting (2008)

4 That passion may not harm us, let us act as if we had only eight hours to live.
Blaise Pascal
Pensées (17th century)

5 Passionate persistence without impertinence produces progress!
Robert Schuller
The Be (Happy) Attitudes (1985)

6 Anything we feel passionate about we can also overdo.
Patrick Morley
Understanding Your Man in the Mirror (1998)

7 One of the things that I've said to God so many times is, never let my zeal in public exceed my zeal in private.
Beth Moore
Life Today article (1996)

8 Don't let me get out there somewhere and get a big thing going that was not true this morning just between the two of us, Lord Jesus.
Beth Moore
Life Today article (1996)

9 It is not the place where we are, or the work that we do or cannot do, that matters, it is something else. It is the fire within that burns and shines, whatever be our circumstances.
Amy Carmichael
Edges of His Ways (1955)

10 O sirs, it is a miserable thing when men study and talk of heaven and hell, and the fewness of the saved, and the difficulty of salvation, and be not all the while in good earnest.
Richard Baxter
The Reformed Pastor (17th century)

11 It's hard to sustain passion for something you believe is unattainable.
Bob Moorehead
A Passion for Victory (1996)

12 No passion is easy to control. But passion should not be allowed to run wild. We must not be angry without restraint. We cannot be

joyful without boundaries. We dare not love without control.
William Coleman
Engaged (1980)

13 This surely is the way we turn to Christ: to desire nothing but him.
Richard Rolle
The Fire of Love (14th century)

14 A man can have enthusiasm in everything else, but the moment that a little fire gets into the Church, people raise the cry, "Ah, enthusiasm—false excitement—I'm afraid of that."
D. L. Moody
The Faithful Saying (1877)

299 PAST, THE

*For a thousand years in thy sight
are but as yesterday when it is past,
and as a watch in the night.*
Psalm 90:4

1 God only looks at your future because He's canceled out your past.
Karon Phillips Goodman
Grab a Broom, Lord—There's Dust Everywhere! (2003)

2 Let us fear being remembered only for the past.
George Verwer
Come! Live! Die! (1972)

3 One of the cardinal rules of the spiritual life is, that we are to live exclusively in the present moment, without casting a look beyond.
François Fénelon and Jeanne Guyon
Spiritual Progress (17th century)

4 The wise and diligent traveller watches all his steps, and keeps his eyes always directed to that part of the road which is immediately before him; but he does not incessantly look backwards to count his steps and examine his footmarks.
François Fénelon and Jeanne Guyon
Spiritual Progress (17th century)

5 Revisiting the past, even unpleasant memories and discoveries, is a privilege. When we look at it as a healthy thing we are able to appreciate what it has to offer. It brings defining insight to the present.
Maxine Marsolini
Blended Families (2000)

6 Our gracious heavenly Father entreats us to confess our mess. And to show us that it's okay to let down our pretenses, His Word is full of stories about unlikely people becoming heroes—a stuttering ex-con who leads God's people out of slavery; an unethical little "IRS agent" who becomes a friend of Jesus; a sleazy woman whose testimony triggers a revival in her hometown. If you're embarrassed by your past, you're in good company!
Lisa Harper
Every Woman's Hope (2001)

7 Ultimately, remembrance is not merely backward-looking. Remembrance as a spiritual discipline gives us strength to live in the present and direction to move forward. When our future seems uncertain, remembrance of God's past trustworthiness gives us hope to carry on.
Albert Hsu
Grieving a Suicide (2002)

8 Don't give away any more of today's energy and promise fretting over the pain or disappointment of the past.
Martha Bolton
Growing Your Own Turtleneck (2005)

9 By revisiting the evidence of our journeys, we remind ourselves that we are more than what we are at any one moment.
Nancy Nordenson
Just Think (2003)

10 History is a marvelous tapestry woven from facts and aspirations and accomplishments, all intermingled with the tragedies of mistaken motives and forgotten truths.
   Donn Taylor
   Rhapsody in Red (2008)

11 I believe the memory is "the worm that never dies"...the memory is never cleansed of obscene stories and unclean acts. Even if a man repents and reforms he often has to fight the past.
   D. L. Moody
   Weighed and Wanting (19th century)

12 The more you hang out where the past is, the more it comes calling.
   Steve Campbell
   "Freedom from Addiction" sermon (2009)

13 Knowing from whence we have come can help us chart where we are yet to be.
   Florence Littauer, Marita Littauer, and Lauren Littauer Briggs
   Making the Blue Plate Special (2006)

14 It's all right to look back and allow ourselves to experience feelings of loss, but eventually we have to look ahead or else miss the adventure God has waiting for us.
   Poppy Smith
   I'm Too Young to Be This Old! (1997)

15 Moments when the well of your soul is empty—these are the times when you need to remember God's power and times in the past when He has sustained you.
   Lois Evans
   Stones of Remembrance (2006)

PASTORS (*see* CLERGY)

300 PATIENCE
For ye have need of patience, that, after ye have done the will of God, ye might receive the promise.
HEBREWS 10:36

1 Patience has its perfect work in the school of delay.
   E. M. Bounds
   The Necessity of Prayer (19th century)

2 It's such a contradiction—we plead for patience when what we really want is the granting of our wishes so we don't have to be patient anymore.
   Karon Phillips Goodman
   You're Late Again, Lord! (2002)

3 Impatience breeds a little bit of arrogance now and then!
   Karon Phillips Goodman
   You're Late Again, Lord! (2002)

4 Patience is the virtue that transforms an angry tongue. Patience takes time to hesitate and evaluate. It rejects anger sins. True patience finds its strength in an unflinching focus on God and an unconditional love toward those who have hurt us.
   Joseph Stowell
   Tongue in Cheek (1983)

5 The time you spend waiting today can become the critical time God uses to prepare you for the answers to your prayers.
   Ginger Garrett
   Couples Who Long for Children (2003)

6 Waiting is, by its nature, something only the humble can do with grace. When we wait for something, we recognize that we are not in control.
   John Ortberg
   If You Want to Walk on Water, You've Got to Get Out of the Boat (2001)

7 Nothing so cultivates the grace of patience as the endurance of temptation.
   Hannah Whitall Smith
   The Christian's Secret of a Happy Life (1888)

8   Our society has become accustomed to instant coffee, microwave meals, and quick access to information via the Internet. We don't like to wait, but sometimes we learn while we're waiting. During the time of waiting, God leads us through the valley and refines our character.

Heather Whitestone McCallum
Let God Surprise You (2003)

9   Do not judge God's ways while they are in progress. Wait till the plan is complete.

F. B. Meyer
The Shepherd Psalm (1889)

10 Maybe we need to practice waiting. After all, if something is foreign to you, you only learn it by practice.

Tracie Peterson
The Eyes of the Heart (2002)

11 There's something about patience that God deems necessary for our life in the age to come.

Russell Moore
Adoption for Life (2009)

12 In this present time we learn to bear with equanimity the ills to which even good men are subject, and to hold cheap the blessings which even the wicked enjoy.

Augustine
The City of God (5th century)

13 When it is said that charity suffers long, we cannot infer from this, that we are to bear injuries meekly for a season, and that after that season we may cease thus to bear them.

Jonathan Edwards
"Charity Disposes Us Meekly to Bear the Injuries Received from Others" sermon (1738)

14 Perhaps one reason God delays his answer to our prayers is because He knows we need to be with Him far more than we need the things we ask of Him.

Ben Patterson
Deepening Your Conversation with God (1991)

15 Our hearts are much distressed and burdened, so we go to prayer and maybe spend much time pouring out our petitions before the throne. And too many times we get up immediately, rush out of His presence and often try to answer the prayer by some efforts of our own.

John Wright Follette
Broken Bread (1957)

16 Learn to enjoy waiting, realizing that waiting is what will deliver your dream.

Joyce Meyer
When God, When? (1994)

17 Patience is a powerful witness to unbelievers.

Joyce Meyer
When God, When? (1994)

18 Waiting silently is the hardest thing of all.
Elisabeth Elliot
Passion and Purity (1984)

19 Patience is love enduring.
Bob Parry
"The Law of Love" sermon (2010)

20 Godly patience is a willingness to wait for God's timing.

David Wilkerson
"Hold on to Your Confidence" article (2010)

21 Impatience. How many of us have ruined rare and unusual opportunities to serve Christ because of impatience? It doesn't seem like

such a big thing and yet—do you know what impatience represents? It is a sign of distrust in the sovereign control of God.
Luis Palau
Heart After God (1978)

22 Wait is the command we must obey whether we want to or not.
Luci Shaw
God in the Dark (1989)

23 Impatience is usually a mark of immaturity.
Warren Wiersbe
God Isn't in a Hurry (1994)

301 PEACE
And the peace of God, which passeth all understanding, shall keep your hearts and minds through Christ Jesus.
PHILIPPIANS 4:7

1 Faith brings great ease of mind and perfect peace of heart.
E. M. Bounds
The Necessity of Prayer (19th century)

2 Believing prayer ushers in God's peace. Not a random, nebulous, earthly peace, but his peace. Imported from heaven. The same tranquility that marks the throne room, God offers to you.
Max Lucado
Come Thirsty (2004)

3 The most striking characteristic of men and women who are doing God's work His way is their lack of stress. Believers who are walking in the Spirit are going to experience peace.
Charles Stanley
The Wonderful Spirit-Filled Life (1992)

4 With God's peace, we can stand firm in distress, disease, destruction, and even death.
Hank Hanegraaff
The Covering (2002)

5 There can never really be any peace and joy for me until there is peace and joy finally for you too.
Frederick Buechner
Beyond Words: Daily Readings in the ABC's of Faith (2004)

6 The peace of God is first and foremost peace with God.
J. I. Packer
Knowing God (1993)

7 Christ brings also peace, but not as the apostles brought it, through preaching; he gives it as a Creator, as his own proper creature.
Martin Luther
Table Talk (16th century)

8 Capitalize on times of peace.
Charles Swindoll
The Darkness and the Dawn (2001)

9 God's peace can break through the bleakest of circumstances, even into those moments when we stare into darkness and the shadow of death.
Virginia Ann Froehle
Loving Yourself More (1993)

10 No tongue can tell the depth of that calm which comes over the soul which has received the peace of God which passeth all understanding.
Charles Spurgeon
All of Grace (19th century)

11 The basic response of the soul to the Light is internal adoration and joy, thanksgiving and worship, self-surrender and listening. The secret places of the heart cease to be our noisy workshop. They become a holy sanctuary of adoration and self-oblation, where we are kept in perfect peace if our minds be stayed on Him.
Thomas Kelly
A Testament of Devotion (1992)

12 Peace with everyone is surely the goal for us as believers. But it is not always possible.
Jan Silvious
Foolproofing Your Life (1998)

13 There will be no peace in any soul until it is willing to obey the voice of God.
D. L. Moody
Short Talks (19th century)

14 We experience peace as we focus our thoughts and our vivid imaginations on the Father—and not on our concerns and worries.
Gigi Graham Tchividjian
Currents of the Heart (1996)

15 The peace we have in Christ refers to an internal order, not the external order of this world.
Neil Anderson and Dave Park
Overcoming Negative Self-Image (2003)

16 Real self-denial makes us more calm and patient. First of all, Scripture draws our attention to the fact that if we want ease and tranquility in our lives, we should resign ourselves and all that we have to the will of God.
John Calvin
On the Life of the Christian Man (1550)

PEACEMAKING
(*see* RECONCILIATION)

302 PEER PRESSURE
Take heed to thyself that thou be not snared by following them...
DEUTERONOMY 12:30

1 The issue is not whether everybody else is doing it. The issue is whether it is right or wrong.
Nathaniel and Hans Bluedorn
The Fallacy Detective (2002)

303 PERFECTION
But the God of all grace, who hath called us unto his eternal glory by Christ Jesus, after that ye have suffered a while, make you perfect...
1 PETER 5:10

1 I met another man who considered himself perfect, but he was thoroughly mad; and I do not believe that any of the pretenders to perfection are better than good maniacs... for, while a man has got a spark of reason left in him, he cannot, unless he is the most impudent of impostors, talk about being perfect.
Charles Spurgeon
Autobiography (1897)

2 Those who put themselves in His hands will become perfect, as He is perfect—perfect in love, wisdom, joy, beauty, and immortality. The change will not be completed in this life, for death is an important part of the treatment.
C. S. Lewis
Mere Christianity (1952)

3 Just as we don't stop loving our children because they aren't perfect, God doesn't stop loving us because we've done things wrong. Some people think they have to get their life totally together before they can say yes to God. But that's getting things backward. He wants to guide us so our lives can be all He created us to be.
Laurie Lovejoy Hilliard and Sharon Lovejoy Autry
Hold You, Mommy (2006)

4 You do not have to be perfect to become a vessel God can use.
Donna Partow
A 10-Week Journey to Becoming a Vessel God Can Use (1996)

5 I am filled with shame and confusion, when I reflect on the one hand upon the great favours which God has done, and

incessantly continues to do; and on the other, upon the ill use I have made of them, and my small advancement in the way of perfection.

Brother Lawrence
The Practice of the Presence of God
(17th century)

6   God knows we won't be perfect today. Complete perfection is reserved for a time in the future. We're not done yet. If we were done, we'd be dead.

Elisa Morgan
Mom to Mom (1996)

7   Nothing is required of man that is not first in God. It is because God is perfect that we are required to be perfect.

George MacDonald
"The Child in the Midst" sermon
(19th century)

8   This is true perfection: not to avoid a wicked life because like slaves we servilely fear punishment, nor to do good because we hope for rewards, as if cashing in on the virtuous life by some business-like arrangement. On the contrary. . .we regard falling from God's friendship as the only thing dreadful and we consider becoming God's friend the only thing worthy of honor and desire. This, as I have said, is the perfection of life.

Gregory of Nyssa
The Life of Moses (4th century)

304 PERFECTIONISM
I have seen an end of all perfection.
PSALM 119:96

1   The perfectionist lives under the Law. He is in bondage to a demand that says, "If you do it right, you'll be loved."

Henry Cloud and John Townsend
Safe People (2005)

2   Some people cannot live with less than perfection, and therefore they cannot forgive, and therefore they cannot love.

John Cowan
Small Decencies (1992)

3   Every man is idealistic; only it so often happens that he has the wrong ideal.

G. K Chesterton
Heretics (1905)

4   It is difficult to attain a high ideal; consequently, it is almost impossible to persuade ourselves that we have attained it.

G. K. Chesterton
Heretics (1905)

5   Perfection doesn't exist on this planet, but that doesn't stop a lot of us from trying to achieve it!

Steve Stephens and Alice Gray
The Worn Out Woman (2004)

6   Probably the greatest source of false guilt is perfectionism—that inner voice that says you can do more, be more, achieve more. Perfectionism is both a driver for great expectations and a reminder that you are not achieving enough. When you compare yourself to this standard of perfection, you can never achieve enough.

David Hawkins
The Relationship Doctor's Prescription for Living Beyond Guilt (2006)

305 PERSECUTION
But as then he that was born after the flesh persecuted him that was born after the Spirit, even so it is now.
GALATIANS 4:29

1   Every true work of God has had its bitter enemies—not only outside, but also inside—just as in the days of Nehemiah.

D. L. Moody
"Revivals" sermon (19th century)

2   The best work usually meets the strongest opposition.
    D. L. Moody
    "Revivals" sermon (19th century)

3   In the midst of persecution, we get a double gift—the blessing of being drawn deeper into the embrace of God and the knowledge of rewards waiting in heaven.
    Angela Thomas
    A Beautiful Offering (2004)

4   When you go through persecution and rejection, it's not always because somebody has it in for you. Sometimes, that's God way of directing you into His perfect will.
    Joel Osteen
    Becoming a Better You (2007)

5   It is easy to be religious when religion is in fashion; but it is an evidence of strong faith and resolution to swim against a stream to heaven, and to appear for God when no one else appears for him.
    Matthew Henry
    Commentary on the Whole Bible (1706)

6   It's impossible to have an impact for the kingdom of God without being slandered.
    Rich Mendola
    "Farthest Horizon: Responding to Personal Attacks" sermon (2009)

306 PERSEVERANCE

Praying always with all prayer and supplication in the Spirit, and watching thereunto with all perseverance. . .
EPHESIANS 6:18

1   The secret of endurance is to remember that your pain is temporary but your reward will be eternal.
    Rick Warren
    The Purpose-Driven Life (2002)

2   Do not pray for easy lives, pray to be stronger men. Do not pray for tasks equal to your powers, pray for powers equal to your tasks.
    Phillips Brooks
    "Going Up to Jerusalem" sermon (1886)

3   God evermore gives power answerable to what He requires of us.
    Thomas Wilson
    Private Thoughts (1828)

4   Watch a baby trying to learn to walk. It doesn't worry about what might happen. It doesn't worry about what people will think. It doesn't worry about how it will look to others as it struggles with the task. It doesn't give up and just lie there. It gets up and falls down and gets up and falls down and gets up again, patiently, doggedly, until the job is done.
    Suzette Haden Elgin
    The Grandmother Principles (1998)

5   Satan can call God a liar, he can flash before our dazzled eyes all the supposed sin-fun imaginable, but if we do not agree to his blandishments, give him the nod, he remains helpless.
    Catherine Marshall
    Something More (1974)

6   As we pass through life, dirt will land on us. How long we let it stay there is up to us.
    Michelle McKinney Hammond
    Why Do I Say "Yes" When I Need to Say "No"? (2002)

7   We can be miserable or we can try to decipher the lesson life is teaching us in all that we encounter.
    Michele Weiner-Davis
    A Woman's Guide to Changing Her Man (1998)

8   Make no mistake, it is intimacy with God when you are willing to wrestle something out with him.
    Beth Moore
    "Wrestling with God" teaching series (2009)

9   Determination fades quickly without endurance.
    Steve Campbell
    "Just Keep Trying" sermon (2009)

10 I refuse to allow defeat to be my legacy.
    Steve Campbell
    "Just Keep Trying" sermon (2009)

11 Determination is the refusal to accept defeat as final.
    Steve Campbell
    "Just Keep Trying" sermon (2009)

12 Getting from big idea to meaningful change is tough.
    Alex and Brett Harris
    Do Hard Things (2008)

13 You must remember when waging war with the forces of hell, endurance is the name of the game!
    Rick Renner
    Living in the Combat Zone (1989)

14 We are called to endure and not grow weary or give up, but to hold fast.
    Benedict of Nursia
    The Rule of St. Benedict (6th century)

307 PERSPECTIVE
I am God, and there is none like me,
Declaring the end from the beginning.
Isaiah 46:9–10

1   The spring would not be so pleasant as it is if it did not succeed the winter.
    Matthew Henry
    Commentary on the Whole Bible (1706)

2   You must have perspective before things make sense.
    Todd Hafer and Jeff Hafer
    Wake Up and Smell the Pizza (2005)

3   If things upset, irritate, or even momentarily bother me, let me think of what Christ endured for me and the contrast will put my troubles in perspective.
    Elisabeth Elliot
    The Music of His Promises (2000)

308 PHILOSOPHY
(*see also* REASON; SCIENCE)
Beware lest any man spoil you through philosophy and vain deceit, after the tradition of men, after the rudiments of the world, and not after Christ.
Colossians 2:8

1   Moral relativism doesn't work. It's a broken system, a bankrupt philosophy, a worldview at war with itself.
    Ryan Dobson
    Be Intolerant (2003)

2   Moral relativism is sin in a toga. It's selfishness and hedonism and rebellion dressed up in philosophers' robes.
    Ryan Dobson
    Be Intolerant (2003)

3   Humanism, of course, is a religion that teaches that man is the measure of all things. There is no supernatural being to whom we are all accountable.
    Ken Ham
    Why Won't They Listen? (2002)

4   Again I warn you, beware of philosophers and great reasoners. They will always be a snare to you, and will do you more harm than you will know how to do them good. They linger and pine away in discussing exterior trifles, and never reach the knowledge of the truth.
    François Fénelon and Jeanne Guyon
    Spiritual Progress (17th century)

5   Humanistic World View: Relative Morality. Christian World View: God Sets Rules.
    Ken Ham
    The Lie: Evolution (1987)

6   One who claims to be a skeptic of one set of beliefs is actually a true believer in another set of beliefs.
    Phillip Johnson
    "Exposing Naturalistic Presuppositions of Evolution" speech (1998)

7   Philosophic argument, especially that drawn from the vastness of the universe, in comparison with the apparent insignificance of this globe, has sometimes shaken my reason for the faith that is in me; but my heart has always assured and reassured me that the gospel of Jesus Christ must be Divine Reality. The Sermon on the Mount cannot be a mere human production. This belief enters into the very depth of my conscience. The whole history of man proves it.
    Daniel Webster (1852)
    Spoken on the eve of his death and carved as his epitaph

8   Overwhelming pressures are being brought to bear on people who have no absolutes, but only have the impoverished values of personal peace and prosperity. The pressures are progressively preparing modern people to accept a manipulative authoritarian government.
    Francis Schaeffer
    How Should We Then Live? (1976)

9   You hear it a thousand times and more growing up in the East—"We all come through different routes and end up in the same place." But I say to you, God is not a place or an experience or a feeling.
    Ravi Zacharias
    What Is Truth? (2007)

10   Pluralistic cultures are beguiled by the cosmetically courteous idea that sincerity or privilege of birth is all that counts and that truth is subject to the beholder.
    Ravi Zacharias
    What Is Truth? (2007)

11   Any philosophy that makes it easier to sin is of the devil.
    Vance Havner
    Messages on Revival (1958)

12   The brutal man never can by analysis find anything but lust in love; the Flatlander never can find anything but flat shapes in a picture; physiology never can find anything in thought except twitching of grey matter.
    C. S. Lewis
    The Weight of Glory (1949)

13   Without the idea that we live in reality with other people who are as real as we are, compassion is impossible and so is any other virtue one could name. Nothing beyond the gratification of the moment matters in such a world, not fairness, not justice, not responsibility, not honor. None of them matters because in such a world none of them exists.
    Lynne Cheney
    Telling the Truth (1995)

14   Repeatedly bombarded with the idea that there is no truth, but only various fictions that must be enforced, one can all too easily decide to adapt, to go along in order to get along.
    Lynne Cheney
    Telling the Truth (1995)

15   We are seeing more and more examples of people treating animals—and even insects—as if they had as much value as humans.
    Chuck Colson
    "I Got the Sucker" article (2009)

16 If all life has equal value, then the logical conclusion is to treat all life the same, no matter how lowly—or how deadly, like mosquitoes carrying the West Nile virus.
Chuck Colson
"I Got the Sucker" article (2009)

17 Christians need to learn to press people to face the logical conclusion of their own beliefs.
Chuck Colson
"I Got the Sucker" article (2009)

18 How do I define right from wrong and what happens to me when I die? Those are the fulcrum points of our existence.
Ravi Zacharias
Christian Worldview article (2008)

19 If the relativist is to remain consistent, he can't legitimately criticize another's point of view.
Paul Copan
"Who Are You to Judge Others?" article (2001)

20 The denial of an objective moral law, based on the compulsion to deny the existence of God, results ultimately in the denial of evil itself.
Ravi Zacharias
"The Undeluded Truth?" article (2008)

21 Our inability to alter what is actual frustrates our grandiose delusions of being sovereign over everything.
Ravi Zacharias
"The Undeluded Truth?" article (2008)

22 What one will allow or exclude as a possible starting point will greatly affect the outcome of the discussion.
Paul Copan
"Atheistic Goodness Revisited" article (2007)

23 First, we want to find as much truth as possible. And second, we want to avoid as much falsehood as possible. These two goals stand in tension with each other.
James Beilby and David Clark
A Brief Introduction to the Theory of Knowledge (2002)

24 It's critical to distinguish truth and knowledge.
James Beilby and David Clark
A Brief Introduction to the Theory of Knowledge (2002)

25 Truth doesn't depend on anyone knowing the truth.
James Beilby and David Clark
A Brief Introduction to the Theory of Knowledge (2002)

26 Truth is independent of human minds.
James Beilby and David Clark
A Brief Introduction to the Theory of Knowledge (2002)

27 The best is perhaps what we understand the least.
C. S. Lewis
A Grief Observed (1961)

28 There is no philosophy that is not to some extent also theology.
Karl Barth
Evangelical Theology: An Introduction (1963)

29 It is obviously useless to discuss any theory until we are agreed as to what that theory is.
Charles Hodge
What Is Darwinism? (1874)

30 Some distinguished naturalists are swinging round from one pole to the opposite; from saying there is no God, to teaching that everything is God.
Charles Hodge
What Is Darwinism? (1874)

31 There is no hope of bringing a man out of his delusion, unless he desires to know the truth.
R. A. Torrey
How to Bring Men to Christ (1893)

32 To further trouble the waters and muddy the distinction between wrong and righteous, we find ourselves surrounded by the intellectual waves of secular humanism.
Ted Engstrom and Robert Larson
Integrity (1987)

33 Is your faith based on godly truth, or is it based on a make-it-up-as-you-go philosophy?
Stephen Arterburn and Jack Felton
Toxic Faith (1991)

34 The starting point for the origin of life is not a question of science but of philosophy or faith.
Terrell Clemmons
"Questioning the Quantum Leap" article (2009)

35 We live in a world where God has been marginalized, and human wisdom has been elevated.
Michael Youssef
"The Perfect Antidote" article (2009)

36 It never occurred to Paul that a gospel might be true for one man and not for another; the blight of pragmatism had never fallen upon his soul.
J. Gresham Machen
Christianity and Liberalism (1923)

37 Not unfrequently it leaves the mind of the student prepossessed with opinions concerning God, man, and the world opposed to those which underlie the Christian faith, so that at least one, if not the principal, function of apologetic must be to deal with anti-Christian prejudices, that Christianity may get a fair hearing.
Alexander Balmain Bruce
Apologetics, or Christianity Defensively Stated (1892)

38 Apologetic, as I conceive it, is a preparer of the way of faith, an aid to faith against doubts whencesoever arising, especially such as are engendered by philosophy and science.
Alexander Balmain Bruce
Apologetics, or Christianity Defensively Stated (1892)

309 PHYSICAL APPEARANCE
(*see also* BEAUTY)
Man looketh on the outward appearance, but the LORD looketh on the heart.
1 SAMUEL 16:7

1 O thou who art gifted with a noble frame, a comely body, boast not thyself therein, for thy gifts come from God.
Charles Spurgeon
"Divine Sovereignty" sermon (1856)

2 Believers are not to use outward appearance as the main criterion by which to evaluate the women of the Bible, or anyone else, for that matter. Though physical appearance is important to people, it is not God's standard for evaluation.
Pat Warren
Weighed by the Word (2009)

3 External beauty cannot hide internal ugliness.
Neil Anderson and Dave Park
Overcoming Negative Self-Image (2003)

PITY (*see* COMPASSION)

310 PLANS
(*see also* ASPIRATIONS; GOALS)
Without counsel purposes are disappointed: but in the multitude of counsellors they are established.
PROVERBS 15:22

1 It is possible that what we see as an inconvenient interruption is a divine appointment.
John Ortberg
God Is Closer Than You Think (2005)

2   Wisdom knows when to abandon one plan in favor of a better one.
Gary Stanley
How to Make a Moose Run (2001)

3   We should live our lives by design rather than by default.
Michele Weiner-Davis
A Woman's Guide to Changing Her Man (1998)

4   What you are today is what you are becoming.
Elizabeth George
A Woman after God's Own Heart (1997)

311 PLEASING GOD
So then they that are in the flesh cannot please God.
ROMANS 8:8

1   God is impressed, not with noise or size or wealth, but with quiet things. . .things done in secret—the inner motives, the true heart condition.
Charles Swindoll
Simple Faith (1991)

2   God's delight is received upon surrender, not awarded upon conquest.
Max Lucado
The Applause of Heaven (1990)

3   We need to simply do what we were created to do: love the Lord our God, obey His voice, hold fast to Him.
Kay Arthur
Our Covenant God (1999)

4   This is the distinctiveness of Christian forgiveness. Every man-made religion ever concocted teaches that there is something the sinner must do in order to appease God. Biblical Christianity alone teaches that God has supplied on the sinner's behalf all the merit that is necessary to please Him.
John MacArthur
The Freedom and Power of Forgiveness (1998)

5   It is possible to please God first and at the same time to please those around us. But if we always try to please those around us first, we will never please God.
Rubye Goodlett
Gathered Fragments (1986)

312 PLEASURE
They shall be abundantly satisfied with the fatness of thy house; and thou shalt make them drink of the river of thy pleasures.
PSALM 36:8

1   The great hindrance to worship is not that we are pleasure-seeking people, but that we are willing to settle for such pitiful pleasures.
John Piper
The Dangerous Duty of Delight (2001)

2   Fun isn't reserved for children, clowns, and fools. Fun provides a stimulus that keeps people going. It is the connection we share with others. When people are having fun, they forget their troubles and concerns, and just enjoy the play. When people are having fun, they create more and begin to see other options.
Anne Bryan Smollin
God Knows You're Stressed (2001)

3   One design ye are to pursue to the end of time—the enjoyment of God in time and in eternity.
John Wesley
A Plain Account of Christian Perfection (18th century)

4   Life affords us only so many genuine pleasures, and being married to a person you cherish, love, and enjoy rates right up there as the most pleasurable of all.
William Coleman
Before I Give You Away (1995)

5   Pleasure in itself is a dead-end street. It never satisfies.
Gene Getz
The Measure of a Man (2004)

POLITENESS (*see* RESPECT)

313 POLITICS

Righteousness exalteth a nation:
but sin is a reproach to any people.
PROVERBS 14:34

1   The political world is waiting for the sunrise. The politicians do not know it, of course. They would try to make the day dawn by their efforts around conference tables. But the hope of a better day rests with only One, The Lord of Glory. Only in Christ can you bring men together.
Vance Havner
Jesus Only (1946)

2   Compassion is the work of a nation, not just a government.
George W. Bush
Inaugural Address (2001)

3   The propitious smiles of Heaven can never be expected on a nation that disregards the eternal rules of order and right which Heaven itself has ordained.
George Washington
Inaugural Address (1789)

4 . It must be felt that there is no national security but in the nation's humble, acknowledged dependence upon God and His overruling providence.
Franklin Pierce
Inaugural Address (1853)

5   In entering this great office I must humbly invoke the God of our fathers for wisdom and firmness to execute its high and responsible duties in such a manner as to restore harmony and ancient friendship among the people and several States and to preserve our free institutions throughout many generations.
James Buchanan
Inaugural Address (1857)

6   It is the high privilege and sacred duty of those now living to educate their successors, and fit them, by intelligence and virtue, for the inheritance which awaits them.
James Garfield
Inaugural Address (1881)

7   If the task I seek should be given me I would pray only that I could perform it in a way that would serve God.
Ronald Reagan (20th century) quoted in
Reagan: A Life in Letters

8   Our nation exists for one purpose only—to assure each one of us the ultimate in individual freedom consistent with law and order. God meant America to be free because God intended each man to have the dignity of freedom.
Ronald Reagan (20th century) quoted in
Reagan: A Life in Letters

9   Government exists to protect rights which are ours from birth; the right to life, to liberty and the pursuit of happiness.
Ronald Reagan (20th century) quoted in
Reagan: A Life in Letters

10 A man may choose to sit and fish instead of working. That's his pursuit of happiness. He does not have the right to force his neighbors to support him (welfare) in his pursuit because that interferes with their pursuit of happiness.
Ronald Reagan (20th century) quoted in
Reagan: A Life in Letters

11 Not only every politician, high or low, but every citizen interested in politics, and especially every man who, in a newspaper or on the stump, advocates or condemns any public policy or any public man, should remember always that the two cardinal points

in his doctrine ought to be, "Thou shalt not steal" and "Thou shalt not bear false witness against thy neighbor."

Theodore Roosevelt
The Strenuous Life (1899)

12 We can afford to differ on the currency, the tariff, and foreign policy; but we cannot afford to differ on the question of honesty if we expect our republic permanently to endure.

Theodore Roosevelt
The Strenuous Life (1899)

13 Honesty is not so much a credit as an absolute prerequisite to efficient service to the public. Unless a man is honest we have no right to keep him in public life.

Theodore Roosevelt
The Strenuous Life (1899)

14 No man who is corrupt, no man who condones corruption in others, can possibly do his duty by the community.

Theodore Roosevelt
The Strenuous Life (1899)

15 Military power is at an end when the honor of the soldier can no longer be trusted; and, in the right sense of the word, civic greatness is at an end when civic righteousness is no longer its foundation.

Theodore Roosevelt
The Strenuous Life (1899)

16 There are always politicians willing, on the one hand, to promise everything to the people, and, on the other, to perform everything for the machine or the boss, with chuckling delight in the success of their efforts to hoodwink the former and serve the latter. Now, not only should such politicians be regarded as infamous, but the people who are hoodwinked by them should share the blame.

Theodore Roosevelt
The Strenuous Life (1899)

17 The moral side of every political question will be considered its most important side, and the ground will be distinctly taken that nations, as well as individuals, are under the same law, to do all things to the glory of God, as the first rule of action.

Charles Sheldon
In His Steps (1896)

POOR, THE (*see* POVERTY)

POPULARITY (*see* FAME)

314 PORNOGRAPHY
*Likewise also these filthy dreamers
defile the flesh. . .*
JUDE 8

1 To combat this X-rated environment in which we live, you need to create your own "department of homeland security."

Adrian Rogers
Family Survival in an X-rated World (2005)

2 Porn can raise its ugly head almost anywhere. You don't have to go looking for it. It will find you.

Adrian Rogers
Family Survival in an X-rated World (2005)

3 Like a spider's web is the sticky trap of pornography.

Adrian Rogers
Family Survival in an X-rated World (2005)

4 Pornography is the ultimate dehumanizing of sex. It is sex wholly and purposefully void of love.

Adrian Rogers
Family Survival in an X-rated World (2005)

315 POSSESSIONS (*see also* MATERIAL THINGS; TREASURE)
And he said unto them, Take heed, and beware of covetousness: for a man's life consisteth not in the abundance of the things which he possesseth.
LUKE 12:15

1 Whenever we have something and we offer it to God—God can do something dramatic with it.
Rich Mendola
"The Acts of the Holy Spirit: Wonders and Good News" sermon (2009)

2 You don't own anything. God gives you the privilege of living in this world for a little while and enjoying its benefits.
Bob and Rusty Russell
Jesus: Lord of Your Personality (2002)

3 To comfort a sorrowful conscience is much better than to possess many kingdoms; yet the world regards it not; nay, condemns it, calling us rebels, disturbers of the peace.
Martin Luther
Table Talk (16th century)

4 Turn loose what you are striving to hold on to and claim Jesus as your portion in this life. Your relationship with Him is your only possession that no one can take from you.
Rubye Goodlett
Gathered Fragments (1986)

316 POVERTY
Ye have the poor with you always, and whensoever ye will ye may do them good.
MARK 14:7

1 We patronize the poor when we give them advice. But Jesus is news, not advice.
Ray Bakke
A Theology as Big as the City (1997)

317 POWER
(*see also* ABILITY; STRENGTH)
But ye shall receive power, after that the Holy Ghost is come upon you.
ACTS 1:8

1 The same power that raised Jesus from the dead is available to lift you up out of your private pit.
Bruce Wilkinson
Beyond Jabez (2005)

318 PRAISE (*see also* WORSHIP)
Praise ye the LORD.
Praise the LORD, O my soul.
PSALM 146:1

1 If you want to praise the Lord Jesus Christ, tell the people about him. Take of the things of Christ, and show them to the people, and you will glorify Christ.
Charles Spurgeon
"Honey in the Mouth!" sermon (1891)

2 One way to drive Satan to distraction, and to overcome him, is through praise of Jesus.
Anne Graham Lotz
Just Give Me Jesus (2002)

3 I must never lose that sense of wonder and awe when I come into the presence of God. He is worthy of my praise, and it is the very act of praising him that changes my perspective and enables me to pray with power.
Marlene Bagnull
Write His Answer (1990)

4 Christ is praised by being prized. He is magnified as a glorious treasure when He becomes our unrivaled pleasure.
John Piper
The Dangerous Duty of Delight (2001)

5 The heartfelt praises of one true believer are more precious to God than all the 220,000 oxen and the 120,000 sheep that Solomon offered to God at the dedication of the temple.
Jonathan Edwards
"Christians, a Royal Priesthood" sermon (1744)

6 God is most beautifully praised when His people hear His Word, love His Word, and obey His Word.
Albert Mohler Jr.
He Is Not Silent (2008)

7 Praise is like a shot of adrenaline that energizes a person. If you want to bring out the best in your mate, give the gift of praise.
Gary Smalley
Making Love Last Forever (1997)

8 Desire not to live but to praise his name; let all your thoughts, words, and works tend to his glory.
John Wesley
A Plain Account of Christian Perfection (18th century)

9 Praise will come, and the Christian, as he is praised, trembles at the thought of God's all-discerning vision.
George Edward Jelf
The Secret Trials of the Christian Life (19th century)

10 For our praise to reach the perfection God wants for us, it needs to be free of any thoughts of reward. Praise is not another way of bargaining with the Lord.
Merlin Carothers
Prison to Praise (1970)

11 Praise is a contradiction of pride. Pride says "look at me," but praise longs for people to see Jesus.
Matt Redman
The Unquenchable Worshipper (2001)

12 Sometimes praise is repetitively desperate, but it is often in these repetitive cries that purer praise is found.
David Crowder
Praise Habit (2004)

13 It is my belief that we were made to praise and that the original intentions for it might have been bigger and sweeter than most of us have dreamed or that a scheduled moment could properly contain.
David Crowder
Praise Habit (2004)

319 PRAYER (*see also* INTERCESSION)

Therefore I say unto you, What things soever ye desire, when ye pray, believe that ye receive them, and ye shall have them.
MARK 11:24

General

1 The purpose of prayer is to get God's will done.
Samuel Gordon
Quiet Talks on Prayer (1904)

2 I must pour out my heart in the language which his Spirit gives me; and more than that, I must trust in the Spirit to speak the unutterable groanings of my spirit, when my lips cannot actually express all the emotions of my heart.
Charles Spurgeon
"The Fatherhood of God" sermon (1858)

3 Every day you have another opportunity to affect your future with the words you speak to God.
Stormie Omartian
Just Enough Light for the Step I'm On (1999)

4 Sometimes a person prays with his tears, even when words are missing.
Bill Gothard
The Power of Crying Out (2002)

5 Daily prayer for daily needs.
E. M. Bounds
The Necessity of Prayer (19th century)

6 Faith thrives in an atmosphere of prayer.
E. M. Bounds
The Necessity of Prayer (19th century)

7 Faith starts prayer to work—clears the way to the mercy seat.
E. M. Bounds
The Necessity of Prayer (19th century)

8 He prays not at all, who does not press his plea.

E. M. Bounds
The Necessity of Prayer (19th century)

9 Humility is an indispensable requisite of true prayer.

E. M. Bounds
The Essentials of Prayer (19th century)

10 Humility must be in the praying character as light is in the sun.

E. M. Bounds
The Essentials of Prayer (19th century)

11 Kneeling well becomes us as the attitude of prayer, because it betokens humility.

E. M. Bounds
The Essentials of Prayer (19th century)

12 What a nobility would come into life if secret prayer were not only an asking for some new sense of comfort, or light, or strength, but the giving way of life just for one day into the sure and safe keeping of a mighty and faithful God.

Andrew Murray
The Prayer Life (1912)

13 Every day is a good day if you pray.

Norman Vincent Peale
The Power of Positive Thinking (1952)

14 When we feel least like praying is the time when we most need to pray.

R. A. Torrey
How to Pray (1900)

15 The prayer that is born of meditation upon the Word of God is the prayer that soars upward most easily to God's listening ear.

R. A. Torrey
How to Pray (1900)

16 There is no question God will duck, no battle He can't win, no topic He doesn't know. You can't make Him uncomfortable. You can't push Him too hard. So go ahead, hit Him with your best shot.

Karon Phillips Goodman
You're Late Again, Lord! (2002)

17 Unless the common course of our lives be according to the common spirit of our prayers, our prayers are so far from being real or sufficient degree of devotion that they become an empty lip-labour, or, what is worse, a notorious hypocrisy.

William Law
A Serious Call to a Devout and Holy Life (1729)

18 Life is short—pray hard.

Bumper Sticker

19 Let not the understanding, but the whole heart set upon the living God as the teacher, be the chief thing, when thou enterest thy closet. Then shalt thou find good understanding. God will give thee an understanding heart, a spiritual understanding.

Andrew Murray
Prayer's Inner Chamber (1912)

20 The more that prayer becomes the untrammeled, free and natural expression of the desires of our hearts, the more real it becomes.

O. Hallesby
Prayer (1931)

21 My prayers, my God, flow from what I am not; I think thy answers make me what I am.

George MacDonald
Diary of an Old Soul (1880)

22 Look deep, yet deeper, in my heart, and there,
Beyond where I can feel, read thou the prayer.

George MacDonald
Diary of an Old Soul (1880)

23 Where I am most perplexed, it may be there
Thou mak'st a secret chamber, holy-dim,
Where thou wilt come to help my deepest prayer.
George MacDonald
Diary of an Old Soul (1880)

24 The benefits of prayer come not from praying but from living what we discover in prayer.
Matthew Kelly
A Call to Joy (1997)

25 Remember, the shortest distance between a problem and the solution is the distance between our knees and the floor.
Charles Stanley
Handle with Prayer (1987)

26 Prayer allows a place for me to bring my doubts and complaints and subject them to the blinding light of reality I cannot comprehend but can haltingly learn to trust.
Philip Yancey
Prayer: Does It Make Any Difference? (2006)

27 Most of us talk too much when we pray, which is really kind of silly when you think about it. If prayer is a conversation with God, how can we hear what He has to say if we're talking all the time?
Bob Buford
Game Plan (1997)

28 For a long while I was a mistress of the art of praying for God to change difficult circumstances. It took years before I learned how to pray for God to change me in the midst of the difficult circumstances.
Karen Burton Mains
The God Hunt (2003)

29 God has given us the gift of prayer. It was never meant to be a burden, but rather, a source of unlimited blessing for us and for those around us.
Ray Pritchard
The God You Can Trust (2003)

30 When we can't pray, when the words won't come, when we don't know what to pray for, we have the Spirit within us, who prays for us. What an honor, what a privilege, what a gift. And what a God, who would make such provision for us!
Ray Pritchard
The God You Can Trust (2003)

31 Prayer is so universal and so natural that its place in our lives needs no defense. We all pray, and we pray because it is a part of our nature.
Robert and Debra Bruce
Reclaiming Intimacy (1996)

32 Prayer enhances unity, transforms attitudes, encourages mutual concern, builds trust, and moves God.
Glenn Daman
Shepherding the Small Church (2002)

33 When people love one another, they pray for one another, and when they pray for one another they learn to love one another more deeply.
Glenn Daman
Shepherding the Small Church (2002)

34 What we want is to press our case right up to the throne of God.
D. L. Moody
Prevailing Prayer: What Hinders It? (1884)

35 All true prayer must be offered in full submission to God.
D. L. Moody
Prevailing Prayer: What Hinders It? (1884)

36 To pray and not act is not only deception but also plain laziness.
Scott Hinkle
Recapturing the Primary Purpose (2005)

37 When we practice a rule of prayer, prayer gradually becomes a holy habit, something we do that is not dependent on feelings or moods or our ability to articulate well. It becomes central to our lives and strengthens our connections to God.

Valerie Hess and Marti Watson Garlett
Habits of a Child's Heart (2004)

38 If we are unwilling to change, we will abandon prayer as a noticeable characteristic of our lives.

Richard Foster
Celebration of Discipline (1978)

39 Fretting magnifies the problem, but prayer magnifies God.

Joanna Weaver
Having a Mary Heart in a Martha World (2000)

40 Prayer never evaporates.

Elisabeth Elliot
The Music of His Promises (2000)

41 Sometimes we need to pray about what to pray about.

Virginia Ann Froehle
Loving Yourself More (1993)

42 Prayer is not trying to manipulate God into doing our will.

Steve Campbell
"Foundations for Answered Prayer" sermon (2009)

43 Not that you should imagine that the purpose of your prayer is to tell the Lord what you want; for he knows well enough what you need. Rather, the purpose of prayer is to make you ready and able to receive as a clean vessel the grace that our Lord would freely give to you.

Walter Hilton
Toward a Perfect Love (1985)

44 Every day as we have prayed, "Thy kingdom come," has our Christian consciousness taken in the tremendous sweep of that prayer and seen how it covers the length and breadth of this great world and every interest of human life?

Henry Drummond
A Life for a Life and Other Addresses (1893)

45 When we pray more we can talk less.

A. W. Tozer
"In Everything by Prayer" sermon (20th century)

46 Ask God to open your heart and kindle in it a spark of his love, and then you will begin to understand what praying means.

Jean-Nicholas Grou
How to Pray (18th century)

47 Why do we pray so much with our lips and so little with our heart?

Jean-Nicholas Grou
How to Pray (18th century)

as Dependence on God

48 True prayer is a spontaneous outpouring of honesty and need from the soul's foundation. In calm times, we say a prayer. In desperate times, we truly pray.

David Jeremiah
A Bend in the Road (2000)

49 True prayers are born of present trials and present needs.

E. M. Bounds
The Necessity of Prayer (19th century)

50 Prayer shows our dependence on God. It honors Him as the source of all blessing, and it reminds us that converting individuals and growing churches are His works, not ours.

Mark Dever and Paul Alexander
The Deliberate Church (2005)

51 Prayer is a declaration of our dependence on God. It isn't something mechanical you do; it is somewhere you go to meet Someone you know.
Jill Briscoe
The New Normal (2005)

52 The very thing that most qualifies us to pray is our helplessness.
David Jeremiah
The Prayer Matrix (2004)

53 Instead of life support, I was on "prayer support"!
Simi Mary Chacko personal testimony (2009)

54 Make no decision without prayer.
Elizabeth George
A Woman after God's Own Heart (1997)

55 Helplessness united with faith produces prayer.
O. Hallesby
Prayer (1931)

56 When all other courses of action have been eliminated, when we stand on the edge of the abyss, when we approach God with empty hands and an aching heart, then we draw close to the true heart of prayer.
Jerry Sittser
When God Doesn't Answer Your Prayer (2003)

57 The prayer of a Christian is not an attempt to force God's hand, but a humble acknowledgment of helplessness and dependence.
J. I. Packer
Evangelism and the Sovereignty of God (2008)

58 Prayers are needed. They are the winged messengers to carry the need to God.
John Wright Follette
Broken Bread (1957)

as Communion with God

59 God knows what's in our hearts. We might as well get right to the point.
Bruce Bickel and Stan Jantz
God Is in the Small Stuff (1998)

60 In prayer man rises to heaven to dwell with God: in the Word God comes to dwell with man. In prayer man gives himself to God: in the Word God gives himself to man.
Andrew Murray
The Prayer Life (1912)

61 The least little remembrance will always be acceptable to Him. You need not cry very loud.
Brother Lawrence
The Practice of the Presence of God (17th century)

62 Prayer provides nourishment for your soul, satiates that "inner" spiritual hunger, and helps you develop your relationship with a loving Father who can heal distraught relationships.
Robert and Debra Bruce
Reclaiming Intimacy (1996)

63 Most of us don't pray on a regular basis because we're aware it will cost us something. . . . Honesty.
Jack Hayford
Prayer Is Invading the Impossible (2002)

64 Prayer is not to get the goods. It is to enjoy the One who is good.
Jon Courson
Application Commentary (2003)

65 The great gift of God in prayer is Himself.
Maxie Dunnam
The Workbook of Intercessory Prayer (1979)

66 Those that think three meals a day little enough for the body ought much more to

think three solemn prayers a day little enough for the soul, and to count it a pleasure, not a task.

Matthew Henry
Commentary on the Whole Bible (1706)

67 To pray is to let Jesus into our lives.
O. Hallesby
Prayer (1931)

68 It is through prayer that we become friends with Christ.
Matthew Kelly
A Call to Joy (1997)

69 The purpose of prayer is not primarily to move the hand of God but rather to hold the hand of God.
Jon Courson
Application Commentary (2006)

70 Thy praying voice is music in God's ears.
Matthew Henry
Commentary on the Whole Bible (1706)

71 I challenge you to shift the focus of your prayer. Don't spend a lot of time describing your mountain to the Lord. He knows what it is. Instead, focus your attention on the mountain mover—his glory, power and faithfulness.
Bill Hybels
Too Busy Not to Pray (1988)

72 Prayer is our being in a constant state of understanding that we are in his presence, talking with him as we would a friend—a father—and being ever intent on hearing his voice as he speaks to us.
Eva Marie Everson
Oasis (2007)

73 The call to unceasing prayer is not an invitation to divided consciousness; it does not imply that we pay any less attention to daily

realities or retreat from life's responsibilities. ... [It] means being consciously constantly conscious of the presence of God amidst the changing complexion of everyday life.
Debra Farrington
A Beginner's Guide to Unceasing Prayer (2002)

74 So many times we try to please God by the length of time we pray. Legislating prayer time becomes as unnatural as legislating conversations or hugs or kisses.
Steve Sampson
You Can Hear the Voice of God (1993)

75 Some people think God does not like to be troubled with our constant coming and asking. The only way to trouble God is not to come at all.
D. L. Moody
Prevailing Prayer: What Hinders It? (1884)

76 When we pray it is far more important to pray with a sense of the greatness of God than with a sense of the greatness of the problem.
Gordon S. Jackson
Destination Unknown (2004)

77 When the appointed times of prayer were past, he found no difference, because he still continued with God, praising and blessing Him with all his might, so that he passed his life in continual joy.
Brother Lawrence
The Practice of the Presence of God (17th century)

78 A little lifting up the heart suffices; a little remembrance of God, one act of inward worship, though upon a march, and sword in hand, are prayers which however short, are nevertheless very acceptable to God.
Brother Lawrence
The Practice of the Presence of God (17th century)

79 His prayer was nothing else but a sense of the presence of God.

> Brother Lawrence
> *The Practice of the Presence of God*
> (17th century)

80 Prayer is related to our inborn hunger for God. And prayer is not for God's benefit, but for ours.

> Robert and Debra Bruce
> *Reclaiming Intimacy* (1996)

81 The heart has been poured out, and now lifted upon the wings of prayer the message is wafted up and away through the silent reaches of space to the Father's throne.

> John Wright Follette
> *Broken Bread* (1957)

82 Why do we not lay open our heart to God and beg him to put into it whatever is most pleasing to him?

> Jean-Nicholas Grou
> *How to Pray* (18th century)

83 The determined fixing of our will upon God, and pressing toward him steadily and without deflection; this is the very center and the art of prayer.

> Evelyn Underhill
> *The Essentials of Mysticism* (1960)

84 Prayer, then, begins by an intellectual adjustment. By thinking of God earnestly and humbly to the exclusion of other objects of thought, by deliberately surrendering the mind to spiritual things, by preparing the consciousness for the inflow of new life.

> Evelyn Underhill
> *The Essentials of Mysticism* (1960)

85 An open life, an open hand, open upward, is the pipe line of communication between the heart of God and this poor befooled old world.

> Samuel Gordon
> *Quiet Talks on Prayer* (1904)

86 The essence of prayer is simply talking to God as you would to a beloved friend—without pretense or flippancy.

> John MacArthur
> *Alone with God* (1995)

87 I think of praying at all times as living in continual God-consciousness, where everything we see and experience becomes a kind of prayer, lived in deep awareness of and surrender to our Heavenly Father.

> John MacArthur
> *Alone with God* (1995)

Power of

88 Prayer and faith are sacred picklocks that can open secrets, and obtain great treasures.

> Charles Spurgeon
> "The Holy Ghost—The Great Teacher" sermon (1855)

89 Prayer is the never-failing resort of the Christian in any case and in every plight.

> Charles Spurgeon
> "The Believer Sinking in the Mire" sermon (1865)

90 Prayer isn't getting your way in heaven; it's getting God's way on earth.

> Greg Laurie
> *Wrestling with God* (2003)

91 If we are to pray with power we must pray with faith.

> R. A. Torrey
> *How to Pray* (1900)

92 More can be accomplished in prayer in the first hours of the day than at any other time during the day.

> R. A. Torrey
> *How to Pray* (1900)

93 Nights of prayer to God are followed by days of power with men.
R. A. Torrey
How to Pray (1900)

94 God will use our simple prayers because of the authority behind them.
Rich Mendola
"The Acts of the Holy Spirit: Wonders and Good News" sermon (2009)

95 Prayer should be the means by which I, at all times, receive all that I need, and, for this reason, be my daily refuge, my daily consolation, my daily joy, my source of rich and inexhaustible joy in life.
O. Hallesby
Prayer (1931)

96 Someone has said that when we work, we work; but when we pray, God works. His supernatural strength is available to praying people who are convinced to the core of their beings that he can make a difference.
Bill Hybels
Too Busy Not to Pray (1988)

97 Scripture insists that God has hard-wired the universe in such a way that He works primarily through prayer.
David Jeremiah
The Prayer Matrix (2004)

98 Prayer is the greatest power God has put into our hands for service—praying is harder work than doing, at least I find it so.
Mary Slessor
Mary Slessor of Calabar (1917)

99 Unless I had the spirit of prayer I could do nothing. If even for a day or an hour I lost the spirit of grace and supplication, I found myself unable to preach with power and efficiency, or to win souls by personal conversation.
Charles Finney
Memoirs of Rev. Charles G. Finney (1876)

100 The devil smiles when we are up to our ears in work, but he trembles when we pray.
Corrie ten Boom
Not Good If Detached (1957)

101 The devil often laughs when we work, but he trembles when we pray.
Corrie ten Boom
Amazing Love (1953)

102 By praying more, we will not work any less, and we will accomplish vastly more.
R. A. Torrey
How to Bring Men to Christ (1893)

103 In your hour of desperation, where do you turn? Do you tell your troubles to anyone who will listen, or do you seek the throne of grace?
Michael Youssef
"A Prayer of Brokenness" article (2009)

104 Prayer brings momentum. It lifts the heart above the challenges of life and gives it a view of God's resources of victory and hope.
John Mason
The Impossible Is Possible (2003)

105 Prayer may not change all things for you, but it sure changes you for all things.
John Mason
The Impossible Is Possible (2003)

106 More is accomplished by prayer than by anything else this world knows.
Ted Engstrom
Motivation to Last a Lifetime (1984)

107 Prayer is the preacher's mightiest weapon.
E. M. Bounds
Power Through Prayer (1906)

108 In Everything by Prayer: An Unfailing Technique for Spiritual Success.
A. W. Tozer sermon title
(20th century)

109   For Christians prayer is like breathing. You don't have to think to breathe because the atmosphere exerts pressure on your lungs and forces you to breathe. That's why it is more difficult to hold your breath than it is to breathe. Similarly, when you're born into the family of God, you enter into a spiritual atmosphere wherein God's presence and grace exert pressure, or influence, on your life. Prayer is the normal response to that pressure.
　　John MacArthur
　　Alone with God (1995)

Answered/Unanswered Prayer

110   Tho' dark the way, still trust and pray, The answering time will come.
　　Mary Wingate
　　"The Answering Time Will Come" (1908)

111   God loves to hear and answer prayers. More often than not, He is the God of "Yes."
　　Dave Earley
　　The 21 Most Effective Prayers of the Bible (2005)

112   Be sure to remember that nothing in your daily life is so insignificant and so inconsequential that the Lord will not help you by answering your prayer.
　　O. Hallesby
　　Prayer (1931)

113   You thought God was to hear and answer you by making everything straight and pleasant—not so are nations or churches or men and women born; not so is character made. God is answering your prayer in His way.
　　Mary Slessor
　　Mary Slessor of Calabar (1917)

114   If we knock, God has promised to open the door and grant our request. It may be years before the answer comes; He may keep us knocking; but He has promised that the answer will come.
　　D. L. Moody
　　Prevailing Prayer: What Hinders It? (1884)

115   I ask Him daily and often momently to give me wisdom, understanding and bodily strength to do His will, hence I am asking and receiving all the time.
　　George Washington Carver
　　George Washington Carver in His Own Words (1941)

116   We need to ask God to take this fragile, selfish, flawed self of ours and make it more like him. God will answer that prayer.
　　Jerry Sittser
　　When God Doesn't Answer Your Prayer (2003)

117   I know what it is to pray long years and never get the answer—I had to pray for my father. But I know my heavenly Father so well I can leave it with Him for the lower fatherhood.
　　Mary Slessor
　　Mary Slessor of Calabar (1917)

118   Unanswered prayer never becomes a significant issue until we really need an answer to prayer, until our life depends on an answer. Then we cry out to God out of a deep sense of need. We pray out of desperation.
　　Jerry Sittser
　　When God Doesn't Answer Your Prayers (2003)

119   God detests the prayers of a man who has no delight in His Word. When we live with a closed Bible, we live with a closed heaven; God will not answer our prayers.
　　Charles Stanley
　　Handle with Prayer (1987)

120 No matter how intense or fervent or long your prayers may be, if you have unconfessed sin in your life, your prayers are really going nowhere.
Greg Laurie
Wrestling with God (2003)

121 The reason why we don't pray more—and probably don't see more answers to prayer—is not because we don't know how to pray but because we don't really need to pray. We are not desperate enough.
Jerry Sittser
When God Doesn't Answer Your Prayer (2003)

122 We are to ask with a beggar's humility, to seek with a servant's carefulness, and to knock with the confidence of a friend.
D. L. Moody
Prevailing Prayer: What Hinders It? (1884)

123 Be specific with God in prayer and he will be specific with you in regard to the answer.
David Wilkerson
Prayer—The Long and Short of It! (2009)

124 We must have a warrant for our prayers. If we have some great desire, we must search the Scriptures to find if it be right to ask it.
D. L. Moody
Prevailing Prayer: What Hinders It? (1884)

125 We cannot be too frequent in our requests; God will not weary of His children's prayers.
D. L. Moody
Prevailing Prayer: What Hinders It? (1884)

126 My life is one long daily, hourly, record of answered prayer.
Mary Slessor
Mary Slessor of Calabar (1917)

PREACHERS (*see* CLERGY)

320 PREACHING

For the preaching of the cross is to them that perish foolishness; but unto us which are saved it is the power of God.
1 CORINTHIANS 1:18

1 God does amazing things when His truth is proclaimed.
Colin Smith
Unlocking the Bible Story (2002)

2 If the truth cannot be fearlessly proclaimed in the church, what place is there for truth at all? How can we build a generation of discerning Christians if we are terror-struck at the thought that non-Christians might not like hearing the unvarnished truth?
John MacArthur
The Truth War (2007)

3 I look upon all the world as my parish; thus far I mean, that, in whatever part of it I am, I judge it meet, right, and my bounden duty to declare unto all that are willing to hear, the glad tidings of salvation.
John Wesley
The Journal of John Wesley (18th century)

4 But this holy function of preaching the Word is, by Satan, fiercely resisted; he would willingly have it utterly suppressed, for thereby his kingdom is destroyed.
Martin Luther
Table Talk (16th century)

5 When warm and fuzzy moral messages, peppered with cute anecdotes and an occasional skit, replace the meat of God's Word, the consequences are devastating.
John MacArthur
Fool's Gold? (2005)

357

6   Predictably, in a church where the preaching of Scripture is neglected, it becomes impossible to get people to submit to the authority of Scripture.
   John MacArthur
   Fool's Gold? (2005)

7   The sermon cannot rise in its life-giving forces above the man. Dead men give out dead sermons and dead sermons kill. Everything depends on the spiritual character of the preacher.
   E. M. Bounds
   Power Through Prayer (1906)

8   It will do no good to preach to you while your hearts are in this hardened, and waste, and fallow state. The farmer might just as well sow his grain on the rock. It will bring forth no fruit.
   Charles Finney
   Lectures of Revivals of Religion (1835)

9   Behind the concept and the act of preaching there lies a doctrine of God, a conviction about his being, his action, and his purpose. The kind of God we believe in determines the kind of sermons we preach.
   John Stott
   Between Two Worlds: The Challenge of Preaching Today (1982)

10   The truth is, the God of modern preaching, though He may perhaps be very good, is rather uninteresting.
   J. Gresham Machen
   Christianity and Liberalism (1923)

PREJUDICE (*see* BIGOTRY)

321 PRESENCE OF GOD
(*see also* INTIMACY WITH GOD; KNOWING GOD)

Let us therefore come boldly unto the throne of grace, that we may obtain mercy, and find grace to help in time of need.
HEBREWS 4:16

1   No creature of his [God's] can creep away out of his sight, and live in a realm in which He has nothing to do.
   Phillips Brooks
   Visions and Tasks and Other Sermons (1886)

2   What an unspeakable honor to come boldly into the presence of the Creator of the universe!
   Dennis and Barbara Rainey
   Two Hearts Praying As One (2002)

3   Living in the constant awareness of God's presence brings peace, security, and guidance throughout life.
   Thomas Blackaby
   Encounters with God Daily Bible (2008)

4   As soon as the soul by faith places itself in the presence of God, and becomes recollected before Him, let it remain thus for a little time in respectful silence.
   François Fénelon and Jeanne Guyon
   Spiritual Progress (17th century)

5   We will never have pure hearts unless we do whatever it takes to consistently get ourselves into the presence of God.
   Angela Thomas
   A Beautiful Offering (2004)

6   One of the greatest tragedies among God's people is that, although they deeply long to experience God, they are encountering Him day after day but do not recognize Him.
   Henry Blackaby
   Experiencing God (2007)

7   When God does His mighty work in the midst of His people in a particular place, it's overwhelming to those who are there to experience Him. Though it often brings much hard work for them, His presence makes everything worthwhile.
   Henry Blackaby
   What the Spirit Is Saying to the Churches (2003)

8   The Spirit of God puts the people of God into the presence of God. And in His presence, the Spirit reveals God's purposes to the church He would use. He then waits for our response.
  Henry Blackaby
  What the Spirit Is Saying to the Churches (2003)

9   He is calling you into His presence so that your life can become a dance for joy.
  Matthew Kelly
  A Call to Joy (1997)

10   The desire to be with God, to know him, and to draw from him is among our most primal. Yet, we do more than desire him. We need him. Just as we cannot live without water, we cannot live without God's presence.
  Eva Marie Everson
  Oasis (2007)

11   I am as sure as I live that nothing is so near to me as God. God is nearer to me than I am to myself.
  Meister Eckhart
  Meister Eckhart's Sermons (14th century)

12   He is always near you and with you; leave Him not alone.
  Brother Lawrence
  The Practice of the Presence of God (17th century)

13   Let us fear to leave Him. Let us be always with Him. Let us live and die in His presence.
  Brother Lawrence
  The Practice of the Presence of God (17th century)

14   Wherever we are, we have the same opportunity for closeness to God. His joy is over all His creation.
  Don Osgood
  Listening for God's Silent Language (1995)

15   When God tells you He will be with you, that means no matter what the circumstances are like, everything will work out all right.
  Joyce Meyer
  Do It Afraid! (1996)

16   The presence of God puts life in perspective.
  Matt Redman
  Facedown (2004)

17   The defining attribute, the identity of God, is "present rescuer." His name holds for us the very promise of presence.
  David Crowder
  Praise Habit (2004)

18   Deep within every mortal heart lies a created hunger for the heavenly mountains of God's presence.
  Michael Phillips
  A God to Call Father (1994)

19   Only the Lord's presence can truly calm our fears. Only Christ can say to our hearts, "Peace, be still."
  Zig Ziglar
  Confessions of a Grieving Christian (1998)

322 PRESENT, THE
(*see also* TIME; TODAY)
*To day if ye will hear his voice,
harden not your hearts.*
HEBREWS 4:7

1   Abandonment is being satisfied with the present moment, no matter what that moment contains. You are satisfied because you know that whatever that moment has, it contains— in that instant—God's eternal plan for you.
  Jeanne Guyon
  Experiencing the Depths of Jesus Christ (1685)

2 The time present, no doubt, is not a time of ease. It is a time of watching and praying, fighting and struggling, believing and working. But it is only for a few years.
J. C. Ryle
Holiness: Its Nature, Hindrances, Difficulties, and Roots (19th century)

323 PRIDE (*see also* SELF-ESTEEM)
Pride goeth before destruction, and an haughty spirit before a fall.
PROVERBS 16:18

1 All man's troubles emanate from his pride.
D. Martyn Lloyd-Jones
The Cross (1986)

2 A man who has not faith proves that he cannot stoop; for he has not faith for this reason, because he is too proud to believe. He declares he will not yield his intellect, he will not become a child and believe meekly what God tells him to believe.
Charles Spurgeon
"Faith" sermon (1856)

3 Pride gets no pleasure out of having something, only out of having more of it than the next man.
C. S. Lewis
Mere Christianity (1952)

4 Throughout our time on this earth, and in every arena of our lives, you and I share a common greatest enemy: pride.
C. J. Mahaney
Humility: True Greatness (2005)

5 Why does God hate pride so passionately? Here's why: Pride is when sinful human beings aspire to the status and position of God and refuse to acknowledge their dependence on Him.
C. J. Mahaney
Humility: True Greatness (2005)

6 At its root, pride is simply independence from God.
David Wilkerson
Revival on Broadway! (1996)

7 Pride is not the opposite of low self-esteem. Pride is the opposite of humility.
Beth Moore
Praying God's Word (2000)

8 The greatest of all disorders is to think we are whole and need no help.
Thomas Wilson
Private Thoughts (1828)

9 When you're full of yourself, God can't fill you. But when you empty yourself, God has a useful vessel.
Max Lucado
Cure for the Common Life (2005)

10 Pride and self-conceit are sins that beset great men. They are apt to take that glory to themselves which is due to God only.
Matthew Henry
Commentary on the Whole Bible (1706)

11 We should take heed of pride; it is a sin that turned angels into devils.
Matthew Henry
Commentary on the Whole Bible (1706)

12 It is of great importance to guard against vexation on account of our faults; it springs from a secret root of pride, and a love of our own excellence; we are hurt at feeling what we are.
François Fénelon and Jeanne Guyon
Spiritual Progress (17th century)

13 Where pride hath possessed itself thoroughly of the soul, it turns the heart into steel, yea, into a rock.
Thomas Brooks
The Unsearchable Riches of Christ (1655)

14 A proud heart resists, and is resisted.
Thomas Brooks
The Unsearchable Riches of Christ (1655)

15 At the deepest level, pride is the choice to exclude both God and other people from their rightful place in our hearts. Jesus said the essence of the spiritual life is to love God and to love people. Pride destroys our capacity to love.
John Ortberg
The Life You've Always Wanted (2002)

16 Nebuchadnezzar's pride invited God's judgment.
Grant Jeffrey
Countdown to Apocalypse (2008)

17 Pride is: Having a stronger desire to do my will than God's.
Neil Anderson and Charles Mylander
Blessed Are the Peacemakers (2002)

18 We can't fight the battle effectively if we don't first deal with our blind spots. Casualties run high when we don't see the enemy coming. We can't expect our churches to grow, our pastors to thrive, our teens to serve the Lord, and our marriages to triumph if we don't ask our brothers and sisters to help us overcome our blind areas.
Bill McCartney
Blind Spots (2003)

19 When God wants to get you further than your road is taking you, he will mostly use people who don't have a ghost of a clue about what is getting ready to happen, because if they did, they'd let their pride destroy what God had in mind. Ego kills the spontaneity of God's grace.
Robert Stofel
God, Are We There Yet? (2004)

20 What is pride? Pride is rooted in self-dependency and self-focus. Pride can be strutting our stuff: "I don't need God. I can do this on my own." Or pride can be disguised as humility: "I'm nothing. I'm nobody. God could never use me." Both of these extremes share a common feature: the focus is on us. God hates it.
Chip Ingram
Holy Ambition (2002)

21 There is only one center of the universe worthy of all our attention, and that center is God. If we make anything other than God the center of the universe, we are engaging in what the Bible calls pride and arrogance. This attitude is neither a minor glitch nor something God merely dislikes. It is not something He overlooks. He loathes pride.
Chip Ingram
Holy Ambition (2002)

22 We can combat pride when we pray that God will never let us become more impressed with the ministry than with Him.
Dutch Sheets
Watchman Prayer (2000)

23 Pride resisteth God, it rejecteth him, it turneth from him, and chooseth to worship and adore something else instead of him; whereas humility leaveth all for God, falls down before him, and opens all the doors of the heart for his entrance into it.
William Law
The Spirit of Prayer (1750)

24 Pride, self-exaltation, hatred, and persecution, under a cloak of religious zeal, will sanctify actions which nature, left to itself, would be ashamed to own.
William Law
The Spirit of Prayer (1750)

PRIDE

25 Be any thing, as to outward profession, so you are lowly in heart; so you resist and conquer every motion of pride, and have that mind in you which was also in Christ Jesus.
John Wesley
The Works of the Rev. John Wesley
(18th century)

26 The knowledge of God, even as it is revealed to us below, is so glorious and so elevating, that we are soon inclined to despise those who, as we think, have it not.
George Edward Jelf
The Secret Trials of the Christian Life
(19th century)

27 How prone we are, as having been endued with power celestial, to act as if we were saying to our graceless neighbour, "Stand by thyself, I am holier than thou."
George Edward Jelf
The Secret Trials of the Christian Life
(19th century)

28 It is so difficult for us, even when we wish to give God the glory, to keep from that comparison of ourselves with others, which S. Paul tells us is " not wise."
George Edward Jelf
The Secret Trials of the Christian Life
(19th century)

29 You can always tell when a man is a great way from God—he is always talking about himself, and how good he is.
D. L. Moody
Best Thoughts and Discourses of D. L. Moody
(1876)

30 If we insist on doing it our way, God will stand back and watch us mess up.
Steve Campbell
"What to Say When You Shouldn't Say Anything" sermon (2009)

31 It should be obvious that the very idea of a self-existent, self-sufficient, totally unique God does not appeal to people who would use the same words to describe themselves!
Stuart Briscoe
What Works When Life Doesn't (2004)

32 The moment we feel we can succeed and attain victory over sin by the strength of our will alone is the moment we are worshiping the will.
Richard Foster
Celebration of Discipline (1978)

33 It's easy to forget who is the servant and who is to be served.
Max Lucado
He Still Moves Stones (1993)

34 Wherever pride is, there the devil is riding in his first fiery chariot.
William Law
An Humble, Affectionate, and Earnest Address (1761)

35 We are always talking about the sin of intemperate drinking, because it is quite obvious that the poor have it more than the rich. But we are always denying that there is any such thing as the sin of pride, because it would be quite obvious that the rich have it more than the poor.
G. K. Chesterton
Heretics (1905)

36 Man will cling to the last rag of his self-respect. He does not part with that when he thrills, admires, sympathizes; but he does when he has to give up his whole self in the obedience of faith.
Peter Taylor Forsyth
The Work of Christ (1909)

37 Be on your constant guard against the least confidence and trust in yourselves.
Samuel Hopkins
"God Working in Men to Will and to Do" sermon (1803)

362

38 If men want to praise us and not God in us, we are not to endure it, but with all our powers forbid it and flee from it as from the most grievous sin and robbery of divine honor.
Martin Luther
A Treatise on Good Works (1520)

39 So long as we do not look beyond the earth, we are quite pleased with our own righteousness, wisdom, and virtue; we address ourselves in the most flattering terms, and seem only less than demigods.
John Calvin
Institutes of the Christian Religion (16th century)

40 Outside of God's light men can be arrogant and haughty; but under the revelation of the light they can only prostrate themselves before Him.
Watchman Nee
The Release of the Spirit (1965)

41 Unteachable people are shaped by their overconfidence.
Jeffery Miller
The Hazards of Being a Man (2007)

42 Loss of position is like a small death.
Jerry White
Dangers Men Face (1997)

43 It's our gratitude for what Christ did for us that strips us of anything as utterly insubstantial and inconsequential as our dinky personal pride.
Stephen Arterburn and John Shore
Midlife Manual for Men (2008)

44 Each of us has the crippling tendency to forget what God has done for us. For a while, we're humbled. Then if we don't guard our hearts and minds, we begin to think God is so good to us because we have done something right.
Beth Moore
Breaking Free (1999)

45 Entitlement is born in each of our hearts the moment soul satisfaction in God is swallowed by self-satisfaction.
Shelly Beach
The Silent Seduction of Self-Talk (2009)

46 Blinded by the glaucoma of our self-importance, we no longer see the Cross's relevance or significance.
Calvin Miller
Once Upon a Tree (2002)

47 It's from our pride we need, above everything, to be redeemed.
Andrew Murray
Humility (1896)

48 Pride has its root and strength in a terrible spiritual power, outside of us as well as within us.
Andrew Murray
Humility (1896)

324 PRIORITIES

Jesus answered and said unto her, Martha, Martha, thou art careful and troubled about many things: But one thing is needful: and Mary hath chosen that good part, which shall not be taken away from her.
LUKE 10:41–42

1 Somehow fixing your eyes on Jesus causes other things to dim in significance. Possessions, people, reputation, opinions, political rhetoric, world wars, death, disease, heartache—all of these and so much more grow strangely dim when we gaze on Him.
Charles Swindoll
So You Want to Be Like Christ? (2005)

2 Do we love the work God has given us to do at the expense of the Giver of it?
Watchman Nee
Changed into His Likeness (1967)

3   Whatever you're involved in, make sure God is a visible part of that activity.
   Jimmy Houston
   Hooked for Life (1999)

4   Scripture calls us to action and to change the priorities in our lives.
   Paul Brand
   He Satisfies My Soul (2008)

5   Earthly things need to be ignored and despised by those of heavenly descent.
   Jonathan Edwards
   "Christians, a Royal Priesthood" sermon (1744)

6   What is it that chiefly makes you desire to go to heaven when you die?
   Jonathan Edwards
   "God, the Best Portion of Christians" sermon (1744)

7   At the end of our life will we really care about all the hours we worked, all the committees we sat on, or even all the money we accumulated? Or will we wish we had spent more time laughing, talking to loved ones, relaxing, and filling our hearts and souls with life-giving memories? My guess is that we would choose the latter.
   Anne Bryan Smollin
   God Knows You're Stressed (2001)

8   A day is coming upon us all when the value of everything will be altered.
   J. C. Ryle
   Practical Religion (1878)

9   A successful life is lived by one who has the right priorities in his life—being obedient to God's Word—and then putting into action what he knows to be true.
   Bob and Emilie Barnes
   Simple Secrets Couples Should Know (2008)

10 To serve God is to make religion the main business of life.
   Charles Finney
   Lectures to Professing Christians (1837)

11 Do not be an amphibian; no man can serve two masters, and, if you only knew it, it is a thousand times easier to seek first the Kingdom of God than to seek it second.
   Henry Drummond
   Stones Rolled Away and Other Addresses to Young Men (1893)

12 The lifestyle we select reflects our needs and preferences and also how we view the needs of other people in our community.
   Ted Engstrom and Norman Rohrer
   Welcome to the Rest of Your Life (1994)

13 "To me to live is—business"; "to me to live is—pleasure," "to me to live is—myself." We can all tell in a moment what our religion is really worth. "To me to live is"—what? What are we living for? What rises naturally in our heart when we press it with a test like this: "to me to live is"—what?
   Henry Drummond
   "To Me to Live Is Christ" sermon (19th century)

14 The time will come when we shall ask ourselves why we ever crushed this infinite substance of our life within these narrow bounds, and centered that which lasts for ever on what must pass away.
   Henry Drummond
   "To Me to Live Is Christ" sermon (19th century)

15 It is deplorable to see everybody deliberating only about the means, never the end.
   Blaise Pascal
   Pensées (17th century)

16 What we most value, we shall think no pains too great to obtain.
Richard Baxter
The Causes and Danger of Slighting Christ and His Gospel (17th century)

17 When God gets relegated to second place behind any bauble or trinket, I have swapped the pearl of great price for painted fragments of glass.
Brennan Manning
The Rabbi's Heartbeat (2003)

325 PROMISES OF GOD

For all the promises of God in him are yea, and in him Amen, unto the glory of God by us.
2 CORINTHIANS 1:20

1 We love to speak about the sweet promises of God; but if we could ever suppose that one of them could be changed, we would not talk anything more about them.
Charles Spurgeon
"The Immutability of God" sermon (1855)

2 Unclaimed promises are like uncashed checks; they will keep us from bankruptcy, but not from want.
Frances Ridley Havergal
Kept for the Master's Use (1879)

3 For every person who lives with the memory of an earthly father who failed, there is a promise of a heavenly Father who will not—who cannot fail.
Ed Young
From Bad Beginnings to Happy Endings (1994)

4 Sometimes there are no easy answers, but His promises remain true.
Bruce Carroll
Sometimes Miracles Hide (1999)

5 To understand covenant is to hear Him say to you, "You are precious in my sight"—and to believe Him.
Kay Arthur
Our Covenant God (1999)

6 God has not given us hundreds of promises simply for us to read and enjoy. God has given us His promises so we might boldly declare them to bring us victory, health, hope, and abundant life.
Joel Osteen
Your Best Life Now (2004)

PROTECTION (*see* DELIVERANCE)

326 PROVISION

I will abundantly bless her provision: I will satisfy her poor with bread.
PSALM 132:15

1 All of my need He freely supplieth,
Day after day His goodness I prove;
Mercies unfailing, new every morning,
Tell me of God's unchangeable love.
Thomas Chisholm
"He Supplieth All of My Need" hymn (1914)

2 Bread for today is bread enough.
E. M. Bounds
The Necessity of Prayer (19th century)

3 It is true that all God requires of us we lack; but it is also true that all we need He supplies.
Evan Henry Hopkins
Thoughts on Life and Godliness (1883)

4 In God's engineering, all goods and services are multipurpose from the start.
Paul Brand
He Satisfies My Soul (2008)

5   When God gives us a commission, He always equips us for the job. God has made provision for our needs before the needs ever arise.

Charles Stanley
Handle with Prayer (1987)

6   Our Father gives us what we don't deserve and could never earn from a throne that never runs low on its provision.

Tony Evans and Jonathan Evans
Get in the Game (2006)

7   If God is the Creator and we are the creation, we have to depend on him for life and provision.

Henry Cloud and John Townsend
How People Grow (2001)

8   Thy best Friend is the Lord of Providence. Thy Brother is Prime Minister of the universe, and holds the keys of the divine commissariat.

F. B. Meyer
The Way into the Holiest (1893)

9   He that feeds his birds will not starve his babes.

Matthew Henry
Commentary on the Whole Bible (1706)

10   Our adequacy comes from God and God alone.

Kay Arthur
Lord, Give Me a Heart for You (2001)

11   You are where God in His providence has put you and kept you.

John Dawson
The Saviour in the Workshop (1868)

12   What do you have that you did not receive? The answer doesn't require higher math—it's nothing! Everything that we have fits in the category of received.

James MacDonald
"The Act of Remembering" sermon (2009)

13   Our God, we will trust thee. Shall we not find thee equal to our faith? One day, we shall laugh ourselves to scorn that we looked for so little from thee; for thy giving will not be limited by our hoping.

George MacDonald
"The Higher Faith" sermon (19th century)

327 PSALMS, THE

*Sing unto him, sing psalms unto him,
talk ye of all his wondrous works.*
1 CHRONICLES 16:9

1   The Psalms propel us into the deepest questions about ourselves, about others, and about God. As we let them expose the depths of our emotion, they will lead us to the God who reveals Himself in the midst of our struggle.

Dan Allender and Tremper Longman III
The Cry of the Soul (1994)

2   In the words of the Psalmist, "As the deer pants for streams of water so my soul pants for the mega church I hope to build. . .so my soul pants for the hit ministry I hope to establish." No. "So my soul pants for You, O God."

Phil Vischer
"When Your Dream Dies" teaching (2008)

PUNISHMENT (see HELL)

328 PURITY
(see also CHASTITY; INTEGRITY)

Let no man despise thy youth; but be thou an example of the believers, in word, in conversation, in charity, in spirit, in faith, in purity.
1 TIMOTHY 4:12

1   A relationship devoid of purity is soon reduced to nothing more than two bodies grasping at and demanding pleasure.

Joshua Harris
I Kissed Dating Goodbye (1997)

2   We aren't victims of some vast conspiracy to ensnare us sexually; we've simply chosen to mix in our own standards of sexual conduct with God's standard. Since we found God's standard too difficult, we created a mixture—something new, something comfortable, something mediocre.
Stephen Arterburn, Fred Stoeker, and Mike Yorkey
Every Man's Battle (2000)

3   To have a pure heart, we must submit all thoughts to the authority of Christ.
Max Lucado
Just Like Jesus (1998)

4   Just as a fire consumes every physical thing that is combustible, just so the love of God burns and consumes all sin and dross from the soul, refining and purifying it, like an intense fire purifying metal.
Walter Hilton
Toward a Perfect Love (1999)

5   There is dullness, monotony, sheer boredom in all of life when virginity and purity are no longer protected and prized.
Elisabeth Elliot
Passion and Purity (1984)

6   The only thing that tarnishes us is our own sin, and we are one simple prayer of repentance away from purity at all times.
Beth Moore
Breaking Free (1999)

329 PURPOSE
The LORD thy God hath chosen thee to be a special people unto himself. . .
DEUTERONOMY 7:6

1   So often our primary ambition is to escape pain or feel good or be delivered from a problem when instead we need to keep our focus on the big picture of what God is doing in our life and the lives of others through pain or problems. Our primary aim should be to glorify God, not be honored or to be healthy or to be happy.
Anne Graham Lotz
Trusting God When You Don't Understand (2004)

2   There is, in every human soul, the need to be part of something much bigger than any earth achievement, or even any earth relationship, can offer.
Ron Hutchcraft
Called to Greatness (2001)

3   If the goal for our Christian young people is merely to survive, they probably won't. Survival is an unworthy goal for a person in whom there lives resurrection power! No, they don't need a survival kit. They need a mission.
Ron Hutchcraft
The Battle for a Generation (1996)

4   Reject low living, sight walking, small planning, casual praying, and limited giving—God has chosen you for greatness.
Anne Graham Lotz
I Saw the Lord (2006)

5   Jesus promised the Spirit's power only as it related to accomplishing our God-given work in the kingdom of God. If you want His kingdom power, you must be living for His kingdom purposes.
Tony Evans
The Fire That Ignites (2003)

6   We exist to exhibit God, to display his glory. We serve as canvases for his brush stroke, papers for his pen, soil for his seeds, glimpses of his image.
Max Lucado
Cure for the Common Life (2005)

7 Think of three things—whence you came, where you are going, and to Whom you must account.
   Benjamin Franklin
   Poor Richard's Almanac (18th century)

8 Simple decisions, such as how you spend your time and money, will become opportunities of great promise. And you will begin to live with an unshakable certainty that everything you do today matters forever.
   Bruce Wilkinson
   A Life God Rewards (2002)

9 As you love people, serve people, point people toward faith in Christ, redirect wayward people, restore broken people, and develop people into the peak of their spiritual potential, you reaffirm your understanding of your primary mission in the world.
   Bill Hybels
   Just Walk Across the Room (2006)

10 A man's purpose is fulfilled when he finds something bigger and better than himself to which to offer up his life.
   Mark Elfstrand
   10 Passions of a Man's Soul (2006)

11 In order to live with purpose, you must determine a cause worth pursuing. Don't expect a burning bush to resolve the issue for you. It is something you seek out as part of your life journey.
   Mark Elfstrand
   10 Passions of a Man's Soul (2006)

12 Just what makes you tick? You want to find a meaningful place to give your life away to others. You want to change the world, even if it's just one person's world. No matter what your age or position in life, if you can get where you regularly give of yourself in significant ways to others, you'll experience God's richest blessings.
   Steve and Janie Sjogren
   101 Ways to Reinvest Your Life (2003)

13 You need to be filled with the desire to fight for a higher and greater purpose than yourself. Spend your energy and use your gifts for the greatest good. Know what it's like to stand and fight on the battlefield of faith—to taste the triumph of victory in your life.
   Claire and Curt Cloninger
   E-mail from God for Teens (1999)

14 From brokenness to mission is the human pattern.
   R. C. Sproul
   The Holiness of God (20th century)

15 Our purpose in life is to know God and become more and more like Him.
   Josh McDowell and Bob Hostetler
   Beyond Belief to Conviction (2002)

16 God's ultimate purpose is to make us more and more like Jesus in faith and character. Our ultimate need to trust in things eternal and not earthly is served as we experience undeserved earthly blessing.
   Bryan Chapell
   Holiness by Grace (2001)

17 The prospect of making a difference for God gives an edge of excitement to even the most ordinary experiences.
   W. Phillip Keller
   What Makes Life Worth Living? (1998)

18 Living life according to God's purpose does not disregard anyone's wish list (though for some it may alter the outcome dramatically!). Living according to His purpose brings meaning to our lives, provides a feeling of fulfillment at our deepest levels, and creates in us an impression of wonderment and trust.
   Cynthia Yates
   Living Well in Retirement (2005)

19 God challenges us in unique and special ways to help us know who we are, despite our handicaps. Most of us are suffering from manipulation. When we have no goals, it is easy for others to impose on us their ideas of who we are and are not, and of what we should and should not be doing. Manipulation is a result of purposelessness. Anytime we don't know and understand our purpose, or who we were created to be, we become vulnerable to manipulation.
 T. D. Jakes
 Loose That Man and Let Him Go! (1995)

20 Anybody can assign his agenda to you if you don't know who you are. Unless you confront your own frailties and map your own vulnerabilities, you will never be prepared for attacks in those areas. When you are not prepared, you will find yourself saying, "But I never thought I would do that! I never believed I could get that angry and hostile! I never ever thought I would have an affair! How could I be that weak?"
 T. D. Jakes
 Loose That Man and Let Him Go! (1995)

21 People who want to live generously are also servants—no more, no less—acting on behalf of a returning Prince. Wealth, resources, influence: these belong to the Prince. We must never forget this. And we put them to use in His name, for His purpose.
 Gordon MacDonald
 Secrets of the Generous Life (2002)

22 It's easy to forget the real purpose of anything that's as habitual as the activities of the spiritual life.
 Donald Whitney
 Simplify Your Spiritual Life (2003)

23 The purpose of our life is to receive the gift of the Savior and offer all we have and are to Him.
 Lloyd John Ogilvie
 Life without Limits (1975)

24 If fate clips your wings and casts you on the humbler plains of life, be a hero there.
 Billy Sunday
 The Sawdust Trail (1932)

25 Peace, potential and purpose are what people are crying for.
 Sarah Jepson
 For the Love of Singles (1970)

26 Being endowed with a divine purpose is nothing less than a precious gift from our loving Creator who wants us to be all that we were meant to be for His glory.
 Richard Abanes
 The Purpose That Drives Him (2005)

27 God reveals His purpose or plans to the world by using us in the world.
 Richard Abanes
 The Purpose That Drives Him (2005)

28 Christians are the only agents God has for carrying out His purposes. Think of that! He could himself with a single breath cleanse the whole of New York or the whole of London, but he does not do it.
 Henry Drummond
 A Life for a Life and Other Addresses (1893)

29 I do not see how it would be possible to find a meaningful life in a meaningless universe. The only purpose that is worthy of life is something bigger than life itself.
 John Ortberg
 Faith and Doubt (2008)

30 If I am to be fulfilled, I must pursue a will that is greater than mine—a fulfilled life is one that has the will of God as its focus, not the appetite of the flesh.
 Ravi Zacharias
 Jesus Among Other Gods (2000)

31 Since the ultimate purpose of our salvation is to glorify God and to bring us into intimate, rich fellowship with Him, failure to seek God in prayer is to deny that purpose.
John MacArthur
Alone with God (1995)

32 People whose lives are packed with meaning are almost always happier.
Jim and Cathy Burns
Closer (2009)

33 There is no reason to feel insignificant or that life is without meaning. You were made on purpose, with purpose.
Dave Earley
The 21 Most Dangerous Questions of the Bible (2007)

QUARRELING (*see* ARGUING; CONFLICT; DISPUTING)

330 QUESTIONS
But foolish and unlearned questions avoid, knowing that they do gender strifes.
2 TIMOTHY 2:23

1 Sometimes God allows us to explore the "why" of His instructions. Other times He wants us to obey "because He said so." Then wait on the Lord to bless your act of obedience, no matter how long it takes. He is faithful.
Beth Moore
Jesus: 90 Days with the One and Only (2007)

2 God is under no obligation to answer our question of why.
Sharon Jaynes
Your Scars Are Beautiful to God (2006)

QUIETNESS (*see* SILENCE)

331 QUIET TIME
It is good that a man should both hope and quietly wait for the salvation of the LORD.
LAMENTATIONS 3:26

1 Whatever else we may gain from his example, we cannot overestimate the priority Jesus gave to communion with his Father.
Jim Reapsome
10 Minutes a Day with Jesus (2008)

2 God often speaks quietly, which suggests we need to be very still in order to hear Him.
Bob Buford
Game Plan (1997)

3 We hunger for quiet times: we find in them a womb to renew our strength.
Virginia Ann Froehle
Loving Yourself More (1993)

4 We are starved for mystery, to know this God as One who is totally Other and to experience reverence in his presence. We are starved for intimacy, to see and feel and know God in the very cells of our being. We are starved for rest, to know God beyond what we can do for him. We are starved for quiet, to hear the sound of sheer silence that is the presence of God himself.
Ruth Haley Barton
Invitation to Solitude and Silence (2004)

5 The truth is that the feelings we receive from our devotional life are the least of its benefits. The invisible and unfelt grace of God is much greater, and it is beyond our comprehension.
John of the Cross (16th century) quoted in
John of the Cross: Selected Writings

6 From these moments of quietness let light go forth, and joy, and power, that will remain with me through all the hours of the day.
John Baillie
A Diary of Private Prayer (1949)

RACISM (*see* BIGOTRY)

332 RAPTURE, THE

In a moment, in the twinkling of an eye,
at the last trump: for the trumpet shall sound,
and the dead shall be raised incorruptible,
and we shall be changed.
1 CORINTHIANS 15:52

1   In case of rapture, this car will be unmanned.
Bumper sticker

2   What would you like to be doing
when He returns? Where would you like
to be when the trumpet sounds, when the
archangel shouts, and when, in the twinkling
of an eye, we are changed and rise into the
clouds to meet Him?
David Jeremiah
What in the World Is Going On? (2008)

3   It is unworthy of strong, mature Christians
to believe that the Rapture will occur before
the Tribulation if our reason for doing so is
because we are afraid to trust Christ to take
care of us during that time of trial. Happily,
that is not the reason we hold such a position.
Tim LaHaye
The Rapture (2002)

333 READING

Till I come, give attendance to reading,
to exhortation, to doctrine.
1 TIMOTHY 4:13

1   We should choose those works for
reading which instruct us in our duty and
in our faults; which, while they point out
the greatness of God, teach us what is our
duty to Him, and how very far we are from
performing it.
François Fénelon and Jeanne Guyon
Spiritual Progress (17th century)

2   Reading a book is an opportunity to
discover wisdom from someone else's
perspective, to expand our horizons, and

perhaps learn to know God from a new
vantage point.
Debra Farrington
A Beginner's Guide to Unceasing Prayer
(2002)

3   Books are to read, but that is by no means
the end of it. . . . They are giving you their
eloquent and inexhaustible silence. They are
giving you time to find your way to them.
Maybe they are giving you time, with or
without them, just to find your way.
Frederick Buechner
Beyond Words: Daily Readings in the ABC's
of Faith (2004)

4   We can liken daily Bible reading to an oil
change for the lawnmower. The fresh oil kept
the lawnmower operating long past the time
it should have quit, and so it is with us. When
we study the Word, we add usefulness and
longevity to our Christian service.
James Scudder
Your Secret to Spiritual Success (2002)

5   The latest statistic is that the average
American watches 1,456 hours of television a
year but only reads three books. So if it's true
that readers are leaders, and the more you read
the further you advance, then there isn't a lot
of competition.
Donald Miller
To Own a Dragon (2006)

6   Studying an ancient text makes a person feel
as though they are living in a complicated but
wondrous reality that is greater than they are.
Donald Miller
To Own a Dragon (2006)

334 REALITY

O send out thy light and
thy truth: let them lead me.
PSALM 43:3

1   If you want realism, come to the Bible.
Martyn Lloyd-Jones
Love So Amazing (1962)

2   Reality may not be pleasant, but no problem was ever solved, no goal ever reached without looking at the situation squarely with no editing or reframing.
John Townsend
It's Not My Fault (2007)

3   Someone once said, "Reality is a tough place to live, but it is the only place to get a good steak." While reality can be tough to handle, it is where the good things of life reside as well.
Henry Cloud and John Townsend
Boundaries with Kids (1998)

4   Mental and spiritual health begins with an acceptance of life as it is.
James Dobson
Life on the Edge (1995)

5   Looking only at the good side of every situation is often a dangerous way of trying to escape the reality of it. When we praise God we thank Him for our situation, not in spite of it.
Merlin Carothers
Prison to Praise (1970)

REAPING
(*see* SOWING AND REAPING)

335 REASON
(*see also* PHILOSOPHY; SCIENCE)
Come now, and let us reason together,
saith the LORD.
ISAIAH 1:18

1   People who say they rely not on faith but on reasoning alone haven't carefully considered what reasoning is. Reasoning itself depends on faith.
Ravi Zacharias and Norman Geisler
Is Your Church Ready? (2003)

2   God has put enough into the world to make faith in him a most reasonable thing, and he has left enough out to make it impossible to live by sheer reason or observation alone.
Ravi Zacharias
The Real Face of Atheism (2004)

3   We reason that we can give in to those seemingly minor temptations—say an emotional attraction to a coworker, or just one drink at the party—because we think we know the boundaries. We think our reason can keep us safe.
Chuck Colson
"The Bewilderment of Sin" article (2009)

4   Dr. Henning asked: "Is reason to hold no authority at all with Christians, since it is to be set aside in matters of faith?" The Doctor replied: "Before faith and the knowledge of God, reason is mere darkness; but in the hands of those who believe, 'tis an excellent instrument."
Martin Luther
Table Talk (1546)

336 REBIRTH
Being born again, not of corruptible seed,
but of incorruptible, by the word of God,
which liveth and abideth for ever.
1 PETER 1:23

1   The Lord never wastes anything. He will take everything old and create for you something new.
Karon Phillips Goodman
Grab a Broom, Lord—There's Dust Everywhere! (2003)

2   I cannot fully praise nor love Him therefore must I die, and cast myself into the divine void, till I rise from non-existence to existence.
Meister Eckhart
Meister Eckhart's Sermons (14th century)

3   While I am here, He is in me; after this life, I am in Him.
Meister Eckhart
Meister Eckhart's Sermons (14th century)

4   In this sense the New Birth of man is the focus towards which all creation strives, because man is the image of God after the likeness of which the world is created.
Meister Eckhart
Meister Eckhart's Sermons (14th century)

5   When something precious comes to an end, it's painful to let go, but that's what you have to do if there is to be a fresh beginning.
Poppy Smith
I'm Too Young to Be This Old! (1997)

337 REBUKE (*see also* CORRECTION)
Them that sin rebuke before all,
that others also may fear.
1 TIMOTHY 5:20

1   Confronting an irresponsible person is not painful to him; only consequences are.
Henry Cloud and John Townsend
Boundaries (1992)

2   The sting of a reproach is the truth of it.
Benjamin Franklin
Poor Richard's Almanac (18th century)

338 RECONCILIATION
God was in Christ, reconciling the world
unto himself, not imputing their trespasses
unto them; and hath committed unto us
the word of reconciliation.
2 CORINTHIANS 5:19

1   Biblically, the stronger person always initiates the peace.
Gary Smalley
Love Is a Decision (1989)

2   Human beings face two fundamental problems: We are alienated from God and separated from each other. God's plan of salvation addresses both of these issues. He reconciles us to Himself through the Cross, and He reconciles us to each other in the church.
Colin Smith
Ten Keys to Unlock the Christian Life (2005)

3   Because reconciliation is the healing of our deepest longing, it is never too late to seek it.
John Ortberg
Everybody's Normal Till You Get to Know Them (2003)

4   Whatever your position in a relationship, if you are aware of a problem, make a concerted effort to create a positive change.
John Maxwell
Be a People Person (1989)

5   Christ's great act of reconciliation erases human distinctions.
Stephen Mosley
Secrets of Jesus' Touch (2003)

6   God has reconciled sinners to Himself. I hope you can begin to appreciate the wonder of this reality. All Christians are forgiven an unpayable debt, not because we deserve it, not as a reward for doing penance by which we somehow pay for our own sins, but solely on the basis of what God Himself has done for us.
John MacArthur
The Freedom and Power of Forgiveness (1998)

7   Reconciliation must always begin where we are.
Gary Chapman
Hope for the Separated (1982)

339 REDEMPTION (*see also* BORN AGAIN; CONVERSION; NEW BIRTH; REGENERATION; SALVATION)
But of him are ye in Christ Jesus, who of God
is made unto us wisdom, and righteousness,
and sanctification, and redemption.
1 CORINTHIANS 1:30

1   Strictly speaking, of course, not one of us deserves redemption. God owes us nothing, but He nevertheless offers His undeserved grace. Though we deserve damnation, He invites each of us to be redeemed.
  Erwin Lutzer
  After You've Blown It (2004)

2   The cost of redemption cannot be overstated. The wonders of grace cannot be overemphasized. Christ took the hell He didn't deserve so we could have the heaven we don't deserve.
  Randy Alcorn
  The Grace and Truth Paradox (2003)

3   Redemption is God's mighty act delivering us from anyone or anything that holds us in bondage.
  Mel Lawrenz
  Jubilee (2008)

4   When the Bible says that you have been redeemed, it means that you have been absolutely freed, fully released, and totally delivered from all that had you bound in the past.
  Roy Lessin
  Today Is Your Best Day (2006)

5   God has a double claim on believer's bodies. First, God made and fashioned them. Then He bought them back. All three Persons of the Trinity had a part in both their creation and their redemption.
  Pat Warren
  Weighed by the Word (2009)

6   What is it to bring the man out of his sepulchre if you leave him dead? Why lead him into the light if he is still blind? We thank God, that He who forgives our iniquities also heals our diseases.
  Charles Spurgeon
  All of Grace (19th century)

7   You are Christ's and Christ is yours. As Adam stood for his descendants, so does Jesus stand for all who are in Him.
  Charles Spurgeon
  All of Grace (19th century)

8   You can never be poor while Jesus is rich, since you are in one firm with Him. Want can never assail you, since you are joint-proprietor with Him who is Possessor of Heaven and earth.
  Charles Spurgeon
  All of Grace (19th century)

9   It was the precious lifeblood, which flowed from our Lord's crucified body on Calvary, which purchased for us redemption from the curse of a broken law.
  J. C. Ryle
  The Upper Room (19th century)

10 Christ's death was not a case of heroism simply, it was a case of redemption.
  Peter Taylor Forsyth
  The Work of Christ (1909)

11 Jesus came not only to teach but to save, not only to reveal God to human beings, but also to redeem human beings for God. This is because our major problem is not our ignorance but our sin and guilt.
  John Stott
  Life in Christ (2003)

12 What greater motivation for becoming a Christian could an unbeliever have, and what greater consolation could a believer have, than to know that in Christ all sins—past, present, and future—are forgiven forever?
  John MacArthur
  1 Corinthians (1984)

13 Faith abases men, and exalts God; it gives all the glory of redemption to him alone.
  Jonathan Edwards
  "God Glorified in Man's Dependence" sermon (18th century)

14 The heart of God hungers to redeem the world.
   Samuel Gordon
   Quiet Talks on Prayer (1904)

340 REGENERATION (*see also* BORN AGAIN; CONVERSION; NEW BIRTH; REDEMPTION; SALVATION)

Not by works of righteousness which we have done, but according to his mercy he saved us, by the washing of regeneration, and renewing of the Holy Ghost.
TITUS 3:5

1 Regeneration, or the new birth, is a subject to which the world is very averse; it is, however, the grand concern, in comparison with which every thing else is but trifling.
   Matthew Henry
   Commentary on the Whole Bible (1706)

341 REGRET

For godly sorrow worketh repentance to salvation not to be repented of: but the sorrow of the world worketh death.
2 CORINTHIANS 7:10

1 Regrets slow you down. Regrets cause you to fail to pay attention to the future.
   Bob Buford
   Game Plan (1997)

2 We will always experience regret when we live for the moment and do not weigh our words and deeds before we give them life.
   Lisa Bevere
   Kissed the Girls and Made Them Cry (2002)

3 Apology is birthed in the womb of regret.
   Gary Chapman and Jennifer Thomas
   The Five Languages of Apology (2006)

4 Regret is a brutal task master.
   Sheila Walsh
   Let Go (2008)

5 We are to find as much bitterness in weeping for sin as ever we found sweetness in committing it.
   Thomas Watson
   The Doctrine of Repentance (1668)

342 RELATIONSHIPS, HUMAN (*see also* FRIENDSHIP)

Can two walk together, except they be agreed?
AMOS 3:3

1 Indifference is the mortar that can solidify a wall between two people.
   Gary and Mona Shriver
   Unfaithful (2005)

2 Personal meaning and human value arise only in relationship. Solitude casts doubt on them. Identity, too, is discovered only in relationship. Lacking companions at the level of the soul, I finally cannot find my soul. It always takes another person to show myself to me. Alone, I die.
   Walter Wangerin Jr.
   As for Me and My House (1990)

3 Important, relationship-defining moments generally don't arrive on cue.
   Tim Clinton and Gary Sibcy
   Attachments (2002)

4 The three most powerful words in any relationship are "I am sorry."
   Wayne and Mary Sotile
   Beat Stress Together (1998)

5 We came into being as needy people in need of companionship and in need of what others have to offer. God never intended us to be self-contained units unable to satisfy our every requirement.
   Maxine Marsolini
   Blended Families (2000)

6 Our personal individuality—who we really are—comes only in relation to others: God, our family and our fellow believers.

Neil Anderson and Charles Mylander
Blessed Are the Peacemakers (2002)

7 No relationship can long endure, let alone thrive, if its members don't consciously and continually make room in their hearts for one another.

Bill McCartney
Blind Spots (2003)

8 Whether you are blessed with soul mates who settle into the most comfortable room inside you, or with those who walk with you just a little while, not one of these people crosses your path by chance. Each is a messenger, sent by God, to give you the wisdom, companionship, comfort, or challenge you need for a particular leg of your spiritual journey.

Traci Mullins
Celebrating Friendship (1998)

9 God desires to be the first stop on the way to understanding our relational needs and having them met.

David and Jan Stoop
The Complete Marriage Book (2002)

10 There is in all of us a sense of incompleteness that can only be eased when we are in relationship with other people.

Rich Hurst
Courage to Connect (2002)

11 Belonging and significance—these needs are common to all of us. As they provide us pictures of our souls, we see both our desire and our capacity for intimacy. We see both the joy that comes with affirmation and the fear of failure and rejection.

Rich Hurst
Courage to Connect (2002)

12 If relationships bring meaning to life, then the ultimate mockery of life is the reality that all relationships are either ruptured by sin or severed by death.

Ravi Zacharias
The Real Face of Atheism (2004)

13 One of the benefits of being honest and vulnerable with another person is that you have an opportunity to be accepted unconditionally for who you are. As a result, you will experience something of what God's unconditional love for us is like through the relationship.

Dick Purnell
Finding a Lasting Love (2003)

14 Requests give direction to love, but demands stop the flow of love.

Gary Chapman
The Five Love Languages (1995)

15 The world in which we live is made up of the interweaving and intersecting between individuals and groups, which we call human relationships. Society exists as a result of these relationships. They provide companionship and communication, and through them we give and receive love and understanding. Through relationships we develop, grow, and learn. And from them we obtain self-esteem, identity, and significance.

Gigi Graham Tchividjian
For Women Only (2001)

16 Everybody is somebody's impossible person some of the time.

Les Parrott III
High-Maintenance Relationships (1996)

17 Letting my favorite people in the world into my struggles not only gives them the opportunity to minister to me, but it also takes the pressure off by lightening the burden a little.

Laurie Lovejoy Hilliard and
Sharon Lovejoy Autry
Hold You, Mommy (2006)

18 People need two sorts of relationships to grow: the divine and the human.
   Henry Cloud and John Townsend
   How People Grow (2001)

19 Good relationships do involve confronting, forgiving, and reconciling.
   Henry Cloud and John Townsend
   How People Grow (2001)

20 It is never our job to fix anyone. It is, however, our job to facilitate an environment in which God and people can work together to heal their every pain and thereby solve their every problem.
   James Richards
   How to Stop the Pain (2001)

21 Expecting to change another person fundamentally is as silly as expecting gold from a lead mine.
   H. Norman Wright
   Let's Just Be Friends (2002)

22 If we presume people know we are sorry after a hurtful incident, we are usually making a mistake.
   Patrick Brennan
   The Way of Forgiveness (2000)

23 It is important to develop a discipline in our relationships in which we express what is going on within. This is true especially for those emotional states that are building blocks for good relationships: affection, appreciation, encouragement, sorrow for sin and hurt.
   Patrick Brennan
   The Way of Forgiveness (2000)

24 In a truly loving relationship, the partners freely choose to be with each other, to be associated with each other, to love each other.
   Thomas Whiteman
   Victim of Love (1998)

25 Good relationships, even among competitive people, have that aspect of encouragement, challenge, and inspiration. When one wins, both win. That's the kind of balance a healthy relationship requires.
   Thomas Whiteman
   Victim of Love (1998)

26 We need to make a conscious effort to widen our circle of support to include other believers. By weaving the threads of relationship with God's people, we can administer our special gifts to one another.
   Skip Heitzig
   Relationships (1997)

27 We need other people—relationships. We need people to expose to us where we fall short of doing the will of God and our moment in need of walking in conscious fellowship with Him.
   Pamela Reeve
   Relationships: What It Takes to Be a Friend (1997)

28 Healthy relationships are not built on dictatorships.
   Kay Arthur
   Lord, Give Me a Heart for You (2001)

29 We haven't yet dreamed big enough dreams of what we could mean to one another.
   Larry Crabb
   Connecting (1997)

30 In connecting with God, we gain life. In connecting with others, we nourish and experience that life as we freely share it.
   Larry Crabb
   Connecting (1997)

31 Our relationships are radically altered as we live in fellowship with Christ and allow the depth of His love to heal us.
   Lloyd John Ogilvie
   Life without Limits (1975)

32 If we can't hear someone who loves us—a son, a daughter, a spouse, or God—maybe we should step closer.
Don Osgood
Listening for God's Silent Language (1995)

33 Commitment. . .an old-fashioned word, but one that can't be outdone in helping produce life's most wonderful relationships.
William Krutza
101 Ways to Enrich Your Marriage (1982)

34 When a relationship is fractured by hurt and anger, an apology is always in order.
Gary Chapman and Jennifer Thomas
The Five Languages of Apology (2006)

35 The motivation in genuine love is to build a relationship primarily for the other person's sake and when we do that, we gain because we have a better relationship to enjoy.
Gary Smalley
If Only He Knew (1979)

36 All of us can fall into the trap of being more interested in the perks than the person.
Jill Briscoe
8 Choices That Will Change a Woman's Life (2004)

37 The cry of the heart is to enter life-giving, love-producing relationships and work to leave a healed and healing legacy on the hearts and lives of those we love and touch in a meaningful way.
Janet Hagberg and Robert Guelich
The Critical Journey (1995)

38 Our souls yearn to unite, to live in concert and connection with other souls.
Sue Patton Thoele
Heart Centered Marriage (1996)

39 Honor is the key that unlocks the door of conflict that leads to deeper intimacy.
Gary Smalley
Secrets to Lasting Love (2000)

40 The goal of intimacy is to hold each other in your hearts.
Bill and Pam Farrel
The Marriage Code (2009)

41 "Denial" is not a river in Egypt, and yet for many of us who are involved with fools, it is our emotional address!
Jan Silvious
Foolproofing Your Life (1998)

42 There is no substitute for knowing and being known by another human being.
Howard and William Hendricks
As Iron Sharpens Iron (1995)

43 Grace that leaves me at peace with God but in broken and dysfunctional relationships with others is less than amazing.
Keith Meyer
Whole Life Transformation (2010)

44 Pain is a very real part of any relationship. It is inevitable when you share yourself with another person.
David Gudgel
Before You Live Together (2003)

45 It is hard for a person to be happy when his or her relationship is built on the need to prove himself or herself.
David Gudgel
Before You Live Together (2003)

46 Relationships are built and maintained upon communication.
Cindi McMenamin
When Women Walk Alone (2002)

47 People were created with a twofold need—fellowship with God and companionship with other human beings.
J. Oswald Sanders
Facing Loneliness (1988)

48 God created us to operate in relationship with Him and with each other. We are not made for isolation.
David Stoop
Seeking Wise Counsel (2002)

49 God's plan is for us to be connected to others. That way, when we are faced with problems, we don't have to face them alone.
David Stoop
Seeking Wise Counsel (2002)

50 The gift of listening offers relief from the exhaustion and hopelessness you feel when your relationship knots become more hopelessly tangled. The longer you work on the relationship, the more tangled the knots. Through the gift of listening, you can untangle the knots and preserve these precious God-given relationships.
Dallas and Nancy Demmitt
Can You Hear Me Now? (2003)

51 When we focus on appearance, performance or social status, we fail to develop the lasting values of character that hold a relationship together.
Neil Anderson and Dave Park
Overcoming Negative Self-Image (2003)

343 RELATIVITY

Jesus answered, "I am the way and the truth and the life. No one comes to the Father except through me.
JOHN 14:6 NIV

1 If nothing is absolute, then we are left with absolutely nothing.
Fawn Parish
Honor: What Love Looks Like (1999)

344 RELIGION

Pure religion and undefiled before God and the Father is this, To visit the fatherless and widows in their affliction, and to keep himself unspotted from the world.
JAMES 1:27

1 It is so easy to get religious instead of godly.
Charles Swindoll
So You Want to Be Like Christ? (2005)

2 Religion moves you to do what you do out of fear, insecurity, and self-righteousness, but the gospel moves you to do what you do more and more out of grateful joy in who God is in himself.
Timothy Keller
The Supremacy of Christ in a Postmodern World (2007)

3 Religion is a matter of our freest choice, and if men will obstinately and willfully set themselves against it, there is no remedy.
John Tillotson
The Wisdom of Being Religious (1819)

4 Men of dissolute lives cry down Religion, because they would not be under the restraint of it.
John Tillotson
The Wisdom of Being Religious (1819)

5 Religious leaders try to add baptism, church membership, faithful living, personal sacrifice or some other human work to the work of Christ to the hope of salvation for the believer. Such philosophies may have filled the coffers of religion but have confused the issue of salvation and thus damaged countless souls.
Lance Latham
The Two Gospels (1984)

6 Religion, or the duty which we owe our Creator, and the manner of discharging it, can be directed only by reason and conviction, not by force and violence; and therefore all men are equally entitled to the free exercise of religion, according to the dictates of conscience.
James Madison
"Virginia Declaration of Rights" 1776

7 It is superstition to put one's hope in formalities; but it is pride to be unwilling to submit to them.
Blaise Pascal
Pensées (17th century)

8   Anyone who claims that all religions are the same betrays not only an ignorance of all religions, but a caricatured view of even the best-known ones. Every religion at its core is exclusive.

Ravi Zacharias
What Is Truth? (2007)

9   At the heart of every religion is an uncompromising commitment to a particular way of defining who God is or is not and accordingly, of defining life's purpose.

Ravi Zacharias
What Is Truth? (2007)

10   Long for nothing, desire nothing, hope for nothing, but to have all that is within thee changed into the spirit and holy temper of the holy Jesus. Let this be thy Christianity, thy church, and thy religion.

William Law
The Spirit of Prayer (1750)

11   You have to overcome your religiosity that substitutes positive thinking for holiness, rituals for repentance, traditions for truth, and orthodoxy for obedience.

Anne Graham Lotz
Heaven, My Father's House (2002)

12   The whole substance of religion was faith, hope, and charity; by the practice of which we become united to the will of God.

Brother Lawrence
The Practice of the Presence of God (17th century)

13   The religion of Jesus has probably always suffered more from those who have misunderstood than from those who have opposed it.

Henry Drummond
Natural Law in the Spiritual World (19th century)

14   Proxy religion involves too great a risk: you had better see to your soul's matters yourself, and leave them in no man's hands.

Charles Spurgeon
All of Grace (19th century)

15   The world's entire morality and that of a large portion of the Church are only a spurious benevolence.

Charles Finney
"Men Often Highly Esteem What God Abhors" sermon (19th century)

16   The highest forms of the world's morality are only abominations in God's sight.

Charles Finney
"Men Often Highly Esteem What God Abhors" sermon (19th century)

17   True religion is supernatural at its beginning, supernatural in its continuance, and supernatural in its close. It is the work of God from first to last.

Charles Spurgeon
All of Grace (19th century)

18   For the creature's true religion, is its rendering to God all that is God's, it is its true continual acknowledging all that which it is, and has, and enjoys, in and from God.

William Law
An Humble, Affectionate, and Earnest Address (1761)

19   The Spirit of God first gives, or sows the seed of divine union in the soul of every man; and religion is that by which it is quickened, raised, and brought forth to a fullness and growth of a life in God.

William Law
An Humble, Affectionate, and Earnest Address (1761)

20   A religious faith that is uninspired, a hope, or love that proceeds not from the immediate working of the divine nature within us, can

no more do any divine good to our souls, or unite them with the goodness of God, than an hunger after earthly food can feed us with the immortal bread of heaven.

William Law
An Humble, Affectionate, and Earnest Address (1761)

21 I appeal to every man, whether popish and Protestant churches need do anything else, than that which they now do, and have done for ages, to prove their faithfulness to such a master, and their full obedience to his precepts.

William Law
An Humble, Affectionate, and Earnest Address (1761)

22 Religion, in the lowest as well as in the highest of its forms is an expression of the relation of the soul to something beyond itself it involves, therefore, not one term, but two; it points to the existence of an object, and implies belief in the reality of that object.

James Orr
The Christian View of God and the World (1908)

23 A religion based on mere feeling is the vaguest most unreliable, most unstable of all things.

James Orr
The Christian View of God and the World (1908)

24 The type of religion which rejoices in the pious sound of traditional phrases, regardless of their meanings, or shrinks from "controversial" matters, will never stand amid the shocks of life.

J. Gresham Machen
Christianity and Liberalism (1923)

25 Religion can turn people away as easily as it invites them.

Timothy Johnson
Finding God in the Questions (2004)

26 Religion, in many circles, has become the business of trying to make people happy.

J. I. Packer
J. I. Packer Answers Questions for Today (2001)

345 RENEWAL

And have put on the new man,
which is renewed in knowledge after
the image of him that created him. . .
COLOSSIANS 3:10

1 Renewal and restoration are not luxuries; they are essentials. Being alone and resting for awhile is not selfish; it is Christlike.

Charles Swindoll
Man to Man (1996)

2 Saints are often drowsy, and listless, and half asleep; but the word and Spirit of Christ will put life and vigour into the soul.

Matthew Henry
Commentary on the Whole Bible (1706)

3 There's nothing better than being "scrubbed clean" by taking on the person of Christ. By being in his word, lifting up praise and worship to his name, and making determined decisions to live as children of the light, we become renewed.

Eva Marie Everson
Oasis (2007)

4 We are not transformed by rising to the occasion. We rise to the occasion because we have been transformed. How are we transformed? By the renewing of our mind. By convincing our heart that God is good, even when our circumstances are not.

Donna Partow
This Isn't the Life I Signed Up For (2003)

5 Transformation is the fruit of a changed outlook. First our minds are renewed, and then

we are transformed, and then everything is different, even if it stays the same.

Mark Buchanan
The Rest of God (2006)

346 REPENTANCE

Despisest thou the riches of his goodness and forbearance and longsuffering; not knowing that the goodness of God leadeth thee to repentance?
Romans 2:4

1   When the Holy Spirit shows us an area that needs repentance, we must overcome the instinct to defend ourselves. We must silence the little lawyer who steps out from a dark closet in our minds, pleading, "My client is not so bad."

Francis Frangipane
The Three Battlegrounds (1989)

2   To be sorry is not enough in repentance. Judas was sorry enough to hang himself. It was an admission of guilt without true repentance.

Billy Graham
Peace with God (1984)

3   When you repent of your sin and are broken before the Lord, He sees you through every step of the painful consequences. His mercy, grace, and goodness enable you to bear it all with hope.

David Wilkerson
Revival on Broadway! (1996)

4   If you have truly repented—which means you have experienced godly sorrow and a subsequent detour from the sin—bathe yourself in the river of God's forgiveness.

Beth Moore
Jesus: 90 Days with the One and Only (2007)

5   The Bible teaches that genuine repentance is evidenced by a change in behavior.

Robert Jeffress
When Forgiveness Doesn't Make Sense (2000)

6   Before ye speak peace to your hearts, ye must be made to see, made to feel, made to weep over, made to bewail your actual transgressions against the law of God.

George Whitefield
"A Sermon, Preached on Sabbath Morning" (1741)

7   Repentance is absolutely necessary for salvation. . . . I hope all my dear relations know the truth of those observations by their own experience.

William Carey (19th century) quoted in
Faithful Witness: The Life and Mission of William Carey

8   Repetition of the hurting pattern causes far more damage than the words "I am sorry" can repair. If I repent, but continue in a pattern of hurting, that pattern will speak more clearly than my words.

Patrick Brennan
The Way of Forgiveness (2000)

9   God will have his servants to be repenting sinners, standing in fear of his anger, of the devil, death and hell, and believing in Christ.

Martin Luther
Table Talk (16th century)

10 Sight of sin doth precede sorrow for sin.
George Swinnock
Works of George Swinnock (17th century)

11 God never cured a spiritual leper but he caused him to fall down first and cry out, Unclean, unclean.

George Swinnock
Works of George Swinnock (17th century)

12 To repent literally means to change the way we think. Thus, repentance is sometimes described as "coming to our senses."

Ken Sande
The Peacemaker (1991)

13 It is the unchangeable law of God, that wicked men must turn or die.
Richard Baxter
A Call to the Unconverted, to Turn and Live (17th century)

14 Repentance always opens the floodgates to healing and love.
Dee Brestin and Kathy Troccoli
Living in Love with Jesus (2002)

15 The only way we can walk in the light is to live in a state of continual repentance. It is the cornerstone of the Christian faith.
Dee Brestin and Kathy Troccoli
Living in Love with Jesus (2002)

16 Repentance and forgiveness are riveted together by the eternal purpose of God. What God hath joined together let no man put asunder.
Charles Spurgeon
All of Grace (19th century)

17 Surely no rebel can expect the King to pardon his treason while he remains in open revolt. No one can be so foolish as to imagine that the Judge of all the earth will put away our sins if we refuse to put them away ourselves.
Charles Spurgeon
All of Grace (19th century)

18 Do not make any mistake about it; repentance is not a thing of days and weeks, a temporary penance to be over as fast as possible! No; it is the grace of a lifetime, like faith itself.
Charles Spurgeon
All of Grace (19th century)

19 All the while that we walk by faith and not by sight, the tear of repentance glitters in the eye of faith.
Charles Spurgeon
All of Grace (19th century)

20 It may seem a strange thing, but so it is— the bitterness of repentance and the sweetness of pardon blend in the flavor of every gracious life, and make up an incomparable happiness.
Charles Spurgeon
All of Grace (19th century)

21 Upon your heart the rainbow of covenant grace has been displayed in all its beauty when the tear-drops of repentance have been shone upon by the light of full forgiveness.
Charles Spurgeon
All of Grace (19th century)

22 The meaning of Christ's death rouses our shame, self-contempt, and repentance. And we resent being made to feel ashamed of ourselves. We resent being made to repent.
Peter Taylor Forsyth
The Work of Christ (1909)

23 Either sin must drown or the soul burn. Let it not be said that repentance is difficult. Things that are excellent deserve labour.
Thomas Watson
The Doctrine of Repentance (1668)

24 Be as speedy in your repentance as you would have God speedy in his mercies: "the king's business required haste" (1 Samuel 21:8).
Thomas Watson
The Doctrine of Repentance (1668)

25 Come boldly into his throne of grace— even when you have sinned and failed. He forgives—instantly—those who repent with godly sorrow.
David Wilkerson
"A Dry Spell" article (2010)

RESENTMENT (*see* BITTERNESS)

347 RESPECT
A son honoureth his father, and a servant his master.
MALACHI 1:6

1   Since God has created each person unique, from his or her fingerprints to hair follicles, he intends that each person be treated special.
    Lynn Anderson
    The Jesus Touch (2002)

2   Faith...teaches us not merely to tolerate one another, but to respect one another—to show regard to different views and the courtesy to listen.
    George W. Bush
    Inaugural Address (2001)

3   Respect is a power. It is a power within a person. It is the gift we can give ourselves or share with others.
    Ralph Ransom Frederick
    Steps on the Stairway (1981)

4   Respecting another person is simply admitting that God is big enough to love him or her just as much as he loves me.
    Stephen Arterburn and Jack Felton
    More Jesus, Less Religion (2000)

5   I want to stand well with God and if I stand well with God, I'm likely to stand well with His best people. And after that, I'm not much concerned.
    A. W. Tozer
    "In Everything by Prayer" sermon
    (20th century)

6   I believe we not only bring defeat into our marriages and our husbands when we don't have respect for them, but it shuts the door to new life in us as well.
    Stormie Omartian
    The Power of a Praying Wife (1997)

7   When men do not fear God, they will not regard man.
    Matthew Henry
    Commentary on the Whole Bible (1706)

348 RESPONSIBILITY

"Yes, I tell you, this generation will be held responsible for it all."
LUKE 11:51 NIV

1   Blame is sort of a comfort food for the soul. It diverts us from the effort of owning responsibility.
    Henry Cloud
    It's Not My Fault (2007)

2   We live in a time of relativistic morality that does not believe in a God to whom men are responsible.
    D. James Kennedy
    Why I Believe (1980)

3   God will reward even the meanest drudgery done from a sense of duty, and with a view to glorify him.
    Matthew Henry
    Commentary on the Whole Bible (1706)

4   Denial is the active process that someone uses to avoid responsibility.
    Henry Cloud and John Townsend
    Safe People (2005)

5   If you want a heritage worth remembering, always connect honor with duty. It isn't enough to do the duty. Honor must go alongside with duty if you're going to be a man of great purpose.
    Mark Elfstrand
    10 Passions of a Man's Soul (2006)

6   You choose to find purpose. You choose to find contentment. You choose to find joy. Your spouse cannot do it for you; neither can your preachers or your friend.
    Ellie Kay
    The Debt Diet (2005)

7   Encouraging responsibility is not a search for scapegoats...it is a call to conscience.
    George W. Bush
    Inaugural Address (2001)

8   There's no way to get our world back together again except as each of us begins with himself and with his own family.
   Catherine Marshall
   Something More (1974)

9   The moment-by-moment events of our lives fall into the soil of our understanding like seeds. Our responsibility, like that of our first parents, is to work the garden. To prepare the soil. To tend the growth. And to take what is offered from its branches as nourishment for our soul.
   Ken Gire
   Reflections on Your Life (1998)

10   We have the responsibility and the power to alter our hearts.
   Rhonda Rizzo Webb
   Words Begin in Our Hearts (2003)

11   Rest not under the expired merits of others, shine by those of thy own.
   Thomas Brown
   Christian Morals (17th century)

12   Allowing others to shoulder the weight of their own responsibilities is right because it restores balance in relationships. Along with that, it eases stress by taking undue pressure off us.
   David Hazard
   Reducing Stress (2002)

13   It is not our responsibility to do the hard job or the whole job all the time.
   David Hazard
   Reducing Stress (2002)

14   Disaster is conceived on a bed of neglect.
   Ted Engstrom and Robert Larson
   Integrity (1987)

15   Responsibility means obligation, and obligation must mean a curtailing of freedom.
   Stephen Arterburn and John Shore
   Midlife Manual for Men (2008)

16   We are each responsible to our Creator for our own life.
   Stephen Arterburn
   Finding Mr. Right (2003)

17   We argue with our mates, declare our innocence, and put the blame on them. We do poorly at school, and blame the professor. And we get fired because "the boss is impossible." Each time we do this, we deny our own responsibility and failings.
   Bruce Narramore
   Guilt and Freedom (1974)

18   God has not given and never will give someone else the job of running your life.
   Joyce Meyer
   Approval Addiction (2005)

349 REST

Take my yoke upon you, and learn of me;
for I am meek and lowly in heart:
and ye shall find rest unto your souls.
MATTHEW 11:29

1   Come and yoke yourself with Jesus Christ. Come and find rest from the burden of your sin. Come and trade your busy life for His, because only by the power of the Son of God will there be rest for your soul.
   Angela Thomas McGuffey
   Tender Mercy for a Mother's Soul (2001)

2   The overcommitter must simply do less.
   Kim Thomas
   Even God Rested (2003)

3   It's the rests that make the difference in the music of our lives. They really are the pauses that refresh.
   Steve and Mary Farrar
   Overcoming Overload (2003)

4   When you have had ample rest, you will have a more positive outlook; you will be eager to move through the day; you'll make better judgments and decisions.
   Bruce Bickel and Stan Jantz
   Simple Matters (2001)

5   In a culture where busyness is a fetish and stillness is laziness, rest is sloth. But without rest, we miss the rest of God: the rest he invites us to enter more fully so that we might know him more deeply.
Mark Buchanan
The Rest of God (2006)

6   May it please God to reveal to His children the nearness of Christ standing and knocking at the door of every heart, ready to come in and rest forever there and to lead the soul into His rest.
Andrew Murray
Master's Indwelling (1895)

7   The cross-shaped yoke of Christ is after all an instrument of liberation and power to those who live in it with him and learn the meekness and lowliness of heart that brings rest to the soul.
Dallas Willard
The Spirit of the Disciplines (1988)

8   Those who take regular breaks actually get more done than those who work unceasingly.
Keri Wyatt Kent
Breathe: Creating Space for God in a Hectic Life (2005)

9   Rest communicates something basic about our relationship with God, and God's relationship with us.
Jane Rubietta
Resting Place (2005)

10   The Bible commands us to rest. . .what a generous and kind God we have. We expect marching orders, or hoops to jump through. But God simply says, "Alright, this will be challenging, but here's what I want you to do: take a break."
Keri Wyatt Kent
Breathe: Creating Space for God in a Hectic Life (2005)

11   Rest is an internal state of soul, a relaxing into God's chest even when dashing through a day or a season.
Jane Rubietta
Resting Place (2005)

12   Thou hast made us for Thyself, O Lord, and our hearts are restless until they rest in Thee.
Augustine
Confessions (4th century)

13   God's purposes may best be accomplished through our inactivity.
Jane Rubietta
Resting Place (2005)

350 RESURRECTION
For if we have been planted together in the likeness of his death, we shall be also in the likeness of his resurrection.
ROMANS 6:5

1   The most important single statement in the Bible is that *Christ rose from the dead.* This is the thing for which the whole Bible was written, apart from which it would mean nothing.
Henry H. Halley
Pocket Bible Handbook (1948)

2   God knows where every particle of the handful of dust has gone: he has marked in his book the wandering of every one of its atoms. He hath death so open before his view, that he can bring all these together, bone to bone, and clothe them with the very flesh that robed them in the days of yore, and make them live again.
Charles Spurgeon
"God, the All-Seeing One" sermon (1858)

3   True Christian congregations are built on the reality of the resurrection of Jesus Christ and the reality of our own coming resurrection through him.
Mark Dever
Twelve Challenges Churches Face (2008)

4 Because of the resurrection, everything changes. Death changes. It used to be the end; now it is the beginning.
Max Lucado
When Christ Comes (1999)

5 The greatest proof of Jesus' uniqueness is His physical resurrection. Jesus Himself intended us to accept or reject who He claimed to be, and what He taught, based on the resurrection.
Alex McFarland
The 10 Most Common Objections to Christianity (2007)

6 Life triumphed over death. Death is no longer the end.
Albert Hsu *Grieving a Suicide* (2002)

7 God is still in the business of resurrecting lives.
Tracie Peterson
The Eyes of the Heart (2002)

8 To deny the truth of the resurrection because its mode is a mystery to us, is to say that a finite mind is equal in discovering and investigating power to all difficulties involved in the existence and nature of any truth, however intimate its relationship to the great infinite, either in being or principle.
William Elbert Munsey
Eternal Retribution (1951)

9 What greater proof could Jesus offer than to rise from the dead?
Ravi Zacharias and Kevin Johnson
Jesus Among Other Gods—Youth Edition (2000)

10 The Resurrection of Jesus was an unparalleled event; the sovereignty of death was at an end; he that had ears could hear the first peal sounding for the general resurrection to usher in the world that was to come.
Paul Wernle
The Beginnings of Christianity (1903)

11 As surely as God awakened Jesus so surely will He awaken us.
Paul Wernle
The Beginnings of Christianity (1903)

12 Only Christ's resurrection power can satisfy our empty hearts.
Michael Youssef
"Making Joy a Priority" article (2010)

13 The evidence for the resurrection of Jesus Christ is more powerful than anything else we believe. By His resurrection Jesus proved He is who He says He is. Be confident in this truth. Stand on the Holy Word of God. Don't sell the world a false bill of goods. Preach the Word. Defend the faith. Live the faith.
Charles Colson
Faith on the Line (1994)

RETALIATION (*see* REVENGE)

RETRIBUTION (*see* REVENGE)

351 REVELATION
(*see also* INSPIRATION)
The Revelation of Jesus Christ...
REVELATION 1:1

1 We need not deny that other men have been illuminated; but the difference between illumination and inspiration is as far as the east is from the west.
F. B. Meyer
The Way into the Holiest (1893)

2 Worship is always in response to revelation.
Matt Redman
Facedown (2004)

352 REVENGE
Dearly beloved, avenge not yourselves, but rather give place unto wrath: for it is written, Vengeance is mine; I will repay, saith the Lord.
ROMANS 12:19

1   You can't get ahead if you're trying to get even.
L. James Harvey
701 More Sentence Sermons (2002)

2   Revenge always results in destruction of some kind.
Mary Southerland
Sandpaper People (2005)

3   Returning evil for evil is the childish attitude of "he did this to me so I'll do this to him."
Jo Berry
Beloved Unbeliever (1981)

4   Retribution has no place in the life of any Christian.
Jo Berry
Beloved Unbeliever (1981)

5   A revengeful spirit is contrary to our heavenly calling.
Thomas Manton
One Hundred and Ninety Sermons on the Hundred and Nineteenth Psalm
(17th century)

353 REVIVAL

*Wilt thou not revive us again:
that thy people may rejoice in thee?*
PSALM 85:6

1   Pentecost isn't over yet!
D. L. Moody
"Revivals" sermon (19th century)

2   Do you sometimes feel that you just can't take one more thing? Even in your misery, be mindful that the very weight of your burdens and the intensity of the pressure may be exactly what God is going to use in your life to trigger an experience of personal revival.
Anne Graham Lotz
I Saw the Lord (2006)

3   If you don't see a revival starting around you, let it begin in your own heart, then let it overflow to others.
Robert Morgan
Then Sings My Soul (2003)

4   Revival normally begins among God's people, but before long, like water surging through a broken levee, revival overflows and spills into our society.
Pat Robertson
Six Steps to Spiritual Revival (2002)

5   Satan trembles at the mere thought of revival among God's people.
Pat Robertson
Six Steps to Spiritual Revival (2002)

6   Revival means self-examination on the part of Christians—repentance, confession of sin, renunciation of sin, restitution, submission to the Lordship of Jesus Christ, separation from the world, being filled with the Spirit.
Vance Havner
Messages on Revival (1958)

7   Revival is a sovereign work of God. Yet He invites us to participate in it.
Henry Blackaby, Richard Blackaby, and Claude King *Fresh Encounter* (2007)

8   God revives people who believe and obey His word.
Henry Blackaby, Richard Blackaby, and Claude King
Fresh Encounter (2007)

354 REWARDS (*see also* HEAVEN)

Behold, I come quickly; and my reward is with me, to give every man according as his work shall be.
REVELATION 22:12

1   One day you and I will have our own awards ceremony in eternity. The halls of

heaven will ring with praise and celebration. Witnesses from every nation and every generation will watch with eager anticipation.
  Bruce Wilkinson
  A Life God Rewards (2002)

2   What you did with your life will endure like gold, silver, and precious stones in a fire. Or it will burn up like straw—not a trace will remain, no matter how sensible, enjoyable, or even religious these activities might have seemed while you were alive.
  Bruce Wilkinson
  A Life God Rewards (2002)

355 RICH, THE
(*see also* MONEY; WEALTH)
And again I say unto you, It is easier for a camel to go through the eye of a needle, than for a rich man to enter into the kingdom of God.
MATTHEW 19:24

1   The problem with the rich young ruler wasn't that he had money—but that his money had him.
  Steve Campbell "The Cost of Following Christ" sermon (2009)

2   God only, and not wealth, maintains the world; riches merely make people proud and lazy.
  Martin Luther
  Table Talk (16th century)

3   The more men have to lose, the less willing they are to venture.
  Thomas Paine
  Common Sense (1776)

356 RIGHT AND WRONG
Woe unto them that call evil good, and good evil; that put darkness for light, and light for darkness; that put bitter for sweet, and sweet for bitter!
ISAIAH 5:20

1   What's wrong today is wrong tomorrow, and what's right yesterday is still right today. Rights and wrongs don't change for one simple reason: God doesn't change. He is truth. He is right.
  Alex McFarland
  The 10 Most Common Objections to Christianity (2007)

2   Conscience naturally gives men an apprehension of right and wrong, and suggests the relation there is between right and wrong, and a retribution; the Spirit of God assists men's consciences to do this in a greater degree, helps conscience against the stupefying influence of worldly objects and their lusts.
  Jonathan Edwards
  A Treatise Concerning Religious Affections (18th century)

357 RIGHTEOUSNESS
(*see also* VIRTUE)
Abraham believed God, and it was accounted to him for righteousness.
GALATIANS 3:6

1   In Christianity, men gain righteousness only by confessing their unrighteousness and being covered by Christ's merit. Every other religion is man working his way to God. Christianity is God working His way to men.
  Randy Alcorn
  The Grace and Truth Paradox (2003)

2   A righteous man will be moral, but being moral does not make a man righteous.
  Kay Arthur
  Beloved (1994)

3   Biblical righteousness does not begin with our preferences. God's righteousness is settled and authoritative. God does not change His standards to conform to us. His standards

are the expression of what is right, and our behavior becomes righteous as we come into alignment with them.

Joseph Stowell
Fan the Flame (1986)

4   It is when we live by the right principles that we begin to love the right principles. Most of the time, we want to fall in love with what is right and then have it happen to us.

John Maxwell
Be All You Can Be (1987)

5   Righteousness is the core of Christianity compressed into a single word.

Hank Hanegraaff
The Covering (2002)

6   We are judged by the righteousness of the Christ who lives within, not our own.

Philip Yancey
The Jesus I Never Knew (1995)

7   Christ's leadings are always along "paths of righteousness."

F. B. Meyer
The Shepherd Psalm (1889)

8   In the original language of the New Testament, the word righteousness literally means "to stay within the lines." These days, no one is really sure where the lines are or who was supposed to draw them. But in a world with no lines, how can we make right choices? . . . Each person will have to find his or her own lines—and hang on tight to them.

John Trent
Making Wise Life Choices (2003)

9   What you should do, and what someone's response is going to be, are two very different issues.

Henry Cloud
9 Things You Simply Must Do (2004)

10   It is important for every Christian to keep in mind the great difference between his position and his practice, his standing and his state. God sees us as righteous, because He sees us through His righteous Son, who has taken our place, and because He has planted in us a righteous new nature.

John MacArthur
1 Corinthians (1984)

358 RISK

Who have for my life laid down their own necks:
unto whom not only I give thanks, but
also all the churches of the Gentiles.
Romans 16:4

1   Avoidance of risk is the greatest risk of all.
Henry Cloud
9 Things You Simply Must Do (2004)

359 ROMANCE

Let him kiss me with the kisses of his mouth:
for thy love is better than wine.
Song of Solomon 1:2

1   Truth is, the most joyful, beautiful, exciting romance is the one that is pure.
Rebecca St. James
Wait for Me (2008)

2   A woman wants to be swept off her feet, while a man may think sweeping the front porch does just that.
Nancy Cobb and Connie Grigsby
How to Get Your Husband to Talk to You (2001)

3   Romantic love is one of those rare human endeavors that succeeds best when it requires the least effort.
James Dobson
Life on the Edge (1995)

4   Sometimes in a relationship, we can be so caught up in our feelings for the other person that we squeeze God into the background.
Eric and Leslie Ludy
When God Writes Your Love Story (1999)

5   Dreaming and envisioning are the essence
of romance!
   Neil Clark Warren
   The Triumphant Marriage (1995)

6   There is romance in the heart of God and
a hunger for romance in the heart of God-
imaging creatures.
   R. Paul Stevens
   Down-to-Earth Spirituality (2003)

360 RULES
(*see also* TEN COMMANDMENTS)
And if a man also strive for masteries, yet is he not
crowned, except he strive lawfully.
2 TIMOTHY 2:5

1   Everyone needs to make some personal
rules to live by. Life is just too complicated for
us to succeed at living it unless we make some
rules for ourselves.
   Lewis Smedes
   Choices (1986)

2   We all live by rules, but the rules we live by
come from many sources. Where they come
from says a lot about how serious we need to
be about keeping them.
   Lewis Smedes
   Choices (1986)

3   There is no such thing as absolute freedom.
Everybody answers to somebody.
   Andy Stanley
   The Seven Checkpoints (2001)

4   Let's face it: To ignore or rebel against
authority is to rebel against God.
   Andy Stanley
   The Seven Checkpoints (2001)

5   Rules focus on behavior. Principles focus
on the heart.
   Scott Turansky and Joanne Miller
   Parenting Is Heart Work (2006)

6   God never instituted anything designed to
make man miserable.
   Gary Chapman
   Hope for the Separated (1982)

7   Love and laws are allies, not enemies.
Don't let anyone deceive you into thinking you
must choose between them. Law needs love as
its driving force, else it degenerates into cruel
legalism. Love needs law as its eyes, for it is
often blind as to how it should honor or please
its object.
   Rubel Shelly
   Written in Stone (1994)

361 SABBATH (*see also* SUNDAY)
Remember the sabbath day, to keep it holy.
EXODUS 20:8

1   Sabbath, in the long run, is as essential to
your well-being as food and water, and as good
as a wood fire on a cold day.
   Mark Buchanan
   The Rest of God (2006)

362 SACRAMENTS (*see also* BAPTISM;
LORD'S SUPPER)
Now I praise you, brethren, that ye remember me
in all things, and keep the ordinances,
as I delivered them to you.
1 CORINTHIANS 11:2

1   The church is generated by the right
preaching of the Word; the church is
contained and distinguished by the right
administration of baptism and the Lord's
Supper.
   Mark Dever
   Nine Marks of a Healthy Church (2004)

2   The ordinances of Christ are the ornaments
of the Church.
   Matthew Henry
   Commentary on the Whole Bible (1706)

363 SACRIFICE

I beseech you therefore, brethren, by the mercies of God, that ye present your bodies a living sacrifice, holy, acceptable unto God, which is your reasonable service.

ROMANS 12:1

1   He is no fool who gives up what he cannot keep to gain what he cannot lose.
Jim Elliot (1949)
quoted in *Through Gates of Splendor* by Elisabeth Elliot

2   There is a secret feeling that all this brings more sacrifice, difficulty and danger, than we are ready for. This is only true as long as we have not seen how absolute God's claim is, how unutterably blessed it is to yield to it, and how certain that God himself will work it in us.
Andrew Murray
Prayer's Inner Chamber (1989)

3   The worship of God has always involved a sacrifice. It began with the blood of bulls and goats and lambs and culminated with the blood of the perfect and spotless Lamb of God—Christ himself.
Josh McDowell
The Last Christian Generation (2006)

4   A man should not sacrifice what he does not esteem.
G. K. Chesterton (20th century) quoted in *The Collected Works of G. K. Chesterton*

5   Sacrifice for a friend is always worth it, even if it's never acknowledged, appreciated, or known. Be assured that Jesus, our example, sees the sacrifices you make for your friends and will reward you in the end.
G. A. Myers
Hugs for Friends Book 2 (2003)

6   I did not engage in a religious life but for the love of God, and I have endeavoured to act only for Him; whatever becomes of me, whether I be lost or saved.
Brother Lawrence
The Practice of the Presence of God (17th century)

7   What's the secret to a lasting relationship? Self-sacrifice. And not just on one side; it applies to both members of any relationship.
Jason Boyett
Pocket Guide to Adulthood (2005)

8   When a man has given away all his goods, he has nothing else remaining that he can give, but himself.
Jonathan Edwards
"The Greatest Performances or Sufferings in Vain without Charity" sermon (1738)

9   I will offer to Him both my tears and my exultation. Nothing we offer to Him will be lost.
Elisabeth Elliot
Be Still My Soul (2003)

364 SADNESS

Sorrow is better than laughter: for by the sadness of the countenance the heart is made better.

ECCLESIASTES 7:3

1   I have yet to find that God ever uses a man who is all the time looking on the dark side, and talking about the obstacles and looking at them, and who is discouraged and cast down.
D. L. Moody
The Faithful Saying (1877)

2   What makes men depressed? Self-concentration, as a rule.
Henry Drummond
Stones Rolled Away and Other Addresses to Young Men (1893)

3   When a man is wrapped up in himself, seeking only his own, he finds he is seeking a very shallow object, and very soon gets to

the end of it; hence all the springs of life have nothing to act upon, and depression follows.
Henry Drummond
Stones Rolled Away and Other Addresses to Young Men (1893)

4   All power is given unto him in heaven and on earth. Why, then, art thou so sad?
F. B. Meyer
The Way into the Holiest (1893)

5   There is no other way into the deep things of God but a broken spirit.
Smith Wigglesworth
Faith That Prevails (1938)

365 SALVATION (*see also* BORN AGAIN; CONVERSION; NEW BIRTH; REDEMPTION; REGENERATION)
For God hath not appointed us to wrath, but to obtain salvation by our Lord Jesus Christ.
1 THESSALONIANS 5:9

1   Are you washed in the blood,
In the soul cleansing blood of the Lamb?
Elisha Hoffman
"Are You Washed in the Blood?" (1878)

2   If you have ever come to God, crying out for salvation, and for salvation only, then you have come unto God aright.
Charles Spurgeon
"Salvation to the Uttermost" sermon (1856)

3   Those who genuinely cry out to the Lord for salvation are instantly born again by the Spirit of God, who then dwells forever within them and energizes them to cry out for further needs.
Bill Gothard
The Power of Crying Out (2002)

4   Our value does not lie in what we possess. It doesn't spring from what we wear, what we drive, or where we live. Our value is wrapped up in the amazing fact that Jesus Christ, the mighty Son of God and Creator of the world,

loved us enough to pay the price for our salvation.
Ron Mehl
Right with God (2003)

5   We can all get to heaven without health, without wealth, without fame, without learning, without culture, without beauty, without friends, without ten thousand things. But we can never get to heaven without Christ.
Corrie ten Boom
He Cares, He Comforts (1977)

6   The ultimate question is not who you are but whose you are.
John Piper
The Passion of Jesus Christ (2004)

7   When we remove all the discussion and debate about man's relationship to God, how he can know Him, and what he must do, it comes down to a person saying, "I believe."
John MacArthur
Nothing But the Truth (1999)

8   God excludes none, if they do not exclude themselves.
William Guthrie
The Christian's Great Interest (17th century)

9   The only proof of true, living, saving knowledge of God; the only proof of not being self-deceived in our religion; of God's love not being an imagination, but a possession, is, keeping his Word.
Andrew Murray
Prayer's Inner Chamber (1912)

10 God became earth's mockery to save his children. How absurd to think that such nobility would go to such poverty to share such a treasure with such thankless souls. But he did.
Max Lucado
God Came Near (1986)

11 Among the voices that found their way into the carpentry shop in Nazareth was your voice. Your silent prayers uttered on tearstained pillows were heard before they were said. Your deepest questions about death and eternity were answered before they were asked. And your direst need for a Savior, was met before you ever sinned.

Max Lucado
God Came Near (1986)

12 God's salvation is not a purchase to be made, nor wages to be earned, nor a summit to be climbed, nor a task to be accomplished; but it is simply and only a gift to be accepted, and can only be accepted by faith.

Hannah Whitall Smith
The God of All Comfort (1906)

13 Christian influence in the home could have a lasting impact on a child's life, but faith could not be passed on as an inheritance, like the family silver. It had to be exercised by each individual.

Billy Graham
Just As I Am (1997)

14 God does not expect or require months of misery-evoking penance or daily sacrifices to appease His anger. Christ's death on our behalf provided the once-for-all payment for sin. Nevertheless, a contrite heart that expresses itself in mourning over wrongdoing results in divine comfort. Count on it.

Charles Swindoll
Simple Faith (1991)

15 If we are trusting in our repentance and faith, we will never have assurance, because our faith and our repentance are never what they might be. Our salvation depends entirely on Christ. Faith is the open hand that receives what He offers, and repentance is the response of a heart that has received.

Colin Smith
Ten Keys for Unlocking the Bible (2002)

16 Salvation brings into the life a new capacity and with it a new ability to think right, to love God, to purpose to do the will of God, to have a changed heart.

Charles Ryrie
Balancing the Christian Life (1969)

17 If my faith hasn't changed me, it hasn't saved me.

James MacDonald
"Are You Saved" sermon (2008)

18 Salvation happens at a moment in time— but salvation is demonstrated over time.

James MacDonald
"Are You Saved" sermon (2008)

19 Since Christ has an infinite power, and also an infinite desire to save mankind, how can any one miss of this salvation, but through his own unwillingness to be saved by him?

William Law
The Spirit of Prayer (1750)

20 Awake, thou that sleepest, and Christ, who from all eternity hath been espoused to thy soul, shall give thee light.

William Law
The Spirit of Prayer (1750)

21 You must be much in the way, or much out of the way; a good soldier for God, or for the devil. O choose the better part'—now!— to-day!

John Wesley
The Works of the Rev. John Wesley (18th century)

22 Your salvation does not depend on what you are but on what He is. For every look at self, take ten looks at Christ.

F. B. Meyer
The Shepherd Psalm (1889)

23 Don't throw any mud at the plan of salvation until you try it and find out that it won't work.

Billy Sunday
The Real Billy Sunday (1914)

24 While he was describing the change which God works in the heart through faith in Christ, I felt my heart strangely warmed. I felt I did trust in Christ, Christ alone, for salvation; and an assurance was given me that He had taken away my sins, even mine, and saved me from the law of sin and death.

John Wesley
The Journal of John Wesley (18th century)

25 That is why we must preach with the urgency of the dying man. It is because human beings are in desperate need of salvation. Time is short, God's wrath is certain, and eternity hangs in the balance.

Albert Mohler Jr.
He Is Not Silent (2008)

26 We receive salvation because of God's mercy and faithfulness toward us, not because of anything we do or say or wear.

Lisa Harper
Relentless Love (2002)

27 You might say the whole plan of salvation is in two words—Giving; Receiving. God gives; I receive.

D. L. Moody
Wondrous Love (1876)

28 This great gift of God, the salvation of our souls, is no other than the image of God fresh stamped on our hearts.

John Wesley
A Plain Account of Christian Perfection (18th century)

29 The Christian good news is not simply a declaration that God has said something. It also affirms that God has done something.

John Stott
Basic Christianity (1958)

30 We must be clear on one crucial point: Being a member of any one church or group does not guarantee automatic membership in the Body of Christ.

Fritz Ridenour
So What's the Difference? (1967)

31 Jesus' shorthand for this perpetual Jubilee life is the cryptic message, "Repent, for the kingdom of heaven is at hand."

Richard Foster
Streams of Living Water (1998)

32 If you have not seen your utter, absolute need of being forgiven by God and being reconciled to Him, then your whole position is wrong, and you have no right to consider anything else.

Martyn Lloyd-Jones
Compelling Christianity (2007)

33 Beware of a false peace: strive to enter in at the strait gate; and give all diligence to make your calling and election sure: remember you are but a babe in Christ, if so much!

George Whitefield
Memoirs of Rev. George Whitefield (1741)

34 If there is any direction in which we are seeking to have our own way and not letting Him have His own way in our lives, our power will be crippled and men lost that we might have saved.

R. A. Torrey
How to Bring Men to Christ (1893)

35 Among those who entertain false hopes, perhaps the largest class are those who expect to be saved by their righteous lives.

R. A. Torrey
How to Bring Men to Christ (1893)

36 It is not so much God who damns men as men who damn themselves in spite of God's goodness because they will not come to Christ and accept the life freely offered.
R. A. Torrey
How to Bring Men to Christ (1893)

37 "Am I saved, or am I lost? " It must be one or the other. There is no neutrality about the matter.
D. L. Moody
Best Thoughts and Discourses of D. L. Moody (1876)

38 The entire salvation plan was founded on legal truths.
Steve Campbell
"Freedom from Addiction" sermon (2009)

39 When we couldn't reach up to heaven, heaven came down to us and welcomed us into the Living Room through the doorway of Jesus Christ.
Joanna Weaver
Having a Mary Heart in a Martha World (2000)

40 It hath been the astonishing wonder of many a man, as well as me, to read in the holy Scripture, how few will be saved.
Richard Baxter
A Call to the Unconverted, to Turn and Live (17th century)

41 How adorable then is the depth of God's wisdom, and the vehemence of his kindness, to have a remedy ready to apply for the cure of fallen nature! God had a salve lying by him for the sore, and provided himself with a remedy for defeating the designs of Satan.
Stephen Charnock
Discourse of God's being the Author of Reconciliation (1652)

42 Now, poor soul! will you come into this lifeboat, just as you are? Here is safety from the wreck!
Charles Spurgeon
All of Grace (19th century)

43 Let us join hands and stand together at the foot of the cross, and trust our souls once for all to Him who shed His blood for the guilty. We will be saved by one and the same Saviour.
Charles Spurgeon
All of Grace (19th century)

44 Salvation is God's business.
Max Lucado
He Still Moves Stones (1993)

45 When you truly believe what the Bible says about Jesus Christ and decide to follow Him, to let Him be your Master, something miraculous happens.
Kay Arthur
God, Are You There? (1994)

46 He did not come to save us because we were worth the saving, but because we were utterly worthless, ruined, and undone.
Charles Spurgeon
All of Grace (19th century)

47 Let me ask you, sinner, how much time will it take you to do the first great duty which God requires namely, give Him your heart?
Charles Finney
"The Sinner's Excuses Answered" sermon (19th century)

48 Dear reader, the salvation which is received by faith is not a thing of months and years; for our Lord Jesus hath "obtained eternal salvation for us," and that which is eternal cannot come to an end.
Charles Spurgeon
All of Grace (19th century)

49 To be kept holy is better than merely to be kept safe.

Charles Spurgeon
All of Grace (19th century)

50 God grant that in that last great day we may stand free from all charge, that none in the whole universe may dare to challenge our claim to be the redeemed of the Lord.

Charles Spurgeon
All of Grace (19th century)

51 If a pardon be sweet to a condemned criminal, how sweet must the sprinkling the blood of Jesus be to the trembling conscience of a law-condemned sinner?

John Flavel
Christ Altogether Lovely (17th century)

52 You must repent (turn from sin) and trust in Jesus Christ alone in order to be saved from eternal justice. This is the type of trust you would have when you put your faith in a parachute to save you—it's more than just a belief.

Kirk Cameron and Ray Comfort
Life's Emergency Handbook (2002)

53 Is not he a fool who minds his recreation more than his salvation?

Thomas Watson
The Doctrine of Repentance (1668)

54 Remember, you have been saved to soar, not sink. Yu have been converted to conquer, not capitulate. You have been won to win!

Bob Moorehead
A Passion for Victory (1996)

55 It is necessary in order to saving faith, that man should be emptied of himself, be sensible that he is "wretched, and miserable, and poor, and blind, and naked." Humility is a great ingredient of true faith.

Jonathan Edwards
"God Glorified in Man's Dependence" sermon (18th century)

56 We cannot know a man's mental processes. This is surely true, that if in the very last halftwinkling of an eye a man look up towards God longingly, that look is the turning of the will to God. And that is quite enough.

Samuel Gordon
Quiet Talks on Prayer (1904)

57 If ever you would be savingly converted, you must despair of doing it in your own strength.

Joseph Alleine
A Sure Guide to Heaven (1671)

58 Every man's vote is for salvation from suffering, but they do not desire to be saved from sinning.

Joseph Alleine
A Sure Guide to Heaven (1671)

59 If the Lord does not save at his own initiative and for his own sake alone, then salvation cannot and will not take place.

Eugene Merrill
Everlasting Dominion (2006)

60 When someone uses the phrase "invite Jesus into your heart," the thought often conveyed is, "Say a prayer that 'invites Jesus into your heart' and you're saved." A person places trust in a prayer that was said instead of the Savior who died on a cross.

R. Larry Moyer
21 Things God Never Said (2004)

61 Spiritual salvation is not behavior modification. It is life modification. It is life saving and life enriching. And it is our only genuine balm for grief.

Zig Ziglar
Confessions of a Grieving Christian (1998)

366 SANCTIFICATION (*see also* GROWTH, SPIRITUAL; MATURITY)

Elect according to the foreknowledge of God the Father, through sanctification of the Spirit, unto obedience and sprinkling of the blood of Jesus Christ. . .
1 PETER 1:2

1   Man's part is to trust and God's part is to work.

Hannah Whitall Smith
The Christian's Secret of a Happy Life (1875)

2   Sanctification grows out of faith in Jesus Christ. Remember holiness is a flower, not a root; it is not sanctification that saves, but salvation that sanctifies.

Charles Spurgeon
"Consecration to God" sermon (1868)

3   To make room for the kind of abundance He created us for, He must first cut away parts of our lives that drain precious time and energy from what's truly important.

Bruce Wilkinson
Secrets of the Vine (2001)

4   Drawing near to God's brightness, we suddenly become aware of our condition. The sin in our lives, which we first accepted as normal, becomes distasteful—and then loathsome.

Pat Robertson
Six Steps to Spiritual Revival (2002)

5   We are "God's workmanship," and God is good, therefore His workmanship must be good also; and we may securely trust that before He is done with us, He will make out of us something that will be to His glory, no matter how unlike this we may as yet feel ourselves to be.

Hannah Whitall Smith
God of All Comfort (1906)

6   God loves us too much to leave us the way we are.

Jonathan and Jennifer Campbell
The Way of Jesus (2005)

7   Never doubt but that God will set you free from all evil passions, if you are steadfast and devout on your part.

Francis de Sales
Introduction to the Devout Life (1608)

8   How are you to meet the swarm of foolish attachments, triflings, and undesirable inclinations which beset you? By turning sharply away, and thoroughly renouncing such vanities, flying to the Saviour's Cross, and clasping His Crown of thorns to your heart, so that these little foxes may not spoil your vines.

Francis de Sales
Introduction to the Devout Life (1608)

9   We come to Jesus as we are, but as someone has said, He loves us too much to leave us that way.

Erwin Lutzer
The Truth About Same-Sex Marriage (2004)

10 No man is called to a life of self-denial for its own sake.

Henry Drummond
Natural Law in the Spiritual World (19th century)

11 The penalty of evading self-denial is just that we get the lesser instead of the larger good.

Henry Drummond
Natural Law in the Spiritual World (19th century)

12 Dying to self is a progressive journey, and I have come to believe it is traveled only through praise.

Merlin Carothers
Prison to Praise (1970)

13 We must not lie loitering in the ditch, and wait till Omnipotence pull us from thence. No, no: we must bestir ourselves, and actuate those powers which we have already received.

Henry Scougal
Life of God in the Soul of Man (17th century)

14 If we desire to have our souls moulded to this holy frame, to become partakers of the

divine nature, and have Christ formed in our hearts, we must seriously resolve, and carefully endeavour, to avoid and abandon all vicious and sinful practices.

Henry Scougal
Life of God in the Soul of Man
(17th century)

15 Sanctification is not a heavy yoke, but a joyful liberation.

Corrie ten Boom
Not Good If Detached (1957)

16 The mortification of indwelling sin remaining in our mortal bodies, that it may not have life and power to bring forth the works or deeds of the flesh, is the constant duty of believers.

John Owen
Of the Mortification of Sin in Believers
(1656)

17 Be humble, and, in a constant sense of your own utter insufficiency, to do the least thing towards your salvation of yourselves, put your whole trust in God at all times for his constant influence and help, by which alone you will be able to work out your own salvation.

Samuel Hopkins
"God Working in Men to Will
and to Do" sermon (1803)

18 Sanctification is the process of becoming progressively more like Christ by cooperating with God to become holy.

Keith Meyer
Whole Life Transformation (2010)

SATAN (*see* DEVIL)

367 SATISFACTION
(*see also* CONTENTMENT)
For he satisfieth the longing soul,
and filleth the hungry soul with goodness.
PSALM 107:9

1 All the human satisfactions of the cravings of body and soul have one defect; they do not satisfy forever. They only serve to deaden the present want; but they never extinguish it. The want always revives again.

Fulton Sheen
Life of Christ (1958)

2 Satisfaction and contentment are marks of a man or woman of God. Combined with a hunger and thirst to know God and enjoy His creation, they create a healthy tension in the Christian life.

Gordon MacDonald
Secrets of the Generous Life (2002)

SAVIOR
(*see* CHRIST; JESUS; MESSIAH)

368 SCIENCE
(*see also* PHILOSOPHY; REASON)
O Timothy, keep that which is committed to thy
trust, avoiding profane and vain babblings,
and oppositions of science falsely so called.
1 TIMOTHY 6:20

1 It may be said that Christ did not teach science. True, but He taught truth.

Charles Hodge
What Is Darwinism? (1874)

2 Scripture, not science, is the ultimate test of all truth. And the further evangelicalism gets from that conviction, the less evangelical and more humanistic it becomes.

John MacArthur
The Battle for the Beginning (2001)

SCRIPTURE (*see* BIBLE, THE)

369 SECOND COMING
For as the lightning cometh out of the east, and
shineth even unto the west; so shall also the
coming of the Son of man be.
MATTHEW 24:27

1   The first time Jesus came to earth, He came in humility: born in a stable, raised in a humble home, and working with Joseph in the carpenter's shop. He came to serve and to give Himself as a ransom. Not so the second time. When He comes back this time, He'll come to be served. He won't be coming back to die, but to sweep His enemies right off the planet. He will be glorified beyond anything on this earth.
   Ken Hutcherson
   Before All Hell Breaks Loose (2001)

2   We have no business letting the world get us down. When I start feeling down, I turn to the last chapter of the book of Revelation. There is no way I can ever, ever stay down when I have read that last chapter.
   Ken Hutcherson
   Before All Hell Breaks Loose (2001)

3   For the Christian, the return of Christ is not a riddle to be solved or a code to be broken, but rather a day to be anticipated.
   Max Lucado
   When Christ Comes (1999)

4   Bodies will push back the dirt and break the surface of the sea. The earth will tremble, the sky will roar, and those who do not know him will shudder. But in that hour you will not fear, because you know him.
   Max Lucado
   When Christ Comes (1999)

5   Christians get excited about the return of Jesus. Oh, happy day! Yes, it is a happy day for the saved, but for the unsaved the return of Jesus is the worst of all conceivable calamities.
   R. C. Sproul
   Saved from What? (2002)

370 SECURITY

And I give unto them eternal life; and they shall never perish, neither shall any man pluck them out of my hand.
JOHN 10:28

1   The objects of everlasting love never change.
   Charles Spurgeon
   "The Immutability of God" sermon (1855)

2   If you square your hearts and lives in all sincerity according to the gospel rule, there is a provision made for your security in the blood of Christ.
   Stephen Charnock
   Discourse on the Cleansing
   Virtue of Christ's Blood (17th century)

3   For most women, security is a more vibrant and common need than success. It isn't that we don't want to succeed; it is simply that we view success as a means for providing security.
   Bill and Pam Farrel
   The Marriage Code (2009)

4   For most men, success is a more vibrant and common need than security. It's not that we don't want to be secure; it is simply that we will sacrifice security in order to do what we are best at. The need to feel successful is the need we feel most often, and it determines the quality of everything in our lives.
   Bill and Pam Farrel
   The Marriage Code (2009)

5   It's a huge shocker to talk to hundreds of women and find that while financial security is nice, it isn't nearly as important to them as feeling emotionally secure—feeling close and confident that you will be there for her no matter what.
   Shaunti and Jeff Feldhahn
   For Men Only (2006)

6   If security can be defined as that sense of confidence, assurance, and contentment with life that comes from knowing God, through Christ, personally, then being really convinced, mentally and emotionally, that God is in control of your life brings contentment with the outcome.

Josh McDowell and Dale Bellis
Evidence for Joy (1984)

7   Living a life based on "security" is living a life based on fear.

Don Howe
Motivational Speech (2010)

371 SEEKING GOD

O God, thou art my God; early will I seek thee: my soul thirsteth for thee, my flesh longeth for thee in a dry and thirsty land, where no water is.
PSALM 63:1

1   Many have sought the Lord but not found Him because they failed to seek Him with their whole heart.

Bill Gothard
Our Jealous God (2003)

2   The process of seeking the Lord with our whole heart really begins with delighting in the Word of God.

Bill Gothard
Our Jealous God (2003)

3   Though God has no other desire than to impart Himself to the loving soul that seeks Him, yet He frequently conceals Himself from it, that it may be roused from sloth, and impelled to seek Him with fidelity and love.

François Fénelon and Jeanne Guyon
Spiritual Progress (17th century)

4   All over the world, people go to unimaginable lengths to find God—which is sad when you consider the unimaginable lengths God has already gone to find us.

Joanna Weaver
Having a Mary Heart in a Martha World (2000)

5   He who seeks God in tangible form misses the very thing he is seeking, for God is a Spirit.

Henry Drummond
"Why Christ Must Depart" sermon
(19th century)

6   We are, by nature, blind and ignorant, at best but groping in the dim light of nature after God.

John Flavel
Christ Altogether Lovely (17th century)

7   If you have an honest heart, an appetite for truth and an openness to God's Spirit, you will be gratified by the results.

Josh McDowell and Dale Bellis
Evidence for Joy (1984)

8   Every person, on coming to the knowledge of himself, is not only urged to seek God, but is also led as by the hand to find him.

John Calvin
Institutes of the Christian Religion (16th century)

9   The more we take the time to study the character of God from His Word, facet by facet, the more He will reveal Himself to us.

Joy Dawson
Intimate Friendship with God (1986)

10 Mind that which is of God in you, to guide you to the Father of life.

George Fox Personal Letter
(17th century)

372 SELF, THE

For no man ever yet hated his own flesh;
but nourisheth and cherisheth it. . .
EPHESIANS 5:29

1   Self must step aside, to let God work.
Hannah Whitall Smith
The Christian's Secret of a Happy Life
(1888)

2   A long, hard look in the mirror will cure
most of us from the notion that we can make
it on our own.
Jeff Walling
Until I Return (2000)

3   The fake self counts on outside experiences
to deliver inner meaning.
Brennan Manning
Posers, Fakers, and Wannabes (2003)

4   When God instilled in your DNA all
that makes you, you, He didn't have a backup
person to play your part if you bailed.
Verla Gillmor
Reality Check (2001)

5   We need to purge our inner Pharisee—our
concern with looking spiritual, our desire to
create the criteria for everyone else's behavior,
our arrogant tendency to have all the answers,
our penchant to perform meaningless religious
rituals.
Lisa Harper
Relenless Love (2002)

6   A healthy self-image is not one of pride or
arrogance, but one that coincides with God's
viewpoint. It is choosing to accept God's
evaluation, learning to see ourselves as God
sees us, agreeing with who we are in His eyes,
and giving Him permission to make us what
He designed us to be. In His eyes, every person
is valuable.
Mary Southerland
Sandpaper People (2005)

7   Whether your handicap is physical or
emotional today can be the day you begin to
chip away at that granite mountain of self-
defeat.
Ted Engstrom
The Pursuit of Excellence (1982)

8   As long as we're in search of ourselves and
our true identity, we will be under pressure.
Lloyd John Ogilvie
The Bush Is Still Burning (1980)

9   Our function is not to label each other or
become junior psychiatrists of other people,
but to analyze ourselves.
Florence Littauer
After Every Wedding Comes a Marriage
(1981)

10 Are you able to ground your identity in God
rather than in the work that you do for God?
Janet Hagberg and Robert Guelich
The Critical Journey (1995)

11 There are many professors who are willing
to do almost any thing in religion, that does
not require self-denial.
Charles Finney
Lectures of Revivals of Religion (1835)

12 Resolve by the grace of God, if you love
life, that you will have regular seasons for
examining yourself, and looking over the
accounts of your soul.
J. C. Ryle
The Upper Room (19th century)

13 I am disgusted with the pettiness and
futility of my unled self. If the way out is not
more perfect slavery to God, then what is the
way out?
Frank Laubach
Letters by a Modern Mystic (1937)

373 SELF-CONTROL (*see also* ABSTINENCE; TEMPERANCE)

But the fruit of the Spirit is love, joy, peace, longsuffering, gentleness, goodness, faith, meekness, temperance. . .
GALATIANS 5:22–23

1   He yet will not deny his Inclinations and Will, will soon lose ye command of his Actions.
Thomas Wilson
Private Thoughts (1828)

2   That man will not hold out long, who Acts, or Resists Sin, on worldly motives only.
Thomas Wilson
Private Thoughts (1828)

3   Stay in charge of the only person you can control: yourself.
Henry Cloud and John Townsend
Boundaries Face to Face (2003)

4   You can expect to be in control of what you do, but what another person does is totally up to him.
Henry Cloud and John Townsend
Boundaries Face to Face (2003)

5   Being a man is all about self-control. Not self-gratification.
Jeffrey Dean
One-Liner Wisdom for Today's Guys (2006)

6   We want to change our out-of-control behavior. The danger in wanting to change, however, is being impatient and naïve about the process.
Karen O'Connor
Addicted to Shopping (2005)

7   Practice self-control, don't be controlled.
Henry Cloud and John Townsend
How People Grow (2001)

8   Your main concern lies in dwelling continually upon the God who is within you. Then, without particularly thinking of self-denial or "putting away the deeds of the flesh," God will cause you to experience a natural subduing of the flesh!
Jeanne Guyon
Experiencing the Depths of Jesus (1685)

9   For gluttony, drunkenness, lying late abed, loafing and being without work are weapons of unchastity, with which chastity is quickly overcome.
Martin Luther
A Treatise on Good Works (1520)

10   There is no end and no limit to the obstacles of the one who wants to pursue what is right and at the same time shrinks back from self-denial. It is an ancient and true observation that there is a world of vices hidden in the soul, but Christian self-denial is the remedy of them all.
John Calvin
On the Life of the Christian Man (1550)

374 SELF-ESTEEM (*see also* PRIDE)

That he would grant you, according to the riches of his glory, to be strengthened with might by his Spirit in the inner man. . .
EPHESIANS 3:16

1   It is only when our spirit turns to God and we see ourselves as one for whom Christ died that we may begin to realize our infinite worth in His sight.
Paul Brand
He Satisfies My Soul (2008)

2   Our value is not dependent on our ability to earn the fickle acceptance of people, but rather, its true source is the love and acceptance of God.
Robert McGee
The Search for Significance (1998)

3 We are deeply loved and completely forgiven by God, fully pleasing to God, totally accepted by God, and complete in Him.
    Robert McGee
    The Search for Significance (1998)

4 The Lord never meant for us to find the fulfillment of our self-worth and significance in the opinions of others.
    Robert McGee
    The Search for Significance (1998)

5 Contrary to popular belief, God wired people to receive our sense of inner-worth by getting outside of ourselves, not from fickle self-absorption.
    Jeff Leeland
    Disarming the Teenage Heart (2003)

6 The truth is, until I truly love myself as God loves me, I'm doomed to be self-centered, self-indulgent, self-absorbed. It's our natural human response to feeling holes in our hearts, our souls, and our psyches. When we feel empty we do all kinds of crazy things, hold all kinds of skewed attitudes, and harbor inane feelings about ourselves and others.
    Robin Chaddock
    Discovering Your Divine Assignment (2005)

7 Our self-talk begins to give definition to our self-esteem. We begin to become who we tell ourselves we are.
    Anne Bryan Smollin
    God Knows You're Stressed (2001)

8 Your identity or self-image is crucial. It affects your relationship with God, with your family, with your dates, how you perform in school or at work, and the choice of a marriage partner. It can also determine what you receive from life.
    H. Norman Wright and Marvin Inmon
    Dating, Waiting and Choosing a Mate (1978)

9 A healthy concept of self is rooted in who we are in Jesus Christ, not in our own accomplishments or success.
    Michael Youssef
    "A Prayer of Humility" article (2009)

10 You have a choice to believe what is true about you or to believe what others say is true about you.
    Paul and Nicole Johnson
    Random Acts of Grace (1995)

11 The only hope believers have for a healthy self-image lies in our concept of God.
    Rory Noland
    The Heart of the Artist (1999)

12 Loving and valuing ourselves makes it possible to truly love and value another.
    Sue Patton Thoele
    Heart Centered Marriage (1996)

13 Loving ourselves is not selfish or unnatural, as we may have been taught. It is, instead, one of our highest and hardest life tasks.
    Sue Patton Thoele
    Heart Centered Marriage (1996)

14 To believe the truth is to see ourselves as God sees us, precious and honored, lovable and loved.
    Virginia Ann Froehle
    Loving Yourself More (1993)

15 The opposite of self conscious is not a "good" self image or self esteem. The opposite of conscious is unconscious. To lose consciousness of one's self happens when we become more conscious or aware of God and His will than we are of self and its will.
    Lisa Bevere
    You Are Not What You Weigh (1998)

16 Though I should come to think meanly of myself, yet I cannot endure that others should think so too.
Henry Scougal
Life of God in the Soul of Man
(17th century)

17 Don't allow who you truly are to be lost, buried, or devalued. What is in you matters. What is most truly you matters. You have learned lessons, experienced pain, known joys, and gained a perspective nobody else has. You have an answer to the world's needs that is yours alone.
Lynne Hybels
Nice Girls Don't Change the World (2005)

18 True self-esteem can come only from experiencing our identity as creatures who are loved and formed in the image of our Creator.
Stephen Arterburn
Finding Mr. Right (2003)

19 A negative self-image is inevitable when the self is the creator of it.
Neil Anderson and Dave Park
Overcoming Negative Self-Image (2003)

375 SELFISHNESS
(*see also* ARROGANCE; BOASTING)
Let nothing be done through strife or vainglory; but in lowliness of mind let each esteem other better than themselves.
PHILIPPIANS 2:3

1 To consume the best for yourself and give the crumbs to God is blasphemy.
Ravi Zacharias
The Grand Weaver (2007)

2 The word "mine" in its fully possessive sense cannot be uttered by a human being about anything.
C. S. Lewis
The Screwtape Letters (1941)

3 One sign of spiritual immaturity is to be selfish; a sign of maturity is to be selfless.
Jill Briscoe
The New Normal (2005)

4 What do I have that I'm not willing to let God have access to?
Steve Campbell
"Nine Pennies" sermon (2008)

5 Self-pity is consumed with its own comforts and constantly asks: Why is this happening to me?
Susie Larson
Alone in Marriage (2007)

6 People who desire to fail forward must turn their attention away from themselves and toward helping others. You could call that process getting over yourself.
John Maxwell
Failing Forward (2000)

7 Every time we pursue self-interest over God's interest, we are inflicting a wound in the heart of God.
Colin Smith
Unlocking the Bible Story (2002)

8 The reason not to live a self-centered, self-seeking life is because living like that will make you miserable. Guaranteed.
Claire and Curt Cloninger
E-mail from God for Teens (1999)

9 A lifetime of putting yourself at the center of your own universe will turn you into a caricature of low ideals and degrading habits. It will sink you into the mire of competition, trap you in a cycle of never-satisfied desires, and steal from you the joys of simple serenity.
Claire and Curt Cloninger
E-mail from God for Teens (1999)

10 You can have your eyes on your own situation and become absorbed in self-pity,

or you can get your eyes on yourself and be puffed with pride or demoralized by insecurity. With your eyes on yourself, you are constantly comparing your life with someone else's. You will never stay balanced while fighting the comparison battle.

> Charles Swindoll
> *Hand Me Another Brick* (1981)

11 Selfishness turns life into a burden. Unselfishness turns a burden into life!

> Robert Schuller
> *The Be (Happy) Attitudes* (1985)

12 In a world where people live self-centered lives, we can point to the defiant beauty of a selfless life.

> Gary Thomas
> *Authentic Faith* (2002)

13 To consider persons and events and situations only in the light of their effect upon myself is to live on the doorstep of hell.

> Thomas Merton
> *No Man Is an Island* (1955)

14 The closer we get to God, the less self-centeredness is a part of our lives.

> Bob Parry
> "The Law of Love" sermon (2010)

15 We all need to overcome the basic egocentricity of life, the inborn feeling that "the world revolves around me." Whenever we view others only in terms of how they affect us, we are in big trouble.

> Henry Cloud and John Townsend
> *Boundaries in Marriage* (1999)

16 One brand of "faith" subtly attempts to use others—or even God—for its own ends. But faith is not manipulation.

> Lynn Anderson
> *If I Really Believe, Why Do I Have These Doubts?* (1992)

17 The sad truth is that the person who is wrapped up in themselves makes for a pretty small package and poor representation of what God wants from us.

> Frank Edelinski
> "Be Blessed" sermon (2010)

18 Selfishness is the very essence of sin.

> Steve Campbell
> "The Blood Speaks" sermon (2010)

19 People whose eyes are riveted on themselves cannot focus upon God. How are we helping people to see beyond themselves?

> George Barna
> *Inside Out Worship* (2005)

20 This is the rat race, the broad path. It is the wide-open pursuit of this world to the exclusion of God. In a nutshell, this broad path always leads to living for self. For self-fulfillment, self-comfort self-preservation. For money, knowledge, popularity, respect, prestige, position, or possessions. It is living to make a living rather than living to make a life. It is the mindless, futile pursuit of this world.

> Steven Lawson
> *Men Who Win* (1992)

376 SELF-RIGHTEOUSNESS
(*see also* CRITICISM; FAULT-FINDING; JUDGING)

For I say, through the grace given unto me, to every man that is among you, not to think of himself more highly than he ought to think; but to think soberly, according as God hath dealt to every man the measure of faith.
ROMANS 12:3

1 One of the most difficult things for any person to see clearly is his own sin.

> Charles Stanley
> *When the Enemy Strikes* (2004)

2 Thou knowest well how to excuse and colour thine own deeds, but thou art not willing to receive the excuses of others.
Thomas à Kempis
The Imitation of Christ (15th century)

3 Sometimes we don't recognize ourselves until we judge another and hear the Holy Spirit resound within our hearts, "You are that person!"
Beth Moore
Daniel (2006)

4 While the necessity of a holy walk is insisted upon, as the effect and evidence of the knowledge of God in Christ Jesus, the opposite error of self-righteous pride is guarded against with equal care.
Matthew Henry
Commentary on the Whole Bible (1706)

5 God's grace freely can justify the worst. But God must utterly reject the self-righteous sinner who thinks he has no need for His mercy and forgiveness.
Lance Latham
The Two Gospels (1984)

6 Any time we exalt ourselves, we are trying to convince not only God, but also ourselves that we are better than we really are.
Robert Stofel
God, How Much Longer? (2005)

7 I could pine and macerate my body, and undergo many hardships and troubles; but I cannot get all my corruptions starved, nor my affections wholly weaned from earthly things.
Henry Scougal
Life of God in the Soul of Man (17th century)

8 No sinner under the light of the Gospel lives a single hour in sin without some excuse, either tacit or avowed, by which he justifies himself.
Charles Finney
"The Sinner's Excuses Answered" sermon (19th century)

9 Unsound hearts pretend to leave old sins, but they do not turn to God or embrace his service.
Thomas Watson
The Doctrine of Repentance (1668)

10 Strong-willed people are convinced their feelings, ways and judgments are always right.
Watchman Nee
The Release of the Spirit (1965)

377 SENSUALITY (*see also* IMMORALITY; LUST; SIN; TEMPTATION)
These be they who separate themselves, sensual, having not the Spirit.
JUDE 1:19

1 'Tis easier to suppress the first desire, than to satisfy all that follow it.
Benjamin Franklin
Poor Richard's Almanac (18th century)

2 Many a man thinks he is buying pleasure, when he is really selling himself a slave to it.
Benjamin Franklin
Poor Richard's Almanac (18th century)

3 Men who value the wrapping (her body) more than the gift inside are bad company.
Shannon Ethridge
Every Woman's Battle (2003)

4 Indulgences of most kinds are often signs that we are avoiding or trying to escape our pain.
Phileena Heuertz
Pilgrimage of a Soul (2010)

378 SEPARATION

Wherefore come out from among them,
and be ye separate, saith the Lord, and touch not
the unclean thing; and I will receive you.
2 CORINTHIANS 6:17

1 If you want power with God, just get as far
from the world as you can.
D. L. Moody
"The Transfiguration" sermon
(19th century)

2 The Christian always lives with tension,
the tension between what is transformable and
that from which he or she must separate.
James Eckman
Biblical Ethics (2004)

SERENITY (*see* PEACE)

379 SERMONS

Preach the word; be instant in season, out of
season; reprove, rebuke, exhort with all long
suffering and doctrine.
2 TIMOTHY 4:2

1 It is not so often a whole sermon as a
single short sentence in it, that wings God's
arrow to a heart.
Frances Ridley Havergal
Kept for the Master's Use (1879)

2 There are times when a sermon has a value
and power due to conditions in the audience
rather than to anything new or startling
or eloquent in the words or the arguments
presented.
Charles Sheldon
In His Steps (1896)

SERVICE (*see* MINISTRY)

380 SEX

Nevertheless, to avoid fornication, let every man
have his own wife, and let every woman
have her own husband.
1 CORINTHIANS 7:2

1 It is the business of these great masters to
produce in every age a general misdirection of
what may be called sexual "taste." This they do
by working through the small circle of popular
artists, dressmakers, actresses, and advertisers
who determine the fashionable type. The aim
is to guide each sex away from those members
of the other with whom spiritually helpful,
happy, and fertile marriages are most likely.
C. S. Lewis
The Screwtape Letters (1941)

2 It is God's desire that every Christian
couple, including you and your wife, regularly
enjoy the best, most intimate, most satisfying
sexual relations of which humans are capable.
We're talking really, really good sex. Marital
intimacy is God's gift to those who enter his
holy covenant of marriage. And what a gift it is!
C. J. Mahaney
Sex, Romance, and the Glory of God (2004)

3 The best sex and the deepest human
intimacy are only possible when, first, sex
takes place within the context of marriage,
and, second, that couple is living in the light
of God's purpose for marriage. That is simply
how God designed it.
C. J. Mahaney
Sex, Romance, and the Glory of God (2004)

4 In order for romance to deepen, you must
touch the heart and mind of your wife before
you touch her body. This, gentlemen, is a truth
that can change your marriage. Nothing kindles
erotic romance in a marriage like a husband
who knows how to touch the heart and mind of
his wife before he touches her body.
C. J. Mahaney
Sex, Romance, and the Glory of God (2004)

5 Sexual intercourse, and those wonderfully
intense passions it brings about, are designed
to help man and wife form a relational bond
of unique, unparalleled richness. When these

divine purposes are experienced and fulfilled, they bring much glory to God.

C. J. Mahaney
Sex, Romance, and the Glory of God (2004)

6 God says, "Sex is to be a part of the marriage relationship." Satan says, "Sex is the relationship."

Charles Stanley
Winning the War Within (1998)

7 Satan cannot get inside a believer, but sexual seduction is one of the most powerful ways the fires of hell can burn the outside of a believer. The sin is forgiven the moment the person repents, but healing from the ramifications can take longer.

Beth Moore
When Godly People Do Ungodly Things (2002)

8 God desires more than anything to restore sexual purity to those who have been sexually seduced, but it takes time to peel away the damaged character. The pain that can be involved in the process demands much trust in a good and loving God.

Beth Moore
When Godly People Do Ungodly Things (2002)

9 A dose of respect beats a dose of Viagra any day!

Emerson Eggerichs
Love and Respect (2004)

10 Sex is not for mature people. Sex is not for ready people. Sex is not for in-love people. Sex is for married people.

Andy Stanley
The Seven Checkpoints (2001)

11 Sexual rapport doesn't just happen. It is created.

Jo Berry
Beloved Unbeliever (1981)

12 Above all, a wife must never withhold sex because her husband doesn't communicate in other areas.

Jo Berry
Beloved Unbeliever (1981)

13 For the Christian there is one rule and one rule only: total abstention from sexual activity outside of marriage and total faithfulness inside marriage. Period.

Elisabeth Elliot
Passion and Purity (1984)

14 God has lovingly placed boundaries around sexual intimacy and declares it to be holy within the lifetime bond of marriage. He longs for us to honor those boundaries.

James MacDonald
"Checkup" article (2010)

15 For a wife, sex comes out of affection. She doesn't want to be affectionate with a man who makes her feel angry, hurt, lonely, disappointed, overworked, unsupported, uncared for, or abandoned. But for a husband, sex is pure need. His eyes, ears, brain, and emotions get clouded if he doesn't have that release. He has trouble hearing anything his wife says or seeing what she needs when that area of his being is neglected.

Stormie Omartian
The Power of a Praying Wife (1997)

16 While it is important for men to talk with one another about sex, it is equally important that we not reduce the act of sex to the equivalent of a game of racquetball.

Jeffrey Miller
The Hazards of Being a Man (2007)

381 SHAME
(*see also* EMBARRASSMENT; GUILT)

*When pride cometh, then cometh shame:
but with the lowly is wisdom.*
PROVERBS 11:2

SHAME

1 At times of greatest shame, we need to do the exact opposite of what we feel like doing. We need to lift our faces to our God, open our mouths in confession, let Him wash us with forgiveness and bathe us with His radiance.
Beth Moore
Daniel (2006)

2 Secrecy's cellmate is shame.
Sheila Walsh
Let Go (2008)

3 Guilt tells me I have done something wrong. . . . Shame tells me I am something wrong.
Sheila Walsh
Let Go (2008)

4 Guilt is the feeling of having done something wrong; toxic shame is the pervasive feeling of actually being wrong and bad.
David Hawkins
The Relationship Doctor's Prescription for Living Beyond Guilt (2006)

5 God weeps over us when shame and self hatred immobilize us.
Brennan Manning
The Rabbi's Heartbeat (2003)

SHARING (*see* CHARITY; GENEROSITY; GIVING)

382 SICKNESS
That it might be fulfilled which was spoken by Esaias the prophet, saying, Himself took our infirmities, and bare our sicknesses.
MATTHEW 8:17

1 It is heartbreaking to watch someone we love suffer with illness. Sometimes it raises difficult questions for us and can even make us feel angry with, or abandoned by, God. Though we can't always know why He chooses a certain path for us, we can trust Him based on what we know of His character. If the situation seems unbearable, reflect on what these hardships are purchasing in eternity. No matter how deep the suffering, the cost is nothing compared to the joy that will be experienced if your loved one comes to know Jesus through this ordeal.
Melody Rossi
May I Walk You Home? (2007)

383 SIGNIFICANCE
If any man's work abide which he hath built thereupon, he shall receive a reward.
1 CORINTHIANS 3:14

1 Here's the Significance Test: "Does what I am about to do contribute to the welfare of others in demonstration of faith, love, obedience, and service to Christ?"
Patrick Morley
The Man in the Mirror (1992)

2 When I die, I want it said that I mattered.
Rich Hurst
Courage to Connect (2002)

3 We cannot make everything pleasurable and easy if we are going to accomplish anything significant.
Bruce Narramore
Guilt and Freedom (1974)

384 SILENCE
A time to rend, and a time to sew; a time to keep silence, and a time to speak. . .
ECCLESIASTES 3:7

1 God is an infinite stillness. Your soul, if it is to be united with the Lord, must partake of His stillness.
Jeanne Guyon
Experiencing the Depths of Jesus Christ (1685)

410

2   There is a time to listen, a time to learn, and a time to do something different, in the beauty of this silent moment.

Don Osgood
Listening for God's Silent Language (1995)

3   We do the praying but not the waiting. Let us not be afraid to be silent before Him thinking it is wasted time.

John Wright Follette
Broken Bread (1957)

4   Quiet is a blessed gift. In this frantic world how we must cherish every moment of it, and carve it out for ourselves every chance we get.

Anne Ortlund
Disciplines of the Beautiful Woman (1977)

5   Solitude and silence are not self-indulgent exercises for times when an overcrowded soul needs a little time to itself. Rather, they are concrete ways of opening to the presence of God.

Ruth Haley Barton
Invitation to Solitude and Silence (2004)

6   Solitude and silence are not, in the end, about success and failure. They are about showing up and letting God do the rest. They are not an end in themselves; they are merely a means through which we regularly make ourselves available to God for the intimacy of relationship and for the work of transformation that only God can accomplish.

Ruth Haley Barton
Invitation to Solitude and Silence (2004)

385 SIMPLICITY

The LORD preserveth the simple: I was brought low, and he helped me.
PSALM 116:6

1   Nothing makes a journey more difficult than a heavy backpack filled with nice but unnecessary things. Pilgrims travel light.

Randy Alcorn
The Treasure Principle (2001)

2   The primary reason to pursue simplicity in our spirituality is to maintain "the simplicity and purity of devotion to Christ."

Donald Whitney
Simplify Your Spiritual Life (2003)

3   We simplify, not merely to save time, but to eliminate hindrances to the time we devote to knowing Christ. All the reasons we simplify should eventually lead us to Jesus Christ.

Donald Whitney
Simplify Your Spiritual Life (2003)

4   Simplicity sets us free to receive the provision of God as a gift that is not ours to keep and can be freely shared with others.

Richard Foster
Celebration of Discipline (1978)

5   To men who are not simple, simple words are the most inexplicable of riddles.

George MacDonald
"It Shall Not Be Forgiven" sermon
(19th century)

386 SIN (*see also* IMMORALITY; LUST; SENSUALITY; TEMPTATION)

All unrighteousness is sin.
1 JOHN 5:17

1   I have no sympathy with the idea that God puts us behind the blood and saves us, and then leaves us in Egypt to be under the old taskmaster. I believe God brings us out of Egypt into the promised land, and that it is the privilege of every child of God to be delivered from every foe, from every besetting sin.

D. L. Moody
"The Ninety-First Psalm"
sermon (19th century)

2   No sin, no matter how momentarily pleasurable, comforting, or habitual, is worth missing what God has for us.

Beth Moore
Believing God (2004)

3   We have a strange illusion that mere time cancels sin.
C. S. Lewis
The Problem of Pain (1947)

4   We've tried calling sin "errors" or "mistakes" or "poor judgment," but sin itself has stayed the same.
Billy Graham
Peace with God (1984)

5   Our situation couldn't be more serious. Prior to our conversion we were sin's prisoners, and even after our conversion we continue to fight the presence of sin, though we are freed from the power and penalty of sin. And if you aren't aware of this danger, you'll never sufficiently appreciate the significance of His death.
C. J. Mahaney
Humility: True Greatness (2005)

6   A strong strand throughout the Bible stresses that you are to give to needs and put limits on sin.
Henry Cloud and John Townsend
Boundaries (1992)

7   To be living in any known sin is to be living in darkness.
Evan Henry Hopkins
Thoughts on Life and Godliness (1883)

8   Sin has sired a thousand heartaches and broken a million promises. Your addiction can be traced back to sin. Your mistrust can be traced back to sin. Bigotry, robbery, adultery—all because of sin. But in heaven, all of this will end.
Max Lucado
When Christ Comes (1999)

9   Sin is a deep-seated, terminal disease that can be cured only by the healing work of the Great Physician.
John MacArthur
Nothing But the Truth (1999)

10   Sin is not rated on a sliding scale, like a report card.
Billy Graham
Facing Death—and the Life After (1987)

11   Sin is the ruin and misery of the soul. It is destructive in its nature, and if God should leave it without restraint, nothing else would be needed to make the soul miserable.
Jonathan Edwards
"Sinners in the Hands of an Angry God" sermon (1741)

12   All sin must be wept over; here, in godly sorrow, or, hereafter, in eternal misery.
Matthew Henry
Commentary on the Whole Bible (1706)

13   Dare we make light of that which brings down the wrath of God?
Matthew Henry
Commentary on the Whole Bible (1706)

14   No matter how cool, sexy, glamorous, accepted, justifiable or right the world makes it look, nothing is ever okay that is out of the will of God.
Jeffrey Dean
One-Liner Wisdom for Today's Guys (2006)

15   One of the reasons that many Christians seem to have no thrill at being forgiven through the gospel is that they have not been brokenhearted over their sin. They have not despaired. They have not wrestled with warranted self-loathing. They have not grieved over their sin because of its moral repugnance, but have grieved only because of guilt feelings and threats of hell.
John Piper
God Is the Gospel (2005)

16   The lack of God-centeredness leads to self-centeredness. Sin celebrates its middle letter—sIn.
Max Lucado
Come Thirsty (2004)

17 Where we might think of sin as slip-ups or missteps, God views sin as a godless attitude that leads to godless actions.
Max Lucado
Come Thirsty (2004)

18 I assure you that no matter what has you trapped, or how strong its hold, Jesus Christ's death on the cross has broken both the penalty and the power of your sin.
Bruce Wilkinson
Beyond Jabez (2005)

19 Sin is choosing to do what I want without doing it in submission to God's will and plan.
Erwin Lutzer
How You Can Be Sure That You Will Spend Eternity with God (1996)

20 Honey confuses the sight, and worldly friendship confuses the judgment, so that men think themselves right while doing evil, and assume their excuses and pretexts to be valid reasoning.
Francis de Sales
Introduction to the Devout Life
(17th century)

21 The decision to sin always includes the thought that I cannot really trust God to watch out for my well-being.
John Ortberg
Everybody's Normal Till You Get to Know Them (2003)

22 There is no such thing as "no fault" sin.
Gina Burgess
"Writing on Stones" article (2009)

23 When sin gets written into our hearts, it becomes engraved on our character.
Colin Smith
Unlocking the Bible Story (2002)

24 While we can all avoid some sin, none of us can avoid all sin.
Colin Smith
Unlocking the Bible Story (2002)

25 Does not sin harden while it deceives?
James Thomas Holloway
The Analogy of Faith (1836)

26 The first sin may be the least but it will not be the last; the end is ruin, loss of character and of peace of mind.
James Thomas Holloway
The Analogy of Faith (1836)

27 It is a fearful thing to sin against God, but still more fearful to be hardened under it.
James Thomas Holloway
The Analogy of Faith (1836)

28 The terrors of the Lord may make us afraid of sin, but the love of the Lord alone, will make us hate it; not the flames of hell, but the love of heaven.
James Thomas Holloway
The Analogy of Faith (1836)

29 Where is the child of God, who has sinned, that has not smarted for it?
James Thomas Holloway
The Analogy of Faith (1836)

30 Let those who will imitate David's sins, in the hope of David's pardon, be prepared to encounter David's calamities.
James Thomas Holloway
The Analogy of Faith (1836)

31 No matter what we choose to call it, sin is sin, and God is not confused about it.
Ed Young
From Bad Beginnings to Happy Endings (1994)

32 The greatest punishment of repetitive sin after forgiveness consists of the consequences sin brings to the person engaging in it.
Patrick Brennan
The Way of Forgiveness (2000)

33 Wherever sin is present, war is raging.
Jan Winebrenner and Debra Frazier
When a Leader Falls (1993)

34 Recognizing and confronting sin in ourselves and in our leaders is as much a part of the ministry of the body as baptizing, preaching, and teaching.
Jan Winebrenner and Debra Frazier
When a Leader Falls (1993)

35 If you think it's really possible to lead a secret life or keep a little pocket of sins concealed, you're just fooling yourself!
Bob Barnes
Walking Together in Wisdom (2001)

36 When you do not assess the potential of sin within, you will not pray against these things. It will inevitably leave you vulnerable to the attack of the enemy.
T. D. Jakes
Loose That Man and Let Him Go! (1995)

37 The guilt of sin is not measured merely or principally by the external act, but by the light and advantages enjoyed by some above others.
Archibald Alexander
The Misery of the Lost (19th century)

38 As the rose is destroyed by the canker which breeds in it, so are the souls of men by those sins in which they indulge.
Thomas Watson and Samuel Lee
The Bible and the Closet (1842)

39 Sin is abashed in the presence of Christ.
Henry Drummond
Stones Rolled Away and Other Addresses to Young Men (1893)

40 Our sins are so deep-dyed, so inveterate, so fast, that nothing but blood could set us free. Blood must atone for us. Blood must cleanse us.
F. B. Meyer
The Way into the Holiest (1893)

41 The way of sin is down-hill; a man cannot stop himself when he will. Suppress the first emotions of sin, and leave it off before it be meddled with.
Matthew Henry
Commentary on the Whole Bible (1706)

42 The root of all sin is acting independently of God, turning to our own way.
Kay Arthur
Our Covenant God (1999)

43 For by sin we were alienated from God, our sin had caused justice to lock up the gates of paradise, and forbid such guilty and polluted offenders to approach to the pure majesty of God.
Stephen Charnock
Discourse on the Cleansing Virtue of Christ's Blood (17th century)

44 Since God had decreed and enacted that whosoever sinned should die, God must either, upon man's sin, destroy him to preserve his truth and justice, or neglect his own law, and turn it upside down for the discovery of his mercy.
Stephen Charnock
Discourse on God's being the Author of Reconciliation (17th century)

45 We must not continue our sinful practices, in hopes that the divine grace will one day overpower our spirits, and make us hate them for their own deformity.
Henry Scougal
Life of God in the Soul of Man (17th century)

46 If sin be such an evil that it requires the death of Christ for its expiation, no wonder if it deserve our everlasting misery.
   Richard Baxter
   A Call to the Unconverted, to Turn and Live (17th century)

47 Recollect the question which flashed into the mind of young Bunyan when at his sports on the green on Sunday: "Wilt thou have thy sins and go to hell, or wilt thou quit thy sins and go to heaven?" That brought him to a dead stand.
   Charles Spurgeon
   All of Grace (19th century)

48 The doctrine of the cross can be used to slay sin, even as the old warriors used their huge two-handed swords, and mowed down their foes at every stroke.
   Charles Spurgeon
   All of Grace (19th century)

49 Our sins are often as dear to us as our children: we love them, hug them, cleave to them, and delight in them. To part with them is as hard as cutting off a right hand, or plucking out a right eye.
   J. C. Ryle
   Holiness: Its Nature, Hindrances, Difficulties, and Roots (19th century)

50 The universality of sin follows as a simple inference from the universality of death.
   Paul Wernle
   The Beginnings of Christianity (1903)

51 Do you mortify; do you make it your daily work; be always at it while you live; cease not a day from this work; be killing sin or it will be killing you.
   John Owen
   Of the Mortification of Sin in Believers (1656)

52 Sin will not only be striving, acting, rebelling, troubling, disquieting, but if let alone, if not continually mortified, it will bring forth great, cursed, scandalous, soul-destroying sins.
   John Owen
   Of the Mortification of Sin in Believers (1656)

53 Sin aims always at the utmost; every time it rises up to tempt or entice, may it have its own course, it would go out to the utmost sin in that kind.
   John Owen
   Of the Mortification of Sin in Believers (1656)

54 It is the case of most sinners to think themselves freest from those sins to which they are most enslaved.
   Richard Baxter
   The Causes and Danger of Slighting Christ and His Gospel (17th century)

55 What do people gain by forgetting God and walking in sinful pleasures? "A little while" and their joy is turned into sorrow.
   The Lutheran Witness (1885)

56 For the short pleasure of sin which flits away like a shadow, men will barter their soul's salvation, and although they know it they nevertheless will do it; "whose damnation is just."
   The Lutheran Witness (1885)

57 Self-love raises a sick-bed vow, and love of sin will prevail against it.
   Thomas Watson
   The Doctrine of Repentance (1668)

58 The eye is made both for seeing and weeping. Sin must first be seen before it can be wept for.
   Thomas Watson
   The Doctrine of Repentance (1668)

59 Loving of sin is worse than committing it.
Thomas Watson
The Doctrine of Repentance (1668)

60 Sin is the Trojan horse out of which comes a whole army of troubles.
Thomas Watson
The Doctrine of Repentance (1668)

61 Sin is a reality. Every one must firmly hold this who regards Christ as He regarded Himself, as a moral physician, and believes that God in the person of Christ entered into the world as a redemptive force with fixed intent to fight with and destroy moral evil.
Alexander Balmain Bruce
Apologetics, or Christianity Defensively Stated (1892)

62 Why is God so extremely severe in dealing with sin? Simply because sin is a broken law, a broken relationship, a broken fellowship, and it produces a broken life.
Judson Cornwall
Let Us Enjoy Forgiveness (1978)

63 Stepping into sin is akin to launching a canoe in the rapids above Niagara Falls.
Judson Cornwall
Let Us Enjoy Forgiveness (1978)

64 The sin in our lives that we fail to conquer will eventually conquer us.
Warren Wiersbe
Be Available (1994)

65 The tendency to sin gathers force with every new commission. So the battle goes on in every one of us. We must either overcome sin, or it will overcome us; we must decide.
D. L. Moody
Short Talks (19th century)

66 The essence of sin is obedience to our own lusts and desires, and disobedience to God.
D. L. Moody
Short Talks (19th century)

67 The worst choice we can make is to enjoy the evil we engage in.
Gregory Spencer
Awakening the Quieter Virtues (2010)

68 We are never better for having sinned.
Gary Chapman
Hope for the Separated (1982)

69 Sin happens whenever you break God's law.
Joe Beam
Getting Past Guilt (2003)

SINGING (*see* MUSIC)

387 SINGLENESS

He that is unmarried careth for the things that belong to the Lord, how he may please the Lord.
1 CORINTHIANS 7:32

1 But so often we focus our energy and our desire on someone else. A person. A crush. We never get to explore that destiny we were designed for because we're so busy trying to get someone to like us.
Justin Lookadoo and Hayley DiMarco
Dateable (2006)

2 Trudging through the trenches of singleness takes perseverance. Sometimes it's perseverance generated by sheer obedience—a gritted-teeth act of submission. I choose to believe that God has put me where I am at this point in time, and then I choose to live in obedience to Him. I hold the hand of God and walk in trust next to my Friend. I want to press on because I'm so in step with the Creator of the universe that walking a difficult road is an

opportunity to sidle a little closer to Him, to hold His hand a little tighter.
Wendy Widder
Living Whole Without a Better Half (2000)

3 Singleness can be a platform, water to walk on instead of a storm to wait out. Without family responsibilities, I am free to pour my energies into local church ministries. With just me and my paycheck, I can sometimes afford to encourage friends with impulsive gifts. Without the encumbrances of someone else's schedule, I can give extra attention to developing reading, writing, and study habits.
Wendy Widder
Living Whole Without a Better Half (2000)

4 Don't ever think for a moment that the worst thing you could possibly be is single.
Beth Moore
"Overcoming Insecurity" teaching series (2006)

5 I beg you if you are not married, you do not make a marital decision out of desperation. That is no way to think. You are not ready to think that through yet. Wait until you can think straight.
Beth Moore
"Overcoming Insecurity" teaching series (2006)

6 Contrary to what most of us believe, our discontentment with singleness can't be solved by finding a guy and getting a ring on our finger.
Leslie Ludy
Sacred Singleness (2009)

7 I am convinced that the ultimate happiness is not equated in singles or doubles, but the ultimate for all is to know the will of God.
Sarah Jepson
For the Love of Singles (1970)

8 The basic problem that single people grapple with is the basic problem in the lives of us all, married or singles—"the pursuit of happiness."
Sarah Jepson
For the Love of Singles (1970)

9 A women who has lost her husband, as well as a man who has lost his wife, feels the loss and knows that no circle of friends is large enough to fill the void.
Sarah Jepson
For the Love of Singles (1970)

10 It is surprising how much some single adults, even in their eighties, are accomplishing in the Divine Purpose.
Sarah Jepson
For the Love of Singles (1970)

11 Singleness is not a second-class, second-best status. It can and should be a fulfilling, satisfying way of life.
Gary Collins
It's OK to Be Single (1976)

12 Scripture has much to teach us about developing a Christian single adult life style. Jesus' paradigm for his own relationships was not marriage but friendships.
Gary Collins
It's OK to Be Single (1976)

13 Remaining single is as appropriate an option as being married.
Gary Collins
It's OK to Be Single (1976)

14 One seldom-discussed reason for remaining single is that many persons choose not to marry.
Gary Collins
It's OK to Be Single (1976)

15 God's promises of joy and peace and satisfaction are not made just to married people.
Bill and Lynne Hybels
Fit to Be Tied: Making Marriage Last a Lifetime (1991)

388 SINNERS

I came not to call the righteous,
but sinners to repentance.
LUKE 5:32

1   We think that we do well to be angry with the rebellious, and so we prove ourselves to be more like Jonah than Jesus.
Charles Spurgeon
"God's Longsuffering" sermon (1886)

2   As sinners, we all have a God-sized problem. Thankfully, there is a God-sized solution.
Erwin Lutzer
After You've Blown It (2004)

3   It concerns me when I hear believers speaking of non-believers as the enemy. According to Scripture, those who do not believe have been taken captive by Satan to do his will—they're prisoners of war. Nonbelievers aren't the enemy; they're the enemy's captives.
Greg Laurie
Wrestling with God (2003)

4   You can tell people they're sinners, but unless they understand what sin is, they will not comprehend the message.
Ken Ham
Why Won't They Listen? (2002)

5   Truth hates sin. Grace loves sinners. Those full of grace and truth do both.
Randy Alcorn
The Grace and Truth Paradox (2003)

6   Sinners are pleased with gods that neither see, nor hear, nor know; but they will be judged by One to whom all things are open.
Matthew Henry
Commentary on the Whole Bible (1706)

7   The principles of religion and the doctrines of the Holy Scriptures are terrible enemies to wicked men.
John Tillotson
The Wisdom of Being Religious (1819)

8   It has been correctly said that the ground is level at the foot of the cross. We all come as needy sinners; we all come with the same need for the pardon that God alone can give us.
Erwin Lutzer
The Truth About Same-Sex Marriage (2004)

9   It is easy to love an individual sinner, especially if he is personally picturesque, or interesting. To love a multitude of sinners, lay distinctly a Christlike quality.
Charles Sheldon
In His Steps (1896)

10   God seemed to have granted the greatest favours to the greatest sinners, as more signal monuments of His mercy.
Brother Lawrence
The Practice of the Presence of God (17th century)

11   Coming from a long line of poor choosers can create a strong internal pull to replicate what we've seen, heard, and experienced. In the Bible, that's referred to as "the sin of the fathers" being passed down from generation to generation.
John Trent
Making Wise Life Choices (2003)

12   God doesn't turn away from sinners in disgust but moves toward us, bringing his redemptive presence.
David Benner
Surrender to Love (2003)

13   For my part, I am a poor sinner, and that I am sure of out of God's Word.
Martin Luther
Table Talk (16th century)

14   Jesus hates hypocrites, but He loves all sinners—even repentant Pharisees—who flee to Him for grace.
Richard Phillips
Tabletalk magazine (2009)

15 If we come to God in ourselves, what are we but as criminals before a judge, stubble before fire?

Stephen Charnock
Discourse of God's being the Author of Reconciliation (17th century)

16 Do you think that you must be lost because you are a sinner? This is the reason why you can be saved.

Charles Spurgeon
All of Grace (19th century)

17 Because you own yourself to be a sinner I would encourage you to believe that grace is ordained for such as you are.

Charles Spurgeon
All of Grace (19th century)

18 I would be glad to talk all night to bona fide sinners. The inn of mercy never closes its doors upon such, neither weekdays nor Sunday.

Charles Spurgeon
All of Grace (19th century)

19 "Oh," said the devil to Martin Luther, "you are a sinner." "Yes," said he, "Christ died to save sinners." Thus he smote him with his own sword.

Charles Spurgeon
All of Grace (19th century)

20 The wicked fare like the people before the flood; like the inhabitants of Sodom and Gomorrah.

The Lutheran Witness (1885)

21 The Biblical fact is that no two persons are compatible, regardless of whether their backgrounds were similar or not. We are all born sinners, and that means that we are by nature incompatible people.

Jay Adams
Christian Living in the Home (1972)

SLANDER (*see* GOSSIP)

389 SLAVERY
Masters, give unto your servants that which is just and equal; knowing that ye also have a Master in heaven.
COLOSSIANS 4:1

1 Mighty minds are from time to time discovered in men whose limbs are wearing the chains of slavery, and whose backs are laid bare to the whip—they have black skins, but are in mind vastly superior to their brutal masters.

Charles Spurgeon
"Divine Sovereignty" sermon (1856)

390 SLEEP (*see also* REST)
Love not sleep, lest thou come to poverty.
PROVERBS 20:13

1 Abide Not in the Realm of Dreams
William Burleigh hymn title (1871)

SMILING (*see* CHEER; ENCOURAGEMENT)

SOBRIETY (*see* ALCOHOL; DRUNKENNESS; SUBSTANCE ABUSE)

391 SOCIETY
Even so shall it be also unto this wicked generation.
MATTHEW 12:45

1 We live in a spiritually deceptive generation in which Satan attempts to divert the attention of believers to focus on celebrity leaders rather than Jesus Christ, God's purpose, and His glory.

Grant Jeffrey
Countdown to Apocalypse (2008)

2 Few influences in life are as dominant as the power of culture.

Ravi Zacharias
Deliver Us from Evil (1996)

3   The soul of a nation is changed one person at a time.
   Ravi Zacharias
   Deliver Us from Evil (1996)

4   We must learn to walk the tightrope of living for God in the context of the postmodern culture. By striking the proper balance we are—by God's grace—living in obedience in the culture, and modeling true, biblical discipleship for all those who come to faith.
   Walt Mueller
   Engaging the Soul of Youth Culture (2006)

5   Our modern culture has. . .dethroned God as the ultimate source of truth and morality, and enthroned man in His place.
   Josh McDowell and Bob Hostetler
   Right from Wrong (1994)

6   We must not expect to change our culture (if indeed we could); we must change the way we respond to it.
   Josh McDowell and Bob Hostetler
   Right from Wrong (1994)

7   As our culture has become increasingly hostile to Christianity, it has become correspondingly open to wickedness.
   Rick Scarborough
   Enough Is Enough (1996)

8   We are now witnessing the proof that the death of God leads to the death of civility.
   Rick Scarborough
   Enough Is Enough (1996)

9   When ethics and morality are confused and mixed, the result is that the culture makes the norms.
   James Eckman
   Biblical Ethics (2004)

10   When wickedness has become general, then universal ruin is not far off; while there is a remnant of praying people in a nation, to empty the measure as it fills, judgments may be kept off a great while.
   Matthew Henry
   Commentary on the Whole Bible (1706)

11   Those differences of high and low, rich and poor, are only calculated for the present world, and cannot outlive time. In the grave, at the day of judgment, and in heaven, there are no such distinctions.
   Thomas Manton
   A Practical Commentary on the Epistle of James (17th century)

12   As our cities swell with immigrants and migrants, I'm reminded that Jesus was born in a borrowed barn in Asia and became an African refugee in Egypt.
   Ray Bakke
   A Theology as Big as the City (1997)

13   Political remedies to our nation's moral ills are no cure for the underlying spiritual problems. Of all people, Christians ought to know that, and the preponderance of our efforts ought to be focused on proclaiming the truth that can genuinely set people free.
   John MacArthur
   Can God Bless America? (2002)

14   Over the past few decades, our incremental acceptance of obscenity and violence has elevated our tolerance for evil.
   Rubel Shelly
   Written in Stone (1994)

392 SOLITUDE

And in the morning, rising up a great while before day, he went out, and departed into a solitary place, and there prayed.
MARK 1:35

1   Mystical though it may sound, it is absolutely essential that those whom God appoints to places of leadership learn to breathe comfortably in the thin air of the Himalayan heights where God's comfort and assurance come in the crushing silence of solitude.
Charles Swindoll
The Quest for Character (1982)

2   It is in lonely solitude that God delivers His best thoughts.
Charles Swindoll
The Quest for Character (1982)

3   Solitude can generate a sense of solitariness that is both creative and motivating.
J. Oswald Sanders
Facing Loneliness (1988)

4   The longing for solitude is the longing for God.
Ruth Haley Barton
Sacred Rhythms (2006)

5   One of the fundamental purposes of solitude is to give us a concrete way of entering into such stillness, so that God can come in and do what only God can do.
Ruth Haley Barton
Sacred Rhythms (2006)

SONGS (*see* MUSIC)

393 SONS
*That our sons may be as plants
grown up in their youth. . .*
PSALM 144:12

1   Building a strong relationship with your son takes effort, although it is enjoyable effort. It requires intentionality. That means we need to set a goal of having strong friendships with our sons, and we have to make sure that our actions,

words, and attitude will get us to our goal.
Jack and Jerry Schreur
Fathers and Sons (1995)

2   It is not easy to say which fathering strength is the most important or which one we should work on the most. All of the strengths are vital and enrich our relationship with our sons in different ways.
Jack and Jerry Schreur
Fathers and Sons (1995)

3   How do we build friendships with other people? We do things with them. We ask them out for dinner, or we play racquetball or golf with them, or we go to movies with them. We share our lives with them by giving them time. If we want to build an enduring friendship with our sons, we need to do the same for them. Friendships are built on shared experiences, so we need to take time to be with our kids if we hope to build a strong, powerful relationship.
Jack and Jerry Schreur
Fathers and Sons (1995)

SORCERY (*see* OCCULT)

394 SORROW (*see also* GRIEF)
*But I am poor and sorrowful: let thy salvation,
O God, set me up on high.*
PSALM 69:29

1   When you are hurting, your head says that God is far away, but Jesus says, in fact, that God is closer than ever.
Angela Thomas
A Beautiful Offering (2004)

2   Sorrow is a refiner's crucible.
F. B. Meyer
The Secret of Guidance (1896)

3   There can be no doubt that some trials are permitted to come to us, as to our Lord, for no other reason than that by means of them

we should become able to give sympathy and succor to others.

F. B. Meyer
The Secret of Guidance (1896)

4   To bear sorrow with dry eyes and stolid heart may befit a Stoic, but not a Christian.

F. B. Meyer
The Secret of Guidance (1896)

5   Each sorrow carries at its heart a germ of holy truth, which if you get and sow in the soil of your heart will bear harvests of fruit as seed-corns from mummy-cases bear fruit in modern soil.

F.B. Meyer
The Secret of Guidance (1896)

6   My attitude as a saint to sorrow and difficulty is not to ask that they may be prevented, but to ask that I may preserve the self God created me to be through every fire of sorrow. Our Lord received Himself in the fire of sorrow, He was saved not from the hour, but out of the hour. . . . If you receive yourself in the fires of sorrow, God will make you nourishment for other people.

Oswald Chambers
My Utmost for His Highest (1935)

7   In the Bible clouds are always connected with God. Clouds are those sorrows or sufferings or providences, within or without our personal lives, which seem to dispute the rule of God. It is by those very clouds that the spirit of God is teaching us how to walk by faith. If there were no clouds, we should have no faith.

Oswald Chambers
My Utmost for His Highest (1935)

8   In God is neither sorrow, nor grief, nor trouble. Wouldst thou be free from all grief and trouble, abide and walk in God, and to God alone.

Meister Eckhart
Meister Eckhart's Sermons (14th century)

9   Verily were there anything nobler than sorrow, God would have redeemed man thereby. Sorrow is the root of all virtue.

Meister Eckhart
Meister Eckhart's Sermons (14th century)

10   If I had really cared, as I thought I did, about the sorrows of the world, I should not have been so overwhelmed when my own sorrow came.

C. S. Lewis
A Grief Observed (1961)

11   Sorrow is one of the things that are lent, not given. A thing that is lent may be taken away; a thing that is given is not taken away. Joy is given; sorrow is lent; . . .then it will be taken away and everlasting joy will be our Father's gift to us, and the Lord God will wipe away all tears from off all faces.

Amy Carmichael
Edges of His Ways (1955)

12   Those whom God uses most effectively have been hammered, filed, and tempered in the furnace of trials and heartache.

Charles Swindoll
Encourage Me (1982)

395 SOUL (*see also* SPIRIT)
And the very God of peace sanctify you wholly; and I pray God your whole spirit and soul and body be preserved blameless unto the coming of our Lord Jesus Christ.
1 THESSALONIANS 5:23

1   The body is but a tabernacle, or tent, of the soul.

Matthew Henry
Commentary on the Whole Bible (1706)

2   Your soul is the place God fashioned for His presence—the place where He intends to abide and to work. Your soul is a holy place. You were made for God.

Angela Thomas McGuffey
Tender Mercy for a Mother's Soul (2001)

3   Think of the worth of a single soul—a soul delivered from eternal death, and made an heir of eternal bliss!
William Carey (19th century) quoted in
Faithful Witness: The Life and Mission of William Carey

4   There is a somewhat in the soul that is, as it were, a blood-relative of God.
Meister Eckhart
Meister Eckhart's Sermons (14th century)

5   Therefore St. Augustine saith that the soul is greater by its love-giving power than by its life-giving power.
Meister Eckhart
Meister Eckhart's Sermons (14th century)

6   As for outward works they are ordained for this purpose that the outward man may be directed to God. But the inner work, the work of God in the soul, is the chief matter.
Meister Eckhart
Meister Eckhart's Sermons (14th century)

7   If the vessel of our soul is still tossed with winds and storms, let us awake the Lord, who reposes in it, and He will quickly calm the sea.
Brother Lawrence
The Practice of the Presence of God (17th century)

8   Heaven and earth, all the emperors, kings, and princes of the world, could not raise a fit dwelling-place for God; yet, in a weak human soul, that keeps his Word, he willingly resides.
Martin Luther
Table Talk (16th century)

9   The soul of man, like the bird in the shell, is still growing or ripening in sin or grace, till at last the shell breaks by death, and the soul flies away to the peace it is prepared for, and where it must abide for ever.
John Flavel
Pneumatologia (1698)

10   "They cannot kill the soul." And though the Almighty power of God, that created it out of nothing, can as easily reduce it to nothing; yet he will never do so.
John Flavel
Pneumatologia (1698)

11   My soul is of more value than ten thousand worlds.
John Flavel
Pneumatologia (1698)

12   The soul was the chief offender, the soul then ought to be the principal sufferer.
Stephen Charnock
Discourse of God's being the Author of Reconciliation (17th century)

13   Surely these are times when we ought often to sit down and "count the cost," and to consider the state of our souls.
J. C. Ryle
Holiness: Its Nature, Hindrances, Difficulties, and Roots (19th century)

14   Your soul is really just a mirror in which you are enabled to see God spiritually. But for this reason you need first to find your "mirror" and then keep it bright and clean from carnal rubbish and worldly vanity.
Walter Hilton
Toward a Perfect Love (1985)

15   It matters to all of life to know whether the soul is mortal or immortal.
Blaise Pascal
Pensées (17th century)

16   To really thrive in life, our soul needs to be transformed—over and over again.
Phileena Heuertz
Pilgrimage of a Soul (2010)

396 SOWING AND REAPING

*Be not deceived; God is not mocked: for
whatsoever a man soweth, that shall he also reap.*
GALATIANS 6:7

1   Establishing boundaries helps codependent
people stop interrupting the Law of Sowing
and Reaping in their loved one's life.
Boundaries force the person who is doing the
sowing to also do the reaping.
Henry Cloud and John Townsend
Boundaries (1992)

2   Sowing in faith results in an eternal crop.
Cowering in fear yields empty fields.
Andy Stanley
Fields of Gold (2004)

3   A farmer doesn't acquire seed to consume
it or hoard it. He only decides where to
plant it. And only when the seed has been
irrevocably cast into the ground is a harvest
returned.
Andy Stanley
Fields of Gold (2004)

4   Whatever exists in a man's moral or
intellectual nature naturally develops and
manifests itself in the life.
William Elbert Munsey
Eternal Retribution (1951)

5   Grace means that in forgiving you,
God gives you the strength to endure
the consequences. It does not mean the
consequences are automatically removed.
Charles Swindoll
"Trouble at Home" sermon (2009)

6   Though sowing wild oats may have a kick
in it, it is the harvest that brings the curse to
the sowers and tears of sorrow to the father
and mother.
Billy Sunday
The Sawdust Trail (1932)

7   As you have brewed, so shall you drink.
Robert Louis Stevenson
Treasure Island (1883)

8   The sweetest graces by a slight perversion
may bear the bitterest fruit.
E. M. Bounds
Power Through Prayer (1906)

9   The wages of sin are the same for the
sinner and the saint.
Judson Cornwall
Let Us Enjoy Forgiveness (1978)

10   For good or for bad we will harvest what
we plant, more than we plant, later than we
plant.
Rebecca Lusignolo
"Immediate Consequences" devotional
(2008)

11   Grant me eyes to see the consequences of
my actions.
Rebecca Lusignolo
Immediate Consequences" devotional
(2008)

12   All of us eat the fruit of our own decision
and choice.
Rick Renner
Living in the Combat Zone (1989)

13   No tree can grow except on the root from
which it sprang.
Andrew Murray
Humility (1896)

397 SPEECH
(*see also* COMMUNICATION; CONVERSATION; LISTENING; TONGUE, THE)

*Let your speech be always with grace,
seasoned with salt, that ye may know
how ye ought to answer every man.*
COLOSSIANS 4:6

1   God intends for the words of His church to touch the world. And when we speak lovingly and respectfully to one another, we literally identify ourselves as His disciples. God knew that loving words, matched with loving deeds, would be the greatest source of evangelism.
Ron Mehl
Right with God (2003)

2   When your mouth is filled with gratitude and thanksgiving, there simply won't be room for false or cynical words.
Ron Mehl
Right with God (2003)

3   Often the most courageous and powerful word in our vocabulary is the word no.
Dennis and Barbara Rainey
Pressure Proof Your Marriage (2003)

4   We often poison and wound each other; especially our children, with words.
Suzette Haden Elgin
How to Turn the Other Cheek (1997)

5   To guard the passion and presence of God in your heart, choose your words the way you choose your friends. . .wisely. Know they will be few but precious.
Lisa Bevere
Kissed the Girls and Made Them Cry (2002)

6   If you can't say something nice, take a vow of silence.
Martha Bolton
If the Tongue's a Fire, Who Needs Salsa? (2002)

7   The only reason that a man should speak at all is because he says things that are not being said.
Henry Drummond
A Life for a Life and Other Addresses (1893)

8   Because words have the power to affect people deeply, it is appropriate to consider how to encourage fellow Christians through what we say. Words can encourage, discourage, or do nothing.
Larry Crabb
Encouragement: The Key to Caring (1984)

9   Our words cause spiritual activity to take place.
Steve Campbell
"Navigating the Storms of Life" sermon (2009)

10   Words always rest on the virtue of the speaker.
Jeanne Hendricks
A Woman for All Seasons (1977)

11   Out of the overflow of a changed heart the mouth most beautifully speaks.
Beth Moore
Breaking Free (1999)

SPIRIT (*see* SOUL)

SPIRITUAL GROWTH (*see* GROWTH, SPIRITUAL)

SPIRITUAL HUNGER (*see* HUNGER, SPIRITUAL)

398 STEWARDSHIP

As every man hath received the gift,
even so minister the same one to another,
as good stewards of the manifold grace of God.
1 PETER 4:10

1   Stewardship involves priorities. When does God get "paid"? Is He the last one? Are you giving to your church and the other ministries only after everything else has been purchased and paid for? Is God getting just the leftovers (if there are any)? God deserves first place in our lives. That means our finances, too. Giving a portion to God first reflects an attitude that God has priority in your family finances.
Bruce Bickel and Stan Jantz
God Is in the Small Stuff for Your Family (1999)

2   The essence of a financial plan is to determine the best way, as a manager, to handle God's money that He has entrusted to you. The real issue is not how much of your money you plan to give to God, but rather how much of His money you will keep for yourself.

Deborah Smith Pegues
30 Days to Taming Your Finances (2006)

3   Every man must render to God the things that are God's, and that, let it be remembered, is all he is and all he possesses.

Richard Baxter
The Reformed Pastor (17th century)

399 STRENGTH
(*see also* ABILITY; MIGHT; POWER)

*God is our refuge and strength,
a very present help in trouble.*
PSALM 46:1

1   Since God Himself is a steadfast Rock, the foundation of all certitude and steadfastness, it must be by faith or holding fast to God that man can become steadfast.

Andrew Murray
Have Mercy Upon Me (1896)

400 STRESS (*see also* BUSYNESS)

And Jesus answered and said unto her, Martha, Martha, thou art careful and troubled about many things: But one thing is needful: and Mary hath chosen that good part, which shall not be taken away from her.
LUKE 10:41–42

1   God will never adjust His agenda to fit ours. He will not speed up His pace to catch up with ours; we need to slow our pace in order to recover our walk with Him. God will not scream and shout over the noisy clamor; He expects us to seek quietness, where His still small voice can be heard again.

Charles Swindoll
So You Want to Live Like Christ? (2005)

2   Get away from stressful situations or commitments and set aside time to listen to God's voice of peace and comfort.

Susan McCarthy Peabody
Alphabet Soup for Christian Living (2007)

3   By itself, stress won't destroy our families; but the way we handle it can.

Sandra Aldrich
Upward Glances (2000)

4   Don't let the cares of the day, the stresses of the moment, and the worries of tomorrow interfere with your communing with and partaking of the love affair that Jesus longs for you to have with Him.

Dee Brestin and Kathy Troccoli
Living in Love with Jesus (2002)

5   When we live life in a hurry, we end up weary. . .in a hurry.

Keri Wyatt Kent
Breathe: Creating Space for God in a Hectic Life (2005)

6   There is no peace in striving with your own strength to hold on to what you may lose.

Rubye Goodlett
Gathered Fragments (1986)

401 STRUGGLES
(*see also* DISAPPOINTMENT; DISCOURAGEMENT; FRUSTRATION)

Watch ye and pray, lest ye enter into temptation. The spirit truly is ready, but the flesh is weak.
MARK 14:38

1   We are designed to function poorly, to feel overwhelmed and alone apart from our relationship with Jesus. We are made to be lost without God.

Angela Thomas McGuffey
Tender Mercy for a Mother's Soul (2001)

2   Without struggle there is no progress, no greatness, making of things to happen.
Ralph Ransom Frederick
Steps on the Stairway (1981)

3   You make your list of all the things you've already told God you could not survive and I bet you, if I were a betting woman, Satan threatens you over those things all the time.
Beth Moore
"Who Do You Trust?" teaching series (2007)

4   Our struggles are not about right or wrong, win or lose, can or cannot—they are often just life as it is.
Leslie Haskin
God Has Not Forgotten About You (2009)

5   What is big to you can only be determined by you.
Leslie Haskin
God Has Not Forgotten About You (2009)

STUDY (*see* LEARNING)

402 STUMBLING BLOCKS

But take heed lest by any means this liberty of
yours become a stumblingblock
to them that are weak.
1 CORINTHIANS 8:9

1   You may pray for the release of some area of life in a friend and find that you are called upon to set right something in your own life that has acted as a stumbling block to him.
Douglas Steere
Prayer and Worship (1978)

403 SUBMISSION
(*see also* OBEDIENCE; SURRENDER)

Submit yourselves therefore to God.
JAMES 4:7

1   To let God be God, of course, means climbing down from my own executive chair of control.
Philip Yancey
Prayer: Does It Make Any Difference? (2006)

2   Before anything that is truly of God can be born, your own preferences have to die.
Ed Stetzer and David Putman
Breaking the Missional Code (2006)

3   Life can be lived only in absolute and disciplined submission to its authority.
Charles Colson
Faith on the Line (1986)

404 SUBSTANCE ABUSE
(*see also* ALCOHOL;
DRUNKENNESS; SOBRIETY)

All things are lawful unto me, but all things are
not expedient: all things are lawful for me, but I
will not be brought under the power of any.
1 CORINTHIANS 6:12

1   In working with an alcoholic we must always go by what he does—not by what he says he's going to do.
Jerry Dunn
God Is for the Alcoholic (1965)

2   This is something you must remember if you are dealing with an alcoholic—he becomes an accomplished liar. He is able to look you straight in the eye and speak with tones of one taking a solemn oath without uttering a single word of truth.
Jerry Dunn
God Is for the Alcoholic (1965)

3   Drugs and alcohol are temporary escapes that will destroy you.
Mike Klumpp
The Single Dad's Survival Guide (2003)

405 SUCCESS

Save now, I beseech thee, O LORD: O LORD,
I beseech thee, send now prosperity.
PSALM 118:25

1   Interestingly, the Bible says little about success, but a lot about the heart, the place where true success originates.
Charles Swindoll
The Quest for Character (1982)

2   Successes can easily become failures. All it takes is letting our guard down.
Charles Swindoll
The Quest for Character (1982)

3   God has eternal purposes for every person in the world. He wants each one to discover those purposes and fulfill them. This is the basis of true success.
Bill Gothard
The Power of Spoken Blessings (2004)

4   Success brings its own set of problems.
John Townsend
It's Not My Fault (2007)

5   Success has ruin'd many a Man.
Benjamin Franklin
Poor Richard's Almanac (18th century)

6   There is no better measure of real success than Jesus' words, "Well done, good and faithful servant."
Mel Lawrenz
Jubilee (2008)

7   What does it signify though we are well able to act our parts in life, in every other respect, if at last we hear from the Supreme Judge, "Depart from me, I know you not, ye workers of iniquity?"
Matthew Henry
Commentary on the Whole Bible (1706)

8   Some men attain great esteem in this world—their accomplishments are significant in the eyes of men. But at the end of their lives, how many of these men rest in peace? How many of these men satisfy that deep hunger each of us has for purpose, meaning, and significance?
Patrick Morley
The Man in the Mirror (1992)

9   Success is accepting God's goal for our lives and by His grace becoming what He has called us to be.
Neil Anderson
Victory Over the Darkness (1990)

10 Paul had been shipwrecked, whipped, beaten, stoned, and imprisoned. Throughout everything, his faith enabled him to maintain perspective. He realized that as long as he was doing what he was supposed to do, his being labeled success or failure by others really didn't matter.
John Maxwell
Failing Forward (2000)

11 The greatest deception is to equate success with wealth.
L. James Harvey
701 More Sentence Sermons (2002)

12 My definition of success: choosing to enter into the arena of action, determined to give yourself to that cause which will better mankind and last for eternity. Success is more than just power or not violating the rights of others; it is the privilege of contributing to the betterment of others.
John Maxwell
Be All You Can Be (1987)

13 You can be deeply involved in your job, become successful, and increase your income and status. At the same time, if you only experience loveless coexistence with others, the satisfaction you might have from your job or other endeavors is spoiled.
Dick Purnell
Finding a Lasting Love (2003)

14 We need to define who we are and what is truly important. Remember, our lives must be directed by what wealth, prestige, and power can never gain—loving others and being grateful for the life God has given us.
Ray and Nancy Kane
From Fear to Love (2002)

15 Nice guys may appear to finish last, but usually they are running in a different race.
Ken Blanchard
Leadership Smarts (2004)

16 True achievement only exists when our confidence comes from God and our gain results from a life of integrity.
Pam Farrel
Woman of Confidence (2001)

17 Each of us in our own humble endeavors can make a noble and beautiful contribution to our generation.
W. Phillip Keller
What Makes Life Worth Living? (1998)

18 Great things aren't just the legacy of unusually gifted great men and women. Great things are what you will accomplish when you put God first and make Him owner of all you care about most.
Bruce Wilkinson
The Dream Giver (2003)

19 In believing that God is in control of everything, we have a tendency to play down man's role.
Ted Engstrom
The Making of a Christian Leader (1978)

20 You can't get to success without risking failure.
Alex and Brett Harris
Do Hard Things (2008)

21 Successful people do not hang on to bad stuff for long. . .they do not allow negative things to take up space in their lives, draining them of energy and resources. If the tooth is infected, they pull it. Immediately. They have little tolerance for nagging pains that are unresolved.
Henry Cloud
9 Things You Simply Must Do (2004)

22 Efficiency is the foundation for survival. Effectiveness is the foundation for success.
John Maxwell
Developing the Leader within You (1993)

23 Greatness hath nothing greater than a heart to be willing, and a power to be able to do good.
Thomas Manton
A Practical Commentary on the Epistle of James (17th century)

24 Success depends entirely and absolutely on the immediate blessing and influence of God.
Jonathan Edwards
"God Glorified in Man's Dependence" sermon (18th century)

25 The real victory in all of this service is won in secret, beforehand, by prayer.
Samuel Gordon
Quiet Talks on Prayer (1904)

26 You are called not to be successful or to meet any of the other counterfeit standards of this world, but to be faithful and to be expended in the cause of serving the risen and returning Christ.
Charles Colson
Faith on the Line (1986)

27 The only way to risk greatness is to trust God with all areas of your life.
Kerry and Chris Shook
One Month to Live (2008)

28 Just three words, Do it now, can propel us on to achievements we never thought possible.
Ted Engstrom
Motivation to Last a Lifetime (1984)

29 Success is won by people who know it can be done.

    Ted Engstrom
    Motivation to Last a Lifetime (1984)

30 Our success doesn't hinge on what the culture at-large says or does, or how others act towards us, or even on the outcome of our circumstances. Our ultimate success totally depends on God: God's Son the Living Word, and God's written Word in us, filling us, directing us.

    Lois Evans
    Stones of Remembrance (2006)

31 We envy the success of others, when we should emulate the process by which that success came.

    William George Jordan
    The Kingship of Self-Control (1898)

32 Success is not a reward to be enjoyed but a trust to be administered.

    Charlie "Tremendous" Jones
    Life Is Tremendous! (1968)

33 Millions of people try to climb the ladder of success, only to discover when they get to the top that their ladder is leaning against the wrong wall!

    Neil Anderson and Dave Park
    Overcoming Negative Self-Image (2003)

34 You are called not to be successful or to meet any of the other counterfeit standards of this world, but to be faithful and to be expended in the cause of serving the risen and returning Christ.

    Charles Colson
    Faith on the Line (1994)

406 SUFFERING

This is my comfort in my affliction:
for thy word hath quickened me.
PSALM 119:50

1 Love sweetens pain; and when one loves God, one suffers for His sake with joy and courage.

    Brother Lawrence
    The Practice of the Presence of God
    (17th century)

2 Regardless of the source of our pain, we must accept that God knows, God loves and God is at work.

    Charles Stanley
    The Blessings of Brokenness (1997)

3 Above all else, He loves you and chose to measure that love out not in words, but in blood. He loves you enough to give you the greatest gift conceivable. Would such a love allow you to suffer without purpose?

    David Jeremiah
    A Bend in the Road (2000)

4 He doesn't exult in your pain, but He delights in your tighter embrace.

    David Jeremiah
    A Bend in the Road (2000)

5 God whispers to us in our pleasures, speaks in our conscience, but shouts in our pains.

    C. S. Lewis
    The Problem of Pain (1947)

6 A season of suffering is a small price to pay for a clear view of God.

    Max Lucado
    In the Eye of the Storm (1991)

7 Your pain has a purpose. Your problems, struggles, heartaches, and hassles cooperate toward one end—the glory of God.

    Max Lucado
    It's Not About Me (2004)

8 Be obedient in the painful times, and trust that God is up to something more grand and wonderful than you can imagine.

    Susie Larson
    Alone in Marriage (2007)

9   If we accept that the results of evil—pain, suffering and death—are not from God, yet He allows them, then we must assume that they play a part in His plan. And since we know that His plan is one of eternal redemption— that the world will be saved—then it's safe to say that pain must play a role in our personal redemption. Pain indeed has a purpose.
Alex McFarland
The 10 Most Common Objections to Christianity (2007)

10   As soon as anything is presented in the form of suffering, and you feel a repugnance, resign yourself immediately to God with respect to it, and give yourself up to Him in sacrifice: you will then find, that when the cross arrives, it will not be so very burthensome, because you have yourself desired it. This, however does not prevent you from feeling its weight, as some have imagined; for when we do not feel the cross, we do not suffer.
François Fénelon and Jeanne Guyon
Spiritual Progress (17th century)

11   Far from being estranged by our suffering and wretched state, it is then that God appears; and if any weakness has been apparent, He gives us some token of his immediate presence, as if to assure the soul for a moment, that He was with it in its tribulation.
François Fénelon and Jeanne Guyon
Spiritual Progress (17th century)

12   For those of us who know God, pain is a process with a certain purpose. We don't make it through tough times. We are made through tough times—made into the beauty of Christ Jesus. And in that perspective, the pain is worth the gain.
Joseph Stowell
Through the Fire (1985)

13   Pain exists, and pain hurts, and pain can slow down even secure, optimistic people. It

may even stop them for a while. But over time, pain eases a bit, and secure people see that as their cue to get up and get going again.
Tim Clinton and Gary Sibcy
Attachments (2002)

14   There are two kinds of pain that we forget. We forget hurts too trivial to bother about. We forget pains too horrible for our memory to manage.
Lewis Smedes
Forgive and Forget (1986)

15   The pains we dare not remember are the most dangerous pains of all.
Lewis Smedes
Forgive and Forget (1986)

16   Pain, more than joy, shapes our lives and motivates us to learn and grow.
Carol Kuykendall
Learning to Let Go (1985)

17   Yet I could not say, "Take thy plague away from me"; but only "Let me be purified, not consumed."
John Wesley
The Works of the Rev. John Wesley (18th century)

18   It is not possible to be significantly used by God in any area of endeavor without suffering.
Ed Young
From Bad Beginnings to Happy Endings (1994)

19   This is the chief significance of the suffering of Christ for us, that we cast all our grief into the ocean of His suffering.
Meister Eckhart
Meister Eckhart's Sermons (14th century)

20   If thou sufferest only regarding thyself, from whatever cause it may be, that suffering causes grief to thee, and is hard to bear. But if thou sufferest regarding God and Him alone,

that suffering is not grievous, nor hard to bear, because God bears the load.

Meister Eckhart
Meister Eckhart's Sermons (14th century)

21 In the meantime, though misfortune, misery, and trouble be upon us, we must have this sure confidence in him, that he will not suffer us to be destroyed either in body or soul, but will so deal with us, that all things, be they good or evil, shall redound to our advantage.

Martin Luther
Table Talk (16th century)

22 When I consider my crosses, tribulations, and temptations, I shame myself almost to death, thinking what are they in comparison of the sufferings of my blessed Saviour Christ Jesus.

Martin Luther
Table Talk (16th century)

23 Our capacity of pain seems to bear an exact proportion to our susceptibility of pleasure.

Archibald Alexander
The Misery of the Lost (19th century)

24 Useless and hateful in itself, suffering without faith is a curse.

Thomas Merton
No Man Is an Island (1955)

25 The shadow of suffering falls across every path, including yours.

Charles Swindoll
The Darkness and the Dawn (2001)

26 Very often in times of deep confusion, pain, selfishness, and anger, we do things that hurt others far more than we can imagine.

Jay Kesler
Is Your Marriage Really Worth Fighting For? (1989)

27 Get your arms around a really, really important truth. God is never more present in your life than when you are suffering.

James MacDonald
"Jesus Stands for You" teaching (2007)

28 Jesus Christ is an experienced sufferer.

James MacDonald
"Jesus Stands for You" teaching (2007)

29 My very relationship with God was made possible because Jesus took responsibility for my sins by suffering. Suffering was at the heart of the gospel message. How had I missed it?

Ruth Graham and Stacy Mattingly
In Every Pew Sits a Broken Heart (2004)

30 Suffering is part of the human condition. All of us have suffered, are suffering or will suffer.

Ruth Graham and Stacy Mattingly
In Every Pew Sits a Broken Heart (2004)

31 Sometimes we have difficulty seeing beyond our pain, but we must try.

Ruth Graham and Stacy Mattingly
In Every Pew Sits a Broken Heart (2004)

32 Circumstances in life often take us places that we never intended to go. We visit some places of beauty, others of pain and desolation.

Kristin Armstrong
Happily Ever After (2007)

33 With Christ as our pinnacle example, we can say with confidence that it is impossible to be of great faith and not endure suffering.

Kristin Armstrong
Happily Ever After (2007)

34 There is a place where our humanity, be it our emotional will or physical strength, simply stops. We come to the end of our personal resources.

Kristin Armstrong
Happily Ever After (2007)

35 We spend our whole lives trying to avoid anything that will hurt or be hard. But there's a better kind of life—a deeper, more fulfilling kind of life—that isn't about avoiding every pain. It's about finding God faithful and powerful in the midst of whatever thorns He allows.
James MacDonald
"Strength in Weakness" sermon (2009)

36 We often treat suffering like a dodgeball game. Anytime anything painful comes at us, we jump out of the way.
James MacDonald
"Strength in Weakness" sermon (2009)

37 The deepest lessons come out of the deepest waters and the hottest fires.
Elisabeth Elliot
A Path Through Suffering (1990)

38 Each time the mystery of suffering touches us personally and all the cosmic questions arise fresh in our minds we face the choice between faith (which accepts) and unbelief (which refuses to accept).
Elisabeth Elliot
A Path Through Suffering (1990)

39 Christ and his church, when they are the lowest, are nearest rising.
Richard Sibbes
The Bruised Reed (1630)

40 Thank God, suffering is always that short period before final victory.
David Wilkerson
"A Dry Spell" article (2010)

41 Satan wants to use suffering to tear us down, but God can use suffering to build us up and equip us to serve him better. However, keep in mind that suffering does not automatically equip the saint. Sad to say, some Christians have gone through trials and have come out of the fiery furnace burned and bitter instead of purified and perfected. It is only when we depend on the grace of "the God of all grace" that the furnace does its equipping work.
Warren Wiersbe
Be What You Are (1988)

42 Like the spine of a good book, scars, by their very nature, imply there's a story to tell.
Sharon Jaynes
Your Scars Are Beautiful to God (2006)

43 We receive scars in two ways: What has been done to us by other people or what has been done through us by our own mistakes and failures.
Sharon Jaynes
Your Scars Are Beautiful to God (2006)

44 We must be courageous enough to let pain do its work, and brave enough to endure so that our hearts become filled to overflowing with God's infinite and complete love.
Kim Moore and Pam Mellskog
A Patchwork Heart (2002)

45 There is no such thing as a saint who has not suffered.
Paul Billheimer
Don't Waste Your Sorrows (1977)

46 We sparkle in the deep, hidden mines of our private sufferings.
Joy Sawyer
Dancing to the Heartbeat of Redemption (2000)

47 If we conceal our wounds, out of fear or shame, our inner darkness can neither be illuminated nor become a light for others.
Brennan Manning
The Rabbi's Heartbeat (2003)

407 SUNDAY (*see also* SABBATH)
And upon the first day of the week,
when the disciples came together to break bread,
Paul preached unto them. . .
ACTS 20:7

1   Sundays observe; think when the bells do chime,
'Tis angels' music.
>   George Herbert
>   *The Church Porch* (17th century)

2   Ah Lord! be thou in all our being; as not in the Sundays of our time alone.
>   George MacDonald
>   "The Higher Faith" sermon (19th century)

408 SURRENDER (*see also* OBEDIENCE; SUBMISSION)

Furthermore we have had fathers of our flesh which corrected us, and we gave them reverence: shall we not much rather be in subjection unto the Father of spirits, and live?
HEBREWS 12:9

1   It is not because of any want of historical data that people do not believe the Scripture or do not believe in Christ. Rather, it is because of a want of a moral disposition to surrender one's life to the Lordship and authority of Jesus Christ.
>   D. James Kennedy
>   *Why I Believe* (1980)

2   We can learn the purpose of God as we fill ourselves with his Word and then look to Him for direction with a surrendered heart.
>   Jim Cymbala
>   *You Were Made for More* (2008)

3   If we walk in the Spirit daily, surrendered to His power, we have the right to expect anything we need to hear from God. The Holy Spirit living within us and speaking to us ought to be the natural, normal life-style of believers.
>   Charles Stanley
>   *How to Listen to God* (1985)

4   Jesus is not just a historical fact. He is an abiding presence, and we can surrender to an intimate relationship with Him.
>   Tony Campolo
>   *How to Be Pentecostal without Speaking in Tongues* (1991)

5   Christ is not after my good works. He desires a surrendered heart that can be filled with His love. The outpouring of a love-filled heart will be righteous actions that bring glory to God.
>   Jack and Dona Eggar
>   *Shaping Your Family's Faith* (2007)

6   There is no autonomy in the fallen world. We are governed by sin or governed by God.
>   John Piper
>   *The Passion of Jesus Christ* (2004)

7   There are many who have accepted Christ as their Lord, but have never yet come to the final, absolute surrender of everything.
>   Andrew Murray
>   *Master's Indwelling* (1895)

8   The discipline of surrender. . .has nothing to do with bondage. It is an expression of freedom.
>   Karen O'Connor
>   *Addicted to Shopping* (2005)

9   If you try to surrender just a little bit to God, He'll know. It's like trying to carry on a conversation with someone who's preoccupied with the newspaper: most unsatisfying and practially useless.
>   Karon Phillips Goodman
>   *You're Late Again, Lord!* (2002)

SYMPATHY (*see* COMPASSION)

409 TALENT

And unto one he gave five talents, to another two, and to another one; to every man according to his several ability. . .
MATTHEW 25:15

1   If you're not stretching yourself and your talents ask yourself why not? And then do something about it.
>   Ted Engstrom
>   *The Pursuit of Excellence* (1982)

2 All that a man has to answer for is for the talent or talents that God has given him.
D. L. Moody
The Faithful Saying (1877)

3 Surely as a little knowledge is a dangerous thing, so are we fearfully responsible for all that we can discover, for all that we can do.
George Edward Jelf
The Secret Trials of the Christian Life (19th century)

4 If you concern yourself with your neighbor's talents, you will neglect yours. But if you concern yourself with yours, you could inspire both.
Max Lucado
He Still Moves Stones (1993)

410 TEACHING

And thou shalt teach them ordinances and laws, and shalt shew them the way wherein they must walk, and the work that they must do.
EXODUS 18:20

1 What a wonderful opportunity it is to teach these little ones to love God with all their heart and to serve fellowman throughout their lives. There is no higher calling than that!
James Dobson
Parenting Isn't for Cowards (1987)

2 The only proper response to false teaching is to shun it.
John MacArthur
Fool's Gold? (2005)

3 Disciplemaking involves more than rubbing shoulders with friends—it is intentionally and actively helping them live on the growing edge of their faith.
Alice Fryling
Disciplemakers' Handbook (1989)

4 If we want to be disciplemakers, then, we must follow Jesus' example and intentionally seek out those who are waiting to grow. We need to communicate that Jesus loves each of us as we are and that he will help us become much more than we think we can ever be.
Alice Fryling
Disciplemakers' Handbook (1989)

5 Disciplemaking, then, is God's idea and based on his ability. It also runs according to his timetable. Some fruit in disciplemaking comes as quickly as squash in a summer garden. Other fruit, like the oak tree in our front yard, takes years to develop. The rate of growth is God's, not ours.
Alice Fryling
Disciplemakers' Handbook (1989)

411 TEAMWORK

We then, as workers together with him. . .
2 CORINTHIANS 6:1

1 The least important word: I—it gets the least amount done. The most important word: We—it gets the most amount done.
John Maxwell
Be a People Person (1989)

2 I will go down, but remember that you must hold the ropes.
William Carey (19th century) quoted in *Faithful Witness: The Life and Mission of William Carey*

3 We must each see ourselves as vital members of the body, each entrusted with the care of the whole.
Jane Winebrenner and Debra Frazier
When a Leader Falls (1993)

412 TEMPERANCE
(*see also* ABSTINENCE; MODERATION; SELF-CONTROL)

That the aged men be sober, grave, temperate. . .
TITUS 2:2

1 Elderly people tend to weigh their thoughts before they respond. That shows maturity and an understanding of what it means to be temperate. Would your family say you're temperate, or would they say you show little restraint when you respond?

Dan Seaborn
26 Words That Will Improve the Way You Do Family (2002)

413 TEMPTATION
(*see also* IMMORALITY; LUST; SENSUALITY; SIN)

There hath no temptation taken you but such as is common to man: but God is faithful, who will not suffer you to be tempted above that ye are able; but will with the temptation also make a way to escape, that ye may be able to bear it.
1 CORINTHIANS 10:13

1 I have a reluctance to say much about temptations to which I myself am not exposed. No man, I suppose, is tempted to every sin.

C. S. Lewis
Mere Christianity (1952)

2 It seems to me that if we get one look at Christ in His love and beauty, this world and its pleasures will look very small to us.

D. L. Moody
"The Transfiguration" sermon
(19th century)

3 It's always easier to avoid temptation than to resist it.

Randy Alcorn
The Purity Principle (2003)

4 By far our most important strategy for defeating the roaring lion is to stay out of the arena.

Bruce Wilkinson
The Prayer of Jabez (2000)

5 Dwelling on a sinful desire is like starting the countdown for the space shuttle—it's just a matter of time until liftoff.

James MacDonald
Lord, Change My Attitude (2001)

6 No one is immune to temptation. Not even a hero. Not even a nobody. Not even people like you and me. Lust is never very far away. And just when you least expect it, there it is again.

Charles Swindoll
Man to Man (1996)

7 Keep your eyes open. You will be tempted.
Bruce Wilkinson
Beyond Jabez (2005)

8 Those who do not mean to entertain guests should take down their signboard.

Francis de Sales
Introduction to the Devout Life
(17th century)

9 It is always good to keep the Lord between you and Satan.

Jon Courson
Application Commentary (2005)

10 Temptation is around us every day. It doesn't usually lurk in the bushes for a surprise attack. Instead it slowly befriends us, convincing us that we have nothing to fear.

Gregg Matte
The Highest Education: Becoming a Godly Man (2000)

11 Satan has a way of setting up situations and temptations that can suck us under like a riptide sucks a swimmer beneath the surface of the sea. But, Satan doesn't push our head under water. It is by choice we ignore the Rip Tide warning sign written in large red print with a flag waving mightily in the wind.

Gina Burgess
"Writing on Stones" article (2009)

12 No matter how enticing the temptation, we are responsible for the choices we make.
Hank Hanegraaff
The Covering (2002)

13 The awful, never-ending process of combating temptation is God's means of maturing us and conforming us to the image of Christ.
Charles Stanley
Winning the War Within (1998)

14 God has set a limit on the intensity of every temptation. God knows you perfectly, inside and out. In accordance with His perfect knowledge He has set a limit on the intensity of the temptations you will face.
Charles Stanley
Winning the War Within (1998)

15 A wise individual prepares for those things that are inevitable in life. Temptation is one of those inevitable things.
Charles Stanley
Winning the War Within (1998)

16 Habit, if not resisted, becomes necessity.
Augustine
Augustine's Conversion (5th century)

17 Temptation is not sin. Yielding is.
Billy Sunday
The Real Billy Sunday (1914)

18 What is it exactly that makes stepping over the line worth the risk? It's the beauty, the appeal, the allure of deception's first cousin. . . temptation.
Michelle McKinney Hammond
Why Do I Say "Yes" When I Need to Say "No"? (2002)

19 Every privilege and blessing has accompanying temptations. People of wisdom understand this, and they do all they can to quickly spot and defeat those temptations.
Gordon MacDonald
Secrets of the Generous Life (2002)

20 God delights in our temptations, and yet hates them; he delights in them when they drive us to prayer; he hates them when they drive us to despair.
Martin Luther
Table Talk (16th century)

21 When we acknowledge temptation and resist it, we make a conscious decision to detach ourselves from sin, and in doing that, we find we are attached more firmly to Christ.
Steven Curtis Chapman
The Great Adventure (2001)

22 When we dwell on desire—yielding is a matter of time.
James MacDonald
Replace My Covetous Attitude (2009)

23 So long as the regenerate man is kept in this world, he must find the old environment at many points a severe temptation.
Henry Drummond
Natural Law in the Spiritual World (19th century)

24 Quit presenting yourself as a willing candidate for addiction.
Steve Campbell
"Freedom from Addiction" sermon (2009)

25 The devil may send the package, but I'm responsible for signing for it.
Steve Campbell
"Freedom from Addiction" sermon (2009)

26 Temptation is a pitiless thing. It goes into the church and picks off the man in the pulpit. It goes into the university and picks off the flower of the class.
Henry Drummond
Stones Rolled Away and Other Addresses to Young Men (1893)

27 Many a man goes through life hanging his head with shame and living without his self-respect because he has never discovered the distinction between temptation and sin.
Henry Drummond
Stones Rolled Away and Other Addresses to Young Men (1893)

28 Those that would not eat the forbidden fruit must not come near the forbidden tree.
Matthew Henry
Commentary on the Whole Bible (1706)

29 The tempter will suffer the punishment he deserves, and the blameless, if true to themselves, will be strengthened and ennobled by the temptation.
F. C. Cook
Bible Commentary (19th century)

30 The trouble with temptation is that it's just so tempting.
Sheila Walsh
Let Go (2008)

31 Necessity is an ill counsellor, and will soon tempt us to some evil way for our own ease, some sinful compliance or confederacy.
Thomas Manton
One Hundred and Ninety Sermons on the Hundred and Nineteenth Psalm (17th century)

32 Let's all wise up. Some of us aren't fighting the fire; we're playing with fire. Flirting with the devil. Stop it! Stop it now before all hell literally breaks loose.
Beth Moore
Voices of the Faithful (2005)

33 We too easily play with the serpent's baits, and are ensnared by his wiles.
Richard Baxter
The Reformed Pastor (17th century)

34 For they who think they make an end of temptation by yielding to it, only set themselves on fire the more.
Martin Luther
A Treatise on Good Works (1520)

35 The strongest defence is prayer and the Word of God; namely, that when evil lust stirs, a man flee to prayer, call upon God's mercy and help, read and meditate on the Gospel, and in it consider Christ's sufferings.
Martin Luther
A Treatise on Good Works (1520)

36 Yet we must not despair if we are not soon rid of the temptation, nor by any means imagine that we are free from it as long as we live, and we must regard it only as an incentive and admonition to prayer, fasting, watching, laboring.
Martin Luther
A Treatise on Good Works (1520)

37 Confusion about your identity makes you a sitting duck for Satan.
Bob Moorehead
A Passion for Victory (1996)

38 Seduction has many voices.
Shelly Beach
The Silent Seduction of Self-Talk (2009)

414 TEN COMMANDMENTS
(*see also* RULES)

And the LORD said unto Moses, Come up to me into the mount, and be there: and I will give thee tables of stone, and a law, and commandments which I have written; that thou mayest teach them.
EXODUS 24:12

1 What Moses brought down from Mount Sinai were not the Ten Suggestions.
Ted Koppel (1987)
Duke University commencement address

2   Take the Ten Commandments, for
instance. People joke about them, do they
not? They even make films of them. They do
everything but keep them!
   Martyn Lloyd-Jones
   Love So Amazing (1962)

3   The sheer brilliance of the Ten
Commandments is that they codify, in a
handful of words, acceptable human behavior.
Not just for then or now but for all time.
   Ted Koppel (1987)
   Duke University commencement address

4   God has his measuring lines and his
canons, called the Ten Commandments; they
are written in our flesh and blood: the sum of
them is this: "What thou wouldest have done
to thyself, the same do thou to another."
   Martin Luther
   Table Talk (16th century)

415 TESTIMONY (*see also* WITNESS)

*I John, who also am your brother, and companion in
tribulation, and in the kingdom and patience of Jesus
Christ, was in the isle that is called Patmos, for the
word of God, and for the testimony of Jesus Christ.*
   REVELATION 1:9

1   I beseech you, do not add to your eternal
misery being a wolf in sheep's clothing. Show
the cloven foot; do not hide it.
   Charles Spurgeon
   "God, the All-Seeing One" sermon (1858)

2   Count upon God, who has seen thee
in secret, to reward thee openly, to give
grace in dealings with men to maintain thy
communion with him, and to make them
know his grace and light are on thee.
   Andrew Murray
   The Prayer Life (1912)

3   The world can get on very well without you
and me, but the world cannot get on without
Christ, and therefore we must testify of Him.
   D. L. Moody
   Secret Power (1881)

4   Jesus says to shine for the world. Shine
your light into the darkness; that's where it
is really needed. Spend less time in your own
well-lighted-all-Christian world and more
time there in the darkness!
   Charles Swindoll
   Simple Faith (1991)

5 Good Christians will be afraid of giving any
occasion to those about them to question their
faith in Christ and their love to him.
   Matthew Henry
   Commentary on the Whole Bible (1706)

6 When we have led them to the living waters,
if we muddy it by our filthy lives, we may lose
our labor, and they be never the better.
   Richard Baxter
   The Reformed Pastor (17th century)

7   So, let your lives preach, let your light
shine, that your works may be seen, that your
Father may be glorified.
   George Fox
   Personal Letter (17th century)

416 TESTING (*see also* ADVERSITY; AFFLICTIONS; DIFFICULTIES; HARDSHIPS; TRIALS; TROUBLES)

*Knowing this, that the trying of your faith
worketh patience.*
   JAMES 1:3

1   Before God can truly use us, in one way or
another, we will pass through a time of threshing.
   Francis Frangipane
   The Three Battlegrounds (1989)

2   You can rest in the knowledge that even
when bad things happen, God is always there.
He is always in charge. Although He may not
always deliver in the way you expect, you will
find His grace sufficient.
   Kay Arthur
   When Bad Things Happen (2002)

3　We must lay our questions, frustrations, anxieties, and impotence at the feet of God and wait for His answer. When we receive it, we must live by faith.

Kay Arthur
When Bad Things Happen (2002)

4　Occasions do not make a man frail, but they shew what he is.

Thomas à Kempis
The Imitation of Christ (15th century)

5　God by his providence will prevent the evils we fear, if that be best for us; or that he will support us under them when they are present.

John Tillotson
The Wisdom of Being Religious (1819)

6　Be not like those who give themselves to Him at one season, only to withdraw from Him at another. They give themselves only to be caressed, and wrest themselves back again, when they are crucified.

François Fénelon and Jeanne Guyon
Spiritual Progress (17th century)

7　The very area where you are most tempted to distrust God is the very place He has most chosen to trust you.

Beth Moore
"Who Do You Trust?" teaching series (2007)

8　God never does anything to us that isn't for us.

Elisabeth Elliot
Be Still My Soul (2003)

9　Just as God allowed Job, John the Baptist, and many other faithful believers to be tested and troubled beyond their human strength, He may test us.

Leslie Haskin
God Has Not Forgotten About You (2009)

10　A Christian is a bird that can sing in winter as well as in spring; he can live in the fire like Moses' bush; burn, and not be consumed; nay, leap in the fire.

Thomas Manton
A Practical Commentary on the Epistle of James (17th century)

11　Oftentimes, the only way for us to know what's in our heart is for God to squeeze it by circumstances. He already knows, it's we who need to be made aware. This revelation isn't meant to condemn us but to give us the opportunity to humbly ask for His help. . .and to recognize our dependence upon Him.

Rebecca Lusignolo
"Squeezed by Life" devotional (2007)

417 THANKSGIVING

I will offer to thee the sacrifice of thanksgiving, and will call upon the name of the LORD.
PSALM 116:17

1　The first great characteristic of the true Christian is always a sense of thankfulness and of gratitude to God.

Martyn Lloyd-Jones
Love So Amazing (1962)

2　May we all be like the one, rather than the nine.

Jennifer Rothschild
Lessons I Learned in the Dark (2002)

3　Physical pain can cloud our convictions about God's benefits, which is why I must continually stir my soul to remember them.

Joni Eareckson Tada
Pearls of Great Price (2006)

4　Aren't you glad that God doesn't give you only that which you remember to thank him for?

Max Lucado
In the Eye of the Storm (1991)

5   If any one would tell you the surest, shortest way to all happiness and all perfection, he must tell you to make it a rule to yourself, to thank God for every thing that happens to you.
  William Law
  A Serious Call to a Devout and Holy Life (1729)

6   If believers are truly chosen by God, they should be grateful.
  Jonathan Edwards
  "Christians—A Chosen Generation" sermon (1742)

7   Gratitude is the attitude that sets the altitude for living.
  James MacDonald
  Lord, Change My Attitude (2001)

8   An attitude of thanksgiving is the clearest indication that the heart recognizes the unmerited love of God.
  Chip Ingram
  Effective Parenting in a Defective World (2006)

9   Maybe it's just me, but in our day it seemed people were far more appreciative of what they had been given. Maybe that was because we, or our parents and grandparents, had gone through times of war, famine, recessions and, for some, a major depression.
  Martha Bolton
  Growing Your Own Turtleneck (2005)

10   It is a rare person who, when his cup frequently runs over, can give thanks to God instead of complaining about the limited size of his mug!
  Bob and Rusty Russell
  Jesus: Lord of Your Personality (2002)

11   When I fail in my duty, I readily acknowledge it, saying, I am used to do so: I shall never do otherwise, if I am left to myself. If I fail not, then I give God thanks, acknowledging that it comes from Him.
  Brother Lawrence
  The Practice of the Presence of God (17th century)

12   He requires no great matters of us; a little remembrance of Him from time to time, a little adoration: sometimes to pray for His grace, sometimes to offer Him your sufferings, and sometimes to return Him thanks for the favours He has given you.
  Brother Lawrence
  The Practice of the Presence of God (17th century)

13   In 1 Thessalonians 5:18, the Bible tells us to give thanks in all things. We may not be able to give thanks for all things, but in every situation we can praise God for His character, His faithfulness, and His promises.
  Gary Oliver
  Made Perfect in Weakness (1995)

14   I believe that when we are in the midst of even the worst life storms, our reaction as children of the King should be to thank God, for it may be that He allowed the very trauma we're going through at the moment for the purpose of preventing us from going through storms that might well destroy us or hinder us in doing what He has called us to do. That, friends, is a miracle in and of itself!
  Mac Brunson
  The Miracle You've Been Searching For (2004)

15   Pausing to thank God for food is a small token of gratefulness. Often enough the prayer gets rattled off so fast that any meaning gets lost. Taking the effort, though, day after day, does say something about God's place in your lives. When you're hungry, when you're in a hurry, even when you don't feel like it, you thank God for the food.
  Tim Stafford
  Never Mind the Joneses (2004)

16 The highest and most precious treasure we receive of God is, that we can speak, hear, see, etc.; but how few acknowledge these as God's special gifts, much less give God thanks for them.
    Martin Luther
    Table Talk (16th century)

17 The most acceptable service we can do and show unto God, and which alone he desires of us, is, that he be praised of us.
    Martin Luther
    Table Talk (16th century)

18 Annihilate not the mercies of God by the oblivion of ingratitude.
    Thomas Brown
    Christian Morals (17th century)

19 How tragic not to be able to say "Thank you" and to live a thankful life.
    William Krutza
    101 Ways to Enrich Your Marriage (1982)

20 Showing gratitude has to do with appreciating benefits received and expressing that thankfulness to others. True gratitude evidences itself by bringing joy to others and alleviating their discomfort.
    Carol Kent
    A New Kind of Normal (2007)

21 We can thank God for everything good, and all the rest we don't comprehend yet.
    Kristin Armstrong
    Happily Ever After (2007)

418 THEOLOGY

And they were astonished at his doctrine: for he taught them as one that had authority...
MARK 1:22

1 Moral relativism actively rejects the faith of the New Testament and strongly recommends you pick another, more "flexible" belief system.
    Ryan Dobson
    Be Intolerant (2003)

2 Every single biblical doctrine of theology, directly or indirectly, ultimately has its basis in the Book of Genesis.
    Ken Ham
    The Lie: Evolution (1987)

3 Let your theology rise above your circumstances.
    John MacArthur
    "The Man Who Would Be Christ" sermon (2009)

4 God's knowledge and His eternal purposes intersect with human choice in such a way that we have real choices to make, and yet those choices fulfill God's purposes to accomplish His goal.
    Tony Evans
    Theology You Can Count On (2008)

5 Everyone acknowledges the expertise of the trained professional until we come to theology. Then, everyone's an expert.
    Jack Hayford
    Prayer Is Invading the Impossible (2002)

6 Theology these days has fallen on hard times. Not just what we would call religious theology, but all realms of philosophical thought.
    Michael Phillips
    A God to Call Father (1994)

419 THINKING (*see also* MIND, THE)

Tell us therefore, What thinkest thou?
MATTHEW 22:17

1 There is an urgent need in the church today for more genuinely Christian thinkers, who have not capitulated to the prevailing secularism, that is to say, for more Christians who have put their minds under the yoke of Christ.
    John Stott
    Life in Christ (2003)

2   The way we think determines what we do, how we do it, and whether we have any motivation to change.
   Jan Silvious
   Foolproofing Your Life (1998)

3   "Honest doubters," sincere inquirers, earnest seekers after God and truth, groping their way amid the darkness of involuntary misapprehensions, how few they are at any time! How much more numerous the contented slaves of opinion, Christian or non-Christian, according to the accidents of birth and education!
   Alexander Balmain Bruce
   Apologetics, or Christianity Defensively Stated (1892)

4   Negative thinking tends to beget negative thinking.
   Gary Chapman
   Desperate Marriages (2008)

5   First we think, then we feel, then we will.
   Evelyn Underhill
   The Essentials of Mysticism (1960)

420 THOUGHTS (*see also* MIND, THE)
Casting down imaginations, and every high thing that exalteth itself against the knowledge of God, and bringing into captivity every thought to the obedience of Christ. . .
2 CORINTHIANS 10:5

1   These thoughts, if you hate them, are none of yours, but are injections of the Devil, for which he is responsible, and not you. If you strive against them, they are no more yours than are the cursings and falsehoods of rioters in the street.
   Charles Spurgeon
   All of Grace (19th century)

2   A man might as well hope to fight a swarm of flies with a sword as to master his own thoughts when they are set on by the devil.
   Charles Spurgeon
   All of Grace (19th century)

3   The poor diseased woman could not come to Jesus for the press, and you are in much the same condition, because of the rush and throng of these dreadful thoughts. Still, she put forth her finger, and touched the fringe of the Lord's garment, and she was healed. Do you the same.
   Charles Spurgeon
   All of Grace (19th century)

4   You are always moving in the direction of your most dominant thoughts.
   Brian Tracy
   Million Dollar Habits (2006)

5   Oh Christians, if you would avoid self-deceit, see that you mind not only your actions but your motives.
   Joseph Alleine
   A Sure Guide to Heaven (1671)

6   Often, we allow our thoughts to shape us, rather than consciously choosing to shape our thoughts.
   Shelly Beach
   The Silent Seduction of Self-Talk (2009)

7   I believe our thoughts sound as loudly in heaven as our words do on earth.
   Joy Dawson
   Intimate Friendship with God (1986)

421 TIME
(*see also* PRESENT, THE; TODAY)
My times are in thy hand.
PSALM 31:15

1   We shall have plenty of time in heaven to say all we have to say to each other.
   Elizabeth Prentiss
   More Love to Thee—The Life and Letters of Elizabeth Prentiss (1882)

2 Eternity depends on the proper use of time.
Jonathan Edwards
"The Preciousness of Time and the
Importance of Redeeming It"
sermon (1734)

3 God has, quite literally, all the time in the
world for each one of us.
Philip Yancey
Prayer: Does It Make Any Difference? (2006)

4 The aim of man is beyond the temporal—
in the serene region of the everlasting Present.
Meister Eckhart
Meister Eckhart's Sermons (14th century)

5 Time that is measured fights against time
that is lived.
Ted Engstrom and Norman Rohrer
Welcome to the Rest of Your Life (1994)

6 Submerge as much of your day as you can,
to make it your invisible keel, by eliminating
less important things. You need time to look
into the face of God, time to read and study
his Word systematically, time to think and
plan for your life, time to praise, time to
intercede, time to get wisdom for handling
people and for making decisions.
Anne Ortlund
Disciplines of the Beautiful Woman (1977)

422 TIMING, GOD'S

He hath made every thing beautiful in his time.
ECCLESIASTES 3:11

1 We can't hurry God, and we can't bribe
Him or force Him to alter the plan He's made.
But we can learn to trust Him not to waste our
waiting time.
Karon Phillips Goodman
You're Late Again, Lord! (2002)

2 The Lord's timing is not ours. His is perfect.
Jon Courson
Application Commentary (2005)

3 Answers to prayer have to be on God's
schedule, not ours. He hears us pray, and He
answers according to His will in His own time.
David Jeremiah
The Prayer Matrix (2004)

4 God's mill grinds slow, but sure.
George Herbert
Jacula Prudentum (17th century)

5 Delays can actually be part of God's
purpose; seemingly unanswered prayer can be as
much a part of God's will as answered prayer.
R. T. Kendall
Total Forgiveness (2002)

6 God is never late, but neither does he seem
to be particularly early. He waits until we
know we need his help, and then he opens his
generous hand.
Dean Merrill
Wait Quietly (1994)

7 I want you to be encouraged that in God's
time you will see the dreams and visions that
God has given you fulfilled.
Joyce Meyer
When God, When? (1994)

8 God has a perfect timetable for meeting
your needs.
Josh McDowell and Dale Bellis
Evidence for Joy (1984)

9 God can grow a mushroom overnight, but
He will take time to grow an oak or a giant
sequoia.
Warren Wiersbe
God Isn't in a Hurry (1994)

10 The best thing you and I can do is to stop
looking at our watches and calendars and
simply look by faith into the face of God and
let Him have His way—in His time.
Warren Wiersbe
God Isn't in a Hurry (1994)

423 TITHING

*Bring ye all the tithes into the storehouse,
that there may be meat in mine house, and prove
me now herewith, saith the LORD of hosts, if I will
not open you the windows of heaven, and pour you
out a blessing, that there shall not be room enough
to receive it.*
MALACHI 3:10

1   The tithe is not an obligation but a
privilege allowing us to have a part in God's
work.
Sandra Aldrich
From One Single Mother to Another (1991)

424 TODAY

*But exhort one another daily, while it is called
To day; lest any of you be hardened through
the deceitfulness of sin.*
HEBREWS 3:13

1   Tomorrow—it is not written in the
almanack of time. Tomorrow—it is in Satan's
calendar, and nowhere else.... Yonder clock
saith "today"; everything crieth "today."
Charles Spurgeon
"Effectual Calling" sermon (1856)

2   Every day is a gift, of course, precious and
worthwhile.
Luci Shaw
God in the Dark (1989)

3   The future has driven the present moment
from our awareness.
Bill Kemp and Diane Kerner Arnett
Going Home (2005)

4   Now is the time to invest in the things that
you will not regret.
Kim Thomas
Living in the Sacred Now (2001)

5   Today unused is lost forever, and tomorrow
may never come.
Ted Engstrom
Motivation to Last a Lifetime (1984)

425 TOLERANCE

*Do not intermarry with them.
Do not give your daughters to their sons
or take their daughters for your sons...*
DEUTERONOMY 7:3 NIV

1   The greatest act of tolerance in all of
human history was the death and resurrection
of God's Son, Jesus Christ. It was not exclusive
for one class or another, for one race or
another, but for all.
Franklin Graham
The Name (2002)

2   Anyone who takes the Bible seriously
knows that it is often intolerant and
discriminatory. It is intolerant of sexual sins
among heterosexuals and homosexuals; it
loudly discriminates against those who do a
variety of evils and those who believe false
doctrine. It especially discriminates against
those who refuse to accept Jesus as Savior and
teaches that they shall be in hell forever.
Erwin Lutzer
The Truth About Same-Sex Marriage (2004)

3   Tolerance has arisen as the sole virtue of
western culture, and intolerance the sole vice.
Josh McDowell and Bob Hostetler
Right from Wrong (1994)

4   Tolerance refuses to judge someone merely
because he or she has judged you.
Stephen Arterburn and Jack Felton
More Jesus, Less Religion (2000)

5   Tolerance in personal opinions is a virtue,
but tolerance when dealing with facts is
ridiculous.
David DeWitt
Answering the Tough Ones (1980)

6   Our culture confuses tolerance with
acceptance, much to our detriment as a society.
Stephen Arterburn
Finding Mr. Right (2003)

7   Be Intolerant—Because Some Things Are Just Stupid.
Ryan Dobson book title (2003)

8   Tolerance is the virtue of those who believe in nothing.
Ryan Dobson
Be Intolerant (2003)

9   True tolerance grants people the right to dissent.
Paul Copan
"Who Are You to Judge Others?" article (2001)

426 TONGUE, THE
(*see also* COMMUNICATION; CONVERSATION; LISTENING; SPEECH)
Even so the tongue is a little member, and boasteth great things. Behold, how great a matter a little fire kindleth!
JAMES 3:5

1   Why does the tongue have such devastating power? Because it speaks the thoughts and feelings of the heart, and our hearts are naturally proud and willing to strike out at others.
Bill Gothard
The Power of Spoken Blessings (2004)

2   Remember, "A closed mouth gathers no foot." We must be cautious about our words.
Kenneth Boa and Gail Burnett
The Art of Living Well (1999)

3   In the end our tongues always betray symptoms of soul sickness.
Karen Burton Mains
You Are What You Say (1988)

4   If the tongue is the member of the body that most inadvertently reveals the condition of the soul (and if it also sets the temperature level for the inner self), what does the national verbal decline in our communal language reveal about the heart of a nation?
Karen Burton Mains
You Are What You Say (1988)

5   All hell can break loose when we don't learn to control our tongues.
R. T. Kendall
Total Forgiveness (2002)

427 TRADITION
Therefore, brethren, stand fast, and hold the traditions which ye have been taught, whether by word, or our epistle.
2 THESSALONIANS 2:15

1   We are bold enough to challenge history, but wise enough to abide by its lessons. . . whenever we discover places where human or church traditions choke simplicity, we examine those practices in the Word, with much prayer.
Jack Hayford
Glory on Your House (1991)

2   Traditions give us a sense of unity and encouragement in the hard times.
David and Claudia Arp
Where the Wild Strawberries Grow (1996)

3   To be disrespectful of tradition and of historical theology is to be disrespectful of the Holy Spirit who has been actively enlightening the church in every century.
John Stott
The Cross of Christ (1986)

4   All tradition must bow in reverence before the clear testimony of God's Word.
A. W. Tozer
"Who Is the Holy Spirit?" sermon (20th century)

428 TREASURE (*see also* MATERIAL THINGS; POSSESSIONS)

*For where your treasure is,
there will your heart be also.*
MATTHEW 6:21

1 The way we honor Christ in death is to treasure Jesus above the gift of life, and the way we honor Christ in life is to treasure Jesus above life's gifts.
John Piper
Don't Waste Your Life (2003)

2 If we give instead of keep, if we invest in the eternal instead of the temporal, we store up treasures in heaven that will never stop paying dividends. Whatever treasures we store up on earth will be left behind when we leave. Whatever treasures we store up in heaven will be waiting for us when we arrive.
Randy Alcorn
The Treasure Principle (2001)

3 Your health can be taken and your money stolen—but your place at God's table is permanent.
Max Lucado
He Still Moves Stones (1993)

4 He who may have a treasure simply by his grasping it will be foolish indeed if he remains poor.
Charles Spurgeon
All of Grace (19th century)

429 TRIALS (*see also* ADVERSITY; AFFLICTIONS; DIFFICULTIES; HARDSHIPS; TESTING; TROUBLES)
Beloved, think it not strange concerning the fiery trial which is to try you, as though some strange thing happened unto you. . .
1 PETER 4:12

1 You do not understand what troubles means; you have hardly sipped the cup of trouble; you have only had a drop or two, but Jesus drunk the dregs.
Charles Spurgeon
"The Immutability of God" sermon (1855)

2 I do not pray that you may be delivered from your pains, but I pray God earnestly that He would give you strength and patience to bear them as long as He pleases.
Brother Lawrence
The Practice of the Presence of God (17th century)

3 You've got to believe that no matter what you're going through, no matter what your burden is, He cares! God is not mad at you. He is not hiding from you. On the contrary, His heart is moved toward you. He cares about everything affecting you.
David Wilkerson
Revival on Broadway! (1996)

4 When "the fog" becomes so thick that we can't see any of the good God promises, we have no choice but to return to His written and living Word to give us the full, big picture of what's going on around us.
Ken Ham
How Could a Loving God. . . ? (2007)

5 Everything God teaches us about Himself is something that will guide us through the trials of our lives. Everything He reveals to us stretches our minds so that we can apply His faithfulness everywhere we need it.
Karon Phillips Goodman
You Still Here, Lord? (2004)

6 Let us enjoy light and consolation when it is his pleasure to give it to us, but let us not attach ourselves to his gifts, but to Him; and when He plunges us into the night of Pure Faith, let us still press on through the agonizing darkness.
François Fénelon and Jeanne Guyon
Spiritual Progress (17th century)

7   Never trouble yourself to inquire whether you will have strength to endure what is presented, if it should actually come upon you, for the moment of trial will have its appointed and sufficient grace.

François Fénelon and Jeanne Guyon
Spiritual Progress (17th century)

8   When God begins to burn, destroy, and purify, the soul does not perceive that these operations are intended for its good, but rather supposes the contrary.

François Fénelon and Jeanne Guyon
Spiritual Progress (17th century)

9   You may have experienced adversity or trials in your past. . .but today is a brand new day.

Joel Osteen
Your Best Life Begins Each Morning (2008)

10   God does at times change our trying circumstances. But more often, he doesn't—because he wants to change us!

David Wilkerson
"Have Faith in God's Faithfulness" article (2009)

11   Every trial has a beginning and an ending.

Rebecca Lusignolo
Devotions for Difficult Days (2006)

12   The word *trial* is defined as a test or examination of our character. When trials come, we are to receive them with joy, recognizing a God-given opportunity to identify those specific character flaws we need to change so that we can love more purely.

Ray and Nancy Kane
From Fear to Love (2002)

13   The purification process for gold requires the fire to become extremely hot so that the impurities will rise to the top. Once these impurities rise, they are scraped off so that the gold remaining will become pure. The trials in our life are like purifying gold. God uses these trials to allow those character issues that are blocking our ability to love to rise to the surface.

Ray and Nancy Kane
From Fear to Love (2002)

14   Sometimes our blessings reach us through the trials they bring. Sometimes God delivers us out of all our trials. Sometimes He keeps us in trials so someone else can be delivered.

Heather Whitestone McCallum
Let God Surprise You (2003)

15   We think we are fully for God until we are exposed to the cleansing fire of pain.

F. B. Meyer
The Secret of Guidance (1896)

16   The severity of the test is exactly determined by the reserves of grace and strength which are lying unrecognized within but will be sought for and used beneath the severe pressure of pain.

F. B. Meyer
The Secret of Guidance (1896)

17   God has a meaning in each blow of His chisel, each incision of His knife. He knows the way that He takes.

F. B. Meyer
The Secret of Guidance (1896)

18   Oh! his grace and goodness towards us is so immeasurably great, that without great assaults and trials it cannot be understood.

Martin Luther
Table Talk (16th century)

19   His shame, and therein is the foretaste of His crown, the promise of the great blessings of heaven.

George Edward Jelf
The Secret Trials of the Christian Life (19th century)

20 Everyone experiences challenges in life. And while some people march through valiantly and seemingly unscathed, others go kicking and screaming. Still, we all do our best to endure. Over the past few years, however, I have come to believe that it isn't as important how we go through, but that we get through.

Leslie Haskin
God Has Not Forgotten About You (2009)

21 God lets trials happen to the Christian just like He lets them happen to the pagans so that the superiority of the life lived in God can be demonstrated through our lives.

James MacDonald
"Turning It Around for Good" teaching (2009)

22 God did not cause the horrible events in your life, but you need to embrace the fact that He allowed them.

James MacDonald
"Turning It Around for Good" teaching (2009)

23 God could not make a world in which we are free and at the same time guarantee that everyone would choose Him. So the world is broken and bad things happen. But God promises that He will be with those who love Him. He will bring us through the fire, and we will come forth as gold.

James MacDonald
"Turning It Around for Good" teaching (2009)

24 God is so sovereign. He's so much in control that even when Satan tries to ruin our lives, God takes the weapon that Satan wants to use to destroy us and turns it into a good thing.

James MacDonald
"Turning It Around for Good" teaching (2009)

25 We all have a thorn. We all have something that God has allowed into our lives that Satan meant for our destruction but that God has turned around to help us grow and change.

James MacDonald
"Turning It Around for Good" teaching (2009)

26 The harder the trial, the closer He moves toward you. Are you feeling crushed today? He is rushing toward you to stand beside you and help you.

James MacDonald
"Jesus Stands for You" teaching (2007)

27 True virtue never appears so lovely, as when it is most oppressed; and the divine excellency of real Christianity, is never exhibited with such advantage, as when under the greatest trials.

Jonathan Edwards
A Treatise Concerning Religious Affections (18th century)

28 Consider, that it is necessary such inward trials should come, to wean us from the immoderate love of sensible devotion, and teach us to follow Christ, not merely for his loaves, but out of a principle of love and obedience.

George Whitefield
Selected Sermons of George Whitefield (18th century)

29 Trials reveal what we think about God.
Jude D'Souza
"From Fear to Awe" sermon (2009)

30 Whatever storm cometh, you will find his bosom the surest place of retreat.

Thomas Manton
A Practical Commentary on the Epistle of James (17th century)

31 Given the grace of God, given your knowledge of God's Word, given your present state of sanctification, given the resources of the Holy Spirit within, there is no trial into which God calls you that is beyond your ability to withstand.
Jay Adams
Christ and Your Problems (1971)

32 The fire of oppression will either cause you to burn up or help you grow stronger.
Mary Nelson
Grace for Tough Times (2006)

33 In the middle of the fire, where the flames are hottest, you meet the Almighty God face-to-face.
Mary Nelson
Grace for Tough Times (2006)

34 As difficult as it may be for you to believe this today, the Master knows what He's doing. Your Savior knows your breaking point. The bruising and crushing and melting process is designed to reshape you, not ruin you. Your value is increasing the longer He lingers over you.
Charles Swindoll
Encourage Me (1982)

35 Those who have faith must bear every disagreeable thing for the Lord, keeping in mind the promise, "But in all these things we shall overcome because of Him who loves us." God shall try us by fire just as silver is tried and purified.
Benedict of Nursia
The Rule of St. Benedict (6th century)

430 TRINITY, THE
Go ye therefore, and teach all nations, baptizing them in the name of the Father, and of the Son, and of the Holy Ghost.
MATTHEW 28:19

1 There is no salvation apart from the Trinity. It must be the Father, the Son, and the Holy Ghost.
Charles Spurgeon
"Honey in the Mouth!" sermon (1891)

2 In God's dimension, so to speak, you find a being who is three Persons while remaining one Being, just as a cube is six squares while remaining one cube.
C. S. Lewis
Mere Christianity (1952)

3 The Scriptures teach that there is essentially but one God, and, therefore, that the essence both of the Son and Spirit is unbegotten.
John Calvin
Institutes of the Christian Religion (16th century)

431 TROUBLES (*see also* ADVERSITY; AFFLICTIONS; DIFFICULTIES; HARDSHIPS; TESTING; TRIALS)
This poor man cried, and the LORD heard him, and saved him out of all his troubles.
PSALM 34:6

1 The darker the night grows, and the fiercer the storm becomes, the better will we remember that he of the lake of Galilee came to them upon the waves in the night when the storm was wildest.
Charles Spurgeon
"Honey in the Mouth!" sermon (1891)
2 When bad things happen, God gets our attention, doesn't He?
Kay Arthur
When Bad Things Happen (2002)

3 Identify the problem. (You'll half-solve it.) Present it to Jesus. (He's happy to help.) Do what He says. (No matter how crazy.)
Max Lucado
A Gentle Thunder (1995)

4   Be patient under all the sufferings God sends; if your love to Him be pure, you will not seek Him less on Calvary, than on Tabor; and surely, He should be as much loved on that as on this, since it was on Calvary that he made the greatest display of love.
François Fénelon and Jeanne Guyon
Spiritual Progress (17th century)

5   One reason we have great problems is that God wants to show us great solutions.
David Jeremiah
The Prayer Matrix (2004)

6   We must take our troubles to the Lord... but we must do more than that: we must leave them there.
Hannah Whitall Smith
The Christian's Secret of a Happy Life (1888)

7   When you are skeptical about the purpose of God, when it looks as if God has abandoned you, when you're not sure that God is really for you, remember that He has gone through infinite disaster so that you can have victory in the midst of your life disasters.
Ed Dobson
Finding God in the Face of Evil (2002)

8   Listen, life will rock and roll you. It is a constant roller coaster. You wake up every morning, you have no idea what will happen that day—but God knows.
Beth Moore
"A Beautiful Mind" teaching series (2009)

9   I need an accurate view of God more than I need my problems solved.
Rory Noland
The Heart of the Artist (1999)

10   There is no problem so small that God is not needed and no problem so big for which He is not adequate.
Rebecca Lusignolo
Devotions for Difficult Days (2007)

11   Trouble will come, but you can be confident the Lord will deliver you from it—all of it.
Joyce Meyer
Do It Afraid! (1996)

12   The real challenge of Christian living is not to eliminate every uncomfortable circumstance from our lives, but to trust our sovereign, wise, good, and powerful God in the midst of every situation. Things that might trouble us such as the way we look, the way others treat us, or where we live or work can actually be sources of strength, not weakness.
John MacArthur
Anxiety Attacked (1993)

13   Problems are the very means by which God changes us, transforms us, and drives us forward. Without problems, there would be no growth.
Tim Hansel
Eating Problems for Breakfast (1988)

432 TRUST
In God have I put my trust: I will not be afraid what man can do unto me.
PSALM 56:11

1   Trust shows itself when it leaves the tip of our tongue and lands on our tennis shoes.
Jennifer Rothschild
Lessons I Learned in the Dark (2002)

2   The times when you and I can't trace His hand of purpose, we must trust His heart of love!
Anne Graham Lotz
Why? Trusting God When You Don't Understand (2004)

3   The kind of trust God wants us to have cannot be learned in comfort and ease.
Anne Graham Lotz
Why? Trusting God When You Don't Understand (2004)

4   God doesn't often reveal the details of where He's taking you because He wants you to trust Him for every step.
   Stormie Omartian
   Just Enough Light for the Step I'm On (1999)

5   We must trust God today, and leave tomorrow with him.
   E. M. Bounds
   The Necessity of Prayer (19th century)

6   Trust always operates in the present tense.
   E. M. Bounds
   The Necessity of Prayer (19th century)

7   Trusting God trumps understanding God. The train will have long left the station and left us on the platform if we determine to ride only with full understanding. Life will have passed us by. I'm choosing to trust the conductor and the track he's laid down for me.
   Terry Esau
   Be the Surprise (2008)

8   Trust is dangerous. Trust requires courage. If trust were easy, we'd never hear another peep from our enemy called Fear.
   Angela Thomas
   Do You Think I'm Beautiful? (2003)

9   Our lives are full of supposes. Suppose this should happen or suppose that should happen; but what could we do and how would we bear it? But, if we are living in the "high tower" of the dwelling place of God, all these supposes will drop out of our lives.
   Hannah Whitall Smith
   The God of All Comfort (1906)

10   It is not your responsibility to explain what God is doing with your life. He has not provided enough information for you to figure it out. Instead, you are asked to turn loose and let God be God.
   James Dobson
   When God Doesn't Make Sense (1993)

11   Trusting in God to care for me frees me from self-interest so that I am able to care for others.
   Joseph Stowell
   Tongue in Check (1983)

12   In order to trust God, we must always view our adverse circumstances through the eyes of faith, not of sense.
   Jerry Bridges
   Trusting God: Even When Life Hurts (2008)

13   Trust is what motivates people to follow leadership whether at work or at home. And trust must be earned.
   Steve Farrar
   Point Man (1990)

14   He who did not spare His own Son, but offered Him up for us all, will also give us what we need to continue trusting and following Him. That may not include answers. We do not really "need" the answers—we only want them, though they would not add to our trust of Him if He gave them to us.
   Ed Dobson
   Finding God in the Face of Evil (2002)

15   I would rather walk with God in the dark than go alone in the light.
   Mary Gardiner Brainard
   "Not Knowing" poem (19th century)

16   Food is scarce just now. We live from hand to mouth. We have not more than will be our breakfast today, but I know we shall be fed, for God answers prayer.
   Mary Slessor
   Mary Slessor of Calabar (1917)

17   Explanations are a substitute for trust.
   Tullian Tchividjian
   Do I Know God? (2007)

18 The trust we put in God honours Him much, and draws down great graces.
   Brother Lawrence
   The Practice of the Presence of God
   (17th century)

19 Working constantly may be visible proof that deep inside we do not trust God.
   Bill Bright
   The Joy of Faithful Obedience (2005)

20 I know how to read the word, I know how to speak it out. I need some healing over my heart in some places where I continue to house distrust.
   Beth Moore
   "Who Do You Trust?" teaching series (2007)

21 It is not enough to trust God that that which we fear the most will not happen.
   Beth Moore
   "Who Do You Trust?" teaching series (2007)

22 This is what we call trust—"I will trust you to do what I say." This is our idea of trust.
   Beth Moore
   "Who Do You Trust?" teaching series (2007)

23 Things happen. Deep hurts happen. If you and I are going to walk in this trust thing, we've got to get down in under all those conditional elements until we can say this, I just trust you.
   Beth Moore
   "Who Do You Trust?" teaching series (2007)

24 Don't we think in some little way, we're a little god and that we're the only ones that keep the things that concern us on His mind?
   Beth Moore
   "Who Do You Trust?" teaching series (2007)

25 Fear strangles our dreams, but trust breaks its grip, setting us free.
   Mary Southerland
   Experiencing God's Power in Your Ministry
   (2006)

26 How does one strengthen the relationship of trust? Not by demanding that the other believe you, but by being constantly believable.
   William Krutza
   101 Ways to Enrich Your Marriage (1982)

27 We might not be able to see the end of the story. But we can trust the Storyteller.
   Joanna Weaver
   Having a Mary Heart in a Martha World
   (2000)

28 Whatever the specifics, if we are saying "Yes, Lord, but," He is saying Trust Me. That is every moment's greatest need.
   Elisabeth Elliot
   The Music of His Promises (2000)

29 Trust is the bridge over the raging river. Trust is how we access God's way for us. Trust is acting on your belief that God will make a way. You will never benefit from your faith in God until you step on the bridge and start walking across. Trust is both an attitude and an action.
   Henry Cloud and John Townsend
   God Will Make a Way (2002)

30 God will do what only he can do, and your job is to do what you can do.
   Henry Cloud and John Townsend
   God Will Make a Way (2002)

31 Is our expectation from Him or from ourselves, friends or circumstances?
   John Wright Follette
   Broken Bread (1957)

32 I have nothing but God, I trust God; I am waiting upon God; my flesh rests in Him;

I have given up everything, that I may rest, waiting upon what God is to do to me.

Andrew Murray
Master's Indwelling (1895)

33 Our glorious, exalted, almighty, ever present Christ! Why is it that you and I cannot trust Him fully, perfectly to do His work?

Andrew Murray
Master's Indwelling (1895)

34 To trust in the favour of princes is to build upon the sands.

F. C. Cook
Bible Commentary (19th century)

35 When circumstances in my life might tempt me to panic, feel terrified, become a nervous wreck, or be filled with dread, I can choose either to give in to those feelings or to trust in God and present myself to Him to be filled with His peace.

Elizabeth George
God's Garden of Grace (1996)

36 After all He's done for me, I realize God deserves my trust even when I can't figure out the, "How could You let this happen?" question.

Becky Lusignolo
"Super Saint?" teaching (2009)

37 Complete pessimism as regards the body is the necessary converse of the optimistic trust in Christ and His Spirit.

Paul Wernle
The Beginnings of Christianity (1903)

38 The truth is that when men speak of trust in Jesus' Person, as being possible without acceptance of the message of His death and resurrection, they do not really mean trust at all.

J. Gresham Machen
Christianity and Liberalism (1923)

39 If, therefore, thou dost believe that God is almighty, why dost thou fear devils and enemies, and not confidently trust in God, and crave his help in all thy troubles and dangers?

Lewis Bayly
The Practice of Piety (1611)

40 If thou dost truly believe that God is most wise, why dost not thou refer the events of crosses and disgraces to him who knoweth how to turn all things to the best unto them that love him?

Lewis Bayly
The Practice of Piety (1611)

41 If I leap, if I trust, I do not know for sure what will happen. What I do know is this: if I don't leap, if I don't trust, if I don't hope, if I don't ask, I will never soar.

John Ortberg
Faith and Doubt (2008)

42 There is only one way the puzzle of life will fit together, and that's God's way.

Maxie Dunnam
Let Me Say That Again (1996)

43 God will often use the desert of quiet faithful service, or the prison of injustice, to permanently transform our self-confidence into Christ-confidence. It is only when control is out of our own hands and we are thrust blindly into God's arms that He is free to teach us that He can be completely relied upon.

Tim Burns
Forged in the Fire (2003)

44 The reasonableness of trust depends on the trustworthiness of the person being trusted, and no more trustworthy person exists than the God who has revealed himself in Christ.

John Stott
Christian Basics (1991)

45 Father God, grant me eyes to see Your hand at work and a heart to trust Your ways. Even as I long for quick action and a short cut through my trials, cause faith to rise within me to recognize Your "scenic route" answers are for my best and Your glory.
Rebecca Lusignolo
"The Scenic Route" devotional (2008)

46 Trust is a beautiful and costly act of worship—an honoring response to the sovereignty of God and to His fatherly heart.
Matt Redman
Facedown (2004)

47 Trust means you anchor your heart in the reality of God's awareness of your situation.
James MacDonald
"I Choose to Trust" devotional (2010)

48 The only place we can safely put our confidence is in God.
Jerry White
Dangers Men Face (1997)

49 Trust and risk go hand in hand.
David Augsburger
Caring Enough to Forgive—Caring Enough Not to Forgive (1981)

433 TRUTH
Sanctify them through thy truth: thy word is truth.
JOHN 17:17

1 Truth is the thread that separates true spirituality from false spirituality. Spirituality does not give relevance to life; rather, truth gives relevance to spirituality.
Ravi Zacharias
The Grand Weaver (2007)

2 The Christian message...is not true because it works. Rather, the reason it works is because it is true.
Ravi Zacharias
Beyond Opinion (2007)

3 Truth is true even if no one believes it, and falsehood is false even if everyone believes it.
Ravi Zacharias
Beyond Opinion (2007)

4 What really matters is not what we think we perceive, or what others tell us is the truth, but what God says is the accurate perception and the truth of any situation.
Charles Stanley
When the Enemy Strikes (2004)

5 The lies of the devil always have a ring of truth to them. The best counterfeit is always as close to the original as possible.
Charles Stanley
When the Enemy Strikes (2004)

6 Absolute truth is divisive truth, separating darkness from light. The humanist knows this is where the real battle is being waged and they will reject us on this point incessantly.
Ken Ham
How Could a Loving God...? (2007)

7 When we speak the truth, we speak Christ's language. When we speak lies, we speak Satan's language.
Randy Alcorn
The Grace and Truth Paradox (2003)

8 Truth, by definition cannot be everything. If it includes everything, there's no such thing as falsehood. If there's no such thing as falsehood—there's no such thing as truth.
Ravi Zacharias
"Is There Not a Cost?" article (2008)

9 Sometimes truth is costly but not nearly as costly as deception.
Beth Moore
Praying God's Word (2000)

10 We begin to recognize lies when we know the Truth.
> Beth Moore
> *Praying God's Word* (2000)

11 It doesn't matter if everyone in the world joins hands and votes unanimously that God's truth is false, it still remains true. It remains true whether I believe in it or I don't believe in it.
> D. James Kennedy
> *Why I Believe* (1980)

12 Truth Is Not Relative. Truth Is Truth.
> Bumper Sticker

13 Christian theism views truth as absolute. If something is "true," that is, if it corresponds to God's perspective, then it is true for all people in all places at all times.
> Voddie Baucham Jr.
> *The Supremacy of Christ in a Postmodern World* (2007)

14 Help me to walk by the other light supreme,
Which shows thy facts behind man's vaguely hinting dream.
> George MacDonald
> *Diary of an Old Soul* (1880)

15 We can live based upon false or misleading input, or we can hear what God says about us and live as if that were true.
> Rich Hurst
> *Courage to Connect* (2002)

16 Truth is that which is consistent with the mind, will, character, glory, and being of God. Even more to the point: truth is the self-expression of God.
> John MacArthur
> *The Truth War* (2007)

17 The opposite of true is false.
> Norman Geisler, Frank Turek, and David Limbaugh
> *I Don't Have Enough Faith to Be an Atheist* (2004)

18 Truth is discovered, not invented. It exists independent of anyone's knowledge of it.
> Norman Geisler, Frank Turek, and David Limbaugh
> *I Don't Have Enough Faith to Be an Atheist* (2004)

19 It is truth that frees us, one that looms larger than all the lies presently surrounding us.
> Lisa Bevere
> *Kissed the Girls and Made Them Cry* (2002)

20 Truth is the dawning of morning where there has been a gross and long night of darkness filled with horrible disappointment and despair.
> Lisa Bevere
> *Kissed the Girls and Made Them Cry* (2002)

21 We should seek the truth without hesitation; and, if we refuse it, we show that we value the esteem of men more than the search for truth.
> Blaise Pascal
> *Pensées* (17th century)

22 The truth is an objective standard of reality that stands outside of our experience and stands above our opinions.
> Tony Evans
> *Tony Evans Speaks Out* (2000)

23 What is true must correspond to reality; otherwise, it is false. Therefore, if truth means anything at all, it must exclude something—namely, falsehood.
> Ravi Zacharias
> *What Is Truth?* (2007)

24 If you want to know what the truth is, look at Jesus Christ.
Ravi Zacharias
Recapture the Wonder (2003)

25 Waiting, for the believer, is not the futile and desperate act of those who have no other options, but rather a confident trust that eventually God will set things right.
Gary Thomas
Authentic Faith (2002)

26 Superstition, idolatry, and hypocrisy, have ample wages, but truth goes a begging.
Martin Luther
Table Talk (16th century)

27 We will never be able to recognize a lie unless we know the truth.
Beth Moore
"A Beautiful Mind" teaching series (2009)

28 Each generation must learn the same truths as every generation that came before.
Vinita Hampton Wright
The Soul Tells the Story (2005)

29 You must know the truth in order for the truth to deliver you.
Steve Campbell
"Why More Aren't Healed" sermon (2009)

30 I design plain truth for plain people.
John Wesley
Sermons of Several Occasions (18th century)

31 Some of you may believe that you cannot discover Truth. If that is true, you have actually discovered a truth.
Thor Ramsey
A Comedian's Guide to Theology (2008)

32 Truth is not based on personal preference, but upon, well, whoever decides what Truth is from the beginning of time. That would be God, by the way.
Thor Ramsey
A Comedian's Guide to Theology (2008)

33 Master the truth to refute error.
John MacArthur
Fool's Gold? (2005)

34 Truth is objective because God exists outside ourselves; it is universal because God is above all; it is constant because God is eternal. Absolute truth is absolute because it originates from the original.
Josh McDowell and Bob Hostetler
Right from Wrong (1994)

35 Eternal truth cannot be found within the confines or reasoning power of mortal man.
Lisa Bevere
You Are Not What You Weigh (1998)

36 It is not love to withhold the truth, no matter how brutal it seems!
Jeff Chapman
"Fishing for Men" article (2009)

37 Few men are apt to believe that which they would not have to be true, and fewer would have that to be true, which they apprehend to be against them.
Richard Baxter
A Call to the Unconverted, to Turn and Live (17th century)

38 Truth unquickened by God's Spirit deadens as much as, or more than, error.
E. M. Bounds
Power Through Prayer (1906)

39 Truth and time walk hand in hand.
James MacDonald
"Wise Up About Wisdom" sermon (2009)

40 Contradiction is a poor sign of truth. Many certain things are contradicted. Many false things pass without contradiction.
Blaise Pascal
Pensées (17th century)

41 Truth fears nothing so much as concealment, and desires nothing so much as clearly to be laid open to the view of all.
Richard Sibbes
The Bruised Reed (1630)

42 How do we know when Satan is lying? Whenever he moves his lips. How do we know when Jesus is telling the truth? Truth is all He is.
James MacDonald
"The True One" article (2008)

43 Taking our stand on biblical truth can be our only defense against our culture's penchant to reduce all issues to simplistic suppositions and glib answers.
Charles Colson
Faith on the Line (1986)

44 To see a truth, to know what it is, to understand it, and to love it, are all one.
George MacDonald
"The Consuming Fire" sermon
(19th century)

45 If it be the truth, we shall one day see it another thing than it appears now, and love it because we see it lovely; for all truth is lovely.
George MacDonald
"It Shall Not Be Forgiven" sermon
(19th century)

46 Ultimate value comes not in reading but in applying truth.
Gary Chapman
Hope for the Separated (1982)

47 Even the greatest truth we know can often lose its vibrancy within us.
Joy Sawyer
Dancing to the Heartbeat of Redemption
(2000)

48 God gives us unique insights into His Word when we ask to receive His truth.
Bettie Youngs and Debbie Thurman
A Teen's Guide to Christian Living (2003)

434 UNBELIEF (*see also* DOUBT)

And he did not many mighty works there because of their unbelief.
MATTHEW 13:58

1 Unbelief is highly contagious.
Beth Moore
Believing God (2004)

2 Unbelief puts circumstances between itself and Christ, so as to not see Him.
F. B. Meyer
The Shepherd Psalm (1889)

3 We say—"If I really could believe!" The point is—If I really will believe. No wonder Jesus Christ lays such emphasis on the sin of unbelief. "And He did not many mighty works there because of their unbelief." If we really believed that God meant what He said—what should we be like! Dare I really let God be to me all that He says He will be?
Oswald Chambers
My Utmost for His Highest (1935)

4 Unbelief is the originator of all other sins.
Thor Ramsey
A Comedian's Guide to Theology (2008)

5 Such as are not settled in the faith can never suffer for it; skeptics in religion will hardly ever prove martyrs.
Thomas Watson
A Body of Practical Divinity (1838)

6 Unsettled Christians do not consult what is best, but what is safest.
Thomas Watson
A Body of Practical Divinity (1838)

7 Unbelief. Instances in which you have virtually charged the God of truth with lying, by your unbelief of his express promises and declarations.
Charles Finney
Lectures of Revivals of Religion (1835)

8   At its core, pessimism is unbelief. It is a lack of faith in God and His ability or desire to keep His promises.
   Michael Youssef
   "Breaking the Power of Pessimism" article (2010)

435 UNDERSTANDING
(*see also* DISCERNMENT; LIGHT, SPIRITUAL; WISDOM)
For this cause we also, since the day we heard it, do not cease to pray for you, and to desire that ye might be filled with the knowledge of his will in all wisdom and spiritual understanding.
COLOSSIANS 1:9

1   No man can understand spiritual mysteries by carnal reason.
   Thomas Brooks
   A Cabinet of Jewels (1669)

2   The great men and the doctors understand not the word of God, but it is revealed to the humble and to children.
   Martin Luther
   Table Talk (16th century)

3   When we turn our expectations into demands, individuality is stifled, freedom is destroyed, and love is damaged. Jesus never forced Himself or His will on another person. We must resist forcing our partners to fit our expectations and projecting our values on them as if somehow ours are pure and theirs aren't. Our demands are not scriptural mandates. Conformity isn't the goal; understanding is.
   David and Janet Congo
   Lifemates (2001)

4   You will understand what God wants you to understand. He will teach you a little bit, and when you understand that, He will teach you a little bit more. The more you continue to study His word, the more you will see and understand.
   Kay Arthur
   God, Are You There? (1994)

436 UNEMPLOYMENT
Why stand ye here all the day idle? They say unto him, Because no man hath hired us.
MATTHEW 20:6–7

1   Unemployment is humbling, as you pray "Give us this day our daily bread" with renewed vigor.
   Stan Guthrie
   "The Spiritual Uses of Unemployment" article (2009)

2   Joseph said to the brothers who sold him into slavery that "what you meant for evil God meant for good." God redeems every circumstance for his children—even unemployment.
   Stan Guthrie
   "The Spiritual Uses of Unemployment" article (2009)

437 UNFORGIVENESS
But if ye forgive not men their trespasses, neither will your Father forgive your trespasses.
MATTHEW 6:15

1   It is pride or self-conceit, that is very much the foundation of a high and bitter resentment, and of an unforgiving and revengeful spirit.
   Jonathan Edwards
   "Charity Disposes Us Meekly to Bear the Injuries Received from Others" sermon (1738)

2   An unforgiving heart is unforgivable.
   David Augsburger
   70 x 7: The Freedom of Forgiveness (1970)

438 UNITED STATES
Blessed is the nation whose God is the LORD.
PSALM 33:12

1   Our fathers' God, to thee,
Author of liberty,
To thee I sing;
Long may our land be bright

With freedom's holy light;
Protect us by thy might,
Great God, our King!
Samuel Francis Smith
"America" (1832)

2 With a good conscience our only sure
reward, with history the final judge of our deeds,
let us go forth to lead the land we love, asking
His blessing and His help, but knowing that here
on earth God's work must truly be our own.
John F. Kennedy
Inaugural Address (1961)

3 What America needs more than anything
else right now is to know she cannot exist
without the worldview that helped bring her
into being. And that was the Judeo-Christian
worldview.
Ravi Zacharias
Christian Worldview (2008)

4 When the Constitution declares that "all
men all created equal," it is not referring to
intelligence, good looks, good humor, height,
weight, or income. It is talking about certain
rights, "inalienable" in that they cannot be
taken away.
Elisabeth Elliot
The Mark of a Man (1981)

5 Certainly God can bless America, but
the necessary prelude to national blessing is
a sweeping spiritual renewal that begins with
individual repentance and faith in the Lord
Jesus Christ. Apart from such a profound
spiritual awakening and a decisive return to the
God of Scripture, we have no right as a nation
to anticipate anything but God's judgment.
John MacArthur
Can God Bless America? (2002)

6 If God is going to bless America, it will
not be for the sake of the nation itself. He
blesses the nation, and has always done so, for
the sake of His people. If we who are called by

His name are not fulfilling the conditions for
divine blessing, there is no hope whatsoever
for the rest of the nation.
John MacArthur
Can God Bless America? (2002)

7 The biblical principle of morality is the
basis of our laws.
Deborah Dewart
Death of a Christian Nation (2010)

8 Religious liberty is our first liberty, not a
constitutional stepchild.
Deborah Dewart
Death of a Christian Nation (2010)

439 UNITY
*Behold, how good and how pleasant it is for
brethren to dwell together in unity!*
PSALM 133:1

1 Christ is the center of the church's unity.
Matthew Henry
Commentary on the Whole Bible (1706)

2 When we take God for our God we must
take his people for our people in all conditions.
Matthew Henry
Commentary on the Whole Bible (1706)

3 Unity and diversity must work together
or one will destroy the other. Unity without
diversity is uniformity, but diversity without
unity is anarchy.
Warren Wiersbe
A Gallery of Grace (2002)

4 Towards this union with God for which it
is created the soul strives perpetually.
Meister Eckhart
Meister Eckhart's Sermons (14th century)

5 Our Christian belief is based upon the
work of Christ; and we hold that human
society can only continue to exist in final unity
upon that same supernatural basis.
Peter Taylor Forsyth
The Work of Christ (1909)

UNMARRIED (see SINGLENESS)

VENGEANCE (see REVENGE)

440 VICTORY

For whatsoever is born of God overcometh
the world: and this is the victory that
overcometh the world, even our faith.
1 JOHN 5:4

1 We live on a broken planet, fallen far
from God's original intent. It takes effort to
remember who we are, God's creation, and
faith to imagine what we someday will be,
God's triumph.
Philip Yancey
Prayer: Does It Make Any Difference? (2006)

2 The victory lies not with us, but with
Christ, who hast taken on him both to
conquer for us and to conquer in us.
Richard Sibbes
The Bruised Reed (1630)

3 It is easier to walk in triumph every day
when we know that the condemnation is gone
and that we're free to live in victory.
Bob Moorehead
A Passion for Victory (1996)

4 Thank God, when we become Christians,
we don't have to check our drive to win at the
front door of the church. We don't have to stop
competing. We just get on the right track and
run a new race, with all the passion and energy
of our soul. We simply redirect our competitive
drive to run His race. So while we don't suppress our will to win, we must let Christ rule
it—and use it for His glory.
Steven Lawson
Men Who Win (1992)

5 If a man wins God's race, it doesn't matter
where else he loses. If a man loses God's race,
it matters not where else he may win.
Steven Lawson
Men Who Win (1992)

6 The best motivation to overcome sin is
not guilt, but a greater and greater love for the
Saviour.
Rubye Goodlett
Gathered Fragments (1986)

441 VIRGIN BIRTH

Therefore the Lord himself shall give you a sign;
Behold, a virgin shall conceive, and bear a son,
and shall call his name Immanuel.
ISAIAH 7:14

1 If the virgin birth of Jesus is untrue, then the
story of Jesus changes greatly; we would have a
sexually promiscuous young woman lying about
God's miraculous hand in the birth of her son,
raising that son to declare he was God, and
then joining his religion. But if Mary is nothing
more than a sinful con artist than neither she
nor her son Jesus should be trusted.
John Piper
The Supremacy of Christ in a Postmodern
World (2007)

442 VIRTUE
(see also HONOR; RIGHTEOUSNESS)
Add to your faith virtue. . .
2 PETER 1:5

1 Virtue is never mere virtue, it is either
from God, or through God, or in God.
Meister Eckhart
Meister Eckhart's Sermons (14th century)

2 Stain not fair acts with foul intentions.
Thomas Brown
Christian Morals (17th century)

3 Whoever pursues true virtue participates in
nothing other than God, because he is himself
absolute virtue.
Gregory of Nyssa
The Life of Moses (4th century)

443 VISION

Where there is no vision, the people perish:
but he that keepeth the law, happy is he.
PROVERBS 29:18

1 When we believe in the Lord and in
the workings of the Father—who sent the
Son—we can fulfill His vision and will because
Christ lives in us.
Juanita Bynum
My Spiritual Inheritance (2004)

2 When we are born again we all have
visions, if we are spiritual at all, of what Jesus
wants us to be, and the great thing is to learn
not to be disobedient to the vision, not to say
that it cannot be attained.
Oswald Chambers
My Utmost for His Highest (1935)

3 When God gives a vision, transact business
on that line, no matter what the cost.
Oswald Chambers
My Utmost for His Highest (1935)

4 Regret looks back. Worry looks around.
Vision looks up.
Jentezen Franklin
Believe That You Can (2008)

VOCATION (*see* CALLING; WORK)

WAITING ON GOD
(*see* PATIENCE; TIMING, GOD'S)

444 WAR

And I saw heaven opened, and behold a white
horse; and he that sat upon him was called
Faithful and True, and in righteousness
he doth judge and make war.
REVELATION 19:11

1 War is one of the most calamitous
consequences of evil. It is catastrophic. It is
always ugly. It should never be glamorized, and
no sane person should ever desire the conflict
or savor the strife of war. There are times,
however, when evil makes warfare absolutely
necessary.
John MacArthur
The Truth War (2007)

2 To make men kill men, is meat and drink
to that roaring adversary of mankind, who
goeth about seeking whom he may devour.
William Law
An Humble, Affectionate, and Earnest
Address (1761)

445 WARFARE, SPIRITUAL

For the weapons of our warfare are not carnal,
but mighty through God to the pulling down
of strong holds...
2 CORINTHIANS 10:4

1 No truce while the foe is unconquered;
No laying the armor down!
Fanny Crosby
"Awake! For the Trumpet Is Sounding"
(19th century)

2 To go into battle without the "full armor
of God" is as foolish as a soldier entering the
front lines dressed for a game of tennis.
Marlene Bagnull
Write His Answer (1990)

3 The problem is that so often we forget that
we are in warfare and that Satan's target is our
mind.
Kay Arthur
Speak to My Heart, God (1993)

4 Thank God for the angelic forces that fight
off the works of darkness. Angels never minister
selfishly; they serve so that all glory may be
given to God as believers are strengthened.
Billy Graham
Angels (1975)

5   No time for self-indulgence,
For resting by the way;
Repose will come at even,
But toil is for the day.
  Claudia Hernaman
  "The Call to Arms Is Sounding" (1886)

6   We have lost the sense that we are at war and that is why we are so often defeated. It's not that Christians don't want to win. They don't even know they are at war!
  David Jeremiah
  Spiritual Warfare (1995)

7   God did not build the church for our safety but to equip us to win at spiritual warfare.
  Bill McCartney
  Blind Spots (2003)

8   A proper perspective on spiritual warfare is focused on the power of God, rather than on the ploys of Satan.
  Hank Hanegraaff
  The Covering (2002)

9   We take up the shield of faith when we take up the truth we "amend" on Sunday and live it out on Monday.
  Tony Evans
  Tony Evans Speaks Out (2000)

10 Your enemy, as well as your God is watching very carefully over the area of your desires because you are volatile there.
  Beth Moore
  "Overcoming Insecurity" teaching series (2006)

11 If the Son of God felt it necessary to respond to Satan's specific lies with specific truths, what does that say about us?
  Andy Stanley
  Louder Than Words (2004)

12 To pray is also to engage in radical warfare.
  Ben Patterson
  Deepening Your Conversation with God (1991)

13 If in this world men persecute and slander you do not let this surprise or distress you, for this is for you no place of rest, but a battlefield.
  Sadhu Sundar Singh
  At the Master's Feet (20th century)

14 If we would therefore behave like good soldiers of Jesus Christ, we must be always upon our guard, and never pretend to lay down our spiritual weapons of prayer and watching, till our warfare is accomplished by death.
  George Whitefield
  Selected Sermons of George Whitefield (18th century)

15 Are you famous in hell? Do demons shudder at the mention of your name?
  Dave Earley
  The 21 Most Dangerous Questions of the Bible (2007)

16 Nothing that changes this lost world and drives back Satan's forces is easy!
  Rick Renner
  Living in the Combat Zone (1989)

446 WATCHFULNESS
Be watchful, and strengthen the things which remain, that are ready to die: for I have not found thy works perfect before God.
REVELATION 3:2

1   We are so good at waiting that we don't wait forwardly. We forget to look. We are so patient that we become complacent. We are too content. We seldom search the skies. We rarely run to the temple. We seldom, if ever, allow the Holy Spirit to interrupt our plans and lead us to worship so that we might see Jesus.
  Max Lucado
  When Christ Comes (1999)

447 WEAKNESS

*And he said unto me, My grace is sufficient for
thee: for my strength is made perfect in weakness.*

2 CORINTHIANS 12:9

1   If you feel helpless, you've become eligible
for the assistance of God.
    David Jeremiah
    A Bend in the Road (2000)

2   There is strength in being weak—God's
strength! Let God step in and do what you
cannot.
    Barb Albert
    *The 100 Most Important Bible Verses for
    Mothers* (2006)

3   When we run out of power to be and to do
what we ought, the Lord has only just begun
to supply us with His strength to live well
beyond what we can do on our own.
    Jill Briscoe
    A Little Pot of Oil (2003)

4   God insists that our spiritual life originate
not from our own strength, but from our
union with him, so the times of isolation. . .
become instruments for God to work in us our
new identity and deeper faith in him.
    Jonathan and Jennifer Campbell
    The Way of Jesus (2005)

5   God meets you in your weakness, not in
your strength. He comforts those who mourn,
not those who live above desperation. He
reveals Himself more often in darkness than in
the happy moments of life.
    Dan Allender and Tremper Longman III
    The Cry of the Soul (1994)

6   Your biggest weakness is God's greatest
opportunity.
    Charles Stanley
    How to Handle Adversity (1989)

7   It is human nature to point to our
inadequacies and let them direct us down the
path of least resistance.
    Ginger Garrett
    Couples Who Long for Children (2003)

8   Our limitations do not speak of our
capabilities—they only whisper of what God
can overcome.
    Ginger Garrett
    Couples Who Long for Children (2003)

9   Weakness is when you know that you are
out of your depth. And that is precisely where
we discover His strength holding us up.
    Colin Smith
    Unlocking the Bible Story (2002)

10   Our weaknesses are never revealed in good
times, but they quickly show up in times of
trial and tribulation.
    Joyce Meyer
    Never Give Up! (2008)

11   In times of temptation and distraction,
remain by faith in the simple presence of Jesus
Christ. You will find an immediate supply of
strength.
    Jeanne Guyon
    Experiencing the Depths of Jesus Christ
    (1685)

12   God has always allowed man's weakness
to validate man's immeasurable need of His
redemption and His sufficiency.
    Mary Southerland
    Experiencing God's Power in Your Ministry
    (2006)

13   God helps not those who help themselves,
but He is the champion of those who cannot
help themselves.
    Frances Roberts
    Come Away My Beloved (1970)

14   No matter what limitation or circumstance
you find yourself up against in life, there is a

God who can empower you and gift you to go past what you thought was possible. . .when you're at the end of yourself, that's the time he can do his best work.

Henry Cloud and John Townsend
God Will Make a Way (2002)

15 God can take every loss or limitation, including every physical loss or limitation, and use it for His glory.

Pat Warren
Weighed by the Word (2009)

16 Christ counted it no humiliation to be able to do nothing of Himself, to be always and absolutely dependent on the Father.

Andrew Murray
Working for God (1901)

17 It's the hard times and the unhealthy times and the hurting times that reveal my weaknesses. And it's also during those times that God shows up strong.

James MacDonald
"Strength in Weakness" sermon (2009)

18 Sometimes prayer, meditation, and contemplation are "death"—a kind of descent into our own nothingness, a recognition of helplessness, frustration, infidelity, confusion, ignorance.

Thomas Merton
Contemplative Prayer (1969)

19 All the human abilities in the world won't bring down a single stronghold of Satan.

David Wilkerson
"Hold on to Your Confidence" article (2010)

20 My honest confession of impotence opens the door to omnipotence.

Jack Hayford
Prayer Is Invading the Impossible (2002)

21 I believe that our greatest problem is our self-limitation. In having a more sane estimate of our abilities, we need to realize the incredible things that God can do in us and through us.

Tim Hansel
Eating Problems for Breakfast (1988)

22 There can be grace hidden in powerlessness.

Patricia Livingston
This Blessed Mess (2000)

23 The Lord doesn't promise to give us something to take so we can handle our weary moments. He promises us Himself. That is all. And that is enough.

Charles Swindoll
Encourage Me (1982)

448 WEALTH
(*see also* MONEY; RICH, THE)
They that trust in their wealth, and boast themselves in the multitude of their riches; None of them can by any means redeem his brother, nor give to God a ransom for him.
PSALM 49:6–7

1 It is not often that God's people get the riches of this world, and that does but prove that riches are little worth, else God would give them to us.

Charles Spurgeon
"God in the Covenant" sermon (1856)

2 The world is not impressed when Christians get rich and say thanks to God. They are impressed when God is so satisfying that we give our riches away for Christ's sake and count it gain.

John Piper
Don't Waste Your Life (2003)

3 The healthiest attitude about wealth is to realize that the happiest people are not those who have suddenly found wealth, but those who have found purpose.

Ellie Kay
The Debt Diet (2005)

4 By finding purpose—bringing it out in ourselves and in others and putting it to good use, we find true wealth—a wealth that stock market downturns or economic slumps cannot take away.

> Ellie Kay
> *The Debt Diet* (2005)

5 God puts greater value on his relationship with us than on our comfort and affluence.

> Gary Thomas
> *Authetic Faith* (2002)

6 Wealth is the smallest thing on earth, the least gift that God has bestowed on mankind. What is it in comparison with God's Word?

> Martin Luther
> *Table Talk* (16th century)

7 When we have our sweet and loving Saviour Christ, we are rich and happy more than enough; we care nothing for their state, honor, and wealth.

> Martin Luther
> *Table Talk* (16th century)

8 Let the fruition of things bless the possession of them, and think it more satisfaction to live richly than die rich.

> Thomas Brown
> *Christian Morals* (17th century)

9 A slave unto mammon makes no servant unto God.

> Thomas Brown
> *Christian Morals* (17th century)

10 The heaped-up treasures of the wicked find their way at last into the hands of better men.

> F. C. Cook
> *Bible Commentary* (19th century)

WELLNESS (*see* HEALTH)

WICKED, THE (*see* SINNERS)

449 WILL OF GOD

*And the world passeth away,
and the lust thereof: but he that doeth the will
of God abideth for ever.*
1 JOHN 2:17

1 Our prayers become part of God's plan and will.

> Maxie Dunnam
> *The Workbook of Intercessory Prayer* (1979)

2 Nothing can happen to a child of God outside the will of God.

> Jill Briscoe
> *The New Normal* (2005)

3 Not a hair of our heads falls to the ground without our heavenly Father's consent.

> Jonathan Edwards
> "The Final Judgment" sermon (1741)

4 Through the will of God, delighted in, and done, lies our only way to the heart of God, his only way to our heart. Keep the commandments. This is the way to every blessing.

> Andrew Murray
> *Prayer's Inner Chamber* (1912)

5 Even in their evil intentions—they were playing out the will of God. Though the chief priests and elders commanded Peter and John to stop teaching in the name of Jesus—the Apostles obeyed God and the Gospel message ignited among the people.

> Tim Walter
> "The Acts of the Holy Spirit" sermon
> (2009)

6 Afresh I seek thee. Lead me—once more I pray—Even should it be against my will, thy way.

> George MacDonald
> *Diary of an Old Soul* (1880)

7 The divine will is preferable to every other good. Shake off, then, all self-interest, and live by faith and abandonment.

François Fénelon and Jeanne Guyon
Spiritual Progress (17th century)

8 Let me no more from out thy presence go,
But keep me waiting watchful for thy will—
Even while I do it, waiting watchful still.

George MacDonald
Diary of an Old Soul (1880)

9 We sometimes discover the will of God through giving heed to the counsel of others if they are definitely committed Christians.

Billy Graham
Answers to Life's Problems (1994)

10 The place where God puts you will not be perfect. Even Eden was exposed to the possibility of evil. But there is no better place to be than where God has set you down.

Colin Smith
Ten Keys for Unlocking the Bible (2002)

11 If I started with the mind and will of God, viewing the rest of my life from that point of view, other details would fall into place—or at least fall into a different place.

Philip Yancey
Prayer: Does It Make Any Difference? (2006)

12 Before Moses went up the mountain, he chiseled out the stones on which God's laws would be written. Our hearts are the new stones. We must bring them to God in our hands, ready for him to write upon them his will for our lives.

Eva Marie Everson
Oasis (2007)

13 We all know what happened to Adam and Eve, but see the element of God's plan that is still the same today: All the trees but one are there for [us]. We've reversed the equation thinking God's plan means we only have one

good tree and the rest bad ones. Therefore we fearfully seek the dot on the map of His will. . . . Don't sell God short. He has a garden for you!

Gregg Matte
The Highest Calling: Becoming a Godly Man (2000)

14 Psalm 37:4 reads, "Delight yourself in the Lord; and He will give you the desires of your heart." Delight comes before desire. What I delight in determines what I desire. If I delight in God, my desire will be to do things according to His will and to ask according to His will. Too often we try to make this principle work in reverse; and we lack desire because our delight is not great enough.

John Maxwell
Be All You Can Be (1987)

15 If God told an angel to go to a tree and pluck caterpillars off it, the angel would be quite ready to do so, and it would be his happiness, if it were the will of God.

Meister Eckhart
Meister Eckhart's Sermons (14th century)

16 It's so much easier for us to change God than it is to conform to His will.

Bill Hybels
Laws of the Heart (1985)

17 When we know God and recognize fully His deep love for us, we will more willingly and freely yield ourselves to His plan for us and our life. Although in our pain we may sometimes ask, "Why?" we can trust that God's plan for us is good.

Elizabeth George
Loving God with All Your Mind (1994)

18 Work Your whole will in my life at any cost.

Elisabeth Elliot
Be Still My Soul (2003)

19 I started to read the Book to find out what the ideal life was, and I found that the only thing worth doing in the world was to do the will of God; whether that was done in the pulpit or in the slums, whether it was done in the college or class-room or on the street did not matter at all.
Henry Drummond
A Life for a Life and Other Addresses (1893)

20 It matters little whether we go to foreign lands or stay at home, as long as we are sure that we are where God puts us.
Henry Drummond
A Life for a Life and Other Addresses (1893)

21 Do not sacrifice yourself to a thing that is disagreeable unless you are quite sure that it is the will of God.
Henry Drummond
A Life for a Life and Other Addresses (1893)

22 Eve was declaring her rights. What she saw as her rights had nothing to do with the will of God and therefore nothing to do, finally, with her happiness, sure as she was that they had.
Elisabeth Elliot
The Mark of a Man (1981)

23 Just as air flooded with the light of the sun is transformed into the same splendor of the light so that it appears to be light itself, so it is like for those who melt away from themselves and are entirely transfused into the will of God.
Bernard of Clairvaux
On the Love of God (12th century)

24 I ask You, Lord, please demolish anything in my life that isn't according to Your specifications or that doesn't merit Your crowning seal of approval.
Dick Eastman and Jack Hayford
Living and Praying in Jesus' Name (1988)

25 There's a place in God's will for you, no matter what your age, no matter what your past.
Jack Hayford
Pursuing the Will of God (1997)

26 If we set our paths to pursue God's will, even amid our muddling failures, the Lord can somehow bring about a net gain of profit, perception, and understanding.
Jack Hayford
Pursuing the Will of God (1997)

27 I feel simply carried along each hour, doing my part in a plan which is far beyond myself. . . . My part is to live in this hour in continuous inner conversation with God and in perfect responsiveness to his will. To make this hour gloriously rich. This seems to be all I need to think about.
Frank Laubach
Letters by a Modern Mystic (1937)

450 WISDOM
(*see also* DISCERNMENT; LIGHT, SPIRITUAL; UNDERSTANDING)
But unto them which are called, both Jews and Greeks, Christ the power of God, and the wisdom of God.
1 CORINTHIANS 1:24

1 It is an honor to believe what the lips of Jesus taught. I had sooner be a fool with Christ than a wise man with the philosophers.
Charles Spurgeon
"Christ Precious to Believers" sermon (1890)

2 The only true wisdom is to be always prepared to meet God, to put nothing off which concerns eternity and to live like men ready to depart at any moment.
J. C. Ryle
Expository Thoughts on the Gospels (1879)

3   The wisdom of this age is folly in view of eternity.
John Piper
The Passion of Jesus Christ (2004)

4   For not that which is approved of men now, but what shall finally be approved by God, is true wisdom.
John Tillotson
The Wisdom of Being Religious (1819)

5   O the blindness of the greater part of mankind, who pride themselves on science and wisdom! How true is it, O my God, that thou hast hid these things from the wise and prudent, and hast revealed them unto babes!
François Fénelon and Jeanne Guyon
Spiritual Progress (17th century)

6   Being wise and being knowledgeable are two different things. But when knowledge begins with an understanding of God's character, our wisdom will continue to grow by merely acting on what we know.
Vicki Kuyper
Be Patient, God Isn't Finished with Me Yet (2003)

7   There are places you are better off not visiting. There are people you shouldn't be alone with. There are circumstances you need to avoid. In your heart, you know what they are. If you're wise, you'll pay attention!
Bob Barnes
Walking Together in Wisdom (2001)

8   Wisdom is repeatedly personified as a woman in the book of Proverbs. That's certainly by design. Wisdom isn't pictured as a testosterone-loaded taxi driver. It doesn't ignore us and drive by as we wave, or finally stop and shove us helplessly into the backseat and race us to an unknown destination. Wisdom is pictured as a woman who uses truthful, caring words—words that call, guide,

encourage, and direct us as we learn to "walk in wisdom." Her words are an extension of the counsel offered by God, the author of wisdom Himself, who also offers to be our Guide.
John Trent
Making Wise Life Choices (2003)

9   There is a standard for right and wrong and a source of wisdom to know it.
John Trent
Making Wise Life Choices (2003)

10 Should we then admire our own wisdom? I, for my part, admit myself a fool, and yield myself captive.
Martin Luther
Table Talk (16th century)

11 All the wisdom of the world is childish foolishness in comparison with the acknowledgment of Christ.
Martin Luther
Table Talk (16th century)

12 When you work with ideas, dreams, visions, intuitions and other soul matters day in and day out, you can't help but grow in wisdom.
Vinita Hampton Wright
The Soul Tells the Story (2005)

13 There is but One, He that sitteth in heaven, who is able to teach man wisdom.
John Wesley
The Journal of John Wesley (18th century)

14 The wisdom of the ancients, where is it? It is wholly gone. A schoolboy to-day knows more than Sir Isaac Newton knew. His knowledge has vanished away.
Henry Drummond
The Greatest Thing in the World (1874)

15 Long ago humanity reached the limit of its wisdom.
Martin Bell
Street Singing and Preaching (1991)

16 We have a right judgment in all things in proportion as our hearts seek to know God.
F. C. Cook
Bible Commentary (19th century)

17 Older men have a responsibility to walk alongside younger men, giving them the benefit of their experience. Likewise, young men should be open—in fact, eager—to receive advice from the more mature members of their sex.
Rick Johnson
That's My Son (2005)

18 I believe that a soul that has truly recognized its own murkiness is not vulnerable to a counterfeit light.
Walter Hilton
Toward a Perfect Love (1985)

19 Christ's eye-salve must clear your sight, or else you cannot make a right judgment: there is no proper and fit apprehension of things till you get within the veil, and see by the light of a sanctuary lamp.
Thomas Manton
A Practical Commentary on the Epistle of James (17th century)

20 Wisdom is the right use of knowledge.
James MacDonald
"Wise Up About Wisdom" sermon (2009)

21 Natural senses do not perceive the worth and price of spiritual privileges.
Thomas Manton
A Practical Commentary on the Epistle of James (17th century)

22 Our wisdom, in so far as it ought to be deemed true and solid Wisdom, consists almost entirely of two parts: the knowledge of God and of ourselves.
John Calvin
Institutes of the Christian Religion (16th century)

23 Since the Lord has been pleased to instruct us, not in frivolous questions, but in solid piety, in the fear of his name, in true faith, and the duties of holiness, let us rest satisfied with such knowledge.
John Calvin
Institutes of the Christian Religion (16th century)

24 We all want our children to be smart. Unfortunately, people have largely forgotten that there is a huge difference between intelligence and wisdom. Intelligence is a measurement of things you know. Wisdom is your ability to discern right from wrong and make moral choices. A wise person will follow God. An intelligent person may or may not.
Sonya Haskins
Homeschooling for the Rest of Us (2010)

25 One generation passes wisdom to the next, wisdom about girls and faith and punctuation. And we won't be as good a person if we don't receive it.
Donald Miller
To Own a Dragon (2006)

451 WITNESS (*see also* TESTIMONY)

But ye shall receive power, after that the Holy Ghost is come upon you: and ye shall be witnesses unto me both in Jerusalem, and in all Judaea, and in Samaria, and unto the uttermost part of the earth.
ACTS 1:8

1 We are the only light the world has. The Lord could come down Himself and give light to the world, but He has chosen differently.
A. B. Simpson
Days of Heaven Upon Earth (1897)

2 God calls you and me to be fragrant aromas of Him and to entice others to "taste and see of the goodness of the Lord."
Paul Brand
He Satisfies My Soul (2008)

3   John Q. Citizen will never be convinced about the credibility of the Christian faith until he becomes personally acquainted with someone who lives out the Christian life.
Erwin Lutzer
The Truth About Same-Sex Marriage (2004)

4   I am convinced that believers who are effective in witnessing have most likely been arrested by grace. Not only do they understand it theologically, they have experienced it firsthand.
Christine Wood
Character Witness (2003)

5   Being a witness means passionately pursuing the lost in love.
Douglas Cecil
The 7 Principles of an Evangelistic Life (2003)

6   We are weaving for God the garment, the only garment, they may ever see by Him.
Amy Carmichael
From Sunrise Land: Letters from Japan (1895)

7   Will you not ask that we may be saved from ever, by word or look or gesture, pushing a soul back into the dark?
Amy Carmichael
From Sunrise Land: Letters from Japan (1895)

8   The changed life of a Christian is the only way that most unbelieving people will encounter Christianity.
Elmer Towns
Core Christianity (2007)

9   Witnessing for Christ is not something we turn on and off, like a TV set. Every believer is a witness at all times—either a good one or a bad one.
Warren Wiersbe
Be What You Are (1988)

452 WITNESSING
(*see also* EVANGELISM; GOSPEL, THE; MISSIONARIES)

Having therefore obtained help of God,
I continue unto this day, witnessing
both to small and great. . .
ACTS 26:22

1   The law is a rough thing; Mount Sinai is a rough thing. Woe unto the watchman that warns not the ungodly!
Charles Spurgeon
"The Immutability of God" sermon (1855)

2   Are you winning souls for Jesus?
Does your life example prove
Him to be the precious Savior
Sacrificed because of love?
Carrie Breck
"Are You Winning Souls?" hymn (1905)

3   Do not underestimate the role you may play in clearing the obstacles in someone's spiritual journey.
Ravi Zacharias
Beyond Opinion (2007)

4   The life-saving strategy of Jesus is based on ordinary people showing and telling about Him in ordinary places.
Ron Hutchcraft
Called to Greatness (2001)

5   Those who say they are followers of Jesus Christ should never be ashamed of speaking his name. Nor should they be hesitant to bless people in his name or invite them to church or to a prayer breakfast or to read and study the Scriptures together. After all, they may be surprised just how interested even presidents, prime ministers, and kings—not to mention their own friends and neighbors—are the hear Christ's message of hope and love.
Joel Rosenberg
Epicenter (2006)

6 We must learn to present the gospel message as the Truth that demands a decision.
Ray Comfort
Hell's Best Kept Secret (1989)

7 The Bible is a basic indispensable tool for evangelists.
John MacArthur
Nothing But the Truth (1999)

8 Are you more worried about what people think of you, or about what God thinks of you? Too many times believers worry what others think. However, when we are witnessing to people, what is the worst thing they can do to us? They can kill us and send us to Heaven.
Mark Cahill
One Thing You Can't Do in Heaven (2002)

9 If knowing everything were a prerequisite for us to share our faith, none of us could ever witness.
Mark Cahill
One Thing You Can't Do in Heaven (2002)

10 The single greatest gift you can give someone is an introduction to the God who asked his Son to go the unthinkable distance to redeem them.
Bill Hybels
Just Walk Across the Room (2006)

11 All around us are people who are lost and separated from their heavenly Father, and we have a responsibility to tell them about Him.
Billy Graham
The Journey (2006)

12 Jesus consistently used word pictures, analogies and illustrations from his culture as tools for communicating unchanging truth.
Walt Mueller
Engaging the Soul of Youth Culture (2006)

13 In talking to a man you want to win, talk to him in his own language.
Henry Drummond
Stones Rolled Away and Other Addresses to Young Men (1893)

14 The goal is not to win the argument. It is to help people see Jesus.
Jim Petersen and Mike Shamy
The Insider (2003)

15 We can make them hear, but cannot make them feel. Our Words stop in the Porch of their Ears and Fancies, but enter not into their inward Parts.
Richard Baxter
The Causes and Danger of Slighting Christ and His Gospel (17th century)

16 When we are willing to open our mouths to speak for Him, we can be sure that He will give us the right thing to say. It is not that we put our minds in neutral but that we submit our minds to Him to use as He sees fit and to empower as He has promised.
John MacArthur
1 Corinthians (1984)

17 Our work is mere service, and we can but persuade; Christ must impose upon the conscience.
Thomas Manton
A Practical Commentary on the Epistle of James (17th century)

18 Too many Christians think they are prosecuting attorneys or judges, when God has called all of us to be witnesses.
Warren Wiersbe
Be What You Are (1988)

453 WIVES

Whoso findeth a wife findeth a good thing, and obtaineth favour of the LORD.
PROVERBS 18:22

1   Loving our husbands with a tender and passionate love is not something that happens automatically in our marriage. Ever since Adam and Eve took that fatal bite of forbidden fruit, our natural human inclination has shifted toward sin. Therefore, we are not naturally prone toward love. We are not naturally inclined to be passionate and respectful toward our husbands. In fact, if we do what comes naturally, it will be wrong most of the time!

Carolyn Mahaney
Feminine Appeal (2004)

2   Behind every man should be an admiring wife.

Willard Harley Jr.
His Needs, Her Needs (1986)

3   We are happiest when our openhearted friendship with our husband is a strong and sturdy vine that carries the nutrients we both need and desire.

Sue Patton Thoele
The Courage to Be a Stepmom (1999)

4   Enormous fortunes have been built on small amounts of money faithfully invested over time. The same is true of relationships. Your husband's sense of worth can be greatly enlarged by your reaction to him. The way you treat him, therefore, affects your own quality of life. There is an irrefutable principle in life that we all know but give little thought to: You get back what you give out.

Nancy Cobb and Connie Grigsby
How to Get Your Husband to Talk to You (2001)

5   There are few things more challenging and more rewarding than becoming a need-meeting woman in your man's life. If your husband is running on empty, or even if you are, watch what happens when you begin to invest in his stock. His emotional portfolio will begin to grow. Value him, and he will begin to feel valuable to you. As a married couple what affects one affects the other. You will begin to see the results in your own life, too. It doesn't take long.

Nancy Cobb and Connie Grigsby
How to Get Your Husband to Talk to You (2001)

6   The lovely, gracious, gentle, submission of a Christian woman to her unsaved husband, is the strongest evangelistic tool she has. It is not what she says, it is what she is.

John MacArthur
"How to Win Your Unsaved Spouse" sermon (1990)

7   Ask of your actions, "Will this help or hinder my husband?"

Elizabeth George
A Woman after God's Own Heart (1997)

8   Decide to make your husband your number one human relationship.

Elizabeth George
A Woman after God's Own Heart (1997)

9   The woman was made of a rib out of the side of Adam; not made out of his head to rule over him, nor out of his feet to be trampled upon by him, but out of his side to be equal with him, under his arm to be protected, and near his heart to be beloved.

Matthew Henry
Commentary on the Whole Bible (1706)

10 If man is the head, she is the crown, a crown to her husband, the crown of the visible creation. The man was dust refined, but the woman was dust double-refined, one removed further from the earth.

Matthew Henry
Commentary on the Whole Bible (1706)

11 Beside every great dad is a great wife.
Ken Canfield
Beside Every Great Dad (1993)

12 If the act of encouraging your husband
is like the sowing of good seed, then
understanding him is like tilling and
cultivating the soil beforehand.
Ken Canfield
Beside Every Great Dad (1993)

13 If a man's wife believes in him, he can
conquer the world—or at least his little corner
of it.
Shaunti Feldhahn
For Women Only (2004)

14 Because our husbands have pledged
their faithfulness for better or for worse,
and because we know "it's what's inside that
counts," we can easily migrate to the idea that
what's outside doesn't matter. But what's on
the outside does matter. And when we seem
to be willfully ignoring that truth, our men—
even godly men who are devoted to us—end
up feeling disregarded, disrespected, and hurt.
Shaunti Feldhahn
For Women Only (2004)

15 If a man feels disrespected, he is going to
feel unloved. And what that translates to is
this: If you want to love your man in the way
he needs to be loved, then you need to ensure
that he feels your respect most of all.
Shaunti Feldhahn
For Women Only (2004)

16 For your husband, sex is more than just a
physical need. Lack of sex is as emotionally
serious to him as, say, his sudden silence
would be to you, were he simply to stop
communicating with you. It is just as wounding
to him, just as much a legitimate grievance—
and just as dangerous to your marriage.
Shaunti Feldhahn
For Women Only (2004)

17 Our feminine hearts do desire men's hearts
turned toward us, delighting in our beauty and
cherishing who we are. We want to be wanted
by them in ways that will reflect God's longing
for His people and Christ's yearning to bless
His Church.
Nancy Groom
Heart to Heart About Men (1995)

454 WOMEN
*Every wise woman buildeth her house: but the
foolish plucketh it down with her hands.*
PROVERBS 14:1

1 We can become women of confidence only
as we grasp a great view of God.
Pam Farrel
Woman of Confidence (2001)

2 Adam had a good life before the woman
was made, but it couldn't hold a candle to his
situation after God sent Eve into his world.
She was just what the doctor ordered, so to
speak. She still is.
Greg Laurie
Marriage + Connections (2002)

3 Untold millions of women have made
a positive impact in their lifetimes—some
famous, others not so well known. Yet each
had a plan and a purpose in this world. Isn't it
wonderful to know that God created you and
me for a plan and a purpose as well?
Karol Ladd
The Power of a Positive Woman (2002)

4 God created a woman's heart to be a
unique and caring reflection of His heart.
Roy Lessin
The Loving Heart (2005)

5 Through a woman's words, ways, and
wisdom we have a richer understanding of the
nurturing of God.
Roy Lessin
The Loving Heart (2005)

6   God has called you to be a woman who trusts in the Lord in all of your ways, for all of your life, with all of your heart.
Roy Lessin
The Loving Heart (2005)

7   Woman, as well as man, was made after the image of God, in the Creation; and in the Resurrection, when we shall rise such as we were here, her sex shall not diminish her glory.
John Donne
"Sermon Preached on Easter Sunday"
(1630)

8   One of the greatest ways we can love our future husbands with unconditional, self-sacrificing love is by carefully protecting that precious gift we possess—our inward and outward purity.
Eric and Leslie Ludy
When God Writes Your Love Story (1999)

9   If the younger women don't learn from the older ones, they run the risk of concentrating on the wrong priorities.
Sandra Aldrich
Upward Glances (2000)

10   A true woman of God has a renewed mind, hands full of God's Spirit-directed work, and a heart on fire for the God she loves to distraction.
Jill Briscoe
8 Things That Will Change a Woman's Life
(2004)

11   Many times a woman doesn't even know what the issue is; she simply can sense there is one.
Bill and Pam Farrel
The Marriage Code (2009)

12   Some feminists treat marriage as if it were a diabolical plot.
Elisabeth Elliot
The Mark of a Man (1981)

13   Whereas a girl of any age lives out the script she learned as a child—a script too often grounded in powerlessness—a woman acknowledges and accepts her power to change, and grow, and be a force for good in the world.
Lynne Hybels
Nice Girls Don't Change the World (2005)

14   In order to learn what it means to be a woman, we must start with the One who made her.
Elisabeth Elliot
Let Me Be a Woman (1976)

15   Be wary of men who are intrigued by the wrapping but fail to see the value of what is in the package.
Shannon Ethridge
Every Woman's Battle (2003)

16   Though every woman is as unique as her own story, we sometimes best understand and interpret our own stories by listening to each other.
Nancy Groom
Heart to Heart About Men (1995)

17   A man's sacrificial love is practically irresistible to us as women, just as Jesus' passion for our hearts draws us compellingly to Himself.
Nancy Groom
Heart to Heart About Men (1995)

18   The first thing Eve received was her identity.
Jeanne Hendricks
A Woman for All Seasons (1977)

455 WONDERS (see also MIRACLES)
Who is like unto thee, O LORD, among the gods?
who is like thee, glorious in holiness,
fearful in praises, doing wonders?
EXODUS 15:11

1   Marvellous are all God's works; but the greatest delicacy and beauty are to be found among those works least exposed to view.
John Dawson
The Saviour in the Workshop (1868)

456 WORD OF GOD
(*see also* BIBLE, THE)
And take the helmet of salvation, and the sword of the Spirit, which is the word of God.
EPHESIANS 6:17

1   God hung the universe with words. Everything you will ever see, touch or taste had its genesis in a word from God. You exist because God spoke.
Fawn Parish
Honor: What Love Looks Like (1999)

2   "The sword of the Spirit, which is the Word of God" is far more powerful than our own arguments.
Corrie ten Boom
Amazing Love (1953)

3   We rob the work of Jesus Christ of its efficacy, and we stand powerless before the adversary, because we doubt the integrity of the Word of God.
Corrie ten Boom
Amazing Love (1953)

4   God will have the last word and it will be good!
Robert Schuller
The Be (Happy) Attitudes (1985)

5   As Christians we have the assurance from the Word of God that suffering is a part of His teaching curriculum for our lives, and that it is not an elective!
Ed Young
From Bad Beginnings to Happy Endings (1994)

6   I have lived to see the greatest plague on earth—the condemning of God's Word, a fearful thing, surpassing all other plagues in the world.
Martin Luther
Table Talk (16th century)

7   If I were addicted to God's Word at all times alike, and always had such love and desire thereunto as sometimes I have, then should I account myself the most blessed man on earth.
Martin Luther
Table Talk (16th century)

8   Once sure that the doctrine we teach is God's Word, once certain of this, we may build thereupon, and know that this cause shall and must remain; the devil shall not be able to overthrow it, much less the world be able to uproot it, how fiercely soever it rage.
Martin Luther
Table Talk (16th century)

9   I have before me God's Word which cannot fail, nor can the gates of hell prevail against it; thereby will I remain, though the whole world be against me.
Martin Luther
Table Talk (16th century)

10   A man's word is a little sound, that flies into the air, and soon vanishes; but the Word of God is greater than heaven and earth.
Martin Luther
Table Talk (16th century)

11   The Word is sure, and fails not, though heaven and earth must pass away.
Martin Luther
Table Talk (16th century)

12   To people just like you and me, God's Word says, "Don't allow sinful kinds of behavior or thoughts to enter your mind, your heart, or your relationships." Why? Because

these words and actions are, at their core, the very opposite of walking in love. They are neither innocent, nor harmless fun, they are destructive.

Chip Ingram
Love, Sex, and Lasting Relationships (2003)

13 God is so faithful to speak to us, through His Word and the words of others. As you read a book or listen to a radio program, your pastor, a Bible study teacher, an inspirational speaker, or to tapes, open your eyes and ears to listen for the still, small voice of God, giving you new insights, directions, corrections, and encouragement. Let God use the gifts and ministries of others to be your mentor when you most need them.

Betty Southard
The Mentor Quest (2002)

14 For God's Word is a light that shines in a dark place, as all examples of faith show.

Martin Luther
Table Talk (16th century)

15 The mere reading of the Word of God has power to communicate the life of God to us mentally, morally, and spiritually.

Oswald Chambers
Approved Unto God (1941)

16 If God says it, let us take our stand upon it.

D. L. Moody
Wondrous Love (1876)

17 We are not living by faith if we believe how we feel more than we believe what God's Word says.

Joyce Meyer
Approval Addiction (2005)

18 Truly the Word of God changes a man until he becomes an epistle of God.

Smith Wigglesworth
Faith That Prevails (1938)

19 The only certain foundation which any person has to believe that he is invited to partake of the blessings of the gospel, is, that the word of God declares that persons so qualified as he is, are invited, and God who declares it, is true, and cannot lie.

Jonathan Edwards
A Treatise Concerning Religious Affections (18th century)

20 God's word is an extension of himself and when uttered comes loaded with all the magisterial authority inherent in his nature.

Eugene Merrill
Everlasting Dominion (2006)

457 WORK (*see also* BUSINESS)
Now them that are such we command and exhort by our Lord Jesus Christ, that with quietness they work, and eat their own bread.
2 THESSALONIANS 3:12

1 Why should God have provided that so many hours of every day should be occupied with work? It is because work makes men.

Henry Drummond
The Greatest Thing in the World (1891)

2 A farm is not a place for growing corn, it is a place for growing character.

Henry Drummond
The Greatest Thing in the World (1891)

3 Work is not the central purpose of our existence on earth. God is the center of life. He's why we exist. He's whom we serve. From Him flow all good things.

Dennis and Barbara Rainey
Pressure Proof Your Marriage (2003)

4 God honors work. So honor God in your work.

Max Lucado
Cure for the Common Life (2005)

5   God had in mind that work would be something sacred. It was meant to be a gift from Him—not just something we do to keep body and soul together. God ordained that a large percentage of our lives would be spent at work, so He sought to make it meaningful and fulfilling to us.
> Steve and Janie Sjogren
> *101 Ways to Reinvest Your Life* (2003)

6   One of man's greatest sources of dignity is found in productive and rewarding work.
> Connie Neal
> *Your Thirty-Day Journey to Being a World-Class Father* (1992)

7   Anytime you concentrate on the difficulty of the work instead of its results or rewards, you're likely to become discouraged. Dwell on it too long, and you'll develop self-pity instead of self-discipline.
> John Maxwell
> *Leadership 101* (2002)

8   Labor is God's education.
> Ralph Waldo Emerson (1841) speech

9   When the precepts and example of Jesus Christ fully interpermeate society, to labor with the hands will be regarded not only as a duty but a privilege.
> Catherine Beecher
> "An Address to the Christian Women of America" (1872)

10   I see more and more of my own insufficiency for the great work I am called to. . . . When I compare myself with my work, I sink into a point, a mere despicable nothing!
> William Carey (19th century)
> quoted in *Faithful Witness: The Life and Mission of William Carey*

11   Some people labor on all their lives, never knowing they're utterly incompetent.
> David Roper
> *A Beacon in the Darkness* (1995)

12   As he proceeded in his work, he continued his familiar conversation with his Maker, imploring His grace, and offering to Him all his actions.
> Brother Lawrence
> *The Practice of the Presence of God* (17th century)

13   We are but the instruments or assistants, by whom God works.
> Martin Luther
> *Table Talk* (16th century)

14   Work is not punishment. The story of Adam and Eve tells how God gave the partners work to do while they were still in the garden. True enough, we experience work as frustrating and tedious, since we work in a fallen world. Yet in spite of that adversity, or through it, work pulls us toward personal fulfillment. God knows we were designed to work. His ideal for his creatures is not perpetual vacation on a beach but a job that challenges our abilities and our strength.
> Tim Stafford
> *Never Mind the Joneses* (2004)

15   All of us want to know that our actions touch others in a positive way and that while working toward worthwhile goals, we are creating a better place for others.
> Jerry Fleming
> *Profit at Any Cost?* (2003)

16   Whether we are aware of it or not, the work we do is also an expression of our character.
> Gordon MacDonald
> *Secrets of the Generous Life* (2002)

17   Work that is unfinished or substandard, that does not reflect our best effort, says something about the character of the person who did the work.
> Gordon MacDonald
> *Secrets of the Generous Life* (2002)

18 When we contribute our time and abilities to our churches or civic communities, we are "at work," pressing the quality of our character into some dimension of reality.

Gordon MacDonald
Secrets of the Generous Life (2002)

19 You are likely to enjoy your life much more if you view your activities in the context of what is important to you.

Bruce Bickel and Stan Jantz
Simple Matters (2001)

20 We lack the discipline to limit our entanglements with the world, choosing instead to be dominated by our work and the materialistic gadgetry it will bring. And what is sacrificed in the process are the loving relationships with wives and children and friends who gave life meaning.

James Dobson
Straight Talk (1995)

21 Striving for excellence in our work, whatever it is, is not only our Christian duty, but a basic form of Christian witness. And our nonverbal communication speaks so loudly that people often cannot hear a single word we say.

Ted Engstrom
The Pursuit of Excellence (1982)

22 My feeling is that there is no use writing about life, in any area of living, unless you are willing to stop writing and live.

Edith Schaeffer
Common Sense Christian Living (1983)

23 Life is too short to spend working for a company or person with values and goals irreconcilably opposed to ours.

Lloyd John Ogilvie
The Bush Is Still Burning (1980)

24 None of the secrets to success will work unless you do.

John Mason
The Impossible Is Possible (2003)

25 The Christian is to approach work as a matter of obedience to God; it is a stewardship from Him that demands a commitment of obedience and a consistency even when the boss is not looking.

James Eckman
Biblical Ethics (2004)

26 Christians in their effectual calling, are not called to idleness, but to labor in God's vineyard, and spend their day in doing a great and laborious service.

Jonathan Edwards
A Treatise Concerning Religious Affections (18th century)

27 Work is not done for its own sake. Its value consists in the object it attains. The purpose of him who commands or performs the work gives it its real worth.

Andrew Murray
Working for God (1901)

28 "My meat and my drink," Christ said, "is to do the will of him that sent me," and if you make up your mind that you are going to do the will of God above everything else, it matters little in what direction you work.

Henry Drummond
A Life for a Life and Other Addresses (1893)

29 If your business be lawful, if you are where God would have you to be, however lowly your occupation, there is nothing in it at all incompatible with a pure heart, a character unsullied, and a life regulated by the fear of God.

John Dawson
The Saviour in the Workshop (1868)

30 If Christ glorified God in the workshop, we also may live for God in any sphere in which He has in His providence been pleased to place us—a lesson this which not a few of us need to have impressed upon our mind.

John Dawson
The Saviour in the Workshop (1868)

31 The mighty God, the Prince of the kings of the earth, in the form of a servant, wrought with His own hands, and so stamped with dignity and honour all honest toil.

John Dawson
The Saviour in the Workshop (1868)

32 Worry is mental poison; work is mental food.

William George Jordan
The Kingship of Self-Control (1898)

458 WORLD, THE
(*see also* HUMANITY)

Now we have received, not the spirit of the world,
but the spirit which is of God;
that we might know the things
that are freely given to us of God.
1 CORINTHIANS 2:12

1 Don't ever expect the world to shine for you. God calls you to shine for the world. The world is a dark place, and God has put us where we are to be lights. That's the challenge for the whole church.

Colin Smith
Unlocking the Bible Story (2002)

2 The world seems to me like a decayed house, David and the prophets being the spars, and Christ the main pillar in the midst, that supports all.

Martin Luther
Table Talk (16th century)

3 Love not the world therefore. Nothing that it contains is worth the life and consecration of an immortal soul.

Henry Drummond
The Greatest Thing in the World (1874)

4 It doesn't take a prophet to look out the window these days and see where we're headed.

Tony Evans
Guiding Your Family (1991)

5 In an ideal world, we'd all spend our working hours—whether at home or away—on pursuits that suit our talents and interests and reflect God's calling. In this fallen world, it's not always that easy.

Steve Stephens and Alice Gray
The Worn Out Woman (2004)

6 The truth is that there is an invisible world that is just as real as the visible world. There are vast numbers of angels, both good and bad—spirits that exist all around us. There are glorious beings that would take our breath away if we saw them, and there are evil beings that would horrify us if we could see them.

Chip Ingram
The Invisible War (2006)

7 The world is no friend to grace. The best we can do with this world is to get through it as quickly as we can, for we dwell in an enemy's country.

Charles Spurgeon
All of Grace (19th century)

8 It is easy to sneer at the simple facts and doctrines of Christianity, and to talk great swelling words about" mind," and "thought," and "intellect," and "reason." But there is no getting over the broad fact that it is the body and not the mind, and the wants of the body, by which the world is governed.

J. C. Ryle
The Upper Room (19th century)

459 WORLDLINESS (*see also* BACKSLIDING; CARNALITY)

For the grace of God that bringeth salvation hath
appeared to all men, teaching us that, denying
ungodliness and worldly lusts, we should live
soberly, righteously, and godly,
in this present world.
TITUS 2:11–12

1 Worldliness is rarely even mentioned today, much less identified for what it is.

John MacArthur
Ashamed of the Gospel (1993)

2   The grand maxims which obtain in the world are, the more power, the more money, the more learning, and the more reputation a man has, the more good he will do. And whenever a Christian, pursuing the noblest ends, forms his behaviour by these maxims, he will infallibly (though perhaps by insensible degrees) decline into worldly prudence.

John Wesley (1759) personal letter

3   He who loses sight of the Word of God, falls into despair; the voice of heaven no longer sustains him; he follows only the disorderly tendency of his heart, and of world vanity, which lead him on to his destruction.

Martin Luther
Table Talk (16th century)

4   We must not regard what or how the world esteems us, so we have the Word pure, and are certain of our doctrine.

Martin Luther
Table Talk (16th century)

5   The man who is animated by no principle higher than those drawn from this world, whatever his station, grovels in the dust; be he peer or peasant, he is of the earth, earthy.

John Dawson
The Saviour in the Workshop (1868)

460 WORRY

Rest in the Lord, and wait patiently for him: fret not thyself because of him who prospereth in his way, because of the man who bringeth wicked devices to pass.

PSALM 37:7

1   There's absolutely nothing you're tempted to worry about that you won't be better off talking to God about instead.

Greg Laurie
Wrestling with God (2003)

2   My determination is to transfer this habit of worry into an instant moment of prayer and leaving it with God.

Charles Swindoll
"Prayer: Calling Out" sermon (2004)

3   I do not believe in worry because I believe in God's place of rest.

George Verwer
Come! Live! Die! (1972)

4   But when we worship and wait on God, worry is rarely an issue, because in God's presence we receive assurance of his sovereignty, wisdom, and care. Though circumstances remain unchanged, we now have an eternal perspective which removes the worry from the heart and replaces it with peace."

John Loftness and C. J. Mahaney
Disciplines for Life (1993)

5   Too often our minds are filled with worries or unnecessary concerns. Our hearts yearn to experience God, we long for peace and deep joy each day, but instead we feel lost. A spiritual attitude changes this, it softens our souls.

Robert Wicks
Everyday Simplicity (2000)

6   Perhaps there is no more unsettling feeling in the world than anxiety. It can grip you so fiercely that you believe you will come apart at the seams.

David Hawkins
When Life Makes You Nervous (2001)

7   We cannot live in violation of the laws of God without a penalty—usually involving anxiety, discouragement, and pain.

David Hawkins
When Life Makes You Nervous (2001)

8   Worry about the future is not simply a characteristic tic, it is the sin of unbelief, an indication that our hearts are not resting in the promises of God.

Kevin DeYoung
Just Do Something (2009)

9 Whatever is worth worrying about is certainly worth praying about.
John Mason
The Impossible Is Possible (2003)

10 Concern draws us to God. Worry pulls us from him.
Joanna Weaver
Having a Mary Heart in a Martha World (2000)

11 Christians who worry believe God can redeem them, break the shackles of Satan, take them from hell to heaven, put them into His kingdom, and give them eternal life, but just don't think He can get them through the next couple of days. That is pretty ridiculous. We can believe God for the greater gift and then stumble and not believe Him for the lesser one.
John MacArthur
Anxiety Attacked (1993)

12 When you or I worry, we are choosing to be mastered by our circumstances instead of by the truth of God. The vicissitudes and trials of life pale in comparison to the greatness of our salvation. Jesus wants us to realize it doesn't make sense to believe God can save us from eternal hell, but not help us in the practical matters of life.
John MacArthur
Anxiety Attacked (1993)

13 Trust is the antidote to anxiety; it's the resolution of worry and the destruction of fear.
James MacDonald
"I Choose to Trust" article (2010)

461 WORSHIP (*see also* PRAISE)
Worship him that made heaven, and earth, and the sea, and the fountains of waters.
REVELATION 14:7

1 To be used by God. Is there anything more encouraging, more fulfilling? Perhaps not, but there is something more basic: to meet with God. To linger in His presence, to shut out the noise of the city and, in quietness, give Him the praise He deserves. Before we engage ourselves in His work, let's meet Him in His Word. . .in prayer. . .in worship.
Charles Swindoll
The Quest for Character (1983)

2 When you recognize God as Creator, you will admire him. When you recognize his wisdom, you will learn from him. When you discover his strength, you will rely on him. But only when he saves you will you worship him.
Max Lucado
In the Eye of the Storm (1991)

3 Worship is a voluntary act of gratitude offered by the saved to the Savior, by the healed to the Healer, and by the delivered to the Deliverer.
Max Lucado
In the Eye of the Storm (1991)

4 If we see God as He really is, and ourselves as we really are, there's only one appropriate response: to worship Him.
Randy Alcorn
The Grace and Truth Paradox (2003)

5 Heaven's calendar has seven Sundays a week. God sanctifies each day. He conducts holy business at all hours and in all places. He uncommons the common by turning kitchen sinks into shrines, cafés into convents, and nine-to-five workdays into spiritual adventures.
Max Lucado
The Cure for the Common Life (2005)

6 Worship should never be ho-hum.
Mel Lawrenz
Jubilee (2008)

7 Nothing keeps God at the center of our worship like the biblical conviction that the essence of worship is deep, heartfelt satisfaction in Him and the conviction that the pursuit of satisfaction is why we are together.

John Piper
The Dangerous Duty of Delight (2001)

8 God will refuse to accept worship that is halfhearted or less than what he deserves. Worship that requires little of us is likewise worth little to God.

Henry and Tom Blackaby
The Man God Uses (1999)

9 The glory of Christ in the power of his resurrection into invincible life and omnipotent authority will be reflected back to him in the joyful worship of his risen and perfected saints.

John Piper
Seeing and Savoring Jesus Christ (2004)

10 We are to worship God, not because his ego needs it, but because without worship, our experience and enjoyment of God are not complete. We worship God not so much because He needs it, but because we do.

John Ortberg
If You Want to Walk on Water,
You've Got to Get Out of the Boat (2001)

11 If you want to know a greater depth of worship in your life, get your Bible open and engage with the truth. Soak your mind in it. The Holy Spirit will use the truth to stimulate a response within your heart.

Colin Smith
Unlocking the Bible Story (2002)

12 Our worship of Christ must always come before our work for Christ.

Anne Graham Lotz
The Vision of His Glory (1996)

13 The end we ought to propose to ourselves is to become, in this life, the most perfect worshippers of God we can possibly be, as we hope to be through all eternity.

Brother Lawrence
The Practice of the Presence of God
(17th century)

14 Worship brings ever deepening and expanding dimensions of God-at-work in our world. Worship, in a very real sense of the word, opens a doorway to the power of His presence, confounding dark powers and overthrowing sin's destructive operations.

Jack Hayford
Manifest Presence (2005)

15 The ancient English word for "worship" is *weorthscipe,* which incorporated the idea of "ascribe worth." It meant fundamentally that a true worship of God is more than an exercise of religious ritual; it is a human expression of a proper value being placed in the Person being worshiped and the personal cost of the practice of worshiping Him.

Jack Hayford
Manifest Presence (2005)

16 Worship is a personal encounter with God in which one expresses love for God, concentrates on His attributes, and brings the focus back to Him.

James Scudder
Your Secret to Spiritual Success (2002)

17 Satan is willing to have us worship anything, however sacred—the Bible, the crucifix, the church—if only we do not worship God Himself.

D. L. Moody
"Weighed and Wanting" sermon
(19th century)

18 Genuine worship of God does not come from religious activates, but is an attitude.
  Bill Bright
  The Joy of Faithful Obedience (2005)

19 God doesn't care where we meet Him, only that we do it.
  John Tesh
  An Invitation to Pray and Worship (2003)

20 In many ways, worship is not created; it is discovered and recreated.
  Brad Berglund
  Reinventing Sunday (2001)

21 Gathering for worship is not for the faint of heart.
  Brad Berglund
  Reinventing Sunday (2001)

22 Through worship, God works on my behalf. He repairs and renews my relationship with him.
  Robert Webber
  Worship Is a Verb (1992)

23 True worship demands our attention and beckons us to put ourselves into it, heart and soul.
  Robert Webber
  Worship Is a Verb (1992)

24 Worship, then, is not only the public acts we do as a gathered community, but our very way of day-to-day life.
  Robert Webber
  Worship Is a Verb (1992)

25 Worship is central to all that we do.
  Robert Webber
  Worship Is a Verb (1992)

26 Worshippers are different from praisers, because they have stepped beyond thanking God for altering their conditions to worshipping Him for their position as His children.
  T. D. Jakes
  Intimacy with God (2000)

27 God takes the matter of worship out of the hands of men and puts it in the hands of the Holy Spirit.
  A. W. Tozer
  Whatever Happened to Worship?
  (20th century)

28 If you cannot worship the Lord in the midst of your responsibilities on Monday, it is not very likely that you were worshiping on Sunday!
  A. W. Tozer
  Whatever Happened to Worship?
  (20th century)

29 As the fire doth mount upwards, and the needle that is touched with the loadstone still turneth to the north, so the converted soul is inclined to God.
  Richard Baxter
  A Call to the Unconverted, to Turn and Live
  (17th century)

30 There is a way of ordering our mental life on more than one level at once. On one level we may be thinking, discussing, seeing, calculating, meeting all the demands of external affairs. But deep within, behind the scenes, at a profounder level, we may also be in prayer and adoration, song and worship and a gentle receptiveness to divine breathings.
  Thomas Kelly
  A Testament of Devotion (1992)

31 It is the nature of God, so terribly pure that it destroys all that is not pure as fire, which demands like purity in our worship. He will have purity. It is not that the fire will burn us if we do not worship thus; but that the fire will burn us until we worship thus.
  George MacDonald
  "The Consuming Fire" sermon
  (19th century)

32 The heart of God loves the offerings of a persevering worshipper. Though overwhelmed by many troubles, they are even more overwhelmed by the beauty of God.
Matt Redman
The Unquenchable Worshipper (2001)

33 The most meaningful and powerful worship always comes at a price—the whole of our lives placed on His altar.
Matt Redman
Facedown (2004)

34 In the life of every worshipper there will come times when worship meets with suffering. And these moments shape what kind of worshippers we will become.
Matt and Beth Redman
Blessed Be Your Name (2005)

35 Worship is the foundation on which the ethical life of the people of God is built.
Rubel Shelly
Written in Stone (1994)

WRATH (*see* ANGER)

WRITING (*see* CREATIVITY)

462 YOUTH (*see also* ADOLESCENCE)
And when the Philistine looked about, and saw David, he disdained him: for he was but a youth, and ruddy, and of a fair countenance.
1 SAMUEL 17:42

1 Teenagers are not interested in hearing about religion, denomination, or lifestyle issues. It is the person of Jesus that will interest a modern young person, not the system of Christianity.
Ron Hutchcraft
The Battle for a Generation (1996)

2 Teenagers cannot find their incalculable worth until they realize who they were made by and made for and how much God spent to pay for them. They have been made by God and paid for by God at the cost of His Son.
Ron Hutchcraft
The Battle for a Generation (1996)

3 Thirty years from now, today's tattoos will not be marks of freedom, but indelible reminders of conformity.
John Piper
The Passion of Jesus Christ (2004)

4 No matter how hardened and trampled our teens' surface-living culture is, no matter how much attention is deflected away from their true inner state, no matter how much "irrational tripe" and image-hype mass media produces—deep yearnings for real things are buried in our teens' hearts.
Jeff Leeland
Disarming the Teenage Heart (2003)

5 Youth culture needs wise caretakers, good teachers to help our youth learn to read the deeper meanings of experience and help them to understand and appreciate the real rewards of a good life.
Jeff Leeland
Disarming the Teenage Heart (2003)

6 Listening opens our eyes to the reality and depth of the needs of young people. And once we know the reality, we can communicate the gospel in ways that can be heard and understood.
Walt Mueller
Engaging the Soul of Youth Culture (2006)

7 Do we want our teens to talk to us? Then nothing is more important than the strength of our own integrity, faith, and character. If our teens trust and respect us and feel secure in our unconditional love they will talk to us.
Connie Grigsby and Kent Julian
How to Get Your Teen to Talk to You (2002)

8   No young man can live in such an
atmosphere of unpunished dishonesty and
lawlessness, without wrecking his character.
    Charles Sheldon
    In His Steps (1896)

9   The generation of young people today
under age thirty-five has never known a world
that puts duty before self.
    Josh and Sean McDowell
    Evidence for the Resurrection (2009)

10 We do not confer self-esteem on children.
We help them discover it. We give them
opportunity to find it in themselves.
    Don Otis
    Whisker Rubs (2007)

11 Youth is a game of blindman's buff, a romp
and a struggle in which we hold on fiercely
and shout loudly, but know less as to whom we
are holding or who is holding us than we shall
ever know again.
    John Jay Chapman
    Learning and Other Essays (1910)

ZEAL (*see* PASSION)

AUTHOR INDEX

Note: Codes with each author name indicate first, the subject number, and second, the quote number. For example, the reference 112-21 after the name "Abanes, Richard" directs you to the 112th subject (Depravity of Man) and the 21st quote in that section.

A

Abanes, Richard 112-21, 114-3, 184-54, 292-3, 292-4, 292-5, 292-6, 329-26, 329-27

Adams, Jay 58-15, 66-40, 68-50, 123-3, 171-10, 186-12, 186-13, 186-14, 214-10, 237-37, 237-51, 260-52, 388-21, 429-31

à Kempis, Thomas 4-1, 8-5, 8-6, 72-2, 81-2, 88-17, 120-3, 120-8, 167-1, 199-1, 250-4, 376-2, 416-4

Albert, Barb 170-13, 447-2

Alcorn, Randy 59-5, 180-2, 180-3, 180-4, 184-120, 184-121, 241-3, 339-2, 357-1, 385-1, 388-5, 413-3, 428-2, 433-7, 461-4

Aldrich, Sandra 64-24, 231-21, 247-1, 247-2, 400-3, 423-1, 454-9

Alexander, Archibald 163-19, 184-181, 240-8, 386-37, 406-23

Alleine, Joseph 66-39, 91-10, 91-11, 96-5, 112-35, 240-18, 262-6, 365-57, 365-58, 420-5

Allender, Dan, and Tremper Longman III 23-7, 58-18, 89-2, 113-2, 254-15, 254-16, 260-89, 295-9, 327-1, 447-5

Anderson, Lynn 9-2, 152-75, 227-4, 227-5, 279-5, 347-1, 375-16

Anderson, Neil 59-7, 107-2, 198-8, 213-4, 213-5, 405-9

Anderson, Neil, and Charles Mylander 68-19, 237-23, 323-17, 342-6

Anderson, Neil, and Dave Park 301-15, 309-3, 342-51, 374-19, 405-33

Anyabwile, Thabiti 71-6, 71-7, 74-4, 189-2, 245-1

Aquinas, Thomas 175-5

Armstrong, Brenda 88-16

Armstrong, Kristin 127-15, 406-32, 406-33, 406-34, 417-21

Arnold, Johann Christoph 64-7, 64-8, 122-8, 170-41, 170-42, 170-43, 170-44, 297-6

Arp, David and Claudia 151-4, 158-16, 158-18, 172-9, 296-13, 296-14, 296-15, 427-2

Arp, David and Claudia, and John and Margaret Bell 170-45

Arterburn, Stephen 88-21, 348-16, 374-18, 425-6

Arterburn, Stephen, and Jack Felton 39-4, 39-5, 152-54, 237-24, 260-42, 260-115, 268-14, 308-33, 347-4, 425-4

Arterburn, Stephen, and John Shore 171-11, 273-19, 323-43, 348-15

Arterburn, Stephen, Fred Stoeker, and Mike Yorkey 212-7, 228-1, 260-81, 273-3, 328-2

Arthur, Kay 20-1, 39-3, 42-7, 42-12, 42-13, 42-14, 42-15, 42-16, 43-20, 43-64, 104-29, 116-3, 127-1, 143-7, 152-9, 152-10, 153-11, 170-48, 170-49, 198-2, 198-3, 198-6, 206-9, 231-6, 241-2, 271-1, 311-3, 325-5, 326-10, 342-28, 357-2, 365-45, 386-42, 416-2, 416-3, 431-2, 435-4, 445-3

Astley, Jacob 184-94

Augsburger, David 45-8, 79-7, 82-4, 170-70, 170-71, 170-73, 170-74, 205-2, 205-3, 206-7, 432-49, 437-2

Augsburger, Myron and Esther 17-5, 99-8, 158-13, 260-22

Augustine 184-157, 184-314, 184-315, 192-13, 209-17, 209-18, 219-1, 260-63, 265-2, 295-3, 300-12, 349-12, 413-16

B

Babington, Thomas 43-30

Backus, William and Candace 257-4

Bacon, Francis 12-38, 30-7

Bagnull, Marlene 99-3, 318-3, 445-2

Baillie, John 116-21, 184-32, 278-41, 291-43, 331-6

Bakke, Ray 71-33, 186-11, 237-50, 316-1, 391-12

Baldwin, Jeff 43-33, 43-34, 112-11, 221-23

Balswick, Judy and Jack 297-14

Barna, George 375-19

D

Daman, Glenn 250-11, 319-32, 319-33

D'Avenant, William 12-32

Dawson, John 12-36, 59-30, 68-45, 88-19, 88-20, 131-6, 131-7, 184-146, 221-45, 237-47, 237-141, 249-6, 283-15, 326-11, 455-1, 457-29, 457-30, 457-31, 459-5

Dawson, Joy 184-126, 234-25, 234-26, 371-9, 420-7

Dean, Jeffrey 104-8, 104-9, 260-4, 373-5, 386-14

DeHaan, Mart 8-7

de Maistre, Joseph 184-263

DeMarco, John 65-10, 163-24

Demmitt, Dallas and Nancy 78-17, 90-5, 256-11, 342-50

DeMoss, Nancy Leigh 52-2, 52-3, 52-4

de Sales, Francis 116-20, 147-4, 159-4, 165-1, 172-6, 190-1, 201-3, 260-48, 260-71, 264-17, 366-7, 366-8, 386-20, 413-8

Dever, Mark 43-11, 48-2, 68-52, 71-11, 152-79, 153-1, 153-14, 184-33, 184-147, 192-56, 212-3, 245-2, 250-1, 250-25, 350-3, 362-1

Dever, Mark, and Paul Alexander 71-8, 71-9, 71-10, 143-4, 319-50

Dewart, Deborah 73-7, 254-14, 438-7, 438-8

DeWitt, David 279-3, 425-5

DeYoung, Kevin 184-275, 184-296, 460-8

Dickens, Charles 118-2, 119-7, 199-8, 219-6, 239-3

Dobson, Ed 184-262, 186-6, 237-61, 431-7, 432-14

Dobson, James 45-1, 68-34, 75-7, 78-10, 113-1, 160-21, 184-42, 264-84, 273-9, 282-8, 285-3, 296-1, 296-34, 296-41, 296-61, 296-62, 296-63, 334-4, 359-3, 410-1, 432-10, 457-20

Dobson, Ryan 308-1, 308-2, 418-1, 425-7, 425-8

Doddridge, Philip 192-1

Donne, John 15-10, 46-16, 60-3, 60-4, 79-2, 79-3, 147-1, 191-8, 198-35, 227-8, 249-5, 454-7

Doughty, Stephen 137-3, 137-4, 296-21

Dowd, Alan 221-41

Downing, David 234-27

Driscoll, Mark, and Gerry Breshears 219-13, 237-27, 237-49, 237-75, 237-103

Drummond, Henry 23-3, 59-29, 66-21, 66-22, 67-1, 67-10, 68-5, 68-30, 68-42, 80-8, 99-21, 104-31, 141-4, 143-23, 146-14, 147-3, 153-6, 173-2, 177-3, 188-8, 189-18, 208-23, 221-35, 229-1, 232-2, 237-25, 237-130, 254-10, 254-24, 254-35, 254-37, 257-3, 260-1, 260-34, 260-35, 260-64, 260-111, 268-10, 277-11, 295-4, 319-44, 324-11, 324-13, 324-14, 329-28, 344-13, 364-2, 364-3, 366-10, 366-11, 371-5, 386-39, 397-7, 413-23, 413-26, 413-27, 449-19, 449-20, 449-21, 450-14, 452-13, 457-1, 457-2, 457-28, 458-3

D'Souza, Jude 66-25, 163-35, 429-29

Duggar, Michelle 296-50, 296-51

Dunnam, Maxie 32-26, 32-27, 32-28, 184-189, 184-286, 188-12, 319-65, 432-42, 449-1

Dunn, Jerry 19-1, 129-1, 130-1, 404-1, 404-2

E

Earley, Dave 92-2, 101-25, 138-11, 170-68, 267-11, 319-111, 329-33, 445-15

Eastman, Dick, and Jack Hayford 449-24

Eckhart, Meister 152-34, 163-12, 165-4, 171-5, 184-228, 188-16, 188-17, 198-26, 202-2, 213-33, 221-26, 227-6, 244-5, 244-6, 245-9, 245-10, 245-11, 260-101, 278-10, 283-8, 321-11, 336-2, 336-3, 336-4, 394-8, 394-9, 395-4, 395-5, 395-6, 406-19, 406-20, 421-4, 439-4, 442-1, 449-15

Eckman, James 144-26, 162-1, 378-2, 391-9, 457-25

Edelinski, Frank 278-29, 375-17

Edwards, David 59-19, 59-20, 59-21, 89-1, 184-24, 184-224, 260-96

Edwards, Dwight 181-8, 184-6, 231-11, 237-55

Edwards, Jonathan 12-31, 27-2, 29-1, 63-4, 66-8, 104-22, 116-16, 120-10, 131-5, 152-67, 155-2, 184-28, 184-56, 184-84, 184-86, 184-214, 184-243, 184-244, 184-246, 184-251, 184-267, 184-333, 192-42, 192-43, 192-52, 192-53, 200-7, 209-10, 209-11, 209-12, 209-28, 212-13, 220-6, 225-12, 225-13, 225-18, 225-19, 225-20, 225-21, 239-11, 240-2, 241-5, 241-6, 255-5, 260-36, 260-128, 260-145, 260-146, 275-4, 278-21, 300-13, 318-5, 324-5, 324-6, 339-13, 356-2, 363-8, 365-55, 386-11, 405-24, 417-6, 421-2,

SUBJECT INDEX

LIST OF CONTRIBUTORS

Janice Brown, Spencer Brown, Mary Beth Buhr, Ashley Casteel, Wendy Connell, Dave Dunham, Joyce Goodwin, Vickie Henman, Amber James, Jewell Johnson, Miriam Keating, Eileen Key, Roxane Kohout, April Lehoullier, Donna Maltese, Rebecca Lusignolo, David McLaughlan, Lisa Miller, Paul Muckley, Jorrie Muniz, MariLee Parrish, Kathrine Quintana, Conover Swofford, Janice Thompson, Dana Udlock, Russ Wight, Laura Young